Hugh Nibley:

A Consecrated Life

I have always been furiously active in the Church, but I have also been a nonconformist and have never held any office of rank in anything. I have undertaken many assignments given me by the leaders, and much of the work has been anonymous: no rank, no recognition, no anything. While I have been commended for some things, they were never the things which I considered most important. That was entirely a little understanding between me and my Heavenly Father which I have thoroughly enjoyed, though no one else knows anything about it. . . . I would rather be a doorkeeper in the House of the Lord than mingle with the top brass in the tents of the wicked.

—Hugh Nibley[1]

---

[1] "The Best Possible Test," in *Brother Brigham Challenges the Saints*, edited Don E. Norton and Shirley S. Ricks, Vol. 13 in *The Collected Works of Hugh Nibley* (Salt Lake City: Deseret Books/FARMS, 1994), 535-37. Hugh is paraphrasing Psalms 84:10.

Hugh Nibley:

A Consecrated Life

Boyd Jay Petersen

Greg Kofford Books
Salt Lake City 2002

© 2002 Boyd Jay Petersen

Cover design copyrighted 2002 by Greg Kofford Books, Inc.

Portrait of Dr. Hugh W. Nibley used on the dust jacket is courtesy of the artist Rebecca F. Everett, who retains all rights of the image.

Published by Greg Kofford Books, Inc.
Salt Lake City, Utah

All rights reserved. No part of this book may be reproduced in any format or in any medium without the written permission of the publisher, Greg Kofford Books, Inc., P.O. Box 1362, Draper, UT 84020. The views expressed herein are the responsibility of the author and do not necessarily represent the position of Greg Kofford Books, Inc.

2006 05 04 03   5 4 3 2

Visit us at www.koffordbooks.com

Library of Congress Cataloging-in-Publication Data

Petersen, Boyd.
  Hugh Nibley : a consecrated life / by Boyd Jay Petersen.-- 1st ed.
    p. cm.
Includes bibliographical references and index.
  ISBN 1-58958-020-6 (alk. paper) -- ISBN 1-58958-019-2 (limited leather: alk. paper)
  1. Nibley, Hugh, 1910- 2. Church of Jesus Christ of Latter-Day Saints--Doctrines. I. Title.

BX8695.N P48 2002
289.3'092--dc21

2002151101

This book is lovingly dedicated to my parents, Verl and Dorothy, who taught me what to look for in a hero; to my wife Zina, who has shared her life (and parents) with me; and to my children Mary Rose, Christian Degn, Nathanael Hugh, and Andrew Reid, who make me smile.

Contents

Preface	xi
Foreword by Zina Petersen	xvii
Introduction: The Man and the Legend	xxiii
1. A Scottish Heritage, 1810-1930	1
2. Early Life in Oregon, 1910-21	17
3. "Speaking in a Prophetic Vein": Hugh Nibley as Social Critic	31
4. Growing Up in Los Angeles, 1921-27	49
5. A Voice for the Wilderness: Hugh Nibley, Naturalist	67
6. A Mission to Germany, 1927-30	85
7. Taking Himself Lightly: The Wit of Hugh Nibley	97
8. Higher Education, 1930-38	105
9. "One Peep at the Other Side": Hugh Nibley's Life of Faith	119
10. Teaching at Claremont, 1938-42	133
11. "The Clown of the Professions": Hugh Nibley and Scholarship	149
12. Army "Intelligence," 1942-43	167
13. War in Europe, 1944-45	183
14. "The Work of Death": Hugh Nibley and War	209
15. Brodie and BYU, Nuptials and Newborns, 1945-50	223
16. "Something to Move Mountains": Hugh Nibley and the Book of Mormon	245
17. Poor-Man's Plato and Paterfamilias, 1950-59	261
18. The Home Dance: Hugh Nibley Among the Hopi	277
19. Fighting Academic Battles and Gaining the Brethren's Trust, 1959-69	289
20. "The Book That Answers All the Questions": Nibley and the Pearl of Great Price	313
21. Politics, Basketball, Patriarchs, and Temples, 1970-79	335
22. "The Source of All Good Things": Hugh Nibley and the Temple	351
23. Consecration and Recognition, 1980-89	365
24. "Joy Lies in Another Direction": Hugh Nibley's Call to Leave Babylon and Build Zion	383

25. One Eternal Round, 1990-Present		397
26. Conclusion: Constancy Amid Change		407
Appendix A	A Chronology of the Life of Hugh Winder Nibley	411
Appendix B	Genealogy of Hugh Winder Nibley	421
Appendix C	Letter from the Front, 1945	423
Appendix D	Letter to Sterling M. McMurrin, 23 August 1967	427
Appendix E	Shalamar	431
Index		439

Illustrations

Charles W. Nibley, ca. 1925	xxxii
Charles W. Nibley at age sixteen, ca. 1865	7
Rebecca Neibaur Nibley, ca. 1866	7
Charles W. Nibley about 1920 with his three wives	10
Joseph F. Smith (left), Charles W. Nibley, and Alexander Nibley at a train stop, ca. 1907	12
The LDS First Presidency ca. 1925	13
Hugh Nibley, age about eighteen months	16
Alexander (El) Nibley, ca. 1907	18
Agnes (Sloanie) Sloan Nibley with baby Hugh, ca. 1910	20
Hugh, age seven or eight	21
Hugh Russell Sloan and Margaret Violet Reid Sloan	24
Somewhere in Oregon, includes Melvin J. Ballard, Joseph F. Smith, Agnes Sloan Nibley, Alexander Nibley & Charles W. Nibley	27
Sloanie Nibley and her four sons, ca. 1918	28
Hugh in his classroom, 1990	30
Hugh, about age sixteen, ca. 1916	48
Page from astronomy journal, 21 November 1923	52
Pen sketch on 25 January 1922	53
BYU Aspen Grove summer camp, 1927	64
Ted Wilson campaign advertisement featuring actor Robert Redford and Hugh Nibley	66
Passport photograph, age seventeen	84
The *Montcalm*	88
The Battle of Leipzig Monument in August 1929	94
A comic pose in living room, ca. 1980	96
1933, just before serving for the summer in the Northwestern States Mission	104
1990, scanning a manuscript with his legendary absorption	118
As a new faculty member, ca. 1940	132
In the Ancient Studies reading room in 1990	148
U.S. Army, at Clearwater, Florida, in 1942 at basic training	166
Official Army photograph at Godman Field, Fort Knox, Kentucky, 1943	182
Patch from Hugh's army uniform	188
Master Sergeant Hugh Nibley in 1945	204
Rifle slung over his shoulder	208
Faculty photograph for Brigham Young University, ca. 1947	222
Phyllis Ann Hawkes Draper, ca. 1943	231
Phyllis Draper ca. 1936	232
Phyllis and Hugh with their newborn son Paul in the summer of 1947	239
Hugh and Sidney Sperry (left) examine copies of ancient manuscripts, ca. 1950	244
Hugh Nibley, ca. 1950	260
Forest Lawn Cemetery near Los Angeles on 1 June 1959, Sloanie Nibley burial	271
At the Hopi "prophecy rock" on 27 July 1996	276
Hugh Nibley, already white-haired in his fifties	288
Family portrait in Berkeley, 1959	291
The Nibley family in 1966	305

Hugh looks over a reproduction of Facsimile #1 from the Joseph Smith Papyri, ca. 1967	312
Hugh Nibley in the 1970s	334
Hugh Nibley and Louis Midgley on 21 May 1974	343
Outside the Salt Lake Temple, May 1984	350
Hugh Nibley, ca. 1980	364
BYU 1983 commencement exercises	370
The filming crew for *Faith of an Observer* on location in Egypt in January 1984	375
The Nibley residence at 285 E. 700 North in Provo	382
Margaret Violet Reid Sloan	384
Cartoon, Sunstone, August 1992, No. 88	394
With grandson, Nathanael Hugh Petersen in July 2002	396
Fiftieth anniversary celebration	403
Ninetieth birthday party in March 2000	404
Outside BYU's Maeser Building in the early spring of 2001	406

A Note About the Cover Artwork

The painting on this book's cover was created by Rebecca F. Everett and was commissioned for the Hugh Nibley Ancient Studies Reading Room, which was dedicated on 14 November 2001. The painting seemed particularly appropriate for this book since Everett designed the portrait as a collage representing many of the ideas and images that are associated with Hugh Nibley—from the Dead Sea Scrolls, the Nag Hammadi library, and the Joseph Smith papyri, to ancient and modern temples, Hugh's office with his ubiquitous note cards, and the BYU campus.

As Everett explains, "placed over the collage is the shape of a large circle representing the sun, the symbol for time, or a day; a reminder of the prayer circle; the disk of the sun god Ra; a ring, Uroboros, the cycle of life; eternity, etc. Up in the bits of sky visible outside the arches and bounded by linear representations of the square and the compass, are constellations, on the left: the Big Dipper, by which most of us orient ourselves to find the North Star; and on the right: Orion, of all the constellations, the one most easily recognized by Anyman, and thus perhaps an entry point, or first step toward a personal and intimate contemplation of the mysteries of God"

"The portrait itself is painted in oils on vellum, which was superimposed over the collage and further developed in many layers of glazes so that the underlying images are secondary to the portrait, yet still discernable. I wanted to portray the nobility of scholarship, the quizzical disinterest in the honors of men, and a subtle but definite twinkle in his eye that speaks of the deep joy derived from the daily study of the gospel, and the surprise and delight of encountering truths

Preface

I came to know Hugh Nibley through his daughter. In January 1983, I had returned to Brigham Young University after serving in the France Paris Mission. There a friend recruited me for his College Bowl team—a sort of game-show version of Trivial Pursuit. I was a lousy addition to the team; but Zina Nibley was also a member. I fell for her brains (it's true) and her blonde hair. She liked me because I didn't know who her father was. She was suspicious of boys who were interested in her only because they wanted to meet her famous father.

I met Hugh first at the blessing of one of his grandchildren in October 1983. And while I really didn't know why Hugh Nibley was famous, I had heard the name many times, had been told that he was the smartest man alive by several friends, and was quite intimidated about meeting him. When Zina introduced us, Hugh endearingly apologized for the suit he was wearing. It was really quite typical of all of his suits, but it was obvious that he was as nervous about meeting me as I was about meeting him. That same day, Zina and I became engaged.

This change in my status brought up a new question. What should I call her father, who, at seventy-three, was old enough to be my grandfather? "Brother Nibley" sounded too stuffy. "Hugh" sounded too chummy. I could hardly call him "Daddy" as Zina did. To avoid the awkwardness, whenever I wanted to talk to him I would just look in his direction and start talking. As long as he looked up, it worked fine. Then one day he called me on the phone. He needed a ride to the garage to pick up his car. I answered the phone and the familiar voice on the other end said, "Hi, Boyd. This is . . . uh . . . Nibley." Obviously, he didn't have any idea what I should call him either. I suddenly felt relieved.

I started reading Hugh Nibley's books soon after Zina and I married in May 1984. I felt that if I was going to be in the family I should know a little about why my father-in-law was a local celebrity. It was in his books that I discovered not only great depth and wisdom about the gospel, but a certain "hipness"—a youth and vitality—that makes reading him fun. Hugh Nibley combines both arcane tidbits from such sources as the Dead Sea Scrolls or the Patrologia with quotes from pop culture like "The Muppet Show" or "Hill Street Blues," sprinkling in references to *Popular Science* or a current fashion magazine. In talks I've even heard him impersonate Beavis and Butthead as examples of light-mindedness. This ability to put old things in context with the new was not only interesting, but entertaining. It helped me see that these ancient texts are really dealing with the same issues we must confront today, reassuring me that they really weren't so strange and that we really aren't so clever.

In fact, sometimes I'm startled by how up-to-date Hugh Nibley really is. In April 1998, I began promoting a folk music house concert series in Utah Valley, bringing acoustic musicians from all over the country to play music in the living rooms of my friends. While the music at our concerts is far from raucous, the music I had heard at the Nibley home was usually piano concertos or violin sonatas. It never even crossed my mind to invite my in-laws to a concert. But it did cross the mind of one of Nibley's colleagues, the late Eugene England, who had been attending these shows. England actually invited the Nibleys to come to a concert, and they graciously accepted. At that point I was terrified. I really didn't know how Hugh or Phyllis would respond to the very contemporary acoustic music. But they loved it. In fact, Hugh raved afterwards that the idea of troubadours traveling from house to house with only their instruments and their music was the oldest form of music in Western culture. That's what I've now come to expect: Hugh Nibley can approach anything in our contemporary world, but he will most certainly do so by comparing it to some ancient text or custom.

Soon after I was married I discovered that the Nibley family had no one archiving materials about the immediate family. I vowed to preserve something of my father-in-law for my children. This vow was the genesis of the biography. Soon I was culling through library materials, writing to Hugh's colleagues and associates, and interviewing family and friends. As I discovered, his books are simply the tip of the proverbial iceberg, I realized that my project had a potential audience beyond my own children.

It is extremely difficult to try to capture any life in writing, but a life as full and complex as Hugh Nibley's presents a staggering challenge. I have tried to meet that challenge by treating the subject not only chronologically but also topically, thereby creating a sort of mosaic. Consequently, this volume consists of a conventional biography, its narrative chapters alternating with topical essays about themes important to Hugh Nibley. In the chronological sections I have tried to give a full historical overview of Hugh's life, occasionally adding my own interpretation of a particular event. (For the most part, Hugh's personal writings serve this purpose better than my amateur efforts at psychoanalysis would do.) In the topical chapters, I have tried to provide a deeper perspective on some of his central beliefs and interests. In effect, I have tried to do for Hugh Nibley what he did for Brigham Young in the essays compiled in his *Brother Brigham Challenges the Saints*. That is, I have assembled examples from Hugh's life and selections from his writings (primarily from his private correspondence) that paint a coherent portrait of the man and his views on particular issues.

Despite the number of autobiographical references in Hugh Nibley's books and the numerous articles published about him, most of the information in this book comes from sources that have never seen print before. The first major source of family correspondence begins with the papers of Hugh's grandfather, Charles W. Nibley. One group of letters has been preserved in the L. Tom Perry Special Collections, Harold B. Lee Library, Brigham Young University, Provo, Utah. This collection, donated by Hugh, consists of letters between Charles W. and his son Alexander ("El")—Hugh's father—as well as many birthday letters to El's children. This collection included a few letters Hugh wrote as a youth or young man to his parents that El, knowing Charles W.'s interest in Hugh, forwarded to him. Another collection of Charles W. Nibley's family correspondence is housed in the Historical Department Archives of the Church of Jesus Christ of Latter-day Saints, Salt Lake City. I was given access only to letters to and from Hugh.

An irreplaceable source of information has been Hugh Nibley's own letters—candid, spontaneous, and witty. I cannot adequately express my gratitude to those individuals who both maintained long-term correspondence with Hugh and who preserved those letters. Although far from completely catalogued, this correspondence includes hundreds of items.

But three correspondents were particularly important: The first was his mother, Agnes ("Sloanie") Nibley, to whom he wrote regular, voluminous, and insightful letters from age fifteen, when he left home for the summer to work at the Nibley-Stoddard Lumber Company, through the late 1940s, when he was married and teaching at Brigham Young University. The second correspondent was Paul Springer, Hugh's housemate at Berkeley, fellow scholar, and kindred spirit. This correspondence spans the period that begins with their meeting at Berkeley in 1934 until the passage of time and different interests resulted in an amiable drifting apart in the late 1960s. The third correspondent was Hugh's son Alex, who saved the letters he received on his mission to Japan 1978-80 and again when he lived in the Guam during the late 1980s and early 1990s. Most of the letters Hugh wrote to Paul and Tom during their missions have unfortunately not survived. The owners of these letters generously either made the originals or photocopies of the originals available to me. They remain in possession of members of the Nibley family and eventually will likely be donated to an archive, quite likely BYU's Perry Special Collections. Likewise, unless otherwise noted, all photographs in this book are in my possession or were generously loaned to me by family members.

In addition to these letters, numerous other letters were made available to me by various Nibley family members and friends, in particular Barbara Nibley Richards, JoAnn Sloan Rogers, and Marguerite Goldschmidt. Thanks to such generosity, I have amassed a large secondhand collection of family correspondence which will ultimately also be archived, most likely in the Perry Special Collections at BYU. Unless otherwise noted, all letters by and to Hugh are part of this collection. Unfortunately, I have not yet found most of the letters that Hugh's correspondents wrote to him, so the conversation is mostly one sided.

The second major type of source material is interviews. In addition to the dozen or so published and unpublished interviews by various individuals, Peter Johnson and Sterling Van Wagenen provided me with the transcripts from the mammoth interviewing project conducted ca. 1983-84 with the enthusiastic support of Hugh's son, Alex, for a video documentary, *Faith of an Observer*. Brian Capener was director and photographer, he and Alex wrote the script, Peter G. Czerny was the film editor, Peter Johnson was executive producer, Sterling Van Wagenen was the producer, and production funding came from Brigham Young University and the Foundation for Ancient Research and Mormon Studies (FARMS). Sterling, Alex, and Brian conducted hours of interviews with Hugh Nibley, Phyllis Nibley, Sloan Nibley, Reid Nibley, Lucien Goldschmidt, Paul Springer, Truman Madsen, Sterling McMurrin, and Neal A. Maxwell. The transcript runs to 552 pages, and I have drawn on it heavily. Other interviewers have generously provided me with photocopied transcripts of their interviews.

I have, with my wife's assistance, also conducted many lengthy interviews with Hugh and Phyllis in addition to numerous short conversations to clarify a particular point. Although Hugh has a scorn of celebrity-seeking and a wariness about vanity that verge on the pathological, he and Phyllis were graciousness itself in answering our questions and recalling past episodes, even when they expressed the utmost skepticism that the results would be either interesting or valuable. It is a blessing indeed that age has not laid its hand heavily on their memories; whenever separate documentation exists on a point covered in an interview, I have been startled at how accurate and complete their recall has been. Phyllis also agreed to read the manuscript in final draft.

I have also conducted many interviews with other relatives, friends, associates, and BYU personnel connected to Nibley projects. Audio cassettes and/or transcripts of all of these interviews are in my possession but will ultimately become part of an archive.

In expressing my profound gratitude to the family for their tolerance of and cooperation with this project, I should also explain to the reader that I have deliberately chosen to maintain my focus on Hugh rather than on the family for three reasons. First, from my position as a son-in-law, I have discovered that there are eight very different perspectives about what it was like to grow up in the Nibley family—each with a different mixture of pride and resentment. Even if it were possible to capture those perspectives, it would detract from the central focus of this book.

Second, I know that my brothers- and sisters-in-law grew up in a goldfish bowl where their last name was often seen as more important than their first names, making it a struggle for their individual identities to emerge in the shadow of the towering reputation of their father. Certainly Hugh never intended this. Nevertheless, school teachers often had unrealistic expectations simply because of the children's last name; family night was more often than not a devotional where crowds of BYU students would gather at the Nibley home to hear Hugh speak; and the children grew accustomed to hearing, as the first question from total strangers, "What was it like to be the son or daughter of Hugh Nibley?" While I have provided some brief background about each son and daughter, I wanted to allow them considerable privacy.

Third, I fully respect their right to tell their own stories about the family should they choose to do so. I do not presume to understand what they experienced and do not want to usurp the authority of their unique position from them. This being the case, while I have talked at great length with my brothers- and sisters-in-law about their experiences (family gatherings often focus on little else), I have included comments from them only where they focus on their father's life.

Nevertheless, to provide one perspective of what it was like to grow up in the Nibley family, I invited my wife to write the foreword to this book. Readers should be aware that hers is only one of eight perspectives; that as the youngest child, her experiences in the Nibley household were quite different from those of the oldest siblings; and that it should not be seen as any more authoritative than the others. I hope it does, however, help to balance the lack of family details contained in the book's narrative.

Having explained my reasons for reticence on the Nibley family life, I cannot refrain from adding that Hugh and Phyllis are doting parents who love and support their children. They are proud of their children's accomplishments, take their failures in stride, encourage independent thinking, and are supportive if not always happy when that independence leads to beliefs or attitudes that differ from their own. While I have come to appreciate how difficult it must have been to grow up in the Nibley home, from my perspective, having grown up in a more typical Utah Valley household, I am somewhat envious. While the name certainly brought unwanted attention, it also eased their entry into discussions and groups that others don't have. Hugh's scholarly obsession and local celebrity undoubtedly left the children without the type of father of more "typical" Mormon families, but it also gave them a house brimming with books, ideas, and conversation.

Even though Hugh may not have been as "present" as some fathers, especially given the long-overdue emphasis on hands-on fathering of our own generation, it is clear that he has greatly influenced his children's lives. Each knows and loves great works of literature (especially Shakespeare), has a love for the arts (especially drama), has a deep respect and love for science (especially astronomy), is politically engaged, and is an individualist who can stand up for his or her ideas and enjoys good conversation. Finally, the gospel was not only taught in their home, it was thought about deeply and it was lived. All in all, Hugh and Phyllis gave their children what any good parents should: a sense of self-worth, the knowledge and tools to become independent, and the support they needed to grow.

I should note that, while I have made relatively few alterations to the documents I quote from in this book, for ease of reading, I have standardized spelling, clarified punctuation where desirable, corrected typographical errors, and spelled out all abbreviations.

Finally, I do not claim to be objective. Not only do I believe that true objectivity is impossible for any writer, but I also know that it would be impossible for me. I freely admit that I love Hugh Nibley's writings, but even more so, I love the man. I revere him not only as the father of my wife and grandfather of my children, but as the father of my spiritual self. I have been deeply influenced by his words and his example. I do believe I have a fairly unique position from which to observe and comment on Hugh. As a family member, I have access to material and to the man that few have. Yet as an in-law, I have some distance that is unclouded by years of family issues. And while I cannot claim to be objective, I have tried to be balanced, showing the human side of a man who has become a legend. It is a perspective that I hope readers will also find illuminating.

This book would not have been possible without the support and encouragement of a multitude of generous people. First on the list are my wife and children. Throughout the entire project, and especially over the past year and a half, they have been fully supportive of my ability and the worth of this project. I am also grateful for the help and assistance of my brothers- and sisters-in-law—Paul, Christina, Tom, Michael, Alex, and Rebecca—who have shared insights, memories, letters, and encouragement.

I am grateful to the many people who have shared letters, stories, and papers, or helped in other ways. In particular, I express thanks to Reid Nibley, Barbara Nibley Richards, Richard Lloyd Anderson, Kevin Assef, Lola Atiya, Miriam Reitz Baer, David and Amelia Bahr, Elouise Bell, Gary James Bergera, Wendell Berry, Mary L. Bradford, Phil Bradford, the late Raymond E. Brown, S. Kent Brown, James H. Charlesworth, Kip Clark, Richard H. Cracroft, Steve Eccles, the late Eugene England, David Noel Freedman, John Gee, Gary Gillum, Marguerite Goldschmidt, Cyrus Gordon, William J. Hamblin, George B. Handley, Elder Marion D. Hanks, Elder Jeffrey R. Holland, Omar Kader, Edward L.

Kimball, Charles Knuth, Suzanne Evertsen Lundquist, Michael Lyon, Fergus MacLeod, Elder Neal A. Maxwell, Raymond Meldrum, Louis Midgley, Jacob Milgrom, Elder Russell M. Nelson, Jacob Neusner, Don Norton, Elder Dallin H. Oaks, Brent Orton, Donald Parry, Susan Petersen, Clayne Pope, D. Michael Quinn, Robert Redford, Marv Roberson, Julie Reynolds, JoAnn Sloan Rogers, Hugh Stocks, Laurie DiPadova Stocks, Brian H. Stuy, Gordon C. Thomasson, Jackie Thursby, Benjamin Urrutia, Sterling Van Wagenen, Kent Wallace, Pat Ward, Johnnie Belle Williams, Ted Wilson, Marian Robertson Wilson, William A. Wilson, Victoria Ann Witesman, and H. Curtis Wright.

The kind people at the Foundation for Ancient Research and Mormon Studies (FARMS) gave me generous financial and logistical support. Special thanks go to Brent Hall, Shane Heath, Stephen and Shirley Ricks, John W. Welch, Daniel Peterson, and Noel Reynolds. I am also indebted to the many librarians who have assisted me: The personnel at the Harold B. Lee Library, in particular Mark Smith and David Whittaker in the L. Tom Perry Special Collections Division of Archives and Manuscripts and Kristi Bell in the Folklore Archives; Ronald G. Watt at the LDS Church Archives; Stan Larson and the other helpful librarians at the University of Utah; Ann Buttars of the Merrill Library's Special Collections and Archives at Utah State University, and John A. Larson at the Oriental Institute Archives at the University of Chicago.

My publisher, Greg Kofford, gave me the financial assistance and encouragement without which this book would not have been possible at this time. Tom Kimball remained my friend while working with me on the initial, frustrating stages of writing. And my editor, Lavina Fielding Anderson, has saved me from much embarrassment, kept me honest, and provided support and encouragement above and beyond the call of duty.

Finally, I am deeply grateful for the trust and support I have received from Hugh and Phyllis Nibley. It would be a frightening thing to allow someone to go through your private papers and publish your life story. For the trust placed in me, I am deeply grateful. This book would have been impossible without their cooperation and support.

Any errors, misreadings, or misinterpretations are, of course, my own.

Foreword

by Zina Petersen

One thing I liked about Boyd Petersen when I met him was that he never asked me what it was like to grow up with Hugh Nibley as a father. But now, after eighteen years of marriage, I find myself answering that initially unasked question for a reading audience at his behest. I never could come up with a satisfying answer because . . . well, as opposed to what? Having had no other circumstance and not necessarily a choice in the matter, I can say I don't know what it was *not* like to grow up with Hugh Nibley as a father, but the flip side is enormous: where to start? In the first chapter of this tome, Boyd has already debunked most of the juiciest folk legends and rumors about Daddy, so I could try to paint a new picture. Would you believe that Hugh Nibley was a meddling, prying, intrusive father with an iron fist, obsessed with meticulously groomed landscaping and cat shows? No, me neither.

But off-the-cuff memory is neither tidy nor trustworthy; I've lived in the same house with the writing of this book and know what care has gone into verifying and documenting its history. It would be an insult to both my husband and my father to casually write a slipshod version of my own autobiography as a foreword. Instead, here are a dozen or so vignettes that *are* accurate, if undocumented. They come in no particular order and offer a glimpse, if not a good look, at the possible response to the impossible question.

Vignette #1. Thanksgiving table spread, blessing finished, food circulating clockwise until everyone has a helping of everything. Daddy says in a louder-than-conversational voice, "There are two kinds of people in this world . . ." He looks around at all of us and catches my eye. "Zina?" he prompts. I swallow a mouthful of food and pick up the game: "Those who divide people into two kinds of people in the world . . ." He smiles, "And those who sell yams!" he finishes. A good one.

Vignette #2. Spring sometime in the early seventies. Martha and I, about eight and six, are walking with Daddy past BYU's tennis courts on our way to the Richards P.E.

Building for a swim. The blossoms are out on the flowering plums, and a pretty copper light slants in from a late sunset. Daddy is half-humming, half-whistling a Chopin piano sonata; it's a fast movement, so I have to hustle a bit on my short legs to keep up with the pace it sets for his walk. He notices. "Here," he says, "take my heavily dimpled hand." When we walk back from the pool, tired and wet-haired, it is dark, but still warm. He gives me a piggyback ride home.

Vignette #3. Martha is in high school; I'm one grade away from it. A rare occasion when Daddy has answered a ringing telephone without saying "Oh, go away" as he raises the receiver to his ear. I overhear his side of the conversation. "Yes, this is Mr. Nibley. Yes, Martha is at Provo High School. She what? She missed what? Seminary?" He holds the phone an inch farther away from his mouth and calls to my mother: "Dear? Is Martha taking *seminary*? I told her *not* to take seminary. Great guns, why is she wasting her time in seminary?!" I don't hear the rest of the conversation. I also don't sign up for seminary.

Vignette #4. A "Family" Home Evening when I'm about twelve. Our little living room is crammed with college students, some of whom I know because they are friends of my older brothers and sisters, some of whom are friends of theirs, and friends of *theirs*. Marv Roberson sits closest to Daddy with a tape recorder going. Daddy is talking about the intersection of nature and super-nature; I am enthralled enough by the lesson this time not to resent the weekly takeover, but I still try to squirm out of having to say the closing prayer in front of all those strangers.

Vignette #5. It's Christmas, and there are all sorts of torn wrappings and bows and new books and other presents lying around the living room. Most of us are there, trying out new gadgets or reading funny bits out loud from joke books. Or talking, loudly—that level of "spirited" just below an intellectual argument which is so common in our house. I glance over through the happy chaos and see Daddy sitting in his favorite chair, the hose attachment to the new vacuum cleaner held up, one end to his mouth, one to his ear. He's saying something, a pleasantly sardonic smile curving just the corner of his lip. "What are you doing?" I ask him, but it's too noisy for him to hear me. I put down the wooden knot puzzle I'm working and move closer to him; it's still too noisy to hear. "Daddy," I say, loudly enough that one of the conversations near us quiets. Suddenly we can understand him. "Bottomless pit of wisdom," he is saying very quietly; "untapped oceans of knowledge, endless circ of unmitigated sagacity . . ." As we laugh, he lowers the hose from his mouth and announces straight-faced: "I'm being academic."

Vignette #6. A couple of groupies come to the house to gawk and worship. I'm in high school, old enough to be calling myself a "daughter of a false god." I think this is funny. I think if I told it to the groupies sitting at Daddy's knees they would not get it. I think I am lots cooler than they are, but it gives me an almost maternal concern for their cluelessness. At one point the conversation turns to politics. Before I can catch Daddy's eye and make desperate slashing motions across my throat, one groupie is saying, "Well, Brother Nibley, I bet you always show those liberal idiots a thing or two!" and my father calmly says "I'm the most liberal of all those idiots, of course." Groupie looks like he's just stepped on a gerbil. Maybe his own gerbil. He stammers. "I'm—I'm sure you're as liberal as the Lord, sir." I wince for him.

Vignette #7. My third child, Nathanael Hugh, is five days old. Daddy is ninety years old, and Mom is just out of the hospital where she received a pacemaker—I'm hardly expecting a visit from the grandparents. But Daddy comes over to our house anyway. He takes the baby gingerly, adoringly, then looks at me in alarm, "But he's so tiny!" he says. "Is he all right?" I remind him: "We all weighed nine or ten pounds. Nate is six pounds five ounces, so yes, for you he's tiny." Still Daddy looks a bit worried. A year later he watches Nate scooting around chewing new toys at his birthday party. "I'm *so* glad you named him Hugh," says Daddy. "He'll redeem the name; he's *so* much smarter than me!"

Vignette #8. At seventeen, I move out, take up residence a whole two blocks away, and begin my academic career at BYU as a fully-fledged on-my-own freshman. It's a good year, but spring term comes and my mother can't think of a really stellar reason for me to continue to pay rent when I have, in theory, a bedroom at home. Actually, as we kids have moved out, Daddy's research has taken over all the upstairs rooms of the house like expansionist Russia picking off weak Euroasian countries. I "have" a room, but he has to clear it out for me to use. Late one night in May, I do what I have been doing since September: I stay out most of the night talking to girlfriends. When I wander home at about 3:00 a.m., I find the front door locked. The light is on in the living room. Daddy is asleep on the couch, head drooping toward his chest. The rattle of my key in the lock wakes him, and he launches in—he'd been out looking for me, was terrified something was wrong. I've never been the object of so much direct anger from him, and I am stunned to realize how much he feels, how much he fears for the welfare of his kids. I apologize, crying, and try to give him a hug. This shocks him as much as his outburst shocked me. We both instantly try to revert to comfortably Victorian detached fondness, but now we both know.

Vignette #9. Two-year-old Natalie, the first grandchild, is visiting Utah with my sister Christina. At age nine, I think my niece is the cutest thing ever. Daddy takes me and "Nanny" to see the fish tanks in the basement of the Widtsoe Building. He walks slowly enough for Natalie to keep up—if she takes his heavily dimpled hand. There are trout and other fresh-water fish, then one tank with a gorgeously dramatic ugly creature in it—a poisonous rock fish. Daddy holds Natalie up to the tank. She can't see it at first—its camouflage is perfect—until it moves. My niece shrieks with delight and fear and buries her head in her grandpa's shoulder, then she pulls back a little and whispers, "That's one meeean gonna-get-you-Nanny fish!" That night as I pass my parents' bedroom on the way to my own, I look in and find Natalie burrowed between them in their double bed. Mom looks at me and whispers, "Nanny didn't want to think about the f-i-s-h." Natalie looks from one to the other of them, pats the covers over her tummy and sighs contentedly, "Nice and cozy." My parents chuckle and Daddy says, "Yes, it is nice and cozy."

Vignette #10. Years of *Potion Magique*, named for the potion in Asterix's Gaulois village that made the tiny hamlet invincible, even against Caesar's legions. Daddy concocts for himself a ghastly mixture of hot water, apple cider vinegar, brewer's yeast, honey, and things I didn't stick around to watch. He doesn't make it for himself any more, and I suspect (having been educated at a Catholic school) that the reason he quit was that his penance was up. I don't know what he thought it did for him, but I have a clear olfactory memory of the swilly stuff. At least he never made any of us taste it. It leads seamlessly into memories of Asterix himself, of course. Daddy bought the big colorful French comics at BYU's bookstore and read them to Martha and me as bedtime stories. He would point to the words and illustration details and talk about them; not just the story plots and the history, but also language, explaining French pronunciation and how much more regular the spelling is in Latin languages that are conservative, compared to English, which, since it borrows words from so many sources, has an irregular spelling system. When I got to first grade, I couldn't read very well, but I sure could misspell.

Vignette #11. Daddy isn't visible in this one, but he is so very present. My first day of sixth grade, the teacher passes out tags to tape to our desks. "Everyone, please put your name on these, big enough that I can read it from the front of the room." I raise my hand. "Can I write mine in Egyptian?" I probably should have been glared at more often as a child.

Vignette #12. Not really a vignette so much as a well-blended series of memories. The low-tech stereo and all the stacks of records. With no TV until I was in eighth grade, any entertainment that didn't involve conversation, toddler-watching, or the radio probably came from the record player. My parents bought books and records as gifts, and some of my best summer and sick days were spent listening to records. These were by no means all classical music, though that is what was on most often when Daddy was home; and if it was a particularly jaunty piece, he would dance a quirky little jig as he listened. I was still a preschooler one year when, for Christmas or my birthday, he gave me a lengthy "Folk Tales for Young People" series. I had folk stories from Africa, from the British Isles, from Native American tribes, from Appalachia and the Great Smoky Mountains. Long before I could read, I could recite. I memorized the stories (and their accented delivery) as unconsciously as I memorized the easy rhymes and lovely neologisms of recorded Dr. Seuss books, or as I memorized the early radical routines of the Smothers Brothers, the Chad Mitchell Trio (Daddy's favorite of theirs was their harsh slam "The John Birch Society"), the Three D's, and the stand-up comedy of Bill Cosby. It was from records Daddy loved that I first noticed the difference between British and American comedy, because I knew all those Bill Cosby records and compared them to all three of Flanders and Swan's collections. Though I have been unsuccessful in giving the same experience to my children (and have thus probably saved them from being glared at) I would not change a second of that listening time for all the sitcom reruns ever shown.

Vignette #13. This one is very specific. I am tiny, too small to climb up onto the swing. Daddy picks me up and settles me on the seat. The swing is enormous, hanging from a branch of a centenarian sycamore tree. He gives me a push and the world drops. With each push, I vault higher until the tips of my red buckle shoes brush leaves. It's exhilarating, giddy, terrifying. Safe? crosses my mind, and I look up and see the thick ropes with their unbudgeable knots around the massive branch and I look down and see my unbudgeable father. Safe. As long as I hang on.

I was about sixteen when I first studied Freud. I decided I disagreed with him. Sixteen-year-olds disagree with almost everything, because they get along with almost no one and of course no one ever ever ever understands them. Even though I was only barely coming to realize that people you disagree with are not necessarily wrong, crazy, or stupid, I thought hard about that part where Freud explains religion by "demonstrating" how someone's "God" is nothing but a projected, amplified, exaggerated version of her or his earthly father. Hmm, I thought philosophically to myself; Freud might have a bit of a point there, even though he's wrong. My "God" is very, very, very, very smart, and funny, and emotionally distant. Sounds like the Huge Niblet himself, and—great Scott—that won't do! Daddy would hate it if he found out I'd cast my god in his image; it would horrify him. Let alone what it was doing to poor God. So I quit it. In my adolescent pensiveness, I systematically, consciously examined the traits of my father on earth and my Father in Heaven that I was convoluting and prayed for help in quitting it. My relationships with *both* those guys got so much better! I began to understand something Daddy had tried to teach—that the gospel of Jesus Christ is big enough for the truth, even truth people can find scary or threatening, even truth that is found in places no one wants to look for it. Growing up with Hugh Nibley as a father, I learned this: the world, with all its exhilaration, giddiness, and danger, is actually pretty safe, as long as you are on a course that has strong ropes and sturdy knots and an unmovable, unshakable faith pushing you higher. Then all you have to do is hang on tight.

Introduction

The Man and the Legend

Once Satan appeared to Hugh Nibley. He told Hugh that he and his forces were going to close down the temple in Manti, Utah, and that there was nothing that Hugh could do about it. Hugh responded that indeed something would be done, and so, teaming up with the Three Nephites (and, according to another version my informant heard, the 2000 stripling warriors from the Book of Mormon), he went to the doors of the Manti Temple, and there held back the forces of evil and allowed the temple to operate undisturbed.[1]

This story is obviously not true. While I have heard speculation that Hugh Nibley himself is one of the Three Nephites (how else could someone know so much?) and have been unable to determine the truthfulness of that claim, I know that the story of Hugh thwarting Satan's plans to close the temple is false. It was transferred to the body of Hugh Nibley lore from an experience of Apostle Marriner Merrill, first president of the Logan Temple (serving from 1884 to 1906). According to Apostle Rudger Clawson, Elder Merrill noticed a group of strangers arrive at the temple, some walking and some on horseback. One man came in, and Apostle Merrill asked him who he was and what he wanted. The person replied that he was Satan and he demanded that Merrill shut down the temple—that he did not like what was going on there. Merrill commanded him to leave. Satan reluctantly obeyed but promised that he and his followers would whisper into everyone's ear "persuading them not to come to the temple." As a result attendance fell off dramatically for a long time after that experience.[2] I suspect that this tale has entered

---

[1] Jeff Hovenier, Interviewed by Boyd Petersen, 21 April 1990. I read an earlier version of this chapter, originally titled "Truth Is Stranger than Folklore: Hugh Nibley, the Man and the Folk Legend," at the Annual Conference of the Folklore Society of Utah, 18 October 1997.

[2] Quoted in N. B. Lundwall, *Temples of the Most High* (Salt Lake City: Bookcraft, 1947): 107-8, and Joseph Heinerman, *Temple Manifestations* (Manti, UT: Mountain Valley, 1974), 83.

the Nibley folklore cycle because Hugh has been a chief explicator of temple rituals and a strong proponent of temple work.

Hugh Nibley has achieved the distinguished status within the Mormon community of becoming a folk legend while he is still alive. Latter-day Saints, especially those who have attended BYU, love telling stories about Hugh as much or perhaps more than reading his books.[3] These narratives are shaped in the telling to accommodate the needs of the audience, and the fact that Hugh Nibley stories *are* told and the *ways* in which they are told really say more about the LDS religious community than about Hugh Nibley.

Many of the stories are, like the story of Hugh defending the temple from the forces of Satan, patently false. However, I have had the unique opportunity to compare the folklore told about Hugh with the documented facts of his life and have found that it is not always easy to disentangle the embroidery of folklore from the core of biographical fact. Folklore is shaped, as Richard Dorson has argued, in two significant ways: "by variant tellings of a more or less verifiable incident, and by absorption of wandering tales that get attached to likely figures."[4] But interestingly, I have discovered that the origins of the "borrowed" narratives are much slipperier than I had assumed. Often, I have discovered there are factual, historical elements behind these borrowed tales, something I hadn't expected. This discovery has made me cautious about concluding that a story is false simply because it is also told about another individual.

For example, one popular story recounts that, while Hugh was serving his mission in Germany, his mission president instructed him to tell the people as he preached that they must repent or be destroyed by fire. Only a few years later during World War II, many German cities were destroyed by Allied firebombings with great loss of civilian life.[5] Hugh did, in fact, serve his mission in Germany and returned to Germany after the war. However, I immediately recognized this narrative as as a popular folktale about Mormon missionaries in general. William A. Wilson's exposition points out that the elders, after being mistreated and mocked by the people in a particular village, are "forced to bring the Lord in to fight the battle for them" by shaking the dust from their feet and pronouncing a curse on the townsfolk.[6] The Lord validates these missionaries' actions by destroying the city. Wilson then gave numerous examples: "Towns are destroyed in South America by wind, in Chile by floods, in Costa Rica by a volcano, in Mexico by an earthquake, in Japan by a tidal wave, in Taiwan and Sweden by fire. In South Africa a town's mining industry fails, in Colorado a town's land becomes infertile, and in Germany a town's fishing industry folds." Wilson also notes that in Norway a city is destroyed by German shelling during World War II.[7]

---

[3]In fact, the stories are so plentiful that one folklorist was able to write an entire thesis about the Hugh Nibley folklore told by BYU professors. See Jane D. Brady, "The Brigham Young University Folklore of Hugh Winder Nibley: Gifted Scholar, Eccentric Professor and Latter-day Saint Spiritual Guide" (M.A. thesis, Brigham Young University, 1996).

[4]Richard M. Dorson, "J. Golden Kimball: Apostle and Folk Hero," review of Thomas E. Cheney's *The Golden Legacy*, *Dialogue: A Journal of Mormon Thought* 8 (Autumn/Winter 1973): 166.

[5]Benjamin Urrutia, Letter to Boyd Petersen, 15 February 1990.

[6]William A. Wilson, "On Being Human: The Folklore of Mormon Missionaries," *Sunstone* 7 (January/February 1982): 32-40.

[7]Ibid., 39.

The resemblance between Wilson's unrepentant Norwegian city and Hugh's German cities, both destroyed by World War II military activities, suggests that the Hugh Nibley tale had been borrowed from the larger cycle of missionary lore. But was it? I discovered the following passage in Hugh's missionary journal: "Tracting in Bruchsal. These people really have had a chance. These many testy attempts to dismiss the subject entirely are plainly the workings of a guilty conscience."[8] I also discovered a letter Hugh wrote to a friend immediately following World War II: "Having visited all the scenes of my missionary labors by jeep, and beheld the painfully literal justifications of the warning word to these foolish people 17 years ago, I speak with confidence of calamities to come. Everything has turned out exactly as I had imagined, so there is no reason to suppose that it won't continue to do so."[9]

The final shattering of my assumption that I could tell the difference between Hugh Nibley fact and folklore came when I interviewed him in 1997, and he described himself as a very fiery missionary: "I was hotter than a firecracker in those days; I was preaching destruction and fire from heaven."[10] When Apostle Melvin J. Ballard set him apart for his mission, he admonished Hugh to warn the German people that, unless they repent, "they will be destroyed by fire from heaven"[11] as prophesied in the scriptures (e.g., D&C 63:34). On one occasion, Hugh said, he stopped at a butcher shop and spoke with the butcher's wife. When he prophesied of fiery destruction to come, the woman got so angry that she chased Hugh away with a meat cleaver. In 1946 when Hugh drove through his former mission area, in one town he came upon a door frame standing alone, the only portion of the house to survive RAF firebombs. He realized that it was the very butcher shop where the woman had threatened him.

Granted, important differences between the historical event and the folklore version remain. There is no evidence, for instance, that Hugh actually cursed any city or house during his mission, nor did he invoke "the Lord to fight his battles for him." Nevertheless, the truth behind the lore is not too far removed: Hugh was instructed by an apostle to warn the people of the wrath to come; he did so in the language of the scriptures (probably more zealously than the average missionary); he was in fact threatened by the butcher's wife; and he later discovered that her house was destroyed by fire "from heaven"—air raids—during the war. Rather than being a simple borrowing, as I first thought, the factual story has been recast using the framework of the more common missionary folktale.

This same phenomenon can be viewed in a few of the variants on the frequently told Hugh Nibley courtship story. (See chap. 15.) The tale has many versions, but the true story is every bit as amazing as the folklore. Following his military service, Hugh worked briefly at the *Improvement Era* where Elder John A. Widtsoe, then the editor, encouraged Hugh to apply for a faculty position at Brigham Young University and recommended him to the president. In May 1946, Hugh accepted a position as assistant pro-

---

[8]Hugh Nibley, Journal, 25 March 1929.
[9]Hugh Nibley, Letter to Paul Springer, late summer 1946. See chap. 13.
[10]Hugh Nibley, Interviewed by Boyd Petersen, 9 October 1997.
[11]Hugh W. Nibley, *Teachings of the Book of Mormon, Semester 3*, transcripts of lectures presented to an Honors Book of Mormon Class at Brigham Young University, 1989-90, 123. I later discovered that Hugh related the whole tale to this class.

fessor of history and religion, with his teaching duties to begin that fall at BYU. Widtsoe and BYU's administrators both expressed concern that Hugh was a thirty-six-year-old bachelor, a certified menace to society. Hugh responded guilelessly that if Widtsoe worked it out with the Lord, "I would marry the first girl I met at BYU."[12]

On 25 May 1946, just two days after he accepted BYU's offer, Hugh walked into the housing office. The almost-twenty-year-old receptionist, Phyllis Draper, was the first woman he met there. On the basis of that encounter, Hugh decided that he would marry her, courted her over the summer, and married her on 18 September 1946.

Most of the folk versions of Hugh Nibley's courtship are fairly faithful to the truth except for exaggerating the speed of the courtship, and most emphasize that Hugh made his marriage a matter of obedience to apostolic instruction rather than following more conventional feelings of romance. Two of the variants, however, show direct borrowing from other sources. In one, Hugh reportedly fasted for three days, then patiently waited in Rock Canyon. Soon the woman whom the Lord intended for Hugh walked up the canyon.[13] This narrative borrows heavily from Old Testament narratives in which a patriarch ascends a mountain to meet with God and obtain divine direction and others where a chosen prophet meets the woman who has been divinely selected for him, usually by a well. In a second version, "an angel came to him and told him to marry or he would cut off his head."[14] This story is borrowed from Joseph Smith's report that he entered polygamy only after an angel with a drawn sword threatened him if he continued to delay.[15] Obviously, the Mormon folk are taking the essential elements of the true Hugh Nibley courtship story, admittedly already unconventional, and combining them with elements from other sources. The purpose appears to be to highlight and accentuate the ideals of obedience to divine command.

In other narratives, the fact remains quite similar to the folklore. For example, one story relates how Hugh took his colleague and former Egyptian teacher Klaus Baer hiking in Utah's red rock country. At one point, they stopped and carved into the sandstone Egyptian characters that read, "Plate #1—I, Nephi, having been born of goodly parents . . ."[16] Although this story sounds wildly apocryphal, Hugh himself confirms its essential truthfulness in a letter of condolence to Baer's widow soon after Klaus's death:

> Once as we hiked through the depths of Chimney Rock Canyon he would stop from time to time to scratch into the red walls such Egyptian graffiti as are found left by travellers and pilgrims at Egyptian tombs or shrines, e.g., "NN visited this place and he found it to be like heaven."[17]

---

[12] Todd F. Maynes, "Nibleys: Pianist, Scholar, Brilliant But Different," (BYU) *Daily Universe*, 1 November 1982, 7.

[13] Collected by Liliane Zmolek in 1973, L. Tom Perry Special Collections, William A. Wilson Folklore Archives, FA4 3.5.2 L (hereafter cited as Folklore Archives by narrative number).

[14] Gerald Smith, e-mail to Boyd Petersen, 20 January 1994.

[15] The angel/sword story is reported in Zina Diantha Huntington Jacobs Smith Young, 23 December 1894, *Collected Discourses*, edited by Brian Stuy (Woodland Hills, UT: BHS Publishing, 1992), 5:3132; History of Joseph Lee Robinson, 13, typescript, Utah State Historical Society, Salt Lake City; Benjamin H. Johnson, *My Life's Review* (Independence, MO: Zion's Printing, 1947): 95-96; Mary Elizabeth Rollins Lightner, 1905 Address, 12, typescript, Perry Archives.

[16] Collected by John Baird, 1973, Wilson Folklore Archives, FA5 4.14.1.3.1.

[17] Hugh Nibley, Letter to Miriam Reitz Baer, June 1987.

The main difference between the folktale and the fact is that Baer did not carve a Mormon text on the stone.[18]

In other folktales, the relationship between truth and folklore is much more difficult to untangle. A story that has me somewhat baffled is the tale about Hugh parachuting behind enemy lines during World War II:

> During World War II at some point, Hugh Nibley was to parachute into Greece for some reason, you know, along with his [Military Intelligence] responsibilities or whatever. And as he was parachuting into Greece, he realized that there were people on the ground who could see him and could shoot at him and who were, at least, it appeared that they were assuming that he was a bad guy instead of a good guy. He didn't know how to indicate to them that he was a good guy instead of a bad guy since he didn't speak any modern Greek. So what he did at least this is the way the story goes was that the only Greek he knew was ancient Greek and it was the Iliad or the Odyssey. And so, to convince them that he was a good guy, he started shouting out, as loud as he could in ancient Greek, either the Iliad or the Odyssey to convince them that he was a good guy and not a bad guy. And they subsequently did not shoot at him and he was able to land successfully and carry out his mission.[19]

While this story is false in a very significant way, Hugh never parachuted into Greece, one element of it is accurate. Hugh did visit Greece after his mission, between November 1929 and early 1930, and was delighted that he could communicate effectively with at least some Greeks on the basis of his skill in classical Greek. While this story is not nearly as exciting as the folktale, it does seem to be the basis for the World War II story. However, I am not aware of a story involving another person from which the World War II version may have been borrowed.

It is even more difficult to separate fact from fiction in the many absent-minded professor stories told about Hugh. Richard Dorson has correctly pointed out that "every college and university in the land possesses some odd faculty member whose behavior makes legends,"[20] and Hugh Nibley has been appointed to that role for BYU. He is the quintessential absent-minded professor, knowing far too much but not being able to remember the mundane, like where he parked the car. As a result, it is quite easy to find Hugh Nibley stories that are also told about absent-minded or eccentric professors throughout the country. In his essay "The Folklore of Academe," Barre Toelken relates a number of these professorial tales, some of which have been attributed to Hugh Nibley. In one such story, the professor "concluded a mid-campus conversation with a student by asking 'Which way was I going when we stopped?' and on being told, answered, 'Oh,

---

[18]Hugh later confirmed that Baer did not engrave the "I, Nephi" text, but rather the traditional Egyptian text to which he refers in his letter to Baer's widow. Hugh Nibley, Interviewed by Zina Petersen, 26 January 2002.

[19]Jeff Hovenier, Interviewed by Boyd Petersen, 21 April 1990. Eric Eliason, e-mail to Boyd Petersen, 27 January 1994, tells a condensed version of the same narrative.

[20]Richard A. Dorson, *American Folklore* (Chicago: University of Chicago Press, 1959), 255.

[21]Jan Harold Brunvand, *The Study of American Folklore: An Introduction* (New York: Norton, 1968), Appendix, 321. Rick Skousen collected the Nibley version of this tale, 1989, Wilson Folklore Archives, FA5 4.14.1.8.1.

then I have eaten lunch.'"[21] In another, the professor writes notes on the board with one hand and erases them with the other.[22] (In the Hugh Nibley version of this tale, he uses his shirt or suit sleeve to erase the board.)

Many of these stories not only emphasize Hugh's absent-mindedness but also his amazing breadth of knowledge, which he sometimes assumes everyone shares. In one story, a student approaches Hugh after a lecture to ask him a question. Hugh recommends a book to him and sends him off to the library. It turns out that the book is not in the library, so the student sends for it through inter-library loan. Finally the book arrives and the student discovers that it is in German, and has not been translated. So he goes back to Hugh and tells him that he got the book "but I don't understand it; it's in German." Hugh replies, "So what? It's a small book."[23] In another tale, Hugh supposedly forgets what language to lecture in and "starts going off" in a "dead language not realizing it."[24]

Another story that emphasizes his absent-mindedness tells about how Hugh took one of his children, a baby at the time, with him to the grocery store. He pushed the baby around the store, went through the check stand, and loaded the groceries into the car. When he got home with the groceries, he realized he had left the baby at the store.[25] Although Hugh never left a baby at the grocery store, Phyllis does remember that she and Hugh once made an excursion to the grocery store with six children in tow. They missed six-year-old Michael in the final head count and accidentally left him behind at the store, but quickly recognized and rectified their mistake. Still, this experience may be the source of the Nibley folktale.

Many of these absentminded professor stories may have been borrowed from the larger tradition of academic folklore; however, many contain a genuine basis in fact. Hugh has actually been caught wearing mismatched shoes or socks. And he has, in fact, walked home on numerous occasions, leaving his car where he parked it. Other stories are impossible to confirm; however, they are consistent with Hugh's personality and, hence, quite plausible.

Hugh himself is not certain about some stories. According to one tale about his mission, a small congregation in Germany took up a collection to buy a new coat for one of the elders. Believing that, since the elder needed a new coat, he probably could also use a new pair of shoes, Hugh chipped in generously, only to discover later that the missionary in need was himself.[26] Certainly, this story seems probable. Hugh's first concern in dress has always been practicality, not fashion. Hugh buys most of his clothes at thrift stores and has frequently worn jogging shoes with his standard J.C. Penney, circa 1945 suits. However, when I asked Hugh about this story, he couldn't say whether it happened or not. "It could be true," he admitted. "It was a long time ago and that sort of thing happened."[27]

---

[22]Brunvand, The Study of American Folklore, 323.

[23]Johnna Benson Cornett, Interviewed by Boyd Petersen, 30 June 1992. Eric Eliason, e-mail to Boyd Petersen, 27 January 1994, relates a similar story about a Greek book; when the student approaches Hugh, he replies, "Don't be silly; everyone knows Greek."

[24]Cornett, Interview, 30 June 1992.

[25]Collected by Susan Madsen, 1980, Wilson Folklore Archives, FA1 576.

[26]Collected by Sondra Jones, 1971, Wilson Folklore Archives, FA1 286.

[27]Hugh Nibley, Interviewed by Boyd Petersen, 9 October 1997.

Perhaps Hugh had an ulterior motive behind his dress standards. Gene England relates walking across campus one day with Hugh "in his mismatched socks and his old sport coat and his crumpled hat." Hugh glanced at the preppily dressed Gene "with this sly grin and said, 'They'll never make me department chairman!'"[28]

Hugh is also known for his witty statements and outrageous comments, many of which have ended up in the cycle of folktales about him. For instance, Hugh reportedly once debated another BYU faculty member who, trying to butter him up, stated, "We, at BYU, lean on every word you say," to which Hugh allegedly retorted, "If you do, you're a damn fool."[29] In another example, Hugh is said to have told a class, "Why, I'd rather have a live cobra in my living room than a television."[30] I'm inclined to believe that these remarks are authentic, especially when we consider that the most commonly repeated remark Hugh ever made is authentic and has changed little in various restatements in the folklore cycle. Giving the opening prayer at the 1960 BYU convocation, Hugh stated: "We have met here today clothed in the black robes of a false priesthood . . ." Hugh explained this invocation twenty three years later when he was awarded an honorary doctorate and delivered the stirring address, "Leaders to Managers: The Fatal Shift." (See chap. 23.)[31]

Legends about Hugh Nibley's eccentric behavior even spill over onto his own front yard. I have heard two folktales about Hugh's lawn. According to both stories, Hugh didn't mow his lawn for a long time, and its unkempt appearance began to irritate his neighbors. According to one account, Hugh buys a goat, "stakes him to the center of his lawn, and lets the goat take care of keeping his grass short."[32] In another, Hugh simply pours gasoline over his lawn and sets fire to it.[33] Both of these tales are false but are based on an authentic Hugh Nibley characteristic: Hugh doesn't think of keeping up his yard as a virtue. In one letter he wrote, "I have not the slightest intention of keeping up the yard in the conventional sense: it looks good to me and I am the guy it is supposed to please."[34]

However, Hugh's respect for the environment is a factor in his apparently eccentric behavior; he dislikes the idea of trimming or cutting down any living thing. His early years in the lush green of Oregon and his concern about his grandfather's timber harvesting policies probably helped to etch this attitude into his psyche. (See chap. 5.) Thus,

---

[28] Eugene England, Interviewed by Boyd Petersen, 9 April 1990.

[29] Alan Witt, Conversation with Boyd Petersen, 1984.

[30] Marilyn Lindsay, Interviewed by Boyd Petersen, Summer 1989, Benjamin Urrutia, Letter to Boyd Petersen, 15 February 1990, tells the same story but says the snake was a python.

[31] Hugh Nibley, "Leaders to Managers: The Fatal Shift," *Brother Brigham Challenges the Saints*, edited Don E. Norton and Shirley S. Ricks, Vol. 13 in *The Collected Works of Hugh Nibley* (Salt Lake City: Deseret Books/FARMS, 1994), 491.

[32] Collected by Kristi Bell, 1977, Wilson Folklore Archives, FA5 4.14.1.6.1.

[33] Michael Fishbach, Conversation with Boyd Petersen, summer 1985.

[34] Hugh Nibley, letter to Agnes Sloan Nibley, 28 April 1950. Tom Nibley, the third of Hugh's and Phyllis's children, has reluctantly admitted to having started a small lawn fire when he was about eight. Perhaps a neighbor saw the smoke and a new folktale was born. The lawn suffered additional damage when newly sustained LDS Church President Spencer W. Kimball encouraged members to plant gardens. According to Phyllis, Hugh immediately went out and dug up a plot of the lawn beside their house; but since he knew nothing about gardening "and never did anything with it, it only ruined the lawn on the side of the house." But he so wanted to obey the prophet that he gave it a good, if short-lived and unsuccessful try. Phyllis Nibley, conversation with Boyd Petersen, 8 April 2002.

the tale about Hugh pouring gasoline on his lawn is not only untrue, it is inconsistent. It emphasizes Hugh's unkempt yard, but doesn't recognize his respect for nature.

Another story relates how Hugh was studying in his office late one evening when a pipe broke in the nearby rest room, causing a minor flood. Warned of the encroaching water, Hugh gathered up the books and notecards which were arranged in tidy stacks on the floor, returned to his chair, put his feet on his desk and continued reading.[35] Again, I have no idea whether this story is true, but it is consistent with Hugh's obsession with learning. He routinely took a book to most faculty meetings before his retirement and still takes one to family functions and sacrament meetings. Furthermore, his ability to concentrate during the most chaotic disruptions is legendary and not overstated. One story that is almost too frightening to be true is that Hugh would prop a book up on the steering wheel while he made the half-hour commute between his home in Glendale and UCLA.[36] It turns out that this story is true—confirmed by two of his brothers.[37]

While looking at the truth behind the folklore can be fun, folklore ultimately tells us more about the community in which it is told than it does about the subject of that lore. And despite the parallels with Hugh's life, this is surely true of the Hugh Nibley folklore. As William Wilson states:

> The bulk of Mormon folklore functions to persuade church members that [their] beliefs are valid and that individuals must devote themselves valiantly to the cause, indeed, may suffer dire consequences if they fail to do so. In brief, this folklore falls into two broad categories: lore that shows how God protects the church in its battle with the world, and lore, remarkably like that of the early Puritans, that shows how God brings about conformity to church teachings by intervening directly in the lives of church members.[38]

Much of the folklore told about Hugh Nibley certainly falls into these categories. It validates the faith and promotes conformity. Some of this Nibley folklore functions like the broader folklore told about academics in general. It helps to compensate for the fact that ordinary mortals are not as brilliant as the professors because the professors lack competency in important life skills that ordinary people take for granted.

However, the other side of the coin is the esteem in which Nibley is held. Mormon culture obviously needed someone who stood for a combination of pure intellect and pure spirituality—"pure" meaning untainted by commercial exploitation, aca-

---

[35] Collected by John Baird, 1973, Wilson Folklore Archives, FA5 4.14.1.4.1. See also Hal Knight, "Behind the Legend, There's a Man," *Deseret News*, 1 September 1976, B-1+. A similar story, collected by Liliane Zmolek, 1973, Wilson Folklore Archives, FA4 3.5.0, relates how a janitor was repairing a leaky pipe in the library at night. Because Hugh was the only other person in the library, he asked Hugh to hold the flashlight for him but found it difficult to repair the pipe because Hugh would get absorbed in the book he was reading and forget to aim the flashlight.

[36] Arnold J. Irvine, "Hugh Nibley: Always Studying, Always Learning, Always on the Go," *Utah Magazine* (weekly insert in *Deseret News*) 15 April 1984, 4.

[37] Sloan Nibley, "Faith of an Observer," 538, compilation of interviews, ca. 1983-84 for a video documentary of the same name aired in 1985, photocopy of typescript in my possession, pagination added; Reid Nibley, ibid., 478-79.

[38] William A. Wilson, "Mormon Folklore," in *Handbook of American Folklore*, edited by Richard M. Dorson (Bloomington: Indiana University Press, 1983), 157.

demic politics, groupieism, or trying to build a following. Hugh not only fills that role but actually *is* that person. It's not a mask. It's not a collusion between a performer and his public. Hugh genuinely is that hero. This book is an effort to preserve the truth that lurks below these stories and to preserve the status of this hero in our culture.

Charles W. Nibley, ca. 1925.

Courtesy Nibley Family Photograph Collection,
Special Collections and Archives, Merrill Library, Utah State University.

Chapter 1

A Scottish Heritage, 1810-1930

In November or early December 1931, Hugh Nibley came to Salt Lake City to visit his ailing grandfather. Charles W. Nibley, who was living in his suite on the seventh floor of the Hotel Utah, was bedfast with a severe bladder infection. Hugh's grandfather had been the Presiding Bishop of the Church, second counselor to President Grant, and a very successful businessman. Now he was eighty-two years old and only days away from death. Hugh was very close to his grandfather; and Charles, who loved Hugh dearly, had always taken a keen interest in his grandson's intellectual development.

Hugh, recalling that last conversation with his grandfather, remembered that the frail old man advised Hugh to stay out of business, then reflected with some grief on some of the actions he had felt compelled to take as a businessman. "He did what he had to do to help people out as much as he could," Hugh remembers his grandfather saying, "but sometimes he had to cut corners. . . . In his business you had secrets and you played tricks and all sorts of things." At one point in that final conversation, Charles turned his head and looked at the Angel Moroni atop the temple, then turned back to his grandson and commented, "You see that window there? If an angel were to come through the door I would jump right through that window."[1] Soon thereafter, pneumonia set in and Charles died on 11 December. But Hugh never forgot that last conversation and the ambiguous legacy of his grandfather.

Charles W. Nibley was born in Scotland where life was bleak for his parents and their neighbors. They worked in Scotland's coal mines, supporting the burgeoning Industrial Revolution. It was a grindingly cruel existence. Most of these working families lived in one-room stone huts built by the government. Typically, they were about fourteen feet long and twelve feet wide with a thatch or straw roof, stone walls,

---

[1] Hugh Nibley, "Remarks about Charles W. Nibley on the Occasion of the Celebration of his 150th birthday, 5 February 1999," transcript, 10.

and dirt floors. Workers usually spent twelve-hour days in the mines, without scheduled breaks even for lunch. Often they would not see the daylight except on Sundays or an infrequent holiday. Both boys and girls were put to labor, some as early as age four, but routinely by age seven or eight. The conditions of both the work and the mines themselves often left the workers with crippling disabilities and dire illnesses.[2] Hugh remembers his grandfather saying that the family "would come home at night so utterly exhausted from working in the mines, you'd just wipe the soot and sweat off your face and flop down on the rags and pass out."[3]

Charles's parents, James and Jean Nibley, had qualities of character that helped the family endure these hardships. According to Charles's reminiscences, James Nibley was born in Bonnyrig, Scotland, just outside of Edinburgh in June 1810 but never knew the exact day of his birth. The family had been farmers but, during the Industrial Revolution, drifted into coal mining. James was tall but walked with "a certain stoop or bend from the lower part of the back" which his son Charles attributed to his work in the coal mines. His hair was curly and brown, his nose prominent, his cheek bones high, and his eyes "pure blue." Labeling his father "a plodder," Charles also described James as being "content with little and never aspir[ing] to have much or to be much of anything—a quiet, God-fearing, hard working, inoffensive man." Undoubtedly what helped James survive was his sense of humor. He had a "dry Scotch wit, keen and incisive, almost sarcastic at times," and enough drive to teach himself to read and write even though he never had any formal education.[4]

He also had great determination. Only one trait about James which "could be condemned," according to Charles, was his indulgence in smoking an old clay pipe. But one day, long after the family had joined the Mormon Church and moved to Utah, his wife commented, "I have no seen you smoking, what have you din wi' your pipe?" James replied, "I've stoppet." "For how long?" she inquired. "Some months past," he stated laconically. But James kept the pipe on the mantlepiece throughout the rest of his life as if to say, "I will show you which is master, you or I."[5]

On 16 March 1836 when he was twenty-five, James married twenty-year-old Jean Wilson from the neighboring village of Musseburgh. "Life was a serious thing with her," described Charles, "an almost desperate thing, in which she had no time for levity or play, but only for work and for prayers and other religious activities." Perhaps some of this relentless focus came from Jean's childhood, spent in the mines carrying coal back from the mining face to the collection point in a large basket on her back. She learned to work before she learned to play, and she was determined to make life better for her family. She was "all energy and push and never seemed to tire of working and scheming to get on in the world," Charles noted.[6] James's wit coupled with Jean's grit helped the family not only to survive the harsh life in Scotland but to seek a better life with a new religion in the new world.

---

[2]Michael Elvin Christensen, "The Making of a Leader: A Biography of Charles W. Nibley to 1890" (Ph.D. diss., University of Utah, 1978), 9-11.

[3]Hugh Nibley, "Remarks about Charles W. Nibley," 3.

[4]Charles W. Nibley, *Reminiscences* (Salt Lake City: Stevens and Wallis, 1934), 5-6.

[5]Ibid., 4-5.

[6]Ibid., 7-8.

By 1844, the Nibleys had three children—Mary, James Jr., and Margaret—and a new religion.[7] Mormon elders visited the town that spring and preached on the village green near the Nibley house. Jean listened to the sermon of Elder Henry McEwan and "drank it all in as though it were living water which was springing up unto everlasting life."[8] She had been brought up Presbyterian, then joined the Baptists, and later still the Congregational Society, but always felt unsatisfied. After hearing this Mormon sermon, she immediately asked for baptism. Elder McEwan cautiously asked her to read some tracts and pray about them. If she still wanted to be baptized, he would perform the ordinance when he came back the following week. Jean, disappointed, took the tracts home and began reading them. She was anxious to be baptized but also wanted James to become a member with her; however, she was afraid of triggering his opposition if she approached the subject directly. James was very stubborn, and had, as his son later stated, "the Scotch faculty of not being able to change his mind."[9] So Jean read the tracts to James night after night when he returned from the mines. After several days, she cautiously asked James his opinion. She was surprised and pleased when James replied, "Aye, but it is true." On the following Sunday when Elder McEwen returned, 28 April 1844, he baptized both. The couple remained the only converts to Mormonism in the counties of Edinburgh and Haddington for the next two months. But by the end of 1844, there were twenty-five members in the area.[10]

One year later, James's and Jean's next son, Henry, was born on 8 July 1845. He lived only six years. By that time, James was president of the small branch, its meetings held in their house. Another son, Charles Wilson Nibley, was born on 5 February 1849. He was so frail and sickly that, by the time he was two, Jean had sewn his burial clothes.[11] But Charles pulled through, despite the family's "frugal circumstances"—a euphemism for acute poverty. Oatmeal porridge with a little sour milk was their main source of nourishment; on Sundays they would occasionally get a little meat.[12]

In the spring of 1855, when Charles was six, his family boarded the American ship *Dreadnought* bound for the New World. At that point, the family numbered eight: forty-three-year-old James, thirty-eight-year-old Jean, seventeen-year-old Mary, fourteen-year-old James Jr., twelve-year-old Margaret, six-year-old Charles, two-year-old Henry Wilson, and newborn Euphemia. Jean Wilson Nibley's sister and her brother-in-law had written encouraging news of abundant jobs and high wages in the woolen and cotton mills of Rhode Island. Twenty-eight days later, the family arrived in New York, took a train for Providence, and settled in Greenville, Rhode Island. James and the three oldest children began working in the mills, and Jean "frugally, almost stingily," saved every available penny. By age nine, Charles was also working at the woolen mill. The family lived in Rhode Island for five years, almost always employed and constantly economizing. Since there was no LDS branch in Rhode Island, the family

---

[7]The couple's first child, a boy also named James, lived only one month.
[8]Charles W. Nibley, *Reminiscences*, 9.
[9]Ibid., 11.
[10]Ibid., 9-10; Christensen, "Making of a Leader," 14.
[11]Charles W. Nibley, *Reminiscences*, 12.
[12]Ibid., 13-14.

attended the local Baptist Church; their relatives were Roman Catholic. Soon the children forgot about their Mormon faith.[13]

By 1860, the impending Civil War raised the specter that James and the older sons would be drafted. With their savings of two or three thousand dollars, supplemented by auctioning off all their belongings, the Nibleys joined a group of Mormon emigrants in Boston. They traveled with this group to Florence, Nebraska, then the staging point for Mormon pioneers. Here the Nibley children were reintroduced to their religion—attending Mormon worship meetings, singing hymns, and working alongside other Mormons. The impact was immediate on eleven-year-old Charles: "The religious enthusiasm and spirit of the people were entirely different from what we had left behind in the east."[14] The Nibley family, thanks to Jean's careful economy, was relatively comfortable compared to many of their fellow Saints. They bought their outfit unassisted by the Perpetual Emigration Fund and traveled in what was called the "Independent Company."

On 17 June 1860, the family began the trek across the plains with a large group of 249 people, 36 wagons, 142 oxen, and 54 cattle. By this time, the Mormon Church had thirteen years' experience in transcontinental migration, so the Nibleys' trip was virtually problem-free.[15] Hugh remembers his grandfather saying that the entire company was joyful while crossing the plains. "We were like kids out of school," he said. "It was a lark all the way; we just laughed and sang." Compared to their life in Scotland, "this was deliverance; this was just fun." Hugh also remembers his grandfather's description of how the company captain got his people energized each day: "Every morning [he] would have every man, woman, and child drink a big, hot, steaming cup of Arbuckle's Coffee." Charles averred thereafter that what brought the Saints across the plains was "faith and Arbuckle's Coffee."[16]

It was certainly an amazing adventure for the urban millboy, Charles. His memoirs include stories of seeing large herds of buffalo which would sometimes cross the trail, forcing the wagon train to wait for up to an hour as the herd thundered in front of them. He tells of using buffalo chips for fuel, eating buffalo meat, seeing stunningly violent lightning storms over the Nebraska plains, and encountering Indians "decked in feathers and paint that would frighten most of us."[17] He also tells of pioneer ingenuity. For example, any extra milk left over from the morning milking went into tin churns strapped to the wagons. By noon, the jolting would have produced butter and buttermilk.

On Monday, 3 September 1860, the family emerged from Parley's Canyon for their first glimpse of the Salt Lake Valley. They had not yet reached the end of their strenuous exertions, however. After camping in the city for two or three days, they made the five-day journey to Cache Valley, where they had been told other Scottish families had settled. Soon the family was setting up housekeeping in Wellsville.

---

[13] Ibid., 15.
[14] Ibid., 17.
[15] Christensen, "Making of a Leader," 19.
[16] Hugh Nibley, "Remarks about Charles W. Nibley," 4.
[17] Charles W. Nibley, Reminiscences, 21.

Their new home town was far different from any the family had previously experienced in Scotland and Rhode Island. Wellsville was rural and agricultural, without mines or mills, isolated, almost a week away from Salt Lake City. The climate was a shock—dry and harsh. The very day of their arrival in Wellsville, Jean took the barefooted Charles out to glean wheat in the sharp stubble of the neighbors' fields. The painful punctuation made the experience, as Charles, with wry understatement called it, "not altogether a picnic." Jean laundered for her neighbors, taking her pay in flour. Mary and Margaret became hired girls in other families. James and the older sons worked to build a house, while Charles became one of the community's herd-boys, tending sheep and cattle. By November, the family had constructed a one-room house, half dugout and half log cabin. An old quilt served as the front door during that long and difficult first winter. Charles remembered, "It was a scramble of the severest kind for a mere existence." Nevertheless, the family survived the winter and, by spring, was busy plowing and planting.[18]

Charles attended school for two years in the town's log meetinghouse; the texts were a Greenleaf math book, a Webster spelling book, and the Book of Mormon. He had received some education in Rhode Island and would later sit in on classes when he could, but these two years in territorial Utah constituted his only formal classroom education. He also became a regular on the stage of the community theatrical company. "I suppose there never was any worse acting on any stage than could be seen there, but . . . it was a step in the direction of culture," he noted.[19]

In 1862, the community decided to graze all of its sheep together, and thirteen-year-old Charles was hired as one of the shepherds. In the mountains above Cache Valley, he became adept at protecting himself from wild animals and Indians, and also learned to hunt, identify edible plants, and cook what he collected. Charles would pass the long hours with the sheep by reading and memorizing the works of Shakespeare and his new favorite, Scotland's poet laureate, Robert Burns.[20] Hugh remembers that his grandfather named all of the sheep, "and they knew their names when he called them. As the scriptures say, 'My sheep know my voice, and they hear me, and they follow me.'" Hugh described this intimate care and knowledge as "uncanny."[21]

By this time, the Nibley family had scrambled up toward a more comfortable life. They owned about an acre and a quarter of property on which James created a luxuriant vegetable garden. Charles stated that "such a garden was rarely, if ever, seen in that part of the country. The land produced immensely and my father worked in it from early morning until late at night. It was slow plodding work, just the kind that suited him and he kept at it all the time." James had also become president of the Wellsville high priests quorum.[22] The family was an integrated part of a thriving community.

---

[18]Ibid., 30.
[19]Ibid., 39.
[20]Ibid.
[21]Hugh Nibley, "Remarks about Charles W. Nibley," 8.
[22]Ibid., 44; Christensen, "Making of a Leader," 48.

In 1864, fifteen-year-old Charles began working as a clerk in Isaac Neibaur's short-lived mercantile establishment in Wellsville. Neibaur's brother-in-law, a Brigham City businessman named Morris Rosenbaum, had sent him to Wellsville with a wagonload of goods. The store was open for only one winter, but those few months as a clerk changed Charles's life in two significant ways. First, Charles made such a positive impression on Neibaur that Rosenbaum hired Charles two years later as a clerk in his Brigham City store. And second, assisting Isaac in his store was his fourteen-year-old sister, Rebecca. Charles fell in love with her and married her four years later.[23]

By age seventeen, Charles was living in Brigham City and working in Rosenbaum's store. He was such a valuable and trusted employee that Rosenbaum confided several speculative enterprises to him. Charles always managed to turn a profit and Rosenbaum eventually made him a partner in the store.[24]

Charles was also courting Rebecca during this apprenticeship. She was born 30 March 1851, the eleventh child of Alexander Neibaur and Alice Breakel Neibaur. Alexander, born in Ehrenbriesten, France (now Germany), in 1808, was Mormonism's first Jewish convert. His parents had hoped he would become a rabbi; but after receiving some religious schooling, Alexander chose dentistry as his profession and, in 1830, moved to England where he set up his practice. There he married Alice, a Christian. As in Nibley's family, it was a woman who first heard and recognized the power of the gospel message. When Alice heard the teachings of Mormon missionaries Heber C. Kimball, Willard Richards, Joseph Fielding, and Orson Hyde, she persuaded Alexander to listen to the message as well. They were baptized in 1838 by Isaac Russell in Preston, England. Three years later, they joined the Saints emigrating to America.

In Nauvoo, Alexander continued his profession as a dentist and also began a close association with the Prophet Joseph Smith. Alexander taught Hebrew and German to Joseph Smith and later became one of the final people to hear and record the story of the First Vision as told by the Prophet himself.[25] The Neibaur family crossed the plains to Winter Quarters in 1847 and arrived in the Salt Lake Valley with Brigham Young's company of 1848. They settled in Salt Lake City Fourth Ward where they raised fourteen children.[26]

In September 1868, nineteen-year-old Charles and seventeen-year-old Rebecca became engaged. Despite their youth, Charles later wrote that he had "assurance enough to make up for lack of years and so went forward, nothing doubting." Thus, on 30 March 1869, Charles married "the best and to me the choicest God-given little woman in all the world."[27] There was no honeymoon for the couple; instead they immediately set up housekeeping in a two-room house near the store. By all accounts,

---

[23]Charles W. Nibley, Reminiscences, 47.

[24]Ibid., 49-54.

[25]Alexander Neibaur, Journal, 24 May 1844, Historical Department Archives, Church of Jesus Christ of Latter-day Saints, Salt Lake City (hereafter LDS Church Archives); see Dean C. Jessee, *The Papers of Joseph Smith*, 2 vols. (Salt Lake City: Deseret Book, 1989), 1:459-62.

[26]"Alexander Neibaur," *Utah Genealogical and Historical Magazine* 5, No. 2 (April 1914): 52-69; and Preston Nibley, *Stalwarts of Mormonism* (Salt Lake City: Deseret Book, 1954), 111-12.

[27]Charles W. Nibley, Reminiscences, 45, 60.

Charles W. Nibley at age sixteen, ca. 1865.   Rebecca Neibaur Nibley, ca. 1866.

Both courtesy Nibley Family Photograph Collection,
Special Collections and Archives, Merrill Library, Utah State University.

their marriage was blissfully happy. Its first interruption came less than seven months later when Charles was called on his first mission.

Because of hardening political opposition against the practice of polygamy, many missionaries were sent East to "counteract these evil prejudices."[28] Charles was called as part of a group of about two hundred elders at the October 1869 general conference, and immediately set off for the mission field, leaving Rebecca, who was two months pregnant with their first child. He visited many cities throughout Massachusetts, Pennsylvania, and New York but with little success. Most people so associated the Church with polygamy that they were afraid of the missionaries. Charles was frustrated by the work and lonely for Rebecca. "We did all the missionary work we could," he wrote candidly in his autobiography, "but really when I look back at it and see how utterly unprepared I was for that kind of work I am not sure but what my mission so far as doing any good to the Cause was concerned was rather more hurtful than helpful."[29]

Fortunately, his mission was mercifully brief. In March 1870, he returned to Wellsville and sold his interest in the store to his partner, Morris Rosenbaum. On 21 April 1870, the first of their ten children, Ellen Neibaur Nibley, was born. She died a year and a half later. With sorrow still fresh after more than sixty years, Charles wrote: "In that time she so grew into our loves and affections that it was like tearing out the very heart strings to part with her."[30]

---

[28]Ibid., 61.
[29]Ibid., 63.
[30]Ibid., 64.

Charles's talent for business operations, good judgment, and assiduous attention to detail meant that he was providing a comfortable living for Rebecca. In 1872 Brigham Young appointed Charles general freight and ticket agent for the Utah Northern Railroad, which eventually ran from Ogden to Franklin, Idaho. The Church had sponsored the Utah Northern's construction in 1871 to link the Mormon settlements in northern Utah and to redirect railroad profits away from the non-Mormon city of Corrine, then the terminus for the northern mining trade.[31]

Charles and Rebecca moved to Logan and began construction on a new home. Their first son, born on 7 April 1872, was named Charles W. Nibley Jr. Another daughter, Jean, born 22 May 1874, died in infancy; but Alexander, born on 7 May 1876, was a healthy one-year-old when Charles's second mission call came. Brigham Young had called thirty-eight-year-old Apostle Joseph F. Smith to preside over the mission in England. Knowing Charles's good business sense and administration skills, Smith called him to manage the business affairs of the Liverpool office, which included mission finances, publishing the *Millennial Star* and other works, and organizing emigration from all over the British Isles and the Continent. Charles left for his new duties on Alex's first birthday.

In contrast to Charles's frustrating first mission, this second call proved to be a great success. In the two years that Charles managed the office, almost three thousand Mormons made the journey to Utah.[32] Perhaps most importantly, it was the beginning of a lifelong friendship with Joseph F. Smith, which Charles later compared to the friendship between Jonathan and David. "From the very first we seemed to understand each other and grew more and more into each other's liking and affection," he recalled.[33] Second, Charles honed his administrative skills and ran the office so efficiently that he singlehandedly did the work that had previously required two men. Furthermore, Charles met the man who would later become his third father-in-law, William Budge. Called to replace Joseph F. Smith in 1878, Budge, according to Charles, was an "excellent president, . . . wise, cautious, prudent, and scholarly and withal filled with the spirit of the Gospel."[34] This mission experience also deepened and matured Charles's faith. Even though he primarily worked in the office, he "did a very considerable amount of preaching in the different conferences [districts]" and "had great joy in my labors and the satisfaction of baptizing several people into the Church."[35]

Charles returned home in 1879 with an emigrating company of Saints. Unlike his first passage to the New World, he crossed the ocean on a steamliner in only eleven days compared to twenty-eight days by sail, and reached Salt Lake City by rail in only eight days, contrasted to the two-and-a-half-month wagon trek.[36] Charles had two job offers waiting for him upon arrival, one to manage the local ZCMI and the other to

---

[31] Christensen, "The Making of a Leader," 78-81.
[32] Ibid., 88.
[33] Ibid., 73.
[34] Ibid., 75.
[35] C. W. Nibley, *Reminscences*, 76.
[36] Christensen, "Making of a Leader," 93.

manage the United Order Lumber Company. Charles felt that lumbering offered a greater chance for "development and growth," a decision whose wisdom was certainly borne out by later events.[37] On 1 March 1880, Rebecca gave birth to their fifth child and third surviving son, Joseph F. Nibley. That same month, thirty-one-year-old Charles married Ellen Jane Ricks, the daughter of Joel and Sarah Ricks, on 30 March 1880. The date was thrice significant: it was Ellen's twenty-fourth birthday, Rebecca's twenty-ninth birthday, and the eleventh wedding anniversary of Charles and Rebecca. Charles provided separate houses for his two families about two blocks from each other in Logan. Charles and Ellen became the parents of three sons and three daughters. Their first, Joel, was born in 1881.

Charles's decision to enter plural marriage was a measure of his devotion to Mormonism. The year before, the U.S. Supreme Court had handed down its ruling in the Reynolds case, denying that the practice of polygamy had the protection of the First Amendment. Thus, Charles knew he was embarking upon a stormy sea where the winds were rising. Most of Charles's close friends were polygamists—Joseph F. Smith married six wives—and it was extremely difficult at that time to become a person of power in Utah, ecclesiastically or politically, without embracing "the principle." Charles's entrance into the practice was not based on romance—Rebecca seems to have held that place in his heart all his life—but he had a strong testimony of plural marriage, which he described as "a principle intended to develop and broaden the mind and soul[,] . . . help us overcome our selfishness and . . . become more like our Father and our God."[38]

Charles continued to be successful in his business dealings. Lumbering became very profitable as more and more sawmills were built to supply the ties for the expanding railroads. In addition to running the United Order company, Charles began to purchase his own mills. By 1881, he owned five mills and employed 160 men. Business eventually expanded from Utah and Idaho into Oregon, and from lumber into sugar production. As a result, he was able to provide well for his families. Perhaps remembering the unrelenting pinch of poverty and his mother's thrifty anxiety, Charles, though not wasteful, felt great satisfaction as he bought the latest in carriages, home appliances, and, eventually, automobiles.

In 1884, after dedicating the Logan Temple, Church President John Taylor called upon the Saints in northern Utah to make the temple "a house of learning as it is also a house of God."[39] To fulfill this commandment, the Saints formed the Logan Temple Association, a sort of religious school for members of the community. Five prominent men from the community were called as instructors; Charles was asked to lecture on political economy. The speeches were not highly theological nor were they particularly brilliant prose, but they do demonstrate that, for a self-educated man, Charles was very well read. They also reveal a great concern for economic fairness:

> In a country where one man can . . . clear over a million dollars every year for twenty or thirty years . . . and where another man, nay, thousands of men, are

---

[37] Charles W. Nibley, *Reminiscences*, 79.
[38] Ibid., 80.
[39] Christensen, "Making of a Leader," 148.

unable to earn bread sufficient for themselves and their families to live on . . . something is radically wrong and needs changing, or it will change itself in a manner not pleasant to behold, nor very healthy to the capitalist.[40]

Charles Nibley, himself a successful capitalist, never forgot the poverty his family came from and championed workers' rights throughout his life. As grandson Hugh Nibley would recall, "The poverty and toil of Scottish miners, which his family experienced, filled him with a strong dedication to the idea of justice and at the same time an absolute horror of poverty."[41]

On 14 October 1885, Charles married his third wife, Julia Budge, the twenty-three-year-old daughter of his former mission president. But pressure from the Edmunds Act (1882), actively enforced by federal marshals, forced Julia and Ellen underground, living in different states and hiding from federal marshals. Rebecca, as the first and only legal wife, according to U.S. law, was relatively free from the threat

Charles W. Nibley about 1920 with his three wives: Ellen Ricks Nibley (left), Rebecca Neibaur Nibley, and Julia Budge Nibley.

Courtesy Nibley Family Photograph Collection,
Special Collections and Archives, Merrill Library, Utah State University.

of being forced to testify against her husband and stayed in Logan. From 1885 to 1895, Ellen and Julia moved from community to community, usually under assumed names, in Idaho and southern Utah. Charles was arrested in 1885 and narrowly escaped prosecution, thanks to a faulty warrant. The judge adjourned for lunch without writing a new warrant, and Charles simply did not show up for the 2:00 p.m. ses-

---

[40]*Logan Temple Lectures* (Logan: Utah Journal, n.d.), 39-40. The speeches were delivered by Moses Thatcher, James A. Leishman, William H. Apperly, John E. Carlisle, and Charles W. Nibley.

[41]Hugh Nibley, *Approaching Zion*, edited by Don E. Norton, Vol. 9 of *The Collected Works of Hugh Nibley* (Salt Lake City: Deseret Book/FARMS, 1989), 469.

sion. The pressure mounted another notch in 1887 with the passage of even more ferocious provisions in the Edmunds-Tucker Act. Under the threat of the proposed Collum Bill in 1890, President Wilford Woodruff sought divine guidance; and the Manifesto, withdrawing public support for new plural marriages, was sustained by the October 1890 general conference. After making other concessions, the Church was able to achieve its long-withheld goal of statehood for Utah in 1896. After a decade of turmoil and threat, life for Charles and his families became calm once more; and all three wives were able to establish themselves and their growing families in comfortable homes in Logan.

At that point, Charles was the father of twenty children. Rebecca's eight living children ranged in age from twenty-four-year-old Charles Jr. to six-year-old Alice with Alexander Nibley, Joseph, James, Merrill, Rebecca, and Grover in between. Five of Ellen's six children had been born by 1896: fifteen-year-old Joel Nibley, twelve-year-old Preston, nine-year-old Esther, six-year-old Edna, and two-year-old Florence. Nathan was born in 1899. The third wife, Julia, was the mother of ten-year-old Julia, eight-year-old Annie, five-year-old Margaret, three-year-old William Budge, and year-old Carlyle. Three more children would be born to their union: David Jesse in 1897, Oliver in 1900, and Ruth in 1905. Ruth was the last-born of Charles's twenty-four children; but in addition to the deaths of Rebecca's Ellen and Jean, Ellen's daughter Esther died in 1889 as a two-year-old, and two of Julia's sons, William and David, did not survive to their third birthdays.

The new state of Utah was now recovering from the economic and political sanctions of the federal anti-polygamy campaign and from the financial stresses caused by the nationwide Panic of 1893. By 1906, Charles had a "nice little bank account" and was in a position to invite his dear friend, Joseph F. Smith, now Church President, to accompany him on an expense-paid tour of Europe. It was the first time a Mormon Church president had toured Europe. President Smith, accompanied by one of his wives, Edna, and Charles W. with Rebecca and two children, visited the British Isles, Germany, Holland, Belgium and France. Charles's son, thirty-year-old Alex, was serving his second mission to Holland at that time. During his father's visit, he was set apart as president of the Holland Mission.

Charles and President Smith traveled abroad together on several other occasions, including four trips to the Hawaiian Islands.[42] They enjoyed each other's company immensely; while Smith was focused so much on spiritual things and Charles on the pragmatic, earthly things, they seemed to provide a needed balance for each other. The two men spent their hours at sea playing checkers and conversing. When Charles reached age sixty-six, he discovered "the ancient and royal Scottish game of golf" and promptly introduced it to his friend. Smith and Charles spent many hours, often in the company of Apostle Reed Smoot, on the links in Salt Lake City and in Santa Monica, California. Charles believed in recreation and felt that the trips and regular games of golf were highly beneficial, "lengthening out our days in more of health and ability to work than we could possibly have done without them."[43]

---

[42]Charles W. Nibley, *Reminiscences*, 114-17. Nibley paid President Smith's way only on the first voyage to Europe.
[43]Ibid., 115-17.

Joseph F. Smith (left), Charles W. Nibley, and Alexander Nibley at a train stop, ca. 1907.

Early in December 1907, President Smith called Charles as the Church's Presiding Bishop by saying, as Charles recalled, "Charlie, the Church of Jesus Christ of Latter-day Saints needs a Presiding Bishop and you have been chosen for that place." When Charles accepted the calling, President Smith "wept tears of joy as he hugged me and blessed me as only he can do."[44] Charles was already a close friend of John R. Winder, who had just been released as Presiding Bishop to serve as a counselor in the First Presidency. Charles suspected that Winder had suggested his appointment. However, a year after he was sustained, he was attending a social function at the palatial home of A. W. and Elizabeth McCune when one of the guests referred to President Smith as a prophet, seer, and revelator. President Smith acknowledged that he held these offices by right of ordination but stated that "President of the Church was all the official title that he cared for" because the others were so sacred. "More than once or twice in my life," he continued, "I have heard the voice which has given revelation to me, and never in my life did I hear it more plainly or clearly than when this man," pointing to Charles, "was called to be Bishop of the Church."[45] It was a humbling moment for Charles.

For over seventeen years, Charles served as the Presiding Bishop. During that time, he modernized how the Church conducted its business affairs. He eliminated the scrip system that had served as a cash substitute from Kirtland days until 1907; he centralized membership records; and he raised the funds necessary to construct the Church Administration Building at 47 East South Temple and the Hotel Utah just west

---

[44]Ibid., 117-18.
[45]Ibid., 121.

A Scottish Heritage, 1810-1930   13

The LDS First Presidency ca. 1925: Anthony W. Ivins (left), Heber J. Grant, and Charles W. Nibley. Photographer, Thomas Studio.

Courtesy Nibley Family Photograph Collection, Special Collections and Archives, Merrill Library, Utah State University.

of it.[46] Finishing Hotel Utah, however, required a loan of $2 million. Charles successfully negotiated the loan with a New York bank, which pleased President Smith until he heard the terms: The money would have to be paid back in two years. "Charley, what have you done?" he exclaimed. "How in the world will we ever pay it back in that time?" Charles had already thought through that problem. "I'm going to build the largest and finest bar in the West in the basement of the Hotel, and will see that we will pay off every penny of that debt," he reassured President Smith. Charles got the bar, and the Church repaid its loan on time.[47]

Charles continued to serve as Presiding Bishop after Heber J. Grant became president in 1918. A skilled businessman with banking and insurance interests and an ardent golfer, President Grant had also developed a close friendship with Charles Nibley. Because Charles ended his Reminiscences in 1921, he did not preserve a firsthand account about his last ten years, but we do know that this final decade contained moments of great joy and great sorrow. His personal fortune grew until he was one of Utah's richest men—a millionaire several times over. However, in 1919 and 1920, suits that a U.S. grand jury filed against U&I and Amalgamated Sugar companies charged them with conspiracy in restraint of trade under the Sherman Anti-trust Act. The suits indicted Charles W. Nibley, who was associated with Amalgamated and general manager of U&I. The companies' resulting financial problems cost Charles a great

---

[46]Thomas G. Alexander, Mormonism in Transition: A History of the Latter-day Saints, 1890-1930 (Urbana: University of Illinois Press, 1986), 105; Christensen, Making of a Leader, 180; Charles W. Nibley, Reminiscences, 126.

[47]Nibley, Approaching Zion, 470.

deal of money and public respect. President Grant took the stand in October 1920 general conference in Charles's defense, stating that an indictment was not proof of guilt and urging members to have charitable feelings toward the Presiding Bishop.[48] And in fact, the indictment never proceeded to a trial, although C. W. complained that he was "put to endless trouble and expense and held up to ridicule and scorn" because of the suits.[49]

President Grant's own support never wavered; and he went even further in 1925 when his second counselor, Charles W. Penrose, died. He called Charles Nibley as his counselor, a final vindication. This calling also made Charles one of the very few men sustained to the First Presidency without first having been ordained an apostle. (J. Reuben Clark Jr., also called to Heber J. Grant's First Presidency, was another; and John R. Winder, though never an apostle, served as a counselor to Joseph F. Smith.)

However, the victory was short lived for the seventy-six-year-old Charles. Only two years later on 2 July 1928, Rebecca Nibley, Charles's first wife and sweetheart, died, leaving a void that no one could fill. The stock market crash of October 1929 was another blow. He had endorsed notes for many of his friends and relatives which, as the stocks dropped, were not sufficiently secure. When lending institutions pressed for payment, the Nibley fortune unravelled. In 1930, he arranged to sell what was left of the Nibley Company's assets. This money paid off all of his debts and provided for his immediate family. He had assured some serenity for the closing months of his life. A moment of personal triumph came in October 1931, only two months before his death, when he was invited to address the Brigham Young University student body. As a self-educated man who had always aspired to learning and greatness, this opportunity was a cherished moment. On 11 December 1931, shortly after his introspective conversation with Hugh, Charles died of pneumonia after a two-week illness.

Charles W. Nibley surely embodied the American dream, coming from a family of poor immigrants and rising to the very pinnacle of wealth and power within his community. Yet despite the wealth and power, Charles never forgot his humble origins. He was a very kind and generous man. "He liked to see everybody happy," remembers Hugh, and money was a convenient way to make people happy. "He thoroughly enjoyed distributing it around. That is the only reason he wanted to make it, is so he could throw it around."[50]

Charles also never took himself too seriously. Hugh remarked that his grandfather's sense of humor was not only keen but kind. He was "always telling Scotch jokes at his own expense," Hugh recalled in his remarks about his grandfather. Charles's lack of pretense also impressed Hugh. Charles always talked to everyone, regardless of social position, and took a real interest in their lives. Hugh saw that his grandfather always made it a point to go into the kitchen and talk with the hired help, never seeing himself as above them. "They were as close to him as anybody else," remembers Hugh. One summer when Hugh worked at his grandfather's

---

[48]Alexander, *Mormonism in Transition*, 79-85.
[49]Charles W. Nibley, *Reminiscences*, 141.
[50]Hugh Nibley, "Faith of an Observer," 27.

logging camp, Hugh saw how, when his grandfather visited, all the workers would stop to shake his hand and talk with him. "Rank or station or importance had nothing to do with it. He just loved everybody," says Hugh. Hugh remembers that every time he drove in a car with his grandfather, Charles picked up every hitchhiker they encountered and was interested in each one's life. "Grandpa had to find out all about him, ask him questions and so forth; was he going to church and all that sort of thing."[51]

When Charles died, Hugh says that "every labor temple in the Rocky Mountains, all the labor halls, were draped in black." Charles had strenuously advocated cutting work hours, giving Sundays off, and assuring other workers' rights that made him "very unpopular with chambers of commerce."[52]

Yet on his deathbed, Charles Nibley confessed to his twenty-one-year-old grandson that he was afraid of meeting an angel. "Now the man who would admit that . . . and to say it to a kid, you know, this was something," declares Hugh. "That's a man with a conscience; that's a man with feeling; a remarkable man."[53]

---

[51] Hugh Nibley, "Remarks about Charles W. Nibley," 5, 6, 11.
[52] Ibid., 6.
[53] Ibid., 11.

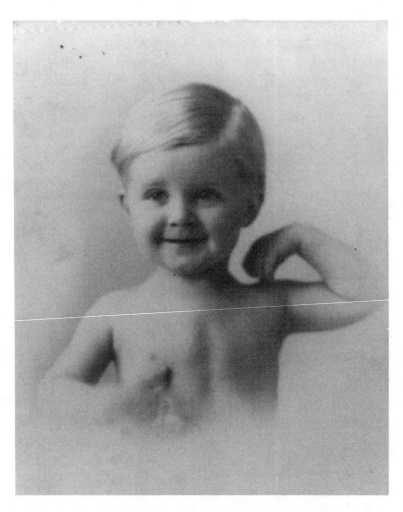

Hugh Nibley, age about eighteen months.

In Portland in 1910 the great rain forests began a few miles from our home on every side, proclaiming in their primal magnificence the kind of world God intended this to be. But the world that men were hewing out of the forest was something else. My grandparents, especially Grandma Sloan, still believed that we were in the Last Days, and could tell us why. Everybody else, including my parents, was cool to that idea—progress and prosperity were the watchword. And what did the signals say? As we stood on the little station platform at Gearhart Beach at the end of our last summer there, the family could hear a lumber company a mile away in the towering woods noisily beginning what was to be the total destruction of the greatest rain forest in the world. My father obligingly explained that the lumber company was only acting in the national interest, since spruce wood makes the best propellers, and a strong air force is necessary to a strong and free America. But it was another message that reached and offended childish ears from that misty battleground of man against nature. A little later I understood better what was going on.[1]

---

[1] Hugh Nibley, "An Intellectual Autobiography," *Nibley on the Timely and the Timeless* (Provo, UT: Brigham Young Press, 1978), xix-xx.

Chapter 2

Early Life in Oregon, 1910-21

Sometime in late 1909 or early 1910, Agnes Sloan Nibley and her husband, Alexander Nibley, traveled from their home in Portland, Oregon, to visit relatives in Salt Lake City. Agnes was in the middle of a difficult pregnancy and went to an endowment session in the Salt Lake Temple to seek some spiritual peace and physical comfort.

There she met an old family friend, John R. Winder, who was then serving both as temple president and as first counselor to Church President Joseph F. Smith. The revered eighty-eight-year-old leader, venerable with glossy white hair and a flowing white beard, smiled at Sister Nibley. His eyes twinkled behind his wire spectacles. "Sister Nibley," he asked, "may I give you a blessing?" Naturally, Agnes consented. President Winder led her into an adjoining room and laid his hands on her head. As he spoke, he not only gave Sister Nibley a blessing of comfort, but also spoke prophetically about the son Sister Nibley would soon deliver, stating that he would accomplish an important work for the Church. A few months later, President Winder died in Salt Lake City on 27 March 1910. On his deathbed, he asked whether Sister Nibley had yet given birth. On that very same day, over 700 miles away in Portland, Agnes Sloan Nibley gave birth to her son. The parents named him Hugh for his maternal grandfather but in honor of President Winder also gave him the middle name of Winder: Hugh Winder Nibley.[2]

Hugh's father, Alexander Nibley, the second son of Charles W. Nibley, was thirty-three years old when his son was born and Agnes was twenty-four. El, as he was known to family and friends, was only one year old when his father, Charles W., left on his mission to Europe; he was three when his father returned. One year later, his father took another wife and then his time was divided between the two families. Years later when Charles Nibley took a third wife, there were three families to provide for. As the anti-polygamy crusades heated up and as his father's business interests grew, El saw less and

---

[2]Hugh Nibley, Interviewed by Boyd Petersen, 9 June 1996.

less of Charles. Most likely the relationship between Charles and El was much like that described by El's brother, Nathan, in a letter he wrote to their father in 1925:

> I . . . believe that you could have helped me greatly with criticism, council and advice, but for some reason you have never counseled with me, or even had a good heart to heart talk. I have regretted the fact that you and I have never been closer to each other. . . . But then, I have received so much from you in the way of example that I don't want you, dear Father, to think, for one minute, that I don't love and revere you a great deal, for I do. In fact I am very proud of you, and it affords me much satisfaction to be known as your son.[3]

Alexander (El) Nibley, ca. 1907.

El's father, Charles Nibley, was thus always an absent-presence in the family; his influence was felt but he was rarely seen. El saw his father try to compensate for his absence at home by giving his family as much monetary help as he could. The children were well provided for, even spoiled, and showered with gifts every time their father came to visit.

The public esteem in which Charles W. Nibley was held may have further compensated El for his lack of personal attention. El wrote his father in 1918: "I have found all along, for many years, that the name Nibley is held in honor by the big men of the land whenever it is known. To me it has always been a magic 'password' gaining admission for me to the offices of some very big and good men."[4] But that name was as much a burden as blessing. Charles's successes in business and in the Church were difficult to live up to, although El tried desperately to do so. Eventually Charles involved all his sons in his various business interests or launched them into businesses of their own. Charles had a great deal of faith in El's talents and abilities and eventually put him in charge of several of his most promising but demanding business ventures.

El attended Brigham Young College and Utah State Agricultural College in Logan, then moved to Baker, Oregon, in 1893 where he worked as a clerk and later as manager of the Oregon Lumber Company's store, maintained for the logging camps. In 1898 when he was twenty-two, he left on a three-year mission to Holland. He returned to La

---

[3]Nathan Nibley, Letter to Charles Nibley, 2 June 1924, quoted in Michael Elvin Christensen, "The Making of a Leader: A Biography of Charles W. Nibley to 1890" (Ph.D. diss., University of Utah, 1978), 185.

[4]Alexander Nibley, Letter to Charles W. Nibley, 19 June 1918, Charles W. Nibley Papers, Box 3, fd. 15, L. Tom Perry Special Collections, Harold B. Lee Library, Brigham Young University, Provo, Utah.

Grande, Oregon, in 1901 and became assistant chemist in another of his father's companies, Amalgamated Sugar. The next year on 17 June 1902, he married Constance Thatcher, a niece of Apostle Moses Thatcher and a granddaughter of Brigham Young. In early 1905, Constance died while giving birth to their first child. The baby, Connie, survived and was raised, as was the custom, by her mother's family.[5]

Almost immediately after his wife's death, El accepted another mission call as a sort of distractive therapy and left for Holland and Belgium in June. Here he served as president of the Liège Conference (District). In the summer of 1906, when his father and Joseph F. Smith visited Europe, El accompanied them on their tour. Before they left Europe, they set him apart as president of the Netherlands-Belgium Mission,[6] a position he served in for only a few months, thanks to another significant event that occurred during this tour. In Berlin, the party met Agnes Sloan, who was there studying piano. Little is known about their courtship, but the two fell in love and Agnes accompanied El's father and President Smith back to Utah to prepare for her wedding. Upon his return, El and Agnes were sealed in the Salt Lake Temple on 27 June 1907 by Joseph F. Smith. Agnes was twenty-one, and El was thirty-one.

Agnes Sloan, known to friends and family as Sloanie, was the oldest daughter of Hugh Russel Sloan's and Margaret Violet Reid Sloan's eleven children. She was born 17 October 1885 in Manti, Utah, but grew up in Cardston, Alberta, Canada, where the family moved in 1896. Sloanie was a gifted musician. After three years of study in Salt Lake City, she had come to continue her studies in Berlin in 1905 and had been there about a year when she and Alexander Nibley met. El was easy-going, quick-witted, and handsome. It was surely a bond that El played the oboe and also the piano. But Sloanie was most likely equally impressed by his family's prestigious name and wealth.[7] As a young woman from the wheat fields of Canada, Sloanie must have seen that El was marked for a life of culture, taste, and wealth. Marriage to him would surely keep her from having to return to the farm.

Following their marriage in 1907, the couple moved to Portland, Oregon, where El took over the duties of directing his father's eighteen-year-old lumber business. In 1899, David Eccles and Charles W. Nibley had entered into a partnership to create the Oregon Lumber Company, which was centered in Baker City and the Sumpter Valley. The combination of "the smooth-talking Nibley and careful-managing Eccles," as one historian has written, "established the organization which made both of them multimillionaires."[8] As the company grew, the directors deliberately gave hiring preferences to Mormons. So many Mormon families moved from Utah to work for the company that the LDS Church soon became one of the most prominent religions in eastern Oregon. The company continued to expand, building saw mills in western Oregon at Hood River and Chenowith. In 1907, the year of El's and Sloanie's marriage, Charles Nibley moved back

---

[5]"Church Worker [Alexander "El" Nibley] Dies at 83 in S.L. Hospital," *Deseret News*, 31 August 1959. Connie married a man surnamed Edwards, and moved to Eldon, Missouri, where she raised her two children. Leo J. Muir, *A Century of Mormon Activities in California*, 2 vols. (Salt Lake City: Deseret News Press, compiled in 1946 and published in 1952), 2:286.

[6]Muir, *A Century of Mormon Activities*, 286-87.

[7]Sloan Nibley, "Faith of an Observer," 541, compilation of interviews, ca. 1983-84 for a video documentary of the same name aired in 1985, photocopy of typescript in my possession, pagination added.

[8]Leonard J. Arrington, *David Eccles: Pioneer Western Industrialist* (Logan: Utah State University Press, 1975), 216.

to Salt Lake City as the Church's Presiding Bishop.⁹ The timing was thus perfect for the newly married El to take over his father's duties in western Oregon.

A biographical sketch of El written in 1946 charts some additional points in his career, although showing considerable vagueness on dates: He "assisted in the promotion of a Portland Cement Company at Oswego, Oregon," and was also "appointed resident manager of the Amalgamated Sugar Company at Grants Pass, Oregon, in 1917."¹⁰ El and Sloanie had a great deal of fun together as one of Portland's young and affluent couples, moving so easily within this elite circle that they could also poke fun at it. At one very formal party in the early 1920s, all the guests duly congregated at the Nibley home, only to find themselves without hosts. While the guests were milling about wondering what was going on, they noticed a couple of tramps wandering about in the yard. Suddenly, the tramps came right in through the French windows and entered the living room. As everyone stood looking astonished and feeling horribly uncomfortable, they suddenly realized that the tramps were El and Sloanie.¹¹

Agnes (Sloanie) Sloan Nibley with baby Hugh, ca. 1910.

While Sloanie was eager to begin a family, she wanted nothing to do with El's two-year-old daughter, Connie. Sloanie loathed polygamy; and even though El was legally a widower, because of his temple sealing to Constance, Sloanie was technically the second wife in a plural relationship that would become operational in the next life. Connie never lived with the family; and Sloanie insisted that, if her own children spoke of Connie, they refer to her as a cousin rather than as a sister. In fact, Hugh's sister Barbara stated that she never knew she had a half-sister until she was fifteen.¹² Sloanie gave birth to her first child, Alexander Sloan, on 23 June 1908. Sloan, as they called him, was fat, healthy, and beautiful with blond curly hair. Sloanie let it grow into long, almost girlish ringlets. When Sloan was almost two, Hugh was born.

As Halley's comet glittered in the night sky in early spring of 1910, the forty-six states of America were only ten years into a new century full of hope and prosperity. Mark Twain, Leo Tolstoi, and William James all died that year. The Model T Ford had been com-

---

⁹Christensen, "Making of a Leader," 179-80.

¹⁰Muir, *A Century of Mormon Activities*, 2:286-87.

¹¹Reid Nibley, "Faith of an Observer," 471-72.

¹²Barbara Nibley Richards, Interviewed by Boyd Petersen, 14 March 1998.

ing off the assembly line for a year. It was the era of the "progressives," with William Howard Taft, the acknowledged successor of popular Theodore ("Teddy") Roosevelt, as president of the United States.

There was likely no place more prosperous or hopeful in 1910 than Portland, Oregon. Employment was keeping pace with a population that was growing by almost twenty thousand each year. Between 1905 and 1910, a building boom had raised the value of new building permits by 400 percent, and the volume of banking transactions increased by 150 percent. The Portland *Oregonian* of 25 September 1910 exclaimed, "Prosperity everywhere apparent and no cloud on the horizon."[13] Hugh was born into a family that fully enjoyed this prosperous period. Though not ostentatious, they lived comfortably.

Hugh was an extremely curious child from the start. Even as a toddler he had, as he later put it, an "abiding conviction that there were things of transcendent import awaiting my attention. So I kept wandering away from where I was supposed to be."[14] One of his earliest memories is of running away from home at age three. "I was determined; I just had to run away; I had to find out what was up there; there would be a rainbow near Mount Hood or something and I would just ache to know what was up there."[15] No doubt this precocity was very troubling to Hugh's young parents, as Hugh off-handedly acknowledged, "Adults find that attitude upsetting."[16]

Early on, Hugh also exhibited an interest in exotic languages. The carpet in the family's living room was a beautiful hand-loomed rug that El had bought for Sloanie on the day Hugh was born. In one corner of the rug, the weaver's name appeared in Arabic

Hugh, age seven or eight.

---

[13] Quoted in Carl Abbott, *Portland: Planning, Politics, and Growth in a Twentieth-Century City* (Lincoln: University of Nebraska Press, 1983), 50-51.
[14] Hugh Nibley, "An Intellectual Autobiography," xix.
[15] Hugh Nibley, "Faith of an Observer," 218.
[16] Hugh Nibley, "Intellectual Autobiography," xix.

script as part of the design. Even as a toddler, little Hugh was fascinated with the script and spent many hours studying the curving letters.[17]

Hugh was precocious in other ways too. He learned to read before he went to school, his first book being *The Fate of a Squash Pie*. It was a sad book, remembers Hugh, because the protagonist "took the squash pie to bed with her. I remember the steel engraving of the little girl coming down the stairs with a squash pie under her arm. But it taught me what to do if you have a squash pie."[18]

Despite his intellectual bent, Hugh's first experience with school was traumatizing. On his first day of school, his mother sent him with the milk man, trusting that he would arrive safely. The milk wagon, "drawn by an old slow horse," meandered along making deliveries, and by the time they got to school young Hugh was quite late. "Then I saw Mr. Brown, the Principal," Hugh remembers, "looking at me out the window from way up there and he called to me." Thinking he was in trouble, Hugh ran home as fast as he could, the principal running right behind. "Mother was on the porch sitting in this hammock and I flung myself at her and clung for dear life."[19]

At school, Hugh was quick to learn, but also quiet. It wasn't until the end of the first term that the teacher found out that he could read. As Hugh recalls, "We were reading the clown book; it was the hardest of them all. No one could do it. So I raised my hand and rattled it off. 'Why Hugh, you didn't tell us you could read!' 'Well, you didn't ask me,'" Hugh replied.[20]

Sloanie and El were devoted parents, but had very different ways of relating to their children. In parenting styles, they had much in common with El's grandparents, James and Jean Nibley. Like James, El was lighthearted and witty; like Jean, Sloanie was stern and businesslike. Hugh's brother Reid later recalled that "Dad was very casual and very loving and very warm."[21] Sloan confirmed that his father was "easy going, a lot of fun. . . . He was a very gregarious person. Everybody liked him."[22] El doted on his children. "Every night," Hugh recalls, "he read to us from the complete works of Mark Twain."[23] El never took anything too seriously, which gave the children emotional security and stability.

An incident illustrating El's playful sense of humor occurred during his second mission to Holland while Apostle Heber J. Grant was serving as president of the European Mission. They toured the various missions together, speaking at district conferences of members and missionaries.[24] Grant frequently spoke on one of his favorite topics—the importance of setting goals and working to achieve them. He gave as one example his own ability to learn how to sing after being born tone deaf. His voice, he reported, had

---

[17] Hugh Nibley, interviewed by Boyd Petersen, 13 October 2000; Hal Knight, "Behind the Legend, There's a Man," *Deseret News*, 1 September 1976, B-12.

[18] Hugh Nibley, interviewed by Boyd Petersen, 18 September 2000.

[19] Ibid.

[20] Ibid.

[21] Reid Nibley, "Faith of an Observer," 471.

[22] Sloan Nibley, "Faith of an Observer," 534.

[23] Hugh Nibley, interviewed by Boyd Petersen, 18 September 2000.

[24] Heber J. Grant, *Conference Report*, April 1924, 154, recalled traveling with Alex Nibley "many years ago" when they called unannounced on King Oscar of Sweden on the Fourth of July.

caused some to say that hearing him sing sounded "like somebody was having his teeth pulled." Undeterred by his impairment, Grant worked and worked, singing the same line of the same song over and over, imitating his voice teacher as best he could. Eventually he learned to sing several hymns. As he stated, "It required a vast amount of practice to learn, and my first hymn was sung many hundreds of times before I succeeded in getting it right."[25] To prove that he had mastered the talent, Grant would then sing for the Saints, accompanied by El on the piano. Hugh recalls his father saying that Grant preferred sentimental old songs like "The Flag Without a Stain" and "I Have Dreamed of a Beautiful City." Over the course of the tour, Grant "sang [these songs] to Dad six or seven hundred times," Hugh recalls. "Oh, it would drive you crazy, as it did him, because his singing was not very good." So El took advantage of Grant's tone deafness and began to play the accompaniment one-half step off, slyly smiling as the congregation tried to contain its laughter. As Hugh states, "You had to hear Grant sing when Dad played, though. It was absolutely horrifying."[26]

Sloanie, in contrast, was very serious and quite moody. "Mother had a great deal of love for her family," Reid states, "but she was so stern. She was the manager and she really ran that place. So we didn't get the same sort of warm feeling that we got from Dad."[27] Sloanie was also temperamental. She "used to have moods where she'd run around cracking heads," Sloan confided. "She'd go through the house imitating a Tasmanian Devil once in a while. Everybody would hide in the storm cellar."[28] Daughter Barbara later recalled: "She was just the most charming person to people outside the family and just a tyrant to people in the family. I think of *Taming of the Shrew*, but she was never tamed."[29]

One of Hugh's earliest memories dates from about 1914. "I remember the day World War I broke out," Hugh would later recall. "I was only four years old, but I remember it vividly, my father coming in and reporting." By the time the United States finally entered the war in 1917, Hugh was playing soldier in the muddy lots behind his house.[30] Hugh's father fully supported the United States's entry into the war and wanted to enlist. Ineligible because he was over forty and had a family, he actively sought some way to contribute to the war effort, finally using his father's influence to land a job with the War Industries Board.[31]

Two people had a great influence on Hugh at this time: his Grandmother Sloan and his Grandfather Nibley. Margaret Violet Reid Sloan had been born to Irish parents John Patrick Reid and Margaret Kirkwood Reid on 16 April 1857 in Edinburgh, Scotland.[32] It was in Scotland that her parents had joined the Mormon Church ten years

---

[25]Heber J. Grant, *Gospel Standards* (Salt Lake City: Improvement Era, 1941), 351-54.

[26]Hugh Nibley, Interviewed by Zina Petersen, 26 January 2002.

[27]Reid Nibley, "Faith of an Observer," 471-72.

[28]Sloan Nibley, "Faith of an Observer," 535.

[29]Barbara Nibley Richards, interviewed by Boyd Petersen, 14 March 1998.

[30]Hugh Nibley, "Faith of an Observer," 165.

[31]Christensen, "Making of a Leader," 179.

[32]Margaret Violet Reid Sloan celebrated her birthday on 27 April and that date is listed on all Church records; however, her birth certificate indicates that she was born on 16 April. Ruth Smith Gifford, *History of William Charles Smith Jr. and Clara Sloan Smith and Family* (Provo, UT: Stevenon's Genealogy Center, 1994), 343.

Hugh Russell Sloan and Margaret Violet Reid Sloan, Hugh's maternal grandparents.

earlier, so Margaret was raised in a zealous Mormon home. Soon after Margaret's birth, the family moved back to Belfast, where Margaret spent most of her youth. In 1862, Margaret's brothers, William Kirkwood Reid and John Kirkwood Reid, emigrated to Utah with their uncle, William Taylor Reid. Her father followed in 1871; and a year later, fifteen-year-old Margaret traveled with her mother and siblings to be reunited with her father and older brothers in Utah.[33] Margaret never had any desire to return to the land of her birth. Her only memories of Ireland were vivid nightmares of the fighting and bloodshed between the British and Irish during the Fenian uprising.

The family eventually settled in Manti, where Margaret was a very popular young lady. At age twenty-one, she married Irish-born Hugh Russel Sloan on 27 September 1878. Although he had lived in Utah for several years, Hugh Sloan was not a member of the Church when the couple married, and Margaret's parents initially opposed the match. Several years after they were married, Margaret became deathly ill and called for the elders to administer to her. When she was miraculously healed, Hugh Sloan was so impressed that he joined the Church in 1882 and became deeply devout. The couple moved from town to town in Utah, where Hugh found work as an artisan. They lived in Manti during the construction of the Manti Temple (1877-88), and Hugh worked on its decoration and trim. Eventually, at the urging of Apostle John W. Taylor, the family moved to Cardston, Alberta, Canada. The couple had eleven children, seven of whom survived to adulthood.[34]

In 1907, following her daughter Sloanie's marriage, Grandma Sloan's health began to deteriorate. She came down from Canada to visit Sloanie in Oregon and felt so much better that she, her husband, and youngest son, Edgar Lloyd, moved to Portland in 1909 and lived there for about five years. Around 1914 they moved to Salt Lake City; and in 1916, they moved back to Canada. During the time the Sloans lived in Portland, Hugh spent many hours with his grandmother, both as a toddler and later on her lengthy, frequent visits. They became very close. Grandma Sloan was known as a very charitable and

---

[33] Accompanying her to America were Margaret's siblings: twelve-year-old Alex, ten-year-old Agnes, eight-year-old Lucy, six-year-old Robert, and four-year-old Sarah.

[34] Their children were John Samuel (1879-1946), William Reid (1881-1961), Hugh Russel Jr. (1883-1963), Agnes (1885-1959), Maggie (1887-88), Clara (1889-1979), Ruth (1891-1928), George Peacock (1894-95), Edward Louden (1896), Rayman Reid (1899), Edgar Lloyd (1902-38). Gifford, *History of William Charles Smith*, 320-56.

practical person with a great sense of humor. "She was a dynamo," remembers Hugh. "And always helping people. She was never so happy as when there was a family sick somewhere."[35] During the flu epidemic of 1918, Grandma Sloan traveled from house to house, nursing the people in Cardston back to health.[36]

Despite her assiduous attentions and genuine concern, her patients were not always grateful. She created "Grandma's oil," a concoction based on a recipe she got from a Chinese doctor in Portland. From a very small bottle, she would pour a drop on the patient's back or chest and cover the spot with cotton. It was obviously some kind of caustic since, in a few days, little pockets formed that itched intolerably and drained pus. This, she believed, drew "impurities" from the body. "When Grandma was at your house you never dared cough in the night," recalled Hugh, "or she'd swoop down on you with that damnable medicine!"[37]

Even though Grandma Sloan had her own residence in Portland, she spent many hours with Sloanie's children—she practically raised them. It is unclear how Sloanie felt about her mother's constant presence in her home; but after her third son, Fred Richard, was born on 29 April 1913, Sloanie was probably grateful for the assistance in raising three boys. Hugh certainly benefited from the time he spent with his grandmother. His love and veneration for her grew deep. Many years later in a birthday greeting to his grandmother, Hugh wrote that she was someone who lived "both wisely and well" and he confessed: "We all love you and something more. It is wonder and veneration on my part. I wish I could become such a person."[38] In another letter to his grandmother, he wrote warmly, "There is nothing about you I don't envy; . . . I know of but one person who is just what we should all be, whose soul from the beginning was as clear and noble and magnanimous as my kind can hope to be only after endless years of painful discipline and ceaseless correction."[39] Clearly, through her visits throughout Hugh's youth, Grandma Sloan kept a very special place in his life.

Part of what made Grandma Sloan so special to Hugh was her discussion of religion. She impressively related prophecies to the children, in particular those of Eliza R. Snow.[40] She frequently reminded the boys that they were living in the last days. In this, Grandma Sloan was being strictly orthodox. As Hugh explains, "In her day everybody talked about that; it was an important part of our doctrine, that these are the last days."[41] This apocalyptic discussion affected young Hugh, especially in light of the changing shape of Portland during the 1910s.

Portland was both submerged in nature and also witnessing its wholesale destruction. Hugh later described the people living in Portland as "the most conservative [and] the most nature minded. People loved nature and because of the great woods . . .

---

[35]Hugh Nibley, interviewed by Boyd Petersen, 18 September 2000.
[36]Gifford, *History of William Charles Smith*, 354.
[37]Ibid., 364-65.
[38]Hugh Nibley, Letter to Margaret Violet Reid Sloan, 27 April 1935.
[39]Hugh Nibley, Letter to Margaret Violet Reid Sloan, 4 October 1938.
[40]Hugh Nibley, *Teachings of the Book of Mormon: Transcripts of Lectures Presented to an Honors Book of Mormon Class at Brigham Young University 1989-90* (Provo, UT: FARMS, n.d.), Semester 4, 282.
[41]Hugh Nibley, interviewed by Boyd Petersen, 18 September 2000.

they wanted to live in it."⁴² But the 1910s were a time of great development, and with development came deforestation. Hugh's grandfather's Oregon Lumber Company—"the biggest lumber company in the world until Weyerhauser came along"—was clearing timber to create railroad ties.⁴³ "I recall how often my grandmother used to say (and we firmly believed it as children)," Hugh would later write: "'It is a sin to kill a fly; much more to harm a greater thing.'"⁴⁴ Hugh's grandmother's abiding respect for life and belief that its destruction was sinful affected Hugh deeply. "What she told me I believed," states Hugh. "And I never had occasion to give it up because it was never exposed [as false] later on."⁴⁵

While she most likely never specifically criticized Charles W. Nibley's lumber company for its destruction of the Oregon forests, Grandma Sloan's words were a striking contrast to Grandpa Nibley's behavior. Nevertheless, Hugh was very close to his Grandpa Nibley. When Charles W. Nibley stopped by the house in Portland, life became jolly. This man who had been distant and remote with his own children would always get down on the floor with his grandchildren, romp with them, and play "very undignified" games.⁴⁶ Charles's love of literature was profound—especially of Burns and Shakespeare—and he would spend many hours discussing poetry and plays with the youthful Hugh. Charles always urged Hugh not to get involved in business: "Hit the Shakespeare, hit the astronomy, and forget the business," recommended this man who was probably one of Mormondom's most consummate businessmen.⁴⁷

Frequently accompanying Charles Nibley to Oregon were equally notable men. President Joseph F. Smith greatly impressed young Hugh, who admired his trait of being neither "subservient" nor "looking down on anyone." This Church president, in a town where Mormons were not a majority, "would get up at 3:00 in the morning and go down to the lower part of town. . . . If some poor old bum had been picked up at the police station, he would come down and try to help him out . . . . He put himself out all the time, and nobody knew about it." On one occasion when there was illness in a ward member's family, President Smith "sat up with him and his little girl all night. He let the business go and everything else. That little sick child and sitting with Brother Westergard were more important to him."⁴⁸

In early 1917 when Hugh turned seven, the family, except for Grandma Sloan, moved to Medford, Oregon, so El could manage his father's sugar company. The year before, Charles Nibley, who was a member of the board of directors in the Oregon-Utah Sugar Company, had financed the construction of a sugar beet processing factory at Grant's Pass in southwest Oregon's Rogue River Valley. Another sugar factory was planned

---

⁴²Hugh Nibley, "Faith of an Observer," 190.

⁴³Ibid., 33.

⁴⁴Hugh Nibley, *Approaching Zion*, edited by Don E. Norton, Vol. 9 of *The Collected Works of Hugh Nibley* (Salt Lake City: Deseret Book/FARMS, 1989), 414.

⁴⁵Hugh Nibley, "Faith of an Observer," 226.

⁴⁶Hugh Nibley, interviewed by Kenneth W. Godfrey and Boyd Petersen, 3 June 1998, 2.

⁴⁷Quoted in Hugh Nibley, "Faith of an Observer," 249.

⁴⁸Hugh Nibley, *Teachings of the Book of Mormon: Transcripts of Lectures Presented to an Honors Book of Mormon Class at Brigham Young University 1989-90* (Provo, UT: FARMS, n.d.): Semester 2, Lecture 38, 5. In the transcript, Nibley incorrectly identifies the Prophet as George Albert Smith; however, it should read Joseph F. Smith, as he has stated elsewhere. These transcripts are paginated lecture by lecture.

This portrait, taken ca. 1910 somewhere in Oregon, includes Melvin J. Ballard (second from left), Joseph F. Smith (fourth from left), Agnes Sloan Nibley next to him in hat with ostrich plumes, then Alexander Nibley. Charles W. Nibley is fourth from the right.

Courtesy Nibley Family Photograph Collection, Special Collections and Archives, Merrill Library, Utah State University.

for Medford, provided farmers could guarantee 5,000 acres of sugar beets in 1917 and 6,000 acres in 1918. Production never reached these goals; and by 1919, the company decided to build in the Yakima Valley instead.[49]

Soon after the family reached Medford, Philip Gordon was born on 25 July 1917, Sloanie's fourth childbirth in nine years. The family's prosperity continued; El was a skilled manager and handled his father's business interests efficiently.

On his eighth birthday, 27 March 1918, Hugh was baptized a member of the Church in Jackson Hot Springs, halfway between Medford and Ashland, Oregon. Hugh remembers that the day was chilly and raining, but the steaming water registered a scorching 108 degrees. "It was just like a visit to Hades to get baptized," he remarked candidly.[50]

When the sugar beet industry folded in Medford in 1919, the family returned to Portland where El continued to represent his father's sugar interests. In the 1920 census, El listed his occupation as purchasing agent for a sugar company. Sloan was now eleven, Hugh was nine, Richard was six, and Philip two. Hugh enrolled in the fourth grade at Irvington Elementary School. It was obvious to everyone that Hugh was very bright, but no one knew how bright until a new principal, a Mr. Barr, was hired. He had been teaching at Columbia University where he had become a disciple of the influential educator John Dewey, who stressed a "pragmatic" approach. Intent on reforming the school, Barr administered the Benet IQ test to all of the students. After seeing Hugh's scores, Barr called him in and told him "Look, if you would go to sleep for nine years and wake up

---

[49]Leonard Arrington, *Beet Sugar in the West* (Seattle: University of Washington Press, 1966), 84-85.
[50]Hugh Nibley, interviewed by Boyd Petersen, 18 September 2000.

Sloanie Nibley with her four sons ca. 1918: from left, Richard, Philip (on Sloanie's lap), Sloan, and Hugh.

you'd still know far more than any of the students in this school." So for the remainder of their time in Portland, Barr privately tutored him. "I didn't go to school," remembers Hugh with some complaisance. "The principal came and tutored me at home. We had some nice times together."[51]

El and Sloanie allowed Hugh great latitude in the educational arrangement. He spent a great deal of time exploring in the woods or riding his bicycle about town. "I would always stop on the Broadway Bridge and look down the river," mused Hugh. "As far as you could see were the masts of ships—three-masters, four-masters. The three-masters were the common ones." Hugh was a very capable artist by age ten and enjoyed sketching the ships and making models out of balsa wood. Hugh also found "exciting" the moments when the steam engines pulled out of the station which was located next to the waterfront.[52]

Hugh's parents supplemented their children's education with all kinds of lessons and tutors. "We had tutors for everything," remembers Sloan. "We had a music teacher that came by every day. Every day!"[53] The piano teacher was a strict old-style instructor named Emma B. Carroll. "She was hell on wheels," remembers Hugh. "You'd get one note wrong, and she'd say, 'That's the most hell-be-damned thing I ever heard.'"[54] A Miss

---

[51] Hugh Nibley, "Faith of an Observer," 97.

[52] Hugh Nibley, *Teachings of the Book of Mormon: Transcripts of Lectures Presented to an Honors Book of Mormon Class at Brigham Young University, 1989-90* (Provo, UT: FARMS, n.d.): Semester 3, Lecture 57, 1.

[53] Sloan Nibley, "Faith of an Observer," 541.

[54] Hugh Nibley, Interviewed by Mark A. Eddington, 22 September 2000.

Binney instructed the boys in French—giving nine-year-old Hugh a head start on his languages.

All four boys slept in "the nursery," heated by an open fireplace, watching the shadows dance on the ceiling until they fell asleep. To amuse themselves after bed time, Sloan and Hugh would tell stories which they made up as they went along. "They usually involved somehow or other falling off the steel bridge [into] the Willamette River," remembered Sloan. "They were pretty slapstick."[55]

On 16 January 1921, the family moved to Southern California.[56] El was having health problems and believed that the move south would help. Charles Nibley had business interests in California that required attention, so the move was doubly convenient. As the family boarded the train for California, ten-year-old Hugh could hear the chain saws roaring. For the forests, the end was near. But for Hugh it was another beginning.

---

[55] Sloan Nibley, "Faith of an Observer," 532-33.
[56] Muir, *A Century of Mormon Activities*, 2:286-87.

Hugh Nibley in his classroom, 1990.

There have been some things said about BYU by others, [but] none of them are as painfully critical as what Nibley occasionally says. And the same goes for the Church, institutionally speaking. He really is its gadfly critic. . . . He is a profoundly sympathetic man who lives in a world that he sees falling apart, who yet has a bright optimistic faith that the outcome—even that of disintegration—will be for the good of mankind. He defies classification. Is he a cynic, a pessimist, with all kinds of negative things to say? Yes. Is he an optimist, an idealist, with great hope for the future? Yes. Some would say you can't get those together. He does.

—Truman Madsen[1]

---

[1] Truman Madsen, "Faith of an Observer," 458, 466, compilation of interviews, ca. 1983-84 for a video documentary of the same name aired in 1985, photocopy of typescript in my possession, pagination added.

Chapter 3

"Speaking in a Prophetic Vein": Hugh Nibley as Social Critic

Eugene England called Hugh Nibley "the finest lay (as opposed to officially called) prophet of the Latter-day Saint people" and has argued that Nibley "most perceptively describes our sins, most courageously and persistently calls us to repentance, and most accurately predicts our future if we will not repent."[2] England may be guilty of hyperbole, but most would agree that Hugh does indeed have a gift for sizing up the spiritual state of the Mormon community and calling us to repentance.

In essays like "Beyond Politics" and "In the Party But Not of the Party,"[3] Hugh has admonished us not to put partisan politics above the interests of God's kingdom; in essays like "Zeal Without Knowledge" and "Educating the Saints,"[4] he has warned us not to allow mindless zeal to substitute for genuine knowledge of the gospel; and in essays like "Brigham Young As a Leader" and his renowned BYU commencement address, "Leaders to Managers: The Fatal Shift,"[5] he has reproached us for placing the image of management over the substance of leadership.

---

[2] Eugene England, "Hugh Nibley as Cassandra," *BYU Studies* 30 (Fall 1990): 104. I read an earlier version of this chapter at the Sunstone Symposium, on 1 August 1998 in Salt Lake City.

[3] "Zeal Without Knowledge," in *Nibley on the Timely and the Timeless* (Provo, Utah: BYU Religious Study Center, 1978), 279-305; "In the Party But Not of the Party," in *Brother Brigham Challenges the Saints*, edited by Don E. Norton and Shirley S. Ricks, Vol. 13 of *The Collected Works of Hugh Nibley* (Salt Lake City: Deseret Book/FARMS, 1994), 105-37.

[4] "Zeal Without Knowledge," *Approaching Zion*, edited by Don E. Norton, Vol. 9 of *The Collected Works of Hugh Nibley* (Salt Lake City: Deseret Book/FARMS, 1989), 63-84; "Educating the Saints," in *Brother Brigham Challenges the Saints*, 306-45.

[5] "Brigham Young As a Leader" and "Leaders to Managers: The Fatal Shift," in *Brother Brigham Challenges the Saints*, 449-90 and 491-508.

Above all, the three themes that dominate his work are the corrupting influence of wealth, which prevents us from fulfilling our covenant to live the Law of Consecration;[6] the destructive attitudes we have toward the environment, which blind us to the Lord's commandment to exercise responsible stewardship over the earth;[7] and the total depravity of war, which frustrates our mission to proclaim peace.[8]

In fact, Hugh is so driven to comment on the social ills of our society and, in particular, our Mormon community that he often does so in writings devoted to other purposes. Hugh's efforts to defend the Book of Mormon or the Book of Abraham are a case in point. While focusing on the scriptural records of these ancient civilizations, he is often simultaneously focusing on the conditions of our present world. For example, in concluding *Since Cumorah*, Hugh calls our attention to two attributes that he says we share with the Book of Mormon peoples. The first is "the Nephite Disease": an obsession with wealth and the ways of Babylon which led to the Nephites' destruction and will likely lead to our own.[9] The second attribute is the Nephite tendency toward polarization which divides the world into camps of "good guys" and "bad guys." Hugh wrote this essay during the frostiest Cold War days of American "good guys" versus Russian "bad guys," but he stressed that "it is by the wicked that the wicked are punished" (Mormon 4:5). Thus, if Americans and Russians are enmeshed in an arms race, he argued, both must be "bad guys," since the true "good guys" of the Book of Mormon were pacifists.[10] In what is, I believe, some of his finest writing, Hugh concludes *Abraham in Egypt* by turning our attention to the scriptures' admonition for us to "do the works of Abraham" and reminds us that this means leaving behind the things of this world and focusing on the things of heaven.[11]

It is not so surprising then, that we find thinly veiled commentary on our society in the articles which Hugh published in secular scholarly journals—his "Gentile exertions" as Hugh calls them, and which he claims were "merely written to set the stage for the [Mormon] stuff."[12] Of the essays compiled in *The Ancient State*, Stephen Ricks writes: "Astute readers will recognize in these essays many now-familiar themes of Hugh's trenchant social commentaries. The foibles of our age are nothing new, repeating what has been done in other eras."[13] For example, when describing the Roman fidelity program in "The Unsolved Loyalty Problem,"[14] Hugh is simultaneously decrying the McCarthy-era loyalty campaign. And when writing of the shift from knowledge to show-

---

[6] See "What Is Zion? A Distant View" and "Work We Must, But the Lunch Is Free," in *Approaching Zion*, 25-62 and 202-51.

[7] See "Man's Dominion, or Subduing the Earth," and "Brigham Young on the Environment," in *Brother Brigham Challenges the Saints*, 3-22 and 23-54.

[8] See "Renounce War, or a Substitute for Victory" and "Brigham Young and the Enemy," in *Brother Brigham Challenges the Saints*, 267-69 and 187-246.

[9] Hugh Nibley, *Since Cumorah*, edited by John W. Welch (1967; reprinted Salt Lake City: Deseret/FARMS, 1988), 354-72.

[10] Ibid., 342-53.

[11] *Abraham in Egypt* (1981; Salt Lake City: Deseret Book/FARMS, 2000), 648-54.

[12] Hugh Nibley, Letter to Paul Springer, 24 May 1958.

[13] Stephen D. Ricks, Foreword, *The Ancient State* (Salt Lake City: Deseret Books/FARMS, 1991), ix.

[14] Ibid., 195-242.

manship in ancient Greece in "How to Have a Quiet Campus, Antique Style,"[15] he is also disparaging the sorry state of contemporary education—which exalts image over substance, careerism over learning, and dress and grooming over moral discipline—in America and especially at BYU. Hugh himself notes that the essay was written as a response to the address given at BYU by then-U.S. vice president Spiro Agnew—whom he characterized as "political, ostentatious, and not overly scrupulous."[16] And in a recent still-unpublished talk, "Roman Satire and Us," Hugh describes the avarice, corruption, and disregard for human suffering depicted in his scathingly satirical commentary on ancient Rome, while simultaneously and subtly encouraging us to note these same tendencies in our own world. As he states, "We have not had the time nor the need to draw modern parallels to the Roman situation. You can find them scattered throughout the weekly news in rich abundance."[17]

I would argue, then, that one of Hugh's primary occupations has been as a social critic. His study of the ancients illuminates their foibles and sins; stringently and repeatedly, he has warned us of similar trends in our modern world. Hugh has continually reminded us of our sins and admonished us that we must all repent: "Even the righteous must repent, constantly and progressively, since all fall short of their capacity and calling."[18]

The Last Days

Hugh's perspective and pungent warnings stem from his deep conviction that these are indeed the last days. His apocalyptic worldview most likely originated in his lengthy youthful discussions with his grandmother Sloan. "My grandparents, especially Grandma Sloan, still believed that we were in the Last Days, and could tell us why," Hugh recorded in his "Intellectual Autobiography."[19] Lucien Goldschmidt, who met Hugh at Camp Ritchie during World War II, described him as "often pessimistic. He altogether regarded that we were at the end of the times and that more disasters were ahead of us."[20] And forty years later in a series of letters to Alex, his missionary son, Hugh explicated the same theme:

> Ever since I was an infant I was taught to think in terms of a Latter-day scenario—certain things would have to happen. I have always believed they would happen, a view shared by very few others within the Church or outside—much too a) drastic and b) alarming, they said. But now I have had time to see whether it has really been work-

---

[15]Ibid., 287-302.

[16]Ibid., 287.

[17]Hugh Nibley, "Roman Satire and Us," 26-27, Lecture to BYU Women, 26 October 1991, photocopy of typescript in my possession.

[18]*Approaching Zion*, 66-67.

[19]In Nibley on the *Timely and the Timeless* (Salt Lake City: BYU Religious Studies Center, 1978): xx. Hugh also noted: "I was raised by a grandmother who was nobody's fool and she knew a great deal. . . . What she told me I believed . . . and I never had occasion to give it up because it was never exposed [to be false] later on." "Faith of an Observer," 226.

[20]Hugh Nibley, "Faith of an Observer," 408.

ing out or not; which scenario has it been? What has happened all along is exactly what I expected to happen. What has happened to people is what they have made to happen, and that is the result of what they have become. I cannot see the remotest possibility of avoiding "the consumption decreed." What irony! No one takes it seriously because it is too unpleasant to accept; and all the time they are working with unflagging industry to bring it about.[21]

It is becoming so startlingly clear all of a sudden that God means business with this generation; the language of the ancient prophets has become flatly relevant—the issues have long been the same as those they faced; and now the scene is becoming like the horrendous backdrops of antiquity.[22]

The fulfillment of prophecy is going right up to schedule, and I have not the slightest doubt that all will be well if our patent recognition of signs long foretold leads to the course of action they admonish.[23]

Everything seems to be just melting away; nothing holds. It's not just me in my old age—it is the fulfillment of all the prophetic expectations in which I believed as a child. . . . Two things make the scene exciting: 1) the completely unpredictable nature of everything that is happening, and 2) the perfect conviction that the Lord is quite aware of everything and how it relates to us.[24]

Rather than foreseeing the apocalypse as doom, Hugh feels that, in our current state, the end of the world is a blessing. As he phrases the situation in a neat paradox, "Unless the end *does* come it is all over with the human race."[25] As early as 1940, he stated wryly: "I am an optimist, expecting the best possible fate to befall our generation, namely, its virtual destruction."[26] Hugh shares Joseph Fielding Smith's belief that the end of our world will be "a day of peace and joy to the righteous, but a dreadful day to the wicked."[27]

As a result of Hugh's dominating worldview, he has observed current events with an apocalyptic eye. Although he never stated it publicly, at one point he was persuaded that the world would end in 1952. To Paul Springer, he wrote with edgy conviction:

Quite a rat-race, but I am convinced that things are going to happen in a very short time. In fact this is the very month in which I have expected the big bang ever since 1945. I may turn out to be a false prophet, but as February runs its course I still cannot free myself from the conviction that early 1952 is the time. I am afraid it is going to be rather exciting and frankly at my age my appetite for excitement has definitely lost its edge.[28]

---

[21] Hugh Nibley, Letter to Charles Alexander Nibley, n.d., ca. 1980.

[22] Hugh Nibley to Charles Alexander Nibley, n.d., ca. May 1980. In another letter to Alex, also ca. May 1980, Hugh explained: "It reminds me of what a Roman historian said of THEIR last days, that it seemed that everybody had simply lost their balance; or as Thucydides put it, Words lost their meaning."

[23] Hugh Nibley, Letter to Charles Alexander Nibley, 27 June 1980.

[24] Hugh Nibley, Letter to Charles Alexander Nibley, n.d., ca. May 1980.

[25] Hugh Nibley, Letter to Charles Alexander Nibley, 10 May 1979. Emphasis his.

[26] Hugh Nibley, Letter to Paul Springer, n.d., ca. 1940.

[27] Quoted in Joseph Fielding Smith, *The Restoration of All Things* (1945; reprinted Salt Lake City: Deseret Book, 1978), 303.

[28] Hugh Nibley, Letter to Paul Springer, 7 February 1952.

In another letter that same month, also to Springer, Hugh stated:

> But I think our old game of trying to predict where and how we will be at a given future date becomes more pointed all the time—just where is the whole shebang going? Wouldn't it be a supreme joke if *nothing* happened and we both enjoyed a sedate old age? Yes it would. It would also be a great joke if you became a Rabbi and I became governor of Kentucky. You see, I rave.[29]

When I asked Hugh about this period, he remembers being convinced that a horrible catastrophe would occur during the 1950s. "I remember there was a long period then during which I worried. I would get up and wander around town at three o'clock in the morning all alone in the nighttime."[30] Part of the reason Hugh says he worried came from his observations of cycles in human history. "It had to do with the patterns of history. Every so many years it would naturally happen." But one of these fears that assaulted him in the deepest hours of the night may have been undiagnosed post-traumatic stress syndrome, a manifestation of the shocks he had suffered in World War II. (See chap. 14.) "There was a long time when I would worry about being recalled to the 101st because people were being called on special missions to Little Rock, Arkansas, and things like that. I was over age and all of that; but under special circumstances they could recall you."[31]

Even though Hugh was wrong about an apocalyptic scenario, international politics were certainly cause enough for nightmarish anxiety. The United States was enmeshed in the unwinnable "police action" of the Korean War. Sino-Soviet demands posed an obvious threat to world peace. The Cold War between the United States and the Soviet Union was confrontational, sprinkled with many violent episodes. By August 1949, the Soviet Union had cracked the secret of nuclear weaponry and had encircled Poland, East Germany, Hungary, Romania, Bulgaria, and Czechoslovakia within what Winston Churchill called its "Iron Curtain." In October 1952, the United States had constructed the B-52 bomber, capable of carrying atomic weapons to the heart of the Soviet Union. In November, the United States tested its first hydrogen bomb, about a thousand times more powerful than the atomic bombs dropped on Hiroshima and Nagasaki. In 1957, the Soviets took a leap into the scientific-technological lead by orbiting the first satellite, Sputnik I, alerting Americans to the possibility that the Soviets could launch a nuclear missile attack on the United States. These were tense times by any standard.

Although the decade of the 1950s quietly passed into history, Hugh's apocalyptic worldview remained unchanged. In 1979, he averred, "Years ago I started cutting relevant items out of the newspapers and magazines. Today there is no point to it: the whole daily paper IS a testament of the times."[32]

---

[29]Hugh Nibley, Letter to Paul Springer, February 1952.
[30]Phyllis does not remember this period of anxiety and finds it unlikely that Hugh could have moved around the small house at night without her knowing it, unless it occurred during the times she was hospitalized.
[31]Hugh Nibley, Interviewed by Zina Petersen, 5 March 2002. Hugh is likely referring to the calling up of a thousand members of the 101st on 25 September 1957 to protect nine black students who were, under court order, attending the newly desegregated Central High School in Little Rock.
[32]Hugh Nibley, Letter to Charles Alexander Nibley, 1 April 1979.

A "most notable" sign of the times, Hugh felt, is the realization by ordinary people that the end of our world is not just a silly joke but a real possibility:

> Heretofore it was the bearded, bedraggled, wild-eyed character in the long night shirt whose lugubrious placard about the End of the World and the Need to Repent brought a touch of humor to city streets. Today—as was not so twenty years ago—it is the most sophisticated and informed who worry about a real end of everything as a distinct possibility.[33]

Hugh did not find Mormons very often to be among these "most sophisticated and informed." He lamented the widespread denial to his son: "I am teaching a Gospel Doctrine class in Sunday School: the Doctrine and Covenants does not miss a thing. Only by carefully circumventing about half the passages in it (with the help of the manual) can we escape recognizing that the time is here!"[34]

To those who point out that many earlier announcements of the end have been, at the least, highly overstated, Hugh has emphasized that the Lord has not delayed His coming but that the Church, which was founded on the belief that these are the last days, has been in existence for a very short time, comparatively speaking. He explained these ideas in a lengthy letter to Alex:

> It is because changes have taken place so rapidly that we fail to feel what a SHORT time it has really been since the founding of the Church. . . . In terms of events and changes we have lived an enormous age since then, but in terms of years and generations it is still very short. If Joseph Smith had lived as long as the late President Joseph Fielding Smith, whom you remember, he could have baptized President Kimball.

That being the case, Hugh's attitude of unsurprised and undiminished expectancy seems altogether appropriate. "The prepared soul, in a state of continual repentance, will anticipate our Lord's return. For "it is not what becomes of men but what they become that is the measure of their happiness or calamity." And it's not where we are in that process of "becoming," but which direction we're headed: "The important thing is not . . . where we stand but in which direction we are moving: the man on the bottom step facing up is a happy man, the one on the top step facing down is miserable."[35]

A Life of Social Criticism

It is astounding to me that Hugh Nibley has had a gift of discerning social ills and a sincere compulsion to call us to repentance ever since he was a teenager. And unlike most of us, Hugh's views have not significantly evolved over that time.

Some of his earliest social commentary is also some of the most insightful. At age seventeen, Hugh was called to serve in the Swiss-German Mission. In letters home, he perceptively sized up the spiritual condition of the German people a decade before World War II. Hugh wrote to his Grandmother Sloan:

---

[33]Ibid.

[34]Hugh Nibley, Letter to Charles Alexander Nibley, 10 May 1979.

[35]Hugh Nibley, Letter to Charles Alexander Nibley, 1 April 1979.

> Nobody [in Germany] believes in a God. The strongest Catholics in Frankenthal are professed atheists. And the suddenness of the thing is unbelievable. One feels a strange spirit like a cloud—a real thing that makes the people every week more testy and intolerant,—you feel [that] spirit closing in on the people; something mean & unpleasant seems to inhabit the average house. Not a spirit of uncertainty but of settled, determined indifference. I often wondered where the wickedness was that the Lord accuses the world of—I suppose it is simply indifference, nobody seems to be really bad—but who has a right to be satisfied? . . . So I must again issue forth to a few hours of intense persuading, decoying, tempting—well-nigh bullying. We are supposed to invite & recommend but nearly all the people are past that stage. I am becoming quite artful.[36]

It is also interesting that Hugh employed then, just as he does, now the same combination of faith and learning to call the German people to repentance. In a letter to his mother, he described some discussions with German clergy:

> Our manipulations are getting under the Holymen's already too-well-filled skins. All these fellows seem to think we know 20 times as much as we do, thanks to my playing around with those primitive English manuscripts, all Catholic writings of course, on which their learning and authority has never been before called into question. . . . Then too, in this land of the free, no two Bibles read at all alike, the interpreters pull most of their crude stuff on some of our best passages; so I have actually been able to turn Greek to account.[37]

Hugh's keen eye has also allowed him to delight in our human foibles. In that same letter, Hugh gleefully reported this anecdote:

> A charming and innocent sight here the other day: Before a festival in the Church the little boys who "fling the golden censer wide," that is the caddies in red who bear the smoke-pots before the altar, were outside in front of the Church awaiting their cue. A crowd of imps (their "lay" friends) assembled to examine the curious stinking things & soon the altar servers, forgetting their celestial offices, converted holy instruments into war clubs, and swinging them wildly, like true brothers of Brunhilde, staged a small battle in the market place. Oh the horror of the good Father when he saw them!—stop the fight he? Rather, like the avenging angel did he baptize the little ones with maledictions. The voice out of the whirlwind became the "still small" when he opened up with a salvo of umlauts and gutturals. That was inspiring.

Hugh's awareness of social ills cannot be attributed either to youthful cynicism (he was never cynical) nor to an unusually astute reading of pre-war German fatalism and materialism. Several years after his release from his mission, he wrote to his grandmother in 1938 in a grim poetic/prophetic evocation of the global spiritual decline:

---

[36]Hugh Nibley, Letter to Margaret Violet Reid Sloan, 31 May 1928, photocopy in my possession courtesy of Barbara Nibley Richards.
[37]Hugh Nibley, Letter to Agnes Sloan Nibley, n.d., ca. July-August 1928, Charles W. Nibley Collection, Box 1, fd. 4, L. Tom Perry Special Collections, Harold B. Lee Library, Brigham Young University, Provo, Utah.

> The brightly-lit and not unpleasant stage on which we live is becoming the scene of a strange commotion which it is impossible to ignore and futile to deny. The lines of the gay and artificial background begin to fade and run together; the lights flicker and the floor begins to melt under our feet. We wish, oh how hard we wish! it were not so, and we denounce with feeling anyone so unadvised as to call our attention to what is going on. That is simply a further application of the very dishonesty which has produced this alarming state of things. And so the world goes down into a time of troubles which is but the reflection of its own love of darkness. All of which we have been taught, but have not learned to expect for a hundred years.
>
> If there is any subject for tears . . . it is those successful ones among us who have found their heaven in rewards of a base conformity, who seek their strength and solace in the buying power of fellows like themselves, whose possessions alone justify them in all things and whose property is their whole sanctification and authority. These will not have to wait to a hereafter to learn their folly; we are soon to see them giving their lives (and especially where they can, other people's lives) to save their treasures, which for all that will vanish like smoke.[38]

As a soldier in the U.S. Army six years later, a role he clearly foresaw, he reflected sorrowfully on his missionary labors:

> I ran like a fanatic through the cities of the Rhine preaching nothing but death and destruction, and though I had no authority for such extravagant behavior (which frequently earned the censure of my fellows) except the Doctrine and Covenants, I expected with perfect confidence the present and violent destruction of Karlsruhe, Mannheim, Ludwigshafen and other such towns, all of which were really rather well warned.[39]

In another letter describing the moral condition of the United States during World War II, Hugh wrote ironically to his mother: "Heigh-ho, Imagine supposing that crisper breakfast foods or faster airplanes will give us the Better World of the Future!"[40] Hugh saw the outbreak of World War II as a natural and even inevitable consequence of the world's moral decay. According to Hugh's brother, Reid, "some years before the war broke out," Hugh had "sized up" the fact that the United States would be going to war.[41] In 1942, just before enlisting in the U.S. Army, the thirty-two-year-old Hugh wrote to Paul Springer:

> There is a good deal of philosophical reflection going on in many quarters these days, following the recognition that we are living in a declining world; that war is nature's way of correcting those sins against abstract justice which is not abstract at all, but which, as Solon of old observed, merely seems to be so because it bides its time. It is really quite overwhelming to think that we are all going to get what we deserve.[42]

Later, from Clearwater, Florida, where Hugh was undergoing basic training, he wrote his grandmother a lengthy lamentation about the spiritual decline in the world. In this let-

---

[38] Hugh Nibley, Letter to Margaret Violet Reid Sloan, 4 October 1938.

[39] Hugh Nibley, Letter to Margaret Violet Reid Sloan, 5 December 1942.

[40] Hugh Nibley, Letter to Agnes Sloan Nibley, postmarked 28 April 1943.

[41] Hugh Nibley, "Faith of an Observer," 479.

[42] Hugh Nibley, Letter to Paul Springer, 7 March 1942.

ter, he articulated clearly his view that war was a battle between two evils rather than a scenario of "good guys" versus "bad guys":

> The pattern of [our world's] feverish and ill-considered career presents some striking features. What strikes one most forcefully from the first is the fact that the people of our world are guilty of the tragic mistake of acting and thinking like animals, like mindless insects or some species of shell-fish, to live and breed for a day and then disintegrate and leave nothing behind but a brief and pestilential odor. For this generation, "life" has come to mean little more than the vicissitudes and processes of one's body—we live in an atmosphere of organic metabolism, of digestion, procreation, assimilation and decay—this and this only is the substance of our life, for which reason we excel in nothing, a shoal of a million jellyfish rotting on a tropic beach at this sultry moment under my protesting nose.[43]

But Hugh is not just engaging in romantic histrionics about the world's evils. Instead, he perceptively pinpoints a source of goodness which remains a hope in countering the world's wickedness:

> There are honorable exceptions to this morbid preoccupation with one's vegetative processes—a few uncompromising idealists who are conspicuously held in awe by their fellows. These men, so far as my experience goes, have turned out in *every* case to be Mormons. Draw your own conclusions. If redemption is to come to this declining world, there is no doubt from which direction it will come. . . . But though I looked for a time "when peace would be taken away from the world and the Devil would have control of his own dominion," I never dared to think the Saints could be *happy* in the midst of such a world. But now I say, "why not?" The Gospel is cut and fashioned to weather the strain of perfectly horrible environments, and wherever you have the Gospel that is heaven—in the awareness of its truth we may have a fullness of joy at any time.[44]

Hugh then continued with soul-stirring optimism:

> One of the most embarrassing qualities of our people—their impulsive ill-considered forwardness and lack of restraint—may presently become a great blessing, for in the last and witless world of the near future, any kind of certitude will carry all before it; it is marvelous how little the people of our time are inclined to challenge and examine anything. It is only because the race has become a pack of sheep that absolute dictators can spring up anywhere without opposition.
>
> But enough of this Jeremiad. If there is no greater distress than to watch the world rushing into ills they know not of, there is certainly no greater comfort than to know that one is in a position to cope with such ills, and to feel ourselves strongly seconded by powers greater than our own. Even if we stood quite alone, it would be enough to know that we are in the right. But we do not stand alone. Certain as I am of the presence of a mighty host, I would beg the other world to withhold its fire, so to speak, till we show them what we can do unaided. I cannot be too grateful to the Lord for allowing us the flattering liberties we enjoy, but I am afraid things have almost reached the

---

[43]Hugh Nibley, Letter to Margaret Violet Reid Sloan, 5 December 1942.
[44]Ibid.

point where we have demonstrated our incompetence to the full—it will soon be time for heaven to intervene, and then we can expect no end of surprises.[45]

Six months later, Hugh wrote to his mother from Camp Ritchie, Maryland, where he was undergoing intelligence training. Again he expressed admiration for the persistence of righteousness in the midst of evil:

> What impresses me (and many others) more than anything else in the army is that the powers of evil in our midst are more than matched by a very real and tangible influence for good, expressed in the persons of a perfectly astonishing number of really honest men. This I must say is less noticeable at Ritchie than anywhere else I have been. Here we have the latest shipment from Continental Europe—a bad and shop-worn lot, for the most part—brash, ill-mannered men, quick to exploit every situation for personal gain. Yet [even] among them are a few a little lower than the angels.[46]

Throughout the war, Hugh persisted in his view that World War II was nothing more than prophecy fulfilled:

> For all that has happened to date, one man [Joseph Smith] only has proven a proper guide. We can do no better than follow him for the future. All that is happening, Joseph Smith described as simply incidental to the working out of the plan of life for this dispensation. One dispensation repeats another pretty closely—that is a fundamental proposition with us, and one which the world has only today and with great reluctance been obliged to concede. But the same authority which has depicted so accurately the true nature of our age in the whole scheme of things also assures us that in certain things it is NOT going to repeat the past. This is what we have been looking for, for herein lies the hope of the world. In every respect our world resembles the world of late antiquity, whose career it is repeating step by step in every detail. There is just one notable difference, and that is that this time the Gospel has not been taken away. . . . It seems to me that I have said all this before, but no matter. I feel more strongly every day that history in our times is not going to run its old familiar course but shall presently strike off at a tangent that will surprise us all.[47]

Immediately after the war, Hugh assisted in some of the mopping-up efforts in Germany. His travels by jeep took him to several cities where he had served on his mission. Somberly, he wrote to Paul Springer: "Having . . . beheld the painfully literal justifications of the warning word to these foolish people 17 years ago, I speak with confidence of calamities to come. Everything has turned out exactly as I had imagined, so there is no reason to suppose that it won't continue to do so."[48]

Perhaps most sobering was his visit to the Nazi death camp at Dachau, where he witnessed the extent and brutality of its effort at genocide. On one of the rare occasions where he singled out the Germans for specific disapprobation—as opposed to merely

---

[45] Ibid.
[46] Hugh Nibley, Letter to Agnes Sloan Nibley, 3 June 1943.
[47] Hugh Nibley, Letter to Margaret Violet Reid Sloan, June 1943.
[48] Hugh Nibley, Letter to Paul Springer, photocopy in my possession. The content of the letter indicates that it was written at the very conclusion of World War II, probably late summer 1946.

being a step ahead of the rest of humankind in plunging toward moral corruption—Hugh wrote: "Other people have their vices as opposed to their virtues, but the Germans' vices *are* their virtues and vice versa; by an act of that will they are forever talking about, they turn good qualities into vicious ones or clothe any crime that suits them in moral garments. They remain, after all, still the most dangerous people in the world—unwilling to distinguish good from bad."[49]

Even though others might see the social degeneration as a result of a world gone mad in war, Hugh unfalteringly continued to attribute the destruction to human immorality—to wrongful choices, rather than circumstances, human nature, bad leadership, or a vengeful God:

> It is only after men have neatly reversed all values, calling black white and vice virtue, that nature follows suit. Nature does not want to be thrown off balance—seventy times seven she will patiently refuse to turn topsy turvy, and then finally one day she reacts to that steady, willful perversity and makes some adjustments of her own. The 4th century BC and the 6th AD are terrible examples. In the times of total confusion which lie ahead let us not forget how clearly our own behavior has foreshadowed the horrible commotion of the earth and the elements. I speak in a prophetic vein, because the signs of an impending readjustment in the face of the whole earth are fairly clear.[50]

The one good thing coming from the war, Hugh argued, is a proper distrust of outward appearances:

> The Nazis have done us the service of showing how complete the depravity can go on year after year enjoying an unchallenged authority, wearing the robes of every office with dignity and ease, professing none but noble motives and going thru all the motions of high governance. After their masterful performance the world may rightly distrust every appearance—flags, hymns, parades, and solemn oaths have been forever discredited by German wickedness.[51]

Despite his abhorrence for German immorality and atrocities, Hugh was equally astringent about the immorality and atrocities committed by Americans. A few months after the Normandy invasion, Hugh responded to some unstated "jeremiads" from his mother about the political climate in the United States by warning succinctly: "Obviously few people are making an effort to win the blessings which the Book of Mormon promises to the promised land; the catch is that the alternative is not an easy decline or gentle corruption but a whacking curse that knocks all the pegs out at once as soon as everything is good and ready."[52] For Hugh, the only "good guys" were those repenting and striving for righteousness; all the rest were "bad guys."

Hugh's skepticism about materialism and moral corruption did not change, even during the prosperous fifties when the USA replaced Great Britain as the bastian of freedom and when a booming economy created the generous Marshall plan for rehabilitating

---

[49]Hugh Nibley, Letter to Agnes Sloan Nibley, n.d. ca. 1945.
[50]Hugh Nibley, Letter to Agnes Sloan Nibley, 5 November 1944.
[51]Hugh Nibley, Letter to Agnes Sloan Nibley, 24 August 1944.
[52]Ibid. I have not yet found the letter to which Hugh is responding, so it is unclear what circumstances prompted this exchange.

the conquered countries, an unheard-of wave of educational opportunities through the G.I. Bill, and unprecedented personal affluence for many Americans. In one letter he commented on the popularity of *A Generation of Vipers* (New York: Rinehart, 1942), an essay of strident social criticism by Philip Wylie. According to Hugh, it "simply preaches a basic Mormon doctrine, namely, that this is a wicked and adulterous generation and well on the way to being destroyed by its own worthlessness."[53] About four years later, he was lamenting to the same correspondent:

> What hurts is not that we and all our neglected possibilities are going down the drain but [that] there is no good reason on earth why we should not be. This poor exploited planet has never had to support a more expensive and pampered race, or one that gave so little in return for the oxygen and carbohydrates it consumes. The Romans on the whole were pretty contemptible, but they had moments of real grandeur, independently of their ability to mass-produce. No such moments for us; when national existence is reduced to the level of merely marking time the show is over.[54]

In another letter, Hugh described the self-satisfaction of the 1950s as a sort of pre-apocalyptic paralysis:

> Good old Ate is taking over in the great Democracy. As you know, I was always yelling about Mme. Ate, the Grecian damsel symbolizing the mental paralysis that grips those about to be destroyed, a sort of hypo that nature kindly administers to her marked victims to spare them the agony of useless struggle; the progressive numbing of the sensibilities is now far advanced, the hypnotic fascination that draws the doomed creature with obscene eagerness to embrace its own undoing has now taken it beyond the point of no return.[55]

In a 1948 letter, written just as the Cold War was heating up, Hugh spoke of the conflict between the United States and the Soviet Union in terms that are now quite prophetic:

> My guess is that neither of the Giant Protagonists is big enough to destroy the other: eventually, weird as it sounds, we are going to have to come to some sort of agreement, whether we want it or not—and it will be the same agreement that we could have made before we lost our pants. Seen from here the American temperament seems to display all the qualities one could ask for but always in the wrong situation—any virtues you have are wasted, says Plato unless you have the great coordinating virtue of Sophrosyne—good sense, a thing notably lacking in our makeup. So we are firm and steadfast in situations where a graceful compliance is indicated. Soft and yielding where the only proper course is not to give an inch. Impetuous and outspoken where silence alone will win the field. Secretive and reserved when outspokenness is everything. Cautious in every situation requiring bold action, very dashing at the time for delicate forbearance. Etc.[56]

---

[53]Hugh Nibley, Letter to Paul Springer, 5 August 1946.

[54]Hugh Nibley, Letter to Paul Springer, n.d., after 17 August 1950.

[55]Hugh Nibley, Letter to Paul Springer, 18 December 1950. More precisely, Ate is the Greek goddess of ruinous and foolhardy impulse.

[56]Hugh Nibley, Letter to Paul Springer, (no day) July 1948.

Even if the superpowers had demonstrated more competence in dealing with their unprecedented perils and opportunities, Hugh was skeptical of a better outcome. As he repeatedly insisted, the basic perspective was fatally flawed: "Some day (soon) we may learn the H-bombs solve nothing and armed might is indeed a joke. The case of the unlamented Adolf should make it clear enough by now that power does not reside where people think it does. As far as I am concerned it's all happening on schedule."[57]

Militarism and materialism were only two manifestations of what Hugh persistently lamented in our declining civilization. Sometime in 1939 or 1940, Hugh visited the Golden Gate International Exposition in San Francisco which was to celebrate the new Golden Gate Bridge and the Oakland Bay Bridge. He was overwhelmed by what he saw as a "reversal" in cultural values:

> In this age of mass-production, a world's fair has nothing to offer but the typical and ordinary: you see how the familiar can of beans is created or how the standard automobile is assembled, or you learn where the average electric-light bulb comes from. As if anybody gave a damn about that. Once fairs were held to display what could be seen nowhere in the world: the unique and the marvelous were worth a journey. The masses have scored again in a complete reversal of the principle: by an incredible perversion the prominence given to exhibits is in direct proportion to their common placeness. Is it possible? The average, the ordinary, the normal, the standard, the ideal, all are at the last the same and find their realization in the single object. Not because all have been raised to the highest level, but because all are brought down to the lowest.[58]

Forty years later, he expressed the same dismay over what U.S. entertainment and diversions communicate about current civilization. "If you ask me the nearest thing I have seen to Hell," he wrote to Alex, his son, then serving a mission in Japan, "I will unhesitatingly reply Disneyland, a schizophrenic nightmare in which nothing is real. With that our anti-culture reaches its peak."[59]

But Hugh was not merely a curmudgeon finding fault with the ways in which other people lived their lives. Rather he saw this collapse of culture as an outward expression of an inward deterioration. People become uninterested in heavenly treasures—the things of the spirit—at the same time they become preoccupied with earthly treasures. "So we [humankind of the future] are going to be a race of sleek naked giants with no inner existence at all," he laments, "waging perpetual warfare for the possession of new planets and things."[60] After the eruption of Oregon's Mount St. Helens in May 1980, Hugh wrote, "Nature is kind and forbearing compared with the relentless drive of corporate and conspiring humanity to further special ends and interests regardless of the price."[61]

---

[57] Hugh Nibley, Letter to Paul Springer, n.d. 1950.
[58] Hugh Nibley, Letter to Paul Springer, n.d., ca. 1940.
[59] Hugh Nibley, Letter to Charles Alexander Nibley, n.d., ca. May 1980.
[60] Hugh Nibley, Letter to Paul Springer, n.d., ca. 1940.
[61] Hugh Nibley, Letter to Charles Alexander Nibley, n.d., ca. May 1980. The letters that Hugh wrote to Alex express a heightened state of Hugh's already constant apocalypticism. They were written between 1979 and 1981 when the United States was in the middle of a military arms race with the Soviet Union and consumed with me-generation avarice.

This deterioration grows directly from the collapse of divine virtues. In 1944, Hugh wrote: "The people of the world for the most part . . . have built up a strong willful indifference to everything: they believe nothing, they hope nothing, they have endured what they had to and hope to be able to get out of enduring anything more."[62] And in 1979, Hugh described "the most ominous of all signs of the times" as "that mentality which is dangerously deficient in faith, hope, and charity."[63]

I think Hugh has at times been overly harsh in his negative assessment of our civilization's achievements. For example, in 1950, he wrote with asperity to Paul Springer, "The question is not, will American civilization collapse? but, rather when *did* it collapse? Answer: it was destroyed in the Civil War, since when no single work of original native greatness has been forthcoming."[64] Despite such overreactions, I still believe Hugh's social criticism is his most valuable contribution to Mormon thought. Across the span of Hugh's adult life, he has perceptively seen the shabbiness of the values governing Western civilization, repeatedly warned against their shallowness, and insisted that a return to gospel principles holds the only hope for human regeneration.

Commitment to the Church

Despite his often biting warnings to his fellow Church members, Hugh Nibley's life is one of staunch commitment to the Church and the gospel. In a day when a mistrust of organizations is widespread, Hugh sees the Church in a very different light. While he is not blind to the foibles and weaknesses of the Church's leaders, he has avoided criticizing them for being human and has also cautioned us to avoid that tendency.

It seems paradoxical to some that Hugh can be so scathing about some aspects of Mormon culture while he simultaneously remains beyond any question a loyal lover of the Church. Interviewed for a documentary video on Hugh Nibley, Elder Neal A. Maxwell singled out Hugh's devotion to the Church for praise. Hugh's "commitment is so visible and has been so pronounced and so repetitively stated that that's not even the issue." In fact, Maxwell sees Hugh's social commentary as "a reflection of his deepened discipleship" and feels that Hugh "is so focused on the things that matter, and is spiritually submissive, that he's impatient with mediocrity; he's impatient with irrelevance."[65]

How does Hugh Nibley achieve and maintain this balance in perspective? I think that he does it in three ways. First, on most occasions Hugh uses his social complaints to stress his testimony of the Church. In one of his most scalding attacks on Mormon culture (his 1983 BYU commencement address), Hugh derided our willingness to sacrifice ethics for wealth, knowledge for training, culture for kitsch, and inspiring leadership for bottom-line management. But in that very talk, he supported his thesis with the examples of Joseph Smith and Brigham Young as divinely inspired leaders and drew from the Book of Mormon his examples of inspired leaders versus immoral managers. He also bore testimony of the Book of Mormon as scripture and as ancient history, of the temple's

---

[62]Hugh Nibley, Letter to Agnes Sloan Nibley, 12 September 1944.
[63]Hugh Nibley, Letter to Charles Alexander Nibley, 1 April 1979.
[64]Hugh Nibley, Letter to Paul Springer, 18 December 1950.
[65]Hugh Nibley, "Faith of an Observer," 525, 522.

importance in setting one's sights on the treasures of heaven, and of the divine appointment of Joseph Smith and his successors as prophets, seers, and revelators.[66]

This combination of perspectives leaves Hugh occupying an oft-ignored and seldom inhabited "middle position" between so-called "liberals" and "conservatives"—those who liked what Hugh said about social issues but didn't like his take on the Book of Mormon vs. those who liked his championship of the Book of Mormon but who shied away from his social criticism. Louis C. Midgley, a BYU professor of political science, observed as early as 1969:

> Hugh Nibley has long been waging a major two front war: his best known campaign is against what might be called "Cultural Mormonism" [Midgley is referring here to those who would like to deemphasize the Book of Mormon and become more like a liberal protestant church]; but an equally significant campaign is now under way against a form of "Sectarian Mormonism" now having some popularity, especially in certain academic circles. Both the Cultural and Sectarian types are eager to effect an accommodation of the gospel with features of the prevailing culture. That Nibley has defended the integrity of the gospel against the Cultural Mormons is rather well known; what is not nearly as well known is that he has evoked the Book of Mormon against the efforts of Sectarian Mormons to align certain American middleclass values with the gospel, as well as the recent attempts of some Mormons to sanctify a radical [rightwing] political ideology by attributing it to God.[67]

Second, Hugh Nibley has never set himself apart or above the rest of us or presumed to speak from a position of moral superiority. Rather, he has established himself as dedicated member of the community of Saints. Where he preaches, he also practices; when he chides us for our sins, he also sets an example. On many occasions I have heard him admit to a sin or weakness, express his regret, and state his firm determination to repent.

Third, Hugh has always held and expressed a deep respect for the General Authorities of the Church, a reverence that is all the more unusual since we might expect him, as the grandson of a General Authority, to see more of their humanness and less of their divine calling. Instead, while he has acknowledged their human weaknesses, he has maintained that they are divinely called and inspired.

He frequently tells a story that he says confirmed his attitude toward the Brethren. During the early 1950s, BYU faculty members accompanied General Authorities to stake quarterly conferences to recruit students. As Hugh accompanied several General Authorities, he was impressed by "how they worked their life-long assignments, living in a goldfish bowl, everlastingly meeting appointments, and carrying out routine duties." In about 1952, he traveled throughout the Southwest with Spencer W. Kimball, then an apostle, a journey rendered memorable by a simple act of meekness. In Los Angeles, Hugh had been visiting a bookstore just prior to the group's departure and had to race for train. He sat down next to Elder Kimball, and the two began discussing Hugh's finds.

---

[66]Hugh Nibley, "Leaders to Managers: The Fatal Shift," in *Brother Brigham Challenges the Saints*, 491-508.
[67]Louis C. Midgley "The Secular Relevance of the Gospel: A Review of Hugh Nibley's *Since Cumorah*," *Dialogue: A Journal of Mormon Thought* 4, no. 4 (Winter 1969): 76.

Brother Kimball casually took an immaculate linen handkerchief from the breast pocket of his jacket, and, stooping over, vigorously dusted off my shoes and trousers. It was the most natural thing in the world, and we both took it completely for granted. After all, my shoes were dusty in the race for the train, and Brother Kimball had always told missionaries to keep themselves clean and proper. It was no great thing—pas d'histoire. Neither of us said a thing about it, but ever since, that has conditioned my attitude toward the Brethren. I truly believe that they are chosen servants of God.[68]

Yet if Hugh was impressed by Elder Kimball, Elder Kimball was also impressed by Hugh. In a letter to his wife, Camilla Eyring Kimball, Elder Kimball called Hugh "a most interesting person"; compared Hugh to her brother, chemist Henry Eyring; attempted to list the number of languages Hugh spoke; and said "he talks like lightning, faster than I do, faster than Henry." In sum, Elder Kimball wrote approvingly, "He seems to know much about many topics and have a great faith with it all."[69] But when Elder Kimball wrote a letter thanking Hugh for accompanying him on the visit, Kimball, though impressed by Hugh as a scholar, focused on his faith: "I personally appreciated very much your sweet spirit and your faith and your humility."[70]

This trio of virtues—his coupling of social criticism with testimony, his willingness to include himself among those he calls to repentance, and his respect for the Brethren—have provided a solid anchoring in the faith for Hugh Nibley.

Hugh's Effectiveness as a Social Critic

In 1990, when Eugene England called Hugh our "finest lay prophet," England pointed out the irony that Hugh's message has been largely unheeded within the Church. England compared Hugh to Cassandra—the Trojan princess who was blessed with the gift of prophecy but cursed with the fate that no one would believe her. Hugh "has been uniquely insightful and yet essentially ineffective" in winning adherents to his "crucial message of repentance to our greedy, militaristic, and environmentally destructive society," stated England.[71] When I asked England several years later if he felt Hugh's status as Cassandra had changed, he responded: "My sense is that, if anything, our culture has become . . . more willing to confuse their cultural convictions with the Gospel."[72]

Hugh himself is neither alarmed nor dismayed by his role as Cassandra. Writing to his son Alex in 1979, he observed: "I have long since learned that my most brash outspeaking leaves the Philistines untouched, because nobody ever thinks any of the criticism applies to him, while gleefully recognizing its delicious pertinence to his neighbors."[73]

Other reasons may partially account for this strange neglect. First, Hugh has never been willing to play the role of pundit and pontificator that has given others access to the media. Second, some may be so used to not understanding Hugh on some top-

---

[68] *Brother Brigham Challenges the Saints*, 444. "Pas d'histoire" is a French phrase that means "nothing to make a fuss over."

[69] Spencer W. Kimball, Letter to Camilla Kimball, 20 May 1952, photocopy courtesy of Edward L. Kimball.

[70] Spencer W. Kimball, Letter to Hugh Nibley, 29 May 1952.

[71] England, "Hugh Nibley as Cassandra," 104-5.

[72] Eugene England, e-mail to Boyd Petersen, 18 November 1997.

[73] Hugh Nibley, Letter to Charles Alexander Nibley, 16 November 1979.

ics—particularly those requiring depth of scholarship—that they simply tune him out no matter what the subject is. Others may assume he is reaffirming their beliefs because that is what he usually does. And still others may simply not hear what he is really saying. For example, I've heard one improbable anecdote that an ROTC officer stated, "Some say Nibley is antiwar, but I just don't see how they get that." And certainly others may hear his words and simply disagree.

Yet I have talked to many individuals who have been deeply moved by Hugh's social commentary and by his challenges to live the gospel more fully. *Approaching Zion* and *Brother Brigham Challenges the Saints* became turning points in their lives. One person told me that Hugh's words decisively influenced him to give up hunting—which was "quite a change for one who grew up in Utah and was often outdoors with a gun in his hands." Several people have confirmed to me that Hugh's environmental essays made them appreciate the natural world more and take action to help protect it. One woman, after reading *Approaching Zion*, cut back her hours at work to spend more time with her family. She also now buys clothes only when she actually needs them. These and other changes, she testifies, have made her life simpler and calmer. Another correspondent took Hugh's warnings about materialism to heart and has stayed in his "starter" home, which is sufficient for his needs, rather than moving up to a larger, more expensive, but no more functional house. Several others identified similar Nibley-influenced lifestyle changes: they buy less, live more modestly, and give more of their income to support the Church, the missionaries, and the poor. As a bonus, several individuals noted that buying less made their children more appreciative and less demanding. In some instances, Hugh's words have given people the courage to leave jobs they didn't enjoy and do work that gives them greater satisfaction even though it provides less income.

I believe that Hugh's social criticism has indeed had a significant impact, if not on the Church as a whole, on the many individuals who feel their lives are better for having headed his counsel. Perhaps that influence will grow as Hugh's *Collected Works* near completion and reach a broader audience.

Hugh Nibley has taught us that the gospel includes much more than most of us ever thought it did, and he has always urged us to take it very seriously. "The Gospel is so devised that you must either go overboard for it or leave it strictly alone."[74]

---

[74] Hugh Nibley, Letter to Paul Springer, n.d., 1957.

Hugh Nibley, about age sixteen, ca. 1916.

    I began my second decade in Southern California as a compulsive reader, memorizing Shakespeare plays and aspiring to add something to the Bard's modest contribution. But English literature I soon found to be derivative, and so took to Old English to find out what was behind it; what was behind it was Latin, and what was behind that was Greek. . . . I began to suspect that the records had something very important to convey to us. . . .

    In the twenties business was booming . . . and I got a good look at some Big Men who played golf [with my grandfather]; dull, profane men they were, who cheated on every stroke, just about. When my admiring father asked one of them at dinner what he considered to be his greatest achievement in life, the man unhesitatingly replied that it was his celebrated filibuster to keep James Joyce's Ulysses (a book of which, as literature, I was very fond) out of the land. . . . I learned that there were kindhearted tramps who knew far more than any teacher I had had—I mean about literature and science—but tramped because they preferred passing through this world as observers of God's works. For such a luxury they paid a heavy price: in any small town in the nation anyone not visibly engaged either in making or spending money was quickly apprehended and locked up as a dangerous person—a vagrant. Everywhere, I learned very well, the magic words were, "Have you any money?" Satan's Golden Question. Freedom to come and go was only for people who had the stuff—in fact you could have anything in this world for it.[1]

---

[1] Hugh Nibley, "An Intellectual Autobiography," *Nibley on the Timely and the Timeless* (Provo, UT: Brigham Young Press, 1978), xx-xxi.

Chapter 4

Growing Up in Los Angeles, 1921-27

Hugh turned ten in 1920. The next seven years—he left on his mission at age seventeen—were years of explosive intellectual growth and almost complete liberty to experience the California environment—both its beautiful woods and its commercial urban landscapes. During these broadening years, he also found the intellectual and spiritual moorings that set his course for the rest of his life.

For an energetic and alert teenager, Southern California offered an unparalleled panorama of experiences to sample. Indeed, its business was booming. Already known as a vacation site, Los Angeles saw thousands of tourists flocking to the area each year. The burgeoning motion picture industry, only a few years old in 1920, became a billion-dollar industry during its first decade. By 1920, Los Angeles had its first aircraft factory and would become home to more before the decade ended. And the Los Angeles harbor, which opened in 1914, had become a major port on the Pacific. Traffic congestion was already a concern in 1920, with 160,000 cars on the road. Some things really haven't changed. But other industries—quite successful then—have since died out in Southern California. For example, oil drilling rigs sprouted at Long Beach, Huntington Beach, and Santa Fe Springs, turning Southern California into the producer of one-fifth of the world's oil supply. Times were good. And with more and more business came more and more people. During the decade, the population of Los Angeles more than doubled and the population of Burbank increased five times. This meant that real estate was booming; 11,608 acres were subdivided in 1923 alone.[2] "Stock was shooting up and everybody was getting rich,"

---

[2]E. Caswell Perry, *Burbank: An Illustrated History* (Northridge, CA: Windsor, 1987), 45.
[3]Hugh Nibley, "Faith of an Observer," 169, compilation of interviews, ca. 1983-84 for a video documentary of the same name aired in 1985, photocopy of typescript in my possession, pagination added.

remembers Hugh. "We thought the Dow Jones would take us right into the Millennium."³

In 1920, a few months before the move, El Nibley had tested the commercial waters in California. His biographical sketch, compiled in the 1940s, states that he and Lon J. Haddock organized the Haddock-Nibley Real Estate Company, "under [the] financial backing of Chas. W. Nibley." Among their major projects were the development of the eighty-acre tract of Glendale Heights, Goldwin Park in Culver City, and Rossmoyne, a tract of 781 acres in northeastern Glendale. El and Charles Nibley generously "gave to the city of Glendale the beautiful property known as Nibley Park. . . . He was well-known in the civic life of Glendale" and served "for many years as a member of the Glendale Park Commission."⁴ In addition, he was vice president and general manager of the Nibley Investment Company. By the mid-twenties, both the real estate and investment companies were benefiting greatly from the economic good times.

The family was living in a comfortable home at 1661 Buckingham Road, Lafayette Square, in Los Angeles, then moved to a frankly luxurious home in Glendale. There Sloanie hosted lavish parties entertaining the posh society of Glendale and, at time, the entire Los Angeles Philharmonic Orchestra. They moved easily among the affluent and cultured in southern California, taking an active part in the state's literature, music, and art scenes.

"There was always an atmosphere of doing interesting things," remembers Reid, who was thirteen years' Hugh's junior. "Going to concerts, going to art galleries, going to where beautiful things were, enjoying beautiful things. And it was always available."⁵ Conversation around the dinner table was always lively, filled with cultural allusions. Conversations became even livelier when they turned to politics. "Dad was the staunch Republican and Mother was the staunch Democrat," Reid later recalled. "The boys tended to have the Democratic viewpoint and so there was this split between Dad and the rest of the family."⁶

While the family was quite refined and sophisticated, they were not snobs. "I had no real consciousness that there was such a thing as wealth and privilege and status or anything like that," says Reid. Nor did they take themselves too seriously. The boys played many games together that required both basic brain-power and wit. As they would ride in the car together, the four boys would often write poetry—what Hugh called "our little moral emblems." They would decide on a poetic meter and then the first player would compose a line. He would then tell the next player the last word of his line, and that player, in turn would write a line that would rhyme with the previous line. And the process continued until they had an entire poem. "It was absolutely nonsense," remembers Reid. "But since the words rhymed at the end of each line . . . , it sounded like the lines were belonging, like the words made some sense, but they were just ridiculous."⁷

---

⁴Leo J. Muir, *A Century of Mormon Activities in California*, 2 vols. (Salt Lake City: Deseret News Press, compiled in 1946 and published in 1952), 2:286-87.

⁵Reid Nibley, "Faith of an Observer," 486.

⁶Ibid., 488.

⁷Ibid., 485, 488-89.

The boys would often play the same game with music. The first player would write a line of music and fold the paper over so that the next player would only see the final note and its value. Then the second player would write another line. Like the poems, the music made no sense, but, as Reid states, "it was hilarious; it was fun." Hugh also composed nonsense lyrics for classical themes. "I've lost my pajamas / I'll have to wear grandma's" fit Mendelssohn's "Fingle's Cave." Beethoven's Sixth Symphony theme was used for: "Oh Uncle Oscar, / what else is there to do, / but sit on the doorstep / and sing to cousin Henry." He seldom went beyond a fragment for the motif, recalled Reid, but Beethoven's choral concerto drew out a lengthier verse, of which Reid remember this much:

> Now that oysters are in season,
> Let us go and bring some here,
> And we'll open them and eat them
> With some pretzels and some beer.
> And if any are left over
> We will put the lot on ice,
> And we'll have them all for breakfast,
> Irregardless of the price.

"The classic of all" was Hugh's text for a theme from Beethoven's Fourth Piano Concerto. It was a rhymed recipe, which Reid laments that he can no longer remember at all: "it was a gem."[8]

Hugh as a teenager also dabbled in playwriting. Most often, he both "wrote and starred in them," according to Sloan, but he also enlisted brothers Phil and Richard for a Greek tragedy that featured a Greek nurse named "Pin-on-didies" (a pun for "pin on diapers") and used the Christmas tree lights as footlights on the makeshift performance area in the family's living room." Sloan confesses that "it took me about three takes to figure it out."[9]

But life for the four Nibley boys was not all fun either. Sloanie Nibley decided early on what she wanted her children to be and pushed them hard. Hugh was to be a novelist, Reid a concert pianist, Richard a concert violinist, and Barbara an opera star. For some reason, the expectations were never as strongly defined for Sloan or Philip. "She was always pushing," remembers Hugh.[10] She pushed them in their school work; she pushed them to learn musical instruments; and she pushed them into particular fields where she thought they would excel. "She had all our lives very carefully planned," recalled Reid, who actually did become a concert pianist, although he chose teaching, rather than performing, as his life's work. "She knew exactly what she wanted every one of us to be, and none of us turned out the way she wanted us to, of course. We were all supposed to be great famous people, and all that, and we didn't care about that."[11] The "great novelist" plan was a bust for Hugh. "Her wanting me to do it, of course, made it an achievement for which I had no desire," confessed Hugh.[12] In fact, he did give it a

---

[8]Ibid., 489, 491.
[9]Sloan Nibley, "Faith of an Observer," 539.
[10]Hugh Nibley, "Faith of an Observer," 107-8.
[11]Reid Nibley, "Faith of an Observer," 483-84.
[12]Todd F. Maynes, "Nibleys: Pianist, Scholar, Brilliant but Different," *Daily Universe*, 1 November 1982, 1-7.

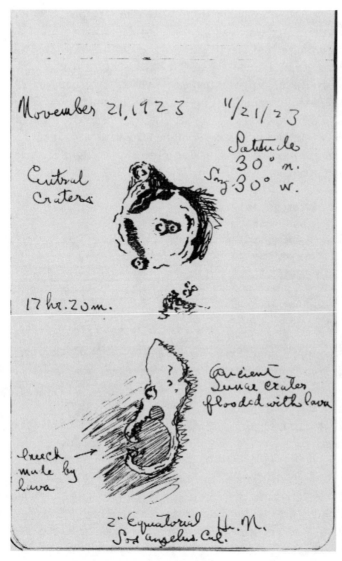

Page from Hugh's astronomy journal, 21 November 1923.

try but just felt "so guilty. What right have I got, making these people up? It's wrong; I shouldn't do it." (One chapter of what was probably a novel dating from his high school days has survived.) In contrast, he loved history: "The real thing is more fascinating."[13]

His own competitive spirit kept him from ignoring academic achievement, and he was a driven learner. "I'd just make myself sick with it," remembers Hugh. "I didn't want to be humiliated by missing a question in a test or anything like that. It had to be over-learned; it had to be overkill."[14]

Although the family continued to hire private tutors, Sloanie also registered Hugh in the public schools. Hugh attended Alta Loma School for his middle school years, from 1921 through early 1923. While private tutors had prepared him academically, they had not prepared him socially. "I was the littlest guy in the whole junior high and [Alta Loma] was a tough place," remembers Hugh.[15] He got in "some fights" but "had no trouble with that because I was a fast learner and my friend Robert Guild was a good fighter." Given this combination, Hugh was soon getting along "fine."[16]

Hugh graduated to Los Angeles High School at the age of thirteen, a year and a half ahead of his age group.[17] "L.A. High School was very tony," remembers Hugh.

---

[13] Hugh Nibley, "Faith of an Observer," 51.
[14] Ibid., 251.
[15] Hugh Nibley, interviewed by Boyd Petersen, 16 June 1996.
[16] Hugh Nibley, "Faith of an Observer," 97.
[17] Los Angeles City School District Certificate of Promotion, 2 February 1923. California and Oregon had half-year schedules, sometimes allowing graduations in winter.

"It was the high school; it was in the most fashionable part of town. And they had an excellent faculty there; they were very choosy about their faculty."[18] He wrote his grandfather in 1924 with qualified approval that LA High lacked "the exasperating red tape that is usually wrapped around every girder, brick, and board. But they take it out on us in study. Every breath is an assignment, every thought a report or composition. 'My heart is in the coffin there, with pleasure.' Ah me! as my Pleasure was ambitious, School slew him but it was all for the good of Hugh Nibley."[19]

Eleven-year-old Hugh made this pen sketch on 25 January 1922.

"He seemed to have interests in nearly everything—music, art, history and science," Reid recalled. However, three interests became consuming for Hugh: astronomy, art, and English. When he received a small telescope as a present, he spent many hours staring into the night sky. "I loved astronomy," remembers Hugh. "I memorized Adam's astronomy and various books."[20] Hugh kept an astronomy journal in which he mapped the constellations and sketched the moonscapes he could make out. Sloan recalls that Hugh was absolutely obsessed with star-gazing and "more than once" would "wake me up at three in the morning and tell me that Venus or somebody was having an occlusion." Sloan added with considerable restraint, "I didn't care to see it particularly."

There was, however, one problem with Hugh's bedroom observatory: a streetlight just outside of the boys' room created distracting light pollution. According to Sloan, Hugh finally became fed up with the troublesome light, hauled out a ladder and some black paint, and painted half of the streetlight out. Hugh's obsession with astronomy was so strong that it sometimes led him to even more drastic lengths. One morning over the breakfast table, the family gazed at Hugh, puzzled by some subtle

---

[18]Hugh Nibley, Interviewed 25 February 2001, by Boyd Petersen.
[19]Hugh Nibley, Letter to Charles W. Nibley, n.d., 1924; Charles W. Nibley Collection, Family Correspondence, LDS Church Archives. He is playing off Shakespeare's, Julius Caesar, III.ii: "My heart is in the coffin there with Caesar."
[20]Hugh Nibley, "Faith of an Observer," 236.

change in his appearance. "Suddenly, one of us noticed that his eyelashes were gone," recalled Sloan. Hugh had cut them off so he could see better through the telescope.[21]

Hugh also discovered a natural ability as an artist. His medium was primarily pencil sketches and his specialty was tall ships. "I must say," Sloan admitted, "he had a real talent there."[22] Despite his ability, Hugh remained humble. Eleven-year-old Hugh wrote his grandfather in 1921, "The other night I stayed up till two o'clock (mainly drawing) while my gentle guardians were out. Drawing is like learning to play the violin. The more you know, the less you think you know. I am positive I know an awful lot."[23]

It was two gifted and devoted high school English teachers—Alma Elizabeth Gunning and Snow Longley—who nurtured Hugh's love and gift for language and literature from his first year in high school. "I was really electrified," remembers Hugh.[24] His first English class, taught by Miss Gunning, gave themselves the name "Mnemosyneians." (Mnemosyne—or memory—is the mother of the nine Muses in Greek mythology.) This class set the goal of memorizing "as many notable passages of literature as possible." And such a course of stocking an agile and retentive mind with great thoughts captured in the best expressions of the English language was meat and drink to thirteen-year-old Hugh. "We read and memorized extensively [Shakespeare's] *Julius Caesar* (which was often dramatized in class, as you will recall), [Sir Walter Scott's] *Ivanhoe*, *Pilgrim's Progress* [by John Bunyan], and even such heavy stuff as *Macbeth*—all in the freshman year of high school."[25]

This wide exposure to English literature prompted Hugh to seek out the texts' antecedents, which, in turn, led him to Anglo-Saxon and beyond:

> The first thing I read was Bede's gospel of John. But then there was King Alfred's *The Book of the Phoenix*, the famous Anglo-Saxon poem, but that's just taken from Lactantius, so I said, "Well, aha, we have to go back to Lactantius." Now Lactantius is the first and, in Latin, the best of all the Christian writers. He is good with Latin, so I had to go back to Latin. But I soon discovered that Lactantius was merely quoting a lot of Greeks . . . , so then it had to be the Greeks. And everybody believed then . . . that it all began with the Greeks, they were the great creators . . . . Well, that's not so at all. [The ultimate literary sources are] much older. It took me a while to find that out, but it's true.[26]

To read these texts, Hugh began to study languages. He had already had some French when he studied with his school principal, Mr. Barr, in Portland. Now he was beginning to learn Old and Middle English, German, Latin, and Greek. Many ministers retired in Pasadena and Santa Monica, and the area's used bookstores were filled

---

[21] Sloan Nibley, "Faith of an Observer," 531.

[22] Ibid., 532.

[23] Hugh Nibley, Letter to Charles W. Nibley, 30 June 1921, Charles W. Nibley Collection, Family Correspondence, LDS Church Archives.

[24] Hugh Nibley, "Faith of an Observer," 52.

[25] Hugh Nibley, *Approaching Zion*, edited by Don E. Norton, Vol. 9 of *The Collected Works of Hugh Nibley* (Salt Lake City: Deseret Book/FARMS, 1989), 545-46.

[26] Hugh Nibley, "Faith of an Observer," 53.

with their libraries, sold by the widows. With an ironic grin, Hugh remembers passing up "a whole series of Gibbons which had belonged to Ralph Waldo Emerson with his commentaries in the margin and his autograph inside the cover. Emerson, I thought, how interesting it's Emerson."[27]

Although Hugh repudiated fiction, he experimented with poetry. His first surviving poem, written just a few days after Hugh turned sixteen, was a tribute to his Grandmother Sloan for her sixty-ninth birthday in April 1926:

> Of Birthdays
> Sun, why do you hurry?
> Why do you clear at one mad bound
> The frail, sweet mist;
> And bursting once in shouting radiance,
> Route [sic] out the lingering muses of the night?
> Why do you scud and slither up your path
> So easily and so cruelly?
> Oh, dumb, relentless sun,
> Is it I who goad you?
> I would fight you, hold you—
> Tie you with sullen weights—dream-wrought and terrible.
> Oh, grant me but a little moment still,
> Before you lash your noon light on the world:
> Before you totter for that awful leap
> That flings you from the zenith, leaving night—
> But stay: your brassy breath is fading now!
> Oh, blind sun, dazzled by your own thin light!
> See now already how you call up little shadows—
> Blue and low, but feeling—gathering,
> They frighten me, they whisper as they creep;
> Sweet Sun, be kind and spare us but an hour.
> The air is purple now the wind is waiting—
> A long sigh from the west
>
> Forgive me, Sun,
> I did forget the glory of thy setting!

Although Hugh presumably gave his Grandmother Sloan a copy of this poem, he did not show it to his parents and apparently swore his grandmother to secrecy as well. Four weeks later on 21 May, El sent a copy of the poem to his father, Charles W. Nibley. In the accompanying letter, El states that Hugh's high school teacher called the poem "a classic." He confesses somewhat sheepishly that "Hugh does not know we have a copy of [the poem] and would have a fit if he thought we were getting his stuff from the High School; he positively refuses to let any of us see what he is doing." The proud father had sent this poem to Will C. Wood, California's Superintendent of Public Instruction, who had responded generously, "I enjoyed it thoroughly and can truly say that it seems remarkable that a lad of 15 [sic] could have philosophized in that fash-

---
[27]Ibid., 52.

ion and constructed his thoughts into such beautiful verse."[28] Hugh's reaction, when the poem appeared in the June 1926 *Improvement Era*, then the official magazine for the Mutual Improvement Associations, has not been recorded; but he probably was not pleased.[29] In fact, the poem is over-exuberant and strains somewhat for effect, nor is the concept—time's flight combined with the consolations of nature—an unusual one; still, it is a remarkable achievement by any standard for a sixteen-year-old.

Also in 1926, Hugh's "The Freight Train" appeared in the literary journal *The Lyric West*.[30]

> The Freight Train
> Color is dead, Romance is dead, and all
> Their retinue—here comes the funeral line,
> Murky and distant things that glimly shine;
> Smothered, obscured in one long dusky pall,
> The wheels and couplings rattle, grip, and brawl;
> Upon the solemn funeral air of pine
> Lies incense blasphemous. Such fate is thine,
> O sweet Romance!—How miserable thy fall!
>
> Ruler of countless ages, now you sleep;
> Shrill and profaning is the funeral song;
> Grunting black horses lug the train of dead.
> There is the throbbing valley, loud and deep,
> I see it coming—coffins jerked along,
> Crude coffins, stencilled, coal-stained, drably red.

Again, the poetic conception—that romance has been strangled by the brutal realisms of the industrial age—is not new, but Hugh, having been classically trained, didn't strive for originality. The image of the jerking, drab freight cars as coffins is vivid and the facility with which he handles the Petrarchan rhyme scheme shows real talent.

During the summer of 1927, seventeen-year-old Hugh wrote a poem that draws heavily on both his interest in astronomy and his deeply spiritual feelings. "Two Stars" was later published in Los Angeles High School's *Anthology of Student Verse*.[31]

> Two Stars
> In the rumbling, steel-smelling murk
> That is night in the city
> Strive two stars—

---

[28] Alexander Nibley, Letter to Charles W. Nibley, 21 May 1926, Charles W. Nibley Collection, Mss. 1523, Box 1, fd. 2, L. Tom Perry Special Collections, Harold B. Lee Library, Brigham Young University, Provo, Utah.

[29] Hugh Nibley, "Of Birthdays," *Improvement Era* 29 (June 1926): 743.

[30] Hugh Nibley, "The Freight Train," *The Lyric West: A Magazine of Verse* 5, no. 5 (1926), 171. This journal was published between April 1921 and 1927 in Los Angeles. Hugh's teacher, Snow Longley, published some of her poetry in the journal, so it is likely that she encouraged him to submit his poem.

[31] Hugh Nibley, "Two Stars," in *Anthology of Student Verse for 1925*, edited by Snow Longley (Los Angeles: Los Angeles High School, n.d.), 10-12. Despite the anthology's title, the note after the poem states that it was composed in the summer of 1927.

Vega and Arcturus—the tale of a life they tell,
For one is pure and glistening—virgin white,
The other warm and glowing;
One is a nervous scintillating light,
The other like slow breathing, warm and close,
Nor ruddy is its spark with light like passion,
Nor yellow which is discontent,
But like music swelling in chords,
Arcturus' glow is love itself—perfumed
With a honey-warm perfume—
A light that tired or frightened things would cling to;
It is friendly, but not hot;
And shines with sublimated laziness—
A light that basks in itself,
And goes and comes with itself,
And dreams its drowsy radiance on the world.
But what was ever drowsiness but sin?
Clear Vega's flashing treble is a goad.
Her light is white—pure white
But for, perhaps, a touch of blue:
Divine; for blue is thought;
The virgin, then, is wise.
Shimmering dizzily, dazzling in her course
Forever nearer, nearer toward the pole,
She flings a passing offer to pursue—
A wild temptation for a wilder joy.
She is the beginning and the end of knowledge—
And she has found the figure one to be
The whole of mathematics, and one motive
The cause for every act of every man!
Oh simple virgin—simple! look ye how
She radiates with every living light.
Look, there the green, and there the red
And there (what mischief here is done!)
Arcturus' sacred charm she playfully shows
For even his deep secret she has pried,
And after having learned the first and last—
Made every spectral hue a part of her,
She has come forth from out her depth of thought,
And laughs and dons a simple robe of white—
But such a white as only one might wear
Who has reached the coldest, clearest height
Of the morning mountain knowledge,
Who has seen the universe and the infinicule spin round.

Oh Vega! do what I will, I feel myself
Hot running after thee—I cannot help it;
Your distance hypnotizes me—
Your coldness is a magnet to me!
Cold and far; and I am blind from looking at thee

> And thinking on thee—
> Oh steady glowing Arcturus, no less bright,
> Your sweet offer of slow wine I now accept;
> To your low song I give my sleepy mind,
> To your calm all-embracing love confide
> My worried, restless tale, and then forget it—
> And you will give me wealths of heady sleep.
> Even as my aching spirit swing
> In that gold fog of half oblivion—
> A last farewell of dizzy, mottled strain,
> A glimmer, half of thought and half of sight—
> A blue-white glimmer in a hole-black void
> Catches my last retreating sense—
> 'tis Vega!
> And she is laughing—
> Her tittering spark is shamelessly amused,
> She laughs at me; and her laugh is indifference itself.
> She does not care—but I!
> Farewell, Arcturus, of all that hints of rest!
> Star! I will pursue thee—
> I will subdue thee—
> For I love thee terribly,
> Though Arcturus sport his sweetest influence
> And tempt me with his singing, overflowing light,
> I will forbear and fiercely follow thee.
>
> Alas: my goal is he whom late I shunned!
> I knew before I first began the race
> Where it would end—but still I struggle on
> I knew I had a million miles before me—
> And yet returned again to Arcturus;
> If this is life, then death is nothing else
> Than running on with Vega—hand in hand.

This ambitious and lengthy poem, in blank verse for the most part, apparently came into Grandfather Charles W. Nibley's hands on publication, and he evidently passed "Two Stars" along to his friend and colleague Orson F. Whitney of the Quorum of the Twelve. Elder Whitney, himself author of an ambitious epic, *Elias*, wrote back enthusiastically to Nibley that the poem "supports the teaching of Joseph the Prophet" by portraying the influences of the "worldly" and "spiritual" over an individual soul. Elder Whitney continued, "It is truly a remarkable production to have been written by one so young. I think it little short of marvelous that a high school 'laddie' could have composed it. It shows lofty imagination, a wealth of language, and a classic up-to-dateness of expression that would do honor to any poet in the land."[32]

On 5 January 1923, the month before Hugh graduated from middle school into high school, Sloanie gave birth to her fourth son—Reid Neibaur Nibley. Almost immediately thirteen-year-old Hugh set himself the task of tutoring the newborn. Undoubtedly, Hugh was as interested in issues of language pedagogy as he was in the

---

[32] Orson F. Whitney, Letter to Charles W. Nibley, 18 May 1926, original in Hugh W. Nibley papers..

development of his new brother. "From what Mother told me," states Reid, "he would take me out in the evenings and he'd put me on his shoulders and we would go for long walks together. And he would tell me all the constellations and teach me the names of the stars and teach me poetry and things like that."[33] By the time Reid was fifteen months old, Hugh, who had turned fourteen three months before, wrote proudly to Grandfather Nibley:

> Reid's mastery of languages is getting uncanny. He can show you "how big he is" in French, English, and German, I think now I'll teach it to him in Spanish. He doesn't even get his foreign languages confused. He can learn how to do things in French with astounding quickness. Go up to any other fifteen-month old baby and say "Est ce que tu a grand, Vee gros as kint (I don't know how to spell it) or how big are you?" and see what he does. . . . Whenever he does anything bright Grandma says "He's an old fashioned boy, all right!" She must think that the only bright babies in history lived at the time she was Reid's age.[34]

While Hugh was going to school at UCLA following his mission, Hugh was also put in charge of teaching Reid piano. "That was a disaster," recalls Reid. "That was the worst mistake possible." At that point, Hugh was less excited about teaching Reid and Reid was not at all excited about Hugh as his teacher. Hugh would sit and read while Reid went through various scales and exercises. One conventional method of learning music at that time was to recite out loud the notes on a page of music. So Hugh would put Reid through this exercise. But Reid knew Hugh was more absorbed in his books than in Reid's music lesson, so he'd just call out miscellaneous letters at random. "I hated every minute of it," Reid stated. "He was my nemesis at that time."[35]

Although Sloanie was quite possessive—and even domineering—she allowed Hugh a remarkable degree of latitude. Hugh remembers that "Dad didn't like it," but Sloanie "was always encouraging it, this independence."[36] The other boys noticed her preferential treatment, and would not have been normal if they hadn't resented it—but somehow they seemed to accept that Hugh was different. "It was rare that we sat down for more than ten minutes without getting a call for some kind of duty," remembers Sloan. "But [Mother] didn't bother Hugh much because I guess she thought what he was doing was more important." Hugh "didn't have to cut lawns or do housework or anything like that."[37] Reid also remembers that "Hugh was always allowed to do his thing, and we sort of worked around Hugh. Things moved around Hugh."[38]

---

[33] Reid Nibley, "Faith of an Observer," 475

[34] Hugh Nibley, Letter to Charles W. Nibley, (no date) 1924, Charles W. Nibley Collection, Family Correspondence, LDS Church Archives. Hugh's enthusiasm outstripped his own mastery. The French sentence he has written means literally: "Is it that you have big" (adjective, not the noun), instead of the idiomatically correct phrase: "Quel taille a tu?"

[35] Reid Nibley, "Faith of an Observer," 475-76.

[36] Hugh Nibley, "Faith of an Observer," 133.

[37] Sloan Nibley, "Faith of an Observer," 531.

[38] Reid Nibley, "Faith of an Observer," 485.

Hugh's discovery of his life's work came as a spiritual experience in his mid-teens. Although the Nibley family did not have formal family scripture reading, they all read the scriptures individually. Hugh cannot remember when he first read the Book of Mormon. "I thought the Book of Mormon and the Pearl of Great Price were absolutely great. And even the dullest Church meeting was productive as far as I was concerned. They'd say something that would mean something, that would be significant, whether the speaker knew it or not. All these things were being suggested, always hints."[39] Then one day when he was fifteen, he was in the attic looking through some old books. As he skimmed through the Pearl of Great Price, he read Moses 1:41 which promised that ancient writings "shall be had again among the children of men." "Oh boy, that hit me," remembers Hugh. "That verse wasn't just purely a mental process." "Absolutely stunned" by this promise, he lifted his head and "stared out the window[;] I was looking out across the sky." Great possibilities dawned in that instant. So "I got into this old stuff,"—ancient literature and history—"and stayed with old stuff ever after that."[40]

Hugh was fortunate that so many of his passions coincided with academics and that, naturally outgoing, his enthusiasms drew friends around him. As Sloan recalls, he struck a fine balance that has eluded many other intellectuals and was neither "a showoff" nor "an introvert."[41] One of Hugh's best friends in high school was John Cage, later one of the twentieth century's most outrageous and controversial composers.[42]

Hugh excelled easily in his studies as long as they held his attention. Absent-minded even as a young man, he confesses to "just wander[ing] away from a gym class" or something similar. (Sloan says Hugh hated gym.) "It was all innocent," Hugh claims. "I just wasn't paying attention."[43]

Perhaps ironically, given that gym class could not hold his attention, Hugh excelled at ROTC. With World War I barely a decade in the past, El and Sloanie saw ROTC as insurance that their sons might get safer positions as officers if another war broke out. That's Hugh's story. Sloan says that it's because boys in ROTC were exempt from gym.[44] Ironically, considering Hugh's later aversion to war, he made an excellent record. "I got proficiency awards: best soldier in the ROTC," Hugh brags wryly.[45] He first participated as a sophomore, and his completion certificate dated in January 1925 showed the fourteen-year-old as scoring "excellent" in conduct and character, "good" in physique, and an impressive 100 percent on physical training, rifle marksmanship, military courtesy, infantry equipment, camping and marching, and gallery practice. Perhaps not surprisingly, his score was a mere 88 percent on infantry drill regula-

---

[39] Hugh Nibley, "Faith of an Observer," 216-17.

[40] Hugh Nibley, interviewed by John W. Welch, May 1986; photocopy of transcript in my possession. See also John W. Welch "The Timelessness of Hugh Nibley," This People, April 1987, 39.

[41] Nibley, "Faith of an Observer," 529.

[42] Cage's composition "433" requires the pianist to sit motionless in front of the keyboard for four minutes and thirty-three seconds.

[43] Quoted in Arnold J. Irvine, "Hugh Nibley: Always Studying, Always Learning, Always on the Go," Deseret News Utah Magazine 15 April 1984, 6.

[44] Hugh Nibley, interviewed by Boyd Petersen, 16 June 1996; Sloan Nibley, "Faith of an Observer," 537.

[45] Hugh Nibley, interviewed by Boyd Petersen, 16 June 1996.

tions.[46] Sloan also has a theory about that low score. Hugh and his group of eight were "well organized and well drilled"; but at the crucial annual review, they "drilled up and down the field . . . like Abbot and Costello . . . doing everything contrary to regulations."[47]

Sloan had no doubt that Hugh both knew better and could do better; and certainly this ineptitude was not the physical incompetence that is the *bête noire* of many intellectuals. Hugh loved nature and spent free afternoons and weekends exploring and hiking California's rugged terrain. During the summer of 1925, fifteen-year-old Hugh spent part of the summer "on vacation" with a friend in the then-primitive area of Big Bear Lake in Southern California. Writing to his father, El comments briefly that the two "took their blankets and some supplies along and are going to camp out under the stars without a tent."[48] "We lived in a cave and had a great time," Hugh recalled.[49]

After this "vacation," Hugh spent the rest of the summer of 1925 working at the Nibley-Stoddard Lumber Company on the Feather River in Cromberg, California. Sloan, who was also working there, remembers that Hugh was assigned to "feed the hog"—meaning that he threw slabs of lumber into the furnace to keep steam going for the saws.[50] "It was tough work," remembers Hugh, "all day long, ten hours a day, six days a week, and I was fifteen years old; there were no child labor laws."[51] Recreation was equally rough. The loggers would egg Hugh and his cousin, sixteen-year-old Joe Nibley, to box with each other. Nothing loathe, Hugh recalls, "we'd get out and box ourselves silly to amuse the men; they'd all stand by and laugh and bet on us and so forth."[52]

The next spring on 2 April 1926, just a week after Hugh turned sixteen, El's and Sloanie's only daughter, Barbara, was born. The parents were thrilled but Hugh and Sloan, wrote El to his father, had wanted another brother.[53] A month later, the family moved into a palatial house at 1016 Rossmoyne Avenue, in the community El was developing. It was not the affluence of the house that El prized but rather its comfort and convenience. In a letter to his father, he says they were finally "very comfortably installed" in their new home, and "Oh! what a difference it makes."[54] One of Hugh's cousins later described the home as a "beautiful 12 room house on about 2 or 3 acres with beautiful shrubbery, flowers and a large rolling lawn." It was the first house in the neighborhood equipped with an elevator. The male members of the fam-

---

[46] Reserve Officers Training Corps, Los Angeles High School, Los Angeles, California, certificate of completion, dated 26 January 1925.

[47] Sloan Nibley, "Faith of an Observer," 537.

[48] Alexander Nibley, Letter to Charles W. Nibley, 29 June 1925, Charles W. Nibley Collection, Mss. 1523, Box 1, fd. 1, Perry Special Collections, Lee Library.

[49] Hugh Nibley, "Faith of an Observer," 181.

[50] Sloan Nibley, "Faith of an Observer," 537.

[51] Hugh Nibley, "Faith of an Observer," 199.

[52] "Faith of an Observer," 199. Joseph Wilson Nibley was born 5 May 1909 to Ada Dusenberry Nibley and Joseph F. Nibley, the fifth child of Charles W. Nibley and Rebecca Neibaur Nibley.

[53] Alexander Nibley, Letter to Charles W. Nibley, 3 April 1926, Charles W. Nibley Collection, Mss. 1523, Box 1, fd. 2, Perry Special Collections, Lee Library.

[54] Alexander Nibley, Letter to Charles W. Nibley, 21 May 1926, Charles W. Nibley Collection, Mss. 1523, Box 1, fd., 2, Perry Special Collections, Lee Library.

ily were expected to don coats and ties when they appeared for dinner in the formal first-floor dining room. Above the garage was a small apartment for the maid. There was a spacious library, and the living room was large enough to provide seating for up to 100 guests at concerts.[55]

Frequent visits from El's father, often bringing political or Church dignitaries also kept the family in touch with Utah's elite. Hugh remembers visits from "Dr. Janz, Senator Smoot, and a lot of big wheels."[56] Charles Nibley always played golf when he came to Southern California, and Hugh was frequently his caddy. Hugh recalls that after each game, the dignitaries "would all go in the clubhouse . . . and have a shot of Scotch. That was part of the game; that was good for you."[57] As a result of seeing these dignitaries up close, Hugh never viewed fame or fortune with any awe. He learned as a boy that people who were considered by others—or who considered themselves—to be very important, were always very human and sometimes hypocritical.

Balancing the clear-eyed Hugh's exposure to the underside of wealth and privilege was comparable exposure to poverty and hardship. Hugh remembers that hoboes would stop by their house almost daily. "Every afternoon, there would be a grimy old tramp or maybe two," remembers Hugh. "Mother's standard handout was bacon and eggs, bread and milk. . . . Mother never turned them down . . . because she learned this from her father . . . [who] just hammered it into them: 'Never, never, never turn anybody away.' Many have been visited by angels unawares. They may be testing you, as far as that goes. So that has always been the policy: Never to turn anybody away."[58]

During the summer of 1926, sixteen-year-old Hugh went to Oregon and spent six weeks alone in the wilderness around the Klamath and Umpqua forests. Hugh took the bus from Los Angeles to Medford, Oregon. Some former neighbors took him the final eighty miles to Crater Lake and dropped him off. This city boy describes an ecstatic reaction to the pristine wilderness and complete solitude.[59] "I was so excited. . . I was just bursting with delight. There was no road around the lake or anything, so I started walking around the lake." In the late afternoon, Hugh began setting up his camp in the deep forest. As he began unrolling his bedroll, he noticed a cougar watching him "with beautiful green eyes, . . . so interested in everything I was doing." Hugh decided to check on the time. He hadn't brought along a watch because "I was really gone for the Concord school, you see. I had to be getting back to nature." He walked out of the dark forest into a clearing and decided it was still too early to go to bed. He returned to his campsite, reassembled his bedroll while the cougar kept

---

[55] Hugh Charles Smith, *Personal History of Hugh Charles Smith* (Provo, Utah: Stevenson's Genealogy, 1991), 48.

[56] Hugh Nibley, "Remarks about Charles W. Nibley on the Occasion of the Celebration of his 150th birthday, 5 February 1999," 7. Janz was a wealthy real estate developer in Los Angeles. He was not a medical doctor but had received an honorary doctorate and thereafter used the title. Reed Smoot, an apostle (1900-41), served as Utah's Republican senator for almost thirty years (1903-32).

[57] Ibid.

[58] Hugh Nibley, *Teachings of the Book of Mormon: Transcripts of Lectures Presented to an Honors Book of Mormon Class at Brigham Young University, 1989-90* (Provo, UT: FARMS, n.d.), Semester 1, Lecture 29, 11.

[59] Hugh Nibley, "Faith of an Observer," 134-35.

watching him, and moseyed on until dusk. When Hugh returned to the lodge to purchase supplies several days later, he learned that an enormous cougar had been killing cattle in the valley. He was sure that the green-eyed cougar with whom he had been so "palsy-walsy" was the identical predator.[60]

Those six weeks in Oregon were no romantic idyll—a salutary shock to his naive adoption of Concord writers like Thoreau and Emerson. "It rained and rained and rained as it does in Oregon," he recalled. He hiked relentlessly, taking shelter when he could for the night in caves where rats nibbled on his crepe-soled shoes. He never saw another human being except for forest rangers and had taken very few provisions—just "a bag of wheat and raisins." His plan to live off nature received quite a setback when he "got myself terribly sick" by overeating "little red huckleberries. . . . But I survived." He concluded triumphantly, "It was quite the adventure."[61]

The cougar was not his only encounter with animals that were tougher than he was, but he did not feel in jeopardy. "Bears would come prowling around," he mused. "They never bothered me, but sometimes they could be rather disturbing. . . . They would snoop into what I had to eat and the like and there was nothing I could do about that very much." A bear came by Hugh's camp site once to play with his canteen hanging from a tree limb. He would "hit it and watch it swing back and forth and then hit it again." Hugh learned to arrange his bedroll on fine nights between two logs, as a kind of "nest," so that the bears "wouldn't want to step on it too much."[62]

One night, waiting out a storm in a cave, he was startled when a timber wolf also came in to seek shelter and glared at him ferociously. Thinking quickly, he broke the teeth out of his celluloid comb and struck a match to the little pile. The flammable plastic flared into a bright flame: "He went out of that cave like a shot and he never came back again," recounts Hugh. On another occasion, he woke up to find a large she-wolf tugging on his blanket. Hugh quickly threw her a piece of bread. "She took the bread in her mouth and trotted off up to a cave . . . and promptly came back. I gave her another piece of bread and she took it up." Hugh realized that she was probably feeding a litter of cubs, so he quickly gathered up his bedroll. When he stood up, the wolf lunged at him, sinking her teeth into his thigh. "She thought I might go in the direction of the cave and might be threatening something up there," he explained. Fortunately, she ran away after biting him and did not follow up the attack. The bite did not become infected, nor was it so serious that Hugh could not continue his solitary hike, "but that bite still hurts sometimes," and a scar remains.[63]

One night as he was walking across the Pumice Desert near Crater Lake, two park rangers drove up in a truck and asked where he was going. With droll literalness, Hugh announced, "Well, I'm going to bed." "Where?" asked the rangers. "Over there in the woods," said Hugh. "You mean you're going to sleep there tonight?," asked one ranger. "Yes, that is what I've been doing," Hugh answered. With that, one ranger turned to the other and said "You know, I wouldn't sleep in there for a hundred dollars."[64]

---

[60] Hugh Nibley, "Faith of an Observer," 135.

[61] Ibid., 131; Hugh Nibley, interviewed by Boyd Petersen, 16 June 1996.

[62] Ibid., 132.

[63] Ibid., 136.

[64] Ibid., 132.

A group at BYU's Aspen Grove summer camp, 1927. Hugh is at the bottom center.

Hugh's adventures in Oregon took him beyond Crater Lake to Diamond Lake and the Three Sisters to the north, and eventually eighty miles back to Medford. His canvas and crepe-soled shoes "were completely worn out and I was barefoot for the last 40 miles," he admitted. Thin, ragged, and unkempt, Hugh boarded a bus for California and arrived home looking "very spiffy," as he reported, tongue in cheek.[65] El wrote thankfully to his father that "Hugh got home safely the other evening, and we were glad to get him back alive particularly after listening to tales of his experiences."[66] Those tales probably lost nothing in the retelling.

The following summer, Hugh opted for a less rugged but even more influential vacation. He spent the summer he was seventeen at Brigham Young Academy's Aspen Grove summer school in the mountains near Provo, Utah. He shared a tent "with all these guys who were going to be future teachers," Hugh remembers. Among them were two future BYU professors, Herald R. Clark and Russel Swensen. "We called ourselves the Brighamites, and [we] would discuss the gospel all night long." During the day "we had very enlightening, very liberal sessions; we had talks with rabbis and priests and so forth."[67] Hugh remembers taking an English class by BYA's renowed Shakespeare scholar P. A. Christensen and was impressed by a lecture from a visiting Rabbi Cohen. But most of all he was dazzled by the Utah landscape. Afterwards "I kept dreaming of mountains."[68] Utah later became an outlet for Hugh Nibley's adventurous side. He would later explore not only the Wasatch Range, which was the setting for Aspen Grove, but also the red rock country of Southern Utah.

Hugh was developing into a young man with great intellectual curiosity and ability. He was also an able outdoorsman and reasonably popular with his high school friends. However, he had now graduated from high school and his father did not see him as competent in "caring for himself among civilized beings." El worried in a let-

---

[65]Ibid., 131.

[66]Alexander Nibley, Letter to Charles W. Nibley, 27 August 1926, Charles W. Nibley Collection, Mss. 1523, Box 1, fd. 2, Perry Special Collections, Lee Library.

[67]Hugh Nibley, interviewed by Alison Clark, June 1996.

[68]Hugh Nibley, "Faith of an Observer," 63. See also Hugh Nibley, *Teachings of the Book of Mormon*, Semester 4 (Provo: FARMS, n.d.), 55.

ter to his own father about this "poor kid" who spent part of his life "wrapped up so in his books" and the rest "perfectly able to take care of himself out in the mountains alone with the bears and the wild cats."[69] El wrote this letter in November when Hugh was no longer in school. His parents began looking for ways to make up for this deficit. A mission seemed just the ticket.

---

[69]Alexander Nibley, Letter to Charles W. Nibley, 1 November 1927, Charles W. Nibley Collection, Mss. 1523, Box 1, fd. 3, Perry Special Collections, Lee Library.

Salt Lake Mayor Ted Wilson (right), campaigning for the U.S. Senate in 1982, used this campaign advertisement featuring actor Robert Redford (left) and Hugh Nibley.

courtesy of (BYU) *Daily Universe*

Hugh Nibley's contributions to an LDS understanding of the environment are not lengthy; but as is characteristic of his work, they are trenchant and to the point. He opens our eyes to the possibility that the responsibility to care for the wellbeing of all creation is a core principle taught in temple worship and in the scriptural declarations of the oath and covenant of the priesthood and of the law of consecration, and that such responsibility constitutes one of the central challenges of our mortal probation. His understanding of this environmental ethic is not ideological or political but deeply doctrinal and profoundly faithful to the teachings of the prophets. So persuasive is his exegesis of the environmental principles of our belief, we can only feel chagrined that we haven't been willing to assume a greater burden on behalf of creation. Meanwhile environmentally minded theologians have in recent years moved closer and closer to principles Hugh Nibley articulated long before such scholarship was fashionable. I think it is not reckless to believe that it is time we too caught up with him.

—George Handley[1]

---

[1]George B. Handley, e-mail to Boyd Petersen, 18 April 2002. George is an associate professor of Humanities and Comparative Literature at BYU, specializing in environmental ethics in literature.

Chapter 5

A Voice for the Wilderness: Hugh Nibley, Naturalist

Hugh Nibley has lived the life of the mind. He has an internal drive and curiosity that will not let him rest. But his curiosity has not been reserved solely for library research. The same drive and determination that have pushed him to learn another language, read another book, or write another article have also pushed him to explore another canyon, climb another mountain, or hike another woodland trail. He has submerged himself in nature as deeply as he has in books. All his life, he has had a deep and abiding love for nature. In nature, he has consistently sought adventure, beauty, and spiritual rejuvenation.

His private writings are preoccupied with nature. "You will think that I harp on the Nature theme with strange persistence," he wrote in one letter, "but it is only because I want to get what I can of the good things of our planet while the getting is possible—absit omen."[2] Hugh's celebrations of nature demonstrate a sensitivity so instinctively poetic that I believe he could have been an environmental writer on a par with Edward Abbey, Aldo Leopold, Annie Dillard, or John Muir.

Hugh's preoccupation with wilderness has, in turn, led him to publicly advocate for environmental concerns long before they became popular issues. Not only has he spoken out for clean air and wilderness preservation, but he has also provided for Mormons a strong theology for environmental stewardship. Yet Hugh's words have, for the most part, been largely ignored by the Mormon community.

---

[2] Hugh Nibley, Letter to Paul Springer, July [no year]. Springer wrote "48" on the first page, but the content strongly suggests 1949 instead. The Latin tag is the pious hope: "May there be no evil omen" or "may no harm result." I read an earlier version of this chapter, titled "A Voice in the Wilderness: Hugh Nibley, Naturalist," at the Sunstone Symposium on 15 March 1998, Los Angeles.

Hugh's Nibley Relationship to Wilderness

Hugh Nibley was born and spent his early childhood in Oregon, where, as he stated in his "Intellectual Autobiography," "the great rain forests began a few miles from our home on every side, proclaiming in their primal magnificence the kind of world God intended this to be."[3] But by the time Hugh left Oregon, the rain forests were coming down. He writes poignantly about waiting to catch the train and hearing, only a mile away, his grandfather's lumber company "noisily beginning what was to be the total destruction of the greatest rain forest in the world." From that "misty battleground of man against nature," conquering man emerged the victor—but Hugh knew it was a hollow and sordid victory.[4]

By the time he was a teenager, Hugh was reading Thoreau and Emerson and had developed a deep passion for wilderness. At age sixteen, he wrote grandiloquently to his English teacher, Miss Longley, "Now I defy poverty to keep me from nature."[5] In the 1920s, "the thing for schoolboys to do," Hugh stated, was either to spend the summer working in mills or ranches or to become "seasonal tramps."[6]

Hugh certainly did his share of tramping. At age fifteen, he and a friend spent the summer of 1925 camping in the vicinity of the Big Bear Lake in California. At age sixteen he camped alone during the summer of 1926 in the Klamath and Umpqua forests around Crater Lake, having both exhilarating and frightening encounters. (See chap. 4.) He reported to his high school English teacher from the woods: "The Klamath Forest is happily the largest and least known of any in the United States. It is teeming and alive in one grand orgy of unmolested wildness."[7]

The year before at age fifteen, Hugh had worked at Charles W. Nibley's family business—the Nibley-Stoddard Lumber Company on California's Feather River. He probably felt motivated by a sense of family obligation but, even more powerfully, by the illusion that it was a way to feed his uncontrollable sense of adventure and his passionate love for nature. He was disillusioned beyond expression. In a memorable letter to his mother, Hugh described the ironic and heart-wrenching opportunity of being surrounded by nature, while witnessing—and, worse, participating in—its destruction.

> Dear Mother:
> What's all this business of coming home? Let me live in Paradise while it lasts. I climbed Jackson Peak Sunday, and when I looked around I saw not the great gray-green expanse of forest I had expected, but hundreds of miles of rocks and stubble broken here and there by well thinned plains of dry pines. This would have been most disappointing had it not been for the presence of one great patch of woods. What a heaven it was to look down onto the blue tops of those great cool firs and know that there in her last stronghold lives Nature with all her great family, for to this citadel have flocked

---

[3] Hugh Nibley, "Intellectual Autobiography," in *Nibley on the Timely and the Timeless* (Provo, UT: Religious Studies Center, Brigham Young University, 1978), xix.

[4] Ibid., xx.

[5] Hugh Nibley, Letter to Miss Snow Longley, summer 1926.

[6] Hugh Nibley, "Intellectual Autobiography," xxi.

[7] Hugh Nibley, letter to Miss [Snow] Longley, (no date) 1926. At the top of the letter, Hugh wrote, "I have honestly forgotten the date. I don't know where I am."

all the hosts of the forest. Here in this cold, green temple, oozing and dripping with a licentious profusity of life, I felt as if I were a trillion years old. Nothing seemed strange or unusual. Badgers, coons, deer, skunks, porcupines, snakes and all only paid me a passing glance, and went on with their business. . . . .

This is the only unlogged tract within half a hundred miles of here—five hundred million feet of it—and owned, "the devil damn it black" (Shakespeare) by the Nibley-Stoddard Lumber Co. Soon it will be leveled to a desert—the streams will dry up and leave it to the sun, the sage brush, the snakes and the lizards.[8]

Hugh has often referred to that pivotal summer at the sawmill and always with the same disdain.[9] When he delivered a speech for the "Last Lecture Series," sponsored by the Associated Students of Brigham Young University in 1971, he spoke of another forest that was leveled by his grandfather:

After my mission I visited a glorious redwood grove near Santa Cruz, California. Only there was no grove there; the two-thousand-year-old trees were all gone: not one of them was left standing. My own grandfather had converted them all into cash. . . . Grandfather took something priceless and irreplaceable and gave in return a few miles of railroad ties.[10]

It is notable that Hugh viewed his grandfather's legacy of wiping out acres of redwoods with the same contempt and horror in 1971 as he had in 1925 and 1931. Time had not imposed any reinterpretation or reevaluation of his grandfather's approach to wilderness since Hugh's youth.[11]

At seventeen, Hugh attended summer school at Aspen Grove, a canyon camp owned by BYU in the North Fork of the Provo River. "I kept dreaming of mountains. I just kept dreaming of them all the time," he recalled. Being near them was one of the advantages of teaching at BYU.[12]

Despite his unquestioned devotion to his missionary labors for the next two years, Hugh found himself unable to resist occasional impulses to plunge deeply into

---

[8] Hugh Nibley, Letter to Agnes Sloan Nibley, 4 August 1925, Charles W. Nibley Collection, Mss 1523, Box 1, fd. 1, L. Tom Perry Special Collections, Harold B. Lee Library, Brigham Young University, Provo, Utah.

[9] See, for example, Hugh Nibley, interviewed in *Faith of an Observer*, video (Provo, Utah: Brigham Young University/FARMS, 1985), 9. This source is different from the lengthy transcriptions of interviews conducted for the video and cited as "Faith of an Observer," cited as an unpublished manuscript by interviewee's name and page. See also his "An Intellectual Autobiography," xxi. He also discusses the sawmill in *Approaching Zion*, Vol. 9 in *Collected Works of Hugh Nibley* (Salt Lake City: Deseret Book/FARMS, 1989), 469-70.

[10] Nibley, "Our Glory or Our Condemnation," in *Approaching Zion*, 10.

[11] Charles W. Nibley left few personal expressions of appreciation for nature. One is a lyrical description of the beauties of autumn which he wrote to his son, El Nibley, on 12 September 1925, just after Hugh had had his shattering encounter with the logging mentality. Charles W. Nibley, however, followed his description with the commercial comment, "There will be a world of money come from the ground this season. After all, the good old farm land is the best and richest gold mine in all the world." Charles W. Nibley Collection, Mss 1523, Box 1, fd. 1, Perry Special Collections. In contrast, even as a boy Hugh saw the earth's beauty as valuable in and of itself, while his grandfather saw it, despite its beauty, as nothing more than a commodity. According to Hugh, "Faith of an Observer," 199, Charles W. Nibley could see "only the feet of timber in a forest and that's all it [was] to him." And because he could not fully appreciate nature, Hugh argued, his grandfather could not experience "a fullness of joy" on this earth.

[12] Hugh Nibley, "Faith of an Observer," 63.

German nature on his bicycle. During his last spring, he recorded in his journal: "The Wanderlust has struck me. It is exactly as with the birds, independent of weather—a quite inexplicable impulse."[13] In late summer, he admitted:

> Last Wednesday I was transported by the romantic appeal of certain delectable mountains "over the River, so early in the morning" I lit out for the Platz. A fantastically beautiful ride thru the woods . . . [I] ride long and hard but fail to glimpse the subject of my desire—those steep, deep hills. So I go back as appointed and bathe in the Rhine. The air was responsible for my not seeing the hills.[14]

Following his mission and his education at UCLA and Berkeley, Hugh taught at Claremont College from 1939 to 1942. These were heady days, teaching bright students and associating with famous scholars. But nature still provided him a sacramental counterpoint to the life of the mind. About 1940, Hugh wrote to his friend Paul Springer about a waterfall he had discovered:

> Yesterday afternoon to get away from it all I pedaled back into one of the canyons behind the town and discovered one of the most exquisite water-falls and bathing-pools I have ever seen. It was like another world, and seems never to have been visited, since it is inconceivable that this plush-bottom generation should of its own accord desert the sterile asphalt which has become the groove of propriety and modern Lebensbahn [path of life].[15]

Significantly, Hugh's standards of natural beauty were not simply those of the conventionally pretty. In a letter to his grandmother during the summer of 1941, Hugh wrote, either about Utah or southern California: "I like to ride out to the hottest and most desolate parts of the country to enjoy nature at her worst: there is infinite comfort in the conviction that the worst in nature is indescribably beautiful."[16]

Just before he enlisted in the army in September 1942, Hugh discovered what would become his favorite desert: the area around Zion National Park. It offered not only spectacular red-rock country but soul-nourishing seclusion. On a postcard to his mother, he wrote: "The place is deserted and the solitude welcome and impressive."[17]

After Southern Utah's geologic austerities, Hugh was ambiguously delighted about the natural vegetation at Clearwater, Florida, his first assignment after enlisting in the U.S. Army: "The vegetation is obscenely exuberant—it looks like Oregon in the Spring all the time; everything you touch or look at turns out to be alive—and usually poisonous."[18] To his mother, he expressed an unqualified delight in "the number and variety of the water birds." He called the region "a naturalist's paradise."[19]

---

[13] Hugh Nibley, Missionary Journal, 5 March 1929.

[14] Ibid., 31 August 1929.

[15] Hugh Nibley, Letter to Paul Springer, ca. 1940, beginning, "Dear Paul, what's the rush . . ."

[16] Hugh Nibley, Letter to Margaret Violet Reid Sloan, 14 July 1941.

[17] Hugh Nibley, Letter to Agnes Sloan Nibley, July 1942. The first digit of the date is "2" but the second is illegible. A second postcard is dated 26 July 1942.

[18] Hugh Nibley, Letter to Paul Springer, 17 Oct. 1942.

[19] Hugh Nibley, Letter to Agnes Sloan Nibley, from Clearwater, n.d. 1942. The first line reads: "Still in Clearwater."

In fact, he worried, "If I stayed here any longer I would turn into a naturalist—which I consider disastrous in view of the superior instruments of knowledge offered as I firmly maintain, by both the written documents and the mathematical skills of the race." He soon succumbed to the lush tropical beauty: "You wouldn't believe how strongly the presence of growing and living nature captivates the whole spirit with a kind of overpowering conviction, a feeling of acceptance and love of whatever is, which is quite Yogi."[20]

In the spring of 1943, Hugh was transferred to Camp Ritchie, Maryland, for training in the intelligence corps. Rather than heading for the nearest city during his leaves, Hugh launched himself on explorations of the region. "I have walked a good deal through the Blue Mountains and the plains just below, which include the field of Gettysburg," he wrote to his mother in April. "The variety and beauty of the rocks in the hills is astonishing—jewel-like quartzes wherever you look, and the way the water springs forth from every direction and play[s] among them is really exquisite. The lowland is Pennsylvania-Dutch country; all rich farm land and quaint old houses."[21]

Similarly, when he was sent to Europe in November 1943, he spent his next summer's leave on "a heavenly week in the Scottish Highlands." In July 1944, he wrote rapturously to his mother of

> . . . simply scrambling aimlessly from one mountain-top to the next, miles from any road or habitation. It was a spell of miraculously fine weather, so completely unexpected, apparently, that not a soul was on hand to take advantage of it. The west coast of Scotland is all forests and streams, the east a world of extremely rugged desert mountains, toned down by the great ice cap to those dramatic and graceful lines which glaciation always gives to mountains. The late sub-arctic spring has covered the ubiquitous spongy blanket of moss and furse with a great variety of wild flowers. If I ever get the chance, my next expedition will be to the Orkneys, which were a tempting sight from northern peaks of the mainland. Not being a biologist, I had the guilty sense of letting much go to waste, but on the other hand there was a good deal to think about.[22]

The war was a devastation to his spirit. He witnessed the atrocities of the European campaign, later visiting Dachau and German cities destroyed by British fire bombings. These scenes left him with memories so horrific that he refuses to talk about them to this day. Prompted by an instinct for healing once he was demobilized, Hugh retreated to the isolation of Hurricane, Utah, and Zion National Park, where he "spent some happy months in hiding."[23] He spent Christmas of 1946 in Hurricane, Utah, with a family he met there (he does not mention their name); but in a lengthy letter to Paul Springer, he wrote of his hunger to return "to my softly howling wilderness." He painted a vivid portrait of this spiritual retreat:

> In the desert south of Zion on the Arizona border is a place where I hang out, gradually setting up on a spot last occupied by the Pueblos some time in the 10th century

---

[20]Hugh Nibley, Letter to Agnes Sloan Nibley, 11 December 1942.
[21]Hugh Nibley, Letter to Agnes Sloan Nibley, postmarked 28 April 1943.
[22]Hugh Nibley, Letter to Agnes Sloan Nibley, 26 July 1944.
[23]Hugh Nibley, Letter to Dr. R., 30 April 1979.

of our era. My rear base is near Hurricane. . . . Do you know we missed all the best stuff around Zion: it is the neighboring terrain that is really staggering once you get into it. I visited Zion a couple of times when I had the car. Why people go there in summer is beyond me—any other season is better, but especially winter. The air is so clear that you can stand in the shadow of a cliff and pick out Mars and Jupiter shining bravely in the mid-afternoon sky. Not a soul in the park and the animals are having a field-day; the snow has lain on the trails for three weeks and the only shoe-tracks on it are mine. The water that seeps through the sandstone covers the cliffs with the most fabulous icicles (you can imagine what the Weeping Rock looks like) but the air is warm and dry—you never have to wear a coat. One of the pleasant surprises was to discover that most of the springs that flow into the canyon are warm-springs—between 70 and 80 degrees (the ranger wouldn't believe it until he investigated in person) and their green borders and pink sands heighten the sense of magic in that wonderful gorge.

Almost as comforting as the long-delayed joys of solitude is the company of the plain and sober people of the area where I live—quite the best I have found yet. And what a contrast to the Armed Forces of the United States of North America![24]

Rejuvenated from these weeks in the southern Utah wilderness, Hugh next went to work as an editor for the *Improvement Era*. There he met Elder John A. Widtsoe, who urged him to teach at BYU. Hugh applied in April 1946—but not because it was a Church school nor for the intellectual stimulation. Instead, he describes his motivation as a hunger to be near his beloved Wasatch Range. Even after two years in Provo, Hugh confided to Paul Springer the soul-deep serenity he received from the mountains: "The savage Himalayan look of our mountains in winter does me much good. Never since I moved to Utah have I had the bored and restless feeling, that haunting urge to get away, which never let me alone in California."[25]

Furthermore, he continued to escape into the wilderness at every opportunity. In the fall of 1946 when he was engaged to Phyllis Draper, it was still the mountains that he singled out as his source of exhilaration: "I am elated beyond description at the local variety of mountains, which present no end of wonders to the curious," he wrote Paul Springer. "Life is a perpetual picnic here."[26] In an undated letter, he wrote, "The weather here is utterly gorgeous and I can't leave the mountains alone; now that I am equipped with a Kodak I have something like a pretext for prowling in the damndest places, and there are really some very impressive shots around here."[27] Phyllis's enjoyment of the mountains, though not as exuberant as Hugh's, was a bond between them. To his mother soon after the wedding in September 1946, Hugh wrote in rapture: "The mountains are still on hand to be viewed whenever necessary, which is approximately five-hundred times a day; we still walk a good deal though we are both very busy, and we don't miss a car at all, since the mountains are only a short stroll away and we could think of no better place to go even if we had a magic carpet, than our canyons."[28]

Phyllis enjoyed the wilderness trips with Hugh when they were first married. After a honeymoon spent exploring the red-rock country of Zion Canyon, they frequent-

---

[24]Hugh Nibley, Letter to Paul Springer, n.d. 1946.

[25]Hugh Nibley, Letter to Paul Springer, n.d. 1948. It begins "Mon Capitaine."

[26]Hugh Nibley, Letter to Paul Springer, 5 August 1946.

[27]Hugh Nibley, Letter to Paul Springer, n.d. The letter begins, "Dear Burnt Njal."

[28]Hugh Nibley, Letter to Agnes Sloan Nibley, n.d. 1946.

ly rented a cabin in Aspen Grove on the North Fork of the Provo River in Provo Canyon. But after the children started coming along, Phyllis's expeditions into the wilderness diminished. She found it trying to tend babies without indoor plumbing and electricity.

Hugh thoroughly explored the Wasatch Range. The trail head for many of his journeys was Rock Canyon, which he stated, "more than satisfies all my esthetic yearnings. It is a tremendously dramatic gap leading back to Windy Pass; I never tire of walking in it."[29] In one letter he describes weekly "walks" in the mountains to the east of Provo:

> Our summer has been very cool until now, and to keep from snapping the thin and frayed thread of our precarious sanity I walked about in the hills on weekends. Surprise, surprise! Every Saturday I got lost—utterly, hopelessly, and completely, that is, taking eight or twelve hours to extricate myself each time. That is because as soon as one gets over the high ridge back of Rock Canyon one is in a trackless wilderness of cliffs and gorges. I never dreamed there was anything like that back there, and if I had not been fortunate enough to be without a car this summer would perhaps never have discovered that wonderful world behind the first range. Which proves that the automobile is not an unmitigated blessing: I bought a car last year with the hopes of discovering such an area, and lo, that was the one thing that stood in the way of its discovery. What surprises me more than anything is the absolute wildness of the country: in all my wanderings I have not met one other person, the Wasatch runs into the Uinta back of Heber (goal and haven of that celebrated flier known as the Heber Creeper) and the whole region is simply a vast lunar emptiness. We have to thank our main highways for this—they are symbolic of our civilization: where the highway doesn't take you isn't worth going; what you see from the highway is all you see and there ain't no more.[30]

Hugh early believed—and still does—that the gem of the Wasatch Range is Mount Timpanogos. "After you see them all you will vote the trail up Timp to be the most beautiful walk in the world," he announced.[31] Eight years after settling down in Provo, his passion was still palpable: "Those Timp trails are still the most beautiful in the Rockies—what a paradise! After all these years I can't stay away from it."[32] Perhaps, for one particularly hazardous hike, he should have done so:

> Last Monday we made the first ascent of Timp this year. The gorgeous terraces on the east side are covered with deep snow-banks lying at a very steep angle of repose; every terrace is delimited above and below by a precipice. In the late morning the sun had softened an inch or two of snow on the surface and so by digging in and hanging on with everything we had we worked ourselves up from ledge to ledge. At noon, however, the sun is thru with the northeast face of the mountain for the day and the wet snow surface, cooled from within, immediately begins to harden so that when we reached the big steps on our way down at 6 p.m. the surface was hard and glassy—one little teeny slip on rubber-soled moccasins and one was vogelfrei [free as a bird] to

---

[29] Hugh Nibley, Letter to Paul Springer, n.d. 1946.
[30] Hugh Nibley, Letter to Paul Springer, 23 July 1949.
[31] Hugh Nibley, Letter to Paul Springer, n.d. ca. 1953. It begins "Thweet Thir."
[32] Hugh Nibley, Letter to Paul Springer, n.d. ca. 1954. It begins "Dear Counsellor Springer."

explore the depths of bottomless chasms of green ice that opened all along the foot of every terrace. I have never had a worse time—utterly terrifying.[33]

As this description shows, Hugh did not hesitate to put himself at risk, both through climbing during chancy conditions and also in climbing without proper equipment. Still, as he stated, "We DO have fun—and then there is the wonder and surprise of getting home alive after all."[34]

Hugh was ahead of his time in his love for camping; and although he has never minded being thought eccentric, his awareness that others may have thought him both idiosyncratic and escapist may account for his slightly defensive tone in this 1948 letter to Paul Springer:

> Any chance to escape the world should be used, I believe—at best we are only here temporarily and if we can get a peep at the world as it should be, even for five minutes, we should drop everything else and comply with our better natures. This by way of saying that I do not entirely apologize for being a bum. I have got in the happy habit of taking the bus in various directions, getting off where the country looks good, and walking a bit.[35]

When Hugh was able to afford a car in 1948, his motivation was, frankly, to facilitate his wanderlust: "The public has chosen—praise the Lord—to think of the Empty Quarter as far more forbidding than it is," he wrote to Paul Springer. "Living right on the edge of the jumping-off place without being able to jump proved to be, as I indicated in my last, more than I could take. Ever since I got my car I have been making exploratory stabs into the area."[36]

Southern Utah's red-rock country continued to be among his favorite haunts. After one 1953 visit, Hugh exulted: "Park Avenue at the Arches, which we visited last week, can be, on a golden afternoon with little white clouds above it, the nearest thing to an opium dream." Even at this early stage, he was aware of wilderness's haunting fragility. "Republican economy has been a blessing in one way," he wrote. "If Mr. MacKay does not give all the stuff away to his personal friends, we can be sure that the natural beauties of national parks, etc. will thrive in an era of salutary neglect: no new roads, and no repairs on the old ones except at the busiest parks, no new construction, signs, or personnel, and as a result the tourists stay away in droves. Goody."[37]

---

[33] Hugh Nibley, Letter to Paul Springer, July 1948.

[34] Hugh Nibley, Letter to Paul Springer, n.d. August 1952.

[35] Hugh Nibley, Letter to Paul Springer, n.d. 1948. It begins "Dear Toots."

[36] Hugh Nibley, Letter to Paul Springer, n.d. 1948. By "char" he may have meant, jokingly, either "chariot" or "charabanc," an excursion wagon. The letter begins "Dear Haunted."

[37] Hugh Nibley, Letter to Paul Springer, n.d. ca. 1953. It begins "Thweet Thir." Douglas McKay (1893-1959) was Secretary of the Interior in the Eisenhower administration. A former car salesman, McKay served as governor of Oregon (1949-52) where his modern Republican views brought him great popularity. This popularity, both in Oregon and the nation, decreased sharply when, as Secretary of the Interior, he supported logging in old-growth forests, selling off segments of the national forest, and transferring public lands to private ownership. This approach was seen as catering to big business, in particular the timber industry. He even proposed building a dam where Dinosaur National Monument stands. McKay characterized conservationists as "long-haired punks" nearly ten years before the hippie movement. The public eventually dismissed McKay as

Enchanted with the minute particularity of U.S. Geological Survey maps, Hugh began buying them in 1950, covering his living room walls with them until he literally ran out of space. "They are splendid maps and our little house looks like the war-room of Shaef [Supreme Headquarters, Allied Expeditionary Forces]," he wrote gleefully to Paul Springer. In fact, retreating to nature was a persistent theme in this constant exchange of letters between Hugh and Paul Springer from 1950 to the early 1960s. These letters show that Hugh frequently took his children along when they grew old enough. Paul was born in 1947, Christina in 1949, and Tom in 1950. Soon after Tom's birth, for instance, Hugh wrote Paul Springer:

> My vacation I must take in installments, and having at last trained my spouse to a reasonable point of view am ready at the drop of a hat to disappear into the wilds that lie about us in all directions. Such behavior may not even be without survival value in a world where it is folly to look for permanence. Zion in the winter is the height of good sense: you can stay at Reeves and have the park absolutely to yourself; the usually hot and throbbing atmosphere of the great corridor is cool and crystalline and the silence is a revelation. Yes, Zion in the winter, by all means.[38]

The following summer, he made his first trip to the High Uintas, which would be declared a wilderness area in 1984. He wrote to Springer:

> After we get back from the Tetons I am concentrating, that is, when I can get away, on the Uintas. They are only 60 miles away, cool, heavenly, full of lakes and minus people. There is an area in the center twenty-five by eighteen miles which they say is still unexplored. What has me drooling from the map is that fabulous Red Castle Lake—never saw a picture of it or ever met anybody who has been there, though the Explorer Scouts go within a few miles of it on the trail to Kings Peak.[39]

Returning from one of these trips, Hugh described the Uintas as "the quietest and wildest retreats" and "a cure for too much society." He added: "It is a long chain of deep cirques, vast ring walls that all look exactly alike and seem to go on without end; in the center of every ring is a very deep and often surprisingly large lake surrounded by forests that run right up to the foot of those appalling perpendicular walls (they often rise above 13,000 ft.)."[40]

The children happily collaborated in these spur-of-the-moment adventures. In 1959, when Paul would have been eleven and Tom nine, Hugh mischievously wrote Paul Springer:

---

the "old car peddler from Oregon." "Governor Douglas McKay: Biographical Note," Oregon Secretary of State, Oregon State Archives, downloaded 17 April 2002 from http://arcweb.sos.state.or.us/governors/McKay/McKaybiography.html; and Marty Jezer, "Rachel Carson's Day," downloaded 17 April 2002 from http://www.sover.net/~mjez/newspapercolumns/rachelcarson.html.

[38] Hugh Nibley, Letter to Paul Springer, after 17 August 1950.

[39] Hugh Nibley, Letter to Paul Springer, n.d. ca. 1954, "Dear Counsellor Springer."

[40] Hugh Nibley, Letter to Paul Springer, 18 December 1950.

On a sudden impulse (especially when there is urgent business to attend to for school, church, home and society) I will let my boys inveigle me (after casually planting the idea in their not too innocent heads—they get the point) into dumping three or four sleeping bags, three loaves of homemade bread, some native cheese, hardboiled eggs, and apples, field glasses, axe, and knives into the back of the car and simply taking off. By determined and skillful reconnoitering we manage to keep a jump ahead of civilization—it has become sort of a game—and it costs almost nothing.[41]

In a 1954 letter to Springer, he wrote:

The more I see of it the more surprised I am by the delightful emptiness of Utah. By the time [Governor J. Bracken] Lee has opened up most of it to pay political debts with fat road contracts I suppose I shall have become so senile that I will be content to remain bumper to bumper on the California assembly line; till then we make the most of golden days. . . . I was up in the Tetons again a few weeks back . . . Still our own mountains do not suffer by comparison when you get to know them; especially the incredibly theatrical Timp and the eery, unearthly Uintas. Must be seen to be appreciated.[42]

As late as 1956, he was still rejoicing: "It is the one advantage of living here that one can escape into real wilderness without any difficulty at all."[43]

Hugh scrambled all over Utah, exploring every trail and mountain he could find. Following his sabbatical to Berkeley in 1960, he exultantly returned to Utah's wilderness:

In other respects [Provo] is decidedly NOT like California: we had all forgotten how very small and quiet everything is in Provo, and how amazingly much empty space there is around it. The kids simply went wild: before we had been home a week we were scattered all over the Uintas—Tommy and I went to a gorgeous canyon with a totally unknown river in it while Paul set out for the Granddaddies. We climbed Wheeler Peak on the Nevada border. Then we dashed down to Bryce. Then we climbed Timp. Then Fivewater. Then Nebo. And now the rapidly worsening social and economic conditions may yet save this from the fat contented hordes that were getting all poised to take it over.[44]

A couple of years later, he reported with apocalyptic overtones:

My brother Reid is teaching at the Y now, and last weekend he with his oldest and I with my two oldest boys went into some of the unexplored parts of Capitol Reef. I was completely bowled over—never dreamed there was anything like that—endless miles of deep winding corridors, STILL largely unexplored. . . . Suddenly I discover that I still haven't grown up—you will probably remember how I gushed about these places fifteen years ago; it is a great relief to discover that many of them are still

---

[41]Hugh Nibley, Letter to Paul Springer, 7 March 1959.
[42]Hugh Nibley, Letter to Paul Springer, n.d. ca. 1954. It begins "Dear Pinkus."
[43]Hugh Nibley, Letter to Paul Springer, June 1956.
[44]Hugh Nibley, Letter to Paul Springer, 12 December 1960. Hugh is alluding to the recession of 1960, which ran from April 1960 to February 1961.

unspoiled—because unknown—and may remain so until THE Crash cuts off the trickle of tourists for good.⁴⁵

Hugh's belief that some kind of "crash" or social calamity was imminent stems from his literal belief that these are the last days (see chap. 3) and from world events that seemed to confirm this view. At the time this letter was written, the United States was enmeshed in the Vietnam War and relations with the Soviet Union were tense. Francis Gary Powers, pilot of the U.S.'s U2 spy plane, had been shot down over the USSR in May 1960, causing an international crisis that did not end until Powers was exchanged for a Soviet spy in February 1962. The Cuban missile crisis would erupt only two months after Hugh wrote this letter.

Throughout his life, Hugh has valued the time he has spent in forests, canyons, and alpine meadows as much as the time he has spent in libraries. As he stated in one early letter, "It is getting so I almost feel ill at ease indoors."⁴⁶ On another occasion he wrote, "Anyone who doesn't avail himself of every possible moment to view the beauties of what remains unravaged of our fair earth should be sentenced to attend a Hollywood preview every day of his life."⁴⁷ In another early letter to Springer, Hugh wrote, "Humbug still rules the world and the whole works is still careening madly downhill. A few days spent in the shadows of the great rocks will do wonders to restore balance and perze. You should try it, little friend."⁴⁸

In 1953, he took a connoisseur's tone: "I have seen a good deal of Arizona and New Mexico by now. They can't compare with Utah—too much monotonous horizontal stuff. In Utah everything is vertical. . . . But as I say, only in Utah can you get away from all traces of our society."⁴⁹ In another letter he wrote, "Speaking of cheap and easy vacations, there is one thing that will probably keep me in Utah until I start acting like one of those Mormons, and that is the dunes and redrock and the canyons."⁵⁰

Springer's letters to Hugh during this period have not yet been found, so it is not possible to know if he was having wilderness experiences of his own in California. He was unquestionably a sympathetic audience for Hugh's effusions over nature, but he does not seem to have joined Hugh on many of these outdoor expeditions, their friendship surviving primarily through letters, rather than visits. Phyllis recognized early in the marriage Hugh's need for such intense periods of solitude and accommodated herself to his sudden disappearances. At least, his letters do not suggest that she resisted his erratic sorties or complained about being left to manage the household and children alone. Hugh frequently took some of the older children with him, reducing some of the turbulence at home. They always returned home in time for church on Sundays, but he was as likely to take off on a Tuesday afternoon when he had no classes as on a weekend.

---

⁴⁵Hugh Nibley, Letter to Paul Springer, 20 August 1962.

⁴⁶Hugh Nibley, Letter to Paul Springer, n.d. 1950.

⁴⁷Hugh Nibley, Letter to Paul Springer, n.d., ca. 1947-48. It begins "My pretty, petulant ptarmigan."

⁴⁸Hugh Nibley, Letter to Paul Springer, n.d. 1949. Springer spent a significant segment of his career working for the San Francisco Superior Court.

⁴⁹Hugh Nibley, Letter to Paul Springer, 7 December 1953.

⁵⁰Hugh Nibley, Letter to Paul Springer, 7 March 1959.

During one extremely stressful period in 1957—unable to work in his office due to interruptions from students and admirers, his life at home disrupted by the visit of his failing mother—Hugh openly fled into the wilderness, reporting in a letter to Springer:

> So I simply got in the car and drove off. I opened your letter in the severest of the Sevier desert, a perfectly desolate waste of reddish-brown sand and huge volcanic blocks: it was indescribably restful. How natural and easy death seems in the quiet anonymity of the dunes! The dry sand drifts with a soft hissing sound in a gentle wind; the bones that lie around beautifully cleaned and polished elicit no pity or remorse, for nothing has any particular identity and everything seems at rest; there is a relaxation and a rightness about everything—after a few hours of sitting or walking about in a perfect emptiness of sand and air one imperceptibly relaxes and begins to soak up certain basic realizations which in any other setting would not be accepted without a struggle. The first is that my being here or not being here doesn't make the slightest difference to anything, one way or the other. The neat white vertebra you kick with your toe might be that of a lame sheep, a coyote, or Alexander the Great—it doesn't make the slightest bit of difference, one is no better than the other as far as this world is concerned. For me this was escape pure and simple, but I came back [after] another day greatly refreshed, having seen some marvelous country that I had never dreamed existed—less than a hundred miles from home.[51]

Hugh was obviously recommending his method of relieving tension to Springer, who was experiencing marital stresses that would end in a divorce.

Throughout his life, Hugh has submerged himself in nature. From it he has drawn peace, comfort, and spiritual strength. And his descriptions of nature in his personal correspondence with Springer are as inviting and poetic as those by any wilderness writer I know.

Hugh Nibley's Theology of Environmentalism

Hugh Nibley's love for wilderness has made him an ardent advocate for environmental protection. As his letters to Springer during the 1950s and 1960s show, he perceived the wilderness as fragile, dwindling under the onslaught of an insensitive and burgeoning materialistic population. Thus, when Rachel Carson's *Silent Spring* launched the ecological movement in 1962, it found Hugh already a convert; and as public concern with environmental issues increased during the 1970s and 1980s, Hugh, who turned seventy in the spring of 1980, willingly and cheerfully spoke out on public occasions.

A local sore point during these decades was the Geneva Steel Mill just six miles northwest of Provo, established in 1941 to boost U.S. steel production during World War II. From the 1950s on, it laid a pall of frequently evil-smelling smoke across Utah Valley, maintained an active public relations campaign to explain the smoke as "steam," and had a reputation—understandable enough considering the expense—of foot-dragging on the installation of scrubbers and other pollutant reducers. Because Geneva was unquestionably a major contributor to the economy of Utah Valley, local people, particularly those who worked at the site, resisted what they saw as politically motivated and highly theo-

---

[51]Hugh Nibley, Letter to Paul Springer, n.d. ca. 1957.

retical interference from BYU students and faculty who espoused the ecological movement.

When USX, Geneva's parent company, decided to shut the mill down in 1987, Joe Cannon and a group of investors stepped in to buy the plant. For the few months Geneva was closed, residents of Utah Valley began to appreciate the resulting clean air. Thus, the debate became quite heated about whether Geneva was an overall benefit in terms of job opportunities or liability in terms resulting from pollution. As the protests rose, the company launched a massive public relations campaign. In 1989, a group of BYU faculty organized a forum to debate the issue, inviting interested parties on both sides for presentations. Hugh delivered one of the best-attended lectures of the forum suggesting that, rather than appeasing the people of Provo by investing in radio and television commercials and giving handouts to the community, as Geneva was doing, "a far better gift would be 'the clear blue sky [arching] over the vales of the free'. . . . But of course there is one serious drawback to that. The clear blue skies cost much more than the highly publicized handouts."[52]

Three years earlier, Hugh had sent testimony to hearings held in Provo by the Bureau of Land Management on conferring "wilderness" designation on some tracts in southern Utah:

> I moved to Utah from California many years ago expressly because I had found the last authentic habitable wilderness in the temperate zone, i.e., in the entire world within reach of pleasant dwelling places. The rest of the world has already become overrun or uninhabitable by nature. So what we have here and here alone is the RAREST commodity in the world, and its rarity can only increase with the passing of time. It is that ultimate blessing, a thing good and desirable in itself, not merely something that can be converted into cash. When it is gone not only the world but our own immediate environment, for which we are responsible, will be a bleaker and poorer one.[53]

Hugh has followed the popular bumper-sticker slogan of "Think globally, act locally" by focusing his actions on his immediate environment. For example, whenever a chain saw was fired up in the botanical gardens on the south side of campus, Hugh was on the phone to the BYU president's office. Setting his words to paper—in a memo to BYU President Jeffrey Holland—Hugh wrote:

> Every year it is the same thing. The young people on the grounds crew protest that it breaks their hearts to destroy all that lovely verdure after it has been so carefully planted and cultivated; but they can do nothing about it—they must obey orders. The botanists and others complain, but go unheeded. President Oaks put a stop to it last spring, but the operation is now going forth with renewed vigor, and with an alarming innovation—the chain saw. In the past week over 100 young trees, after having been

---

[52] Hugh Nibley, "Stewardship of the Air," *Brother Brigham Challenges the Saints*, edited Don E. Norton and Shirley S. Ricks, Vol. 13 in *The Collected Works of Hugh Nibley* (Salt Lake City: Deseret Book/FARMS, 1994), 70. The quotation is from Charles W. Penrose's hymn, "O Ye Mountains High." Ironically, after Hugh's public statement, Geneva began to sponsor the video presentations of Hugh's Book of Mormon classes on KBYU each Sunday during the early 1990s.

[53] Prepared testimony written for the Bureau of Land Management Hearings on Wilderness Designation, 7 May 1986, read by Hugh's daughter, Zina Petersen at the hearings in Provo.

carefully nursed for some years, have been cut to the ground. The extremely clumsy job of paving the "Nature Trail" last year, and the thorough cutting of bushes and tearing up of the grass cover by hand has produced serious erosion problems on the west side. Where a short time ago a large variety of fruits and berries, aromatic plants, and asparagus helped balance the diets of many a poor student, today the scene is as sickly and as barren as a back lot. The south side of campus was President Harris's favorite project: what other school could match the delights of the now ruined nature trail? Can't we do something to save what is left?[54]

Above all, I believe that Hugh's most significant contribution has been to establish a Mormon theological foundation for environmental stewardship. Few, if any, preceded him in this and, sadly, few are following in his footsteps. In his 1972 essay "Subduing the Earth," Hugh argued for an environmentally sensitive interpretation of Genesis 1:28, in which God commands Adam to have dominion over all the earth. Hugh argued that there are two opposing types of "dominion"—one God's and one Satan's. Satan's version of dominion pits man against the natural world to get financial gain, thereby rendering the earth uninhabitable. In contrast, God's version of dominion requires man to cooperate with and care for nature. In Hugh's words, "Man's dominion is a call to service, not a license to exterminate."[55]

Drawing on the Mormon doctrine that all living things have spirits and will be resurrected,[56] Hugh has little sympathy for any attempt to profit from exploiting natural resources or from animal life. For example, he described his grandfather's destruction of the redwoods as "a form of murder." Hugh stated, "I mean this was taking life of various sorts. Because remember, this is a doctrine we do not emphasize, that we believe that all living things . . . are spiritual beings too and shall have their resurrection."[57]

Hugh has also been one of the few brave souls along the Wasatch Front to raise his voice against the popular sport of hunting. He quoted President Joseph F. Smith's strong words against hunting: "I think it is wicked for men to thirst in their souls to kill almost everything which possesses animal life"—and stated that "there is a practice designated by the President and Prophet of the Church as abominable. . . . And yet there are men today engaging in such practices who at the same time speak piously of building up Zion."[58] In Utah culture, even in the urbanized area along the Wasatch Front until the last generation, boys frequently received Daisy bee-bee guns or air rifles at about age eight with which they hunted birds, graduated to .22 rifles at twelve or thirteen, practiced "potting rats" at the city dump, went with their Boy Scout troops on night-shoots in which they blinded jackrabbits with headlights on the desert, and

---

[54]Hugh Nibley, Letter to Jeffrey R. Holland, 9 April 1981.

[55]Hugh Nibley, "Man's Dominion, or Subduing the Earth," in *Brother Brigham Challenges the Saints*, 18.

[56]In Joseph Smith's inspired translation of the Bible (our Book of Moses in the Pearl of Great Price), he bridges the two creation accounts of Genesis 1 and Genesis 2 (which the documentary hypothesis identifies as written by two different authors: P and J) by stating that the first creation was a spiritual creation: "For I, the Lord God, created all things, of which I have spoken, spiritually before they were naturally upon the face of the earth" (Moses 3:5).

[57]Hugh Nibley, "Faith of an Observer," 33.

[58]Hugh Nibley, "Our Glory or Our Condemnation," in *Approaching Zion*, 19; see also Nibley, "Man's Dominion, or Subduing the Earth," 4.

waited impatiently to be old enough to accompany their fathers and uncles on the traditional first day of Utah's deer-hunting season. In the fall of 1952, Hugh expressed his dismay to Springer: "The way the he-man cult of the hunter has blossomed forth since the II phase of the War bodes ill for the future of the great republic: not only does our male population escape brain-work en masse to play Daniel Boone in the back yard, but they don't even learn to be good woodsmen in the glamorous and expensive process."[59]

In early winter, he returned to the theme of hunting. He had accompanied a group of students that fall on the bow hunt; however, he was rooting for the deer:

> One evening not long ago some students came by and swept me off, unprotesting, on a deer-hunting trip with bow and arrow. Nobody got anything—in fact not a single deer was shot with bow and arrow in the state this year. That is because the very late fall provided a magnificent coverage of leaves so that you could walk right through a herd without seeing a single animal. Though you could hear them exchanging snide remarks about people who play Robin Hood at that age. . . . This passion for indiscriminate slaughter is disturbing. The primary concern of the primitive hunter is the preservation, not the destruction, of game—it is strange how softness and cruelty go together. The same generation that insists that animals exist only to be killed is almost pathologically impatient of the slightest discomfort and will not under any conditions walk more than a mile or two from the car to get their game.[60]

Hugh also found support for environmental sensitivity in the example Brigham Young set when colonizing Utah: "The idea that everything in the West is up for grabs was one which Brigham Young found particularly offensive. The idea that people should actually clamor for a decade or so of boomtown construction at the price of rendering the land uninhabitable for 10,000 years to come seems perfectly insane, yet it is an example of how far things can go when greed becomes the motive."[61]

According to Hugh, Brigham Young felt that the physical state of the natural environment mirrored the spiritual state of its occupants: "For Brigham, moral and physical cleanliness and pollution are no more to be separated than mind and body."[62] The physical and the spiritual are interdependent—if you pollute one, you pollute the other.

He often quoted with appreciation President Spencer W. Kimball's encouragement in 1976 to reflect on the spiritual dimension of natural beauty:

> I have travelled in the Four Corners country and over wide parts of the Southwest with the late Spencer W. Kimball, who wrote on the occasion of the Bicentennial, speaking of that part of the world, "I would sometimes ask myself, 'If you were going to create a world, what would it be like?' Now with a little thought the answer seems so natural: 'Just like this one.' . . . This is a marvellous earth on which we find ourselves. . . . When I pass through the lovely countryside . . . I compare these beauties with many

---

[59]Hugh Nibley, Letter to Paul Springer, n.d. ca. 1952.
[60]Hugh Nibley, Letter to Paul Springer, 16 December 1952.
[61]Hugh Nibley, Testimony at BLM Hearing, 7 May 1986.
[62]Hugh Nibley, "Brigham Young on the Environment," 24.
[63]Hugh quotes Kimball's address in the following published essays: in 1981, "The Prophetic Book of Mormon,"

of the dark and miserable practices of man; and I have a feeling that the good earth can hardly bear our presence upon it."[63]

Hugh summarized this quotation by denouncing yet again what he calls "the intolerable pollution of our surroundings," resulting from the perverted urge to exploit natural resources for quick profits.[64]

Fruitfully, Hugh weaves his environmental theology into a philosophical model based on the concepts of Zion and Babylon. Zion, a garden paradise like Eden, is juxtaposed to Babylon—the city where you can have "anything in this world for money" but which produces nothing more than a large, smelly, rotten garbage heap. Soberly he warned, "The world we have made and are making is not the world God meant us to have, and the world he made for us in the beginning is the world we must have."[65]

In a 1986 letter to a correspondent, Hugh aptly summed up his perspective: "As far as abusing the earth, the 49th section of the D&C is specific enough—you take what you need, but wo to whoever takes more. The earth is there for the use of man, and as Brigham Young taught, if he uses it properly it will give him ever increasing benefits; if he does not it will withhold its strength as it did from Cain when he took to seeking gain."[66]

Although Hugh leaves to others the crucial tasks of organizing and lobbying, his prophet-like stance of sounding the alarm has been an indispensable contribution. It was Hugh's 1972 essay "Brigham Young and the Environment" that caught the attention of actor-activist Robert Redford, who believes that Hugh's environmental essays have "played an important role at critical junctures in Utah's history."[67] Wendell Berry, the farmer-poet-essayist of Kentucky whose writing, I believe, bears comparison both in style and substance to Hugh's, quoted Hugh's assertion from "Subduing the Earth" that "dominion is a call to service."[68] In later correspondence with me, Berry added approvingly that this statement was "well said, and exactly right." He took away from an early 1980s meeting with Hugh a fond impression of a man "full of energy and purpose and intelligence and humor."[69]

Two recent publications provide hope that a Mormon appreciation for the environment is emerging. *New Genesis: A Mormon Reader on Land and Community*, edited by Terry Tempest Williams, William B. Smart, and Gibbs M. Smith (Salt Lake City: Gibbs Smith, 1998) is a collection of essays by many Mormon authors, including Marilyn Arnold, Eugene England, Thomas G. Alexander, Emma Lou Thayne, and General Authorities Vaughn J. Featherstone and Hugh W. Pinnock. Hugh Nibley's essay, "Stewardship of the

in *The Prophetic Book of Mormon*, edited by John W. Welch, Vol. 8 of *The Collected Works of Hugh Nibley* (Salt Lake City: Deseret Book/FARMS, 1989), 452; in 1982,"Deny Not the Gifts of God," in *Approaching Zion*, 141; in 1983, "Leaders to Managers: The Fatal Shift," in *Brigham Young Challenges the Saints*, 507; in 1984, "We Will Still Weep for Zion," *Approaching Zion*, 366; in 1986, "The Law of Consecration," *Approaching Zion*, 480 and in 1986 in "Last Call: An Apocalyptic Warning," in *The Prophetic Book of Mormon*, 531; and 1987, "But What Kind of Work?" in *Approaching Zion*, 354.

[64]Hugh Nibley, "Brigham Young on the Environment," 24.

[65]Hugh Nibley, "Our Glory or Our Condemnation," 17, 22, and "Law of Consecration," 483-84, in *Approaching Zion*.

[66]Hugh Nibley, Letter to Russell Stewart, 24 January 1986.

[67]Robert Redford, Letter to Boyd Petersen, 6 December 1996.

[68]*What Are People For?* (San Francisco: Northpoint Press, 1990), 99.

[69]Wendell Berry, Letter to Boyd Petersen, 13 March 1998.

Air" is also included. George Handley's essay, "The Environmental Ethics of Mormon Belief, *BYU Studies* 40, no. 2 (2001): 187-211, picks up where Hugh's work leaves off by seeking to outline the ethical implications of Mormon ecological theology.

But sadly, I believe that Hugh's impact on most members of the Church has been negligible. For the most part, they have shrugged aside his warnings and instead concentrate on "business as usual." In 1986, Hugh characterized Utah's Congressional delegation as "the most anti-environment in the nation," accurately perceiving this attitude as reflecting a larger Mormon callousness. For example, during the debate over the snail-darter, "the ultimate expression of contempt for life came from a senator from Utah who with heavy sarcasm asked, 'Why not declare the smallpox virus an endangered species?' Where business interests are concerned, small living things are to be esteemed as no more than viruses."[70] Certainly, little has changed as far as the Utah congressional delegation is concerned. The uproar over U.S. President Bill Clinton's creation in September 1996 of the Grand Staircase-Escalante National Monument has been deafening. And in Congress, the sponsors for the most generous bills on Utah wilderness designation are a representative from New York and a senator from Illinois.

Hugh's words at the BLM Wilderness hearing in 1986 are poignant:

> Meanwhile, simply to know that [wilderness] is there, a unique feature of America and America alone . . . is a strength and a consolation—this last region of the earth that remains congenial to humans and as pure as God made it. The mere thought of it rests and reassures the mind between visits, and the actual sight of it is invariably exhilarating and restorative. While my eight children grew up we frequently visited what was then an even wilder world (today you must make reservations everywhere that is how the ante is rising!); this gave them a sense of well-being and faith in a good world, a love of their land, that they still have, and that is widely missing in the present day youth who must escape from the drabness and boredom and monotony of urban and suburban life by taking to drugs for their thrills. The proliferations of campers and RVs in the land is testimony enough to the increasing yearning people everywhere are feeling for the healthiest of all forms of escape, and what is getting to be the hardest to find, thanks to the relentless commercialism which spreads its blight everywhere. Industrialization and pollution are inseparable, and the knowledge of an unpolluted area has almost become a dream.[71]

Hugh Nibley has raised a voice in the wilderness for the wilderness. It's a voice *immersed* in the wilderness. His is also a voice *devoted to* the wilderness. His preoccupation with nature has made him an advocate for environmental issues, urging us to rethink our attitudes about the earth and repent of our destructive ways. But, sadly, it's also a voice *lost* in the wilderness. Like the voices of the ancient Jewish prophets, Hugh's words have gone largely unheeded by his people and the Mormon attitude toward the environment is still largely destructive.

---

[70]Hugh Nibley, "Law of Consecration," 480, and "How Firm a Foundation! What Makes It So," 167, in *Approaching Zion*.

[71]Hugh Nibley, Testimony at BLM Hearing, 7 May 1986.

Hugh Nibley's passport photograph when he left on his mission, age seventeen. He has signed it on the right.

Within a year the tramping continued, this time among the amused or resentful villagers of the Black Forest and the Rhine Plain. President Tadje, one of the few great men I have known, allowed me to do it my way. By bicycle in summer and afoot in winter I went alone (my companions thought I was overdoing it) carrying the gospel to Catholic, Lutheran, and Calvinist (they were the toughest) villages. The people were still peasants in those days, living in the Middle Ages in their wildly picturesque storybook towns. Surprising enough, the work was not entirely unsuccessful—the gospel message readily leapt the immense cultural gap, passing through the ever-so-tenuous medium of faith that is common to all cultures and all religions. It was a different story when I knocked on the doors of professors and industrialists in the university and factory towns. German Wissenschaft had long since severed all ties with any gospel but its own proud, self-contained positivism; literally they were without a culture and without religion. The hints were clear enough: the infernal machine of our age was made in Germany.[1]

---

[1] Hugh Nibley, "An Intellectual Autobiography," *Nibley on the Timely and the Timeless* (Provo, UT: Brigham Young Press, 1978), xxi.

Chapter 6

A Mission to Germany, 1927-30

Hugh graduated from high school in 1927 at age seventeen. While college was the obvious next step, Hugh's parents were more concerned with his social development than with his intellectual development. As his father put it in a letter to Charles W. Nibley, "What he needs now is contact with people." And Hugh's parents did not believe college was the best place for him to get that contact. With Hugh's brother Sloan preparing for his mission to Germany, his parents began to think a mission would be perfect for Hugh too. "It will be the finest experience in the world for him to get out tracting from door to door rather than going to college this winter," El wrote.[2] At that time, the Church had no set standards on how old missionaries had to be, so on 11 August 1927 El wrote to his father, then serving in the First Presidency, asking him whether it would be possible for Hugh to receive a call.[3] Hugh's grandfather replied, "We have had many good missionaries who have gone out when they were only seventeen years of age, although it would be preferable if they were eighteen or nineteen. I will try to look into the matter."[4]

By August 20, Sloan had received his mission call to the German-Austrian Mission.[5] Evidently Hugh was given special consideration, because by September 12, his bishop had interviewed him, and the letter of calling had arrived from the Church president. Hugh would leave for the Swiss-German mission in November. Hugh must have been thrilled with this news, for his father wrote that, "He is studying hard all the time for his mission and is most excellently equipt [sic] and prepared.[6]

---

[2]Alexander Nibley, Letter to Charles W. Nibley, 12 September 1927, Charles W. Nibley Collection, Family Correspondence, Mss. 1523, Box 1, fd. 3, L. Tom Perry Special Collections, Lee Library, Brigham Young University, Provo, UT.

[3]I have not been able to find a copy of this letter; however, Charles W. Nibley refers to it in his response.

[4]Charles W. Nibley, Letter to Alexander Nibley, 13 August 1927, Charles W. Nibley Collection, Mss. 1523, Box 1, fd. 3, Perry Special Collections.

[5]Alexander Nibley, Letter to Charles W. Nibley, 20 August 1927, Charles W. Nibley Collection, Mss. 1523, Box 1, fd. 3, Perry Special Collections.

[6]Alexander Nibley, Letter to Charles W. Nibley, 12 September 1927, Charles W. Nibley Collection, Mss. 1523,

Just before he left for Salt Lake to enter the mission home, Hugh and his parents accompanied a youth choir from the Los Angeles and Hollywood Stakes to the Mesa Temple dedication ceremonies.[7] El wrote his father before they left: "I think it is a trip that we will all get a great deal out of and it might be very beneficial to Hugh."[8] The temple was dedicated by President Heber J. Grant in two sessions—morning and evening—on 23 October 1927. The Nibley family attended both ceremonies; Hugh remembers sitting directly behind President Grant. The entire family was spiritually moved by the proceedings, as El later reported to his father: "The services were very impressive and lovely in every respect."[9]

It was at this temple dedication that Hugh first met Elder John A. Widtsoe. Norwegian-born, Elder Widtsoe had received his doctorate from the German University of Göttingen and took a keen interest in mentoring young Church members with intellectual promise. At the time, Widtsoe was serving as the President of the European Mission which supervised all of the missions in Europe including the Swiss-German Mission. According to Hugh's father, Elder Widtsoe immediately took "a great liking for Hugh" and believed he had "all the ear marks of a genius." Widtsoe also agreed with Hugh's parents that "the mission will be the very finest thing that can happen to Hugh at this time" and "will develop him along the lines that he now needs developing before he becomes any older." Reassuringly, Widtsoe promised "to do what he could to help him get started on the right lines in the missionary field."[10]

On 25 October Hugh gave his missionary farewell talk to the Mutual. His father described the talk as "a gem," adding more ambiguously, that Hugh "has a very unusual philosophy and the manner in which he delivered himself of it last night was highly amusing."[11] In a reflective passage a few days later, El evaluated Hugh's strengths and weaknesses: "We are very proud of [Hugh] and know that if he keeps well he will amount to something worthwhile. . . . Hugh has well-defined ideas as to what he is going out for and I am sure he will accomplish anything he sets his mind to."[12] Then on Saturday, 29 October, Hugh took the train from Glendale to Salt Lake City. He was due to arrive by noon on Sunday the 30th; however, a severe winter storm delayed the train and it didn't arrive until early the next morning. Hugh poignantly described his arrival in that "cold blustery snowy November [actually 31 October]. It was dismal out when we came into the station there, and the place was empty—nothing in it except one lone man standing out on the station platform waiting for me: Charles W. Nibley, wearing a long black coat. Such a heart that man had."[13]

Box 1, fd. 3, Perry Special Collections.

[7]El's letter does not mention whether Hugh was in the choir.

[8]Alexander Nibley, Letter to Charles W. Nibley, 18 October 1927, Charles W. Nibley Collection, Mss. 1523, Box 1, fd. 3, Perry Special Collections.

[9]Alexander Nibley, Letter to Charles W. Nibley, 26 October 1927, Charles W. Nibley Collection, Mss. 1523, Box 1, fd. 3, Perry Special Collections.

[10]Alexander Nibley, Letter to Charles W. Nibley, 1 November 1927, Charles W. Nibley Collection, Mss. 1523, Box 1, fd. 3, Perry Special Collections.

[11]Alexander Nibley, Letter to Charles W. Nibley, 26 October 1927, Charles W. Nibley Collection, Mss. 1523, Box 1, fd. 3, Perry Special Collections.

[12]Alexander Nibley, Letter to Charles W. Nibley, 1 November 1927, Charles W. Nibley Collection, Mss. 1523, Box 1, fd. 3, Perry Special Collections.

[13]Hugh Nibley, "Remarks about Charles W. Nibley on the Occasion of the Celebration of his 150th birthday, 5 February 1999," 10.

Hugh went directly to the Salt Lake Mission Home. The large mansion at 31 North State Street near the Church Administration Building had originally been built for one of Brigham Young's daughters. Under the direction of LeRoi C. Snow, son of President Lorenzo Snow, the Church began a one-week missionary training program at the home in 1925. By the time Hugh arrived in 1927, missionaries were spending two weeks at the center. More than thirty teachers, many of them General Authorities, instructed the missionaries "in the gospel, Church organization, the standard Church works, English and foreign languages, singing, genealogy, priesthood and auxiliary work, personal health and hygiene, gymnasium exercises and swimming, table etiquette and manners."[14] During their stay at the home, the missionaries also went to the temple three times, received their patriarchal blessings from the Church Patriarch, and had close contact with Church Authorities. The "greatest good" done by the home, according to its director, was to help the new missionaries "obtain the missionary spirit."[15] While the home provided some of the basic training a missionary needed, it was small in scope and size compared to today's Missionary Training Center.

Nor were the mission rules as strict as they are today. Missionaries from the Salt Lake area lived at home during these two weeks, and those who stayed at the Mission Home were allowed to come and go freely. Hugh often visited his grandfather, who reported to Hugh's father: "Hugh seems to be enjoying himself immensely. I do not see much of him, but he manages to get down to the house every day or two and Mama gives him a good feed and a lot of instructions, all of which he seems to rather like."[16]

On 9 November, Hugh was set apart for his mission by Elder Melvin J. Ballard. The blessing admonished Hugh to warn the German people in strong terms. Hugh remembers Elder Ballard's words: "Tell these people that [unless they repent] they will be destroyed by fire from heaven."[17] While Ballard's words may have been severe, they were based on scripture (e.g., D&C 63:34). Throughout his mission, Hugh was conscious of Elder Ballard's admonition. "I went around all inflamed with this," remembers Hugh.

Soon Hugh was on a train, making his way to Montreal, Quebec, Canada, where he boarded the *Montcalm*, a ship on the Canadian-Pacific line.[18] The ship took two and a half days to travel through the St. Lawrence Seaway, emerging into the Atlantic near Nova Scotia. Despite the ship's serene name, the voyage was "quite rough," Hugh remembers. "At one

---

[14]LeRoi C. Snow, "The Missionary Home," *Improvement Era* 31 (May 1928): 553.

[15]Ibid. See also Richard O. Cowan, *Every Man Shall Hear the Gospel in His Own Language: A History of the Missionary Training Center and Its Predecessors* (Provo, UT: Missionary Training Center, 1984), 5-8.

[16]Charles W. Nibley, Letter to Alexander Nibley, 3 November 1927, Charles W. Nibley Collection, Mss. 1523, Box 1, fd. 3, Perry Special Collections.

[17]Hugh W. Nibley, *Teachings of the Book of Mormon*, Semester 3, transcripts of lectures presented to an Honors Book of Mormon Class at Brigham Young University, 1989-90, 123.

[18]The *Montcalm* and its partner ship the *Montclare* were built by John Brown & Company in Clydebank, Scotland, in 1922. The two ships were 575 feet long and 70 feet wide and displaced 16,418 and 16,314 tons respectively. Steam turbines geared to twin screws gave a service speed of 16 knots. They could each carry 1,810 passengers (542 cabin class, 1,268 third class). Built for Canadian-Pacific Steamships, the ships were used for Liverpool-to-Canada service. When the Great Depression cut into the Atlantic trade, both became cruise ships, the *Montcalm* in 1932 and the *Montclare* the following year. In 1939, both ships were requisitioned for war duty. The *Montcalm* became the armed merchant cruiser HMS *Wolfe*, and later a troopship. The *Montclare* was also converted to an armed merchant cruiser. They were both sold to the British government in 1942 and converted to depot ships. The *Montcalm* was laid up in 1950 and scrapped in 1952. The *Montclare* was laid up in 1955 and scrapped in 1958. Rob Betz, "Re: Canadian-Pacific Liner," e-mail to Boyd Petersen, 14 December 2000.

Hugh sailed to Liverpool on this ship, the Montcalm, then continued on to Germany.

point they thought the boat was going to tip over. I was there in the dining room and everything slid over to one side of the room. The big buffet tipped over; the tables all slid. The sea was not calm that day."[19] After about a week at sea, the ship docked in Liverpool. Hugh then travelled from England to Germany and arrived in Cologne on 27 November.[20]

Hugh's first mission president was Hugh J. Cannon, but Cannon was soon replaced by Fred Tadje, a native-born German whom Hugh described in his mission journal as "the only great man I have ever known" (13 Oct. 1929). "He was a great speaker, a powerful speaker," remembers Hugh. "He was a very simple and very honest person and he had a powerful testimony."[21] Hugh spent the first three weeks of his mission at the mission's own training center in Cologne, where, along with the other new missionaries, he was drilled in basic German in the morning and sent out tracting in the afternoons. Winslow Whitney Smith, a contemporary missionary who later taught in the local mission home, joked, "In the evening people would show up and ask, 'Who were those two nice young men who brought us this tract, and what were they trying to say?'"[22] Hugh, with his penchant for acquiring languages, probably did better at learning German than most missionaries, but German life and culture were certainly an adjustment even for him.

Following his time in Cologne, Hugh was transferred to Ludwigshafen where he spent the remainder of December and all of January 1928.[23] Ludwigshafen was a big

---

[19]Hugh Nibley, interviewed by Boyd Petersen, 1 December 2000.

[20]The Swiss-German Mission Quarterly Report, LDS Church Archives, indicates that Hugh arrived on 27 November. Hugh recorded in his Tagesberichtbuch that he arrived on the 31st—although November has only thirty days. This Tagesberichtbuch (Daily Record Book), titled "Missionary Work in the Swiss-German Mission of the Church of Christ of Latter-day Saints," is a small red appointment book preprinted for missionaries in the Swiss-German Mission. Hugh Nibley dictated its contents to his secretary on 7 July 1999; photocopy and original of dictation in my possession. Hugh kept this very sketchy daily record throughout his mission but, during the latter portion of his mission, recorded more detailed musings in a small notebook, which I cite as "Journal," by the date; typescript of selected entries in my possession.

[21]Hugh Nibley, Interviewed by Boyd Petersen, 1 December 2000.

[22]Quoted in Mary Lythgoe Bradford, Lowell L. Bennion: Teacher, Counsellor, Humanitarian (Salt Lake City: Dialogue, 1995), 35.

[23]The Swiss-German quarterly report states that he was assigned to Frankfurt, but Hugh's Tagesberichtbuch's

industrial city, where Hugh says they claimed to be making fertilizer but were really making munitions. In February, he was transferred, this time to Frankenthal near the Pfalz Mountains, where he spent most of the year tracting in the villages along the Rhine. Hugh's missionary companion at this time was a big coal miner from Pennsylvania with a low opinion of Germans. "He didn't speak German very well," recalls Hugh. "He'd say, 'You can't learn these people anything.'"[24] Hugh next served for over five months with Douglas Cutler, "whose sterling qualities," Hugh quipped in a letter to his mother, "can be no more fitly extolled than by remarking how for that time he has abode my company with perfect grace. Not everyone can, I think you know, do that."[25]

The baptism rate in Germany was quite high in the early 1920s, but by 1928 it had tapered off. In a letter to his grandmother, Hugh quoted some mission statistics to his grandmother: "to convert a soul," wrote Hugh, in 1925, it took 78 hours of tracting and 442 tracts; in 1926, it took 254 hours of tracting and 679 tracts; and in 1927 it took 378 hours of tracting and 2033 tracts. "In 1928, it seems things are harder than ever."[26]

Hugh rode his bicycle, often alone, to villages along the Rhine valley. "It was hard," Hugh later stated. "It was grim. The Calvinist villages were the toughest. The Catholics were next. The Lutherans were rather kind. But it was rough. It was a clash of minds, you see, because immediately these people were tremendously hostile." During World War II, Hugh would visit some of the same cities where he served on his mission. "I would think time and again, this is so much easier than trying to confront these people eye-to-eye. Shooting at a distance was much nicer and much safer."[27]

Hugh recorded one amusing incident that occurred at the Catholic Cathedral in Frankenthal. A stork had built its nest on top of cathedral, which the residents saw as a sign of good luck. During a procession on 29 March 1928 the stork flew over and dropped a frog right on the bishop's head. This must have been a droll sight for a young missionary.

When he wasn't tracting, Hugh would occasionally do some sight-seeing in Germany. On 6 May 1928, Hugh records in his *Tagesberichtbuch* that he walked to Limburg where he visited some ancient ruins which were "cut into a mountain of red sandstone." Hugh described the ruins as "a long series of stairs leading to a chamber supported by natural columns of rock," at the end of which were "three thrones, one large and two small ones." He was impressed. "That was the most dramatic place I have ever been. There were no tourists or anything; nobody ever went there."[28]

On 1 July 1928, Hugh came down with the mumps, an experience he described as "not pleasant."[29] The illness kept him indoors for a couple of weeks, and he employed the time, as he wrote in a letter to his mother, in "examin[ing] what I have learned." What he determined from his enforced contemplation was that Western literature and philosophy was "a skeleton to build affects and attitudes onto, justifying much filthy fuss and

---

tracting record goes straight from Cologne to Ludwigshafen without mentioning Frankfurt.

[24] Hugh Nibley, Interviewed by Boyd Petersen, 1 December 2000.

[25] Hugh Nibley, Letter to Agnes Sloan Nibley, ca. July 1928.

[26] Hugh Nibley, Letter to Margaret Violet Reid Sloan, 31 May 1928.

[27] Nibley, *Teachings of the Book of Mormon*, Semester 3, 122.

[28] Hugh Nibley, Interviewed by Boyd Petersen, 1 December 2000.

[29] *Tagesberichtbuch*, typescript, 2; Nibley, Interviewed by Boyd Petersen, 1 December 2000.

hypocrisy." According to Hugh, "Kant and Socrates found themselves beating their wings in a vacuum" because they did not have "the fulcrum" of faith as "the base for operations."[30]

As he explored his own "fulcrum" of faith, Hugh was impressed by the writings of Brigham Young. He also found Brigham's advice to missionaries important. In a letter to his family, Hugh quoted Brigham Young's counsel about the attitude a missionary should have toward his family at home: "'If they live, all right; if they die, all right; if I live, all right; if I die, all right; don't carry your wives or your children in your heart or in your affections with you one rod.' That's the spirit!" stated Hugh.[31]

When Hugh's parents asked him whether he would like to stay in Germany to pursue his college education, Hugh responded forcefully: "I am not here to become [an] educated darling. Getting into a German University is no harder than walking through the door." Focused instead on his mission work, Hugh continued, "I must spend the whole time telling these people something they don't want to hear."[32] In the summer of 1928, Hugh returned again to this theme:

> The willfulness of these people—their enthusiastic indifference—is nothing short of sinful. The missionaries are working five times as hard as they ever did—I will answer for it, that there is not one in this conference who does not grow surer and graver every day—with almost negligible results. The sad part of it is no one will get any enjoyment out of the chagrin of the poor devils when they wake up. The Lord suffers from their punishment more than they can.[33]

In the same letter, Hugh had urged his mother to quit sending him so much money. "We have rich missionaries in the field, but none manages to spend over $40.00 a month," wrote Hugh. "I have enough money in Basel now to keep me going for at least six months."[34] It's true that Hugh had abstemious habits; but inflation was out of control in Germany, and hard American currency was very valuable. "A German mark was worth nothing then," he explained. "A billion marks for a dollar was what it was going for on the market. And naturally, when they'd send me fifty dollars a month what would I do with that? I could support the entire branch. I had no use for it, so I'd stick it in books and do everything else."[35] Hugh's practice of using dollar bills as book marks proved beneficial to his more financially strapped missionary companions. One of them reported

---

[30]Hugh Nibley, Letter to Agnes Sloan Nibley, 16 July 1928, Charles W. Nibley Collection, MSS 1523, Box 1, fd. 4, Perry Special Collections.

[31]Quoted in Alexander Nibley, Letter to Charles W. Nibley, 24 July 1928, Charles W. Nibley Collection, Mss. 1523, Box 1, fd. 4, Perry Special Collections. See John A. Widtsoe, ed., *Discourses of Brigham Young* (Salt Lake City: Deseret Book, 1954), 324.

[32]Hugh Nibley, quoted in Alexander Nibley, Letter to Charles W. Nibley, 24 July 1928, Charles W. Nibley Papers, MSS 1523, Box 1, fd. 4, Perry Archives.

[33]Hugh Nibley, Letter to Agnes Sloan Nibley, ca. July 1928, Charles W. Nibley Papers, Mss 1523, Box 1, fd. 4, Perry Special Collections.

[34]Ibid. The missionaries did their banking in Basel.

[35]Hugh Nibley, Interviewed by Boyd Petersen, 16 June 1996. Hugh also recalled that his mother would complain about opening books that he mailed back from the mission field "and there would be a few dollars stowed away. . . . I didn't have any use for it." Hugh Nibley, "Faith of an Observer," 32, compilation of interviews, ca. 1983-84 for a video documentary of the same name aired in 1985, photocopy of typescript in my possession, pagination added.

that when any of the missionaries needed money they would leaf through Elder Nibley's books, pilfering his bookmarks.36

When one of Hugh's companions sent some photos to Hugh's family in the summer of 1938, El wrote to Charles W. Nibley that Hugh was "as fat as a little German pig and looks wonderfully well in the pictures."37 Two weeks later, he added to his father that Sloan and Hugh "seem to be getting along as well as the average although I think Hugh is above average while Sloan is not doing anything to brag about."38

In December 1928, Hugh was transferred to Bruchsal in Baden. There and in the neighboring city of Karlsruhe, he spent most of his remaining mission. His missionary book becomes sparse, recording little more than the town names where he worked. However, from March 1929 on, a fairly detailed journal has survived, preserving both Hugh's activities and his musings for the last eight months of his mission.

While most missionaries occasionally feel guilty because they are distracted by sightseeing, spend their time on trivial things, and fail to work as hard as they could, Hugh's occasional battles with guilt came from being distracted by his studies. "Can one hour of Greek a day be playing the devil with my mission?" Hugh wrote on 16 March. The Book of Mormon was a refuge, providing study without guilt. "I am marking Nephi up elaborately," Hugh confided to his journal that same day. A week later, he was fighting with his conscience about studying secular materials during his mission. "I am trying to let up on foreign matter as study," he wrote on 24 March and, the next day, "The Book of Mormon is giving me greater joy than anything ever did."

Even though Hugh experienced a genuine sense of conflict, he was, nevertheless, driven in his studies and intellectual development by a sense of mission. On 15 March, he was concerned that health problems he was experiencing might keep him from being able to "accomplish my purposes. They are the Lord's purposes; most of them have only been acknowledged reluctantly." One of these problems had been resolved only four days earlier in a somewhat humorous way: "A vertebrae has been causing me agony for weeks. Feeling moved to pray for the alleviation of this persistent and dangerous disorder, I hopped into bed." When Hugh's companion, Orson Whitney Young got home, he "pounced in after me, delivering a terrific poke, quite accidently, with his elbow—and right on the spot. That vertebrae got perfect—though violent adjustment. Nothing else would have done the trick, for the ailment was of long standing, and for the moment was stunned."

Hugh also recorded one of his chief methods of study: "My recently adopted method of learning is proving itself the only thing—I give lectures—good, plain, orderly treatises on various subjects, to the atmosphere," he wrote on 9 March. In one of these soliloquies addressed to no one, Hugh noted that he had developed "a new angle on authority" and exulted innocently: "New angling is my especial gift; I must develop it. It staggers all opposition" (29 March). Unfortunately, he neglected to record what this "new angle on authority" was.

36Victoria Ann Decker Witesman, telephone conversation with Boyd Petersen, 6 November 1997; transcript in my possession. Witesman heard this story several times from Winslow Whitney Smith, a family friend and former Swiss-German missionary, now deceased.

37Alexander Nibley, Letter to Charles W. Nibley, 9 August 1928, Charles W. Nibley Collection, Mss. 1523, Box 1, fd. 4, Perry Special Collections.

38Alexander Nibley, Letter to Charles W. Nibley, 25 August 1928, Charles W. Nibley Collection, Mss. 1523, Box

Coupled with these lofty intellectual activities were all-too-earthy experiences. While visiting a small town, Hugh accidentally let two pigs out of their sty. "I got a run for my money with the whole town looking on. If the old man hadn't come out with a whip to help, those animals would still have been loose—and I chasing them." While Hugh was most certainly embarrassed by the incident, he made it work to his advantage. "It gave the spectators a fine spirit, and they took tracts with interest" (13 March 1929).

Hugh continued to experience frustration sharing the gospel with the German people. After a day tracting in the primarily Catholic town of Karlsdorf, Hugh analyzed the experience: "Catholic men are good but the Father likes to work on the perverse nature of people, and it is a keen enjoyment for Catholic women to act like the devil and feel themselves most holy in their entirely negative enthusiasm" (18 March 1929). And after a day spent tracting in Bruchsal, Hugh wrote with some exasperation, "These people really have had a chance. These many testy attempts to dismiss the subject entirely are plainly the workings of a guilty conscience" (25 March 1929). But Hugh also felt concern about his own abilities, especially about speaking to a large group of people. On 24 March, he was "planning a meeting for Heidelsheim and the Orwisheims." Next to that he wrote a one-word summary: "scared."

On his nineteenth birthday, 27 March 1929, Hugh wrote in his journal, "I arose early, feeling superb. The morning was salubrious. I remembered it was my birthday." He describes the day with poetic rapture as being "most Marchy: Grey, cool-cold, high-sweet with new grass and soft . . . earth. . . . Daffodils in the air. It was my day. Late March takes me into its confidence." Hugh's feelings of joy for his birthday coupled with the cool reception he received from the people he spoke with that day prompted a rare outburst of self-righteousness: "Tracting was fun. Never has the joyless self-satisfaction of the people so seemed like blindness. They didn't know it—the ninnies! dunces! The joke was all on them and I enjoyed it thoroughly."

In April, Hugh's brother Sloan visited, and the two made a brief sightseeing trip to the university town of Heidelberg. Such sight-seeing excursions, like cultural exposure, were encouraged for missionaries as part of providing broader educational experience and sophistication. Although he had scoffed the summer before at the suggestion that he might stay in Germany to attend school, "since visiting Heidelberg I haven't got the school idea out of my head," he admitted to his journal. "I am not humble—I haven't even faith enough to trust my education to the Lord" (15 April 1929).

On 22 April in Karlsruhe, Hugh "paid a nauseating visit to the slaughterhouse," where he witnessed a Jewish rabbi perform a kosher slaughter of a cow. "They hung it upside down and cut its throat," remembers Hugh. "It was a bloody mess, but it was very instructive." The rabbi performed the ritual killing wearing his robes, "and when he comes out all bloody and they know that the atonement has been made, they cheer; they've been washed in the blood of the lamb."[39]

Apparently during this second year, Hugh's very intensity began to work against him. The spring before in March 1928, he had noted that he was "very sick, especially headache," which he attributed the red cabbage he had eaten. "They cook it in vinegar," Hugh remembered, "and it was so sour that my stomach was upset." (To this day, Hugh

---

1, fd. 4, Perry Special Collections.

[39] Hugh Nibley, Interviewed by Boyd Petersen, 14 December 2000. This experience gave Hugh great insight into Old Testament temple ordinances and their relationship to Christ's atonement. Nibley, "The Meaning of

cannot eat red cabbage.)⁴⁰ His solution was simple—to eliminate anything from his diet that he disliked, a simple ruthlessness that extended to most foods that required any preparation time. One missionary reported that Hugh's mission diet for a considerable time consisted mostly of wheat that he stashed in his pockets, chewing while he was studying or tracting.⁴¹ Although El had called Hugh "fat" in photos sent home the previous spring, his strenuous missionary work, eccentric eating habits, and other ailments that he noted without describing made his weight plummet dangerously.

In the summer of 1929, Hugh's mother paid a visit to her missionary sons. Dreading the distraction, Hugh wailed in his journal on 20 June,"Mother sails on the 27 of June! What shall I do?" Sloanie toured Europe for a few weeks before reaching Germany. On 20 July, El Nibley wrote to his father that he had received Sloanie's letter, "written on the boat as they were going along the Coast of Ireland" and expected another letter any day "telling of her meeting with the boys."⁴² On 24 July, Hugh received a telegram from his mother who was in Paris. "She will be here tomorrow at five!" Hugh exclaimed with more anxiety than joy. He met Sloanie at the train station the following evening, and Sloanie immediately set about correcting her son's shabby appearance. Hugh tersely recorded the activities of their first day together: "Get up late. Get me a new suit" (26 July 1929). One missionary who served with Hugh said that, at one point—he can't remember exactly when—President Tadje assigned him to "locate Elder Nibley and help him buy a new suit."⁴³ This elder does not say if Hugh agreed to cooperate; apparently he had not by the time Sloanie showed up.

Interviewed seventy years later, Hugh's ambiguous feelings about his mother's two-week-long visit were still apparent. On the one hand, he said, it was "quite nice" because she was "high fashion and all the girls loved her." However, he also admitted that "it was strenuous to have Mother there."⁴⁴ Her imperious presence was an undeniable distraction from missionary work, and he fretted over it. Sloan was supposed to join them on 29 July but, through a misunderstanding, was not at the station. Hugh and Sloanie spent many hours trying to track him down. He finally showed up on 1 August. Eventually, the three toured the cities of Baden Baden, Heidelberg, Frankfurt, and the surrounding countryside. On 3 August, Hugh recorded briefly in his diary: "Sloan and Mother came over. Washing not done. Missionary meeting."

Furthermore, Sloanie had come equipped with Grandma Sloan's oil, the cure-all that raised horrendous blisters wherever it was applied on the body. On 5 August, Hugh recorded despairingly that "she doped the kids [children in a member family] up with 'the oil.'" Two days later, it was his turn: she "paved my bowels with oil." Even after seven decades, he shuddered at the caustic memory: "Oh, . . . it was a horrible remedy."⁴⁵

---

the Atonement," *Approaching Zion*, edited by Don E. Norton, Vol. 9 of *The Collected Works of Hugh Nibley* (Salt Lake City: Deseret Book/FARMS, 1989), 578-83.

⁴⁰*Tagesberichtbuch*, typescript, 1; see also Hugh Nibley, Interviewed by Boyd Petersen, 1 December 2000.

⁴¹Richard Stratford, Letter to John W. Welch, 11 December 1984, photocopy in my possession courtesy of John Welch.

⁴²Alexander Nibley, Letter to Charles W. Nibley, 20 July 1929, Charles W. Nibley Collection, Mss. 1523, Box 1, fd. 5, Perry Special Collections.

⁴³Quayle Cannon, quoted in Donald Q. Cannon, Letter to Boyd Petersen, 27 February 1990.

⁴⁴Hugh Nibley, Interviewed by Boyd Petersen, 1 December 2000.

⁴⁵Ibid.

Hugh (left) and his brother Sloan, also a missionary in Germany, visited the Battle of Leipzig Monument in August 1929 while their mother was with them.

Sloanie had taken the drastic measure of applying the oil internally because Hugh had become seriously ill that day. He had been tracting in the small town of Ettlingen, preceded, door to door, by a Catholic priest who, Hugh surmised, was warning the people not to listen to the young Mormon missionary. At the last house, the family offered Hugh a bowl of soup. Hugh politely declined, but the family insisted so Hugh ate the bowl of soup. Afterwards he became so violently nauseated that he vomited repeatedly in the woods near the village. He wondered if he had been poisoned and was too weak to get out of bed for the next two days (7, 8 August 1929).

He was better on 13 August when Sloanie finally left Germany. "I was not broken hearted," confessed Hugh candidly in his journal. Sloanie was upset by his thinness, which was only made worse by his illness. He weighed only 117 pounds; and even Hugh, generally cavalier about his own well-being, admitted to his journal that branch members on 28 September were "alarmed at my thinness." "Mother made quite a fuss about the way I looked and Brother Tadje was concerned too," recalls Hugh.[46] Sloanie insisted that Hugh be transferred to the mission home where he could regain his strength. Apparently because he remained excessively thin, the mission president took this action two months after Sloanie's departure. On 13 October, Hugh wrote gloomily in his journal: "I talk with Bro. Tadje and am to go to Basel." Richard Stratford, who worked in the mission office in Basel, reported: "In Basel he had three good meals a day and became very bored." Hugh staved it off in a typical way. He discovered, on his companionless tracting expeditions, that "many of the people in Basel could speak only French. As a result, he . . . purchased a French grammar book, and in approximately ten days he was able to do his tracting speaking French and have some excellent conversations with the French speaking people."[47]

Two weeks later, despite a less strenuous schedule and regular meals, Hugh's health problems had not relinquished their hold on him. By the end of October, President Tadje decided to give him an early release. Missionaries who had to learn a foreign language were usually called on two-and-a-half-year missions, but Hugh was released after

---

[46]Ibid.
[47]Stratford, Letter to Welch.

two years, on 6 November 1929.⁴⁸ In his journal he wrote unenthusiastically, "Go enquiring about visa. Get a great wad of bills ($394) from Br. Stratford and discuss with Br. Tadje. Receive my release (damn!) and make my adieu."

Hugh was, however, given "very special consideration" upon his release and was allowed to travel to Greece for six weeks before going home.⁴⁹ Hugh was thrilled to be able to visit what he then thought of as the cradle of civilization; but he also had a quasi-official assignment to call on a Sister Liechti, a member of the branch in Baden Baden who had married a Greek tycoon, and also to visit a "whole slew of saints [who] had landed upon the evacuation of western Turkey."⁵⁰

When Hugh got off the boat in Greece, he was delighted to find that the vocabulary and grammar he had learned from classical Greek primers enabled him to communicate with modern Greeks. And in a wholly improbable coincidence, at the stall of a money-changer and trinket-seller, he discovered a "great big nickle plated watch with a massive copper chain" that he had lost months earlier "in the Black Forest." He bought it back.

In his "Intellectual Autobiography," Hugh sums up his days in Greece:

> At the end of my mission President Tadje let me go to Greece to carry messages to some native members of the Church and to make contact with some who had recently migrated from Turkey in a great influx of refugees. Those marvelous Greeks, cheerful and courteous, exuding the spirit of good will, with nothing to eat and nowhere to live! I took long walks, sleeping in the hills, and had a shock from which I never recovered. While I was circulating among displaced persons (under surveillance, of course) my stuff was stolen from the flea-bag hotel where I was staying. That made me an outcast among the outcasts. I spoke English, but also German and French, and my clothes were certainly not American—how could suspicious officials know where I really came from or what I might be running away from? My passport turned up at the American Express, but that was not the problem. By what right did I lay claim to affluence and security while all the people around me had none? How could a few rubber stamps place me in an exalted station? True, the stamps were only symbols, like money, but symbols of what? Hadn't those others worked as hard as I? Worse still, what was I if my sacred identity depended on who somebody else said or believed I was? If a bored petty official had decided not to make some phone calls, I could have become a nonperson forever. Legal fictions had supplanted intrinsic worth and faith in God and man; it was the papers that everybody was grabbing for in those desperate times. And what were the papers really worth?⁵¹

Hugh set sail from Antwerp on a German steamer which was carrying animal manure to South America. He passed through the Panama Canal and arrived in Los Angeles on New Year's Day, 1930. And there, he found the answer to his question as he learned "how many thousand American millionaires had just become paupers overnight." He did not realize at that moment that his own family would be among the casualties.

---

⁴⁸Swiss-German Mission Quarterly Report, 5 November 1929, gives Hugh's release date as 5 November.

⁴⁹Stratford, Letter to Welch. Stratford arranged Hugh's transportation. Elder Jack C. Jenkins, Letter to President Fred Tadje, *The Accelerator* (Swiss-German Mission newsletter), 1 May 1930, LDS Church Archives, visited Sister Liechti and her daughter in Greece after his mission and reported that "Brother Hugh Nibley had paid them a short visit two months before, and they certainly appreciated it, as they were mighty homesick for Basel" and "considered it a true privilege to see `Mormons' in far away Athens."

⁵⁰Hugh Nibley, Interviewed by Boyd Petersen, 1 December 2000.

⁵¹Hugh Nibley, "Intellectual Autobiography," xxi-xxii.

Hugh strikes a comic pose for the camera, ca. 1959.

Mark Twain had it wrong: there is laughter in heaven. If it were otherwise, would Hugh Nibley have generated so much of it on earth? Nibley understands, right down to the most obscure footnote, how life could and should be lived, but he also has a razor-sharp perception of how it most often is lived. The incongruity between the two rarely escapes his ironic notice. Now many good people, when they begin to suspect this incongruity, in others or in themselves, respond with fear. They tighten up, tense up, batten down the hatches, glower and groan. The tighter they get, the greater the fear becomes. But Nibley knows that laughter, that heaven-sent gift, uncoils the tense springs within. It loosens the spiritual muscles, unlocks the spiritual joints, and frees the frozen heart. Nibley not only celebrates the humor of human incongruity, he sometimes provides a living visual aid so we wouldn't miss it. Why else the battered hat, the lone suspender, the notes and clippings flying every which way, the carefully nurtured absentminded professor pose? Nibley is among the least locked down, up-tight, tightly wound Mormons of the twentieth century. His humor was releasing, revivifying, and recreational. To every Mormon, it gave permission to face the incongruities of life with a chuckle. Somewhat like Twain, Nibley frequently shares his amusement with us in a throwaway line at the end of an especially deep and fast-paced patch of exegesis, or a word mumbled under his breath as he does the "searchingforalost noteamongthestack" shtick. If we miss the joke, we must blame our own slow wit. But if we get it, ah, how brightly we feel ourselves shine in our brother Hugh's reflected light! How fortified for the race, how disdainful of the potholes along the way!

—Elouise Bell[1]

---

[1] Elouise Bell, e-mail to Boyd Petersen, 13 April 2002. Elouise, an emeritus professor of English at BYU, is the author of two collections of essays: *Only When I Laugh* (Salt Lake City: Signature Books, 1990) and *Madame Ridiculous and Lady Sublime* (Salt Lake City: Signature Books, 2001).

Chapter 7

Taking Himself Lightly: The Wit of Hugh Nibley

One day in the early 1950s, Hugh Nibley's teaching assistant Curtis Wright found Hugh leaning over his desk, reading from the Book of Mormon, and laughing. Wright asked Hugh Nibley what was so funny, and Hugh responded that he had discovered an error in the Book of Mormon.

"You did, huh?" Wright asked. "That's interesting. Let me see it."

Hugh handed the scriptures over to Wright and pointed to Alma 42:10, which says that humans are "carnal, sensual, and devilish, by nature." Wright read the passage and demanded, "Well, what's the matter with that?" Having taken classes from several BYU professors who had a very secular approach, Wright was beginning to think that Hugh might be ridiculing the Book of Mormon. "So I got a little defensive," says Wright. Unable to conceal his contempt, Wright demanded, "How's it a mistake?"

Hugh responded, "Well, look at Alma, he says that all mankind is carnal, sensual, and devilish by nature. And he should have said they were carnal, sensual, devilish, and *stupid*."[2]

Carnal, sensual, and *devilish* are dramatic, even melodramatic, adjectives. They are seriously and scarily sinful. By adding *stupid*, Hugh instantly stripped them of glamour and illustrates an important truth about human nature that he has emphasized throughout his life—his refusal to take any mortal being, including himself, very seriously. He believes that humans are stupid by nature. As he stated once during an interview: "Nobody's very clever, nobody's very brave, nobody's very strong, nobody's very wise, we're all pretty stupid. That's why we're not tested in those things." What we *are* tested on

---

[2]Curtis Wright, interviewed by Boyd Petersen, 24 September 2001.

are what Hugh considers to be the two most important "moral qualities": "We can forgive and we can repent, so three cheers. Let's start repenting as of now."³

It is evident that while Hugh may not take himself or anyone else very seriously, he does take the gospel seriously. In fact, he suggests that it is this very fact that allows him to take himself lightly. "If you take yourself seriously, you won't take the gospel seriously and the other way around. If you take the gospel seriously then you will say, 'Now I know that man is nothing,'" stated Hugh in an interview in 1974. "Oh, the nothingness of man. We can joke about ourselves once we take the gospel seriously and once we know its blessings and promises. Then we can relax and breathe easily and have some fun."⁴

Hugh's perspective may seem counterintuitive. After all, the Doctrine and Covenants instructs us to avoid "light-mindedness" and "loud laughter" (D&C 59:15; 88:69, 121). It would appear that the gospel requires seriousness and solemnity. Yet, as Hugh points out, Joseph Smith was "the merry prophet. He often was amused by the thought of the figure he must cut before the eyes of the world . . . and he could laugh and enjoy things." Brigham Young was likewise not a melancholy prophet. "His sermons were very humorous; also very cutting," Hugh maintains.⁵ In fact, Hugh claims that the reason that Joseph Smith never selected his brother Hyrum to be an apostle was because Hyrum, "as he explained in a nice way, being humorless lacked a sense of proportion."⁶

Hugh understands the Doctrine and Covenants' commandments concerning light-mindedness and loud laughter a bit differently. "Humor is not light-minded," Hugh insists. "It is insight into human foibles." He continues: "There is nothing light-minded about the incisive use of satire often delivered with an undertone of sorrow for the foolishness of men and the absurdity of their pretenses. Such was the cutting humor of Abinadi addressing the priests of King Noah. There was nothing light-minded about it, though it might raise a chuckle."

Instead, Hugh insists that what is light-minded is "kitsch, delight in shallow trivia, and the viewing of serious or tragic events with complacency or indifference." Hugh also believes, as he maintains Brigham Young did, that it is light-minded to become obsessed with styles, fashions, and fads, which are "passing and trivial, without solid worth or intellectual appeal."⁷

In Hugh's view, the Doctrine and Covenants proscription against "loud laughter" is not against laughter per se, but against a certain type of laughter. He notes that Doctrine and Covenants 88:69 links "idle thoughts" with "excess of laughter." Hugh believes that what we are being cautioned about is "the hollow laugh, the bray, the meaningless laugh of the soundtrack or the audience responding to prompting cards, or routinely laughing at every remark

---

³Hugh Nibley, "Faith of an Observer," 230, compilation of interviews, ca. 1983-84 for a video documentary of the same name aired in 1985, photocopy of typescript in my possession, pagination added.

⁴"Nibley the Scholar: An Interview with Hugh Nibley by Louis Midgley," transcript, 2. This interview was the BYU Forum assembly, 21 May 1974.

⁵Hugh Nibley, "Faith of an Observer," 385.

⁶Hugh Nibley, Letter to Charles Alexander Nibley, 22 October 1979. Although it is true that Hyrum was not one of the original Twelve Apostles, he was sustained as second counselor in the First Presidency to his brother on 7 November 1837 and was simultaneously "given all the priesthood formerly held by Oliver Cowdery," whom he was replacing "(including apostle)." (no editor), *Deseret News 2001-2002 Church Almanac* (Salt Lake City: Church of Jesus Christ of Latter-day Saints, 2000), 56-57.

⁷Hugh Nibley, "On the Sacred and the Symbolic," in *Temples of the Ancient World: Ritual and Symbolism*, edited by Donald W. Parry (Salt Lake City: Deseret Book/FARMS, 1994), 552.

made, no matter how banal, in a situation comedy." Hugh continues, "Joseph Smith had a hearty laugh that shook his whole frame; but it was a meaningful laugh, a good humored laugh."[8]

Like Joseph, Hugh loves to laugh. Regardless of whether he finds humor in works by Roman satirists like Horace and Petronius, in the French comic-book series featuring Astérix and Obélix, or in *Mad Magazine*, Hugh loves a good laugh. When he finally allowed a television to enter his home in the late 1970s, Hugh loved to watch *Monty Python's Flying Circus* and *The Muppet Show*. He still enjoys British comedies on PBS.

But far oftener he delights in making others laugh. Those who read Hugh's writings know that he is very often successful. His spontaneous wit effortlessly generates quips like calling the phrase "Do you have any money?" "Satan's Golden Question"[9] or when he said that graduation robes cause "the well-known greenhouse effect."[10] Yet he can also create lengthy, sustained satire—as, for example, in *Sounding Brass* and *The Myth Makers*. As a result, Hugh's audience has come to expect not only knowledge but sharp, even caustic, humor in his writings and speeches.

His most scathing humor takes the form of satire and parody, appearing most brilliantly in *Sounding Brass* and *The Myth Makers*, Hugh's anti-anti-Mormon books. Some, as David Whittaker has maintained, have dismissed these works as "flippant,"[11] while others see them as somewhat mean-spirited. Nevertheless, Hugh was employing "the critics' own rhetorical standbys, such as ridicule and caricature" in his response to anti-Mormon attacks. His chapter "How to Write an Anti-Mormon Book (A Handbook for Beginners)" from *Sounding Brass* is a classic.

Not nearly as well-known is Hugh's essay "Bird Island," which was read to a small group of BYU Religion Department faculty and later published in *Dialogue*. There he argued, in a tone of exquisitely droning pomposity, that, based on archaeological and philological evidence, the Hill Cumorah's location had been definitely proved to be the north end of Bird Island in Utah Lake. The archaeological evidence Hugh cited was the discovery of ancient Nephite zippers. "Since at the time of the discovery nothing whatever was known about the use of the zipper among pre-Columbian Americans, it was necessary to offer a course in the subject at Brigham Young University," Hugh wrote. Part of the philological evidence runs as follows:

> The Egyptian word for bird is *apid*. If we drop the vowel, which is expendable, and change the consonants only slightly—such as to be hardly perceptible to the Egyptian ear—we get the Hebrew word *zippur*, *zippor*, which by a remarkable coincidence means "bird." The feminine form is of course *Zipporah*, but the Hebrews wrote from right to left, as we learn in our third year Hebrew class. Read Zipporah from right to left and what do you get? Haroppist. The "o" can be conveniently dropped since Hebrew doesn't write the vowels. This then is an unmistakable allusion to the psalms of David. But since the Hebrews wrote from right to left, and David himself was a Hebrew, we must read his name too in the correct direction. The result is the word Divad, or Divot. This can only refer to the violent removal of the hill by the forces of nature.

---

[8]Ibid.

[9]Hugh Nibley, "Educating the Saints," *Brother Brigham Challenges the Saints*, edited Don E. Norton and Shirley S. Ricks, Vol. 13 in *The Collected Works of Hugh Nibley* (Salt Lake City: Deseret Books/FARMS, 1994), 329.

[10]Hugh Nibley, "Leadership vs. Management," video tape. This spontaneous quip was not included in the printed version of the talk.

[11]David J. Whittaker, Foreword, to Hugh Nibley, *Tinkling Cymbals and Sounding Brass*, edited by David J. Whittaker, Vol. 11 of *The Collected Works of Hugh Nibley* (Salt Lake City: Deseret Book/FARMS, 1991), xiv. Both *The Myth Makers* and *Sounding Brass* have been combined with several similar works in *Tinkling Cymbals and Sounding Brass*.

In concluding, Hugh, still with a straight face, proposed a future lecture about "Jaredite eggbeaters and their designation in the Adamic language."[12] The talk is a wonderfully humorous parody of his own as well as other LDS thinkers' unbalanced zeal in seeking linguistic and archaeological "evidences" for Mormon scripture.

A even less well-known example of Hugh's satire occurred in 1970 when Hugh teamed up with Richard H. Cracroft to produce a skit for the Brigham Young University Women's Program. Cracroft had recently been hired at BYU after obtaining his Ph.D. from the University of Wisconsin.[13] A committee from the Women's Program invited him to "help out" with a skit that Hugh had written—described as wonderful, but a bit too caustic. Hugh had agreed that it needed to be "toned down" some, and so Cracroft agreed to help. "I don't know how much I rewrote it," recalled Cracroft, "but I do know that the script was still essentially Hugh's; all I did was to gentle and broaden some of the humor a bit."

"Shalamar" had Hugh and Cracroft playing bumbling Middle-Eastern savants named Ali and Hadji who spun off a scathing commentary on the BYU administration, faculty, and student body.[14] Taking a particularly sound roasting was President Ernest L. Wilkinson, who had attended this particular session with his wife, Alice. Remembers Cracroft with a twinkle in his eye, "The object was to slow-burn President Wilkinson as much as we could without evoking lightning from on high." The skit presents Wilkinson as "Ernest the King," who proclaims: "The faculty that decays together stays together." Yet this monarch is so humble "he will even admit that he went to that awful Harvard—in fact, he has been known to admit it as much as forty times a day."

At another point, Hugh (a.k.a. Hadji) looks out on the audience and marvels, "Look, Ali, how different from the unwashed, grimy, sullen, long-haired, red-eyed, sneering, pot-smoking, dirty-footed, guitar-playing, naked, drug-conked, bead-wearing, hop-heads that make up the faculties of other universities. All it would take is a little learning to make them a model faculty." The skit also took a shot at the College of Religion: "Broad minded isn't the word for it—the college is a very haven for the unemployables and the dropouts from the effete-ologies of other institutions." Although sharp-edged, the effect of such opinions, delivered by two men draped in flowing oriental robes, turbans, and turned-up shoes, was hilarious.

Nor does the skit spare Hugh. The skit describes him as "the august, the magnificent, bottomless Sea of Wisdom, Fountain of Charity, unplumbed Sink of Sanctity." "We got lots of laughs," recalls Cracroft, "many of them at seeing Hugh act so uninhibited and so wisely innocent about the lines he was delivering. My biggest memory is of seeing Ernest L. Wilkinson on the front row, howling with genuine laughter at the jabs and the jibes. He seemed honored and pleased to be the object of persecution."[15]

Hugh's humor is likewise evident in his private correspondence. The irony and playfulness in his letters to Paul Springer are delightful. The two address each other with

---

[12]Hugh Nibley, "Bird Island," *Dialogue: A Journal of Mormon Thought* 10, no. 4 (Autumn 1977): 120-23.

[13]BYU Women is a cultural and social organization open to BYU faculty women and spouses of male faculty members. The group hosts periodic lectures and social functions. Richard H. Cracroft retired in 2001 after teaching at BYU since 1963. He served as English Department chair, as dean of the College of Humanities, as director of the university's Center for the Study of Christian Values in Literature, as founding member and past president of the Association for Mormon Letters, and has been a bishop, stake president, and mission president.

[14]"Shalamar," skit written by Hugh Nibley and Richard H. Cracroft; presented at the BYU Women's Program, 24 April 1970. See Appendix E.

[15]Richard H. Cracroft, e-mail to Boyd Petersen, 30 November 2001.

such titles as "Mon Colonel," "Buttons," and "Champ," and Hugh signs his letters with phrases like "goobers of love," "hogs and cusses," and "hubba-hubba."

But that playfulness often carries over into Hugh's correspondence with others, even with people he does not know at all. On one occasion when he was belatedly answering a query about changes in Church doctrines, Hugh deftly mocked his own tardiness: "I have delayed in answering your letter to see whether if I waited long enough any of the Church doctrines would change."[16] Likewise, when someone wrote him asking a particularly vague question, Hugh responded, "My knowledge is apparently weakest of all in communications since I haven't the vaguest idea what you are talking about," then added tartly, "I suspect that goes for both of us."[17]

Often Hugh's humor calls attention to some absurd aspect of our culture that we had never noticed before, as in this passage from a letter to his son, Alex, then serving a mission in Japan:

> If you were here now you would pay $1.10 a gallon for gas, and find the cheapest movies (the SCERA, of course) would let you in to see a lot of explosions for $4.00. Explosions, because that is the only thing that sells these days—whenever you see a little house in the prairie or a mighty high-rise or a fish-cart or a diamond necklace or a planet or a galaxy or a stick of gum you can be sure that it will only be a matter of seconds before it explodes with terrific impact, balls of flame in a towering inferno ending in absolutely nothing. For some reason the current public finds that immensely satisfying—won't settle for anything else: if it does not blow up, we are not interested. I sense a message in that attitude.[18]

In that same letter, Hugh endearingly and sensitively calls attention to the awkwardness of his changing relationship with his son who is now an adult; he signs the letter, "Love, what ARE you supposed to call another adult? Father is too pompous, Dad too folksey, Pater too affected, how about the Old One?"[19]

This same playfulness is evident in the autographs he inscribes in his books. Most authors, when asked to autograph their books, are content to sign them with a simple "thank you" or a "sincerely yours." But Hugh has almost always used the occasion to write something pithy. For example, in one copy of *An Approach to the Book of Mormon*, his Melchizedek Priesthood manual for 1957, Hugh wrote "Sweet Sunday Morning Sleep in the '50s, Courtesy Hugh Nibley." And on one copy of *Tinkling Cymbals and Sounding Brass* he wrote, "How to feel nice being nasty." Another copy of *An Approach to the Book of Mormon* was inscribed, "They tell me approaches are the most dangerous part of the flight. Let's all hold our breath and shut our eyes!" In our own copy of this book, Hugh inscribed it, "To Boyd and Zina, just in case they get terribly bored with TV." On a copy of *Messages of the Joseph Smith Papyri*, he wrote an ambiguous message, referring equally well to the book's subject or the author's age: "From the ancient of days, Hugh Nibley." Hugh inscribed one copy of the Nibley quotation book compiled by Gary Gillum, *Of All Things*, with the words "or *Is That All?*"

My favorite autograph is in my copy of *Since Cumorah* which he sent to me for my birthday in 1984. Hugh inscribed it: "Official Presentation to Boyd from the diligent compiler

---

[16]Hugh Nibley, Letter to Gordon H. Moffat, 22 May 1985. Although the letter to which Hugh is replying is often missing, Hugh usually typed his letters and kept carbon copies.

[17]Hugh Nibley, Letter to A. E. Gygi, 26 June 1981.

[18]Hugh Nibley, Letter to Charles Alexander Nibley, n.d., ca. 1979. Letter begins "How were we to know."

[19]Ibid.; emphasis Hugh's.

and plagiarist H. Nibley." Next to the inscription, he drew a little picture of a ribbon with the initials "HN" in the center. Next to the "H. Nibley" he put a small footnote which read "Authentic Signature H.N." Next to the "H.N." he put another footnote which read "Authentic initials H. Nibley." Finally, he footnoted the "H. Nibley" with "Authentic certification Hugh N. . . ." For a man unparalleled in Mormon circles by his use of footnotes, this is a wonderful self-mockery.

One of the most amusing examples of Hugh's wit is found in his response to a reader's letter. Just after reading *The Myth Makers*, she wrote to call Hugh's attention to a *Harpers'* article titled "The Footnote-and-Mouth Disease."[20] The article discusses the way historians rely too heavily on second-hand sources and, as a result, often repeat information that is wrong, garbled, or embroidered, a theme Hugh treats in *The Myth Makers*. In response, Hugh mocked his own reliance on other sources by sprinkling the entire letter with footnotes:[21]

> September 5, 1961
>
> Dear Myrtle McDonald[1]
>
> You[2] could hardly have done worse than to mention me[3] in any connection with the footnote menace.[4] My articles are noted[5] for their massive,[6] pompous,[7] redundant,[8] enigmatic,[9] recondite,[10] footnotes.[11] Nobody steals from me[12] they just pilfer my footnotes, and they are welcome to them all.
>
> Yours truly,[13]
>
> H. Nibley[14]
>
> [1]Mrs., Miss, or Sister. The author here betrays uncertainty as to the identity and status of the recipient.
>
> [2]See supra, n. 1.
>
> [3]See below, n. 14.
>
> [4]H. Hanff, "The Footnote-and-Mouth-Disease," *Harpers*, Vol. So-&-so (Jn., 1961), pp. such to such.
>
> [5]This assumes that they have readers, a hypothesis never confirmed.
>
> [6]See H. Nibley, Cl. Jnl., Vol. XL, No. 9 (June, 1945), pp. 515-543.
>
> [7]See H. Nibley, J.Q.R., Vol. L, No. 2 (Oct., 1959), pp. 97-123, and ibid., No. 3 (Jan., 1960), pp. 229-240.
>
> [8]See H. Nibley, *Wstn. Speech*, Vol. XX, No. 2 (Spring, 1959), pp. 57-82.
>
> [9]See H. Nibley, Ch.Hst., XXX (Jn.61), 131ff.
>
> [10]See H. Nibley, *Wstn.Pol.Qt.*, II, No. 3, (1949), 329-345.
>
> [11]Actually these footnotes were stripped to the bone—the nasty things are expensive. But none of these little gems would have been accepted without at least five times that much documentation in the original version.
>
> [12]Cf. W. Shakespeare, "Othello," Act III, Sc. iii, line xxx (concordance, s.v. "trash").
>
> [13]In a formal sense. See Knigge, *Umgang mit Menschen*, passim.
>
> [14]Supra, n. 3

As those who have spent any time around him know, Hugh is just as quick-witted in conversation. When Jack Welch was at the Nibley home explaining a contract that

---

[20]Myrtle McDonald, Letter to Hugh Nibley, 21 July 1961, photocopy in my possession. The article referred to was Helene Hanff's "The Footnote-and-Mouth Disease," *Harpers*, July 1961, 58-61.

[21]Hugh Nibley, Letter to Myrtle McDonald, 5 September 1961.

he had worked out between FARMS and Deseret Book to publish Nibley's *Collected Works*, he showed them some of the legal language he had drafted that would protect Hugh's work in some way. Both Phyllis and Hugh were pleased with Jack's efforts and said how good it was to have a lawyer around. Jack responded, "Well, I'm not a lawyer for nothing." To which Hugh immediately responded, "I've never known one who was."[22]

Many on the BYU campus have overheard Hugh make some witty remark in passing. One former BYU student who worked in the Cougareat, the former name of the cafeteria in the student center, recalled that Hugh came through his line once and asked for a hamburger "with all manner of vegetation on it."[23]

One summer, Phyllis asked me to paint their house. As I was applying to the front porch ceiling a coat of the swimming-pool green that Hugh prefers, Hugh walked out and announced, "You know that it's not doctrinal for angels to have wings."

Once I walked into a room and caught Hugh doing a little jig to some particularly jolly Christmas music that was on the stereo. For a scholar who writes of serious things, Hugh doesn't mind being quite undignified. At the Christmas and Thanksgiving feasts, he intones the official rule governing Nibley table manners: "Don't scratch your glass eye with your fork." He also articulates the official Nibley signs for determining when you've had enough to eat: the first is a blinding flash; the second is that everything goes black.

The hallmark of wit is its ability to simultaneously make us laugh and reveal something true about our world that may have been previously hidden. In fact, the word *wit* comes to us from the Old High German *wizzan*, through the Old English *witan* which means "to know." Both *wit* and *wisdom* come from this same root. To "have wit" originally meant to have knowledge; but during the eighteenth century, it came to mean a truth that was well-expressed in language. As Alexander Pope's famous couplet defines it, "True wit is nature to advantage dressed, / What oft was thought but ne'er so well expressed." This type of wit is what readers have come to expect in Hugh's writings: to learn something and to find it expressed in a highly original, often humorous way. In particular, they expect Hugh to point out the disparities in our world—with the administration of BYU, the mores of our Mormon culture, the function of our government and politics, or the way we live our lives. Wherever reality veers from the ideal, Hugh has been there to call attention to these contradictions, with humility and good humor. As Richard Cracroft has stated, Hugh's "humor informs his vision of the world, thriving as that vision does on Great Incongruities. Hugh is an Incongruity-Detector par excellence. The Big Incongruity is Mortal Life in contrast with Real/Eternal Life."[24]

In a letter to his son Alex, Hugh once stated: "Nobody takes me seriously—which has been my salvation."[25] I gained a better understanding of what he meant by that when I heard Hugh say that he was grateful that the Lord had made him "small and insignificant": that way no one would take him too seriously. The context of the conversation made it clear that he wanted people to take his message seriously; however, his lack of physical and worldly stature has kept him humble and kept others from becoming his disciples. Yet this is the very thing about Hugh Nibley that I think we must take seriously. The only one Hugh sees as worthy of having disciples is the Savior. All that the rest of us are worth is a good laugh.

---

[22] John W. Welch, e-mail to Boyd Petersen, 27 November 2001, print-out in my possession.

[23] Lance Harding, Letter to Gary Gillum, n.d.; photocopy in my possession courtesy of Gary Gillum.

[24] Cracroft, e-mail to Petersen.

[25] Hugh Nibley, Letter to Charles Alexander Nibley, 16 November 1979.

Hugh Nibley in 1933, just before serving for the summer in the Northwestern States Mission.

At UCLA I quickly learned the knack of getting grades, a craven surrender to custom, since grades had little to do with learning. Still, that was during the Depression, when people of little faith were clinging to institutions for survival, and so I went along, as timid and insecure as the rest of them. What sort of thinking went on there? The man I worked for as an assistant refused to read Spengler, "because he is not even a full professor!" Staggering, isn't it? I have never thought of an answer to that one. Nobody stood alone; the only way they all stayed on their feet was by leaning on each other for support, like a stand of toothpicks. Berkeley was more of the same, with one difference—they had a library. I decided to put it all together in the stacks beginning at the southwest corner of the ninth level and working down to the northeast corner of the first level, book by book, stopping whenever something significant caught my eye. It took four years, and then one day a cardboard tube came in the mail. It contained another passport, this time even more magical than the one with the rubber stamps. I may have forgotten the very names of the courses and teachers that qualified me as a Ph.D., but this pretty document assured me that from here on it was all safely stored in steel filing cabinets in the registrar's office.[1]

---

[1] Hugh Nibley, "Intellectual Autobiography," *Timely and the Timeless* (Provo, UT: BYU Religious Studies Center, 1978), xxii-xxiii.

Chapter 8

Higher Education, 1930-38

In January 1930, Hugh returned from his mission at age nineteen, currently the standard age at which young men depart on their missions. The home town he came back to had changed significantly in the time he had been away. The crash of October 1929 crippled the burgeoning Southern California economy, which was heavily steeped in speculation. Los Angeles experienced the highest bankruptcy rate in the nation at the close of 1930. Building construction valuations dropped over one million dollars between 1929 and 1932. And as the nation's economy worsened, floods of homeless people poured into California, seeking "the Promised Land" but finding instead more of what they had left behind. The population of Burbank reached 34,090 by 1939, more than doubling over the course of the decade. Burbank's employment rate rose to 75 percent in 1936. Nationwide, unemployment peaked at 25 percent in 1933, rising again to 20 percent in the recession of 1938. It was also a decade of natural disasters: the devastating Long Beach earthquake of 1933 and the floods of 1933 and 1938. The bright spot, however, was the film industry. As people throughout the nation flocked to movie theaters to escape the gloom of their daily lives, that sector of the Southern California economy did well during the 1930s.[2]

Even though real estate was hard hit by the crash, El had cannily "sold his real estate interests and entered mining activities." He and Sloanie were still moving in elite circles in Glendale society, where El served "for many years as a member of the Glendale Park Commission." If he served in Church positions as well, they have not apparently been recorded. Sloanie's musical talents had often been employed in callings as ward and stake chorister and organist in the LDS auxiliary organizations. In Oregon, she had been

---

[2]E. Caswell Perry, *Burbank: An Illustrated History* (Northridge, CA: Windsor, 1987), 55-59. National unemployment statistics are based on data from the National Bureau of Economic Research as reported by Dr. Roger A. McCain, Professor of Economics, Drexel University, Philadelphia, Pennsylvania, on his web page on "Cyclical Unemployment" downloaded in spring 2001 from <http://william-king.www.drexel.edu/top/prin/txt/probs/cycunN.html>.

YWMIA president and Relief Society president on the ward level; and four years after the family's move to California, she was again called as the Relief Society president of Adams Ward.³ In 1932, El successfully diversified into mining, which kept the family living in their now-accustomed luxury. That luxury wouldn't last.

Soon after his return, Hugh began attending the University of California at Los Angeles,⁴ where he initially majored in sociology. The school had been known as the Southern California Normal School from 1882 until 1919, when it became the southern branch of the University of California system. Third and fourth year classes were added soon thereafter, and in 1925 the school graduated its first four-year students. At the time Hugh attended the school, it had recently moved to its new home on "the barren chaparral-covered hills of Westwood, the four original buildings—Royce Hall, Powell Library, Haines and Kinsey Halls—formed a lonesome little cluster in the middle of 400 empty acres."⁵ At the time Hugh enrolled, UCLA's student body numbered a little over 5,000, and it had no graduate programs.⁶ The faculty, remembers Hugh, were "just a very minor group of normal school teachers." Quick-witted and challenging, Hugh found them a disappointing bunch—"very mediocre." Candidly he summed up his impressions: "Without any change of their knowledge, [they became] people with enormous pretensions . . . and they didn't know a damn thing." On his first day on campus, Hugh attended an orientation at which one of the administrators pompously stated, "You are now a member of the elect minority." Hugh was not impressed. "UCLA was a complete waste as far as I was concerned. Though they did have a big collection of Scandinavian books."⁷

Despite his recollection of UCLA's faculty as mediocre, Hugh's first year of college was not a stellar performance. He got mostly B's in his course work with C's in physical education, ROTC, and chemistry. Hugh never liked gym in high school, so it is no surprise that he didn't do well in college gym class, and ROTC was likewise a required class that he didn't especially enjoy. "UCLA was a land-grant college at the time, and they required it," Hugh remembers.⁸ After that first year, he continued to get B's and even C's in PE and ROTC but a string of A's in everything else with the exception of B's in three classes: an upper-division German class, an upper-division Latin class, and a two-semester economics class. Hugh's course work focused on history and languages, including Greek, French, German, Latin, and Spanish.⁹

Hugh and his brother Sloan, who was also attending the school, would drive the sixteen miles each day from Glendale to the UCLA campus in Westwood in a Model T Ford. Initially, Hugh and Sloan had planned to take turns driving. That way the passen-

---

³Leo J. Muir, *A Century of Mormon Activities in California*, 2 vols. (Salt Lake City: Deseret News Press, compiled in 1946 and published in 1952), 2:286-87.

⁴The "at" in UCLA's name would become a comma in 1958.

⁵(no author), "A Brief History of UCLA," n.d., downloaded 12 January 2001 from http://www.ucla.edu/about/history.html.

⁶Ibid. UCLA's first master's degree was established in 1933, with the first Ph.D. program following three years later.

⁷Hugh Nibley, "Faith of an Observer," 259-61, compilation of interviews, ca. 1983-84 for a video documentary of the same name aired in 1985, photocopy of typescript in my possession, pagination added.

⁸Hugh Nibley, interviewed by Boyd Petersen, 16 June 1996.

⁹Hugh Nibley, Student Record, Official Transcript for Fall 1930-Spring 1934, University of California at Los Angeles; certified photocopy made for me on 31 January 2002.

ger would have an extra hour of study time every other day. "I took the first day and everything went all right," remembers Sloan. "And [Hugh] took the second day, except he put a Greek grammar or something like that on his lap and he spent much more time looking at the Greek grammar than he did the traffic, so I was glad to get out of there alive and from then on I did all the driving."[10] Combining reading and driving was a habit Hugh retained for at least a few more years. Reid remembers one summer when he was enrolled in an experimental grade school at UCLA. Hugh, who was still enrolled at UCLA at the time, would drive Reid to school in the morning and then pick him up in the afternoon. "He'd sit with a book on the steering wheel and he'd study all the way as we were driving to UCLA," Reid recalls. "We'd go through stop signs or whatever and I guess the guardian angels were watching us because we never cracked up."[11]

While Hugh's time at UCLA may not have been as intellectually challenging as he would have liked, he had one experience that strengthened his testimony of the gospel. As a sociology major, in spring 1932 he did a research project on churches in Glendale, California, based on "quite frank and revealing" interviews with many of the local pastors. He gathered statistics "such as, that church attendance dropped sharply on rainy Sundays and increased proportionately at the movies." These interviews reinforced Hugh's testimony of the restored gospel. "With every one, the strength of the Latter-day Saint position became more apparent to me."[12] Hugh felt that the gospel Joseph Smith had restored, with its acceptance of revelation, spiritual gifts, priesthood authority, temple ordinances, and personal testimony, was adaptable to all peoples and was not created by culture or social forces. "The thing that impressed me in talking to the ministers was that our gospel is not culturally conditioned."[13] He was also impressed at how the LDS Church gives answers to questions other churches cannot answer, found in scriptures others do not have. He recalled that "to talk with the priests was more unsatisfactory to me then than it now is to talk with lawyers."[14]

While attending UCLA, Sloan worked at a gas station; however, Hugh never had a job outside of school. "I was more of a social butterfly anyway," remembers Sloan, "so I had to have a buck once in a while."[15] Hugh spent most of his time buried in books, his social life centered on the library. Hugh switched his major to history, where he focused on ancient history. He also continued to study Greek and Latin, which he had first begun in high school. His French, which he had studied under a tutor in grade school, was helpful as he took a year of Spanish at UCLA. The German, which he learned on his mission, helped him to diverge into Scandinavian languages. As he added new languages, he kept up on the previous languages by rotating through texts. "I would study them in this order, you see, chronologically, in a cycle. Because that's the way the Renaissance scholars studied. That's the way Scaligar studied them. Start with Greek, go

---

[10] Sloan Nibley, "Faith of an Observer," 538.

[11] Reid Nibley, "Faith of an Observer," 478-79.

[12] Hugh Nibley, "How Firm a Foundation! What Makes It So," in *Approaching Zion*, edited by Don E. Norton, Vol. 9 of *The Collected Works of Hugh Nibley* (Salt Lake City: Deseret Book/FARMS, 1989), 149.

[13] Ibid., 151.

[14] Ibid., 150.

[15] Sloan Nibley, "Faith of an Observer," 535.

to Latin, etc."[16] His single-minded devotion to studying paid off in superior grades—not that he cared—and summa cum laude status at graduation on 22 June 1934.

It was while Hugh was an undergraduate at UCLA that his grandfather, Charles W. Nibley, died after a short illness on 11 December 1931. Hugh never talked about how he felt at this death. Brought up in an era when people did not talk about their emotions, Hugh frequently becomes more silent in direct proportion to the depth of his feelings. However, at a family gathering commemorating Charles W. Nibley's 150th birthday on 5 February 1999, Hugh recalled his grandfather, a "remarkable man," with great emotion. Through tears, he stated: "I don't know that I'll ever know anybody like Charles W. Nibley. Let the Lord bless his name."[17] Certainly, his grandfather's death was tragic for Hugh. Even more traumatic was the prolonged illness of Hugh's brother Philip, seven years his junior. By 1930, thirteen-year-old Philip was spending much of his time in bed. El frequently mentions Philip's heart rate as a matter of concern in letters. Hugh thinks it was a weak heart that caused his illness. However, Barbara says they never really knew what was wrong with her brother.

He was basically bedfast from February 1930 through July.[18] On 4 April 1930, after writing that Philip was "decidedly better" from a long illness, El reported to his own father that Philip "has never been despondent or discouraged, but [has] always been full of faith, knowing he is going to get well. . . . Yesterday he lay flat on his back, barely able to speak out loud. He smiled and said, 'My Dad, but the Lord has been good to me, and this will always be a testimony to me.'"[19] Philip's day was brightened in June of 1930 when his father brought world champion wrestler Ed ("the Strangler") Lewis to visit him. "Ed sat on the bed and kidded Phil for half an hour and both of them got a great kick out of it."[20] By September, Philip was able to get up and dress. El and Sloanie frequently took him for short car rides.[21] On 30 September, El wrote Charles Nibley that Philip's "recovery is a miracle if there ever has been one."[22] By November, El reported that Philip "is not strong yet and has to conserve strength, but he is gaining all the time, for which we are sincerely grateful to the Lord."[23] Charles's death in early 1931 ended El's reports on Philip's health. However, he must have recovered significantly thereafter, because Hugh remembers that Philip accompanied the ward Scout troop on a strenuous hike in 1932. "They were up the mountains and the Scoutmaster kept pushing them and pushing them,

---

[16] Hugh Nibley, interviewed by Boyd Petersen, 15 November 2000.

[17] Hugh Nibley, "Remarks about Charles W. Nibley on the Occasion of the Celebration of his 150th birthday, 5 February 1999," 11, transcript in my possession.

[18] Alexander Nibley, Letter to Charles W. Nibley, 18 July 1930, Box 1, fd. 6, L. Tom Perry Special Collections, Harold B. Lee Library, Brigham Young University, Provo, Utah.

[19] Alexander Nibley, Letter to Charles W. Nibley, 4 April 1930, Charles W. Nibley Papers, Mss 1523, Box 1, fd. 6, Perry Special Collections.

[20] Alexander Nibley, Letter to Charles W. Nibley, 11 June 1930, Charles W. Nibley Papers, Mss 1523, Box 1, fd. 6, Perry Special Collections.

[21] Alexander Nibley, Letter to Charles W. Nibley, 9 September 1930, Charles W. Nibley Papers, Mss 1523, Box 1, fd. 6, Perry Special Collections.

[22] Alexander Nibley, Letter to Charles W. Nibley, Charles W. Nibley Papers, Mss 1523, Box 1, fd. 6, Perry Special Collections.

[23] Alexander Nibley, Letter to Charles W. Nibley, 7 November 1930, Charles W. Nibley Papers, Mss 1523, Box 1, fd. 6, Perry Special Collections.

the way scout masters do," remembers Hugh.[24] Whether accurately or not, this hike is remembered as the precipitating event in Philip's long spiral downward, and he died on New Year's Eve, 31 December 1932, at age fifteen.

At the time of Philip's death, seven-year-old Reid, already a prodigy on the piano, was learning Mendelssohn's "Song Without Words." Reid had been especially close to his older brother, Philip, and took his death hard. To this day, Hugh has never talked about the emotional impact of Philip's death on him. The Victorian training simply ran too deep. But his eyes well with tears and his voice cracks when he hears Mendelssohn's "Song Without Words."[25]

It seems likely that Hugh sought solace in his studies. For one thing, it was at this point that his grades improved dramatically. For another, even though he was still living at home, it is doubtful if he found much emotional stability there. Naturally obsessed with Philip's spiral toward death, El and Sloanie were not emotionally present for Hugh at this time. El was also trying to keep one step ahead of the Depression, investing in one risky business deal after another, which also must have caused Sloanie considerable anxiety. Grandma Sloan was in Canada. In short, the library likely offered a welcome and socially acceptable way for Hugh to absent himself from both the emotional stresses of his parental home and the grim economic realities pressing upon them.

Philip's death must have also helped remind Hugh of the spiritual side of his education. The following summer, he served a short-term mission in the Northwestern States, where his uncle, William Reid Sloan, was mission president. President Heber J. Grant issued the call in a letter dated 24 June 1933.[26] The letter may have simply been catching up with actual events, for LeGrand Richards, then president of the Hollywood Stake, set Hugh apart, and he and his Grandmother Sloan arrived in Portland, Oregon, on the 12:45 A.M. bus, less than twenty-four hours after the letter was typed.[27]

Hugh, who had cannily foreseen that shorthand and typing would increase his note-taking speed, had picked up both skills at a business school soon after his return from Germany. He promptly began working as mission stenographer.[28] Evidently, Hugh had not changed much since his mission to Germany. According to Joann Sloan, his cousin, he still did not worry about food and survived on wheat which he carried in his pockets.[29] Hugh was released on 10 September 1934, in time to register for the fall semester.

Several years later when Apostle Rudger Clawson asked William Sloan to identify and report on the "four outstanding missionaries" he had encountered during his eight years as mission president, Sloan named Hugh as one of them. He described Hugh as

> undoubtedly the most intellectual missionary who ever came into this mission. . . . Elder Nibley has mastered thirteen languages, and his knowledge of the standard works

---

[24]Hugh Nibley, Interviewed by Boyd Petersen, 16 June 1996.

[25]Reid has recorded Mendelssohn's "Song without Words," Opus 19, No. 1, on his CD *Quiet Classics: Piano Meditations* (Salt Lake: Bonneville Classics, 1995).

[26]Letter in possession of Hugh Nibley; photocopy in my possession.

[27]William Reid Sloan, Mission Journal, 25 June 1933, photocopy of selected pages in my possession; original in possession of Beverlee Sloan Smith.

[28]Ibid., 27 June 1933.

[29]Joann Sloan Rogers, Letter to Boyd Petersen, n.d., 1996.

of the church by far surpasses that of any missionary I have ever contacted. He has the sweetest faith in the divine mission of the prophet Joseph and the restoration of the priesthood, and his educational career is built around these divine truths. . . . He completed a four year course in Spanish in one year. His knowledge of Hebrew, Greek, Latin, and Assyric stands out, and I am sure that the Church would do well to keep its eyes on this young man.[30]

The following year during the summer of 1934, Hugh accompanied his father on a business trip to Berkeley. While El was meeting some business associates at the Shattuck Hotel, Hugh decided to pick up some information at the university registration office. There was no staff in the office, but Dean Whitman, who was the dean of the graduate school, saw Hugh and they began talking. He must have been impressed with Hugh, for, at the end of the conversation, he telephoned UCLA, filled out the paper work, and admitted Hugh directly into the Ph.D. program on the spot.[31]

When Hugh arrived at Berkeley that fall, his family still had plenty of money. In fact, two years later, his family moved to an even bigger house on Normandie Avenue in Hollywood. The title, registered on 10 February 1936, was legally owned solely by Agnes (Sloanie), probably so that it would not count as a liability in El's increasingly speculative business ventures. Thanks to his family's money and the good scholarships he was receiving, Hugh was able to stay on the top floor of International House, a place where foreign students and U.S. students interested in foreign languages could live and intermingle. The top floor was "the expensive floor," recalls fellow student Paul Springer.[32]

It was in the International House that these lifelong friends first met. Springer was four years younger but equally brilliant. As a youngster, Paul had been chosen to participate in a gifted student program at Stanford University. At Berkeley, he was majoring in economics and German, but also enjoyed studying classical Arabic.[33] The two became best friends, despite diametrically opposed views on money, politics, and religion. Paul was very concerned about making money and keeping it, while Hugh couldn't care less about it. "He was where the money was," Hugh says about Paul.[34] Paul says that, for Hugh, "money just simply didn't mean anything."[35] Hugh remembers that Paul's politics were right-wing, almost fascist, while his own veered to the left. "Until the war began," Hugh recalls, Paul "was pro-Hitler right down the line, so we disagreed on that."[36] And unlike straight-arrow Hugh, Paul was a lady's man and a bootlegger. "He was into all sorts of corrupt stuff; he knew what was going on everywhere," Hugh states.[37] Perhaps the biggest point of difference was the two men's attitudes about God. "One thing that he

---

[30] William Reid Sloan, Letter to Rudger Clawson, 10 September 1937, typescript photocopy courtesy of Joann Sloan Rogers, Hugh's cousin.

[31] Hugh Nibley, interviewed by Boyd Petersen, 15 January 2001.

[32] Paul Springer, "Faith of an Observer," 505.

[33] Paul E. Springer, obituary, *Independent Journal* (Marin County, CA), 6 June 1993, B-2.

[34] Hugh Nibley, "Faith of an Observer," 104.

[35] Paul Springer, "Faith of an Observer," 505.

[36] Hugh Nibley, "Faith of an Observer," 102.

[37] Hugh Nibley, "Faith of an Observer," 104. What Hugh means by "corrupt stuff" is difficult to determine. He dislikes business and politics so much that he may have branded quite normal activities with this label.

has that I would give anything to have is the gift of absolute faith," stated Paul in an interview in 1984. "He has it, and I don't."[38]

The differences between them created conversation, not contention. Hugh staunchly lived by his principles but never let Paul's lifestyle come between them. Hugh was, however, openly critical of Paul's behavior. "The trouble with you," Paul remembers Hugh telling him, "is [that], confronted with a situation . . . you can do the smart thing or you can do the right thing, but you inevitably do the easy thing."[39] Typical are Hugh's words in a letter he wrote to Paul in 1938: "Occasionally, one thinks of you . . . with a despairing shake of the head and a muffled curse in one's beard. . . . Did ever a son of man have so much mischief written all over him and so little within him? Is there another man alive who stubbornly presents his worst side to the world and hides his virtues as carefully as other creatures do their defects?"[40] Yet while Hugh never shied away from talking about his religion, he never pushed his religion on Paul. Paul later recalled how one time, after considering the way Mormons actively proselyte, he asked Hugh why he hadn't tried to convert him. Hugh replied with a wink, "Well, the Church has some rights in this too." Paul added, "I couldn't help but agree with him."[41]

What they did share were common interests in languages, philology, theology, history, and nature. "We usually disagreed," remembers Paul, "which is, of course, the thing that made it interesting."[42] Perhaps even more bonding than their intellectual interests was an indefinable compatibility of mind, a similarly keen wit, and a shared sly sense of humor. Their correspondence is filled with erudite humor and witty repartees.

Hugh and Paul both studied Arabic under the very able but highly tyrannical Professor William Popper. Popper was a short man, about four foot, six inches, remembers Hugh, with a fierce temper. If you made a mistake, "he'd bang the book down, and if you made two mistakes he'd bang the book [shut] and stomp into his [office]. You would not see him the rest of the [class]."[43]

Paul, a year ahead of Hugh in Arabic, remembers Popper's exams as grueling. "I won't say [they were] impossible, but very near to it," says Paul. He remembers a midterm examination in advanced Arabic with around three hundred questions. "I think I got 290 and he stretched a point and gave me a B." Following that exam, Paul confesses, "I made a resolution, I was going to get an A out of that course; and if I had to cheat to do it, I was going to cheat. It was the only examination I ever cheated on in four years of college and four years of law school, but I felt I had moral justification." The final was given on a rainy day, so Paul wore a big gray overcoat in which he smuggled a dictionary, a grammar, and every other book that would help him on the test. A year later, Hugh took

---

[38] Paul Springer, "Faith of an Observer," 508.

[39] Hugh Nibley, "Faith of an Observer," 495.

[40] Hugh Nibley, Letter to Paul Springer, 19 August 1938. Hugh also shared his opinion about Paul with Paul's mother: "To me it has always been a source of delight and amazement to behold one of our species persistently and deliberately on all possible occasions putting his worst foot forward—doing everything to conceal his great gifts and magnanimous nature. To know Paul is to know the worst: one is treated to a full view of all his faults in a moment, and from then on nothing remains to be discovered but good, inexhaustible springs of it jealously guarded by a hyper-intelligent and almost morbidly sensitive nature." Hugh Nibley, Letter to Mrs. [Emma?] Springer, 7 January 1941.

[41] Paul Springer, "Faith of an Observer," 508.

[42] Ibid., 492.

[43] Hugh Nibley, "Faith of an Observer," 55.

the exam for the same class, and Paul asked him how it went. "It was wonderful," Hugh replied, "Dr. Popper said, 'Feel free to use any book in the library that will help you with this.'" Paul marched over to Dr. Popper's office and demanded, "It's a funny thing, Dr. Popper, when Hugh Nibley took your examination . . . you tell him he can use any grammar, dictionary, or book in the library, me you tell nothing!" Paul remembers Popper's chilly reply: "I knew he wouldn't bring his own."[44] Despite Popper's assistance, Hugh still received B's in that class. Paul graduated from Berkeley and began studying law at Golden Gate University not long after meeting Hugh, but the two remained close friends through the 1950s before drifting amicably apart.[45]

At Berkeley, Hugh also studied with Werner Jaeger, a scholar visiting from the University of Chicago who was working on his trilogy about classical Greek culture.[46] The two men hit it off, and Hugh spent many hours in the professor's apartment discussing Greece and its relation with a Middle Eastern milieu.[47] Jaeger was not only impressed by his Hugh's knowledge but also by his refusal to drink tea, based on his religious principles.

Paul Springer recalls that Hugh's "academic record was unbelievable." And Hugh was not a show-off or snob about his achievements. "If anything he had a rather retiring nature and what people might take for showing off was a faculty he had of becoming enthusiastic about whatever subject was at hand."[48] But Paul remembers that Hugh's thinking was, even then, "strongly influenced by his religious feelings. . . . I never caught Hugh questioning the Book of Mormon, or any tenet of the Book of Mormon," continued Paul. "I remember his saying to me one time [that the Book of Mormon] is like a football. You can kick it around all you want, but in the end it's still there."[49]

Toward the end of his graduate program, two events seriously tried Hugh's faith. Both times he received powerful reaffirmation. For the 1936-37 school year—his final year of graduate work at Berkeley—Hugh received a university fellowship. The cash award provided for all of Hugh's school and living expenses but came with one stipulation: he could not seek any employment off campus. By this time, the Depression was beginning to catch up with Hugh's family. When Hugh received the fellowship money, his father approached him for a loan. "Dad said he needed the money just over the weekend," Hugh recalls, "to rescue one of [his] mining deals." Hugh's mother pressured him too, assuring him that the money would all be back by the following Monday. But "I never saw the money again."[50]

---

[44] Ibid., 496-98.

[45] Springer, obituary.

[46] Werner Jaeger, *Paideia: The Ideals of Greek Culture*, 3 vols. New York: Oxford University Press, 1943-45. Jaeger was born in Lobberich, Germany, in 1888, received his Ph.D. from the University of Berlin and later became chair at the University of Basel in Switzerland, a position once held by Friedrich Nietzsche. While his works on Aristotle and Gregory of Nyssa, the Cappadocian church father, were more scholarly, he is best known for his *Paideia*, which looks at the educational, intellectual, and spiritual interests of the Greeks. Jaeger taught at the University of Chicago (1936-39) and Harvard (1939-58) and died in 1961.

[47] Hugh Nibley, "Faith of an Observer," 75; Hugh Nibley, "Goods of First and Second Intent," in *Approaching Zion*, 540.

[48] Paul Springer, "Faith of an Observer," 498.

[49] Ibid., 500-501.

[50] Hugh Nibley, "Faith of an Observer," 29.

Hugh later remembered this period of his life as a "desperate" time when "the bottom of the world fell out."⁵¹ Hugh was not certain that he would be able to continue his studies, and he had literally nowhere to turn for help. While he had certainly suffered emotional pain and grief during the 1930s, this event hit Hugh in a very personal way. Certainly, it strained his relationship with his parents. Hugh was able to forgive his mother for her part in the loss of his fellowship, but he never regained his trust in his father. As Hugh's wife, Phyllis, later put it, "As far as any relationship between them was concerned, that sort of scotched it."⁵²

But even more emotionally terrifying for Hugh—although he does not talk about it in these terms—was the threat to his education. When his grandfather and brother died, when his parents were distant and distressed about Philip's health and their own financial survival, and throughout the stress and strains of the decade's economic and political conditions, Hugh had been able to retreat into his studies. There he found both a welcome distraction and great satisfaction. And now that one remaining source of constancy and comfort was jeopardized.

In an undated letter to his parents which he must have written during this time, Hugh's upbeat tone betrays an underlying cynicism and a pointed reproach:

> We are nicely settled down now, living on apples and brown bread, a monotonous diet, you say, but—let me remind you—a philosophic one. What a lucky person! Already I would have blown $40 at the International House but as it is I have spent virtually nothing, having precisely that amount to spend. . . . I have applied for everything from pearl-diving to travelling fellowships (I honestly think the former would be the pleasanter job to land) and eventually & surely I shall *succeed*! In the meantime I am pleased much at being able to feed handsomely on $2 a week if I had the $2, which I have not.⁵³

But Hugh was not certain that he would succeed. In fact, he was beginning to despair. "I'd been around everywhere looking for work and I couldn't get any," remembers Hugh. "I thought, 'Great guns, this is where it ends!'"⁵⁴

God came to Hugh's rescue in the form of Professor Herbert Bolton.⁵⁵ Right in the depths of Hugh's despair, Bolton called him into his office to discuss some Jesuit manuscripts that the school had recently acquired. "He said, 'I want someone to translate all this Latin stuff,'" recalls Hugh jubilantly. "So I was in business again." After Hugh accepted the job, Bolton rang a bell to call his secretary, so she could get Hugh on the payroll. In that moment as the bell rang, Hugh said, his faith in the gospel was restored. "I felt there was a power there." It proved to him that the Lord can and will provide.⁵⁶

---

⁵¹Ibid., 220.

⁵²Phyllis Nibley, "Faith of an Observer," 437.

⁵³Hugh Nibley, Letter to Agnes Sloan and Alexander Nibley, n.d., ca. 1936.

⁵⁴Hugh Nibley, "Faith of an Observer," 220-21.

⁵⁵Born in 1870, Herbert Bolton became a leading historian of Spanish influences in frontier American culture, taught at Berkeley (1911-40), and was a prolific author. He is widely revered for his explorations in the U.S. Southwest, his extensive archival research, and his application of a comparative approach to historical analysis. He died in 1953. Brigham D. Madsen, a notable western historian at the University of Utah, discusses Bolton's influence on his own graduate studies at Berkeley immediately after World War II. See his *Against the Grain: Memoirs of a Western Historian* (Salt Lake City: Signature Books, 1998), chap. 8.

⁵⁶Hugh Nibley, "Faith of an Observer," 220.

This translation job gave Hugh the funding to continue his education without violating the stipulation of his fellowship that he not take any off-campus employment. But even though he could continue his education, Hugh's budget was very tight. He was forced to move out of the International House and move into a very tiny, cheap apartment on Milvia Street, where the rent was a mere eight dollars per month. Paul Springer, in a practical joke that was not appreciated at the time, "celebrated" Hugh's moving out of the International House by sneaking in during Hugh's absence. He melted a dozen boxes of colored marshmallows, took all of Hugh's neckties, and "festooned the whole room" with neckties and marshmallow goo. Before Hugh could get home, his father dropped by unannounced, bringing with him some business colleagues—"very important big shots, you know, these fat cats," reminisced Hugh. "They come in and here's my room . . . a holy mess."[57] It is typical of Hugh to remember the shock to conventional sensibilities but not what he said, either to his father or to Springer.

Despite his new apartment's modest accommodations, the room had one enormous advantage to Hugh: He was living near Egyptian students—which meant that he had Arabic-speaking neighbors.[58] In a letter he wrote to Paul Springer in 1938, while working on his dissertation, Hugh writes, "Didn't you sense the dim pulse of the East in your throbbing buzzing ears when you reached the top of this minaret [his apartment]? The attic is full of Arabs! That's why I'm here: Assam and Hasan hold forth in the next room and by sitting against the wall . . . I can drink my exhilarating fill of their limpid and heady talk."[59]

As usual, Hugh also economized on food. He ate large quantities of cabbage and other cheap vegetables. Paul Springer remembered one week during that period when Hugh lived on pigeon wheat. "You could buy pigeon wheat very cheaply. You could boil it, and the kernels would swell up, and then you could fry it. It's full of proteins and everything else," Paul stated.[60]

But Hugh was not completely on his own. Reid, who turned fourteen in 1937, remembers driving up with his mother to visit Hugh at Berkeley, take him clean clothes and groceries, and pick up his laundry. "He'd forget to eat," says Reid. Reid and Sloanie would usually stay for a couple of days, and Hugh would break away from his studies long enough to take them to a museum or art gallery or wander with them around San Francisco. "It was always so fascinating to just be around and listen to him talk," remembers Reid.[61]

But Hugh was still emotionally reeling from his losses and disappointment when he returned to his parents' home in Hollywood for the Christmas vacation at the end of 1936. "Those were desperate times," remembers Hugh. "This was not only the Depression, but this was when all the world was going bad." He was getting by—it was not easy, nor was it pleasant—but it was a new reality that he felt he had to face. "I had been feeling that I would have to be entirely independent and I didn't want to depend on any-

---

[57]Ibid., 222.
[58]Ibid., 221.
[59]Hugh Nibley, Letter to Paul Springer, 19 August 1938.
[60]Paul Springer, "Faith of an Observer," 513.
[61]Reid Nibley, "Faith of an Observer," 476-77.

body."[62] That fact left Hugh discouraged. It also led him to see "certain flaws in the gospel," as he put it.[63] One Sunday afternoon, he went up to Mount Wilson and slogged around in the heavy snow, brooding about theology. "I was terribly bothered about this afterlife business and that sort of thing. I had no evidence for that whatever."[64]

That evening, he attended sacrament meeting in the Hollywood Ward with his family. It was Hugh's first visit since his family had moved into the ward after he went to Berkeley, but he was impressed by the speaker that night: Matthias F. Cowley. Cowley, ordained an apostle in 1897, had "resigned" under pressure in 1905 and then had his priesthood suspended in 1911 for his adherence to the principle and practice of post-Manifesto polygamy. He returned to full fellowship, though not to his former office, in April 1936.[65] "He had never denied the brethren or anything," recalls Hugh. Cowley was seventy-eight, but he struck Hugh as much younger—possibly fifty. "He had a big crop of black hair like [Ronald] Reagan and had a beard," remembers Hugh. Following the meeting, Hugh's mother took him up to the front of the meeting hall to meet Brother Cowley. "As soon as he took my hand, he said, 'Come with me,'" Hugh says. "He took me into the back room there and he said, 'I want to give you a blessing.'" In the blessing, Cowley stated that the Lord was aware of his questions and "would give me an answer immediately."[66]

Within the week, Hugh was stricken with appendicitis and taken to the Seventh-day Adventist Hospital in Loma Linda, not far from San Bernardino. Dr. Raymond Weyland, the family physician, was in charge of the operation. When he turned the ether on, Hugh swallowed his tongue and stopped breathing. The staff scrambled for the resuscitator, panicking when it was nowhere to be found. Meanwhile, Hugh could hear everything that was going on and was aware of a sensation of increasing cold:

> I remembered Socrates, the turning cold of the feet, icy, incredibly cold, and it got higher, higher, higher, and (pause) I couldn't believe anything could get that cold. Absolute numbness, absolute nothing, but curiosity all the time. Something big's going to happen, and sure enough. Then, pop! Then it happened. Then all of a sudden, down this thing like a tube . . . and you come out. . . . Boy, I know everything, everything is there and this is what I wanted to know, three cheers and all this sort of thing, and I started solving problems. . . . But all I wanted to know was whether there was anything on the other side; and when I came out there, I didn't meet anything or anybody else, but I looked around, and not only was I in all possession of my faculties, but they were tremendous. I was light as a feather and ready to go, you see, and above all I was interested in problems. I had missed out on a lot of math and stuff like that. . . . Well, five minutes and I can make up for that.[67]

Although Hugh was no longer interested in what was happening to his body, the medical staff resuscitated him and successfully performed the operation. This experience

---

[62]Ibid., 221.

[63]Ibid., 222.

[64]Ibid., 227.

[65](no editor), *Deseret News 2001-2002 Church Almanac* (Salt Lake City: Church of Jesus Christ of Latter-day Saints, 2000), 66.

[66]Hugh Nibley, "Faith of an Observer," 227-28.

[67]Ibid., 228-29.

had a profound influence on Hugh. Certainly, education remained important to him throughout the rest of his life. However, this experience was a "higher" form of education that helped him recognize that the most important tests in this life are not administered in the classroom. As Hugh put it, this knowledge helped him focus on life as a period when we are "tested for our moral qualities."[68] It was a pivotal experience that has served as a balance wheel for his entire life.

With these biggest of big questions answered, Hugh threw himself into academic pursuits with renewed vigor. He returned to school in January 1937 and took his final semester of course work during the fall of 1937. He again focused on history and languages: Arabic, Hebrew, Greek, and Latin.[69]

By the spring of 1938, Hugh was doing research for his dissertation. His original proposal was to write about mobs in ancient history; however, his committee vetoed the project, saying that it had no relevance. Hugh sums up their position: "'We have sensible government and we're civilized people today. We'll not allow ourselves to be moved by mobs. . . . We have controls now and we're sophisticated and educated people. . . .' So they wouldn't even consider the thesis possible."[70] Nazi groupthink proved them horrifyingly wrong; and a generation later during the social upheaval of the 1960s in the United States, Hugh permitted himself the small luxury of hoping that some members of his committee were still alive to reflect on the experience.

Hugh dutifully began research on another topic and soon had several shoeboxes containing "thousands" of 3x5 note cards for his dissertation, all "in perfect order." While he was carrying his boxes from one place to another, he tripped, the boxes went flying, and the cards flew helter skelter. "That wasn't a good subject anyway," Hugh said to himself. "I think I'll write on something else." So he resorted his note cards and wrote a different dissertation.[71] On 19 August 1938, he reported to Paul Springer that he was working on "ever more and more foot-notes to a thesis that is a song without end. As a matter of fact, the work is done, and with a little of your political acumen and audace, toujours l'audace! I might be a success in the world of men."[72]

In an undated letter sent soon thereafter, Hugh's mood had darkened. In a combination of exultation and urgency, he described himself: "Here we are—all pounding down the home-stretch in the triumphant finish. The unremitting toil of years is about to be laid at the feet of an enraptured committee. We can't stop; we can't breathe." But at the same time, he accurately read the shape of the war in Germany. "I want to finish this damn thing before they have me reviewing German grammar on the inside of a Cyclone Super-charged Fence at the instance of one N. Chamberlain," he wrote feverishly. Neville Chamberlain, then Prime Minister of England, had been making calculated concessions to

---

[68] Ibid., 230.

[69] Hugh Nibley, Student Record, Official Transcript.

[70] Hugh Nibley, "Faith of an Observer," 37. Hugh's chair was John James Van Nostrand (1884-1966), a classics professor. His four readers were legal historian Max Radin (1880-1950), classicist Arthur Ernest Gordon (1902-), classicist Henry Roy William Smith (1891-1971), and medieval historian James Westfall Thompson (1869-1941). Radin was later nominated to the California State Supreme Court, but Earl Warren, then California's attorney general, blocked the nomination. Warren later served as Chief Justice of the U.S. Supreme Court (1953-69).

[71] Hugh Nibley, "Faith of an Observer," 88.

[72] Hugh Nibley, Letter to Paul Springer, 19 August 1938.

Hitler in an effort to stave off the coming war. In September 1938, probably just when Hugh wrote this letter, Britain, under Chamberlain's leadership, and France signed a pact with Germany and Italy allowing Germany to partition Czechoslovakia. It was likely this issue that upset Hugh so intensely that he ended his letter with: "Gott strafe England"—"May God punish England."[73]

Hugh wrote his thesis in a six-week marathon. "I couldn't leave the room," he recalled. After he wrote it, he then "typed the whole thing myself on the old Underwood [typewriter]. It had to be five copies, which was pretty dim carbon and so forth, but I typed every bit of it and I did it in about two weeks, about three hundred pages, bibliography and everything."[74] While Hugh worked on his thesis, he says he lived on wilted carrots "for a penny a bunch" and canned milk at "eight cents a can."[75]

In December 1938, the triumphant but exhausted Hugh took the thesis around to his committee. "They all signed it without reading it," recalls Hugh scornfully. "Nobody wanted to be bothered." Nevertheless, it was "a darn good thesis."[76] "The Roman Games as a Survival of an Archaic Year Cult" was filed with the university, and he received his Ph.D. on 16 December 1938.[77]

Hugh had his "magical passport," as he called it; but the kingdom of scholarship to which it admitted him was being crowded to the wall. Enrollment was decreasing because of the Great Depression, which Hugh had barely survived, and also because of the calamitous war toward which the United States was heading. Hugh had a short respite before entering its turmoil, but he would soon need all the faith, determination, and grit he had learned during the 1930s to survive the 1940s.

---

[73]Hugh Nibley, Letter to Paul Springer, n.d., ca. fall 1938. Chamberlain's efforts to appease Germany eventually failed when Hitler invaded Poland on 1 September 1939. Chamberlain resigned, Winston Churchill formed a new government, and Great Britain declared war against Germany.

[74]Hugh Nibley, "Faith of an Observer," 88.

[75]Ibid., 29. Perhaps this spartan diet was due not only to Hugh's straitened finances but also to his absorption in his studies.

[76]Hugh Nibley, "Faith of an Observer," 87-88.

[77]The library at UC Berkeley did not catalogue the work until early 1939.

Hugh Nibley in 1990, scanning a manuscript with his legendary absorption.

The one thing that he has that I would give anything to have is the gift of absolute faith. He has it and this you can't acquire. You either have it or you don't. He has it and I don't.

—Paul Springer[1]

The one thing I do know without a shadow of a doubt is that he believes in the gospel and in Joseph Smith as a prophet.

—Phyllis Nibley[2]

---

[1] Paul Springer, "Faith of an Observer," 508, compilation of interviews, ca. 1983-84 for a video documentary of the same name aired in 1985, photocopy of typescript in my possession, pagination added.
[2] Phyllis Nibley, "Faith of an Observer," 432.

Chapter 9

"One Peep at the Other Side": Hugh Nibley's Life of Faith

Leonard J. Arrington, former LDS Church Historian, once named Sterling McMurrin, Lowell Bennion, and Hugh Nibley as the three "leading Mormon intellectuals" of the late-twentieth century. He characterized each man's work: "McMurrin is concerned with ideas, Bennion with people, and Nibley with the faith."[3] Although this characterization suffers from over-simplification, I believe that Arrington correctly identified the central preoccupation of each man. Since his 1946 response to Fawn Brodie, *No, Ma'am, That's Not History*, Hugh has established himself as an ardent and vocal advocate for the gospel. He has produced evidence to show that the Book of Mormon, the book of Moses, and the book of Abraham are ancient texts; he has argued that the Church was established by revelation; and he has professed his belief that prophetic inspiration continues to guide the Church today. As Louis Midgley, a BYU professor of political science, once put it, "With the passing of B. H. Roberts, Nibley more than anyone else has assumed the role of defender of the faith and the Saints."[4] Hugh has always maintained, however, that a true testimony of the gospel comes, not through argument, but through the whisperings of the Holy Ghost to each individual. Just after he turned seventy in 1980, Hugh wrote to his son, Alex:

> I am trying to increase in faith, having become sort of a specialist in evidences for the Gospel. They turn up everywhere—some are convincing to others, and some are not, but I am besieged all day long by people seeking reassurance. It is infinitely

---

[3]Leonard J. Arrington, "The Intellectual Tradition of the Latter-day Saints," *Dialogue: A Journal of Mormon Thought* 4, no. 1 (Spring 1969): 24.

[4]Louis Midgley, "Hugh Nibley: A Short Biographical Note," *Dialogue: A Journal of Mormon Thought* 2, no. 1 (Spring 1967): 119.

satisfying to be able to speak to them with absolute assurance. Of course the real knowledge does not come from any source but one.[5]

Faith, however, is not just something Hugh talks about. I have witnessed how in his personal life he has allowed the Spirit to direct his actions and words. He fully anticipates personal revelation, and he regularly expects miracles.

Hugh's reliance on heavenly direction and intervention led Sterling McMurrin to label Hugh's thought as having "a strong mystical element" in that "he is one of those who holds that there are special avenues to the truth."[6] Hugh might quibble with the term "mystical"[7]; nevertheless, I believe it is true that he believes in and has taken advantage of the "special avenues to truth" that McMurrin refers to. Hugh would, however, likely call this type of thinking "mantic" or "eschatological." "Mantic" thinking, as Hugh has described it in one of his most influential lectures, denotes that which is "inspired, revealed, oracular, prophetic, or divinatory."[8] And Hugh best described "eschatological" thinking with a parable which not only ably defines the word, but which also, I believe, points to one of the moorings of Hugh's own faith:

> Imagine, then, a successful businessman who, responding to some slight but persistent physical discomfort and the urging of an importunate wife, pays a visit to a friend of his—a doctor. Since the man has always considered himself a fairly healthy specimen, it is with an unquiet mind that he descends the steps of the clinic with the assurance, gained after long hours of searching examination, that he has about three weeks to live. In the days that follow, this man's thinking undergoes a change, not a slow and subtle change—there is no time for that—but a quick and brutal reorientation.[9]

This reorientation takes the businessman from a world obsessed with career, status, and material possessions to a world obsessed with nature, knowledge, family, and personal salvation. "His values [have become] all those of eternity, looking to the 'latter end' not only of his own existence but of everything and everybody around him," continues Hugh. "In a word, his thinking has become eschatological." Later, after another series of tests, doctors determine that the man's diagnosis was wrong: "He

---

[5] Hugh Nibley, Letter to Charles Alexander Nibley, 27 June 1980. Likewise, in the conclusion to *Since Cumorah*, Hugh writes, "One can never prove the Book of Mormon to another, but one can go far enough to ask for a testimony for one's self, and get it" (406).

[6] Sterling McMurrin, "Faith of an Observer," 548.

[7] In his essay on "Prophets and Mystics," Nibley, *The World and the Prophets*, edited by John W. Welch, Gary P. Gillum, and Don E. Norton (1954; reprinted Salt Lake City: Deseret Books/FARMS, 1987), 98-107, Nibley argues that, unlike revelation, most of Western mysticism has been socially conditioned, and described in vague terminology, has produced little that is unique, and was founded on neoplatonic thought.

[8] Hugh Nibley, "Three Shrines," in *The Ancient State*, edited by Donald W. Parry and Stephen D. Ricks, Vol. 10 of *The Collected Works of Hugh Nibley* (Salt Lake City: Deseret Books/FARMS, 1991), 382. See generally "Three Shrines: Mantic, Sophic, and Sophistic" and "Paths That Stray: Some Notes on Sophic and Mantic" in *The Ancient State*, 311-79 and 380-478 respectively.

[9] Hugh Nibley, "The Way of the Church" in *Mormonism and Early Christianity*, edited by Todd M. Compton and Stephen D. Ricks, Vol. 4 in *The Collected Works of Hugh Nibley* (Salt Lake City: Deseret Books/FARMS, 1987), 302-3.

may live for many years." Nevertheless, he does not revert to his former perspective. "'This,' he says, 'is no pardon. It is but a stay of execution. Soon enough it is going to happen. The situation is not really changed at all.'"[10]

The description of "eschatological thinking" that Hugh gives in this parable is consistent with the way Hugh has lived his life. He has been as unconcerned with the transient and worldly as he has been obsessed with the permanent and celestial. Furthermore, the source of Hugh's eschatological thinking is, I suspect, similar to that of the businessman's thinking in his parable. In fact, a dear friend of mine who had been given his own "sentence of execution" by a medical doctor assured me prior to his death that Hugh's description of the change in thinking that occurs when one confronts imminent death "is so real that Nibley must have experienced something similar to have written this."[11]

What Hugh had experienced was his glimpse of life after life when he stopped breathing during an appendectomy during Christmas holidays in 1936.[12] (See chap. 8.) Penniless, his graduate fellowship thrown into the receding tide of his father's financial disaster, and struggling with a crisis of faith, Hugh's doubts about the afterlife were dramatically and instantly resolved by this experience. "My land," he exclaimed, "I could no more doubt that than I could doubt that I am here now."[13] Hugh's life was permanently reoriented, just like that of the businessman in his parable.

Two years after the experience, Hugh expressed this certainty in a letter he wrote to his Grandmother Sloan, only a few weeks after the death of her youngest son, Hugh's uncle Edgar.[14] Hugh wrote: "It makes precious little difference whether we work on this side or the other—we are all engaged in the same project, a project which is drawing us nearer together day by day." Hugh felt that death, in this instance, witnessed that his uncle had passed the test of mortality and that his talents were better suited to work on the other side of the veil. "All the worthy ones who leave us now are those whose condition has so overshadowed their abilities, whose great usefulness has been so vitiated by the exigencies of a profoundly corrupt system, that their lives had become virtually a bondage."[15]

Hugh wrote a similar letter some forty-nine years later to the widow of his former Egyptian teacher, Klaus Baer: "If ever there was an unfinished chapter, it is the life of Klaus Baer, and I am perfectly convinced that it is not over," Hugh wrote. "To take this segment of existence, a temporary quarantine for testing purposes, for the whole reality, is to throw away the untried gifts and unlimited capacities that we

---

[10] Ibid., 305, 304, 306-7.

[11] Jeff Hardyman, Response to Boyd Petersen, "The Clown of the Professions: Hugh Nibley and Scholarship," Sunstone Symposium, 9 August 1997, transcript in my possession.

[12] Hugh Nibley, "Faith of an Observer," 220.

[13] Ibid., 227.

[14] Edgar Lloyd Sloan, Hugh's grandmother's eleventh and youngest child, died 12 September 1938 at age thirty-six.

[15] Hugh Nibley, Letter to Margaret Violet Reid Sloan, 4 October 1938.

know are in us, which is the height of absurdity. If so, it can only be a carefully contrived absurdity, and that is really absurd."[16]

Hugh's life-after-life experience so changed his view of death that it became, not the ultimate end, but the ultimate miracle. "To come out on the other side of the wall intact—THAT will be a miracle. But a miracle which I confidently expect," Hugh wrote his missionary son in the late 1970s.[17] This perspective not only left Hugh calm about death, but caused him to view each day of life as a divine gift. As he wrote some time after his seventieth birthday, "The nice thing about being 70 is that the individual from then on is timeless: he can't GET old because he IS old, and any years added from then on are pure gravy, undeserved and received with thanks and surprise."[18]

This reorientation, as rare and strange as it may seem, is one that all individuals should make after accepting the gospel, Hugh argues:

> Anyone who has accepted the Gospel should be a wholly different type of being from one who has not—as well as from the nature of his former self. To be buried in the water and born again changes everything. Granted that every experience changes us for life—one could argue that eating an oyster or bathing in a hotspring for the first time means that one will never be the same again—the acceptance of a celestial order of existence is something that goes far beyond the normal accretion of experience. A miraculous healing should put one into a new life—but how often does it? The ten lepers were all dead—worse than dead, enjoying none of the advantages, social or physical, of being alive. The Lord healed them all, restoring them to life again. And only one of them even bothered to say thank you. The number is significant: we take our glorious transformation about 10% seriously, as we do the law of consecration, for which we conveniently substitute tithing—keeping a nice 90% for ourselves.[19]

The reason Hugh believes that we don't take our "transformation" seriously—that all our lives aren't changed by our acceptance of and commitment to live the gospel—is that we are afraid. "Satan has us all scared stiff," Hugh wrote. "People insane with the futility and boredom of our present routines act as if they were much afraid that the Millennium would be a drag [and] rush to the TV to relieve the *tedium vitae* with prime-time crime. One begins to think that anyone who really belongs in our world must be crazy."[20]

Not only was Hugh's perspective about life and death greatly affected by the experience, but he also developed a renewed vision about the purpose of life. While from a very early age Hugh has been unconcerned with, even suspicious of, wealth, this attitude deepened. (See chap. 24.) And Hugh's concern about careers was great-

[16] Hugh Nibley, Letter to Miriam Reitz Baer, n.d., ca. June 1987; photocopy in my possession courtesy of Mrs. Baer; emphasis Nibley's.

[17] Hugh Nibley, Letter to Charles Alexander Nibley, n.d., ca. 1979; emphasis Nibley's. It begins "How were we to know."

[18] Hugh Nibley, Letter to Charles Alexander Nibley, n.d., ca. 1980; emphasis Nibley's. It begins "On the matter of letter writing."

[19] Hugh Nibley, Letter to Charles Alexander Nibley, n.d., ca. 1980. It begins "From your last letter."

[20] Ibid.

ly reduced. In the same letter he wrote to his grandmother upon the death of her son, Hugh reaffirmed that the true "subject for tears" is not the "fortunate" one who, like his uncle, dies in a state of righteousness but rather those who found "strength and solace" in their purchasing power and "whose property is their whole sanctification and authority." Presciently, he foresaw that they would soon be "giving their lives (and especially where they can, other people's lives)" in a vain effort to save their vanishing treasures.[21] Hugh's words here hauntingly predict the U.S. entry into World War II three years later and foreshadow the disillusioning discoveries he would make after the war about U.S. corporations doing business with the Germans.[22]

Having planted his loyalties firmly in the world of eternity, Hugh was thereafter suspicious of the credo that we must live "in the world but not of the world." As he wrote to a friend who was going through marital problems, "Common ground does not exist" between the two worlds. "As the Scriptures keep repeating over and over again: we must all choose between This World and That World, and there is no compromise possible." Furthermore, neither world can understand the other world but sees the other as an oddity. Hugh continued:

> What [Phyllis and I] just cannot understand is the state of mind of far more than 99% of our fellows, who are firmly convinced that we live for this life only, and therefore should make the most of it, seeking the pleasures of things and the honors of men—to hell with all that. But of course we are the freaks in this, so much so that we have learned . . . to be rather cautious in how we express our real sentiments and in whom we confide. We are in the eyes of society the dangerous ones who should be put under observation.

Hugh concluded his letter with a sly and mischievous austerity: "The Gospel is so devised that you must either go overboard for it or leave it strictly alone."[23]

If we do "go overboard," Hugh believes, we do not find ourselves struggling in overpowering waves but rather discover that God is intimately involved in our everyday lives. Hugh firmly expects personal revelation and divine intervention in his own life. The miraculous is common to him, and likewise, the common is often miraculous. Once when a three-year-old daughter contracted pneumonia, Hugh's priesthood blessing confidently called for a miraculous cure:

> Within a few hours the little nipper was healthier than she has ever been. The alleviation was instantaneous (she was fighting for breath) and the cure complete between midnight and early morning. I have never known this power to fail, it is not a case of asking for a favor from the Lord with a chance that something may happen or not: if the power has actually been put at our disposal there is no ques-

---

[21] Hugh Nibley, Letter to Margaret Violet Reid Sloan, 4 October 1938.
[22] For a scathing critique of U.S. business involvement in World War II, see Charles Higham, *Trading with the Enemy: An Exposé of the Nazi-American Money Plot, 1933-1949* (New York: Delacorte, 1983), chap. 13.
[23] Hugh Nibley, Letter to Paul Springer, n.d., 1957.

tion of whether it will work or not. Leave us not speak of miracles, since we are interested in having the Lord's help, and not eyewash.[24]

But it is far more common for Hugh to see the miraculous in something most would take for granted. In one instance it was the bumper crop he got from his three dwarf fruit trees: "Against all expectations my magnificent estate is yielding tons of fruit. While conscientious farmers with much pruning and spraying have lost all their pears this year, nothing I can do will discourage our little tree from showering down its blessing with almost obscene abundance. That is what comes of paying tithing, my boy."[25]

Hugh also expects and receives personal revelation to direct his life. From a very early age, Hugh sought guidance from the Lord in his education and life's work and struggled to let his will be subsumed in God's will. "I was told that the Holy Ghost directs the investment of one's talents where they will do the most good," wrote Hugh, "not necessarily in the individual's own opinion but in the vast providence of God."[26] One of the earliest records of this battle between his will and God's will is found in his missionary journal. While visiting the city of Heidelberg, Hugh wandered around its great university, confiding to his diary: "Since visiting Heidelberg I haven't got the school idea out of my head." He does not elaborate about the "school idea." Likely he was tempted to consider matriculating there upon completing his mission, since his parents had encouraged him to think about attending a European university. However, he reproached himself for even mulling over the idea: "I am not humble—I haven't even faith enough to trust my education to the Lord."[27]

Hugh did develop that faith, and no better example exists than the story of his courtship of Phyllis. (See chap. 15.) After several serious relationships and an engagement, Hugh was still unmarried when he was hired at BYU. Counseled by Elder John A. Widtsoe to find a wife, Hugh confidently asked Elder Widtsoe to "work it out with the Lord" while, on his part, he promised to marry the first woman he met at BYU. That woman was Phyllis Draper, and they married only months after they met. In many ways they were not well matched. Phyllis was sixteen years younger than Hugh and came from a very different background. But almost fifty years after their marriage in a letter to a son, Hugh expressed gratitude that he had followed the Spirit's promptings in selecting his wife. He testified that faith had held them together and that he expected faith to sustain them:

> As the world's worst businessman I have been royally ripped off (Provo is the place for that). Only your mother saved the day. We were told by a No. 1 Social Psychologist (who achieved glory in the East) that we were a badly matched couple. He was right, of course, but we are perfectly matched on one thing—we have always seen absolutely eye to eye on the Gospel. Nothing else matters—I love her more every day. She is having a hard time getting around—I am going to have to

---

[24] Hugh Nibley, Letter to Paul Springer, n.d. August 1952.
[25] Hugh Nibley, Letter to Paul Springer, autumn 1950.
[26] Hugh Nibley, Letter to Charles Alexander Nibley, n.d., ca. 1980. It begins "From your last letter."
[27] Nibley, Missionary Journal, 15 April 1929.

use more of my own faith-and-prayer treatment. I can assure you with absolute certainty that it never fails.[28]

Hugh has been keenly attuned to the promptings of the Spirit in less dramatic, but just as important ways. In each project he has undertaken, he has always sought guidance from the Lord. In some cases, he has rearranged his priorities to accommodate a prompting: "I had certain projects all planned out for the summer, but the Spirit has been urging me to do other things, and that with such irresistible force that I have been devoting every bit of time to projects I would not have considered on my own. But I am being blessed and abetted in these strange researches which I am certain will have a telling impact somewhere."[29]

Hugh has always taken the advice he gave to one person that, when seeking direction we shouldn't "bother the authorities," since we can "go all the way" to the top:

> Ask for the direction of the Holy Spirit everyday and learn to recognize its whisperings. Then you will know exactly what steps to take and all the rest. Not but what you will have to walk by faith "in fear and trembling," because that is the way we are tested. But do not hesitate to do it that way. The Lord will guide you and in time you will find that our present-day Babylon will be but a distant memory.[30]

Hugh has always maintained that while the direction we receive from the Lord does provide great comfort, it does not remove challenges or free us from pain. Pain is just as much a part of life as joy. When one of his best friends was going through an emotional crisis, Hugh wrote him sympathetically that "life IS tragic—almost unbearably sad from beginning to end" because "the things of this world have a way of lousing everything up." But Hugh offered the advice that "prayer is better comfort than liquor, and an occasional revelation is the best of all. We are our own jailers and if we know whom to trust we can break out from time to time. Let's do."[31]

The key to living peacefully amid the clamor of life, according to Hugh, is to "cultivate a sort of bio-feedback with the Spirit." Then, he states, "you can walk as calmly and confidently as if all the uproar and confusion of compulsory moving-day were behind us all." Hugh continues:

> When the Saints were driven . . . out of Nauvoo in the middle of night and the dead of winter, Joseph appeared to Brigham and said to him repeatedly just two things: "Tell the Saints to get the Spirit of the Lord," and "Don't be in a hurry!" On the few occasions when I have been willing to take that advice seriously I have flourished like the green bay tree—the rest of the time has been a struggle, and no need for it.[32]

---

[28] Hugh Nibley, Letter to Charles Alexander Nibley, 28 August 1993.
[29] Hugh Nibley, Letter to Charles Alexander Nibley, 27 June 1980. He was then working on his as-yet-uncompleted *One Eternal Round*.
[30] Hugh Nibley, Letter to Craig F. Kinghorn, 14 April 1980.
[31] Hugh Nibley, Letter to Paul Springer, 29 April 1957.
[32] Hugh Nibley, Letter to Charles Alexander Nibley, n.d., ca. 1980. It begins "On the matter of letter writing."

From my perspective as someone who joined the Nibley family as an adult, I have observed Hugh carefully. My conclusion is that he has been more attentive to the promptings of the Spirit and more obedient to those promptings than anyone I know. This sensitivity has given him much joy, but it has also required him to tune some things out entirely. As he advised one individual:

> Let the Spirit be your guide from hour to hour, do what it tells you and do not concern yourself with other things. This is my advice to everyone else. There are vitally important issues which concern us all but to which I pay no attention unless so directed by the Spirit. This is because: 1) There is altogether too much for anyone to handle. 2) The time is too short to undertake certain things unless one is emphatically directed to. 3) God moves in a mysterious way—you can count on surprises. The important thing is to know that what you are doing today is what God wants you as an individual to be doing.[33]

In addition to direction, however, Hugh has asked the Lord for special "gifts" to help him in his life. "So I ask the Lord to give me—simply as a bonus, unearned and unmerited, a special favor—this gift and that gift, because these things at present are simply beyond my reach. And according to faith it is done."[34] Asking for such gifts, Hugh believes, is not a burden on the Lord, but is actually what He wants us to do. Thus, it is irresponsible not to ask freely. As he wrote to his son Alex: "I have found that there is just one thing that lets the demon loose—my stupid, pig-headed, willful hesitation to accept the Lord's promise and capacity to give me EVERYTHING I ask for. That is, if I have ever felt I was missing out on some exhilarating experience of mind or body, I have had only to ask."[35]

In a 1982 address, Hugh remarked that most members of the Church ask for only one of the spiritual gifts promised in the scriptures: the gift of healing. God is willing to grant us many others, but "we rarely ask for these gifts today—they don't particularly interest us."[36] Hugh "feels very strongly" that, paraphrasing Moroni 7:26, "whatsoever we ask in faith, believing, will be granted." His personal witness is: "The Lord will grant me anything I ask for; he's done it again and again. And I only ask for things that I can't acquire by my own efforts."[37] Being granted such gifts does not excuse us from work, in Hugh's perspective. "They leave us free to do the real work. The instrument is given to you; it is up to you to show what you can do with it."[38]

Living under a system in which he asks and instantly receives any "gift" he has desired has given Hugh great happiness. "We here go on asking and seeking and instantly finding—a nice arrangement."[39] The gift he has asked for in his old age has

---

[33] Hugh Nibley, Letter to William Clark Bartley, 14 April 1980.

[34] Hugh Nibley, Letter to Charles Alexander Nibley, n.d., ca. 1980.

[35] Hugh Nibley, Letter to Charles Alexander Nibley, n.d., ca. 1980; emphasis Nibley's.

[36] "Work We Must, But the Lunch is Free," in *Approaching Zion*, edited by Don E. Norton, Vol. 9 of *The Collected Works of Hugh Nibley* (Salt Lake City: Deseret Book/FARMS, 1989), 234.

[37] (No interviewer identified), "Hugh Nibley in Black and White," *BYU Today*, May 1990, 41.

[38] Hugh Nibley, "Gifts," in *Approaching Zion*, 101.

been to have an active and reliable mind. This request too has been granted. "The feeble old brain, by special request, is as clear and active as it ever was, and the memory was never more reliable."[40] I have witnessed this phenomenon personally while working on Hugh's biography. He responds to questions about his life and work with astonishing detail; and when I have either known or been able to find corroboration, the tally has been almost invariably exact. For the entire time I have known him, Hugh has been actively engaged in writing what will surely be his magnum opus, *One Eternal Round*. In our frequent family and individual visits, he often shares a stream of new insights about Abraham and the Pearl of Great Price. While Hugh's physical strength has diminished as he has entered his nineties, his mind has remained active, his mental processes coherent, and his memory acute.

While Hugh's faith is the result of a very personal relationship with the Lord, he also has faith that the Church was established and continues to be led by inspired leaders. His testimony of past prophets has come from studying Church history. As he wrote to his son Alex in 1979, "I have been reading the autobiographies of those around the Prophet Joseph—Heber C. Kimball, Brigham, Parley P., Wilford Woodruff, etc. Nothing is more exciting reading, because any critical student is forced to admit that those things they all talk about REALLY HAPPENED." Hugh continues, "It is quite inconceivable that such events should take place in the course of normal human history; but then the events of our day would be equally inconceivable to them—but in both cases it has all been according to prophecy."[41]

Hugh's testimony of contemporary Church leaders has been a result of his personal associations with them from an early age, beginning with his grandfather, Charles W. Nibley. First the Presiding Bishop and later a counselor in the First Presidency to Heber J. Grant, C. W. frequently visited Hugh's family both in Oregon and California, usually accompanied by other Church leaders. During those visits Hugh witnessed first-hand their imperfections: how they would sometimes cheat at golf, how their political beliefs occasionally overruled their religious duties, and how they sometimes disagreed with one another. Hugh could not be disillusioned by the actions of Church leaders because he was never illusioned to begin with. He knew they were human. Yet he also heard his grandfather tell inspiring stories about his encounters with Brigham Young.[42] He saw a compassionate Joseph F. Smith personally nurture the needy and grief-stricken during his visits to Oregon. (See chap. 2.) And he came to respect the variety of talents, interests, and pursuits of Church leaders. As a BYU faculty member, Hugh accompanied at least three General Authorities to stake conferences where they encouraged parents to send their children to BYU. His first-hand experience with Spencer W. Kimball, then an apostle, showed him the conscientious and unpretentious attitude of men whom Hugh came to see as servants of the Lord. (See chap. 3.)

---

[39] Hugh Nibley, Letter to Charles Alexander Nibley, 28 August 1993.
[40] Ibid.
[41] Hugh Nibley, Letter to Charles Alexander Nibley, 22 October 1979.
[42] See, for example, the story Hugh recounts about Brigham's black leather chair in "Educating the Saints," in *Brother Brigham Challenges the Saints*, edited by Don E. Norton and Shirley S. Ricks, Vol. 13 in *The Collected Works of Hugh Nibley* (Salt Lake City: Deseret Books/FARMS, 1994), 307.

But it was not because of the leaders that Hugh gained a testimony that the Church is true. In fact, Hugh made no bones about it that he found the Church true in spite of the humans involved in its management. Hugh's friend Paul Springer eventually investigated the Church, was baptized, and then fell away after being offended by his bishop. Hugh responded bracingly to the disillusioned Springer: "Didn't you know that Mormons are as dumb as other people? They are not stupider only because that is impossible. Have you perchance never heard of Gov. J. Bracken Lee—not a Mormon, thank God, but elected by them? Need I say more? This is the Lord's work, buster, and if it were not I would give it three years to survive at the outside."[43]

Hugh knows that, like other churches, the Church of Jesus Christ of Latter-day Saints is led by imperfect people, but unlike other churches, it has revelation, additional scripture, and authorized ordinances:

> The things in which the Mormon Church resembles and sometimes excels other churches could be dispensed with and never missed. But the prophetic mission of the Prophet Joseph Smith and the scriptures and the ordinances are worth everything the world has to offer—without them the Church would be nothing at all. . . . It is the everlasting gospel from eternity to eternity and the only plan by which mankind can be saved here and hereafter.[44]

But salvation depends on the "only TWO things that human beings can do well; and for the blessed opportunity of exercising those peculiar talents they are envied by the angels," as Hugh puts it. "Those two things are 1) to repent, and 2) to forgive."[45] Whether we are engaged in repenting and forgiving determines, according to Hugh, whether or not we are righteous. As Hugh stated in the address he delivered at the funeral of his friend Don Decker, who taught at Ricks College prior to his death: "Who is righteous? Anyone who is repenting. No matter how bad he has been, if he is repenting, he is a righteous man. There is hope for him. And no matter how good he has been all his life, if he is not repenting, he is a wicked man. The difference is which way you are facing."[46] This testing, Hugh has noted, is not complete until we die. "The gospel of repentance is a constant reminder that the most righteous are still being tested and may yet fall, and that the most wicked are not yet beyond redemption and may still be saved."[47] In sum, repentance is the most important task we have here in mortality and the "good news" of the gospel is that the possibility of repenting is open to all:

> Repentance is the prerogative only of those who are neither wholly saved (no need) nor damned (no hope), but who are in between, where we all are. God

---

[43] Hugh Nibley, Letter to Paul Springer, n.d., 1954.

[44] Hugh Nibley, Letter to Carol Turner, 3 February 1980.

[45] Hugh Nibley, Letter to Charles Alexander Nibley, 1 April 1979. Although the topic of forgiveness seldom figures in Hugh's writings, I have never seen him hold a grudge, even when he has, by any measure, been badly treated. In fact, he actively tries to turn such experiences to good.

[46] "Funeral Address," in *Approaching Zion*, 301-2.

[47] Nibley, "The Prophetic Book of Mormon," in *The Prophetic Book of Mormon*, edited by John W. Welch, Vol. 8 of *The Collected Works of Hugh Nibley* (Salt Lake City: Deseret Book/FARMS, 1989), 461-62.

knows perfectly well where we stand . . . and admonishes us not to despair: what matters is the direction we are facing—the person at the bottom of the stairs facing up is more pleasing to the Father than the one at the top of the stairs facing down.[48]

Furthermore, repentance is an ongoing process that continually calls on us to rearrange our will with God's. In a letter to his son, Alex, Hugh dealt with the specific problem of how to repent:

> On that the Word of the Lord is clear and specific: They shall "repent and call upon God in the name of the Son forever more." Call upon him for what? For instructions on what to do. He will surprise you by sending you from time to time ever greater light and knowledge, things you never had supposed. As soon as the impulse of repentance hits you, that is, you go down on your knees and call upon God, asking HIM what you are to do. And he promises to send you just that light and knowledge, when and as you need it. But you must ask, with honest intent, a firm mind, in faith believing, for that which is expedient. And keep it up.[49]

Faith is as difficult to define as it is to exercise. But for Hugh, that very difficulty makes it all the more real. "I have tried long and vainly to define faith to myself—for me that proves its reality, for we can rationalize and verbalize anything we please into existence, like lawyers, but faith can't be touched by the sophist and his tricks."[50] Nevertheless, faith not only sustains us with direction and comfort in our lives, but it also gives boundless joy. As Hugh stated during his forum appearance with Louis Midgley in 1974, "The gospel is one long shout of hallelujah."[51] If the Saints take advantage of the Atonement by repenting and forgiving, they should be the happiest people of all. "If we remain gloomy after what [Christ] did for us, it is because we do not accept what he did for us," stated Hugh in 1954 during a weekly radio lecture.[52]

Hugh has continually taken stock of the world around him and has not been naive about its problems. But peace can be found in the midst of the worst trouble. Hugh has been very successful in this endeavor. "In this world ye shall have tribulation—that is the word," wrote Hugh in 1993. "Everybody always on the edge, the rich as apprehensive as the poor. What an arrangement! But I have never been happier."[53] In another letter, Hugh wrote that, even during times of distress, "we have nothing to worry about": "We are perfectly free to have joy and rejoicing without limit whenever we are ready, enjoying to the fullest the faith that brushes aside every dark and foreboding cloud of gloom, the hope that leads us on with never a moment's boredom since we are always seeing something wonderful ahead, and above all the luxury of charity towards all."[54]

---

[48] Hugh Nibley, Letter to Charles Alexander Nibley, 22 October 1979.

[49] Hugh Nibley, Letter to Charles Alexander Nibley, 1 April 1979.

[50] Hugh Nibley, Letter to Charles Alexander Nibley, 28 August 1993.

[51] "Nibley the Scholar," BYU forum, 21 May 1974, transcript, 3.

[52] Hugh Nibley, "Prophets and Glad Tidings," in *The World and the Prophets*.

[53] Hugh Nibley, Letter to Charles Alexander Nibley, 28 August 1993.

The key to his "joy and rejoicing" is faith. In poetic language, Hugh described the joy he has experienced:

> How can one express the surge of emotion that comes out of the earth and swoops down from the sky whenever the plan of life and salvation and all that it implies—the endless vistas of joy and excitement, of an expanding spirit and ever-widening identity—is suddenly brought to one's awareness as if from some forgotten adventure in the bosom of time? To me it happens three or four times a day, and then I can say with Brigham Young, I feel that my bones will consume within me if I don't do something about it.[55]

The result of such joy is thanksgiving. "I want to burst with joy and gratitude all the day long as I feel and see the workings of goodness and mercy on every side," wrote Hugh to his son in 1980. "Most delightful of all is to know that [God] loves every other creature just as much as he does me—that being so, what a tumultuously joyful condition awaits us after the present miseries have been corrected!"[56]

In May 1978, Krister Stendahl, an eminent professor of New Testament studies, visited BYU to deliver a paper comparing the Sermon on the Mount to the account in Third Nephi.[57] During his visit to Provo, Stendahl had several conversations with Hugh. In one of these encounters, Hugh mentioned to Stendahl that he agreed with Joseph Smith's statement that, "No man was ever damned for believing too much."[58] Hugh recalls that these words were "the only thing I said that angered him in several days of conversation." Hugh later clarified his position:

> It was no abdication of reason, I insisted, because 90% of what we believe today as scientifically established will probably turn out to be wrong, as it has ever in the past; in which case we should all be damned now for believing too much. Stendahl would rest his faith on certainty, whereas mine begins with uncertainty—the awareness that we do not know everything. His position amounts to insisting that we must never believe in what we do not know for sure. But that is not faith at all, but what Paul would call faith without faith (Heb. 11:1). As to gullibility, that is not faith, which is an effort of the mind—the ultimate effort; gullibility makes no effort and does not bother to understand what it is asked to believe.[59]

In contrast, Hugh has learned to respond instantly when the Spirit whispers. While he was working absorbedly in his office in BYU's Joseph Smith Building one

---

[54] Hugh Nibley, Letter to Charles Alexander Nibley, 1 April 1979.

[55] Hugh Nibley, Letter to Charles Alexander Nibley, n.d., ca. 1980. It begins "On the matter of letter writing."

[56] Hugh Nibley, Letter to Charles Alexander Nibley, 27 June 1980.

[57] Krister Stendahl, "The Sermon on the Mount and Third Nephi," in *Reflections on Mormonism*, edited by Truman G. Madsen (Provo, UT: BYU Religious Studies Center, 1978), 139-54. This event was part of BYU's first Religious Studies Symposium, held in March 1978. Krister Stendahl was dean of the Harvard Divinity School and a New Testament scholar of international renown.

[58] Joseph Fielding Smith, ed. and comp., *Teachings of the Prophet Joseph Smith* (Salt Lake City: Deseret Book, 1976), 374.

[59] Hugh Nibley, Letter to Miriam Reitz Baer, n.d., ca. June 1987; photocopy of original in my possession courtesy of Mrs. Baer. See also Hugh's account in "The Meaning of the Atonement," in *Approaching Zion*, 601.

day in the mid-1960s, he suddenly dropped his book, bolted from his office, and ran down the hill from campus. He arrived at the small irrigation ditch on the south side of campus just as his three-year-old daughter Zina was tumbling in, rescuing her from probable drowning. This incident is typical of many during Hugh Nibley's life where he placed his trust in a prompting from the Lord and responded to it quickly and without questioning. I am personally very grateful that he has. This trusting and obedient relationship with our Heavenly Father resulted from a reorientation of Hugh's life. He has tuned out worldly concerns of career, status, and material things, while maintaining a clear focus on the things that matter most—to him as well as to his hypothetical businessman under a death sentence: knowledge, nature, family, and repentance. As he stated in a letter to Paul Springer, probably in alluding to his life-after-life experience: "One peep at the other side and this show looks too cheap for anything."[60]

---

[60]Hugh Nibley, Letter to Paul Springer, 2 February 1964.

Hugh Nibley as a new faculty member at Claremont Colleges, ca. 1940.

At Claremont Colleges I taught everything under the sun, including American Civilization on alternate days with Everett Dean Martin (who was still famous then) and Junior Humanities alternating with Ed. Goodspeed, retired from the University of Chicago. I also taught the History of Education and received the most sinister vibrations of all: it took no prophetic gift to see that no good could come of the highly successful efforts of [John] Dewey, William Heard Kilpatrick, and the rest, to supplant all religion and culture by their own brand of the new, emancipated, manipulated society. At the request of President Russell M. Story (the second great man I have known) I took notes when a few celebrities would gather at his house in connection with the work of a committee on war objectives and peace aims. There we would talk with such notables as Lewis Mumford, T. V. Smith, Thomas Mann, and Edward S. Corvin. It was heady stuff, but very soon I was getting a much more instructive view of the scene from closer up.[1]

---

[1] Hugh Nibley, "Intellectual Autobiography," *Nibley on the Timely and the Timeless* (Provo, UT: BYU Religious Studies Center, 1978), xxii-xxiii.

Chapter 10

Teaching at Claremont, 1938-42

By the beginning of 1939, Europe was on the verge of war. Repudiating the Treaty of Versailles which ended World War I, Germany had remilitarized, occupied the Rhineland, annexed Austria, partitioned Czechoslovakia, and begun its campaign against the Jews. In August 1938, Britain had warned that it would go to war if Germany invaded Poland. This firmness bought only a year of respite. On 1 September 1939, Germany tempted fate and invaded Poland. Britain declared war; but within a year, Germany had invaded Holland, Luxembourg, Belgium, and France, and was bombing London.

The United States remained neutral. After World War I, most Americans felt that the nation should not get involved in overseas strife. Besides, America had its own problems, most significantly, the lingering effects of the Great Depression which had begun with the spectacular stock market crash of October 1929. Despite the highly acclaimed New Deal of President Franklin D. Roosevelt, which created massive public works projects, deficit spending, and government regulation designed to stimulate the economy, the nation struggled for normalcy. By 1939, the unemployment rate was still 15 percent.

The Depression brought in its wake a resurgence of anti-Semitism across the world, including America. The America First Committee, created in July 1940, lobbied hard to keep the United States out of any European "entanglements," but it also subscribed to a philosophy of militant anti-Semitism. Many of its supporters, including Father Charles Coughlin, Henry Ford, and the nation's hero Charles A. ("Lucky Lindy") Lindbergh, delivered hate-filled speeches against the supposed "Jewish conspiracy" controlling banking, government, and the motion picture industry.[2] From the Depression years through World War II, "anti-semitism had never been worse in the United States, nor would it be again."[3]

---

[2]Leonard Dinnerstein, *Anti-semitism in America* (New York: Oxford University Press, 1994), 128-49. See also Spencer Blakeslee, *The Death of American Anti-semitism* (Westport, CT: Praeger, 2000) and Charles Herbert Stember et al., *Jews in the Mind of America* (New York: Basic Books, 1966).

[3]Blakeslee, *The Death of American Anti-semitism*, 36.

Thus, while Hitler was preparing his "final solution" for the Jews and other social "undesirables" of German-occupied territory in Europe, Americans were retreating into a defiant xenophobia, insisting that the nation's social and economic problems were serious enough that the country should not be meddling in problems abroad. Ironically—and Roosevelt probably realized this—it was America's full industrial mobilization for World War II that finally ended the Depression, fueled a roaring wartime production economy, and founded the prosperity of the 1950s and 1960s. It also—though tragically late—awakened the conscience of Americans and made them aware in new ways of the poison of prejudice.

For Hugh, the conflict in Europe was personal. He had given two years of his life to his mission in Germany. And even though he had been unsparingly critical of German materialism and religious indifference, his love for the language, culture, and people was unfeigned.[4] He also retained many friends in the Church branches where he had served. Undoubtedly the events in Europe caused a great deal of internal conflict for Hugh. Thus he was torn between his mixed feelings for Germany and the German people, concern for the Saints, dread of involvement in a conflict that would certainly disrupt his life and perhaps kill him, uneasiness with the virulent anti-Semitism around him, an ancestral connection with the beleaguered British Isles, and sympathy with the American desire to stand aloof from Continental problems. In a letter to Paul Springer around 1939, Hugh stated that his position about "the international situation" was like that of most Americans: "I remain neutral," wrote Hugh, but, "more against the allies than the Germans."[5] By 1942—after the Japanese attack on Pearl Harbor in December 1941—Hugh had changed his mind. On 28 September, he enlisted in the U.S. Army. Given his knowledge of German, he could predict that he would be sent to the European theater.

Hugh's attitudes about the Jews were even more complicated. Since El's mother was half-Jewish, Hugh would have been considered Jewish under Hitler's Nuremberg Laws of 1935. For Hugh's mother, her children's Jewish ancestry was a source of both pride and shame. Though proud, in the Mormon context, that the Neibaurs had been among the few Jews to accept the gospel, she was also jealous of the gifted Jewish children in Los Angeles with whom they competed. "I think Mother had a fixation about that," states Reid Nibley, "—that her boys should be just as well known and do just as well as any of those little Jewish boys. And she didn't realize that we *were* little Jewish boys!" Reid states that Sloanie wouldn't openly acknowledge her sons' Jewish ancestry most of the time. "She had a problem with that," says Reid. "She definitely had a problem."[6] Yet simultaneously, "she'd go around pinching your nose to make it better, bigger"—more Jewish-looking, Sloan remembers.[7] This incoherent attitude must have affected the sons on some level, giving them a love-hate relationship with their own heritage.

Hugh's best friend, Paul Springer, was every bit as schizophrenic in his attitudes. His right-wing, border-line fascist politics led him to sympathize with the Germans dur-

---

[4]"The willfulness of these people—their enthusiastic indifference—is nothing short of sinful," wrote Hugh to his mother. Hugh Nibley, Letter to Agnes Sloan Nibley, n.d., ca. July 1928, Charles W. Nibley, Mss 1523, Box 1, fd. 4, L. Tom Perry Special Collections, Harold B. Lee Library, Brigham Young University, Provo, Utah.

[5]Hugh Nibley, Letter to Paul Springer, n.d., ca. 1939.

[6]Reid Nibley, "Faith of an Observer," 482, compilation of interviews, ca. 1983-84 for a video documentary of the same name aired in 1985, photocopy of typescript in my possession, pagination added.

[7]Sloan Nibley, "Faith of an Observer," 542.

ing the period before the United States entered the war. "He was a Nazi," Hugh says. And with that political stance came anti-Semitic rhetoric. "He was sort of faking most of it," remembers Hugh, "but he poured it on. He couldn't stand the Jews; he hated Jews. He made a big show of it."[8] Nevertheless, Hugh recalls that Springer's attitudes didn't stop him from having many Jewish friends. Occasionally, some of the same anti-Semitic rhetoric that was passing through the nation and which he heard from his mother and Paul Springer would pop up in Hugh's letters to Paul. While Hugh was never as extreme as his mother or Paul Springer and certainly never came close to the kind of invective that was heard from the likes of Father Coughlin, Charles Lindbergh, Henry Ford, and the America First Committee, it is still startling to come across views that are at such marked variance with those of the mature gospel scholar. He once referred to the "Jewish Question" as "largely aesthetic," since the Jews take any dialect "and turn it into a thing of sheer unloveliness."[9] In another letter he quipped that the Germans hated Jews, while he liked them because, "unlike poles attract each other, and like poles repel each other." He quickly added, paradoxically: "I promise immediate violence to the unfortunate who mistakes me for one of them [a Jew]."[10] In 1939 or early 1940, Hugh stated rather dismissively that he would "endure them willingly if they could manage somehow or other either (1) to remember their religion or (2) to forget their race. So far all their effort is in the opposite direction."[11]

However, his keen eye did not miss the hypocrisy inherent in the German anti-Jewish crusade, and he delighted in pointing out such inconsistencies to check Paul's over-fondness for the Germans. In one letter, he joked that the German swastika was a variant of the Star of David, while the German outstretched-arm salute was passed down from the "Hand of God" greeting of the ancient Hebrews.[12] He amusingly said that a "poizinal friend" was working in the Copenhagen city archives when Joseph Paul Goebbels, Hitler's minister of propaganda, who had Danish ancestry, was told that his genealogy could be found, not in the city archives, but at the synagogue.[13]

By 1942, Hugh's attitudes toward Jews had moved in a markedly tolerant direction. In March, after receiving an anti-Semitic letter from his mother, he wrote sternly: "Your polemic on the Jews is very depressing." He assured Sloanie, based on "inside information," that the Jewish presence in the war was every bit as great and every bit as dedicated as the allies' and concluded: "I beg of you to let up on that hysterical theme."[14] Although there is no record of how Sloanie took this rebuke, there is nothing more that could be considered even remotely anti-Semitic in Hugh's correspondence after this point.

This change in attitude resulted from first-hand conversations with exiled Germans about the realities of Hitler's Germany and with some of Germany's most influential and gifted Jews about the lethal realities of German anti-Semitism. This opportunity came not from living in Germany, but from teaching at the small campuses of

---

[8]Hugh Nibley, interviewed by Boyd Petersen, 17 February 2001.
[9]Hugh Nibley, Letter to Paul Springer, n.d., ca. 1940. It begins "Dear Paul, what's the rush."
[10]Hugh Nibley, Letter to Paul Springer, n.d., ca. 1940. It begins "Dear Sol."
[11]Hugh Nibley, Letter to Paul Springer, n.d. ca. late 1939 or early 1940. It begins "Dear Springerlein."
[12]Hugh Nibley, Letter to Paul Springer, n.d., ca. 1938. It begins "Suh."
[13]Hugh Nibley, Letter to Paul Springer, n.d., ca. 1940. It begins "Dear Sol."
[14]Hugh Nibley, Letter to Agnes Sloan Nibley, 27 March 1942.

Claremont Colleges, located some fifty miles east of Los Angeles, where Hugh had been attached to the faculty since 1939.

The Claremont Colleges comprise a cluster of undergraduate colleges and a graduate school on adjoining campuses. Based on the Oxford model, each campus is independent, with its own faculty, student body, administration, and curricular emphasis. Pomona College was founded in 1887 by the Congregational Church. As the student body grew, rather than expanding Pomona the board of directors decided in 1925 to create a consortium of colleges surrounding central administration and library facilities. The consortium would allow the school to become a serious intellectual center while maintaining its small-college atmosphere. When Hugh was hired in 1939, the campus consisted of Pomona College, Scripps College (a private liberal arts college for women), and the Claremont Graduate School. "It was a very small school," remembers Hugh. "Only 800 students, mind you, so you get to know everybody pretty well there . . . The graduate school was even smaller. We only had about a hundred [students]."[15]

Upon graduation from Berkeley in December 1938, twenty-eight-year-old Hugh sought employment at the Claremont Colleges. When he approached the school's president, Russell Story, about teaching, Story noted that Hugh had no experience teaching, nor did he have a teaching certificate. Hugh volunteered to teach for free, as he stated, "just for the experience, because then I could have an inside [track]. . . . So I did teach for nothing the first year"—probably the 1939-40 academic year. "I didn't get any pay at all at Claremont the first year."[16] During this period when Hugh had no income, he subsisted on oranges, which would drop off the trees around Claremont, and cabbage which cost only a few pennies.[17] The reality which modifies this picture of direst poverty is that Sloanie, accompanied by Reid, would drive out to Claremont every couple of weeks to bring Hugh "a bag of food" and clean laundry, as they had when Hugh was a graduate student at Berkeley.

Barbara, who turned thirteen in 1939, like Reid, remembers driving over to Claremont from Hollywood with her mother "to pick up Hugh's dirty clothes and clean out the wilted old cabbage leaves, orange and grapefruit peels, and other odds and ends that were lying about. She'd take the clothes home, wash them, and then we'd take them back and clean out the old wilted cabbage leaves and orange and grapefruit peels again." The fastidious Sloanie must have been beside herself, both because of Hugh's slovenliness and also because of his death-defying disregard of nutrition. Barbara agrees, "I don't think he bothered to cook anything—just lived on raw whatever."[18]

Probably beginning in the fall of 1940, Hugh was employed as a lecturer in history and social philosophy. At Pomona, he taught modern European history, at Scripps he taught humanities, and at the graduate school he taught U.S. history, the history of education, Greek, and German. In a letter to Paul Springer during that academic year, Hugh, who had taken to referring to himself in the first person plural very early—a mockery of academic affectation that became habitual—reported on his heavy schedule:

---

[15]Hugh Nibley, "Faith of an Observer," 259.

[16]Ibid., 29. Payroll records for the school have not been preserved earlier than the 1960s, so it is impossible to verify Hugh's status.

[17]Ibid.

[18]Barbara Nibley Richards, e-mail to Boyd Petersen, 21 February 2002.

We are in a state of total dither: our first class meets at 7:30 a.m., from which time until noon I talk, talk, talk at an ever accelerating speed until the torrid finale sounds like the whirlwind finish of Appasionata. I am giving, for example, a five-weeks cram course in (di meliora!) the Intellectual History of the Western World, and find that the only way to cover the ground is to exhaust the subject, myself and my auditors at the rate of one century a day. After one of these bouts, I feel as if I had done a month on a rock pile—and there is another century coming up for tomorrow. This fantastic schedule runs six days a week.[19]

Hugh also became an active member of the local LDS branch, which met in the Women's Ebell Club on Holt Avenue in Pomona. According to Brooks Wasden, also a member of the branch, only three of its ninety-eight members were "inactive. All others would either show up for meetings or send a reason for absence."[20] On Hugh's first day in the branch, Sunday School teacher Jack Smith noticed the new face and assumed Hugh was no more than a high school senior. Wanting to make him feel welcome, the instructor decided to draw him into the discussion with a simple question. The lesson was about "sin," so the teacher asked Hugh, "What is sin?"—which the lesson manual defined succinctly as "the transgression of the law." Hugh "seemed to draw in a slight breath, leaned back," and "gave a complete dissertation on sin, laws, and human behavior." Brother Smith "choked and watched [his] whole easy lesson go up in smoke." That evening, Hugh spoke in sacrament meeting. "He had so much to tell us [that], when he couldn't get it out in English he would quote from the original language and translate for our benefit," described Wasden. The small branch listened, half baffled, half amazed, as Hugh delivered "a treatise that would qualify for a college course."

Soon the branch let the young college professor take the reins as Sunday School teacher. Every Sunday thereafter, Hugh would "wheedle an exceedingly heavy and unreliable bicycle thru air as bright and hot as the cozy confines of an electric furnace to Pomona to cozen the sodden minds of a wilting Sunday School class. Then . . . return to Claremont, which is a thousand feet higher than Pomona, by the same lovely conveyance."[21] The branch soon grew accustomed to Hugh's intellectual excursions and learned to accept his sometimes cutting wit. On one occasion when a man walked up to the podium to give the invocation, Hugh noticed that he was chewing gum. With "eyebrows furrowed like [he] was taking aim on a grizzly bear, [he] drew in his breath like the near whistle of a boiling tea-kettle, and [he] hissed 'If the Prophet Joseph Smith had known about chewing gum in his day it would have been in the Word of Wisdom.'"[22]

Hugh's intellectual breadth and witty repartee likely fared better at Claremont than they did in the ward. Russell Story came to admire and enjoy Hugh's company, and Hugh, in turn, greatly admired Story. Story, an intellectual in his own right and a professor of political science at Pomona College, had graduated from Monmouth College in Illinois and received his Ph.D. from Harvard. He had taught at Clark University in

---

[19]Hugh Nibley, Letter to Paul Springer, n.d. ca. 1940. It begins "Dear Paul, what's the rush."
[20]Brooks Wasden, Letter to Gary Gillum, 3 February 1984; photocopy in my possession courtesy of Gary Gillum.
[21]Hugh Nibley, Letter to Paul Springer, n.d. ca. 1940. It begins "Dear Paul, what's the rush."
[22]Wasden, Letter to Gillum.

Massachusetts; Monmouth; the University of Illinois; and Syracuse University before his appointment to Pomona. He was described as "an able teacher whose questioning mind, at its best in seminar discussion, stimulated thought and independent work."[23] In 1937, Story received a two-year leave from Pomona College to serve as acting president of the Claremont Colleges, a post he assumed in full in 1939. In this position, Story "made important contributions in the establishment of graduate work, particularly in the social sciences."[24] Hugh remembers Story as "a wonderful man, a great man."[25] Hugh believed Story created a strong intellectual climate at Claremont that was always open, honest, and effectual. In November 1941 after Hugh had been teaching for about two years, he wrote to his mother, "As long as Story waves, truth will go for more than appearances here at least; but for the rest of the land, opportunism, exploitation and inertia remain the rule."[26] Not only was Story a capable scholar, but he was also a very effective administrator. "He initiated and organized and it always worked," remembers Hugh. "He was the type of administrator that you need. He was very self-effacing."[27]

Hugh also credits Story with getting some very impressive intellectual talent at Claremont. However, Story's achievement might be more realistically appraised as his ability to seize a once-in-a-lifetime opportunity. As a result of the Nazi takeover in Germany, many scholars—Jews and others critical of Hitler's Reich—were forced to flee, many of them to American universities. Some eminent German scholars gained permanent positions at Claremont; others visited Claremont to give lectures. Their presence energized the young Hugh. "We used to have people like Thomas Mann and the like come and visit us; Dr. Einstein would give a lecture."[28] During Thomas Mann's visit, the novelist reported on his work in progress, *Joseph in Egypt*. He "told us . . . he was wondering what he would do with Joseph next," recalled Hugh with relish.[29]

With the many Germans emigrés at Claremont, it was perhaps inevitable that some would turn out to be spies; but Hugh expressed disgust at their ineptness, rather than concern. In the spring of 1942, he reported to Paul Springer that "two of my particular friends on the Scripps staff turn out to be big-time Nazi agents," a fact that "perhaps three people at Claremont" hadn't already "suspected steadily for the past two years. As spies these two are the prize ninnies: I could carry it off more subtly in darkest Japan."[30]

Another source of intellectual talent came from the many scholars who retired to Southern California and taught part-time in their fields. On at least two occasions, Hugh co-taught classes with eminent retired professors. "For four years at Claremont, I taught a course alternately with Everett Dean Martin. He would teach on Tuesdays, and I on

---

[23] E. Wilson Lyon, *The History of Pomona College, 1887-1969* (Pomona, CA: Pomona College, 1977), 217.
[24] Ibid., 363.
[25] Hugh Nibley, Interviewed by Boyd Petersen, 17 February 2001.
[26] Hugh Nibley, Letter to Agnes Sloan Nibley, n.d., postmarked 3 November 1941.
[27] Hugh Nibley, interviewed by Boyd Petersen, 17 February 2001.
[28] Hugh Nibley, "Faith of Observer," 258-59.
[29] Hugh Nibley, Interviewed by Boyd Petersen, 17 February 2001.
[30] Hugh Nibley, Letter to Paul Springer, n.d. Springer has written "Spring 1942" on the top of the letter.
[31] *Teachings on the Book of Mormon, Semester 1* (Provo, Utah: FARMS, n.d.), lecture 5, p. 2. The first-semester transcripts are not numbered consecutively, but by lecture.

Thursdays."³¹ Martin was the founder of Cooper Union, a college for the underprivileged in New York, and, as Hugh put it, "a great student of the Constitution."³² "We taught absolutely opposite points of view," Hugh recalls. Story confessed to Hugh that he specifically arranged for Martin and Hugh to teach the class together, "because [Martin] was extreme right-wing and I could be as left wing as I wanted. And we just canceled each other out."³³ At Scripps, Hugh taught humanities on alternating days with Edgar J. Goodspeed, a famous New Testament scholar who had retired from the University of Chicago.³⁴ On another occasion, Hugh attended the party celebrating the eightieth birthday of German Egyptologist Georg Steindorff, who had retired to the Claremont area. Hugh considered Steindorff "the dean of all Egyptologists."³⁵

Hugh also met many "celebrity" intellectuals who came specifically to speak to the Committee on War Objectives and Peace Aims, financed by the Rockefeller Foundation, which was based at Claremont and whose meetings were usually held in Story's living room. Hugh, who was by this time skilled at shorthand from one post-high school class, attended these private meetings as secretary. "We'd sit around and wisely discuss, with some pretty high-powered people," Hugh recalls.³⁶

However, Hugh maintained a tempered skepticism about intellectualism for its own sake. After describing Steindorff's party to his mother, Hugh summarized, with flamboyant understatement: "It is not uninteresting to be able to pass muster among the very highest men in a field," but commented: "Awful vanity! let us temper it with the gospel that a man is only worth what he produces. . . . So far I rate zero."³⁷ A year earlier, Hugh had expressed a more jaundiced view to Paul Springer, confessing that he was "dead sick of these text-book humanists. The emigrés with the big names are worse than the others: humbugs for the most part."³⁸

Hugh also reported one experience that underscores the lack of esteem he could expect to find for his own interests in Mormon scholarship. Frances Hart Breasted, the widow of James Henry Breasted, the distinguished Egyptologist who founded the Oriental Institute at the University of Chicago,³⁹ lived next door to Hugh. "And since we both rode bicycles, we got to be pretty good friends." Hugh relates. Mrs. Breasted told him that her husband had once decided to "do the world a good deed and save a lot of people the trouble of mixing themselves up and being confused in their ignorance and hope-

---

³²Ibid.

³³Hugh Nibley, Interviewed by Boyd Petersen, 17 February 2001.

³⁴Hugh Nibley, *Teachings of the Book of Mormon: Transcripts of Lectures Presented to an Honors Book of Mormon Class at Brigham Young University 1989-90* (Provo, UT: FARMS, n.d.), Semester 3, 210. Born in Quincy, Illinois, in 1871, Edgar Johnson Goodspeed was a biblical scholar and educator at the University of Chicago from 1902-37. Renowned for his expertise in biblical exegesis and Greek papyrology, Goodspeed achieved fame for his relatively more vernacular *New Testament: An American Translation* (1923). Goodspeed died in 1962.

³⁵Hugh Nibley, Letter to Agnes Sloan Nibley, n.d., postmarked 21 November 1941. Steindorff was born 1861 and died in 1951.

³⁶Hugh Nibley, "Faith of Observer," 164.

³⁷Hugh Nibley, Letter to Agnes Sloan Nibley, n.d., postmarked 21 November 1941.

³⁸Hugh Nibley, Letter to Paul Springer, n.d., ca. fall 1940.

³⁹James Henry Breasted was born in Rockford, Illinois, in 1865. Regarded as the first teacher of Egyptology in America, he was assistant in Egyptology (1895), assistant director of the Haskell Oriental Museum

lessness by taking a few hours off and going through the Book of Mormon (and that was all it would take, a few hours) and showing them it was a fraud." Hugh asked Mrs. Breasted what happened to her husband's "public service." Her reply was that "he just dropped it, that was all."[40]

Hugh energetically attended academic conferences and began publishing academic articles. During the Christmas holidays of 1940, Hugh read a paper titled "The Origin of the Roman Dole" at the annual meeting of the Pacific Coast Branch of the American Historical Association at Stanford.[41] In April 1941, he attended conferences in Oakland and Berkeley.[42] Also in 1941, Hugh read a paper titled "Acclamatio" at the annual convention for the Southwest Archaeological Foundation, in San Diego. The paper discussed the politics of ancient mobs, a topic he originally researched for his dissertation, but which his committee forced him to table.[43]

The library at Claremont was not yet up to the standards Hugh had enjoyed as a college student, so he would occasionally bicycle off to UCLA to look up sources. In June 1941, he wrote Springer, "Last Monday for the sake of checking up on one little foot-note and a bit of exercise I cycled in to UCLA, over 50 miles from here, against a strong headwind, in a little more than 3 hours. Thus we wisely atone for long periods of completely sedentary work by violent fits of over-exertion."[44] Hugh had actually purchased a car the year before; but no doubt wartime rationing of gasoline was another incentive to keep on using the bicycle.

Hugh had not lost his childhood faculty of becoming so absorbed in his work as to lose all track of external reality, a gift he has retained all his life. He wrote Sloanie on his thirty-second birthday, "I have been working very hard on a project—on a number of projects, I should say, and so pull myself out of Old Stuff only with the greatest difficul-

---

(1895), instructor in Egyptology (1896), and professor of Egyptology and Oriental history, all at the University of Chicago (1905-35). He founded the Oriental Institute in 1919. He is best known for his monumental Ancient Records of Egypt (1906-07), previously unpublished inscriptions with translations, and his translation and editing of the Edwin Smith Surgical Papyrus (1930), often referred to as the earliest known scientific document. Breasted died in 1935 and his widow relocated to Claremont.

[40] Nibley, The Prophetic Book of Mormon, edited by John W. Welch, Vol. 8 of The Collected Works of Hugh Nibley (Salt Lake City: Deseret Book/FARMS, 1989), 239-40.

[41] Annual Report of the American Historical Association, 1940, 90. This is probably the paper that Hugh mentioned in an undated (ca. fall 1940) letter to Paul Springer: he had "a speech all ready to give at Stanford during the Holidays." Hugh's vita, which he sent to BYU President Howard S. McDonald on 28 April 1946, lists this conference and the title of the paper.

[42] Hugh Nibley, Letter to Paul Springer, 1 April 1941. Hugh Nibley, Letter to Howard S. McDonald, 28 April 1946, lists these two papers: "Nimrod," submitted to (but not published by) the American Journal of Philology, and "Gog and Magog" which he described as "to be published by Claremont Col., now undergoing alterations."

[43] Hugh would return to this theme many years later in his essay "Acclamatio (Never Cry Mob)" which was published in Toward a Humanistic Science of Politics: Essays in Honor of Francis Dunham Wormuth, edited by Dalmas H. Nelson and Richard L. Sklar (Lanham, MD: University Press of America, 1983), 11-22. See Louis Midgley, "Hugh Winder Nibley: Bibliography and Register," in By Study and Also by Faith: Essays in Honor of Hugh W. Nibley, 2 vols., edited by John M. Lundquist and Stephen D. Ricks (Salt Lake City: Deseret Book/FARMS, 1990), 1:lxvii.

[44] Hugh Nibley, Letter to Paul Springer, 18 June 1941.

[45] Hugh Nibley, Letter to Agnes Sloan Nibley, 27 March 1942.

ty: it is an atmosphere that envelopes you like a dream and is very hard to shake for a few minutes while trying to write something like this."⁴⁵

Hugh's efforts began to pay off as he began to see his work published in scholarly journals. The *Classical Journal*, a publication of the Classical Association of the Midwest and South, published two essays by Hugh. The first was a short piece, "New Light on Scaliger," responding to an earlier article. Joseph Justus Scaliger, the Italian-born physician and scholar of the sixteenth century, had an encyclopedic knowledge, which caused Hugh to refer to him, somewhat extravagantly, as "the greatest scholar who ever lived." Hugh noted three facts about his intellectual hero that had apparently escaped the notice of previous scholars. First, from reading some Arabic script in a contemporary portrait of Scaliger, Hugh determined that the scholar's name was pronounced with a hard "g" rather than the then-accepted soft "j". Second, contrary to tradition, Scaliger was not "a self-taught recluse" but had sought out some of the finest teachers of his time. And third, even in Scaliger's day, he had a reputation for being a "bottomless pit of learning" and "a sun among the learned."⁴⁶

Hugh has long admired Scaliger, not only for his intellectual breadth, but also for his deep humility. When Scaliger was learning Hebrew, Hugh says, he "went to the ghetto and the children made fun of him, correcting his Hebrew." Meanwhile, scholars wouldn't speak to him. "They were indignant," Hugh summarizes. "Anyone who would allow himself to be laughed at by children and corrected by children was just not worthy of our profession. Unless you become as a little child you are not intelligent, you see; you're stupid.... They blocked it because of their haughtiness, their pride, and that pride is stupidity, that is what it is." It was Scaliger's willingness "to humiliate himself and become as a little child in order to learn" that Hugh admired and which he would emulate in his own language studies.⁴⁷

The second essay published by the *Classical Journal* was "Sparsiones" (meaning "to spread around" or "to asperge" or "sprinkle," as in Catholic baptism). Summarizing research from Hugh's dissertation, the article discussed the ancient Roman practice of throwing small gifts to the masses "to be scrambled for in scenes of wild disorder."⁴⁸ In August of 1942, Hugh jubilantly announced to Paul Springer that this article, which he redundantly called "my grand magnum opus," had been accepted for publication in 1944. "Just think what things will be then, with the world rushing from worse to worse in the meantime," he mused.⁴⁹ In fact, the article would not appear in print until 1945, after Hugh had seen first-hand the worst the world could offer.

While at Claremont, Hugh continued to hone his language skills. His office calendar for May 1941 notes his systematic rotation through texts in Latin, Hebrew, Egyptian, Greek, and Arabic. But he also continued to learn new languages. In June 1941, he wrote to Springer, "I have made a considerable dent in Irish." In early 1942, he was not only "going to town on Egyptian," but Babylonian was "thawing out nicely." In March

---

⁴⁶Hugh Nibley, "New Light on Scaliger," *Classical Journal* 37 (1942): 291-95, responding to Warren E. Blake, "Joseph Justus Scaliger," *Classical Journal* 36 (1940): 83-91. Nibley's essay was reprinted in The *Ancient State*, edited by Donald W. Parry and Stephen D. Ricks, Vol. 10 of *The Collected Works of Hugh Nibley* (Salt Lake City: Deseret Books/FARMS, 1991), 303-10. For Nibley's admiration of Scaliger, see "Faith of an Observer," 94, and "New Approaches to Book of Mormon Study," in *The Prophetic Book of Mormon*, 114.

⁴⁷Hugh Nibley, "Faith of an Observer," 94, 12-13.

⁴⁸Nibley, *The Ancient State*, 148.

⁴⁹Hugh Nibley, Letter to Paul Springer, 5 August 1942.

1942, he was "getting my hand in at Russian, and speak rather fair Italian." The next year in June, he claimed: "In this country [southern California] it is impossible not to learn Spanish, which I have come to speak, I flatter myself, rather fluently."[50]

Although he certainly concentrated on the bookish aspects of language learning, Hugh also took considerable pains to seek out native speakers and rejoiced in the war's silver lining: that it brought immigrants to California: "Starving Syrians, Greeks and Hebrews are foregathering in great numbers in these parts and we are commanding their services at a figure low enough not to strain our still pedestrian economy," he wrote Springer in 1941.[51] Somewhat extravagantly, he claimed to his mother that he was able to learn more about "the Mind and Speech of the Gorgeous East . . . in the bosom of Claremont than I could have in the slums of Beyrut."[52] Although these immigrants were probably looked down on in rarefied academic circles and there is, in fact, no way of knowing what social level of language Hugh learned from them, his diligence was unflagging.

He reported to Springer that he had "attached myself like a leech" to a Syrian named Lawand. "He speaks only Arabic and recites endlessly from the Koran and an enormous repertoire of Bedawin songs and tales."[53] In 1940, Hugh even bought a car,

> just so I could satisfy [Lawand's] insatiable yearning for desert places—for any dry gully or rocky hillside where he can feel like an Arab. You get him out in the open and he will start reciting and singing and wailing like a *majnun*, editing each verse with a long and often very enlightening commentary on the customs and manners that gave rise to it. Every rock is a quotation, every plant a memory, every odor a song.[54]

With satisfaction, Hugh reported the results of these immersion sessions: English "sounds so flat and brittle and even foreign after a few hours of Lawandian recitative."[55] He also joked that he exhausted his tutor: "I find it useful with my Syrian [tutor] to let him take three deep breaths, after the bucket of water has revived him, before continuing the lesson, and to relax my questioning whenever he shows signs of impending hysterics."[56]

He was apparently sincere in telling Springer that the car was primarily a means to enhance his language study, for he also explained to his mother: "It was the means of establishing contact and ingratiating myself with various Orientals, mostly Lebanese, living throughout the valley."[57] Before enlisting in the army in September 1942, Hugh sold this "powerfully-throbbing Dodge." Already used when he bought it, it had suffered

---

[50]Hugh Nibley, Letters to Paul Springer, 18 June 1941, n.d. ca. 1942; 7 March 1942; 21 June 1942.

[51]Hugh Nibley, Letter to Paul Springer, n.d., ca. 1941.

[52]Hugh Nibley, Letter to Agnes Sloan Nibley, 27 March 1942.

[53]Hugh Nibley, Letter to Paul Springer, n.d., ca. 1940. It begins "My dear Springer Minor."

[54]Ibid. Hugh is alluding to the Middle Eastern love story *Layla and Majnun*, in which Majnun goes mad with love and longing for the beautiful Layla. Unable to unite with his beloved, he becomes a masterful poet who wanders the desert. This tale was most artfully captured by the twelfth-century Persian poet Nizami and inspired Eric Clapton's "Layla." See Colin Turner's prose translation, *Layla and Majnun* (London: Blake, 1997).

[55]Ibid.

[56]Hugh Nibley, Letter to Paul Springer, n.d., ca. fall 1940.

[57]Hugh Nibley, Letter to Agnes Sloan Nibley, 27 March 1942.

somewhat at his hands. In 1941 when he broke off his key in the door lock, he broke the window to get in and did not bother to repair it, claiming, "It runs better, I find, with a broken window."[58]

When Lawand was not available, Hugh frequented the home of an Arabic-speaking family named Simon, "who are the cutest peasants (with the cutest daughters) you would care to meet."[59] Hugh was so dedicated to learning Arabic that in the summer of 1942 he actually moved to a different apartment so he would be nearer one of his Arabic tutors, of whom Hugh wrote, "Nothing else matters when he starts talking—every *sukun*, every *hamza*, yes, every *tanwin* is there, with a full, soleful [sic] enjoyment which makes you want to weep. I now understand him perfectly when he talks; it only remains to learn how to answer him in kind."[60]

Oddly enough, Hugh never studied Far Eastern languages, even though Claremont had been investing a great deal of scholarship in Japanese and Chinese cultures since 1929. Russell Story himself taught courses on political problems of Eastern Asia.[61] Hugh acknowledged, "There is a great emphasis laid at this institution on Far Eastern studies, for which we have a really splendid library." But he chose to concentrate on Western civilization: "I have always maintained that it is enough for a man to understand his own culture, which in the case of our own composite heritage is an overwhelming task."[62]

Despite his absorption in teaching and studying, Hugh, who turned thirty in the spring of 1940, was aware of and dissatisfied with his bachelorhood. In late 1940, he preened himself: "This IS news: I have become a ladies man! It started out when my advances to a highly respectable young woman were received not at all coldly. So I decided I should get married since dames ingenious enough to go for little me don't grow on trees." He did not bother to propose to this unnamed young woman, however, since he discovered that other women were also interested in him. Bemusedly he claimed: "Now we are running about with the hottest numbers in town: we take long hikes, we attend concerts, we swim in reservoirs, we eat at toney joints, and lo! there are plenty of beauties to attend us. So now I am wondering, why bother to marry the first one? It is a pleasant confusion."[63]

By early 1941, still in a mood of high exultation, Hugh chanted the hymn to Hymen, classical god of marriage: "Hymen o Hymenaee, Hymen ades o Hymenaee! Who knows but what I shall get married one of these days? Who knows? Who? Ignorance, thy ubiquity is wide-spread!"[64] And in April 1941, Hugh announced jubilantly to Paul Springer: "It has finally happened: I am formally, legally, ritually engaged to be married!" His fiancée was a twenty-seven-year-old German emigrée named Herta Pauly, whom Hugh described as "petite, exquisite, an incredible combination of unaffected elegance and volcanic energy," and "absolutely perfect in all respects (allowing for a pardonable

---

[58]Hugh Nibley, Letter to Agnes Sloan Nibley, n.d., postmarked 29 November 1941.

[59]Hugh Nibley, Letter to Paul Springer, early 1942.

[60]Hugh Nibley, Letter to Paul Springer, 21 June 1942.

[61]Lyon, *The History of Pomona College*, 312-14.

[62]Hugh Nibley, Letter to Paul Springer, 18 June 1941.

[63]Hugh Nibley, Letter to Paul Springer, n.d., fall 1940.

[64]Hugh Nibley, Letter to Paul Springer, n.d., ca. 1941.

sympathy with the German cause in the present debacle)." Herta, who was teaching at Scripps, had taken Greek from Hugh at the Graduate School. Hugh wrote that the wedding day would be "sometime in December," and signed the letter, "Love and kisses from an expert, HN, junker-to-be by marriage."65 Still, the engagement was short-lived. Hugh found himself ultimately unable to tolerate Herta's Nazi sympathizes; furthermore, she was a Lutheran. But most decisively, he lost patience with her temperament. On 21 November, Hugh abruptly wrote his mother: "The affaire Pauly is washed up and that's that."66 He did not elaborate. However, in a letter to Paul Springer in the spring of 1942, Hugh added a few details: "*Sturm and Drang*—24 hours of it a day with my Teutonic passion-flower; it got very tedious. We called it off; she is utterly wonderful, but as you know I am a person of definite limitations."67

Hugh bounced back from the breakup; and at almost the same time, in March 1942, he ecstatically wrote Springer about his "latest passion flower—and I swear the true one," a young Arab woman named Hind 'Abdu-Nur, whom he described as, "a full-moon of beauty, more sweet and complacent and wise than Shaharezade herself."68 Despite Hugh's assurance that this woman was "the true one," the relationship also came to nothing.

Meanwhile, the Nibley family fortunes had taken a decided turn for the worse. Although El and Sloanie had continued to live lavishly through the worst of the Depression, their finances were not stable. Despite the ill-fated mining venture in 1936 that had swallowed Hugh's fellowship money, at least one such venture had paid off. Hugh remembers that Paul Springer's father, who was the director of the U.S. Mint in San Francisco, told him that one of El's mines sent in twenty to thirty thousand dollars worth of gold every week. "So they did all right," says Hugh. "But Dad was ripped off. He was always playing tricks on people and having tricks played on him; he wasn't meant to be a businessman at all."69

Although the stock market crashed in October 1929, it was not until a decade later that the Nibley fortune finally vanished. On 29 November 1938, a notice of default was filed about the house on Normandie Avenue, showing that El and Sloanie were not keeping up on their mortage payments. Eight months later on 26 July 1939, a trustee's deed transferred the house from Sloanie to Mortgage Guarantee Company. The next step was a forced sale at auction of the house itself and the furniture. Chattel mortgages on several of the more expensive pieces of furniture document the presence of a grand piano, a grandfather clock, a dining room set, and bedroom sets, one of which had served as

---

65Hugh Nibley, Letter to Paul Springer, n.d., 1941. Springer wrote "3 April 1941" at the top of the letter; however, Hugh's letter to his mother announcing the engagement was postmarked 10 October 1941. In that letter, Hugh writes, "H.P. leaves nothing to be desired: having observed all her motions with a lively and interested curiosity for over a year, it was with considerable complacency that we learned that we ourself were more than an object of unmixed aversion on her part." *Junker* was the term by which Prussian aristocratic families referred to themselves.

66Hugh Nibley, Letter to Agnes Sloan Nibley, n.d., postmarked 21 November 1941.

67Hugh Nibley, Letter to Paul Springer, n.d. Springer dated this letter "Spring 1942." *Sturm and Drang* (storm and stress) was a late eighteenth-century German literary movement emphasizing rousing action and high emotionalism.

68Hugh Nibley, Letter to Paul Springer, n.d. Springer wrote "7 March 1942" at the top of the letter.

69Hugh Nibley, Interviewed by Boyd Petersen, 17 February 2001.

70Los Angeles County Recorder Grantee and Grantor Books, 1932-41, searched by Steve Eccles and Phil

security for a $2,550 loan.⁷⁰ On 14 July 1941 in a letter to his grandmother, Hugh described Sloanie "moving all our effects to a near-by garage for storage." He added critically that it was "not an unmixed evil" to have Sloanie's "whirlwind tempo" checked by worsening arthritis. "I cannot without qualification accept her view of life as a perpetual Blitzkrieg."⁷¹

Hugh took the family's financial collapse without any hand-wringing, even though his cosigning of some undefined document with his mother "having to do with the old house" required him to pay $133 that he could ill afford. In a letter to his mother in November 1941, he reported making the payment, then added, "Hope that's the last of it."⁷² It is not clear what the documents were that Hugh cosigned with his mother, nor does Hugh remember. Sloanie apparently then sought his advice on purchasing a smaller home. Hugh replied, "You are asking the wrong person for financial advice. But I must say—if you would be paying no more than rent anyway, what could you lose? Of course it is a real obligation, and paying for houses is one thing we have hardly proven to be our favorite sport."⁷³

Although Hugh was stoical, Sloanie was shattered. "With Mother it was very, very difficult to lose all that," remembers Barbara. "She was a beautiful woman, she married a well-known, handsome man, into a family that was wealthy, she had everything, all the money she wanted to spend, beautiful jewels, beautiful paintings, beautiful everything; and when that was lost, I think it really, really embittered her."⁷⁴ The family moved to a much smaller house on nearby Winona Boulevard, Sloanie began to sell hearing aids, and El spent the rest of his life trying to mount one unsuccessful get-rich scheme after another. The relationship between Sloanie and El was so strained that, although they never divorced, they lived apart for most of the rest of their lives, often in different cities.

Less than two weeks after Hugh offered Sloanie his view on buying a house, the lives of all Americans were decisively changed when the Japanese attacked Pearl Harbor on 7 December 1941. Germany unexpectedly declared war on the United States three days later, effectively ending all discussion about whether the United States would enter the war. The Selective Training and Service Act (PL 76-783) had been signed into law on 16 September 1940, requiring men to register with the Selective Service as a precaution in case the United States could not avoid the European war. The first registration of men ages twenty-one to thirty-five took place on 16 October—thirty-year-old Hugh would have been included in this group—and the first national lottery was held on 29 October to determine the order in which they would be drafted.⁷⁵

Hugh had applied for a deferment based on his age; but as of June 1941, he had received "no word from Uncle Sam, not even a questionnaire." The next month he added, "For some reason the local draft board seems to have taken a shine or a violent aversion

---

Bradford; additional title search courtesy of Kevin Assef; documentation in my possession.

⁷¹Hugh Nibley, Letter to Margaret Violet Reid Sloan, 14 July 1941. This may have been the garage where Sloanie stored many of the books Hugh sent back from Europe while he was in the army; he assumed for several years that they were lost. See chap. 15.

⁷²Hugh Nibley, Letter to Agnes Sloan Nibley, n.d., postmarked 3 November 1941.

⁷³Hugh Nibley, Letter to Agnes Sloan Nibley, n.d., postmarked 29 November 1941.

⁷⁴Barbara Nibley Richards, interviewed by Boyd Petersen, 14 March 1998.

⁷⁵By 27 April 1942, the date of the fourth registration, the age range also extended to men ages forty-five to sixty-five.

to me, I cannot tell which; at any rate they are stubbornly averse to deferring me, even tho I am safely beyond the 28 year mark—seem determined to see what I look like in a uniform."[76]

Reinforcing the suspense about his draft status came a personal loss with professional consequences. On 26 March 1942, the day before Hugh turned thirty-two, Russell M. Story died of a massive heart attack.[77] Hugh lamented to his mother: "The only strictly honest man I have ever known, President Story, died last night of a stroke. I find the circumstances significant; suppose I shall soon be moving on." He added: "I hear a report that I have been reclassified in the local draft-board to 1-A." Hugh felt that he would not longer be welcome at Claremont because "I could not keep my feet out of that; I could not leave the gospel alone. I had to drag the scriptures in no matter what, no matter what I was teaching. And that would sometimes get raised eyebrows."[78] Other faculty members felt Hugh's religious perspective was not appropriate at a school with a Congregationalist heritage and a decidedly liberal orientation. The Claremont Board of Fellows decided not to immediately appoint a successor to Story and instead named Robert J. Bernard as Claremont's "administrative director."[79] Hugh "got along famously" with Bernard, but another administrator named Bird "knew not Israel," as Hugh put it. Bird approached him soon after Story's death and told him, "You know you are not one of us." "I could feel the tension growing," said Hugh, in a considerable understatement.[80]

A month later, Hugh wrote that he had been investigating his options if he enlisted and had concluded: "I have rather a good line-up with the government."[81] "My only care," he confided gloomily, is "what's to be done with all these books."[82] By late May, the uncertainty was beginning to tell, and he complained: "The war has brought everything in Claremont very nearly to a dead stop. Since Story went there is little interest in the place. Right now I am working desperately to make the most of a lull between two storms: the school is washed up and the war is still waiting."[83] His attitude was more resignation to the inevitable than either patriotic fervor or war fever. As late as June 1941, he had writ-

[76]Hugh Nibley, Letter to Paul Springer, n.d. Springer wrote "July 1941" at the top of the letter. Hugh's confusion about his eligibility may spring from confusion in the Selective Service itself. My two inquiries produced both a document stating that Hugh would not have been exempt from the draft and another stating that he was eligible for deferment.

[77]Lyon, *The History of Pomona College*, 362-63; Frances Bernard Drake, *Two Men and an Idea* (Claremont, CA: Claremont University Center, 1996), 64.

[78]Hugh Nibley, Letter to Agnes Sloan Nibley, 27 March 1942.

[79]Lyon, *The History of Pomona College*, 364. Robert J. Bernard attended Pomona College as an undergraduate, during which time he became a protégé of former President James Blaisdell, who served from 1909 to 1928. Soon after graduating in 1917, Bernard became Blaisdale's assistant, established himself as an invaluable fundraiser for the school, and then in 1922 became the college's executive secretary, the administrative director (1941-59), and ultimately president (1959-63). Ibid., 206, 364, 384, 524, 528.

[80]Hugh Nibley, "Faith of an Observer," 67. I have been unable to find an administrator named Bird at Claremont; but since the school is a consortium, he may have been an administrator on one of the many other campuses.

[81]Hugh Nibley, Letter to Agnes Sloan Nibley, n.d., postmarked 22 April 1942.

[82]Hugh Nibley, Letter to Agnes Sloan Nibley, 27 March 1942.

[83]Hugh Nibley, Letter to Agnes Sloan Nibley, n.d., postmarked 29 May 1942.

ten tellingly to Paul: "The astounding alignments in the present debacle all but forbid one to take sides."[84]

In June 1942, Hugh resigned his position at Claremont. He wrote to Paul Springer late that month:

> As you no doubt know, the war has simply decapitated the education business, especially in the graduate field. A few weeks ago the president of this institution died—the only thoroughly honest man I have ever known—and that was the final inducement for me to break ties with Claremont. Like you, I am now in a moment of ambrosial serenity, but without the slightest doubt that the storm is shortly to follow, à la Beethoven VI.[85]

Hugh had not firmly decided on a course, for he speculated in the same letter: "If I didn't hate boats and get strange diseases on the water I would join the navy. It might be wise to dicker with various government agencies, but I strongly feel that salvation does not lie in that direction. Come what may, our concern is to do the right thing and let the opportunists do the smart thing—in the end we shall see which course is the wiser."

Paul had recently married; and though still in suspense, Hugh wrote a letter in July, urging him and his wife, Nell, to join him on a trip to Zion Park in southern Utah: "Verily He who placed before our feet the expansive (lit. 'stretched-out') Deserts and they are full of sand and plant and animal creatures without number and they are creeping and running and flying in the air. . . ."[86] The trip turned out to be a calm and rejuvenating vacation for Hugh. He was back in the Utah wilderness that he had come to love and had the good conversation of an old friend. From Zion, Hugh wrote his mother a postcard: "I am again among the rocks of Zion, absolutely alone but for the Springers. The place is deserted and the solitude welcome and impressive."[87] A few days later, he wrote, "Still in Zion. . . . It is very hard to tear away from these burning rocks so we are doing it by degrees."[88] After this trip, Hugh happily wrote to Paul: "We have explored pretty well in the last decade of days that bright and happy, albeit narrow, vale in which our opinions do not clash."[89]

Upon his return from Zion, Hugh found that "the draft board is still marking time and the whole situation is as ever teeming with quiet fun."[90] Even though men from age twenty-eight up were deferred for the draft between August 1941 and September 1942, Hugh, who had turned thirty-one in March 1941, took matters into his own hands. On 28 September 1942, he enlisted in U.S. Army and was inducted at Fort MacArthur about ten miles west of Long Beach, California. The wait was over. From the ivory towers of academe, Hugh was marching out to confront the storms of war.

---

[84] Hugh Nibley, Letter to Paul Springer, 18 June 1941.

[85] Hugh Nibley, Letter to Paul Springer, 21 June 1942. He is referring to the thunderstorm sequence in Beethoven's famed Sixth ("Pastoral") Symphony.

[86] Hugh Nibley, Letter to Paul Springer, n.d. Springer wrote "16 July 1942" at the top of the letter.

[87] Hugh Nibley, Letter to Agnes Sloan Nibley, n.d., July 1942. The postmark is illegible.

[88] Hugh Nibley, Letter to Agnes Sloan Nibley, n.d., postmarked 26 July 1942.

[89] Hugh Nibley, Letter to Paul Springer, 5 August 1942.

[90] Ibid.

Hugh Nibley in the BYU Ancient Studies reading room in 1990 at age eighty.

    Few students can talk coherently about their first class from Brother Nibley. For some it was simply a rite of passage, the academic equivalent of a social-unit initiation. For many it was, at best, a brisk blur edged with random flashes of insight. For a few it was an intellectual implosion, from which they will never recover.

—Robert K. Thomas[1]

    As a teacher, [Nibley] is, at least at the outset, terrifying. He does not lecture; he explodes. He brings source materials in the original to class, translates them on the spot, and lapses into spasms of free association as he sees linguistic connections. He teaches whatever he is working on that day, allowing students to look over his shoulder. His long paragraphs go by at approximately the speed of light. . . . Most of the time he talks as if everyone present has just read everything he has. This is less Germanic or Olympian detachment than a temperamental unwillingness to put anyone down.

—Truman G. Madsen[2]

---

[1] Robert K. Thomas, "The Influence of Hugh Nibley: His Presence in the University," In *By Study and Also by Faith: Essays in Honor of Hugh W. Nibley on the Occasion of his Eightieth Birthday, 27 March 1990*, 2 vols. (Salt Lake City: Deseret Book/FARMS, 1990), 1:45.

[2] Truman G. Madsen, "Foreword," *Nibley on the Timely and the Timeless* (Provo, UT: Brigham Young University Religious Studies Center, 1978), xii-xiii.

Chapter 11

"The Clown of the Professions": Hugh Nibley and Scholarship

On 23 March 1955, a crowd gathered in the Orson Spencer Hall at the University of Utah campus to hear a debate between two men who were polar opposites within the Mormon community in everything except their intellectual gifts and rich Mormon heritage. Sterling McMurrin, professor of philosophy at the University of Utah and ardent skeptic, met Hugh Nibley, professor of religion and history from Brigham Young University and ardent defender of the Mormon faith. Their topic was: "Do History and Religion Conflict?" Sterling and Hugh unstintingly expressed their respect for each other. Sterling said he had "great admiration" for Hugh's "superb intellectual talents and scholarly attainments" as well as for his "high degree of independence of thought and action," while Hugh admired the fact that Sterling remained always charitable and "never lost his temper."[3] Despite their profound respect for each other as individuals, however, they saw the world from completely different perspectives. For his entire life, Hugh was impatient with theology, which he saw as an attempt to replace revelation with philosophy, while McMurrin found Hugh's work both anti-intellectual and antirational. This debate was no exception.

During his part of the debate, Hugh was critical of historical endeavors, stating that historians face many obstacles in reconstructing the past. He cited as examples contradictions within the discipline as well as the all-too-human nature of the historian. Despite these obstacles, Hugh argued, history is often accepted with as little thought and every bit as dogmatically as religion: "History is as much what a man

---

[3]Sterling McMurrin, Letter to Hugh Nibley, 30 January 1986, Sterling McMurrin Papers, Special Collections, J. Willard Marriott Library, University of Utah, Salt Lake City; Hugh Nibley, Interviewed by Boyd Petersen, 2 August 1997. I read an earlier version of this chapter at the Sunstone Symposium on 9 August 1997 in Salt Lake City.

believes as his religion is," stated Hugh. Following the prepared remarks, McMurrin asked about Hugh's own historical writings, to which Hugh responded that they are "nothing but a game."[4] McMurrin and Hugh were known to disagree on most things, but the fact that Hugh made this statement is something neither disputes.

Readers of Hugh have often heard him refer to others' scholarly endeavors as a game, but here is an instance where Hugh actually referred to his own work as a game. What did Hugh mean by this statement? Some have interpreted the statement as disingenuous—that what he states publicly is not what he believes privately. In fact, in a later exchange of letters, McMurrin commented: "The unfortunate thing is that some of your Church readers have taken your stuff seriously."[5] What did Hugh mean by the comment?

Ironically, even though Hugh Nibley is almost certainly the most respected scholar in Mormonism, few scholars in or outside of the Church have been as critical of academe as he has been. As Hugh wrote from the war front: "Scholarship is as usual the clown of the professions—its practitioners are either dealing in things so abstruse as to place them beyond criticism (in which case they are almost bound to be phonies) or else they are chewing old familiar cuds—in which case they are wasting their time."[6]

Yet Hugh has also spent his entire life engaged in scholarly activities and receiving his salary from universities. It is obvious that he has a love-hate relationship with academic life. His comments about Brigham Young University, the locale in which he has spent by far the majority of his professional life, reveals much about his attitude toward academia in general:

> I can see two totally different pictures of the BYU, each one a reality: From one direction I see high purpose, sobriety, good cheer, dedication, and a measure of stability which in this unquiet world is by no means to be despised. Then by shifting my position but slightly I see a carnival of human vanity and folly to which only Gilbert and Sullivan could do justice, with solemn antics before high heaven that make the angels weep. Why take sides or contend? Both of the pictures are genuine![7]

Understanding what Hugh refers to as the "carnival" is the key to appreciating his comment that his own work is a "game." One of Hugh's most consistent and loudest criticisms of the academy is its authoritarian tendency to stress credentials rather than quality of work. He dismissively commented in one letter: "I have always maintained that displays of titles and credentials, to say nothing of disputes and wrangles about them, are entirely irrelevant."[8] He also observed: "If you are alert in

---

[4] Sterling McMurrin, Letters to Hugh Nibley, 1 November 1960 and 30 January 1986, McMurrin Papers. Hugh Nibley, Interviewed by Boyd Petersen, 2 August 1997.

[5] Sterling McMurrin, Letter to Hugh Nibley, 1 November 1960, McMurrin Papers.

[6] Hugh Nibley, Letter to Agnes Sloan Nibley, n.d. ca. late 1944 or early 1945. From internal evidence, Hugh wrote this letter from Europe after the Normandy invasion.

[7] Hugh Nibley, "Some Reasons for the Restored Gospel," 5, unpublished typescript, 1975; photocopy in my possession.

[8] Hugh Nibley, Letter to Barbara Ellsworth, 18 December 1980. Ellsworth seems to have been a Church mem-

the ways of scholarship you should know that people are to be judged only by what they produce, and that is to be judged not by the credentials of the author but by your own estimate of what he says."[9]

Credentials, according to Hugh, have only a coincidental connection with what a person knows. He scoffed to a correspondent: "You would be surprised how many Egyptologists . . . who made a great show of learning couldn't read Egyptian at all, and how many humble students of which I know several can read it far better than most professional Egyptologists. That, you say, remains to be proved but it *can* be proved; just bring your documents or send them with somebody else and request a performance."[10]

Administrators like "a president or a dean or a department head," he pointed out, "can be made by appointment, a breath can make them and a breath hath made, as far as that goes. . . . But . . . since the beginning of the world nobody ever became an artist or scientist or a scholar by appointment."[11]

In fact, Hugh argues, the credentials, offices, appointments, and honors bestowed upon an individual may actually have an inverse relationship to his or her actual academic production: "The first rule of success in the scholarly as in the military world is not to make waves," he observed, "versus the first rule of discovery in the scholarly and victory in the military realms: . . . do unorthodox and surprising things."[12]

Hugh found in the life of Albert Einstein, whom he had heard lecture at Claremont, an inspiring example of solid amateur scholarship: "Einstein was an amateur mathematician and an amateur astronomer," he pointed out to a correspondent. "He failed to gain admission to college and his Ph.D. thesis was rejected; professionally he was a clerk in the patent office, in which position he had to let the evidence speak for itself. There are no Einsteins around today but the point of this is that credentials are worth nothing."[13]

Although Hugh had expressed his misgivings about the U.S. educational system privately for many years, it was not until the 1960s that he began to speak forcefully in public. There are likely two reasons for this: first, Hugh's sabbatical at Berkeley showed him real scholarship, but it was marred by academic games, one-up-manship, and turf wars. Hugh loved studying with Klaus Baer, but he didn't like the big-name scholars who were desperately clinging to their rank without adding much to their scholarship base. He saw the same game-playing at BYU but without the genuine scholarship. He resented the far-right conservativism that manifested itself among some faculty members and was outraged that they turned the Book of Mormon into a tract against socialism. But he also thought that many more liberal

---

ber with a question, not an acquaintance.

[9] Hugh Nibley, Letter to David L. Parkos, 2 December 1983. Parkos seems to have been another nonacquaintance.

[10] Hugh Nibley, Letter to Della Smith, 26 June 1981.

[11] Hugh Nibley, "Faith of an Observer," 41, compilation of interviews, ca. 1983-84 for a video documentary of the same name aired in 1985, photocopy of typescript in my possession, pagination added.

[12] Hugh Nibley, Open Letter to John W. Welch and other contributors to his festschrift, 20 September 1978.

[13] Hugh Nibley, Letter to Brother Ball, March 1979.

faculty members failed to take the gospel—especially the Book of Mormon—seriously.

A further source of uneasiness for him was the turn toward competition and utilitarianism that American education took during the Cold War. After the Soviet Union launched Sputnik I in 1957, the U.S. Congress passed the National Defense Education Act (NDEA) to pour money into projects to close the "space gap." Areas considered crucial to national defense and security included mathematics, modern foreign languages, and science. Education, in short, was valued for its utility—what the country could gain from it—rather than as valuable in itself.

Despite Hugh's downplay of credentials, surely he has the intellectual training to be taken seriously by those who do look to credentials. His curriculum vita shows one solid academic achievement after another. Still a teenager, he laid the foundation of stunning multilingual competencies, ancient and modern. He graduated summa cum laude from UCLA with a bachelor's degree in history. He took his Ph.D. from Berkeley, where he was a university fellow, an honors designation that brought with it a merit-based scholarship. Then within the University of California college system, Hugh simultaneously taught modern European history at Pomona College, humanities at Scripps College, and U.S. history, history of education, Greek, and German at Claremont College. At Brigham Young University from 1946 on, he was a sort of one-man classics department, teaching courses in Greek, Russian, early and medieval Christianity, and ancient and classical history.

Hugh was particularly unsparing when he saw academic games slopping over into the study of the gospel. When students complained of being bored by their religion classes, he fumed to a correspondent in the early 1980s:

> The [BYU] department of Religion holds a position of unrivaled privilege but abysmal prestige in the university. Young people are being more critical today than ever before; they complain that they feel that they have a right to something more than rather average Sunday School teaching in classes in which they are compelled to spend some of the most valuable (and expensive) hours of their lives. Meaning that they have a right to be exposed occasionally to learning on the same level as that provided by departments of physics or biology.[14]

Although Hugh is a man to whom awards mean little, Phyllis and Christina have hung an entire wall of his home with honors he has received from BYU and other institutions. Among these are an award from the Political Science Honor Society at the University of Utah in 1964; BYU Professor of the Year in 1973; an Honorary Doctor of Letters degree from BYU in 1983; and the Exemplary Manhood Award from Associated Students at BYU in 1991. Hugh received a Fulbright to spend the 1959-60 school year in Libya; however, the United States cancelled all Fulbright aid to Libya that year and he spent those months instead at Berkeley.

Hugh's gift of languages is amazing. One of the most common questions I've been asked about Hugh Nibley is, "How many languages does he actually speak?" The problem with this question is that language is derivative—that is, once you know the

---

[14]Hugh Nibley, Letter of Recommendation for Avraham Gileadi, 16 February 1982.

basic root languages, you can get by in many of its offshoots. I know that Hugh Nibley is comfortable listing the following languages on his vita: German, French, Arabic, Spanish, Latin, Greek, Russian, Dutch, Italian, Old Norse, Hebrew, Coptic, and Egyptian. Having served his mission in Germany, it is probably the one he knows best, but he has spent more time with Arabic than any other. A friend, Kent Wallace, told me that shortly after returning from his mission to Norway, he was invited to the Nibleys' family home evening. At one point during the evening, he asked Hugh if he spoke Norwegian. Hugh replied that he didn't but that he did know Old Icelandic and had read several Norwegian books. According to Kent, he then "rattled off a fairly long list of titles that ended with the name of Norway's most popular encyclopedia." Kent asked him if he'd looked up articles in the encyclopedia. "Brother Nibley replied offhandedly that he had read the entire Norwegian encyclopedia—all twenty-nine volumes."[15]

Hugh has published hundreds of articles and the compilation of his *Collected Works*, which is not yet finished, is now up to thirteen hefty volumes. They include articles for many non-Mormon journals, including the *Classical Journal*, *Western Political Quarterly*, *Western Speech*, *Jewish Quarterly Review*, *Church History*, *Revue de Qumran*, *Vigililae Christianae*, *The Historian*, the *American Political Science Review*, and the *Encyclopedia Judaica*. (See chap. 19.) Hugh commented breezily in a letter to Paul Springer in 1958: "I have got some important communication from some big shots in the business, but none of them were in response to any of my Gentile exertions (which are merely written to set the stage for the other stuff)."[16]

The esteem of Hugh's non-Mormon colleagues is visible at a glance at the contents of the two-volume *Festschrift* published in his honor in 1990. Among the contributors are some of the top scholars in biblical and ancient studies, including James Charlesworth, Cyrus Gordon, Jacob Milgrom, Raphael Patai, Jacob Neusner, and the late Aziz Atiya. Professor James Charlesworth, of Princeton Theological Seminary, has called Hugh "a philological genius"[17] and stated that "he has an incredibly gifted mind, especially with languages."[18] Berkeley's Jacob Milgrom admires Hugh's "catholic reading and his wry humor."[19] Cyrus Gordon is impressed with Hugh for "inspiring a generation of disciples with a love of learning and with the dedication to devote their lives to it,"[20] adding that Hugh's contribution to scholarship has been that "he bridged the gap that used to separate Mormon scholarship from the mainstream of Near Eastern Studies."[21] Jacob Neusner has called Hugh "a first-rate intel-

---

[15] Kent Wallace, e-mail to Boyd Petersen, 5 August 1997.

[16] Hugh Nibley, Letter to Paul Springer, 24 May 1958. See Chapter 15 for a scholarly exchange on Hugh's "Baptism for the Dead in Ancient Times," which was serialized in the *Improvement Era* and reviewed in the *Catholic Biblical Quarterly*.

[17] James H. Charlesworth, "From the Philopedia of Jesus to the Misopedia of the Acts of Thomas," *By Study and Also by Faith*, edited by John M. Lundquist and Stephen D. Ricks (Salt Lake City: Deseret Book/FARMS, 1990), 1:46.

[18] James H. Charlesworth, Letter to Boyd Petersen, 12 February 1997.

[19] Jacob Milgrom, Letter to Boyd Petersen, 13 February 1997.

[20] Cyrus H. Gordon, "A Hebrew Inscription Authenticated," *By Study and Also by Faith*, 1:67.

[21] Cyrus Gordon, Letter to Boyd Petersen, 8 February 1997.

lect"[22] and predicts that "when he receives his audience, [Nibley] will be seen as one of the fecund intellects of the study of religion in our century."[23]

Egyptologist Klaus Baer, during an interchange with Grant Heward over the Abraham papyri, appraised Hugh's scholarship:

> I have considerable respect for the scholarly studies of early Christian Church history that Prof. Nibley has published in places where they will be read and scrutinized by professionals in the field and in which he demonstrates that the beliefs and practices of the very early Church may well have been considerably closer, in some respects, to those of the Mormon Church than to those that became orthodox later.[24]

One of Hugh's former students, Gordon Thomasson, was a graduate student reader for Mircea Eliade when that scholar was a visiting professor at the University of California at Santa Barbara. When Thomasson "saw the thread of his seminar going in the direction of Nibley's 'The Expanding Gospel,' I gave Eliade a copy. The next week [Eliade] was nearly jumping out of his skin." He demanded: "Who is this Hugh Nibley? . . . He knows my field better than I do, and his translations are elegant." Thomasson said he pointed out to Eliade that there was an LDS subtext to the essay, to which Eliade replied impatiently, "Who cares? His evidence and logic are faultless." Eliade even asked whether he could get Hugh to teach at Chicago; but when he heard that Hugh had been at the rival department at Chicago, the Oriental Institute, Eliade lost interest in hiring Hugh. Still, he spent the rest of the semester requesting, reading, and discussing with Thomasson every Nibley article Thomasson could provide.[25]

Even Fawn Brodie, whom Hugh critiqued with his first Mormon publication, *No, Ma'am, That's Not History*, recognized Hugh's brilliance. Commenting on his "Intellectual Autobiography" to Everett Cooley, the University of Utah's archivist, Brodie wrote: "I found the mini-autobiography fascinating in every way. This man surely had a touch of genius, and a great linguistic talent. What a pity that he was emotionally trapped by his allegiance to Joseph Smith and the Book of Mormon."[26]

Hugh has, however, run from any attempt to place him in any academic committee or directorship, preferring instead the grind and lower pay of the professor. "I deplore the authoritarian, Baconian structure on which the entire edifice of modern learning is built . . . ," he proclaimed unhesitatingly "and have always been a passionate devotee of the open-ended discussion in which nothing is ever proven except for the individual. Whenever anything is proven it is because some individual has

---

[22]Jacob Neusner, Letter to Boyd Petersen, 10 February 1997.

[23]Jacob Neusner, "Why No New Judaisms in the Twentieth Century?," *By Study and Also by Faith*, 2:552.

[24]Klaus Baer, Letter to Grant S. Heward, 26 August 1966.

[25]Gordon C. Thomasson, "Was There an Apostasy?" Internet discussion on SAMU-L, 26 August 1994; Gordon C. Thomasson, e-mail to Boyd Petersen, "Re: Nibley and Scholarship," 21 September 1997.

[26]Fawn M. Brodie, Letter to Everett Cooley, 23 August 1978, Fawn McKay Brodie Papers, Special Collections, Marriott Library, University of Utah. She was responding to Nibley, "Intellectual Autobiography," *Nibley on the Timely and the Timeless* (Provo, Utah: BYU Religious Studies Center, 1978): xix-xxvii.

been convinced, having acquired a personal, non-communicable testimony of the truth of the proposition."[27]

Hugh has similarly lamented what he sees as the academy's privileging image over substance and the pompous showmanship that has become rampant in education today. This game of deceit, whether staged for the masses or for a single classroom, hides substance and mocks actual learning. Hugh once referred to BYU's convocation as the "pompous fireworks of the local commencement . . . a day of ghastly rhetoric in rented (9 bucks yet!) mummery."[28] Given this attitude, it is no surprise that Hugh often plotted to avoid commencement exercises.

Hugh's denunciations of typical classroom instruction did not mince words: "The only thing that keeps [the Humanities] alive today is 'theatromania,' that is, turning it all into show business—journalism, TV, or peddling videos. You must be able to get in on some kind of sensationalism. If that sounds drastic, it is exactly where the ancient world ended up in the 4th century, as the empty shell of a civilization."[29] Although plenty of his own students have lurched out of his classroom, both dazed and dazzled by polyglot lectures delivered at machine-gun speed, Hugh eschewed such ear-tickling entertainment treats as movies, videos, sentimental stories, or electronic games.

Hugh genuinely mourned the lack of substance in the classroom that left students impoverished: "The ignorance of this generation of students is staggering, where the tradition of the race is concerned, just as their knowledge of the lyrics of TV commercials is often broad and detailed."[30]

Another area where Hugh has criticized the academy has been its modern focus on narrow, career-driven training, in contrast to broad, general, classical education. Hugh once counseled that, it is "wise to lay a broad and general foundation, refusing, even at a risk, to specialize before the right time." He continued: "Once you go down to work in the fields you lose that power to survey the whole scene and move when the time comes in any direction; you sacrifice that breadth of view and freedom of action which is essential, I suspect, to doing the most good, or perhaps even for survival itself, in our world."[31]

Although specialization is often justified on the basis of economic efficiency, Hugh argues for the flat opposite, rebuffing what was apparently his mother's inquiry during his first teaching job at Claremont about his career plans: "It should be perfectly clear to you by now what has always been perfectly clear to me, that anyone is a damn fool who prepares for a particular career in this great world of ours. It just doesn't work that way, thank heaven."[32]

---

[27] Hugh Nibley, Letter to Sterling McMurrin, 23 August 1967. McMurrin was planning a book on significant Mormon philosophers and had asked Nibley for a statement of his position. This letter was Nibley's response. See Appendix D.
[28] Hugh Nibley, Letter to Paul Springer, n.d. 1949.
[29] Hugh Nibley, Letter to Robert N. Seaver, 9 May 1986.
[30] Hugh Nibley, Letter to Charles Alexander Nibley, n.d., ca. 1979. It begins "How were we to know."
[31] Hugh Nibley, Letter to Mrs. [Emma?] Springer, 7 January 1941.
[32] Hugh Nibley, Letter to Agnes Sloan Nibley, fall 1941.

Hugh saw as criminal the negligence which modern education treated the classical world: "Apparently our present-day education has forgotten the ancient world, to our loss, for theirs is the history we are even now repeating."[33]

Hugh certainly cannot be accused of having specialized too narrowly. Again, it is illustrative to glance through his *Festschrift* where scholars who consider him their peer came together from many different departments, disciplines, universities and religions.

Closely related to the problem of image over substance is academe's pursuit of eminence rather than "truth." Writing to his mother in deep disillusionment from Claremont less than three years after finishing his dissertation, Hugh commented: "I think I shall find a chance to break with the despicable and corrupt teaching profession. Claremont is the only place in the country where it is not unspeakably degraded."[34] Hugh's comment may be something of an exaggeration, since he was a new professor teaching in his first position. However, he made substantially the same comments much later in his life after teaching at Claremont, BYU, and Berkeley, where he had known some of the best scholars in the country.

This was the same view—and virtually the same vocabulary—Hugh used over forty years later in an interview: "A university is nothing more nor less than a place to show off.... Everybody's after eminence.... Their whole objective is eminence. They have nothing else to live for."[35] Having witnessed what became of those who had achieved that goal, Hugh had little desire for it. As a graduate student at Berkeley, he observed that "the faculty had but one objective in life—to achieve eminence—and all labored under the pathetic illusion that mere association with a prestigious institution was the nearest thing to human satisfaction that this life could offer."[36]

Hugh was also disillusioned by the "great minds" he came in contact with over the years. The influx of European professors fleeing the Nazis during World War II had raised his anticipation at Claremont because

> ... they included some of the biggest names in the business. I was elated, because Claremont was very small then and I was in daily contact with all of them.... I thought I was in for a treat, but I should have known better. Berkeley at that time was crowding Harvard in all fields and surpassing it in many, and I had been with some Big Names there and been properly disillusioned: even the great Jaeger had nothing to say, though he said it impressively. I was sure that a flock of No. 1 Noodles from the Old World would have the edge even over Berkeley, but they were all duds—every single one of them. It sounds like an outrageous thing to say, but it is true. I split classes with Everett Dean Martin and Edgar Goodspeed (i.e., they would take the class one day and I would take the same class the next) and had a hard time keeping a straight face. It is as if such people had lost all contact with

---

[33] Hugh Nibley, Letter to Leslie G. Francis, 29 September 1987.
[34] Hugh Nibley, Letter to Agnes Sloan Nibley, fall 1941.
[35] Hugh Nibley, "Faith of an Observer," 259.
[36] Hugh Nibley, "An Intellectual Autobiography," in *Nibley on the Timely and the Timeless* (Provo, UT: BYU Religious Study Center, 1978), xix-xxviii.

reality: "And even as they did not like to retain God in their knowledge, God gave them over to a reprobate mind . . ." (Romans 1:28). I have been impressed more recently in dealing with Egyptologists that it is literally true that they are not in the least interested in the Egyptians but only in the remuneration and prestige of being Egyptologists.[37]

Hugh returned to Berkeley for a full-year sabbatical in 1959-60. After its completion, he wrote from Provo about "the all-pervading disillusionment of Great Men who have arrived and have no where to go." He continues, "There is a dungeon-like quality about things—dampness, hopelessness and gloom. . . . Can't blame my eminent colleagues for hitting the bottle."[38] In a memorandum describing his sabbatical to BYU's President Ernest L. Wilkinson, Hugh lauded Berkeley for its academic rigor but lamented the *angst* of the faculty:

They are all dissatisfied and many of them are afraid; they are beset by a sense of futility—they have arrived; they aren't going any place, and they know it; they study what they study because it is their job, not because they find it particularly interesting or significant. In fact, the best of them boast of writing dull studies "that only six men in the world will read." The sense of disillusionment and resignation is at times quite overpowering. What they lack is the gospel. That makes all the difference in the world, and I returned eagerly to Provo resolved to teach and study nothing else from here on.[39]

Hugh's goal has never been eminence. Rather, even as a graduate student, he stated that his goal was the Platonic ideal of "excelling yourself."[40] However, that goal has been shaped by and coupled with his zeal to proclaim the gospel. He rebuffed encouragement to teach elsewhere for that reason, responding on one occasion:

Of course you are right, but not all right. If I knew what you knew I wouldn't be here, and if you knew what I knew you wouldn't be there and weeza woiza, as the Immortal [Krazy] Kat would say. . . . I have found that no matter where I go I promptly subside into a groove of gospel declamation which displeases people everywhere but here and which is by no means viewed with approval by all the local brains. . . . Where fourteen or fifteen ineffectual *Stubemenschen* read my articles, hundreds of thousands have read Lehi in the form of a priesthood manual, and I get communications all the time telling how one way or another some of the stuff I have ground out has changed the life of this person or that and they are not all fools.[41]

---

[37] Hugh Nibley, Letter to Charles Alexander Nibley, 27 June 1980.

[38] Hugh Nibley, Letter to Paul Springer, 12 December 1960.

[39] Hugh Nibley, Letter to Ernest L. Wilkinson, 18 July 1960, Wilkinson Presidential Papers, L. Tom Perry Special Collections, Harold B. Lee Library, Brigham Young University, Provo, Utah.

[40] Hugh Nibley, "Faith of an Observer," 253.

[41] Hugh Nibley, Letter to Paul Springer, 24 May 1958. *Stubemenschen* means literally "parlor people," with the implication that these individuals lead sheltered lives, engaging in parlor games, but without the ability to deal effectively with real life.

In another letter he stated, "I manage to let the gospel into every situation. Let it, that is, not drag it—it is like the pressure of water on a dam: the only way it can be kept out of any context or issue is to block it out forcibly."[42]

Another problem Hugh sees with academics—one he has had to fight himself—is pride. In one interview, he conceded that in his youth he was "an insufferable little show off" and that, throughout his life, vanity has been "a plague.... I've prayed against it for years and years and whether the prayer works or not, I don't know."[43]

Hugh fought the demon of vanity by keeping things in perspective. From his insider's view, he knew that even some of the "great names" of Mormondom had an all-too-human side; and the collapse of his family's fortune had proved how quickly wealth could vanish. He was equally skeptical of over-reliance on his own gifts and achievements, indubitable though they were.

As already discussed (see chap. 10), Hugh had no hesitancy about asking refugees and children to tutor him in languages. He befriended native speakers of Arabic, Russian, and Greek, disregarding their economic and social status. Such an approach manifests the humility of the true student. Furthermore, Hugh has always quickly recognized and highly prized humility in others. When Klaus Baer died, Hugh wrote a tender letter of condolence to his Baer's widow, extolling Klaus: "There was no academic barrier between him and anyone else, not the slightest trace of stuffiness or pretense—as gracious, frank and open as an angel, Klaus was incapable of the usual feuding and intrigue that flourishes in graduate schools."[44]

Hugh has repeatedly stressed that knowledge changes while truth, which remains constant, also remains elusive. In scholarship, answers reveal more questions. Furthermore, the accepted rules and the accepted winners change with the times. Speaking of two astronomers who were well-known during his youth, Hugh commented:

> As a boy I thought they were wonderful. And yet today their life's work has been effectively wiped out by a few photographs. Well, what's the loss? Science moves on, and I am not too badly broken up about my heroes. But what if I had followed them to the point of rejecting the gospel—the point of no return? I used to spend long hours listening to old Dr. Larkin talking about the wonders of astronomy and the absurdities of "ancient Jewish mythology." Today his astronomy sounds pathetically old-fashioned—he was wrong on almost everything—and ancient Jewish "mythology" has received a new lease on life. What if I had become his disciple to the point of rejecting religion, as he often urged me to? THERE ARE THOUSANDS OF PEOPLE OUTSIDE OF THE CHURCH TODAY BECAUSE OF SOME SCIENTIFIC TEACHINGS WHICH HAVE NOW BEEN EXPLODED, ARE NOW BEING EXPLODED, AND ARE YET TO BE EXPLODED, while the gospel remains unscathed.[45]

---

[42] Hugh Nibley, Letter to Charles Alexander Nibley, n.d., ca. 1979. It begins "How were we to know."

[43] Hugh Nibley, "Faith of an Observer," 137, 250.

[44] Hugh Nibley, Letter to Miriam Reitz Baer, June 1987.

[45] Hugh Nibley, Open letter to "Mr. W.," 16 September 1965, emphasis Hugh's. This is his letter to Lorin Wheelright. See chap. 19.

Hugh has also consistently applied this rule to his own work. He has stated that his work "should be heard critically and stringently questioned. I, for one, welcome such criticism."[46] In 1979, Edward H. Ashment presented a paper at a Sunstone Symposium to which Hugh was supposed to respond. Ashment's presentation attempted to prove that some of Hugh's earlier conclusions about the Book of Abraham were not sound. Hugh's response at the time was agitated but mature: "I refuse to be held responsible for anything I wrote more than three years ago. . . . I would say about four-fifths of everything I put down has changed."[47]

Hugh has consistently downplayed the permanence of his own scholarly corpus: "What is worth saving will probably be saved, but that can't be very much and in this world it is vain to pin one's hopes on the survival of anything for long. What belongs to the eternities will not be lost; the rest does not interest me very much."[48]

One of Hugh's intellectual anchors, paradoxically, has been spiritual. His own abiding faith has been a counterbalance to assigning excessive importance to his own and his colleagues' contributions to scholarly discussion. He has consistently maintained that the serious nature of the gospel—the literal life-and-death claims of faith—makes the world of scholarship irretrievably trivial and insignificant by comparison. As Hugh wrote to Sterling McMurrin:

> I find for one thing that there are some things that I simply cannot take seriously and other things which I must take seriously even at the risk of giving offense to my more rational colleagues. It is surprising how many people have thought me to be merely spoofing—just having a little fun, like Joseph Smith when he got up the Book of Mormon. I wonder if they realize what a price one must pay for that kind of fun? I say to hell with careers and the things of the world, but if I thought there was the remotest possibility that this was my only life and my only world I would most assuredly NOT say it, and I would not throw away invitations to serious accomplishment for the sake of a monotonous series of pranks. . . . I am stuck with the gospel, I know perfectly well that it is true; there may be things about the Church that I find perfectly appalling—but that has nothing to do with it. I KNOW THE GOSPEL IS TRUE.[49]

This letter is significant. It is a private expression of profound faith, made to a respected but nonbelieving colleague, who, like Hugh, was a privileged and extremely bright scion of an old-time Mormon family and who, like Hugh, had a General Authority for a grandfather. If Hugh had any private doubts about the gospel, surely Sterling McMurrin would have been as safe to confide them to as Hugh's startlingly candid opinion about deficiencies in the Church. But instead, he insists, metaphorically at the top of his voice, in the truth of the gospel.

This point needs to be stressed. In Mormon terms, Hugh has a testimony. Some have speculated that Hugh is disingenuous—that he doesn't believe privately

---

[46] Hugh Nibley, Letter to Louise Wrathall, 15 October 1979.

[47] Hugh Nibley, "The Facsimiles of the Book of Abraham: A Response," *Sunstone* 4, nos. 5-6 (December 1979): 49.

[48] Hugh Nibley, Letter to David H. Mulholland, 26 June 1981.

[49] Hugh Nibley, Letter to Sterling McMurrin, 23 August 1967. For full text, see Appendix D.

what he writes publicly. Those who doubt Hugh's sincerity are frequently people who no longer accept the truth claims of the Church and express skepticism about Mormon theology. For example, Everett Cooley, archivist at the University of Utah library, once told Fawn Brodie that he had catalogued "some interesting correspondence of [Hugh's] with Sterling McMurrin. . . . Among other things, [Hugh] states that he can, does, and will argue any topic on either or both sides if need be."[50] My search of the McMurrin and Brodie papers has failed to find any letter from Hugh in which he makes anything even remotely close to this statement, nor does such a statement appear in the correspondence between Hugh and Sterling, copies of which are in my possession. Because there is no context in which to consider Cooley's comment, I can only say that Hugh was not known for arguing "either or both sides" of any issue—and certainly not where the gospel was concerned.

If Hugh was ever tempted by his own all-too-lively awareness of the human limitations of General Authorities, Church bureaucracy (including BYU's), or short-sighted ecclesiastical politics to seek comfort with the equally bruised, I found no evidence that he ever succumbed. On the contrary, he considered such comradeship to be yet another opportunity to bear his testimony. At some point before his 1955 debate with Sterling McMurrin, Hugh was invited to speak to a meeting at the University of Utah, of the "Swearing Elders"—a group of liberal Mormons associated with Utah universities.[51] After giving his presentation, Hugh says they took him aside and told him "You're among friends now, you can say what you really feel about the Book of Mormon." Hugh simply bore his testimony that the Book of Mormon is, in fact, a true record of an ancient people and that Joseph Smith was a prophet. "Oh, were they mad," Hugh states. "They were just boiling."[52] He recalls one member of the group launching into a harangue about the Book of Mormon and how "we have to get rid of it. It's driving the best minds out of the church! You can't see it, but with my training, I know it. Joseph Smith was a deceiver, but he was a sly deceiver." Hugh was chilled by such reactions: "They had a real active hatred of the Book of Mormon."[53] These were, for the most part, members of the Church in good standing. Today, such attitudes would place them at the fringes of the Church.

---

[50]Everett Cooley, Letter to Fawn Brodie, 31 August 1978, Fawn Brodie Papers, Special Collections, Marriott Library.

[51]For an overview of the group's activities, see Thomas A. Blakely, "The Swearing Elders: The Birth of the Mormon Intelligentsia," *Sunstone* 10, no. 9 (January 1986): 8-13; Richard D. Poll, "The Swearing Elders: Some Reflections," ibid., 14-17; and Sterling M. McMurrin and L. Jackson Newell, *Matters of Conscience: Conversations with Sterling M. McMurrin* (Salt Lake: Signature Books, 1996), 181-84. The group met between 1949 and 1955.

[52]Hugh Nibley, interviewed by Allison Clark, June 1996, photocopy of transcript in my possession. This incident does not appear in other accounts of the Swearing Elders, and perhaps Hugh is exaggerating their reaction or generalizing from several incidents. However, Hugh was listed as a speaker in several reminiscent histories of this group and has consistently identified O. C. Tanner to me as being the individual most upset at his defense of the Book of Mormon. Because McMurrin likewise did not accept the historicity of the Book of Mormon, it seems probable that several individuals in the group held similar views and were genuinely flabbergasted that Hugh, whose intellectual status was unquestionable, had such an orthodox view of the book. Phyllis remembers that Hugh told about this incident as soon as he reached home on the day it happened and was "visibly rattled" by the response his presentation had generated. Phyllis Nibley, conversation with Boyd Petersen, 8 April 2002.

[53]Ibid.

As another example, in the late 1940s, Hugh wrote a letter to Stanley S. Ivins, responding to his critique of Hugh's *No, Ma'am, That's Not History*, which in turn was a critique of Fawn Brodie's highly critical biography of Joseph Smith, *No Man Knows My History*. (See chap. 15.) With unmistakable impatience, Hugh challenged Ivins:

> What are you trying to do? If it is a heroic nonconformity you are after, why don't you champion some unpopular cause instead of whooping it up with the Big Boys Back East? If you feel that your career has been blighted and your talents ignored, why not drop a note to Time Magazine, hinting that you may soon be taking the Road to Rome—that will get you national attention over-night. Only you had better make up your mind, so that your bemused correspondents will know whether they are dealing with a Mormon, an honest nit-wit, or a Benedict Arnold.

In that same letter, Hugh characterized our current age as a time of "extreme emergency" where our assignment is to "warn the world of 'the calamity which should come upon the inhabitants of the earth.'" In such a context, Hugh warned, the "game of hair-splitting and sniping at the Prophet [is] not merely silly but downright criminal."[54]

In his 1955 debate with McMurrin, he took a similar tone: "We should stop playing this game of naughty boys behind the barn, smoking corn-silk and saying damn and hell to show how emancipated we are. It is much too easy to be a 'swearing elder': knowledge is not so cheaply bought."[55]

In a recent conversation with a Mormon historian in which I described this biography project, I was somewhat taken aback that his first question was, "What does Hugh *really* believe?" From the context, it was clear he was asking whether Hugh really had a testimony or whether he was just defending the Church. It is perhaps not a compliment to my questioner to wonder why he seemed to assume that Hugh would say one thing but believe another. Hugh Nibley, in point of fact, says exactly what he believes.

Over the past fourteen years, I have collected, studied, and archived Hugh's correspondence. Most of these letters are written to close personal friends and family. Many are written to non-Mormon friends. I can say without equivocation that there is no difference between the public and the private Hugh Nibley. Not only are his personal views consistent with his private views, but his stated views are consistent with the way he lives his life.

Beyond the issue of Hugh's personal faith is the issue of how it relates to his work. Some have taken the position that because Hugh's work is apologetics it cannot be taken seriously as scholarship. Elder Neal A. Maxwell brushes that argument aside: Hugh's "commitment is so visible and has been so pronounced and so repetitively stated that that's not even the issue. So shall we get on to what is Hugh saying?"[56] It seems improbable that any of Hugh's criticisms of Mormon culture would be heard if his commitment to the gospel were not so explicit and if his ability to put

---

[54] Hugh Nibley, Letter to Stanley Ivins, 3 June 1946, Stanley Snow Ivins Collection, Utah State Historical Society, Salt Lake City.

[55] "Do Religion and History Conflict?" in *Temple and Cosmos: Beyond This Ignorant Present*, Vol. 12 in *Collected Works of Hugh Nibley*, edited by Don E. Norton (Salt Lake City: Deseret Book/FARMS, 1992), 448.

his finger on weaknesses in living up to its lofty standards were not so uncannily accurate:

> I thought of resigning [from BYU] a number of times and discussed this matter with President Joseph Fielding Smith and Brother [Marion G.] Romney. They urged me to stay on. When I said I was bound to offend certain parties if I continued to speak too freely a number of General Authorities, including members of the First Presidency, assured me that they considered my dissenting opinions not only valuable but indispensable to maintaining a healthy academic climate in Provo.[57]

Furthermore, equating apologetics with bad scholarship overlooks the long-respected tradition of scholarly apologetic literature. Perhaps the clearest articulation of the strength of Hugh's approach comes from Carl Mosser and Paul Owen, two young non-Mormon scholars. In their article, published in Trinity Journal at Trinity Evangelical Divinity School in Deerfield, Illinois, they call Hugh

> the pioneer of LDS scholarship and apologetics. . . [who] has produced a seemingly endless stream of books and articles covering a vast array of subject matter. Whether writing on Patristics, the Dead Sea Scrolls, the Apocrypha, the culture of the Ancient Near East, or Mormonism, he demonstrates an impressive command of the original languages, primary texts, and secondary literature. . . . No doubt there are flaws in Nibley's work, but most counter-cultists [i.e., anti-Mormons] do not have the tools to demonstrate this. Few have tried. . . . Whatever flaws may exist in his methodology, Nibley is a scholar of high caliber.[58]

Others see Hugh as being driven by his conclusions to muster corroborating evidence. Hugh has been aware of such criticism, but he has never denied starting his research with a preconceived notion. In fact, he argues he has no other choice:

> An agonized cry goes up from the faculty: "How can you be so narrow, so biased, so prejudiced as to *begin* your researches by assuming that you already have the truth!" While in Berkeley I got a letter from a BYU professor who gave me to know that because I believe the Book of Mormon I am not really qualified to teach history, and who ended his harangue with the observation that while I claim to know the truth, the gentlemen of the History Department, like true scholars, claim only to be searching for it. A noble sentiment, truly, but a phony one—are they really searching? For one thing, they don't believe for a moment that the truth of the gospel *can* be found, and have only loud cries of rage and contempt for any who say they have found it—they are as sure that it doesn't exist as we are that it does; which is to say, our dedicated searchers for truth are dead sure that they have the answer already![59] As if to prove that they have no intention of pursuing serious investigations, these people have conspicuously neglected to prepare themselves for

---

[56] Neal A. Maxwell, "Faith of an Observer," 525.

[57] Hugh Nibley, Letter to David B. Rimington, 4 March 1980.

[58] Carl Mosser and Paul Owen, "Mormon Scholarship, Apologetics, and Evangelical Neglect: Losing the Battle and Not Knowing It?" Trinity Journal 19, no. 2 (Fall 1998): 179-205. Mosser holds master's degrees in theology, New Testament, and philosophy of religion from the Talbot School of Theology in La Miranda, California. Owen is a Ph.D. candidate at the University of Edinburgh, Scotland, studying New Testament languages, literature, and theology.

any but the most localized research; they are like a man setting out to explore a wonderful cavern without bothering to equip himself with either lights or ropes. We respect our local *Gelehrten* [savants, scholars] for that knowledge and proficiency which they have demonstrated to the world, but when they go out of bounds and attack the Church with specious learning they invite legitimate censure. They are like dentists who insist on performing delicate brain surgery, because that is more interesting than filing teeth. Nice for them—but what about their patients?[60]

If articulating an explicit belief and desiring to support it with corroborating evidence lacks intellectual rigor, then I agree that Hugh is guilty. However, I believe that he was simply, once again, in advance of his times. The postmodern movement, despite its many inadequacies, has thoroughly dismantled the assumption that one can be truly "objective," setting aside personal biases and perspective. In the past generation, readers have learned to regard with well-justified suspicion contemporary scholarship—both Mormon and non-Mormon—that feigns objectivity but reveals an unstated agenda between the lines. Hugh's explicitness about his own stance is a refreshing call to readers to understand and factor in his perspective in tackling the ideas and evidence he presents.

Hugh has also been accused of "parallelomania"—improperly citing parallels without regard to the date, provenance, or applicability of the documents. The latest writer to level this criticism against Hugh is Douglas F. Salmon. Although somewhat critical of lapses in Hugh's scholarship, Todd Compton has characterized those who dismiss Hugh with this charge as "shallow critics of Nibley who merely shout 'Parallelomania,' as if it were a magical incantation, and reject his whole methodology and corpus out of hand."[61] Nevertheless, in Hugh's preface to *Since Cumorah*, he has conceded that "the same evidence which convinces one expert may leave another completely unsatisfied." And he reminds us that no one can prove the Book of Mormon, or any other truth claim of the Gospel, with such parallels. "When, indeed, is a thing proven? Only when an individual has accumulated in his own conscience enough observations, impressions, reasonings, and feelings to satisfy him personally that it is so."[62]

---

[59] In Hugh's "Some Reasons for the Restored Gospel," 3, he expands this point further: "If there is anything that has been fully established in recent years it is that all scientists form their opinions and select and interpret their evidence on the basis of personal predilection and interpretation, no matter how loudly they may proclaim their dispassionate objectivity and devotion to total truth. This must be permitted since it cannot be avoided, and indeed is a useful procedure as long as all conclusions are regarded as tentative."

[60] Hugh Nibley, Letter to "Brother Bergen," 29 July 1960, 1. This ruthless nine-page appraisal of education, especially at BYU, was titled "Nobody to Blame." Hugh circulated it with a cover letter addressed to "Dear Brother" dated 3 August 1960. I have not found Bergen's letter that generated this response.

[61] Douglas F. Salmon, "Parallelomania and the Study of Latter-day Scripture: Confirmation, Coincidence, or the Collective Unconscious?" *Dialogue: A Journal of Mormon Thought* 33, no. 2 (Summer 2000): 129-56. Gerry L. Ensley responded to this article in a letter to the editor, "Non-Canonical Sources as Almost Conclusive Proof of LDS Religious Truth, Ancient Apostasy, and Joseph Smith's Divine Calling," *Dialogue: A Journal of Mormon Thought* 33, no. 3 (Winter 2000): v-viii. See also Todd Compton, "Review of *Lehi in the Desert, The World of the Jaredites, There Were Jaredites; An Approach to the Book of Mormon*; and *Since Cumorah*," *FARMS Review of Books on the Book of Mormon* 1 (1989): 115.

In short, for someone who has spent his entire life in scholarship, Hugh Nibley demonstrates a startling lack of enchantment with either its ends or means. He respects scholarship, enjoys it, and employs it well, but he is not enamored of it. Nor does he view the segment of American society that he knows best—higher education—through rose-tinted glasses. From graduate school to retirement, Hugh has seen American education as highly defective. While teaching at Claremont in 1942, he wrote: "Certainly I can never remain at ease in the stifling atmosphere of the American College, an institution which I hope with all my heart will go the way of the buffalo and the spittoon. It already survives only as a curio."[63] During World War II, he compared the modern education system with the literal mud at his military intelligence training camp: "Mud like manure has great possibilities, but of itself is simply loathsome. The same holds true of our educational system—a vast sluggish sea of uniform primordial ooze out of which we fondly expect marvelous trees of knowledge to emerge, even though we have already waited 50 years for a single butter-cup to appear."[64]

After attending a convention for the American History Association in the late 1940s, Hugh wrote: "The one solid comfort I get out of such conferences is the reassurance that if I am a fool there are bigger ones."[65] To Paul Springer in the late 1950s, Hugh lamented: "Scholarship in America is as dead as the dodo and has been for at least 30 years: go to their conventions if you don't believe they are a bunch of ineffectual zombies; they are simply marking time waiting for nothing to happen."[66]

Describing the depressing state of education at BYU, Hugh wrote to Klaus Baer in the early 1960s, "So we are not going anywhere, and I cultivate mon jardin [my garden] and say what the hell. For that matter I am not at all enthusiastic to go where the world is going just now."[67] And in another letter, he writes, "It is the same here as in Berkeley institution-wise—the University is part of a world that is passing away; the whole show is so unreal it gives you gooseflesh."[68] In 1987, he wrote impatiently: "Education: What a waste of time! It's sort of required to show that you have been under surveillance for a certain time."[69] Throughout the 1970s and 1980s, Hugh publicly reiterated these themes in speeches and essays like "Educating the Saints" (1970), "The Day of the Amateur" (1971), "Zeal Without Knowledge" (1975), "More Brigham Young on Education" (1976), "Goods of First and Second Intent" (1987), and, most forcefully, in "Leaders to Managers: The Fatal Shift" (1983).[70]

---

[62]Hugh Nibley, *Since Cumorah*, edited by John W. Welch (Salt Lake City: Deseret Book, 1967; reprinted (Salt Lake City: Deseret/FARMS, 1988), xiv.

[63]Hugh Nibley, Letter to Agnes Sloan Nibley, postmarked 14 February 1942.

[64]Hugh Nibley, Letter to Agnes Sloan Nibley, 13 April 1943.

[65]Hugh Nibley, Letter to Agnes Sloan Nibley and Alexander Nibley, 4 January 1948.

[66]Hugh Nibley, Letter to Paul Springer, 24 May 1958.

[67]Hugh Nibley, Letter to Klaus Baer, 1 June 1964.

[68]Hugh Nibley, Letter to Paul Springer, 12 December 1960.

[69]Hugh Nibley, Letter to "Pres. Smartt," 3 August 1987.

The games of the academy—placing credentials over production, image over substance, careerism over learning, eminence over truth, and pride over humility—have turned education into what Hugh referred to as "the clown of the professions." The ways of the academy are too much the ways of the world, while Hugh has been much more interested in the ways of God.

---

[70]Four of these essays appear in *Brother Brigham Challenges the Saints*, edited by Don E. Norton and Shirley S. Ricks, Vol. 13 in *The Collected Works of Hugh Nibley* (Salt Lake City: Deseret Books/FARMS, 1994): "Educating the Saints," pp. 306-45; "The Day of the Amateur," pp. 301-45; "More Brigham Young on Education," pp. 346-79; and "Leaders to Managers: The Fatal Shift," pp. 491-508. The other two are in *Approaching Zion*, edited by Don E. Norton, Vol. 9 of *The Collected Works of Hugh Nibley* (Salt Lake City: Deseret Book/FARMS, 1989): "Zeal Without Knowledge," pp. 63-84, and "Goods of First and Second Intent," pp. 524-53.

Hugh Nibley, U.S. Army, at Clearwater, Florida, in 1942 where he received basic training.

In high school I had won the Proficiency Medal as the best soldier in the ROTC. Now I was a master sergeant doing paper work in military intelligence at every level and keeping my eyes open. Mr. Tucker used to come down from Washington to Camp Ritchie with exciting news of what went on in High Places; for example, there was the fabulous Miss Crawford in the British War Office who knew every secret of the German Army; and in time behold it was I who ended up as Miss Crawford's assistant, she being a fussy red-headed spinster who got all her information from newspapers and magazines and kept all the clippings stirred up in a shoebox. That is how it is done. The army is correctly defined (by R. Heinlein) as "a permanent organization for the destruction of life and property."[1]

---

[1] Hugh Nibley, "Intellectual Autobiography," *Nibley on the Timely and the Timeless* (Provo, UT: BYU Religious Studies Center, 1978): xxiii-xxiv.

Chapter 12

Army "Intelligence," 1942-43

Despite any misgivings Hugh had about the conflict with Germany, he knew several years before World War II actually broke out that he would be in the conflict. "I can remember very clearly," states Hugh's brother Reid, "one day he had a huge steamer trunk which was filled with shoe boxes which contained his note cards, and he was going through this and either filing or setting them up somehow." Their mother asked Hugh what he was doing. He answered: "Oh, I'm just getting ready; I'll be going to war." Reid remembers that this was in 1938 or 1939, when most Americans were still resolved to stay out of this "European" conflict, "but he had sized that up pretty early."[2] While Hugh was not "a wild haired patriot," as Paul Springer puts it, "the idea of being drafted was very unpleasant to him." The mood in America was that going to war was at least a manly duty and at most a glorious adventure. "After Pearl Harbor you were a heel if you didn't want to. The expression was: Break the Nazi line and set the rising sun."[3]

So on 28 September 1942, Hugh Nibley was inducted into the U.S. Army at Fort MacArthur, which was situated on the coast just south of Los Angeles. Built in 1914 to defend the Los Angeles harbor, this emplacement was named after Lt. Gen. Arthur MacArthur, Civil War Medal of Honor winner, commanding general in the Philippines during the Spanish-American War, and father of General Douglas MacArthur, already well-known for his dramatic retreat in the Far East from the advancing Japanese and equally dramatic vow to return. The fort had served as a training center in World War I, was the center of all army activities in Southern California during the 1920s and 1930s, and became a chief induction center during World War II. The atmosphere at the fort when Hugh reported for conscription was electric. War anxiety was tangible throughout the nation, but particularly in Southern California where several enemy submarines had been sighted off the coast during the early months of 1942. Hundreds of men were being

---
[2]Reid Nibley, "Faith of an Observer," 479, compilation of interviews, ca. 1983-84 for a video documentary of the same name aired in 1985, photocopy of typescript in my possession, pagination added.
[3]Paul Springer, "Faith of an Observer," 495-96.

processed the same day as Hugh in a scene of confusion and haste, as a mass of additional tunnels were being constructed simultaneously to turn the base into an underground fortress. A year later new gun batteries were also erected along the seacoast.[4]

Induction is a dehumanizing process. The army wants to effect an immediate and absolute transition from man into soldier, from individual to platoon. As one of Hugh's fellow recruits at Fort MacArthur later wrote of his induction:

> We handed in our personal effects, our last physical link to civilian life, to be shipped back to relatives or friends. Our fears of failing the physical proved quite unfounded. With the Army in dire need of bodies, a vertical corpse pushed along the recruit line would have had a fair chance of passing. There was a psychological exam, but I should guess only a flagrant deviate would have flunked that. By early evening we had taken the oath and been supplied with a Service record and Form 20, detailing our biographical data and civilian qualifications. As enlisted wards of the Army we had been issued our new olive-drab uniforms and personal effects free of charge. We now were OD from the skin outward. This standardization, together with the new title of Private indiscriminately granted to all, should at least have inspired in us a feeling of esprit de corps. What keeps up morale under such circumstances is that everyone is in the same, shall we say, to reflect the general mental state of most, leaky ship.[5]

Additionally, that first day brought an initiation into the army mess hall chow line and training in making a bunk bed with blankets so tight that a dime would bounce to attention.[6]

On the second day at Fort MacArthur, all recruits were given the two-hour Army General Classification test, an IQ test that determined where each soldier would be placed within the various services. Soldiers who received high scores on the exam went into the Army Air Corps.[7] Not unsurprisingly, Hugh received a high score and was soon on the train to the Army Air Force's 586th Technical School Squadron at St. Petersburg, Florida.

In addition to Hugh's still-vivid memories of the war years, the best source about his experiences is his letters to his mother. Throughout the war, he wrote every two or three weeks, as circumstances allowed. When he had access to a typewriter, he used that; otherwise, his letters are handwritten. Most were written on regular stationery; however, after he arrived in Europe, about half used light-weight Army V-mail forms. Sloanie saved all of these letters, and Hugh must have acquired them on her death in 1959. I discovered them in a box in the Nibleys' garage. Unfortunately, I have not found any letters from Sloanie to Hugh. If Hugh wrote to his siblings, none of those letters have survived; but it seems more likely that they all wrote to Sloanie, who relayed the family news to each.

This correspondence begins with a short postcard Hugh wrote Sloanie from New Orleans on 5 October, describing the trip as "very leisurely and relaxing" and the South

---

[4]Fort MacArthur Museum Association, "A Brief History of Fort MacArthur," 1998; downloaded on 9 May 2001 from http://www.ftmac.org/Fmhist.htm.

[5]Max Oppenheimer Jr., *An Innocent Yank at Home Abroad: Footnotes to History, 1922-1945* (Manhattan, KS: Sunflower University Press, 2000), 135. Oppenheimer, who like Hugh would later train at Camp Ritchie and become a member of an Order of Battle (OB) team, was inducted at Fort MacArthur one month after Hugh on 24 October 1942.

[6]Ibid., 135.

[7]Ibid. 135-36.

as "sultry and picturesque."⁸ A few days later from the base, Hugh described the train trip as "by all odds the pleasantest journey I ever made" and joked about his first encounters with Southerners: "The Southern mind and the Southern soul are yours for the asking—anyone who can count up to 4 or spell two out of ten common words is a damn Yankee."⁹ The relaxed atmosphere continued at St. Petersburg, even though "the last few days have been nothing but a round of tests, from which no results are as yet available. Easy and pleasant." Hugh added, "I find myself rather surprisingly in a non-combatant branch of the air-force, but one which promises to be anything but unexciting. More time than ever for study—It looks as if I would at last have a pretext for devoting more time to mathematics." Hugh would indeed have time to study mathematics, a much-loved but neglected subject; but he would also see plenty of combat.

By 13 October, Hugh had been transferred again, this time to the 413th Technical School Squadron twenty miles to the north at Clearwater, Florida. There he lived in the elegant Bellevue Hotel, which the army had purchased and converted into a barracks. Hugh described the hotel to his mother as "very deluxe—set in a wilderness of lagoons and islands, it is indescribably lovely and restful." He had "a deluxe cottage on the lagoon" which he shared with a single roommate, "and with the original hotel beds." Furthermore, even though gripes about chow practically came with the army uniform, Hugh had no complaints: "The food is as elegant as the surroundings."¹⁰

The scores from the St. Petersburg tests were sufficiently high that Hugh was told he could choose any technical school in the air force. He selected weather observer school, primarily because it would give him the best opportunity to study math. "Since I must be a scientist for a while, I am gobbling up mathematics in an ecstacy of zeal—it is a long pent-up appetite which I had almost despaired of ever satisfying. It is heavenly stuff, but I can see now that I really took the wiser course. Languages, especially ancient . . . must be learned over decades—they grow organically and never reach fullness. Science, on the other hand has its limits for all but a few geniuses." Yet because of his on-going interest in languages, Hugh also applied for intelligence school, and reported in the same letter: "My application with the Intelligence is still cooking—they are all satisfactorily impressed. I may get a whack at the Near [Middle] East before you think." Meanwhile, a grueling course of basic training lay ahead, but Hugh's attitude was quite optimistic. "Very jolly and picturesque amid these tropic lagoons with their odd fishes and fowl and stunning exuberance of vegetation." He ended his letter by reassuring his mother somewhat callously that she need not bother to write—"letters in fact are a distinct nuisance."¹¹

Basic training, which was supposed to take twenty-one days, consisted of doing plenty of calisthenics, running obstacle courses, learning to march in field and parade formation, and performing close-order drills with and without rifles. There was also KP duty and guard duty.¹² And while basic training was quite likely much more strenuous than Hugh divulged in his off-handed letters to his mother, his experience was likely less strenuous than some. After all, he was in a unit with educated men training to become air force

---

⁸Hugh Nibley, postcard to Agnes Sloan Nibley, 5 October 1942.

⁹Hugh Nibley, Letter to Agnes Sloan Nibley, postmarked 9 October 1942.

¹⁰Hugh Nibley, Letter to Agnes Sloan Nibley, 17 October 1942.

¹¹Hugh Nibley, Letter to Agnes Sloan Nibley, postmarked 13 October 1942.

¹²Oppenheimer, *An Innocent Yank at Home Abroad*, 136.

technicians, rather than paratroopers. "Lawyers and artists and journalists are thought to have brains (and God knows it does take a modicum of skill for most of them to give that impression) and so they are put in the air force," he wrote. There, "they are banded together in a common band of technical ignorance and worldly wisdom which makes their society the most delightful in the world." Hugh summed up his experience at Clearwater as "pleasant company in a pleasanter setting" and concluded, "So far I have had nothing but fun in the army."[13]

Soon the army evidently began taking advantage of Hugh's language ability. "My business here, and perhaps elsewhere, will be teaching languages," Hugh wrote his mother. Apparently he was teaching French because he asked her to send along one of his French language books, lamenting: "Before I get through I will need a trailer for my library, but the books are really necessary." Hugh added with innocent arrogance: "Clearwater enjoys the presence of quite a lot of really good noodles. The dumb soldier is still a reality, but a cultivated minority can have its way every time."[14]

Almost three weeks later, Hugh wrote to his mother that conditions at Clearwater remained the same. "The food is good and sleep is abundant; I have put on 7 lbs. and never get tired—there is no excuse for weariness in such pleasant weather. Since the first week, life has been strenuous but easy—our problems are purely physical—much running about and shouting and tampering with gadgets ancient and modern."[15] In a letter a week later, he added breezily, "Our training is not considered easy even by good standards, and yet I am always fresh as a daisy."[16] In fact, many of Hugh's letters from Clearwater could come more appropriately from a vacation resort than an army base: "Getting lots of sun, rest, swimming, and whatnot."[17]

By 13 November, basic training was finished, and most of Hugh's cohort left for their assigned technical schools, but "weather-men will be the last to go," which meant that "all the work around the place has to be done by the same small and devoted group." Hugh now had "more free moments than ever before," he reported to his mother and planned "to study Russian for all I'm worth." But even while he was writing, word came that all of the men assigned to weather school would be shipped out—except for him. "This means very probably that I am no longer a weather bird," he speculated.[18] It would be another month before he was transferred, but Hugh would in fact go to weather school.

Hugh later recalled that he had spent Thanksgiving eve at Clearwater "scrubbing these latrines out with a big scrubbing brush." An officer came up and ordered him to

---

[13] Hugh Nibley, Letter to Agnes Sloan Nibley, 17 October 1942.

[14] Hugh Nibley, Letter to Agnes Sloan Nibley, n.d., ca. October 1942.

[15] Hugh Nibley, Letter to Agnes Sloan Nibley, postmarked 6 November 1942.

[16] Hugh Nibley, Letter to Agnes Sloan Nibley, 13 November 1942. Several weeks later, Hugh gave a similar report to his grandmother: "While one commonly hears that complaint of long and tedious hours, I must confess I have never had so much free time, nor used it so profitably. Nine weeks in Florida have been a carnival—all the strains and shocks of training have been nothing but fun." Hugh Nibley, Letter to Margaret Violet Reid Sloan, 5 December 1942.

[17] Hugh Nibley, Letter to Agnes Sloan Nibley, n.d., ca. December 1942.

[18] Hugh Nibley, Letter to Agnes Sloan Nibley, 13 November 1942. Hugh wrote 1943 as the date, but the context makes it clear that this letter was written in 1942.

"come with me, and bring the brush," then took him to the officers' mess hall and ordered him to clean a huge pile of celery. "With this brush?" demanded Hugh, appalled. "I just used it for cleaning toilets." The officer didn't want to hear any excuses. Hugh metaphorically shrugged: "So there I was cleaning the celery for the officers the next day for their Thanksgiving dinner with a toilet brush. That's so typically Army. I mean, it is marvelous."[19]

Now almost finished with his second month, Hugh was showing new soldiers the ropes. "Things had just begun to get easy here, what with little me being put in charge of various groups of new and eager soldateska, but as this is only a post for basic training there is no point to hanging around any longer," he reported to his mother on 11 December 1942, the day that he received word he was being "shipped alone—not with any group"—for almost three months of weather observer school at Chanute Field, near Chicago. Hugh was glad to be moving on, even if he was surprised to still be in weather school.[20]

In appraising his stay at Clearwater, Hugh was most pleased with the time he had spent honing his math skills. "We have become quite the little mathematician," he boasted in a letter home, "and work great big problems sometimes passing within view, almost, of the right answer."[21] He had also greatly enjoyed Florida's lush flora and was awed by its unique fauna. In the same letter in which he reported his new assignment, Hugh told his mother about an encounter with a rattlesnake that "for size and brilliance could pass for a python" and then how, that very same day while he was "bumping merrily down a swamp road on a bicycle," he "collided with 'Old Joe' the alligator." Hugh boasted that he was "the only one around here who has been able to get at all intimate with Joseph—alligators are quite shy and very quick—they move like jack-rabbits when they are making for the water." Hugh groped for words in trying to express "the presence of growing and living nature"; rather than filling him with a desire to dominate or exploit it, he instead felt his soul opening to "a feeling of acceptance and love of whatever is."[22]

Despite the absolute contrast between Florida and Illinois in December, Hugh described the weather in the "bleak and vigorous North" as "gorgeous"—"very icy and windy and grey, with bare trees and bleak expanses of perfectly flat white plains." The base, too, was much different from Clearwater's Bellevue Hotel. "This place is vast; such an endless expanse of very 'technical' looking buildings and such seething masses of uniforms of every type and denomination—all very 'World of Tomorrowish,'" wrote Hugh.[23] But a weatherman's duties struck him as arcane. "Among other things we have to learn endless lists of code symbols and code numbers, and rattle them off in minute and complex diagrams of infinite diversity and confusion," reported Hugh. "Some of the codes are so ingenious that they can be learned with almost no effort at all, and the others I would find exceedingly easy if only they weren't such an intolerable bore! That is,

---

[19] Hugh Nibley, "Faith of an Observer," 141-42.
[20] Hugh Nibley, Letter to Agnes Sloan Nibley, 11 December 1942.
[21] Hugh Nibley, Letter to Agnes Sloan Nibley, 18 December 1942.
[22] Hugh Nibley, Letter to Agnes Sloan Nibley, 11 December 1942.
[23] Hugh Nibley, Letter to Agnes Sloan Nibley, 18 December 1942.

they have no deeper meaning. There is no 'so what' to all this clerical clap-trap; and that, I fear, is what work is becoming in most fields."[24]

Worse, "for once in the army I have no spare time at all," lamented Hugh. Describing the army as divided between those who think "effective fighting is what counts" and those who are more interested in "shiny buttons and snappy salutes," Hugh found both attitudes at Chanute in equal numbers. "Everyone must be a full-time technician and at the same time a full-time grenadier," he groused.[25]

In his final letter written from Chanute Field, Hugh described his routine: "Six days a week it is up at four a.m.—which I never find at all unpleasant—and then very high pressure classes till three in the afternoon, after which an hour of calisthenics and a brisk cross-country run. Then scrub the barracks and try to get ready for two or three examinations the following day. . . . Life is busy and merry and absurd." Hugh also reported that when he got a rare day pass, he spent it doing research at the library of the University of Illinois at Urbana. He also mentioned that he had applied "to my surprise" for both Intelligence and Officers Candidate School. "Both of these are pure punishment as far as work is concerned, but so far I thrive under all pressure that has been brought to bear. I do not relish the idea of being an officer, but it would certainly be an improvement on the fussy, complex, ultra-accurate triflings of the weather school."[26]

On 2 March 1943, Hugh graduated and received his diploma as an Army Weather Observer.[27] One week later he was transferred to the 99th Air Base Squadron at Godman Field, near Fort Knox, Kentucky. Godman had only six weather observers instead of Chanute's forty-six, "but there is quite as much weather," wrote Hugh. "A steady stream of reports and charts must pour out twenty-four hours a day, which means going like mad in twelve-hour shifts. What makes things merry is that the traffic is heavy and the weather is vile." Once more, he found "the best men in the army—mostly older men with something like a monopoly on brains," wrote Hugh. "The most remarkable thing about the weather men is the high tone of their discourse. Anything like vulgarity of language (unless of course it is clever vulgarity) is strictly out." Hugh also noted that weather observers, because they were "rabid—often picturesque—individualists," were "regarded as a lot of crackpots and given wide lee-way" in the army. Slyly, he added, "It is very profitable for us to encourage this attitude, as it allows us liberties and privileges unknown to the rest of the army."[28]

Hugh noted that upon arrival at Godman Field, the commanding officer could not understand how Hugh ended up a weather man instead of an officer. "It is the same story here as at every other base—the minute my papers arrive everyone wonders how on earth I ever got into this mess. Just as at St. Petersburg and Chanute Field, the commanding officer is much interested in changing my status, but in this case I really think something will come of it."[29] By the end of the month, however, Hugh reported that "the

---

[24]Hugh Nibley, Letter to Agnes Sloan Nibley, 25 January 1943.

[25]Hugh Nibley, Letter to Agnes Sloan Nibley, n.d., postmarked 18 February 1943.

[26]Hugh Nibley, Letter to Agnes Sloan Nibley, n.d., postmarked 2 March 1943.

[27]U.S. Army Air Forces Technical School, Diploma awarded to Private Hugh Nibley for "satisfactorily complet[ing] the course for Weather Observers" at Chanute Field, Illinois, 2 March 1943.

[28]Hugh Nibley, Letter to Agnes Sloan Nibley, 8 March 1943.

[29]Ibid.

colonel yesterday told me they have 'done what they could' here about my commission—the rest is up to Washington, which, of course, will do nothing at all about it. So that's that."[30]

In that same letter, Hugh teased his mother for including a description of California weather: "By the way, this is a weather office, which means that at every hour of the day we get complete reports on the weather in every inch of the country. I know exactly the condition of air, sky, soil, wind, water, tide, and what-not in Southern California and any time I want to. Let me commend you on the accuracy of your reports." This letter was interrupted by a phone call giving him new orders. "Hey! The phone for me—very confidential—it seems (tho you mustn't breathe a word) that I am quitting weather sometime next week and going into intelligence."[31] His commanding officer at Godman assured him, "You'll be a major tomorrow, my boy," and he wrote his mother that the transfer to intelligence "means I will be an officer."[32] It was a turning point, not only in Hugh's military activities, but for his career.

On the train to the Military Intelligence Training Center at Camp Ritchie in western Maryland, Hugh scribbled that he was "writing in great haste from Cincinnati, never knowing but what every syllable from now on will be censored without mercy" and joked "thanks for the c-n-d-y."[33] Despite his mockery of this elite and secret world, he probably had an overinflated vision of his future. Military Intelligence training was new to the army, and no one in or out of the army really knew what it involved.[34]

Despite the fact that Ritchie was supposed to be a secret army installation, all of the local Marylanders openly referred to it as the "Spy Camp," perhaps because the main entrance was marked: "Military Intelligence Training Center." In fact, Camp Ritchie was listed in the Hagarstown, Maryland, telephone directory.[35] Nevertheless, a cloak of censorship enveloped the internal workings of the camp. "I can't tell you anything about this place," Hugh declared to his mother. "It's just mud and the army." To further burst his bubble, no commission awaited Hugh. He was still a private. And to top it off, he was immediately sent to the hospital with bronchitis—"a mere trifle for which I am being allowed to rest my head off," complained Hugh in mid-April. "Once the army gets you

---

[30]Hugh Nibley, Letter to Agnes Sloan Nibley, postmarked 30 March 1943.

[31]Ibid. Retelling this story forty years later, Hugh confused the order of events slightly. In 1984, Hugh stated that one night while he was on duty at Godman, "some officer took off and flew into Bear Mountain. He was drunk. He smashed up his plane and got himself smashed up or killed, I don't remember which. I think it was killed. So at three o'clock in the morning I get this call and I thought, 'Oh boy, this is it. Court martial at least.' But it wasn't that at all. A letter had come from Camp Ritchie . . . —a five-star notice because they found that I had studied Arabic and spoke German and things like that. And I was to be transferred to Camp Ritchie immediately." Nibley, "Faith of an Observer," 142. However, his letter written when he learned about the transfer makes it clear that he learned about the transfer before the plane went down: "There! we get a flash notice at this very moment. One [officer] has just cracked up a P-38," Hugh wrote after announcing his transfer. He likely worried that someone would blame him for the crash since he was on duty at the time.

[32]Hugh Nibley, "Faith of an Observer," 142; Hugh Nibley, Letter to Agnes Sloan Nibley, 30 March 1943.

[33]Hugh Nibley, Letter to Agnes Sloan Nibley, 1 April 1943.

[34]Oppenheimer, *An Innocent Yank at Home Abroad*, 147.

[35]Ibid., 147-48; George R. Allen, *To Bastogne for the Christmas Holidays* (N.p., 1944), 4.

in a hospital you have to be violently healthy before they even smile at the thought of letting you out."[36]

Cradled in the Catoctin Mountain Range near the Maryland-Pennsylvania border, Camp Ritchie was remote, picturesque, and rugged. During the early twentieth century, the area had been a fashionable summer resort for wealthy families from Philadelphia, Baltimore, and Washington, D.C. The base itself was built in 1926 as the 638-acre summer training camp for the Maryland Army National Guard. When the United States entered World War II, the army leased it from Maryland and converted it into a year-round training base for intelligence personnel in language proficiency and intelligence gathering and analysis. At a cost of $5 million, 165 buildings were built, including classrooms, theater, chapel, headquarters, and barracks to house 3,000 men. During the war, 10,000 men graduated from its intelligence training program.[37]

The bizarre ambiance of Ritchie was not lost on the appreciative Hugh. "A more strange and wonderful assortment of people never gathered than the gang at this almost too-too dramatic place. A combination of a Tibetan monastery and Noah's ark it is, with Grand Hotel and the Magic Mountain quite out of the running."[38] Despite the concentration of language experts, typically no one knew exactly how they would be used by or integrated into the army. Another Camp Ritchie alumnus, George Bailey, later wrote that the camp "harbored every conceivable—and in some cases inconceivable—kind of immigrant: there were barracks housing Russians, Greeks, French, Italians, Spanish, Indians (American and Hindu), Icelanders, Laplanders, Mexicans, Albanians, Ruthenians, Macedonians, Slovenians, Wends, Hungarians, Welsh, Algerians, Syrians, Montenegrins, Ceylonese, Eskimos, Tunisians, Turks, Georgians, Azerbaijani, Uzbeks, Chuvash, Cossacks, Kozakhs, Mongolians, Basques—to name but a few."[39] Bailey described the base as resembling "the Tower of Babel after construction had been discontinued" and said it was common at the base to hear "an Icelander reciting a saga in Old Norse over a strawberry milkshake" or "passages from the Upanishad in the original Sanskrit" recited by "GIs refreshing themselves after a field exercise." Some GIs frequented the PX to test their ability to identify the many languages spoken there. To baffle such people, several soldiers devel-

---

[36] Hugh Nibley, Letter to Agnes Sloan Nibley, 13 April 1943.

[37] "Fort Ritchie Background," Military District of Washington Home Page, August 2000. Downloaded 14 May 2001 from http://www.mdw.army.mil/fs-i12.htm.

[38] Hugh Nibley, Letter to Agnes Sloan Nibley, n.d., postmarked 5 August 1943. *Grand Hotel* (*Menschen Im Hotel* or *People in a Hotel*, 1929) is a novel written by Vickie Baum, a Jewish-Austrian popular novelist. The book was a literary sensation in Germany and became best known in America after Hollywood turned it into an Oscar-winning film in 1932 under the same title, starring Greta Garbo, Joan Crawford, Wallace Beery, and Lionel Barrymore. The novel is set in the lavish Grand Hotel in Berlin, a place described as "Always the same. People come, people go. Nothing ever happens." That statement is proved false as a ballerina, a dying man, a jewel thief, a businessman, and a stenographer pass through the elegant setting in one weekend. *Magic Mountain* (1924; translated 1927) is Thomas Mann's novel about a young man from the bourgeoisie who visits his cousin in a mountain sanitarium where he "falls ill" and struggles with the opposing forces of rationalism, faith, aestheticism, and common sense embodied by the other patients. The novel ends with the protagonist rushing into World War I. Throughout, Mann examines the psychological proclivities of Europe prior to World War I.

[39] George Bailey, *Germans: The Biography of an Obsession* (New York: Times Mirror, 1972), 15-16.

oped an artificial language with a vocabulary of 200 words which they dubbed "Upmanshipad."[40]

Not only were the soldiers at Ritchie multilingual, they were also highly educated, a veritable "hodgepodge of European intellectuals."[41] Writers and poets, musicians and choreographers, dancers and singers, directors and stage producers, psychiatrists and psychologists, professors and engineers, sportsmen and playboys were all to be found among the ranks at Ritchie. While famous people like writer Stefan Heym and Thomas Mann's son Klaus were at Ritchie, "this didn't prevent them from having a Ukranian bartender from the lower East side," remembers Lucien Goldschmidt, a native of Brussels, Belgium, who was educated at the Collège Royal Français in Berlin. Lucien, who became a good friend to Hugh, worked for a rare-book dealer named Pierre Berès in Paris and, at age twenty-five, came to New York in 1937 to open a branch of this bookstore.[42] When a commanding officer noticed a soldier reading a book "with words as long as the page," he demanded skeptically, "Can you read that?" to which the soldier replied, "I wrote it."[43] "There were famous men from Germany and all over," remembers Hugh. "That was a wonderful atmosphere to be in."[44]

Yet even at Ritchie, where multiglots and intellectuals were abundant, Hugh stood out. In his book, Bailey noted that Hugh "spoke sixteen languages tolerably well" and had a "nodding linguistic acquaintanceship [which] included twice that number."[45] The most common language of all at Ritchie was German. Many German refugees, most Jewish, had been sent to Ritchie. And for German speakers, training centered on German intelligence.

One of Hugh's first assignments after being released from the hospital was almost as silly as the celery-cleaning episode. When it was discovered that he knew shorthand, he was recruited by "some weasel-faced officer" who was under orders from Colonel Charles Banfill, the commanding officer of Ritchie, to crawl underneath the officers' club and tap the phone lines. The officer enlisted Hugh to take notes of the conversations. Colonel Banfill was "bucking for a star," remembers Hugh. He wanted to know any criticisms his officers might have, so he ordered the weasel-face to listen in on the other officers' conversations and "take down everything that was spoken by the officers over the officers' telephone booth." "That is how he trusted the officers there," stated Hugh sardonically.[46]

Training at Ritchie was intense, but Hugh was up to the challenge. "This is another high-pressure camp like Chanute," wrote Hugh after a month.[47] The training was "in some ways like weather, but in every way more sinister and more challenging. . . . I have been in a very fever of mental activity since my second week in the army. Who could have dreamed of such a strange shape of things—escape from a too-studious to a far more stu-

---

[40] Ibid., 17-18.
[41] Ibid., 16.
[42] In *New York Times*, 18 December 1992; *New York Times Biographical Service* 23 (December 1992): 1626; Lucien Goldschmidt, "Faith of an Observer," 414.
[43] Bailey, *Germans*, 16.
[44] Hugh Nibley, "Faith of an Observer," 143.
[45] Ibid., 18.
[46] Ibid., 143.
[47] Hugh Nibley, Letter to Agnes Sloan Nibley, postmarked 28 April 1943.

dious life!"[48] The main course of study at Ritchie was Interrogation of Prisoners of War (IPW), an eight-week course in interrogation techniques, German and Italian army organization, military terms, and uniform identification, along with basic instruction in map orienteering, Morse code, and related subjects. Hugh remembers spending a lot of time translating "fascinating" German documents from World War I.[49] Several times during the course, on moonless nights the men would be loaded into the backs of tarp-covered two-and-a-half-ton trucks, driven six to twelve miles into the surrounding countryside, and dropped off. The men would be given a map in a foreign language with only a rendezvous point circled. If they did not make it to the rendezvous by midnight, the trucks would leave, and the soldiers would have to find their own way back to the base.[50]

To test their skills in interrogation, the men role-played with a group of fluent German speakers who would dress in German uniforms and pretend to be freshly captured German soldiers. Trained to act like the various types of German soldier an interrogator was likely to encounter in Europe, each one responded to different approaches. Some would immediately spill their guts, others would have to be browbeaten, and still others would respond to a legalistic reinterpretation of their military oath. Lucien Goldschmidt remembers, too, that a contingent of Native Americans once arrived at the camp dressed as German soldiers, evidently under some strange army rationale that, like Germans, they were different. Dressed in full German uniforms, they would goose-step around the camp in formation. Other "Germans" were Americans dressed in German uniforms; still others were Germans cooperating with the U.S. Army. Having "German troops" parading around the base not only added authenticity to the training, but also gave the men the opportunity to test their knowledge of German rank and branch insignia. "We would be asked to identify what weapons they had, what units they might represent, whether they had given any secrets away by passing through that forest," remembered Lucien Goldschmidt.[51] These "Germans" were so much a part of life at Ritchie, commented George Bailey ironically, that some believed that the best way a German spy could infiltrate the camp undetected would be to "march through the main gate wearing the standard uniform of the German *Wehrmacht* with full field pack and armed to the teeth."[52]

Ritchie did not follow a five-day work week. Instead, school ran seven days a week, after which the men were given a free day. They also got periodic furloughs. While most men caught a train for the bars and brothels of Philadelphia, New York, Baltimore, or Washington, D.C., Hugh spent his free days and furloughs wandering through the countryside alone. "I have walked a good deal through the Blue Mountains and the plains just below, which include the [battle] field of Gettysburg," Hugh told his mother. In the same letter, he described the beauty of the rugged landscape, the "rich farmland" of the

---

[48]Hugh Nibley, Letter to Agnes Sloan Nibley, 3 June 1943.

[49]Hugh Nibley, *Teachings of the Book of Mormon: Transcripts of Lectures Presented to an Honors Book of Mormon Class at Brigham Young University, 1989-90* (Provo, UT: FARMS, n.d.): Semester 2, Lecture 32, 10.

[50]Leonard J. Nevis, "Orienteering," letter to editor, Smithsonian, August 1992, 15; Oppenheimer, *An Innocent Yank at Home Abroad*, 154.

[51]Lucien Goldschmidt, "Faith of an Observer," 409.

[52]Bailey, *Germans*, 19-20.

Pennsylvania Dutch and their "quaint old houses."[53] When he did go to the big cities, Hugh spent his time in the library. "The Enoch Pratt Library in Baltimore beats the Library of Congress," Hugh wrote his mother after one excursion to this large public library.[54] Hugh also visited the Metropolitan Museum in New York to view the Egyptian collections. "The Egyptians are so different from every other ancient people that one hardly knows what to make of them," wrote Hugh. "They had one abiding passion—to conquer time and nullify its power."[55] There is no question that Hugh consciously used these excursions into nature and culture as he used his reading—to construct reminders of an alternate, saner reality than the "darkness and craziness" that had assaulted him "since I entered the hall of crooked mirrors we call Intelligence."[56]

Just as at the other army bases, Hugh was quite impressed by the calibre of men at Ritchie. "The powers of evil in our midst," wrote Hugh:

> . . . are more than matched by a very real and tangible influence for good, expressed in the persons of a perfectly astonishing number of really honest men. This I must say is less noticeable at Ritchie than any where else I have been. Here we have the latest shipment from Continental Europe—a bad and shop worn lot, for the most part—brash, ill-mannered men, quick to exploit every situation for personal gain. Yet among them are a few a little lower than the angels.[57]

The men Hugh admired most shared their admiration for him, and their portraits of Hugh the soldier are consistent with the Hugh of today. Also at Ritchie was Max Oppenheimer, a professor of foreign languages at SUNY, Fredonia, and military consultant to the CIA. He grew up in Germany and Paris but lived mostly in New York after the war. He described Hugh as "a very scholarly and dedicated Mormon" and "a good man!" who was "never seen without a book in his hands. Waiting in line for chow, on the road, during breaks, no matter what the occasion, he was always oblivious to the world around him, absorbed in his reading."[58] Lucien Goldschmidt noticed early on that Hugh was not among the men who told dirty jokes, that he traded the coffee served in the mess hall for powdered lemonade, and that he carried around the Koran in Arabic and Thucydides in Greek.[59]

Goldschmidt also remembered the rather ludicrous episode when he first became aware of Hugh's "depth of knowledge." During a map-reading exercise using an Arabic map, a hapless Lieutenant Church asked Hugh to define the Arabic word *wadi*. "All Lieutenant Church undoubtedly wanted was for him to say 'it's a stream that's dry much of the year, and then other times there is a riverlette or a river,' but once launched, [Hugh] began to say that . . . one had to understand it properly, that the root indicated that it really meant to be with one foot on the dry land and with one foot in the water, and this had,

---

[53]Hugh Nibley, Letter to Agnes Sloan Nibley, postmarked 28 April 1943.

[54]Hugh Nibley, Letter to Agnes Sloan Nibley, 26 June 1943.

[55]Hugh Nibley, Letter to Margaret Violet Sloan, n.d., ca. June 1943.

[56]Hugh Nibley, Letter to Agnes Sloan Nibley, 3 June 1943.

[57]Ibid.

[58]Oppenheimer, *An Innocent Yank at Home Abroad*, 248.

[59]Goldschmidt, "Faith of an Observer," 410.

historically the following explanation, and Lieutenant Church got increasingly concerned about the scholar delivering a lecture when all he had wanted obviously was a simple answer." Lucien concluded: "You could see that if challenged [Hugh] would rise to the occasion."[60]

On 2 June 1943, Hugh completed the "the Seventh Course" of IPW training at Ritchie. The following day he wrote his mother: "For the next week or so [I] must be engrossed in a series of problems to decide whether I am a total loss or whether perchance some of my more appealing qualities may be salvaged for military purposes." Hugh continued, his tone more sober than usual: "Hope for the best, but never try to decide what the 'best' may be. . . . Expect no lucid communications for a time yet."[61]

On 12 June, Hugh received his diploma.[62] He had over two months between graduation and his next assignment. He spent the time relaxing on the base and visiting New York with Lucien Goldschmidt. "We have a lake in the camp (an old resort) and I swim almost every day," wrote Hugh. "My spare time is all spent in New York, where I know quite a number of people including a young lady of indescribable perfection, of whom you will hear more later."[63] This woman was Anahid Iskian, a young Armenian employed in Goldschmidt's bookstore. Goldschmidt returned to the city as often as he could to check on the store. Hugh would tag along, at first to browse among the books but soon to spend time with Anahid.

By August, he was writing to his mother: "I am working hard on the New York Deal, which I regard as a Sure Thing, though Rome was not built in a day." His mother was obviously pestering him for more information, but Hugh put her off: "I hesitate to describe the many perfections of the lady-love until I can be sure of success. She is quite a miracle—almost too much to hope for."[64] Perhaps even on the same day, Hugh wrote to Lucien, who had been shipped off to Italy, that he had undergone "a long and dazzling series of rebuffs" from Anahid. "I have made a couple more trips to New York, but get exactly nowhere with your Able Armenian Assistant," Hugh lamented.[65] But within the month, Hugh stated confidently to his grandmother: "I am getting married very soon."[66]

Hugh evidently felt a great deal of conflict about becoming an interrogator. As Hugh's friend Lucien Goldschmidt stated, "The idea of pressing others, soldiers, who were under orders not to reveal information and to press them to reveal it seemed morally unpleasant to him."[67] Soon he would be given an out. On the outskirts of camp, a small, obscure building was being used by a colonel, a major, and a tech-sergeant for some mysterious training. Rumors were spreading about the super-secret instruction when, on 25 August 1943, Hugh along with seventeen officers and enlisted men, was enrolled in the second Order of Battle (OB) course offered by the U.S. Army. A civilian ana-

---

[60]Ibid., 414.
[61]Hugh Nibley, Letter to Agnes Sloan Nibley, 3 June 1943.
[62]War Department, Military Intelligence Training Center, Camp Ritchie, Maryland, 12 June 1943, graduation of Pvt. Hugh Nibley, from the Seventh Course, by order of Colonel Banfill, Hugh Nibley Papers.
[63]Hugh Nibley, Letter to Agnes Sloan Nibley, 26 June 1943.
[64]Hugh Nibley, Letter to Agnes Sloan Nibley, postmarked 5 August 1943.
[65]Hugh Nibley, Letter to Lucien Goldschmidt, 4 August 1943.
[66]Hugh Nibley, Letter to Margaret Violet Sloan, n.d., ca. August 1943.
[67]Goldschmidt, "Faith of an Observer," 410.

lyst at the Pentagon, Mr. Tucker (no one seems to remember his first name) had come up with the idea of OB training and had written a "little red book" which contained detailed information about all units, commanding officers, weapons, and positions of the German and Italian military. All OB students were to memorize the book.[68] Hugh's superior memory and aggressive ambition to "be at the head of the class," as he put it, had already made "overkill in preparation for examinations" his *modus operandi*. So when faced with the challenge of memorizing lists of German military units, Hugh poured it on. "I was the head for the first four or five times, my name was right at the head of the list; I was the best of all in recalling all these numbers." After he proved to himself and everyone else that he could do it, Hugh lost interest. It was silly to try to remember details that would change so quickly, especially when the point of doing so seemed terminally obscure. Hugh shrugged, "'What the hell,' and let it all go." But by then he had proved his worth to the army.[69]

Additionally, OB students received detailed lectures on German strategy, tactics, military documents, personnel records, and Karl von Clausewitz's theories on war.[70] On several occasions Tucker lectured at Ritchie and at least once the class visited Tucker's office in the Pentagon.[71] Hugh remembers that during these briefings, Tucker often mentioned a woman named Miss Crawford in the British War Office. "She knew more about the war than anybody in existence," Hugh remembers Tucker saying. "We heard a lot about the mysterious Miss Crawford." Soon Hugh would meet the mysterious Miss Crawford.

It was likely after the visit to the Pentagon that Hugh dropped by the Senate Office Building and listened to a hearing before an unspecified committee, where, to his shock, "the whole time was spent in an eager discussion of the next war!"[72]

Some time after beginning the four-week OB course, Hugh wrote to his grandmother, apologizing elaborately for his negligence in letter writing: "For the past months I have been engaged in work of so confidential a nature as to make any kind of a communication about myself an object of suspicion to my superiors." Although he could not reveal much about his studies, Hugh announced in sardonically stilted prose: "The peculiar nature of my own activities shows me much more of the actual workings of war than the average soldier or officer ever gets to see. In this there is one constant and recurring moral, namely that military force is a poor solution to any problem: at best the triumph of negation." Hugh then confessed: "The rough, restless, and unscrupulous ways of Combat Intelligence are rather well suited if not actually agreeable to my temperament. This is a way of life that does not pretend to be a finer thing than it is. Our peace-time life, of which we have suddenly grown so sentimental, was too often a drab and embittered domesticity or a meanly acquisitive manipulation of others, a la Dale Carnegie, for what we could get out of them."[73]

---

[68] Oppenheimer, *An Innocent Yank at Home Abroad*, 158.

[69] Hugh Nibley, "Faith of an Observer," 379.

[70] Karl Philip Gottlieb von Clausewitz (1780-1831) was born in Burg, Germany, served with distinction in the Prussian and Russian armies, and ultimately became director of the Prussian Army School and chief of staff. He is best known for his posthumously published *Vom Kriege* (On War), published in 1833, which advocated the then-revolutionary policy of total war.

[71] Oppenheimer, *An Innocent Yank at Home Abroad*, 158.

[72] Hugh Nibley, Letter to Margaret Violet Sloan, n.d., ca. August 1943.

[73] Ibid.

Despite "living behind a seven-walled barricade of censorship," Hugh told his mother: "The work has been interesting and may become exciting and that is all I can tell you about it." Mocking both the censor and his brief career as a weather observer, Hugh added poetically: "I think it is fairly safe to let you know that the hills around Ritchie are turning to brilliant autumn colors, which I had hoped I would remain long enough to see. Also this marvelous country-side has taken on an atmosphere so deeply autumnal that you can simply swim in it—corn-shocks, pumpkins, old stone houses, smoke in the air, and all the rest." But he returned to a gloomy note in concluding the letter, "I am more convinced than ever that this war will bring about no good."[74]

On 23 September Hugh graduated from the German Order of Battle course and received his diploma.[75] The next day, Hugh wrote to his mother: "Yesterday we went through another graduation ritual—my third Army diploma—it represents some extremely intensified and specialized work—not too hard but very exhausting; also very revealing. It has been a year since we got into this mess and as yet we have acquired neither rank nor honors. But the year has been anything but wasted: it is no small thing to get access to the main-spring of the whole machine." He also owed to the army his encounter with that "work of perfection," Anahid Iskian, whom he finally described: "She is extremely sought after because she is beautiful, vivacious, brainy and generous, with a boundless fund of know-how and a joyous sense of humor. Anahid is quite perfect, as you will agree the instant you meet her. One of those creatures that everybody loves to pieces and vice-versa. As a side-line she conducts the Armenian Congregational Choir, which does not prevent an active and growing interest in the gospel."[76]

However, by late October, things between Hugh and Anahid had frozen. "Thus ends a strange and eventful furlough," a disheartened Hugh wrote to his mother. "After a couple of days among the Amish in the Pennsylvania Dutch country (the autumn colors were incredibly brilliant) I ended up in New York where a whirlwind courtship culminated in a flat refusal."[77] He did not discuss the reasons for this refusal nor his reaction to it.

However, some good news greeted Hugh's return. He and all other OB graduates would automatically achieve the rank of master sergeant. Since OB teams were new to the service, the army chain of command knew that they would be greeted with suspicion. "Can't you see such an officer welcoming with open arms a uniformed individual approaching his desk, . . . smiling, self-satisfied and with supreme confidence, saying with a thick accent, 'I shpeak zeven languitges, und Tjerman da best,'" joked Oppenheimer.[78] The promotions would provide a modicum of credibility and prestige. Later Hugh asserted that this rank was the best in the army. As a noncommissioned officer, he had much of the status of an officer but he also could drive a jeep—a lowly task forbidden to officers.

In preparation for departure for Europe, the OB teams received additional training on the rifle range and in cleaning and assembling a Colt .45 caliber pistol. (After much dithering, the army decided to recommend pistols rather than rifles for OB spe-

---

[74]Hugh Nibley, Letter to Agnes Sloan Nibley, postmarked 24 September 1943.
[75]Certificate of graduation from "Special Course in Order of Battle Intelligence."
[76]Hugh Nibley, Letter to Agnes Sloan Nibley, postmarked 24 September 1943.
[77]Hugh Nibley, Letter to Agnes Sloan Nibley, 29 October 1943.
[78]Oppenheimer, *An Innocent Yank at Home Abroad*, 156.

cialists, since they would be spending more time studying papers than stalking the enemy.) Another physical examination and more vaccinations followed. Hugh designated his mother with his power of attorney, telling her lightheartedly that he was going to "take the liberty to saddle you with all my financial affairs on this continent."[79] On 14 November 1943, Hugh and the other eighteen members of OB teams I-VI sailed from New York City. After almost a year and two months in the army, seven months of it at Camp Ritchie, Hugh was now going to witness first-hand what he had spent all that time studying. As salve for a bruised heart, combat was, at the very least, an attention-getting distraction.

---

[79]Hugh Nibley, Letter to Agnes Sloan Nibley, 29 October 1943.

This official Army photograph of Hugh was taken while he was attending weather observation school at Godman Field, Fort Knox, Kentucky, 1943.

    The business of the 101 A/B Division, to which I was attached through the winter of '43 and all of '44, was to search out and destroy; all the rest of the vast military enterprise was simply supportive of that one objective. "Good hunting!" was the general's stock admonition before takeoff. My business was to know more about the German Army than anyone else and to brief division personnel at every level on that meaningful subject both before and during operations. What I saw on every side was the Mahan Principle in full force, that "great secret" of converting life into property—your life for my property, also your life for my promotion (known as the Catch-22 Principle). Attached to army groups and various intelligence units during 1945, I took my Jeep all over western Europe and beheld the whole thing as a vast business operation. I well remember the pain and distress expressed at headquarters as the war wound down and twilight descended on brilliant military careers, high-living, and unlimited financial manipulation; and how great was the rejoicing when the new concept of "brush-fire wars" was announced to the staff—a simple plan to keep the whole thing going, safely contained and at a safe distance. O peace, where is thy sting? The Mahan Principle was still in full force and remains so to this day.[1]

---

[1] Hugh Nibley, "Intellectual Autobiography," *Nibley on the Timely and the Timeless* (Provo, UT: BYU Religious Studies Center, 1978): xxiv. For a more comprehensive treatment of Hugh Nibley's war years, see Alexander Nibley, *Sergeant Nibley, Ph.D.* (Salt Lake City: Deseret Book, forthcoming).

Chapter 13

War in Europe, 1944-45

After Pearl Harbor, Americans were united and determined to crush Japan. However, after negotiations with England in December 1941, President Roosevelt promised to focus the war effort on Germany. In reality, America was engaged in two wars simultaneously. While the allies focused their attention on the European front, America was fighting, mostly on its own in the Pacific. And for the first year, the United States and its allies were losing both wars.[2] The British surrendered Singapore in February 1942, and by March, Japan had conquered or was on the verge of conquering much of the territory in the Pacific, including Malaysia, New Guinea, the Mariana and Caroline Islands, Admiralty Island, the Gilbert Islands, the Solomon Islands, Burma, Borneo, and others. The Philippines fell two months later, and the Japanese delivered a massive blow to U.S. morale when they forced the 78,000 American and Filipino troops who had surrendered in Bataan to walk sixty-five miles without food or water while being constantly beaten and tortured. More than 5,000 Americans died on that death march. By the winter of 1941-42, America was in full retreat throughout the Pacific.

Europe was not faring much better. By the beginning of 1942, Germany controlled Austria, Poland, Belgium, Luxembourg, Yugoslavia, Norway, Denmark, Holland, Greece, France, and much of Eastern Europe. The one bright spot was that the German drive into the Soviet Union had stalled. Germany also controlled the seas. In the first quarter of 1942, German U-boats sank more than a million tons of goods, 860,000 tons in November alone. In March 1943, 400 U-boats sank 120 ships. On 19 August 1942, an experimental invasion force of 5,000 Canadian, 1,000 British, and 50 American troops attacked the French port of Dieppe, fifty miles up the coast from Le Havre. The invasion was planned to gain experience and intelligence for landing a force

---

[2]The discussion that follows is drawn from Gerald Astor, *The Greatest War*, 3 vols. (New York: Warner, 1999); Mitchell G. Bard, *The Complete Idiot's Guide to World War II* (New York: Alpha Books, 1999); and Antony Shaw, *World War II Day by Day* (Osceola, WI: MBI, 2000).

on the continent. The operation accomplished what it set out to do—gain experience, acquire more intelligence, test equipment, and convince Hitler that the allies would be landing in Calais-Boulogne. However, the success came at a great price.[3] More than 2,000 men were taken prisoner and 1,000 more were killed.

But after this shattering year, 1943 saw a significant change. Colonel James Doolittle's bombing raids on Japan in April 1942 were not a huge success, but they boosted American morale and unsettled the Japanese, who had been assured that their homeland would be immune from attack. In June, the United States turned the tide in the Pacific, taking the Japanese fleet by surprise and crippling it in the Battle of Midway. Japan's navy lost four aircraft carriers, 3,500 men, and nearly 300 planes. Although the United States lost a destroyer, 150 planes, and 307 men, the balance shifted to America's advantage since it had greater resources and could afford to replace more men and matériel.

Technology came to the rescue in the Atlantic. High Frequency Direction Finders (nicknamed Huff Duff) were eventually able to find German submarines by picking up their radio signals. By May 1943, the Allies were sinking a U-boat a day. The U-boats remained a threat, but their effectiveness was greatly reduced. In February, Germany surrendered at Stalingrad in the first major defeat of Hitler's armies. By May, German and Italian troops had surrendered in North Africa. And on 8 September, Italy's surrender was announced and the new government declared war on Germany. While the Japanese population had only seen one brief encounter with war when Doolittle's raiders bombed Tokyo, Germany had been under fire for over three years. In November the British began bombing Berlin. The Battle of Berlin, as it came to be known, left over 6,000 civilians dead and 1.5 million homeless over the course of three and a half months.

The U.S. entry into the war effected radical changes on the home front. Military expenditures in 1942 were $100 billion; by the war's end, that figure had tripled. The government was forced to raise taxes and raise deficit spending, increasing the national debt from $49 billion in 1941 to $259 billion in 1945. The economic expansion offset some of the costs of this buildup as the nation's gross domestic product more than doubled, but as the war buildup forced increased government management of the economy, price controls, wage controls, and production controls became a reality. Congress was also compelled to enact legislation to ensure that striking workers could not hamper production of critical industries. The military buildup ended the Great Depression as the wartime economy swiftly ended unemployment. However, the Depression-developed habits of thrift and economy became even more crucial as home-front rationing, recycling, and conservation measures took effect. Meat, sugar, butter, and other staples were all rationed. So were gasoline, rubber, leather goods, and clothing. Even silk stockings became scarce (nylons were not yet invented) since the silk was needed for parachutes and glider cords. Of course this rationing led to black markets on certain goods, but overall the American public enthusiastically supported the troops.

The war was no less demanding on the Nibley family, but they were fortunate. Three of the boys were in the Armed Forces, and all three escaped injury. Sloan, who

---

[3]William Stevenson, *A Man Called Intrepid: The Secret War* (New York: Ballantine, 1976), 414-32.

enlisted in the Navy, was a junior-grade lieutenant stationed in Washington, D.C., where he wrote scripts for Navy training films, a job that eventually led to his post-war profession as a Hollywood script writer. Sloan and his wife, Gail Sheridan Nibley, had a two-year-old son, Philip. When Hugh was stationed at Camp Ritchie in 1943, he visited them, commenting wistfully to his mother, "All the children around fuss over [Philip] just like they did our Philip."[4]

Richard had married Erna Mary Roberts in 1940, leaving home to serve in a tank division that drove the Axis powers out of Northern Africa. Reid, whose foot had been injured when he was young, was classified ineligible for the draft and was devastated that he couldn't join his older brothers. He spent the war years in New York City where he was a concert pianist. Barbara, who was only fifteen when the war began, matriculated at Los Angeles City College at age sixteen. She defines her main contribution to the war effort as entertaining the troops stationed in the Los Angeles area with a college drama group. El remained in the California area but spent a lot of time traveling to Utah to recruit workers for the Southern California aircraft factories. Sloanie did volunteer sewing for the Relief Society's war efforts, and her late-1930s job of selling hearing aids allowed her to claim a better ration ticket for gasoline.[5]

On the night of 14 November 1943, when Hugh and the other eighteen members of the newly formed OB teams reported to New York harbor, they had no idea that they would be sailing on the legendary *Queen Mary*, bound for Great Britain. It was no luxury cruise, however. The ocean liner that had accommodated 1,957 passengers in deluxe comfort had been converted into a troop ship that accommodated 15,000 soldiers. All the elegance and extravagance of the ship—the recreation areas, dining halls, ballrooms, and salons—had been replaced by spartan sleeping quarters with bunks stacked five deep. Still the ship did have an advantage over other ocean-going vessels. The *Queen Mary* cruised faster than any German submarine.[6] It could be intercepted, but not outrun.

To simplify work assignments, the British crew had attached signs to each cabin listing the detail assigned to its occupants for the duration of the voyage. The master sergeants of the six OB teams remained together in the same cabin, while their officers occupied slightly more comfortable quarters. Hugh and his associates were outraged to discover that they were on kitchen police—setting tables, serving food, and cleaning up after meals. In the U.S. Army, such grunt work was reserved for enlisted men, not for sergeants. Max Oppenheimer recounted: "In shocked disbelief we began scurrying about, attempting to tell officers or the British that in our grade we could not possibly pull KP duty. Our efforts failed. Consequently, the troops were treated to the sight of six Master Sergeants pulling KP at each meal. I am sure they thought a new world order had arisen."[7] Their humiliation was mercifully brief, since the voyage took only four days and sixteen hours.

---

[4]Hugh Nibley, Letter to Agnes Sloan Nibley, 29 October 1943. Gail was Sloan's second wife. An earlier marriage to Marjorie Doolittle had lasted only a short time. He and Gail divorced in the mid-1940s, and he married Linda Stirling on 22 December 1946.

[5]Barbara Nibley Richards, telephone conversation, 20 February 2002; notes in my possession.

[6]Max Oppenheimer, Jr. *An Innocent Yank at Home Abroad: Footnotes to History, 1922-1945* (Manhattan, KS: Sunflower University Press, 2000), 162.

[7]Ibid., 163.

When the ship docked at Glasgow, Scotland, on 21 November 1943, Hugh found that the constant air raids, blackouts, and food shortages were exacting a great toll on the British; nevertheless, morale was high and victory anticipated. The sheer number of American troops must have helped buoy up the British spirits. U.S. troops had begun landing in England in January 1942; by the spring of 1944, 2 million American soldiers were stationed in a country the size of Colorado. The English welcomed the American troops in their homeland and into the conflict. If somewhat suspicious of the Yanks' ability to deliver, they were nevertheless eager to have their help in the war against the Germans.[8]

Hugh and the entire group from Ritchie were posted at Whittington Barracks near Lichfield, Staffordshire. Formerly an ancient Roman military encampment, Litchfield served as the barracks for the South Staffordshire Regiment. The "dank and draughty splendors of tall, medieval barracks," as Hugh described them, were a series of gray stone buildings surrounded by a stone wall.[9] Hugh later added that the barracks were "very cold, dark and stony, with a 150-years' deposit of coal smoke and Empire tradition."[10] The weather was damp, misty, and dreary; but soon after arriving at the base, Hugh wrote his mother that "the bloom of health which suffuses my saucy cheeks is the authentic product of the English countryside."[11]

By 6 December, Hugh was stationed in the open fields near Lichfield. He described the weather as "the most perfect I have discovered. It neither blandishes nor bludgeons, it forces you neither indoors nor out-of-doors, but lets you strictly alone. The eternal Easter of Claremont was as hard to fight against as the merciless succession of cold- and heat-waves that paralyses the spirit over most of the American Continent. Here you can go out walking any time—provided you keep moving."[12]

Despite his upbeat tone, Hugh was still brooding over his failed relationship with Anahid. "I am still mad about not getting married," he confided to his mother, adding sarcastically, "but so many things bemuse me at this stage that any rational or predictable event would mar the perfect confusion of existence and might even bring about a reversion to some sort of reasoned thought—a thing totally out of keeping with present activities and highly detrimental to military peace of mind."[13] He consoled himself in the same letter with anticipations of an assault on London bookstores for Arabic documents. "I devoutly hope it shall soon be possible to follow through with some really impressive bundles of Orientalia, this country being very rich in Near Eastern materials." A few weeks later, Hugh delightedly reported that he had found the motherlode and alerted Sloanie: "You shall presently receive a large package of exceedingly valuable books, the likes of which are nowhere available in the West—Oriental stuff."[14]

---

[8]Ibid., 165; *D-Day: The Total Story*, produced by Greystone Communications and A&E Network, History Channel, 1994. Videocassette in my possession.

[9]Hugh Nibley, Letter to Agnes Sloan Nibley, 6 December 1943; see also Oppenheimer, *An Innocent Yank at Home Abroad*, 166.

[10]Hugh Nibley, Letter to Agnes Sloan Nibley, n.d., ca. summer 1945.

[11]Hugh Nibley, Letter to Agnes Sloan Nibley, 22 November 1943.

[12]Hugh Nibley, Letter to Agnes Sloan Nibley, 6 December 1943.

[13]Ibid.

[14]Hugh Nibley, Letter to Agnes Sloan Nibley, 23 December 1943.

By 23 December 1943, Hugh had been transferred to the headquarters of British Intelligence at Hyde Park Corners in London. All OB personnel were placed under the temporary command of British Intelligence, who put them through another OB course which was sniffily announced to the Ritchie graduates as "the real thing, highly classified, and much more up-to-date." During the week of training, the American OB teams were expected to learn the current designations, strengths, and locations of all German units then in France.[15] Hugh spent Christmas "in the bosom of an English family—wonderful people, such abounding energy and good spirits."[16]

Nor did he slacken his collecting efforts. On 8 January, he again warned his mother that "a great pile of Arabic books should reach you: two of the foremost English Arabists have just been good enough to die and their great collections have been systematically plundered by me and the British Museum."[17] A week later, he mailed off a receipt for a third batch of books, half-apologizing: "If all this stuff I send is a horrible nuisance, take comfort in the thought that someday it may be an inestimable boon." Hugh added, "It certainly puts you in control of the only decent Arabic collection in the West, which is worth a good deal more than it cost me."[18]

Hugh was able to attend LDS Church services at "a number of places" while stationed in England. On these occasions, Hugh said he was "bowled over by the vividness and affection with which Grandfather Nibley is remembered. A simple man, they say, devoid of eloquence, but given to doing good in secret . . . on the sly, almost as if he was ashamed of it, and thereby [he] won a permanent place in their affections."[19]

Following the British OB training course, Hugh was attached to the British War Office and assigned to work with the secret weapon of the British war effort, "the mysterious Miss Crawford." Hugh showed up at the War Office at Whitehall "first thing in the morning with my pass, all my identification, and everything." By nine o'clock he was still waiting; Miss Crawford finally "bustled in" at ten o'clock. "She had a huge mop of frizzy red hair," remembers Hugh. "She was an old maid and very, very fussy." She lectured Hugh about showing up so early. "Well, I know nine o'clock is the hour, but we don't come at that time," Hugh recalls Miss Crawford saying. "That wasn't the proper time to come in the British way of doing it." Hugh was equally surprised when everyone in the office quit what they were doing at eleven o'clock for tea. Then at noon it was time to go to lunch. "This was the way they ran it," Hugh shrugged.[20] The British Army "didn't take anything seriously. They'd say, 'Well, it's going to be a long war; we might as well enjoy it,' and everybody did exactly as he pleased."[21] Despite his deliberately cultivated attitude of casualness, Hugh was more disillusioned than he let on. "The more you see of this sort of thing the clearer it becomes that the 'Empah' is

---

[15] Oppenheimer, *An Innocent Yank at Home Abroad*, 168.

[16] Hugh Nibley, Letter to Agnes Sloan Nibley, 23 December 1943. Hugh did not mention the family's name.

[17] Hugh Nibley, Letter to Agnes Sloan Nibley, 8 January 1944.

[18] Hugh Nibley, Letter to Agnes Sloan Nibley, 15 January 1944

[19] Hugh Nibley, Letter to Agnes Sloan Nibley, 8 January 1944.

[20] Hugh Nibley, *Teachings of the Book of Mormon: Transcripts of Lectures Presented to an Honors Book of Mormon Class at Brigham Young University*, 1989-90 (Provo, UT: FARMS, n.d.): Semester 3, Lecture 68, 132.

[21] Hugh Nibley, "Faith of an Observer," 143.

nothing but a cheeky bit of window-dressing," he confided to his mother. "Top to bottom, it is pure eyewash."[22]

During the month that Hugh was stationed at the War Office, he worked with Miss Crawford to compile the catalogue of German general officers for the June 1944 Order of Battle Book.[23] This top-secret book, called the *Vade Mecum* (Latin for "come with me") was given a brilliant red cover as if to draw attention to itself. Intelligence personnel began to refer to it as the *invade mecum*, "invade with me." Naturally, the work was top secret, so Hugh wrote Sloanie only that "as to the type of work I am doing, you are free to exercise your imagination."[24] But there is no way anyone could have imagined how the *vade mecum* was compiled. The book was supposed to give detailed information on the location, positions, and strength of each German unit. To do this, they would track the German officers who commanded these units, whose locations were most readily available in the newspapers and popular magazines. "That was our sole source of information," remembers Hugh. Miss Crawford did her research by looking through newspapers and magazines. "She would clip [articles] out, and all her information was kept in a shoebox. It was all messed up, and she would go through trying to find things. She had no filing system or anything. This was the way we composed the *vade mecum*. This is the way we kept our thumb on the pulse of the German army—little Miss Crawford there with her red frizzy hair going through a shoebox full of scraps. It's too funny for words."[25]

This patch from Hugh's army uniform is the "screaming eagle" insignia worn by members of the 101st Airborne.

In January, the OB teams, each composed of two master sergeants and a lieutenant, were given their assignments. Hugh was assigned to OB Team 5 with a Lieutenant Braun, a German Jew who spoke with a very thick German accent, and a Sergeant Weigner, "a very rich Jew from New York." Each team was to be attached to an army group "a hundred miles from the front," recalls Hugh. "That was as high and as safe as you could get." But there would be one exception. One team would be attached to the 101st Airborne Division and therefore be among the first to land in Normandy. When Lieutenant Braun came out of the British War Office after having received the team's assignment, Hugh remembers him announcing, "We are it; we got the dirty assignment." Upon hearing the news, Weigner

---

[22]Hugh Nibley, Letter to Agnes Sloan Nibley, n.d., ca. summer 1945.

[23]Army of the United States, Separation Qualification Record [for Hugh W. Nibley], n.d., Hugh Nibley Papers.

[24]Hugh Nibley, *Teachings of the Book of Mormon*, Semester 3, Lecture 68, 132; Hugh Nibley, Letter to Agnes Sloan Nibley, 15 January 1944.

[25]Hugh Nibley, *Teachings of the Book of Mormon*, Semester 3, Lecture 68, 132-33.

turned "as pale as a sheet." With "sweat streaming down his face," he "leaned up against the wall gasping, 'Mama mia, mama mia. We are it.'"[26] Weigner's panic never subsided, and he "dragged me around to half the fortune tellers in London to get some sort of assurance from them," recalled the much more philosophical Hugh. Weigner was "haunted . . . terribly" by a premonition of death. Hugh "kept telling him to forget about it," but his reassurances failed to have the desired effect. For his part, Hugh had just the opposite impression. He felt confident that he would survive the ordeal.[27]

Team 5 reached the headquarters of the 101st Airborne at Grenham Lodge near Avebury, near Marlborough in Wiltshire County, on 21 January 1944, an "unbelievably dark and stormy night." A year later, Hugh described camp conditions to his mother: "We lived in tents without light or heat on top of a very windy hill with gliders tied down all around us. The mud was pelagsic, the food unspeakably vile and very scarce."[28] At the time, however, Hugh endured conditions stoically, the only exception being his plea to his mother, after a month at Grenham Lodge, for "something—anything—sweet." Hugh continued, "Food is not bad here but quite scarce. What the English, who are not without humor, call a 'sweet' gives nothing to the hopeful palate but the sensation of a local anaesthetic." He described the surrounding countryside with forced good cheer: "The country is wonderfully beautiful; a world of very ancient trees and thatched villages: there is nothing on the Continent to compare with it for 'atmosphere.' Of course everything is wet, cold and gray, but that is what makes it so veddy English. Somehow damp moss and dripping lichens go with potato-and-beet sandwiches and beans on toast."[29]

The surrounding countryside offered more than just beauty to the professor turned soldier. Hugh was thrilled to be near Avebury, where the largest stone circle, prehistoric mound (Silbury Hill), and burial mounds in Europe are located. Stonehenge stood about twenty miles to the south. During glider training, he flew over the area, getting a bird's-eye view of the ancient structures; and on days off, Hugh inspected the sites, an experience that "electrified" him.[30]

After he himself was briefed on the division's role in the upcoming invasion, Hugh was placed in charge of, as he put it, "wising everyone up on the strength, disposition, and honest intentions of the Germans."[31] Hugh's discharge papers document that during the months of January through May of 1944, he "gave extensive instruction

---

[26]Hugh Nibley, "Faith of an Observer," 145. compilation of interviews, ca. 1983-84 for a video documentary of the same name aired in 1985, photocopy of typescript in my possession, pagination added.

[27]Ibid., 172, 380. Weigner effected a transfer out of the 101st but was apparently killed anyway, since Hugh's discharge papers identify him as "the sole living member [of OB Team 5] throughout the Normandy campaign." Weigner's replacement, whose name Hugh could not recall, was evidently killed with Lieutenant Braun during D-Day operations; the OB team replacements, Kipness and Burger, were both wounded in Holland. As related, Hugh's replacements at Bastogne were both killed. Neither Hugh nor Allen mentions a third man in that ill-fated OB team; they may have been short of staff at that point in the war.

[28]Hugh Nibley, Letter to Agnes Sloan Nibley, n.d., ca. summer 1945. The Pelasgians were an ancient people mentioned by classical Greek writers; Hugh uses the adjective here to mean something like "primeval."

[29]Hugh Nibley, Letter to Agnes Sloan Nibley, 28 February 1944.

[30]Hugh Nibley, *Temple and Cosmos: Beyond This Ignorant Present*, edited by Don E. Norton, Vol. 12 of *The Collected Works of Hugh Nibley* (Salt Lake City: Deseret Book/FARMS, 1992), 163-64; see also 169, 382.

[31]Hugh Nibley, Letter to Agnes Sloan Nibley, n.d., ca. summer 1945. See Appendix C for the full text. Unless otherwise noted, all citations of an undated letter written during the summer of 1945 refer to this item.

to large classes (40-150) [of] Officers and Men of 101st A/B division on German Strategy and Tactics, German Army Organization, Insignia, Weapons, etc."³² Hugh later recalled that these briefings were something of a grind—two hours of intensive and technical material that he was supposed to transmit to already weary officers every Thursday night. "You can imagine how popular that made me with them," Hugh states. And when he had to brief the regular troops, "it was very sad because they were very eager to know what chances of survival they had, which is fair enough you know. But some of them, like the Pathfinders, didn't have a prayer, actually. They were practically suicide business. And we knew it was going to be bad stuff."³³

Hugh's own faith was sorely tested by General Maxwell Taylor's introduction to his lectures, in which he assured the men that "Sergeant Nibley will be going in among the very first, so he's not going to just give you cold comfort." As a result, the men "would listen with some respect."³⁴ In a letter to his mother at the end of the war, Hugh confessed that he "was wistfully envious of the simple linesmen who had no idea what they were in for. I gave lots of lectures to all the units about the German army, and the questions the boys asked on those occasions called for all the comfort I could give them—I lied until I even cheered myself up."³⁵ Of course, at the time all this was strictly top secret, so Hugh wrote his mother only that "my branch of hurlothrumbism is strictly nobody's business, so what can I write but metaphysics, and who cares about them these days? Or is metaphysics plural? 'Ta metaphysika' says Aristotle, but Greek neuter is always singular, so there you are."³⁶

In April, Hugh spent a short furlough exploring the Scottish highlands. He called the experience "heaven." Surely it was a welcome escape from the war plans, for he encountered "not a soul in uniform, the people unbelievably kind and generous, as if the last remnant of a better world had taken refuge in those lost volcanic coastlands." He also found more bookstores to explore: "Books were abundant and fabulously cheap (like everything else) in Edinburgh," wrote Hugh. "I feel myself more drawn to the East than ever."³⁷

---

³²Army of the United States, *Separation Qualification Record*, n.d.

³³Hugh Nibley, "Faith of an Observer," 146.

³⁴Ibid., 367. Maxwell Davenport Taylor (1901-87) was born in Keytesville, Missouri, graduated from West Point (1922), helped set up the army's first airborne units, and assumed command of the 101st division in the spring of 1944. The first general to land in Normandy on D-day, he was promoted from brigadier general to major general (two stars). Except for a week during the Battle of the Bulge, Taylor commanded the 101st during all its World War II combat. After the war, he served as superintendent of West Point (1945-49), as military governor of Berlin (1949-41), as commander of the U.S. Eighth Army (1953-55) during the Korean War, then as commander of the U.S. and United Nations Far East commands, as army chief of staff (1955-59), as John F. Kennedy's chair of the Joint Chiefs of Staff (1962-64), and as ambassador to South Vietnam (1964-65). Regarded as more cosmopolitan than the average army officer, he was fluent in several languages and the author of four military books.

³⁵Hugh Nibley, Letter to Agnes Sloan Nibley, n.d., ca. summer 1945.

³⁶Hugh Nibley, Letter to Agnes Sloan Nibley, 28 February 1944. Hugh is alluding here to Samuel Johnson's comic parody of Italian opera, *Hurlothrumbo*, which ran for fifty nights to favorable reviews at the Haymarket Theatre in 1729. Historians regard it as mildly amusing nonsense, and the term passed into English as a synonym for "an inconsequential thing."

³⁷Hugh Nibley, Letter to Agnes Sloan Nibley, 8 April 1944.

Although by 1944 Italy had formally surrendered, the northern half of the country remained under German control. On 22 January 1944, American forces landed at Anzio, just south of Naples. The troops secured the beachhead and slowly advanced northward against the Germans. By May 1944, the fall of Monte Cassino opened the road to Rome. The Allies took that city on 4 June, but it was another year—five days before the war ended—before American troops swept the Germans out of Italy. On the eastern front, Germany was locked in a war of attrition with Russia but could do little to halt the Russian advance into Poland on 6 January.

In the Pacific, U.S. forces began an "island-hopping" campaign, focused on taking only the most strategic locations but bypassing many Japanese-controlled islands that were less important. The purpose was to save American lives and isolate the defensive Japanese forces. In January 1944, American troops began invading the Marshall Islands. By June, they were at the Marianas. Despite saturation bombing and shelling to "soften up" resistance, the hand-to-hand combat at each new island was bitter and desperately costly.

Around the end of April 1944, the troops of the 101st were rehearsing the D-Day invasion in war games staged near the coastal town of Torquay in England. There Hugh was thrown into repeated contact with General Maxwell Taylor. "I can't say we were quite chummy, because he was very aloof," recalled Hugh,[38] but Taylor was a student of military history, and Hugh's mastery of ancient history must have proved fascinating. "We'd walk back and forth in the woods chatting intimately like a couple of grand dukes," remembers Hugh with self-deprecating humor. The officers looked on in amazement as Hugh, a noncommissioned officer, held confidential discussions with "the unapproachable Max Taylor."[39]

A month before the invasion, Hugh wrote to his mother thanking her for sending the longed-for box of sweets. War rationing allowed an individual about a cup of sugar per week, so sending any kind of candy or cookies to a GI required not only sacrifice but often creativity, and Hugh's appreciation was appropriately fervent: "There was something unreal about the candy and dates—pure Arabian Nights for these parts; they disappeared in the pious ecstasy of a Kolleridian love-feast. More! More! The Angels cry. 'Let us kick out the windows of heaven that its golden treasures descend as the Dews of Carmel.'" Hugh concluded the letter with the comment: "Within a week I shall have been in this censored-censored Army for a longer time than the country itself was engaged in the last war. Which melancholy reflection brings us to the bottom of our page and our spirits."[40] It was one of his few surviving dispirited confessions.

Hugh was originally scheduled to land in Normandy by glider. The large, plywood Horsa gliders used in the Normandy invasion did not inspire a lot of confidence. They were towed two at a time on a silk cable behind a C-47 Dakota and could barely get off the ground once the C-47 reached a speed of 55 miles per hour. Hugh, who

---

[38] Hugh Nibley, *Teachings of the Book of Mormon: Transcripts of Lectures Presented to an Honors Book of Mormon Class at Brigham Young University, 1989-90* (Provo, UT: FARMS, n.d.), Semester 3, Lecture 65, 101.

[39] Hugh Nibley, "Faith of an Observer," 147.

[40] Hugh Nibley, Letter to Agnes Sloan Nibley, 4 May 1944. Recipes for "war cakes" that required little or no sugar circulated freely. Chocolate was also a rationed item. Despite the strange spelling, Hugh is referring

had a tendency to get nauseated in flight, states that their inventor himself "wouldn't go into one for a thousand pounds. They'd barely fly and most of them smashed up." Their desperate undependability "was a real tragedy."[41] However, only weeks before the invasion, Hugh was required to yield his seat on the glider to Brigadier General Don F. Pratt and was told that he would be driving a jeep ashore. "I didn't argue about it," states Hugh. "You don't argue with a general, and I was not exactly sick at heart being told that I would have to come by sea and land on the beach."[42]

It was a classic case, however, of "out of the frying pan into the fire," since the jeeps would be driving straight into the teeth of the German artillery emplacements on the beach. Before departure, Hugh spent several days waterproofing his jeep under the supervision of the motor pool mechanics. He coated the underside of the jeep and all the electrical wires under the hood with handsful of Harbutt's plasticine, a putty-like grease. It was a messy and time-consuming job; but because his life depended on it, he was naturally motivated to do an excellent job. He attached an exhaust vent and air intake for the carburetor, a vertical pipe that allowed the jeep to drive through some five feet of water.[43]

The generals planning D-Day knew that conditions had to be perfect during the invasion. It had to be during low tide so the landing craft could dodge the obstacles placed on the beach by the Germans. It needed to begin at dawn so the parachute and glider troops would have a cloak of darkness to cover them. They needed some moonlight for the planes to find their drop zones but not so much that the troops would be immediately spotted. They needed good weather to navigate the sometimes treacherous waters of the English Channel. The operation also needed to begin in late spring or early summer to assure at least four months of fighting before winter set in. These conditions coincided only three times in 1944: the first days of May, the first week of June, and toward the end of June. The Allies could not be prepared in time for the May date and choosing late June left no time for a second chance if the weather was bad. Hence, the date was set for 5 June.

On 4 June, Hugh was among the troops on a small transport ship at Bristol, England. Assembled in the English Channel was a huge armada of 139 major warships, 221 smaller combat vessels, over a thousand minesweepers and auxiliary vessels, 4,000 landing craft, 805 merchant ships, 59 blockships, and 300 small craft. It was an awesome sight. The invasion, originally scheduled for 5 June, was postponed for twenty-four hours by a ferocious storm. Winds were blowing at fifteen to twenty knots, while six-foot waves tossed the ships from side to side. "They said they had never had a storm like that since the day World War I began," said Hugh.[44] All the ships remained in the tossing channel,

---

to the English Romantic poet Samuel Taylor Coleridge (1772-1834), whose fragmentary poem "Kubla Khan" is a fantasy about the exotic and luxurious East.

[41]Hugh Nibley, "Faith of an Observer," 146-47.

[42]Ibid., 147. Pratt served as assistant division commander of the 101st Airborne and his glider was among the first to land in Normandy. However, probably because it was overloaded with protective armor plate to protect Pratt, it slid on the wet grass on landing and smashed into a tree. The copilot and Pratt were killed instantly, and the pilot was badly injured.

[43]Gordon Jones, quoted in *Eye-Witness to D-Day: The Story of the Battle by Those Who Were There*, edited by Jon E. Lewis (New York: Carroll & Graf, 1994), 15; Oppenheimer, *An Innocent Yank at Home Abroad*, 181.

[44]Hugh Nibley, "Faith of an Observer," 149.

their decks covered with vomit from the seasick men. Relying on meteorologists' reports that the weather would clear, Eisenhower gave the go-ahead for 6 June.

As dawn broke, the huge guns on the battleships accompanying the fleet began pounding the coast of France; soon the German .88s were responding to the fury. Hugh stood on the deck of the ship watching the bombardment and talking with the army chaplain. Satirizing his own thirst for being "first" he pointed out that he had more than enough of it on this experience:

> Our ship headed the convoy and as if that were not enough our party was to be the first ashore when contact was made with the division. The ship was bombed repeatedly but never hit. I stood at the head of the rope ladder for half an hour and then went down to the LCT without orders. Presently the very spot where I should be waiting was hit by an .88 and half a dozen tankmen blown up; the chaplain with whom I had been talking was wounded.[45]

Ernest Hemingway, then a war reporter, described the LCT sinisterly as a small "coffin-shaped, steel boat."[46] Hugh does not say what he thought as he descended into it alone. Eventually, the rest of the men assigned to the LCT were ordered to board. While the storm had calmed somewhat, the sea was rough and cold, increasing the dangers. Soldiers in full gear struggled to climb "down this slippery, cold net . . . in the pitch-black dark" while the small craft was "bouncing up and down." They tangled themselves in the fouled nets, clinging desperately as the craft rose on a wave almost halfway to the ship's rail, then dropping down in a trough almost out of sight.[47] A crane had already lifted Hugh's jeep from the deck to the LCT. The LCT's 225-hp high-speed diesel engine meant the men would have had to shout to be heard, but they were mostly silent as it pulled away from the ship and headed toward the French coastline.

At low tide, Utah Beach was a 300-400 yard coastline approximately twenty miles west of Omaha Beach. A low concrete wall rose several yards inland, backed up by German fortifications. The German .88 shells "tried hard to stop us, first landing in front and then behind," remembers Hugh, but he could also see "geysers of sand going up all over the place" on Utah Beach from the Allied bombardment. The ship their LCT had just pulled away from took a ferocious series of hits and sank. As the LCT neared the beach, the massive steel drawbridge-door on the front of the craft swung down to allow the troops to drive into the surf. A "command car driven by a big, red-headed Kentuckian" was the first vehicle out. It disappeared into the sea and was never seen again. Next came Hugh, his jeep loaded with sandbags and men clinging on to give it as much weight as possible so that it would gain purchase on the sandy bottom. "All I had to do was press on the gas and it would go straight ahead," remembers Hugh. "And everybody was yelling, 'Go it, Nibs! Keep going, keep going!'" Only Hugh's head and shoulders stuck out of the water as he wrestled the tough little jeep through the surf onto the beach.[48]

---

[45]Hugh Nibley, Letter to Agnes Sloan Nibley, n.d., ca. summer 1945.
[46]Quoted in Lewis, *Eye-Witness to D-Day*, 97.
[47]Gerald Astor, *The Greatest War: D-Day and the Assault on Europe* (New York: Warner, 1999), 2:349-50.
[48]Hugh Nibley, "Faith of an Observer," 148-49.

In a strange episode of double consciousness, Hugh hit Utah beach with Book of Mormon cadences spinning inside his head, like a Greek warrior going to battle chanting Homer. But rather than celebrating the glories of war, Hugh heard the heavy threnody of fulfilled prophecy. Two months before the invasion, he wrote his mother: "Of course, there is little time to relax in the Airborne at a time like this, but when I can snatch a moment or two off it is devoted to a single engrossing item: at this late date I have discovered the Book of Mormon, and live in a state of perpetual excitement-that marvelous production throws everything done in our age completely into the shadows."[49]

Thus, it is not surprising that the Book of Mormon should be on his mind during the landing on Utah Beach. "As I was going down the ladder, going down the rope ladder into the jeep," he described in a 1984 interview, "I had one thing that troubled me—you see, it worried me. I said, Joseph [Smith] slipped up on this one: it was having elephants in the Book of Mormon. Indians didn't have elephants. Then it suddenly occurred to me, that the elephants are only mentioned in the Book of Ether. That's the archaic period. They could have been around then. . . . They're not mentioned in the Nephite story at all. They don't occur. That suddenly corrected my perspective on it."

In a second Book of Mormon intrusion, headed toward the beach with his hands gripping his jeep wheel and his foot on the accelerator, a couple of feet underwater, he remembered that "it really hit me how astonishing the Book of Mormon truly is. It had never occurred to me before, but all I could think of all that day was how wonderful this Book of Mormon was." Like an obsessive strain of music throughout the fighting of the next few days, Hugh was "constantly preoccupied with the Book of Ether." The Germans "were shelling the hell out of the beach." Although the setting was modern, the destruction, devastation, and death that he was witnessing were similar to that ancient scene of ruin and tragedy described in Ether, and the book seemed to be asking the same questions he was: "Why all this nonsense, this vast waste of life, everybody destroyed?"[50]

Making his way from the beach to headquarters at Hiesville was not easy. The Germans had the men pinned down for some time, and Hugh recalls taking refuge in a foxhole. "I was about to eat a chocolate bar . . . and I jumped into the foxhole and it was full of—ah—spattered with brains, a helmet full of brains, and so forth, and it was just a bloody mess there, and I immediately lost my appetite; and then after a few minutes I got hungry and ate the chocolate bar just as unconcerned as anything. I never thought I could do a thing like that. I never thought I could. But apparently you can shut off certain parts of the brain."[51]

When Hugh reached headquarters, which was set up in a small farm house, he found "everybody dirty and frightened and gone." Many of the men had been killed; everyone was confused. Lieutenant Braun had been killed within minutes of the landing. He remembered that there were "just half dozen of us." The men set up a perime-

---

[49]Hugh Nibley, Letter to Agnes Sloan Nibley, 8 April 1944.
[50]Hugh Nibley, "Faith of an Observer," 369, 148, 377; John W. Welch, "Hugh Nibley and the Book of Mormon," *Ensign*, April 1985, 50-56.
[51]Hugh Nibley, "Faith of an Observer," 156.

ter around the farm and dug in for the night. Hugh dug his foxhole with unfortunate precision—right where the family privy had been. And then a cow stepped on his canteen so he had no water to drink that night. "It was a miserable night," remembers Hugh. Around midnight, the gas alarm sounded. Someone had smelled new-mown hay, which resembled the scent of phosgene gas, and sounded the alarm. The men fumbled their gas masks on; but because they had waterproofed them for the trip across the Channel, "you couldn't breathe." They eventually calmed, once they figured out that it was a false alarm, but "what a wild night that was!"[52]

The first day of the invasion was utter confusion. The paratroopers who had been dropped earlier that morning—those who had not been dropped in swamps where they drowned—were scattered all over the Norman countryside, miles from their drop zones. This inadvertent randomness confused the Germans but also isolated the paratroopers, reducing them from a united fighting force to individuals who were easier to kill or capture. There was similar confusion on the beach. "Some craft landed late, others early, all of them a kilometer or so south of the intended target." When he realized that his troops had been landed in the wrong place, General Teddy Roosevelt (son of the former president) gallantly declared, "We'll start the war from right here."[53] Still, despite this early chaos, the landing at Utah Beach turned out to be quite successful. The 23,000 men who went ashore suffered fewer than 300 casualties. In contrast, the Americans landing on Omaha Beach met stiff resistance from German mines, machine-gun fire, and fortified gun emplacements that quickly accounted for more than 2,000 casualties. Tons of supplies and equipment sank in the sea, were destroyed by shell-fire, or were ruined by sand or blood.

When Hugh awoke the next morning, he looked out of his foxhole and saw "beautiful red poppies waving in the breeze." The sight reminded him irresistibly of John McCrae's poem "In Flanders Fields," which describes the poppies blowing between the rows of white crosses so evocatively that wearing a poppy had been as much a part of Armistice Day as the moment of silence since the end of World War I. Hugh, of course, had memorized this poem in his grade school days and found it an eerie experience to wake up, metaphorically, among the graves of World War I. In uncannily apt clichés, he exclaimed, "I said, 'Great guns! What am I doing here? This is where I came in.'"[54] Later, thinking back on the first few weeks of the invasion, Hugh admits soberly, "It was very bad. We were not only hopelessly outnumbered, we were getting no supplies. We were in a desperate situation."[55]

When not bogged down in a foxhole, Hugh spent his time wading through documents, correspondence, pay books, maps and other papers confiscated from German POWs and dead soldiers. He would sift through this mass of paper for any information that might help determine German troop positions, mine fields, or gun

---

[52]Ibid., 149.
[53]Quoted in Stephen Ambrose, *D-Day: June 6, 1944* (New York: Touchstone, 1994), 275–79.
[54]Nibley, *Approaching Zion*, edited by Don E. Norton, Vol. 9 of *The Collected Works of Hugh Nibley* (Salt Lake City: Deseret Book/FARMS, 1989), 303. McCrae's poem is one of the most famous World War I poems. McCrae was a surgeon attached to the 1st Field Artillery Brigade and had spent seventeen days treating the wounded in the battle in the Ypres salient in the spring of 1915. He composed the poem following the death of one of his former students.
[55]Hugh Nibley, "Faith of an Observer," 372.

emplacements. He would also receive G-2 intelligence reports from other units which would help the OB team get the big picture of German war operations. Additionally, he would receive unedited POW interrogation reports. Since he knew the German Order of Battle by heart, he could swiftly extract useful information, feeding the stream into the constantly updated Allied OB files.[56] Hugh's knowledge of Russian also found him doing double duty as an interrogator when the Allies captured Russian conscripts who were manning the gun emplacements on the beach. Being on an OB team meant that Hugh had a grip on the constantly shifting elements of battle, while being assigned to headquarters company meant that he also saw firsthand the bloody work of war. In a letter to his mother, he praised the valor of the 101st Airborne:

> No reports can exaggerate the merits of the boys of the 101st. That exalted zeal that usually invests a few rare souls in the heat of action seemed to hold whole battalions for days on end, so that if just one paratrooper was in a place we could say that position was ours. I am all admiration for these chaps whom you can count on in every situation, this emotion I share even with those horribly conceited German officers who, when pressed, will finally admit our moral superiority.[57]

At the same time, these men were not saints. Some of them had joined the 101st, recalled Hugh, because the alternative was the penitentiary. "They were pretty rough and tough characters."[58] He added, at the war's end, "When you are fighting fire with fire, a gang of cut-throats can be very useful."[59] That was the reality of war, but war also unleashed a darker side. Early in the invasion, one platoon held a French wedding at gun point while the men took turns raping the bride. General Taylor "was very much upset," when he learned of the incident. "He said 'Boys, don't you ever do things like that.' But that's absolutely typical, and I know much worse things than that that happened."[60] And whether Taylor ever punished those responsible has not made it into the official record.

On 11 June, Hugh wrote to his mother, reassuring her that he had survived the invasion. "You know nothing can keep me from Telling All, only the censor has first priority and last say. But here goes for running the blockade: I am in utter health and my usual high spirits." His only complaint—a scholarly form of bravado—was that "at present I am neglecting both Hieroglyphic and Cuneiform."[61]

On 30 June, twenty-four days into the invasion, Hugh wrote again: "I know you would not worry on my behalf: not that there has been no cause for alarm, but rather because of the assurances you mentioned in your last." He continued:

> The "late-great" Justice Holmes called war an "organized bore"; even the fastest-moving situation somehow lacks any sense of freshness or novelty, and the noisiest battles are the stupidest, I am told. As Order of Battle man . . . I am supposed to know what goes on and to preserve an eery secrecy in all things. "Sees all, knows all, tells

---

[56] Oppenheimer, *An Innocent Yank at Home Abroad*, 186.
[57] Hugh Nibley, Letter to Agnes Sloan Nibley, 19 July 1944.
[58] Hugh Nibley, "Faith of an Observer," 158.
[59] Hugh Nibley, Letter to Agnes Sloan Nibley, 3 February 1945.
[60] Hugh Nibley, "Faith of an Observer," 167-68.
[61] Hugh Nibley, Letter to Agnes Sloan Nibley, 11 June 1944.

nothing." . . . This is a strange timeless part of the world—the people, the buildings, the profuse, shaggy foliage, all are dateless and nameless, and everything in a cool, neutral light, seems of the stuff that dreams are made on. . . . Nothing so incongruous to such a setting as the incessant noise. Rich and his crowd will be most welcome if and when they get here.[62]

On 13 July, replacements took over the areas secured by the men of the 101st Airborne—the region from Utah Beach to Ste. Mère Eglise to Vierville, and, after one of the bloodiest battles of the invasion, Carentan. Hugh accompanied the survivors back to England. From the relative comfort of his barracks at Grenham Lodge, Hugh wrote his mother: "All serene again in my department. After some fuss we are at last able to view the situation again with some measure of detachment. Viewing situations with detachment is my peculiar business, and the only interesting job in the War. Only when the View becomes more important than the Detachment, interest tends to give place to alarm and, as you know, I scare easily."[63]

Unfortunately, the serenity Hugh felt at being back from the front did not last long. On 13 June 1944—the very day of Hugh's rotation—the Germans began a series of V-1 "Buzz Bomb" raids on London. The pilotless jet rockets were loaded with explosives and aimed at the city; and in nine months, more than 6,000 died and 75,000 buildings were destroyed. Ironically, men from the 101st Airborne who had just returned from Normandy were among the casualties. "Some of our paratroopers celebrating their return from the Normandy campaign," Hugh wrote his mother, "were killed at a Red Cross Club right in the middle of London. Oh what a pretty world."[64]

For his part, Hugh left London soon after the bombings and spent his well-deserved furlough again in the "heavenly" Scottish highlands, "simply scrambling aimlessly from one mountain-top to the next, miles from any road or habitation." Still, thoughts of the war were not far away. "The War is a problem, but it is a problem to which we have the solution—all that remains now is the spade-work of carrying out the operation. How different is the rest of the picture! The Fourth Century all over again, with its desperate yearning for quiet security running against an insuperable and mounting inclination to moral degeneracy." Hugh concluded, "Since we are in for another Age of Migrations there is no better preparation than to join the Airborne and travel light."[65]

The letters that Hugh wrote immediately after D-Day betray an altogether normal desire to distance himself from the war. Even without his obedience to censorship requirements, he gives few details of the actual fighting or even of GI life on the front. Instead it is more typical of him to write forebodingly about the precarious position of Western culture. It does not take any particular expertise in psychology to deduce that Hugh had turned from the details of death and destruction before his eyes to the larg-

---

[62] Hugh Nibley, Letter to Agnes Sloan Nibley, 30 June 1944. Hugh's brother Richard was a member of a tank battalion.

[63] Hugh Nibley, Letter to Agnes Sloan Nibley, 19 July 1944.

[64] Hugh Nibley, Letter to Agnes Sloan Nibley, 12 [sic] September 1944. From the letter's content, it is obvious that Nibley was writing from Holland, where operations began on 17 September.

[65] Hugh Nibley, Letter to Agnes Sloan Nibley, 26 July 1944.

er questions of significance and meaning. He later lamented about "the wrongness of what we were doing." This sense of futility and madness was "so strong that everybody would cry. . . . It was so sad you could hardly stand it—that people would do such things to each other. Everybody felt that way—the wrongness of it."⁶⁶ His contrasting euphoria at being in Scotland accurately measures the depth of his misery on the battlefield. "When I was in Scotland, I was really happy," he affirmed repeatedly in an interview. "I was enormously happy to get away from the war. I was so happy to be away from the battle."⁶⁷

Upon his return from Scotland, Hugh was involved in "a period of frantic preparation" for the next operation and the frustrations of the ever-changing plans: "The objective would be chosen, the whole operation rehearsed, everyone resigned to fate and all set for the take-off, and then would come word that Patton had already reached the place, or was so near it that we would not have to go in. This happened again and again and was very trying."⁶⁸ Characteristically, Hugh reacted with irritation, rather than relief, to this series of reprieves. Also characteristically, he relied on Church teachings to give structure to a time of terrifying amorphism and anomie. "There has been no occasion for the slightest deviation from the Word of Wisdom—even the early to bed clause goes not unheeded," he reassured his mother. "And how can it be otherwise with double, I repeat double daylight savings in effect? For the rest what I am doing and naturally what I am thinking would never pass the censor."⁶⁹

In the Pacific theater, the Battle of the Philippine Sea in June 1944 saw U.S. forces sink three Japanese carriers and seventeen submarines while sustaining only minor losses. By mid-August, the Marianas were controlled by Americans, opening the way for General Douglas MacArthur to land in the Philippines in October. Although Allied forces had secured Normandy in June and July 1944, efforts to push into the French interior met heavy German resistance. On 25 August, the Allies liberated Paris, and Patton's army pressed on toward Germany. But the offensive soon ran out of steam.

Then, on 17 September 1944, the largest airborne operation in history took place, Operation Market-Garden, an Allied air invasion of Holland. The mission of the 101st was to parachute into or land by glider in Holland in broad daylight, secure the road to the Rhine River, and make it possible for the British to cross into Germany. This time, Hugh took a glider:

> The first flight went late on September 17 and the pilots came back with the worst possible news: terrible weather, murderous flak and waiting for us in the landing zone a division of German tanks. But it was too late to turn back—regardless of weather we would have to make a try for it at dawn the next day. Again I was No. 2 man in No. 1 glider on the right—the one the Germans always try for. . . . Of course I became very sick as I always do in a glider. There was an old piece of armor plate lying on the floor and out of curiosity I wondered how it would be to sit on: just as

---

⁶⁶Hugh Nibley, "Faith of an Observer," 158.

⁶⁷Hugh Nibley, interviewed by Zina Petersen, 22 February 2002.

⁶⁸Hugh Nibley, Letter to Agnes Sloan Nibley, n.d., ca. summer 1945.

⁶⁹Hugh Nibley, Letter to Agnes Sloan Nibley, 24 August 1944. His comment about "early to bed" is an allusion to Doctrine and Covenants 88:124: "Retire to thy bed early, that ye may not be weary; arise early, that your bodies and your minds may be invigorated."

I slipped it on my little chair with a characteristically witty remark it absorbed three machine-gun bullets while another went between my feet. This particular escape became proverbial in headquarters company.[70]

Because of this as well as other narrow escapes, the soldiers all but developed a superstition: "Everything happens to Nibley, and nothing ever happens to him."[71]

Prior to take off, paratroopers and glider men were allowed to load their fatigues with as much ammunition, medical supplies, and morphine syrettes as they could carry.[72] Unlike other soldiers, Hugh loaded himself up with books. Somehow—he does not explain how—in the landing, he lost "every other possession" except for two books: "an Arabic Koran in my right-hand pocket and Gogol's 'Greatcoat' in Russian in the left."[73] Nevertheless, these two books proved a great comfort in the prolonged confrontation and allowed Hugh to engage in one of his favorite pastimes. "I am cheating like mad, still plugging away at Arabic and Russian when no one is looking," wrote Hugh soon after landing in Holland.[74]

Operation Market-Garden was just as chaotic as D-Day had been, but even larger German forces were waiting for the Allies than they had foreseen. The campaign was "touch and go with our people scattered all over the land and surrounded and outnumbered most of the time," recalled Hugh. The other sergeant in Hugh's three-man OB team was "run over by a tank while he was bringing in our jeep"; the lieutenant was wounded but refused to go to the rear.[75]

Ten days after the Holland operation began, Hugh wrote to his mother. "I have had considerable occasion to think of [Father] in the last some days," Hugh mused. (El Nibley had served two missions to Holland and was, for a short time president of the Holland Mission.) "For lo we are in Holland. The Old World changes very slowly and I am sure this is the same world that he visited on a happier mission many years back."[76]

The Holland mission that Hugh was engaged in was not only horrific and chaotic, but at times quite absurd. "The radio is making all things present," wrote Hugh from the front. "What will it be when television is perfected? To hear Schubert quartets amid the noise of battle or catch the loud expensive commonplaces of Jack Benny while a town is being shot to pieces seems perfectly natural. And if the homeland is moving to the front (how the Germans thrill to those words!) the reverse is also taking place." Holland was also wet, as Hugh noted in the same letter. "The earth here is a rich loam ideally suited to the construction of fox-holes but not conducive to gracious living once they have been built. For Holland it is damp and Holland it is cold, and the water comes from the heavens above and the earth beneath and from all sides

---

[70] Hugh Nibley, Letter to Agnes Sloan Nibley, n.d., ca. summer 1945.
[71] Hugh Nibley, "Faith of an Observer," 173.
[72] Donald R. Burgett, *The Road to Arnhem* (New York: Dell, 2001), 32.
[73] Hugh Nibley, Letter to Lucien Goldschmidt, 8 December 1944.
[74] Hugh Nibley, Letter to Agnes Sloan Nibley, 12 [17] September 1944.
[75] Hugh Nibley, Letter to Agnes Sloan Nibley, n.d., ca. summer 1945.
[76] Hugh Nibley, Letter to Agnes Sloan Nibley, 27 September 1944. Although Hugh addressed the letter to both parents, he speaks only to his mother in it, possibly betraying the rift between father and son that remained from El's losing Hugh's Berkeley fellowship eight years earlier.

round about. Nevertheless, our faith waxeth strong, knowing that these are the last days and that there is much more to come." What made the campaign bearable was the "pleasant drizzle of ripe apples and pears" from the orchards surrounding the battlefield.[77]

Hugh's language skills made him much in demand. Hugh wrote to Lucien Goldschmidt right after the Holland campaign that "Dutch, to which I had been exposed for years, came to me with a rush, and sent me into strange and at times unquiet places on missions of interpreting."[78] Hugh's discharge papers state that he was involved in gathering information "by personal interrogation of prisoners of war, examination of captured documents, and special contacts with civilians, [and] underground personnel." Even though OB teams were not supposed to interrogate prisoners of war, Hugh, who had had IPW training, ended up with the job on more than one occasion. "Like men in a trance even the firmest of them [the German POWs] will suddenly break out with the abrupt admission (which always comes as a surprise) that they knew all along it was only make-believe and never actually believed all that stuff"—by which he meant the Nazi ideology.[79]

By mid-October, a month into what Hugh called "the brown horrors and melancholy shades" of the Holland campaign, it was obvious to everyone that the operation had been a failure.[80] It was bleeding the Allied forces of troops, and they had achieved nothing but a stalemate. On 23 October, Hugh waxed philosophical as he watched the war of attrition continue into its fifth week. "The interesting thing about our age is that not many people are really fooled—we are going into perdition with our eyes open; the separation of the tares and the wheat is to be strictly a free-will affair." The only piece of good news he related was that his health continued to be "disappointingly rugged." "The one virtue of Life in the Field," Hugh continued, "is that it fits you preeminently for Life in the Field."[81]

Just the day before, on 22 October 1944, Margaret Violet Reid Sloan, Hugh's grandmother, died near Cardston, Alberta, Canada, at age eighty-seven. When Hugh learned the news almost two weeks later, he paid her an eloquent tribute: "Grandma's departure marks the end of a lot of good things. For us she is the last of the pioneers. Living clear through the soft, spoiled second generation, she survived to see the third moving into another time of restless motion like her own—a restlessness which she never outgrew."[82]

Finally, on 27 November 1944, Hugh and the troops of the 101st Airborne left the front lines in Holland. They had spent seventy-two days in battle, most of them in muddy foxholes. During that time, the 101st Airborne suffered 3,792 casualties. On 28 November, the troops were trucked to France for rest and recuperation from the

---

[77] Hugh Nibley, Letter to Agnes Sloan Nibley, 12 [17] September 1944.

[78] Hugh Nibley, Letter to Lucien Goldschmidt, 8 December 1944. Hugh had never studied Dutch formally; but he knew German and his father spoke Dutch. Hugh had undoubtedly read some of his father's Dutch books and compared languages with him.

[79] Hugh Nibley, Letter to Agnes Sloan Nibley, 23 October 1944.

[80] Hugh Nibley, Letter to Lucien Goldschmidt, 8 December 1944.

[81] Hugh Nibley, Letter to Agnes Sloan Nibley, 23 October 1944.

[82] Hugh Nibley, Letter to Agnes Sloan Nibley, 5 November 1944.

ordeal of Holland and to prepare for redeployment. This camp, Mourmelon-le-Grand, located twenty miles south of Rheims, had been a battlefield for centuries. Julius Caesar had legions there in 54 B.C. The French had occupied it during World War I, the Germans after June 1940, and now the new legions of the Americans had arrived. Another member of the 101st Airborne remembers that "eroded trenches and shell holes still scarred the old battlegrounds. The barracks with their damp concrete floors and "battle-scarred stucco" walls punctured by bullet holes, were equally dilapidated.[83] Hugh remembers that the encampment was near the World War I battlefield of Sedan, still marked by foxholes, trenches, shell holes, and tangles of barbed wire. "It was very gloomy," recalls Hugh. "It was right back to World War I, right back where we started."[84] It was another reminder that the wisdom of man continued to run in a cycle of foolishness and deadly destruction.

Hugh was now the only uninjured survivor of his OB team; so in early December, he set up an office with interrogator George Allen, whom he had met at Camp Ritchie.[85] The classics scholar and the Philadelphia bookstore owner began to plot the location of the Allied and German troops. Soon Hugh deduced that the Germans were planning to break through the lines at Bastogne. "I predicted it right on the button," notes Hugh. To him it "was obvious exactly where the breakthrough would come . . . who would be there; how strong it was."[86] However, headquarters ignored these reports.

Then 17 December, new information on German positions came into the OB section. George Allen called out the changes in the coordinates as Hugh plotted them on the map. As Allen relates: "In a minute or two we realized that a serious breakthrough had been made in the Allied lines in the area known as the Eiffel on the eastern edge of the Ardennes. . . . The attack had begun about 0400 on the morning of Saturday, 16 December but this was our first knowledge of what was taking place."[87] Soon Generals Tony McAuliffe and Gerald Higgins were in the OB Team's situation room, staring at the map. "Nibley showed [them] the situation as well as he could from the knowledge we had from the map," Allen recalls.

But in the way of bureaucracies, the story was left dangling where Hugh was concerned. On that same day, two replacements, a French-Canadian from Maine named Benoit and a New York City native named Herren, showed up with orders that Hugh was to go to Paris. He showed these two excited replacements "the ropes and they took over." As Hugh headed for Paris, the men of the 101st moved out to

---

[83] Donald R. Burget, *Seven Roads to Hell: A Screaming Eagle at Bastogne* (New York: Dell, 1999), 7; see also Burgett, *The Road to Arnhem*, 214; George R. Allen, *To Bastogne for the Christmas Holidays, 1944* (N.p., n.d.), 5.

[84] Hugh Nibley, "Faith of an Observer," 154.

[85] Hugh Nibley, Letter to Lucien Goldschmidt, 8 December 1944.

[86] Hugh Nibley, "Faith of an Observer," 154.

[87] Allen, *To Bastogne for the Christmas Holidays*, 6. Allen incorrrectly states that it was General Maxwell Taylor who entered the briefing room. However, Taylor was then conferring with superiors in Washington, D.C. In his absence, McAuliffe, who was the divisional artillery commander of the 101st, served as the acting divisional commander. McAuliffe assured himself a place in world history when he answered German demands for American surrender at Bastogne with the four-letter word "Nuts!" on 22 December 1944. Gerald Higgins was chief of staff of the 101st Airborne Division.

Bastogne. Benoit and Herren set up their OB station there in a barracks formerly used by the Hitler Youth. Four days later, a flat-trajectory shell from a tank hit the barracks and killed both. Again, Hugh had narrowly escaped death. George Allen wrote that the men's deaths "made me sadder than I had ever been before. It was the realization of a dream for Benoit and Herren to join an airborne division and their stay lasted just four days. They owed their deaths to their enthusiasm to be with a fighting unit and I owed my life to them for coming when they did."[88] Hugh was now the lone survivor of OB Team #5, a fact noted on his separation papers. Hugh summed up the debâcle sharply: "The big boys at Army Group insist that the breakthrough took them totally by surprise." Although he usually shrugged off most of the manifestations of official stupidity, he characterized this face-saving maneuver as "an unpardonable state of affairs."[89]

Soon after leaving Mourmelon, Hugh reported briefly to his mother that "I was very 'lucky' in the Holland campaign and even luckier in what followed." One of the secrets of his mental resilience emerged in his next sentence: "I don't even believe I have wasted much time in the last year—the art of doing things on the run has become second nature. One doesn't wait till things quiet down any more, because things simply don't quiet down."[90]

The Battle of the Bulge—the Germans' last offensive—ended in collapse. The Allies had pushed the Germans back and restored the original line by 12 January. Warsaw fell on 17 January to the Russians, who then drove all the way to the Oder River by 23 January and began their march to Berlin. Meanwhile the Americans took Cologne and Dusseldorf while the British pursued the Germans in Holland.

From Paris, Hugh was "sent on a safe but quite melodramatic" counter-intelligence mission right back to where he had been, in the Ardennes. At the beginning of the breakthrough, the Germans had parachuted "a lot of people in false uniforms and others dressed up as civilians" behind the lines. Because Hugh spoke both French and German, his job was to help weed out these infiltrators and also spot caches of German equipment hidden in the Ardennes' caves. Hugh was thrilled to scramble around in what he then thought were "the oldest inhabitations in the world."[91]

While the Allied successes at the Battle of the Bulge and elsewhere were cause for military optimism, Hugh saw no moral reason to rejoice. In early February, he wrote, "We can expect no security any more—too many people misbehaving."[92] He was alarmed by the Germans who, he said, "have changed—much for the worse—after their intensive course in autoinfatuation." But he was also alarmed by the Americans. The end of the war became the "high tide for the opportunists," as Hugh called it.

---

[88]Ibid., 13. In a letter Hugh wrote to his mother immediately after the war, Hugh tells of Benoit's and Herren's death, dating it as the day after he left for Paris. Allen's account says their deaths occurred four days into their duty. Allen's account is likely more accurate on this point, since he was in Bastogne when it happened while Hugh would have heard the story second-hand.

[89]Hugh Nibley, Letter to Agnes Sloan Nibley, n.d., ca. summer 1945.

[90]Hugh Nibley, Letter to Agnes Sloan Nibley, 19 December 1944.

[91]Hugh Nibley, Teachings of the Book of Mormon: Transcripts of Lectures Presented to an Honors Book of Mormon Class at Brigham Young University 1989-90 (Provo, UT: FARMS, n.d.): Semester 2, Lecture 37, 3.

[92]Hugh Nibley, Letter to Agnes Sloan Nibley, 3 February 1945.

"One would like to ignore them, but they are going to wreck everything, just wait and see."[93]

In March, Hugh was given another furlough. Again he returned to the Scottish Highlands. "I am almost tempted to call them 'my' Highlands," wrote Hugh, "I know them so well, though there is certainly nothing cozy or intimate about them."[94] Upon returning from the restful trip, Hugh wrote to Paul Springer, giving the Highlands the highest praise possible. "There are valleys in the Scottish Highlands which move me almost as deeply as [Zion National Park] itself."[95]

By April 1945, Hugh was transferred to the 6th Army Group and was stationed in Luxembourg with a great deal of unoccupied time. It was another upscale assignment: "We live in sumptuous quarters and have a club that makes the pavilions of the Golden Horn look like something on the wrong side of the tracks," Hugh wrote breezily to his mother.[96]

On 25 April, the Russians took Berlin. The following day, American troops met Russian troops at the Elbe River near Torgau. German resistance was crushed. Hitler's suicide was announced on 1 May, and Berlin fell to the Russians on the following day. the formal act of surrender occurred at Allied headquarters at Reims, France, on 7 May. Soon after the German surrender, Hugh was stationed in Heidelberg. There he spent four months studying Russian with a native Russian tutor.[97] He also found more books which "are too good to miss at the present give-away prices."[98] He reassured his mother that he was not being extravagant: "[Don't] let the books I keep sending give you wrong ideas—I simply keep picking them up because they are both very rare and very cheap."[99]

The military documents in Heidelberg that Hugh was processing with other intelligence teams revealed new depths of war's depravity. He wrote bitterly to Paul Springer: "During the past few months I have had some extremely interesting documents in my hands, for Heidelberg is the official depository of all German war documents; invariably these paper loving boors waited until too late to destroy documents, and the result is that you had better not try to tell little old me who started the war."[100]

Even worse than the documents implicating German leaders in war crimes was the clear involvement of several U.S. corporations in the profiteering schemes that had led directly to the war.[101] Hugh later wrote: "The tension, suspicion, and sheer despair that filled the air of Heidelberg were at times simply unbearable."[102] Several days after

---

[93]Hugh Nibley, Letter to Agnes Sloan Nibley, 17 April 1945.
[94]Hugh Nibley, Letter to Agnes Sloan Nibley, 3 March 1945.
[95]Hugh Nibley, Letter to Paul Springer, postmarked 5 May 1945.
[96]Hugh Nibley, Letter to Agnes Sloan Nibley, n.d., ca. summer 1945.
[97]Hugh Nibley, Letter to Paul Springer, n.d., ca. 1946.
[98]Hugh Nibley, Letter to Agnes Sloan Nibley, n.d., ca. summer 1945.
[99]Hugh Nibley, Letter to Agnes Sloan Nibley, n.d., ca. August 1945.
[100]Hugh Nibley, Letter to Paul Springer, n.d., ca. August 1945.
[101]Hugh Nibley, "Faith of an Observer," 77-78; 159-60; Nibley, *Teachings of the Book of Mormon, Semester 3*, Lecture 65, 94. See also Charles Higham, *Trading with the Enemy: An Exposé of the Nazi-American Money Plot, 1933-1949* (New York: Delacorte, 1983), esp. 32-62.
[102]Hugh Nibley, Letter to Paul Springer, n.d., early summer 1946.

Master Sergeant Hugh Nibley in 1945 near the end of the war near Heidelberg, Germany.

the German concentration camp of Dachau was liberated on 29 April 1945, Hugh visited it. To this day it is the one war memory Hugh refuses to discuss.

This blow drove him deeper into disillusionment. "The major change in my constitution," wrote Hugh distractedly in August to Paul Springer, "has been the development of a deep and chronic dislike for anything German. After three months in lovely Heidelberg, the only undamaged city in Germany, . . . I am fed up. . . . It is a wicked world and one in which there is little to choose between one group and another—but one of the few things that is clear is that the Germans, by their own choice, are a world apart, whose monumental humbug is only equalled by their zeal for dehumanizing everything they touch."[103]

All of the Allied soldiers were disgusted by discovery of German atrocities at the end of the war. But Hugh, who wrote that his "adolescent thinking was all cast in the German mold," had served his mission in Germany and knew first-hand the

---

[103]Hugh Nibley, Letter to Paul Springer, n.d., ca. August 1945. Nibley then quoted in German a lengthy passage—over a thousand words—from Friedrich Hölderlin's *Hyperion*, a lyric epistolary novel first published in 1797. It was a stinging denunciation of Germans as "barbarians from the remotest past, whom industry and science and even religion have made yet more barbarous, profoundly incapable of any divine emotion, spoiled to the core for the delights of the sacred Graces, offensive to every well-conditioned soul through the whole range from pretense to pettiness, hollow and tuneless, like the shards of a discarded pot." Struggling to understand how the Germans had become a people "at odds with themselves," Hölderlin accused them of a "niggardly anxiety" about an endless round of chores and labors undertaken so unimaginatively and so joylessly that he found it no wonder that he saw "so much botched work among them and so little that is free, that gives any genuine pleasure." He summarized: "The virtues of the Germans are glittering vices and nothing more; for they are but forced labor, wrung from the sterile heart in craven fear, with the toil of slaves, and they impart no comfort to any pure soul. . . . They leave nothing pure uncorrupted, nothing sacred untouched by their coarse hands. . . . Life with them is stale and burdened with cares and full of cold, silent discord, because they scorn the Genius, which brings power and nobility into human endeavor, and serenity into suffering, and love and brotherhood to towns and houses." Without imagination, they feared death so terribly that they "bear every indignity, for they know nothing higher than the bungling job that they have made of things." Willard R. Trask, trans., *Hyperion and Selected Poems*, edited by Eric L. Santner, Vol. 22 of *The German*

potential goodness of the German people. He was emotionally shattered by the revelations at the war's end as he had not been during the war itself. "I was particularly miserable because I knew the fundamental excellence that lay beneath the rubble-heaps of folly and ruin, and that a vast and admirable intelligence was being dedicated to wanton destruction. Why must the Germans behave that way?" In the same letter, Hugh related how he had been walking behind a German couple in the woods one day as they spoke about Hitler, calling him "a sordid opportunist—and they might have known it all along, fools that they had been, for couldn't anyone see that he had *dark* hair instead of blond!" Hugh bitterly concluded, "It is the Germans themselves who have not been true to their great tradition—you have no idea how sterile and immoral the Nazi mind was, or do you?"[104]

Nor could Hugh take comfort from the ideals of his own countrymen. As the American army settled into occupation mode, both morale and morals declined sharply. "The God of Battles has become the God of Brothels," wrote Hugh in revulsion. Looting, drinking, and whoring were the chief activities of the American soldier in post-war Germany. Hugh grew deeply depressed as he watched some of "those whom I knew for the best of Saints" give up "their good works in weary disgust and turn to the ways of the world in the worst possible sense. I don't know a single exception. The Army is exacting a frightful toll for its noisy services."[105]

As Hugh found himself a lonely hold-out in his morals, he also found himself alone in apparently reaping no rewards from his patriotic service. He remained a master sergeant while others he had worked with in military intelligence received commissions. Perhaps the tang of sour grapes was on his tongue when he wrote: "Careers are a dime a dozen these days—you should see the 'brass' around here! We are not impressed. Their power and authority is a very little thing, and if you must take it seriously, then the men themselves become ridiculous."[106] He also wrote of how these officers, most of whom had been "worlds removed from the war," were spending "all their time pinning decorations [on] each other, the Lord knows for what."[107] Someone who was completely uninterested in rank and decorations probably would not have noticed such silliness, so it is likely that being passed over for a commission really did bother Hugh. After all, at age thirty-five, he was older than most of the men his rank, he had his doctorate and had been a college professor before the war; but most of all, he had more battle experience than most of his superiors. On the other hand, Max Oppenheimer, who ran into Hugh at the conclusion of the war, wrote that Hugh, although he "performed his duties well," really "had no interest in the military" and was simply "awaiting the day he could return to his beloved teaching and research."[108] In a coincidence of cosmic irony, OB Team #5 received a Presidential Citation for valor; but by then, Hugh had been reassigned and

---

Library (New York: Continuum, 1990), 127-30.

[104]Hugh Nibley, Letter to Paul Springer, n.d., early summer 1946.

[105]Hugh Nibley, Letter to Agnes Sloan Nibley, n.d., ca. summer 1945. This letter, which begins "Since my last note," is different from that in Appendix C.

[106]Hugh Nibley, Letter to Agnes Sloan Nibley, 3 February 1945.

[107]Hugh Nibley, Letter to Agnes Sloan Nibley, n.d., ca. summer 1945.

[108]Oppenheimer, *An Innocent Yank at Home Abroad*, 248.

it went to a later group that had seen little action "after the shooting had stopped." He dismissed it as "just typical army."[109]

However, Hugh enjoyed his chief benefit as a master sergeant: use of an army jeep. He seized every opportunity to travel around Europe a great deal during the summer of 1945. He wrote his mother a hasty itinerary, "After Luxembourg, Belgium for a few weeks and then Paris again. Paris becomes a terrible habit. For the past month I have been in Heidelberg, which has not been scratched by the war. [But] Mannheim and Ludwigshafen have simply ceased to exist."[110] (He had spent a month and a half—part of December and all of January 1928—in Ludwigshafen on his mission.) For a short time, Hugh was detailed to escort Vladimir Kirillovich Romanov, the Grand Duke of Russia, whose family had been in exile (apparently in Germany) since the execution of Nicholas II and his family on 16 July 1918.[111] "We drove around to visit various dignitaries and his family, finally ending up in their family castle in Odenwald where his sister was." As they traveled around the German countryside, Vladimir, an unassuming man of twenty-six, became terrified every time they ran into a Russian soldier. Hugh, in contrast, was very impressed by the Russian soldiers he met. "Most of the Russians I have talked to are simply bursting with energy and good spirits and an honest desire to better themselves—there is nothing 'negative' about them; the salt of the earth, I say."[112] In another letter, he stated warmly: "I think the Lord has big things in mind for them."[113] The future horrors of Stalinism were a crime he could not anticipate at this time.

After the war ended in Europe, Hugh gloomily assumed that he would "end up in the Far East, though I don't relish the prospect."[114] However, the war with Japan ended shortly thereafter when the United States dropped atomic bombs on Hiroshima on 6 August and, three days later, on Nagasaki. On 14 August, Japan surrendered. Despite his personal relief, Hugh darkly predicted that the new bomb "has already made the next war inevitable and perhaps final." He resignedly commented: "If we must act with the high-handed immorality of the gods, it is only right to have our bluff called and the reins thrust into our hands—but of course there can only be one end to the farce."[115]

On 27 October 1945 Hugh sailed for the States, arriving on 9 November 1945. On 19 November at Fort MacArthur, California, the very place where he had begun his

---

[109] Hugh Nibley, "Faith of an Observer," 155. Hugh's discharge papers confirm, however, that he "received a special Presidential Citation early in 1945."

[110] Hugh Nibley, Letter to Agnes Sloan Nibley, n.d., ca. summer 1945.

[111] Hugh Nibley, "Faith of an Observer," 159-60; Hugh Nibley, interviewed by Zina Petersen, 22 February 2002. As the son of Grand Duke Kirill Romanov, Vladimir was the eldest cousin of Nicholas II and great-grandson of Alexander II. In 1922, he proclaimed himself heir to the throne, a claim that the Soviet rulers naturally ignored. He died in Miami on 21 April 1992 but was buried in the Peter and Paul's Fortress, St. Petersburg. Hugh noted that he had read, in the 1970s or 1980s, that Vladimir had joined the LDS Church in New Zealand, but I have been unable to confirm this memory.

[112] Hugh Nibley, Letter to Agnes Sloan Nibley, 3 March 1945.

[113] Hugh Nibley, Letter to Agnes Sloan Nibley, n.d., ca. summer 1945.

[114] Hugh Nibley, Letter to Paul Springer, n.d., ca. August 1945.

[115] Hugh Nibley, Letter to Agnes Sloan Nibley, n.d., ca. August 1945.

military service three years, one month, and twenty-two days earlier, he was given an honorable discharge.

Rifle slung over his shoulder, Hugh snatches a moment to immerse himself in his edition of Mikhail Yuryevich Lermontov (1814-41) a gift from a Russian woman. Lermontov, a Romantic, was inspired by the scenery of the Caucasus and was killed at age twenty-seven in a duel.

While driving to Salt Lake one day in 1967 in Hugh's decrepit chalky red Volkswagen, for a day searching through Brigham Young's manuscript histories in the Church Historian's office, I discovered that I was not alone in Provo opposing the Vietnam War. Hugh, like Holocaust survivors and other real victims of war takes no joy in re-living, or in dragging others through our man-made Hells. But bear witness Hugh does. It is normal that, following World War II's trauma, Hugh felt repulsed and fatigued by the war histories in the Book of Mormon. But as America's Vietnam metastasized, the professional historian's lens he had kept focused at a safer distance—on raiding in Lehi's desert, the ancient Jaredites, and ritual in battle—was no longer adequate to the present world of real and senseless evil, pain, and tragedy. Hugh responded, studying the Book of Mormon in precisely the way he had avoided for decades, as an extraordinarily trained soldier and witness of the Order of Battle on the broadest scale. Whatever the effort cost him, we are blessed by that work, and not because of its obvious apologetic utility or its technical sophistication. His writings sustain and turn us again to the scriptures, through Kuwait, Afghanistan, and whatever lies beyond.
—Gordon Thomasson[1]

---

[1] Gordon C. Thomasson, e-mail to Boyd Petersen, 7 May 2002. Gordon is on the world history faculty at Broome Community College (SUNY), at Binghamton, New York. He wrote *War, Conscription, Conscience, and Mormonism* (Santa Barbara, CA: Mormon Heritage, 1971) during the heat of the Vietnam War.

Chapter 14

"The Work of Death": Hugh Nibley and War

During Operation Market-Garden, the seventy-two-day, bloody, and ill-fated invasion of Holland, Master Sergeant David Harmon was on patrol with Colonel Howard R. Johnson when they saw a car being driven by a German officer. Johnson ordered Harmon to shoot the German since he might be carrying information that would help the Allies. It was a moving target but only medium range. Harmon lifted his rifle and fired, hitting the driver in the head and killing him instantly. Sure enough, in the car they found a briefcase crammed with secret documents. Although he had obeyed an order during a wartime patrol, Harmon was deeply troubled by having killed the German officer in such a calculated way. "He'd done a lot of shooting," Hugh remembers, but for some reason, the fact that he had shot this officer in the head "preyed on his mind." Following the withdrawal of U.S. forces to Mourmelon-le-Grand on 28 November 1944, Hugh was sharing a tent with Harmon. Harmon gave Hugh the German officer's briefcase, locks broken and its fine leather stained with blood, but still functional. One night, Harmon came into the tent, sat down on the bunk next to Hugh, and asked, "Nibley, if I want to kill myself, it's my own goddamn business, isn't it?" As calmly as he could, Hugh tried to assure Harmon that killing himself would affect a lot of other people and was really not a good solution. But "suddenly he whipped out a little Beretta automatic that he had in his pocket, a little Italian Beretta. Shot himself right through the head. Blood splattering all over the place. I put towels around his head and then ran over to the medics but he was dead before that. He just couldn't stand living with it."[2]

---

[2]Hugh Nibley, "Faith of an Observer," 155, compilation of interviews, ca. 1983-84 for a video documentary of the same name aired in 1985, photocopy of typescript in my possession, pagination added. In this quoted passage, I have silently removed the transcriber's ellipses which indicate, not omitted material, but pauses in the narration.

For more than thirty years, Hugh carried that stained briefcase while teaching at BYU. It invariably bulged with books and papers, but its real purpose was to serve as a lasting and tangible symbol of the evils of war.[3]

Hugh Nibley knows warfare, ancient and modern, better than most. As a young boy, he heard long discussions about World War I around the dinner table at his home in Portland. In California, he received proficiency awards for his involvement in the high school ROTC program; his instructor had served in the Spanish-American War. Hugh studied ancient warfare in his classical history courses at UCLA and Berkeley. At Military Intelligence School in the U.S. Army, he learned not only the tactics, disposition, and make-up of the German army, but he also read von Clausewitz and other theoretical texts on warfare. While in training at Camp Ritchie, Hugh had visited the Civil War battlefields of Antietam and Gettysburg, and his voracious reading had given him an impressive knowledge of Civil War history. And finally, Hugh was given what he called a "grand-stand seat" from which to view the enterprise of World War II in the European theater.[4] "I was in the perfect position to observe," states Hugh.[5] As part of an Order of Battle team, his job was to see the war in overview, to be "the hotly detached observer," and to know the strength, disposition, and location of all units of both armies.[6] "I had to know what was going on right from the very beginning," remembers Hugh. "I kept the situation maps."

But being attached to the 101st Airborne, he also saw combat up close from inside a foxhole, "face all blackened, and clusters of grenades on," carrying his "trusty carbine."[7] War was anything but theoretical. He drove one of the first jeeps onto Utah Beach on D-Day, landed in a glider in Holland during operation Market-Garden, predicted the German breakthrough at Bastogne, helped apprehend German infiltrators throughout the Battle of the Bulge, and witnessed the ultimate demise of the Nazi war machine. Truly Hugh is an authority on warfare.

And the result of that very expertise is an unshakable cynicism about war. At the time of World War II, Hugh's knowledge of ancient history made him skeptical about the effectiveness of war as a solution to the world's problems, but his involvement in World War II left him convinced that war in general is a "nasty and immoral business." In the men who fought on both sides in the conflict, Hugh discovered both heroism and unspeakable cruelty. While affirming that "the heroism and sacrifice were real," Hugh has unsparingly denounced the situation of war as "utterly satanic and shameful."[8]

It was Hugh's knowledge of ancient history coupled with his careful reading and deep understanding of the scriptures that shaped his view of world events in the 1940s. Many times in letters written from the front, he compared the world crisis to historical incidents, citing scriptural prophecy to bring home his point. In France six weeks after D-Day, Hugh wrote that the events reminded him of "the Fourth Century all over again, with its desperate yearning for quiet security running against an insuperable and mounting

---

[3]Ibid., 155.

[4]Hugh Nibley, Letter to Agnes Sloan Nibley, n.d., ca. summer 1945. See chaps. 12 and 13.

[5]Hugh Nibley, "Faith of an Observer," 164.

[6]Hugh Nibley, Letter to Agnes Sloan Nibley, n.d., ca. summer 1945.

[7]Hugh Nibley, "Faith of an Observer," 164.

[8]Hugh Nibley, "Beyond Politics," originally published in BYU Studies 9, no. 1 (Autumn 1974): 3-28; reprinted in Nibley on the Timely and Timeless (Provo, UT: BYU Religious Studies Center, 1978): 300.

inclination to moral degeneracy."[9] Since the censorship regulations would not allow Hugh to describe the Market-Garden fiasco, Hugh instead used what amounted to an erudite code: "More I cannot tell, so we must needs talk about the fifth century to fill up space." Then he compared the moral state of 400 A.D. with the one he was experiencing in 1944:

> Truth has the face of a creditor whom no one alive has ever completely paid up—so none of us have the courage to look her in the eye. By the fifth century the people of the West had run up such colossal arrears to the lady, thanks to various types of moral, mental and economic misbehavior, that they just couldn't face it. They settled instead for the poor shabby philosophy of St. Augustine—sit tight, don't ask questions, do like the rest do, and you will be at least as safe as anybody else.[10]

Several months later while he was still in Holland, Hugh described the reversal of values he saw around him—of "calling black white and vice virtue"—which he again compared to an earlier time: "The 4th century BC and the 6th AD are terrible examples," he warned. "In the time of total confusion which lies ahead let us not forget how clearly our own behavior has foreshadowed the horrible commotion of the earth and the elements."[11]

This historical perspective would not allow Hugh ever to view war as a sane answer to the world's problems. War had never worked in the past, and it could not work in the present. Additionally, the scriptures teach that war is nothing more nor less than Satan's tool. Soon after joining the army, Hugh wrote, "I can't possibly see how anything can be settled by the war or after it until somebody gets more sense than we have. This time of troubles is going to outlast all of us, but in that case we will simply be in the same boat with the human race that has preceded us."[12] Similarly, from Camp Ritchie he foresaw:

> I think you will agree by now that the war will be a long one, with the Devil enjoying increasing "control over his own dominion," and everybody getting into a progressively nasty state of mind, until the whole world-society locks itself up to sulk and starve behind Medieval walls. The only comfort in this is that we deserve what we are going to get; of course we will learn to take whatever comes and end up in a mood of Oriental resignation which, if history means anything, is the natural, sorry, stable state of man.[13]

As he learned more about the inner workings of war at Camp Ritchie, he became even more convinced about its insanity. At the end of his first course of intelligence training, Hugh wrote: "I still stick to my original conception of the present mess as a long

---

[9] Hugh Nibley, Letter to Agnes Sloan Nibley, 26 July 1944.
[10] Hugh Nibley, Letter to Agnes Sloan Nibley, 27 September 1944.
[11] Hugh Nibley, Letter to Agnes Sloan Nibley, 5 November 1944.
[12] Hugh Nibley, Letter to Agnes Sloan Nibley, postmarked 6 November 1942.
[13] Hugh Nibley, Letter to Agnes Sloan Nibley, postmarked 28 April 1943. Evidently, Hugh is alluding to Moses 6:15: "And in those days Satan had great dominion among men, and raged in their hearts; and from thenceforth came wars and bloodshed; and a man's hand was against his own brother, in administering death, because of secret works, seeking for power."

series of heartless and joyless engagements, of endless significance for the future, but very saddening to live through."[14] After completing his Order of Battle training, Hugh reiterated the same theme: "I am more convinced than ever that this war will bring about no good."[15]

Soon Hugh saw his predictions become realities. His years of combat taught him six things.[16] First, he learned that the men on both sides of the conflict were basically good. "A fantastically large proportion—I'd say around 10%—of our soldiers are surprisingly high-minded and well-behaved," wrote Hugh from the war front.[17] The German soldiers likewise impressed Hugh. As he later wrote, "The POWs we rounded up to interrogate were men just as good as we were, the victims of a terrible circumstance that the devil's game of power and gain had woven around them."[18]

Second, Hugh learned that men on both sides were capable of great evil. In Normandy, he was sickened to discover that "our boys were acting worse than the Germans, . . . as far as atrocities were concerned." To the nation's shame, "the French were soon preferring them to us as a matter of fact and told us that quite frankly."[19] Cynically, he quoted Jacob Christopher Burckhardt: "Behold the soldier—when he is hungry he steals, and when he is full he fornicates. . . . That covers everything."[20] And any hopes he may have had for German virtue died when he saw Dachau.

Third, Hugh learned that, in the military, careers are built chiefly on the battlefield. As a result, ambitious men longed for the continuation of war. Hugh remembers the gloom that pervaded the upper echelons as the war was drawing to a close: "The war was ending too fast, recalls Hugh. "It meant the end of quick promotions. It meant the slowing down of careers."[21] He later drew on this situation to illustrate the "Mahan Principle"—by which he meant Cain's "great secret" from the Book of Moses "of converting . . . your life [into] my promotion."[22] Just before the Battle of the Bulge, Hugh

---

[14]Hugh Nibley, Letter to Agnes Sloan Nibley, 3 June 1943.

[15]Hugh Nibley, Letter to Agnes Sloan Nibley, postmarked 24 September 1943.

[16]It is interesting to compare Hugh's attitudes about war with those of J. Reuben Clark, who served as counselor in the First Presidency to Heber J. Grant, George Albert Smith, and David O. McKay. Clark felt that the Treaty of Versailles had been a "vengeful and unjust punishment of Germany for all of Europe's mistakes" and the ultimate origin of World War II. He argued for American neutrality as the European conflict broke out. In 1939, he authored a First Presidency statement that condemned war in general; and in 1944, he encouraged America to strive for "a peace based on justice rather than might." Despite his anti-Communist sentiments, Clark would also later oppose the U.S. military's entrance into the Korean and Vietnamese wars. D. Michael Quinn, *Elder Statesman: A Biography of J. Reuben Clark* (Salt Lake City: Signature Books, 2002), 277-317.

[17]Hugh Nibley, Letter to Agnes Sloan Nibley, 3 March 1945.

[18]Nibley, *Nibley on the Timely and the Timeless*, 300.

[19]Hugh Nibley, "Faith of an Observer," 167.

[20]Hugh Nibley, Letter to Paul Springer, n.d., ca. December 1945. Burckhardt (1918-97) was a professor of history at Basel University (1858-93), best-known for his works on the Italian Renaissance and on Greek civilization.

[21]Hugh Nibley, *Teachings of the Book of Mormon: Transcripts of Lectures Presented to an Honors Book of Mormon Class at Brigham Young University*, 1989-90 (Provo, UT: FARMS, n.d.): Semester 3, Lecture 67, 119.

[22]Hugh Nibley, "Intellectual Autobiography," xxiv. Hugh is alluding to Moses 5:31: "And Cain said: Truly I am Mahan, the master of this great secret, that I may murder and get gain. Wherefore Cain was called Master Mahan, and he gloried in his wickedness."

wrote Lucien Goldschmidt: "The whole world today is paying the price of a few careers. I have never objected to being the simple-minded implement of other men's greatness, but one can hardly submit to that without becoming the foil of their spite; for when the mighty fight, the mighty clash by proxy. We are the humble abrasive that polishes their armor."[23]

Fourth, Hugh discovered an even more frightening example of the Mahan Principle, that of "converting life into property—your life for my property."[24] Some businesses were profiting from the war by maintaining interests on both sides of the conflict. "I had to snoop into everything," remembers Hugh. "And I found out all sorts of things I shouldn't have found out. The whole thing was being run as a game for profits." In particular, Hugh discovered incriminating evidence while "mopping up" in Heidelberg at the end of the war that Standard Oil and I. G. Farben "had an equal part on both sides in the war." To a class of students later, he hinted: "I could tell you stories that would amaze the faculties of eyes and ears, 'chill your young blood, and cause each particular hair to stand on end, like quills upon the fretful porpentine.'"[25]

Fifth, Hugh gained a firm knowledge that the military is able to control few things but is also capable of supreme chaos and large-scale blunders. On D-Day, Hugh saw first-hand how the weather threw off the carefully planned landing. "They couldn't move on the 5th. They had to move on the 6th. That threw everything out for us, but it saved our lives because the Germans were expecting us on the 5th." When the Allied troops finally did land, "everything went foul, people being landed on the wrong beach, the wrong things being landed at the wrong time, . . . all sorts of confusion, not getting the things you wanted and the like."[26] As he wrote from Heidelberg at the end of the war, "The Army is no more incompetent than it ever was, only during operations its blunders are strict military secrets: oy! could I write a book, me with my grand stand seat—always the hotly detached observer."[27]

Finally, the most important lesson Hugh learned from his war years was that war is wasteful and wrong. "I remember General Bradley said, 'War is waste!' And that's what it is, you see. The utter wastefulness of the thing. But the wrongness of what we were doing was so strong that everybody would cry. People would cry; they would weep! It was so utterly, unspeakably sad! It was so sad you could hardly stand it. That people would do such things to each other."[28]

---

[23] Hugh Nibley, Letter to Lucien Goldschmidt, 8 December 1944.

[24] Nibley, "Intellectual Autobiography," xxiv.

[25] Hugh Nibley, *Teachings of the Book of Mormon*, Semester 3, Lecture 65, 94. Hugh is quoting Shakespeare's *Hamlet*, Act 1.5.

[26] Hugh Nibley, "Faith of an Observer," 374.

[27] Hugh Nibley, Letter to Agnes Sloan Nibley, n.d., ca. summer 1945.

[28] Hugh Nibley, "Faith of an Observer," 158. General Omar Nelson Bradley (1893-1981) graduated from West Point (1915) and rose slowly through the grades in the peacetime army. A protégé of Army Chief-of-Staff George C. Marshall, Bradley succeeded George C. Patton commanding the Second Corps in 1943, leading it through the Tunisia and Sicily campaigns. He commanded the U.S. First Army in the Normandy landings on 6 June 1944 and the Twelfth Army group in France (with 1.4 million combat troops, it became the largest field command in U.S. history) until the German surrender in May 1945. A hardworking, unassuming officer, known as the "GI general" because of his concern for the welfare of ordinary soldiers, he also served as head of the Veterans Administration (1945-47), as U.S. Army Chief of Staff (1948-49), and as first chair of the Joint Chiefs of Staff (1949).

Despite Hugh's relief at the war's ending, he had little faith that the peace would be permanent. His knowledge of history and scripture forbade such an idealistic conclusion. "Meanwhile we are moving with unerring compliance to prophecy straight into the Next War: nobody seems to believe even halfheartedly that the peace is permanent. We never will learn that there is no point to being clever."[29] Unfortunately, Hugh was correct in his prediction. Within months, the United States and the Soviet Union were squaring off in the cold war, while hot wars broke out in Korea in the 1950s and in Vietnam in the 1960s.

As Hugh watched these conflicts, he could not remain silent. In a 1971 letter to the editor criticizing the Vietnam War, he specified: "This is not a protest, just a timely reminder that we may remember when it happens that we have been warned and forewarned."[30] He strongly warned Church members that their mission was to be engaged in peace, not war. He first articulated this anti-war message in his 1967 *Since Cumorah*. It was published when 380,000 U.S. troops were stationed in Vietnam, and U.S. casualties in the war had reached 6,664 dead with 37,738 wounded. *Since Cumorah* was, like his previous books *Lehi in the Desert* and *An Approach to the Book of Mormon*, devoted to surveying the evidence for the truth claims of the Book of Mormon. But in it, Hugh seized the opportunity to brilliantly outline the Book of Mormon's approach to war.[31]

From the start, Hugh confessed that he was always repulsed and fatigued by the 170 pages of "wars and alarms" in the Book of Mormon and that he always felt "inclined to rush through the military parts of the Book of Mormon as painful reminders of an unpleasant past." But he admitted that this had been the wrong approach. For the Book of Mormon paints war in very authentic terms which would be inconsistent with the type of romanticized fiction circulated in frontier America. For Hugh, the depictions of war in the Book of Mormon are further proof of the book's authenticity as he notes in *Since Cumorah*:

In an insightful response to my reading a version of this chapter at the Mormon History Association annual conference, 17 May 2002, at Tucson, Arizona, John W. Welch proposed several additional lessons Hugh had learned or should have learned from his war experience: (1) that we never know enough or all we ought to know (e.g., the army did not have all of the information it needed about German strengths and positions in Holland); (2) that sometimes one's sense of duty must override one's personal distaste (e.g., Hugh interrogated prisoners despite his moral reservations); (3) that one should be critical of everything in this world; (4) that providence is real and God frequently intervenes in the affairs of humans; (5) that the divine plan is both inexorable and repeating; (6) that just as there was a final "revelation" of all of the German documents at Heidelberg, there will be a final revelation of our own lives' deeds; (7) that one should not make absolute judgments based on generalizations or caricatures (e.g., even though Hugh wrote of America's "moral superiority," he witnessed how Americans could stoop to very immoral levels); (8) that we cannot very well judge others—only weep with them; (9) that comic relief is also divine; and (10) that it is not a cure to hide out in hieroglyphics; Hugh could seek temporary relief in his studies, but he could not avoid the reality at hand.

[29] Hugh Nibley, Letter to Agnes Sloan Nibley, n.d., ca. summer 1945.

[30] Hugh Nibley, "Renounce War, Or a Substitute for Victory," *Brother Brigham Challenges the Saints*, edited Don E. Norton and Shirley S. Ricks, Vol. 13 in *The Collected Works of Hugh Nibley* (Salt Lake City: Deseret Books/FARMS, 1994), 269.

[31] Hugh examined Book of Mormon warfare in his 1957 priesthood manual, *An Approach to the Book of Mormon*, chap. 17, "A Strange Order of Battle," and chap. 30, "Strategy for Survival." However, he did not discuss the ethics of war until *Since Cumorah*, edited by John W. Welch (1967; reprinted (Salt Lake City: Deseret/FARMS, 1988).

> War is anything but glamorous in the Book of Mormon; the campaigns and battles are described not as a writer of fiction would depict ancient warfare with all its excitement and color; all that a romantically inclined young American of the 1820s would imagine as the gaudy trappings of heroic derringdo is conspicuously missing. It is real war that we see here, a tedious, sordid, plodding, joyless routine of seesaw successes and losses—brutally expensive, destructive, exhausting, and boring, with constant marches and countermarches that end sometimes in fiasco and sometimes in intensely unpleasant engagements. The author writes as one would write—as only one could write—who had gone through a long war as a frontline observer with his eyes wide open. Everything is strictly authentic, with the proper emphasis in the proper place. Strategy and tactics are treated with the knowledge of an expert: logistics and supply; armaments and fortifications; recruiting and training; problems of morale and support from the home front; military intelligence from cloak and dagger to scouting and patrolling; interrogation, guarding, feeding, and exchange of war prisoners; propaganda and psychological warfare; rehabilitation and resettlement; feelers for peace and negotiations at various levels; treason; profiteering; and the exploitation of the war economy by individuals and groups—it is all there.

Hugh challenges Book of Mormon critics: "Let the reader judge whether anyone writing in the peaceful world of the 1820s could have faked this complicated and swiftly moving history of the distinguished military career of Captain Moroni." But Hugh sees the presence of wars in the book as more than just evidence. The wars are there to warn us.

> The whole point of Alma's (or rather Mormon's) studies in "the work of death" as he calls it, is that they are supposed to be revolting, they are meant to be painful. It is Mormon and Moroni, the tragic survivors of a nation destroyed in a senseless war, who are editing this book, and they put into it whatever they think might be useful as a warning to us. It is not their purpose to tell an entertaining or reassuring tale.

Hugh concludes that for the Book of Mormon's authors, war is "nasty, brutalizing, wasteful, dirty, degrading, fatiguing, foolish, immoral, and above all unnecessary."[32] Furthermore, he argues that the Book of Mormon shows war as the inevitable fruit of true wickedness on both sides. Contrary to conventional thinking, Hugh argues that war "is never a case of 'good guys versus bad guys.'" Rather, it is always a case of the wicked destroying the wicked, exactly as Mormon 4:5 puts it: "It is by the wicked that the wicked are punished.... Whenever Nephites and Lamanites fight it is because both have rebelled against God.[33] Righteousness for its part invariably brings peace. "Whenever the Nephites were truly righteous, ... the old polarization broke down or vanished completely."[34] In *Since Cumorah*, Hugh not only broke new ground in Book of Mormon scholarship by examining warfare but also warned his Mormon audience in stinging terms that war is wicked and wasteful.

In the late sixties and early seventies, Hugh began to examine the sermons, published and unpublished, of Brigham Young, and there he found more support for his

---
[32] Nibley, *Since Cumorah*, 291-92.
[33] Ibid., 342-43.
[34] Ibid., 340.

views on war. In 1970, *The Young Democrat*, published by the Young Democrats of BYU, ran Hugh's essay "Brigham Young and the Enemy."[35] It explored Brigham Young's views on war, showing how in his prophetic role he consistently advocated peace, even in the face of approaching U.S. troops or conflicts with the Indians. "How then do we deal with the enemy?" queried Hugh. "Brigham Young, who knew as much about as large a variety of enemies as any man who ever lived, has laid it on the line: If we show our Heavenly Father that we trust him to the point of putting aside all feelings of malice and revenge towards our fellowmen, no matter who they may be or how they feel toward us, he will see to it that 'the wicked shall destroy the wicked' (cf. Mormon 4:5)."[36]

By 1971, the Vietnam conflict was becoming increasingly divisive, with large anti-war protests erupting throughout the nation. The revelation in late 1970 of the My Lai massacre of civilians on 16 March 1968 left many Americans sickened. In March 1971, support for President Richard M. Nixon's conduct of the war was at an all-time low of 34 percent, and 51 percent of Americans felt that the conflict was "morally wrong."[37] At other campuses throughout the country, protesting the war was common. At BYU, the combination of a authoritarian administration and a largely conservative student body kept political protest to a minimum.[38]

On 23 to 26 March 1971, the Young Americans for Freedom, a conservative political student group, cosponsored with the Academics Office screenings of the film *No Substitute for Victory*. Hollywood personalities John Wayne and Martha Raye appeared in the production with a host of military and political leaders. Perhaps most significant to BYU students was the appearance of Apostle Ezra Taft Benson, in his role as former Secretary of Agriculture. The film argued that the United States could win the Vietnam conflict quickly if military, rather than political, leaders were put in charge. Several students wrote letters to the *Daily Universe*, complaining that the film was propaganda and that documentaries critical of the war were forbidden. On the last day of the film's showing, the *Universe* published a letter by Hugh Nibley. He argued that there was indeed a very good "substitute for victory," and cited Doctrine and Covenants 98:16-17 which commands the Saints to "renounce war and proclaim peace." "Renounce is a strong word," continued Hugh. "We are not to try to win peace by war, or merely to call a truce, but to renounce war itself, to disclaim it as a policy while proclaiming (that means not just announcing, but preaching) peace without reservation." He warned, "If we do not take this course 'the whole earth' will be cursed, and all flesh consumed,'" thus leaving only two choices: "either to renounce war or to be totally destroyed—there is no third choice." Hugh ends his letter with the chilling warning, "If we persist in reversing the words of the Savior, 'Who takes up the sword shall die by the sword' (cf. Revelation 13:10) to read,

---

[35]Nibley, "Brigham Young and the Enemy," *The Young Democrat*. The essay ran in two installments, one of four pages and one of eleven pages, in 1970; however, no publication date is given. It was reprinted in *Brother Brigham Challenges the Saints*, 187-246. The BYU Young Democrats' president at the time was Omar Kader, who, with his brothers, had helped Hugh to practice Arabic in the 1950s and 1960s. Kader had solicited Hugh's essay.

[36]Ibid., 238.

[37]Stanley Karnow, *Vietnam: A History* (New York: Viking, 1983), 632.

[38]Gary J. Bergera and Ronald Priddis, *Brigham Young University: A House of Faith* (Salt Lake City: Signature Books, 1985), 184-89.

perversely, 'who does not take up the sword shall perish by the sword,' we shall deserve what happens to us."[39]

Less than a week later on 31 March 1971, Hugh delivered a speech on campus entitled "Victory to Victory—Prelude to the Millennium," as a formal response to the film. The Daily Universe announced that he would give "a calm and detached view of things without taking sides," citing authorities like von Clausewitz and Joseph Fielding Smith.[40]

If anyone questioned Hugh Nibley's loyalty to the Church for speaking against the Vietnam war, particularly when he was taking a position different from that of a senior apostle, it was moot after the Ensign published his anti-war essay "If There Must Needs Be Offense" in July 1971. One of his most compelling points is his interpretation of scriptural commandments concerning war. Hugh mentioned that he had recently received from a fellow BYU professor a list of scriptural passages that forbid war with a parallel list of scriptural passages that command it. "This seems like a deadlock, a basic contradiction," wrote Hugh. But in actuality, the passages forbidding war represent "general principles" while those commanding it represent "special instances."[41]

Following the botched withdrawal of U.S. forces from Vietnam, the cold war with the Soviet Union continued, and Hugh himself continued to warn members of the Church against a confrontational path. In 1977, he submitted an essay entitled "Uses and Abuses of Patriotism" for a special edition of the Ensign celebrating the bicentennial of Declaration of Independence. Evidently, the approach Hugh took was not seen as patriotic enough, because it was rejected by the editors. The essay appeared in the textbook for BYU's American Heritage class that same year. In the essay, Hugh noted how the noble emotion of patriotism can be abused by conspiring politicians to create conflicts. "There is something wrong with this patriotism, which is based on conflict," argued Hugh.[42] He termed "patriotism of this type" the "principal weapon used against the Prophet and the Saints" as they were driven from their homes in Ohio, Missouri, and Nauvoo.[43] This patriotic zeal occurs on both sides of a conflict, and "all we can be sure of is that there will be waste and destruction, and the greater the victory, the greater the destruction on both sides."[44]

In a 1979 talk at BYU, "Gifts," Hugh described Satan's plan of presenting us with two equally bad choices and making us believe that we must choose one. "So we have always been told we must join the action to fight against communism, or must accept the leadership of Moscow to fight fascism, or must join Persia against Rome (or Rome against Persia—that's the fourth century)," wrote Hugh. But "there is only one real choice between accepting the gifts of God for what they are on his terms and going directly to him and asking for whatever you need, or seeking the unclean gift, as it is called, of power

---

[39] Nibley, "Renounce War, or, A Substitute for Victory," Brother Brigham Challenges the Saints, 267-69.

[40] I have been unable to locate any transcript of this address. The BYU Daily Universe announced the talk on 31 March 1971 (p. 5), but did not report it.

[41] Nibley, "If There Must Needs Be Offense," Brother Brigham Challenges the Saints, 272.

[42] Ibid., 250.

[43] Ibid., 252.

[44] Ibid., 254.

and gain." He concluded, "The Saints took no sides in that most passionately partisan of wars, the Civil War, and they never regretted it."[45]

That same year, in preparation for the Church's sesquicentennial in 1980, Hugh delivered the speech "How Firm a Foundation! What Makes It So," as part of the Sesquicentennial Lectures on Mormon Arts. In it he noted that we commonly point to the prophecy on war in Doctrine and Covenants 87 as evidence for the truthfulness of the Church without bothering to read it. He continued:

> It still comes through loud and clear with a prophetic message: the consummation of the whole thing is to be "a full end of all nations" (D&C 87:6), not a full end of some or a partial end of all, but a full end of all; and that by war, not as a possibility or contingency, but as a "consumption decreed"it must happen. "Wherefore" the special instructions with which it ends, "stand ye in holy places, and be not moved." (D&C 87:8)[46]

In Hugh's 1984 address, "We Will Still Weep for Zion," he cited, as he did on many occasions, President Spencer W. Kimball's First Presidency message, "The False Gods We Worship." The same editors who rejected Hugh's "Uses and Abuses of Patriotism" in 1977, had been faced with an even less "patriotic" essay for their June 1976 edition celebrating the nation's bicentennial when President Kimball's essay became the First Presidency Message. Kimball decried our becoming too concerned with wealth, our lack of respect for the environment, and our reliance on "gods of stone and steel, ships, planes, missiles, fortifications" to defend ourselves. He stated that "when threatened, we become anti-enemy instead of pro-kingdom of God."[47] Hugh delighted in the essay, since it was quite similar in content to his own views. He was, however, dismayed by how little attention it received: "And how did the Saints, who never tire of saying, 'The Prophet! The Prophet! We have a prophet!' receive his words? As might be expected, reaction has ranged from careful indifference to embarrassed silence and instant deep freeze." Furthermore, President Kimball's message has not only had been ignored, but transgressed: "It can be shown with cruel documentation that Utah leads the nation, at least through its representatives, in outspoken contempt for the environment, unabashed reverence for wealth, and ardent advocacy of military expansion."[48]

In 1986, Hugh delivered a chilling essay entitled, "Last Call: An Apocalyptic Warning from the Book of Mormon" at the Sunstone Theological Symposium in Salt Lake City.[49] In it, Hugh again returned to the theme of warfare in the Book of Mormon. War creates false polarizations, persuading people that "everything evil [is] on one side and everything good on the other. No problem remains for anybody on either side but to kill people on the other side." The Book of Mormon pattern begins when the people become,

---

[45]Nibley, "Gifts," in *Approaching Zion*, edited by Don E. Norton, Vol. 9 of *The Collected Works of Hugh Nibley* (Salt Lake City: Deseret Book/FARMS, 1989), 112-13.

[46]Hugh Nibley, "How Firm a Foundation! What Makes It So," in *Approaching Zion*, 155-56.

[47]Spencer W. Kimball, "The False Gods We Worship," *Ensign*, June 1976, 6.

[48]Nibley, "We Still Weep for Zion," in *Approaching Zion*, 367.

[49]Nibley, "Last Call: An Apocalyptic Warning from the Book of Mormon," *Sunstone* 12, no. 1 (January 1988): 14-25; reprinted in *The Prophetic Book of Mormon*, edited by John W. Welch, Vol. 8 of *The Collected Works of Hugh Nibley* (Salt Lake City: Deseret Book/FARMS, 1989), 498-532.

first, *privatized*, having nothing in common; then becoming *ethnicized*, learning to hate the other nations; then becoming *nationalized*, serving ambitious men's careers; then becoming *militarized*, storing up weapons; then becoming *terrorized*, developing organized crime; then becoming *regionalized*, forming organizations for protection and profit; then becoming *tribalized*, abolishing the central government; then becoming *fragmentized*, forming wandering groups, paramilitary organizations, and family shelters; then becoming *polarized*, creating great armies; finally becoming *pulverized*, wiping each other out as the great armies clashed. "It is left for a future generation to take the final step and become *vaporized*."[50]

In a mid-eighties issue of *This People*, a general interest magazine aimed at the Mormon market, an article titled "Blessed Are the Peacemakers" glorified LDS servicemen, referring to them as "peacemakers," "warriors for peace," and "gospel missionaries."[51] A letter to the editor in the next issue, signed by Hugh Nibley and nine other scholars, condemned the article for its "dangerously glorified" view of the military and called for a more balanced view of war which acknowledged such "adverse consequences of military life" as post-traumatic stress syndrome, alcoholism, immorality, crime, and depression. "Contrary to the Orwellian title of the article," the letter continues, "the military's primary mission is to kill and destroy. Those of us who have served have not forgotten basic training."[52] While the writing style is not typical of Hugh's, its contents well express his sentiments.

On 24 March 1989, the Foundation for Ancient Research and Mormon Studies (FARMS) sponsored a conference to explore an area that Hugh had opened for research thirty years earlier. Hugh addressed the conference by comparing dicta in von Clausewitz's *Vom Kriege* (On War) with how war is portrayed in the Book of Mormon. Concluding his speech, Hugh asked, "So where does that leave us today? Well, short of Zion. It seems that war is inevitable, according to Clausewitz. President Benson is right—he says [the Book of Mormon] all applies to us."[53] After the speech was published in the FARMS volume *Warfare in the Book of Mormon*,[54] one reviewer, Kurt Weiland, took Hugh to task for "imposing his own agenda" on the audience and letting "his biases interfere with his discussion." He criticized Hugh, among other things, for condemning General Maxwell Taylor for being elated that he had discovered brush-fire wars, and chides Hugh for providing "no references, no documentation. Just a cheap shot at a well-known (and generally well-regarded) soldier."[55] The problem with Weiland's review is that he obviously didn't know that Hugh *is* the source for this story. Hugh was there when he heard General Taylor say this. Not only was Hugh on close terms with Taylor during the war, he also had

---

[50] Ibid., 530-31.

[51] JoAnn Jolley, "Blessed Are the Peacemakers: LDS in the Military," *This People*, June/July 1984, 66-73.

[52] (No headline), *This People*, February/March 1987, 8-9. Those who signed it were Pierre Blais, Bart Tippetts, Thomas F. Rogers, Eugene England, Lynn B. Jensen, Steve Hildreth, Edwin B. Firmage, Steven E. Compton, Hugh Nibley, and Edward J. Jordan.

[53] Nibley, *Brother Brigham Challenges the Saints*, 296.

[54] Nibley, "Warfare and the Book of Mormon," in *Warfare in the Book of Mormon*, edited by Stephen D. Ricks and William J. Hamblin (Salt Lake City: Deseret Book/FARMS, 1990), 127-45. Also published in *Brother Brigham Challenges the Saints*, 278-97.

[55] Kurt Weiland, Review of Stephen D. Ricks and William J. Hamblin, eds., *Warfare in the Book of Mormon* (Salt Lake City: Deseret Book/FARMS, 1990), in *Review of Books on the Book of Mormon* 3 (1991): 145.

a great deal of respect for the man. But he did disagree with Taylor, strongly feeling that keeping wars going solely for the purpose of advancing one's military career was both unethical and immoral. This is no cheap shot. A friendlier review by Eugene England of BYU's English Department praised Hugh as the only person in the collection who "does not hesitate to make modern applications of Book of Mormon pacifism." Taking up Nibley's theme, England insists that the wars in the Book of Mormon are not provided "to prove [that] the Book of Mormon is *inspired* but, if we will let them, to be *inspiring*."[56]

Then in the middle of the Gulf War in 1991, Hugh participated at the "Gulf War Teach In" at BYU, a mild protest consisting of lectures by such vocal BYU faculty members as Eugene England, Sam Rushforth, Tomi Ann Roberts, and Cecelia Konchar Farr. On 21 February, speaking to a large audience in the Varsity Theater, Hugh again turned to the Book of Mormon for evidence that war is contrary to God's laws. "Whoever chooses war must break most of the Ten Commandments," Hugh argued. Since the object of war is to win, "warriors justify any means necessary." He further took the position that war is absolute; one cannot condone part of it without condoning everything that it entails. He also stated that military leaders purposely lie to the public. "To ask a military man not to lie is like asking a lumberjack not to cut trees." Revenge is what sustains the public in a war; therefore, stories about atrocities committed by the other side will constantly be recounted, but stories about atrocities committed by our side will be suppressed. In sum, Hugh stated, "The great lesson of the Book of Mormon is not to seek a military solution."[57]

On several occasions, Hugh has related an incident that happened in Normandy where another man was also ordered to shoot a German. On 11 June 1944, the 502nd Regiment took the bridge into Carentan with a bloody bayonet charge. Soon thereafter, as the men of the 101st Airborne were "mopping up," searching through the town for any remaining Germans, someone noticed someone suspicious looking out of a factory window. Intelligence Officer Major Paul Danahy ordered a small patrol to go into the factory and capture the man, and they soon came back with the man in tow. Major Danahy assumed that, since the man was German he must be a spy, so he ordered Sergeant David Bernay to take him out and shoot him. Bernay was, as Hugh remembers, "a fiery little Jew who won a silver star with two clusters; he was no friend of the Nazis." As Bernay escorted the German, they came to a ditch. "Step over the ditch," Bernay ordered in perfect German. Surprised, the German asked, "Do you speak German?" David responded, "Yes." "Where are you from?" the German demanded. "I come from Maximiliansau," Bernay replied. "Maximiliansau! That's just a little place on the Rhine. There was a celluloid factory there," exclaimed the German. "Yes," Bernay said. "Did you know Herr Bernay?" asked the German. "He is my father," replied Bernay. The German said, "This must be little David!" Hugh pressed the punch line: "It turned out that this man he was about to shoot was his father's close friend. He had managed the factory for David's father, and he was the one who made it possible for the [Jewish] family to escape from Germany and

---

[56] Eugene England, "Novels and Nicenes, Chaos and Killing: Mormon Fiction Runs the Gamut," *This People*, Fall 1990, 68.

[57] Rebecca M. Taylor, "War No Solution, Nibley Says," (BYU) *Daily Universe*, 22 February 1991, 1; Tracy E. Farr, Letter to Boyd Petersen, 22 February 1991. I have been unable to find a transcript of this talk; however, it appears from the *Universe* report and from the summary in Farr's letter that Hugh primarily restated themes he had discussed before.

get to New York." The two men "threw themselves at each other" and embraced. Instead of shooting the German, Bernay took him back to the camp and the German became a valuable source of intelligence for the Allies.[58]

Incidents like this convinced Hugh that war diabolically forces us to create divisions, rupturing the essential unity that should bind us to each other as sons and daughters of God. Hugh's knowledge of ancient history, his careful reading and understanding of the scriptures, and his first-hand experience in World War II left him convinced that war is an unnecessary evil. This has led him to raise a warning voice. And while he decries war, he always reminds us that there is hope. Hugh has pointed out that the Book of Mormon sets up the Ammonites as being the perfect example of what to do when faced with a conflict: refuse to take up arms. "In the end the most desperate military situation imaginable is still to be met with the spirit of peace and love."[59]

Is there a point at which war is justified? A point at which the evil caused by war would be less than the evil war would remedy? The Hugh Nibley of today doesn't seem to think so. When I asked Hugh recently if he would join the army if he had it to do over again, Hugh responded with a firm and definite, "No." However, as a young man, Hugh had criticized Chamberlain's policy of appeasement and voluntarily enlisted in the army. It is also interesting that Hugh still does not discuss his visit to Dachau. Perhaps this is because it represents the one piece of data he has not been able to process in his anti-war philosophy. Perhaps genocide is the one crime Hugh would be willing to go to war to prevent. Certainly, events and age have shaped Hugh's attitudes. He was not immune from the widespread cynicism about war as a solution that was part of the legacy of the Vietnam conflict. However, as he noted during his 1984 visit to Utah Beach, every conflict must sooner or later be settled by discussion, so "why not have the discussion now" and avoid the senseless conflict?[60]

---

[58] Hugh Nibley, *Teachings of the Book of Mormon*, Semester 1, Lecture 7, 10. The transcript of this narrative misspells Danahy's and Bernay's names; the spelling I use is from a list in my possession compiled by George Koskimaki from the official rosters of the 101st Airborne, dated 31 May 1944, just prior to the D-Day invasion. Photocopy in my possession.
[59] Nibley, "But What Kind of Work?", in *Brother Brigham Challenges the Saints*, 276.
[60] Hugh Nibley, "Faith of an Observer," 369.

Hugh Nibley's faculty photograph for Brigham Young University, ca. 1947.

Courtesy L. Tom Perry Special Collections,
Harold B. Lee Library, Brigham Young University

After the War I worked for the *Improvement Era* on the top floor of the stately Church Office [Administration] Building on South Temple Street in Salt Lake City, and came to know another kind of headquarters. I also got to know some of the General Authorities quite well. There were scientists, scholars and even poets among their number. One useful thing on the premises was a good collection of anti-Mormon literature. So when Mrs. Brodie's highly fictitious biography of Joseph Smith appeared I became involved in that direction: what I said about Mrs. B. and her methods is exactly what more competent reviewers have said about her more recent *Life of Jefferson*. The bona fides of the Prophet center around the Book of Mormon—another happy coincidence: on the eve (week) of the Normandie [sic] invasion I had in London blown all my savings on Arabic books from the collections of Howells and Ellis, both of whom had conveniently died at that point in time. Lacking other sources, I turned to my own books for an Old World approach to the Book of Mormon that kept me going for years.[1]

---

[1] Hugh Nibley, "Intellectual Autobiography," *Nibley on the Timely and the Timeless* (Provo, UT: BYU Religious Studies Center, 1978), xxiv-xxv

Chapter 15

Brodie and BYU, Nuptials and Newborns, 1945-50

Following his discharge from the army, Hugh went to visit his mother. Sloanie and Hugh's sister, Barbara, were living in a one-room efficiency apartment just down the street from the palatial home in which they had lived five years earlier. Hugh's father was living in a separate apartment. Barbara remembers that Hugh arrived, pulled off his uniform, and slept for three days straight.[2] Obviously, there was not space to accommodate Hugh in either place, so he soon retreated into the "softly howling wilderness" of Utah's red-rock country, where he could "get as far from the post-war world as circumstances will allow." He camped in an area "last occupied by the Pueblos some time in the 10th Century of Our Era," and bought supplies, received mail, and found the only society that he cared for in the small town of Hurricane, Utah. He confessed to Paul Springer, now married and working for the courts in San Francisco: "Almost as comforting as the long-delayed joys of solitude is the company of the plain and sober people of the area where I live—quite the best I have found yet. And what a contrast to the Armed Forces of the United States of North America!"[3]

After witnessing the horrors of war, Hugh was likely suffering from what we would now call post-traumatic stress disorder.[4] Immersing himself in wilderness and soli-

---

[2]Barbara Nibley Richards, Telephone conversation with Boyd Petersen, 20 February 2002, notes in my possession.

[3]Hugh Nibley, Letter to Paul Springer, n.d., ca. December 1945.

[4]Post-Traumatic Stress Disorder (PTSD) did not become a recognizable diagnosis until after the Vietnam War. However, the symptoms were identified in earlier wars as "soldier's heart" in the Civil War, as "shell shock" in World War I, and as "combat fatigue" in World War II. According to the National Center for Post-Traumatic Stress Disorder, it is "a psychiatric disorder that can occur following the experience or witnessing of life-threatening events such as military combat, natural disasters, terrorist incidents, serious accidents, or

tude undoubtedly provided a transitional space during which he could deal with his memories of combat without repressing them in his haste to resume another role that was expected of him; and almost certainly, his simultaneous immersion in the Book of Mormon gave him a structure within which he could assign meaning both to the trauma of violence and to his own participation.

One indication of his own readjustment is that he openly confessed his loneliness and dejection over Anahid's rejection of him in 1943. There is no evidence that Hugh visited her after the war, and no letters between them (if they wrote) have survived. While other soldiers found easy comfort in alcohol and women, Hugh had plunged into solitude, not only those rare days of physical solitude in Scotland but also, by plunging into his books, creating a psychic space for himself. But at some point, the very act of seeking out the healing solitude of Utah's wilderness after his return underscored its negative side: his profound loneliness. His parents were no longer maintaining a home, and there was no room for him in the spaces they were currently occupying. He was thirty-five, and most men his age had been married for a decade or longer. Paul Springer, his best friend, was also married. Under circumstances of what must have been acute and painful loneliness, Hugh undoubtedly revisited in memory his relationship with Anahid, experiencing anew his suffering that his affections were not reciprocated.

Although he had mentioned Anahid's rejection only briefly and only twice in surviving letters to his mother, he now wrote more candidly to Paul Springer, "Another cause of frustration . . . is the reluctance—to put it mildly—of a certain fair Armenian damsel . . . to concur with the most honorable suggestion of which my far from courtly nature is capable." And typically he dealt with this frustration by immersing himself anew in his studies. The extent to which he sublimated his sexual loneliness in his intellectual activities emerges from a revealing metaphor: "We have taken an old love back to our bed, namely Icelandic, and find the reading of the sagas (of which we now possess the whole collection) more exciting than ever." Hugh lamented, however, that "only half the books I sent *ex partibus infidelium* [from the lands of the unbelievers] ever got here, but that still gives me a noble Arabic collection, from which I daily derive joy and some knowledge."[5]

---

violent personal assaults like rape. People who suffer from PTSD often relive the experience through nightmares and flashbacks, have difficulty sleeping, and feel detached or estranged." Sometimes such reactions are "severe enough and last long enough to significantly impair the person's daily life." PTSD can result in troubled interpersonal relationships, emotional and physical exhaustion, depression, headaches, gastrointestinal complaints, immune system problems, dizziness, chest pain, or other discomforts. World War II veterans came home to a hero's welcome, a booming postwar economy, and the assumption that everything was now "normal." Few veterans wanted to talk about the atrocities they had witnessed, and few on the home front wanted to listen. The commonly held assumption, shared by the veterans themselves, was that they should put the war behind them and get on with their lives. Downloaded from the center's web page http://www.ncptsd.org/facts/general/fs_what_isptsd.html and http://www.ncptsd.org/facts/veterans/fs_older_veterans.html, on 23 February 2002.

[5]Hugh Nibley, Letter to Paul Springer, n.d., ca. December 1945. Unbeknownst to Hugh, his cherished books had all arrived safely but his mother had stored them in a garage and forgotten to tell him. On 1 April 1949, Hugh wrote excitedly to Springer: "I had thought [the Arabic library] to be feeding Atlantic fish these five years, but it turns up feeding silver fish in a garage in Los Angeles. This is certainly the best if not the only good thing that ever came out of that dull, damp, drab, dopey community. . . . I now have my Arabic library in proper, chronological order, and it presents a not unimposing sight—some 150 volumes."

Hugh's wilderness sojourn, probably punctuated by brief visits to Los Angeles, lasted for three or four months. In the spring of 1946, Hugh moved to Salt Lake City and began working at the *Improvement Era*, being hired, as he recalled, after an informal conversation with Apostle Richard L. Evans, then the magazine's managing editor. "I have been moving around like mad," wrote Hugh. "Going to be stuck in Salt Lake for the summer. I am an editor, no less. Also doing quite a bit of hack-writing."[6] In addition to the "hack-writing," Hugh was also working on a response to a new biography of Joseph Smith written by Fawn McKay Brodie, *No Man Knows My History: The Life of Joseph Smith* (New York: Knopf, 1945). Brodie was the daughter of President David O. McKay's brother, Thomas E. McKay, a former president of the German Mission who was sustained in 1941 as one of the first group of the five Assistants to the Quorum of the Twelve. A bright and creative woman, Brodie had lost her faith, married a secular Jew at the University of Chicago, and written a literate but thoroughly disparaging biography of its founding prophet. She was excommunicated a few months after it was published.

Among other things, her book hypothesized a naturalistic origin for the Book of Mormon, arguing that it was written by Joseph Smith and reflected the concerns of nineteenth-century America. With the Church Administration Building's comprehensive library of anti-Mormon books and his own extensive library, Hugh began to prepare a response to Brodie's charges, a volunteer project that he did without assignment or supervision.

Hugh worked on his Brodie review throughout much of the spring, titled it *No, Ma'am, That's Not History: A Brief Review of Mrs. Brodie's Reluctant Vindication of a Prophet She Seeks to Expose*,[7] and sent the sixty-two-page monograph to Bookcraft while he took another excursion into southern Utah. When he returned, he discovered that the press had printed the review before letting him see the proofs. "There are a number of bad mistakes," wrote Hugh, "and they toned the thing down a good deal, but still it seems to satisfy." In fact, Hugh discovered more evidence that supported his position on Brodie's book after the monograph was printed. For instance, Brodie had made the case that the First Vision was a later fabrication of Smith's, but Hugh notes: "For the past week I have been looking up stuff in the historian's office: I never dreamed how weak La Brodie's case really is; for example, today I came across an article in a newspaper dated 1832 in which an outsider mentions the first vision as a basic belief in the Church from the time of its founding."[8]

Hugh criticized Brodie's methodology and pointed out many errors and inconsistencies in her findings. He acknowledged that Brodie was "not animated by violent hatred" but he still found her tone condescending, summarizing her position as: "Joseph Smith is a complete imposter . . . but he meant well" (4). Hugh's defense of Joseph Smith was developed in enthusiastic prose and buttressed with many examples. First, Brodie's interpretation of Joseph Smith "takes a beating from the law of parsimony" (i.e., the simplest explanation must be preferred to more elaborate ones). Second, Brodie had "made

---

[6] Hugh Nibley, Letter to Paul Springer, n.d., early spring 1946.

[7] The title, obviously, puns on Brodie's title. It is reproduced in *Tinkling Cymbals and Sounding Brass*, edited by David J. Whittaker, Vol. 11 of *The Collected Works of Hugh Nibley* (Salt Lake City: Deseret Book/FARMS, 1991), 1-52. Citations which follow parenthetically in the text are from *Tinkling Cymbals*.

[8] Hugh Nibley, Letter to Agnes Sloan Nibley, 23 May 1946. I have not been able to locate a newspaper article that fits this description.

up her mind about Joseph Smith and then proceeded to accept any and all evidence, from whatever source, that supports her theory" (6). Third, Brodie did not allow revelation any role in Mormonism's origins; rather, Joseph Smith had borrowed freely from his nineteenth-century environment to create Church doctrine. For example, Brodie assumed that Joseph had borrowed the practice of footwashing, instituted in the Kirtland Temple, from the Baptists, while Hugh argued that Brodie was overlooking the more obvious New Testament source (32). "Brodie's Joseph picks up ideas like a thieving magpie, throws them together haphazardly, and sells them from the pulpit. He is therefore not the man whose teachings are so well-knit and perfectly logical that they have never had to undergo the slightest change or alteration during a century in which every other church in Christendom has continually revamped its doctrines," wrote Hugh (36).

Hugh's analysis accurately points out many weaknesses in Brodie's biography, chief among them that Brodie's "psychologizing" often reads more into the sources than they will allow. When No, Ma'am was reprinted in 1991, Hugh added a note pointing out that Gary Wills's critique of her Thomas Jefferson biography also describes her approach to the Joseph Smith biography: "Typical of Ms. Brodie's hintandrun method [is] to ask a rhetorical question, and then proceed on the assumption that it has been settled in her favor, making the first surmise a basis for second and third ones, in a towering rickety structure of unsupported conjecture."[9]

Nevertheless, Hugh sometimes overstates his point. For instance, it is certainly not true that Church doctrines have not changed since 1830. Furthermore, Hugh's accusation that Brodie marshalled sources to support a preconceived theory is a point that would later be applied with some accuracy to Hugh's own work. LDS Book of Mormon scholar Kent P. Jackson points out that Hugh sometimes works "from the conclusions to the evidence."[10] But unlike Brodie, who feigned objectivity, Hugh openly admitted and energetically advocated the stance he took toward his work. Still, despite No, Ma'am's problems, it represents an important point of Hugh's work, even at this immature stage: It established him as a defender of the faith; and to counteract Brodie's evolutionary theory of Mormon origins, it pushed Hugh to begin what would turn into an obsession with finding ancient parallels for the Book of Mormon.

The response to Hugh's review was mixed but robust, placing him squarely on one side of a polemical debate. Those who were critical of the Church were also critical of Hugh's review. For example, Stanley S. Ivins, whose father, Anthony W. Ivins, had served in the first Presidency with Hugh's grandfather, Charles W. Nibley, wrote a three-page single-spaced letter to Hugh that strongly criticized No, Ma'am. Ivins, who had seen his father perform many post-Manifesto plural marriages in Mexico, became disillusioned after serving a mission and spent considerable time researching and critiquing Mormon polygamy. At this point, he was openly antagonistic toward the Church, which made him and Hugh automatic adversaries. "It seems to me," wrote Ivins, "that you have fallen into a number of errors."[11] He objected to a few places where Hugh had misrepresented

---

[9] Gary Wills, "Uncle Thomas's Cabin," New York Review of Books, 18 April 1974, 26-27, as quoted by Nibley in "A Note on F. M. Brodie," Tinkling Cymbals, 49-52.

[10] Kent P. Jackson, "Review of Old Testament and Related Studies," BYU Studies 28 (Fall 1988): 114-19.

[11] Stanley S. Ivins, Letter to Hugh Nibley, 25 May 1946, Stanley S. Ivins Collection, Utah State Historical Society, Salt Lake City.

Brodie's words and another where Hugh cited Brodie's source and attributed it to Brodie—certainly valid criticisms. He also explained that Brodie's reason for not accepting the historicity of the First Vision is that the Mormon accounts—not just non-Mormon newspapers, the issue Hugh addressed—did not discuss this vision until much later. He took Hugh to task for claiming that we "have whole volumes of Joseph's own words" since "we have nothing that I have ever seen that can be said to be a true specimen of his exact language."[12] Ivins also argued that Hugh's dismissal of all anti-Mormon sources as "unreliable" is naive since no source "can always be relied upon." And he accurately criticized Hugh's statement that the "gospel sprang full-grown from the words of Joseph Smith" and "has never been worked over or touched up in any way."

Utah historian Dale Morgan, who advised Brodie on both the content and style of her biography, privately appraised *No, Ma'am* as "something of a slapstick performance, and the irony of it is, Nibley is much more intoxicated with his own language than you, the 'glib English major' are."[13] Brodie herself dismissed Hugh's critique in a 27 May 1946 letter to her parents as "a flippant and shallow piece."[14] While Hugh's essay was undeniably a bit glib and seems hastily constructed, his main analysis of Brodie's method is sound.

Church leaders, for their part, were pleased with Hugh's monograph. Elder John A. Widtsoe, then senior editor of the *Improvement Era*, wrote to Howard S. McDonald, president of Brigham Young University, urging him to make sure the school's bookstore and library had copies of *No, Ma'am*. "The Brodie book has added nothing new to anti-Mormon literature," wrote Widtsoe, "but published and publicized as it has been, it is misleading many people who do not have a background of knowledge sufficient to know what is true or false."[15] And President David O. McKay wrote warmly to Hugh: "Your comments disclose clearly not only [Brodie's] immature, prejudiced thinking, but also the superficiality of the critics who have referred to her book as 'scholarly.' . . . I congratulate you on your clear exposure of her manifest unfairness, her vindictive insinuations. . . . You do yourself credit, and the Church honor!"[16]

A more balanced response came in a personal letter from Mormon historian Juanita Brooks, who gently critiqued *No, Ma'am*, stating: "I may be wrong. I often am. But it seems to me that in [your] zeal to answer Mrs. Brodie, [you] make some statements almost as far fetched as hers." Changes in the doctrinal interpretation of polygamy, consecration, and the United Order were obvious correctives to Hugh's ill-advised generalization that nothing had altered since Joseph Smith's day. She added reflectively: "[I am] not defending Mrs. Brodie's book; in fact, I think we have been entirely too hysterical about it and have given it an importance greater than it deserves." Furthermore, Brooks

---

[12]Although it is true that the vast majority of words attributed to Joseph Smith come through scribes or the memories of others, a few holograph documents have survived. It is probably true, however, that Ivins had not seen them.

[13]Dale Morgan, Letter to Fawn M. Brodie, June 1946, in *Dale Morgan on Early Mormonism: Correspondence and A New History*, edited by John Phillip Walker (Salt Lake City: Signature Books, 1986), 125.

[14]Quoted in Newell G. Bringhurst, *Fawn McKay Brodie: A Biographer's Life* (Norman: University of Oklahoma Press, 1999), 111.

[15]John A. Widtsoe, Letter to Howard S. McDonald, 10 May 1946, John A. Widtsoe Collection, Historical Department Archives, Church of Jesus Christ of Latter-day Saints, Salt Lake City.

[16]David O. McKay, Letter to Hugh Nibley, 16 May 1946.

was unconcerned about the effects Brodie's book would have on Church members' testimonies. "I think Joseph Smith stands as untouched by Mrs. Brodie's attack as his monument does by the pecking of sparrows."[17]

Hugh seemed to take both kinds of reactions in his stride, moving on quickly to other projects. He gained an appreciation for writing on Church topics and he enjoyed working with and getting to know the General Authorities of the Church who were very involved in the production of the *Improvement Era*. Hugh wrote his mother in mid-April: "I have been doing some interesting work here. Have a very good room and an excellent place for books and stuff. . . . In the meantime we labor mightily and yearn for the desert."[18] Hugh's "very good room" was in the attic of a boarding house at 715 East South Temple that had formerly been the governor's mansion. He roomed there alone until one day when he came out of the Church Administration Building and met "a little wrinkled-up sort of guy" whose accent revealed his Russian origin. Hugh offered to share his room with the man if he would speak only Russian. "I agreed to pay him one penny for every Russian mistake I made and two cents for every English word I spoke. That was the agreement," remembers Hugh.[19] He recounted the bargain in a letter to Paul Springer: "I pay the room-rent of a very well-educated, middle-aged Ukrainian, who shares my quarters under the condition that he shall speak not a syllable of any language but Russian. That works wonders." Hugh continued, "I tried to do the same thing in Arabic with the venerable Lawand [his Arab friend and teacher at Claremont] and was just making a good start when the Army intervened. If there is any language that simply must be heard to be learned it is Russian."[20] In commenting on the same point to his mother, he added: "That has come to be the established Nibley method for learning languages under pressure."[21]

Hugh's stay at the *Improvement Era* is difficult to document, since the date he commenced working there is not known, nor is it clear how much time he spent on *Improvement Era* projects given the amount of time that researching and writing *No, Ma'am* would have taken. He would have technically worked under Elder Widtsoe's supervision, but it is not possible to determine from available documents how close the two men were.

---

[17]Juanita Brooks, Letter to Hugh Nibley, 7 November 1946. Born in 1898, Brooks earned a degree from BYU in English and a master's from Columbia. She taught at Dixie College in St. George after her first husband died. At the time she wrote this letter, she had published a couple of articles about Mormonism in *Harpers* magazine and was working on a book that would be as controversial as Brodie's: *The Mountain Meadows Massacre* (Stanford, CA: Stanford University Press, 1950). Unlike Brodie, however, Brooks was a committed Mormon. The two had met in the summer of 1943, while both were doing research and had a relationship of mutual support if not agreement, sharing documents and critiquing each other's work. Brooks had candidly written Dale Morgan that she felt *No Man* was "needed," "scholarly," and "literary," even though she rejected the idea that Joseph Smith was a deliberate fraud: "The things that were real to him may not seem so to [Brodie] or to you or to most other people, but I think they must have been to him. I have felt that it was his own deep and sincere convictions that attracted and held his following. . . . Men, catching the spark from him, were willing to sacrifice too much to further his cause." Juanita Brooks, Letter to Dale L. Morgan, 9 December 1945, quoted in Bringhurst, *Fawn McKay Brodie*, 11415. After *Mountain Meadows Massacre* appeared, many castigated and shunned Brooks, but the threatened excommunication never materialized. Newell G. Bringhurst "Juanita Brooks and Fawn Brodie: Sisters in Mormon Dissent," *Dialogue: A Journal of Mormon Thought* 27, no. 2 (Summer 1994): 10527.

[18]Hugh Nibley, Letter to Agnes Sloan Nibley, 14 April 1946.

[19]Hugh Nibley, Interviewed by Boyd Petersen, 15 November 2000.

[20]Hugh Nibley, Letter to Paul Springer, n.d., early summer 1946.

[21]Hugh Nibley, Letter to Agnes Sloan Nibley, 23 May 1946.

Widtsoe may have determined quickly that Hugh, a scholar's scholar, was not going to settle down well to the kind of housekeeping chores that make up much of an editor's life and that he would fit much better into an academic environment. In any event, on 14 March 1946, only four months after Hugh's discharge and possibly only a few weeks after he reached Salt Lake City, Widtsoe was writing a letter warmly recommending Hugh for a faculty position at Brigham Young University.

BYU was then experiencing the same post-war boom in student enrollment that was flooding all of the nation's universities. In the 1944-45 school year, enrollment was around 1,500, and most of the students were women; but fall quarter 1945 saw more than 2,700 students report for the first day of classes. In 1946, the school saw almost that many incoming freshmen, 30 percent of them veterans.[22] In 1946, the campus consisted of four buildings huddled together on the block now known as Academy Square: the Education Building (now the Provo Library), College Hall to the east, the BYU Laboratory Training School in the northeast corner, and the Arts Building on the northwest corner. (The latter three were all razed in 1999.) A fifth building, the Women's Gym, still stands to the west across University Avenue. "Upper campus" on the bench above the city consisted of a cluster of four buildings: Maeser, Brimhall, Joseph Smith, and Grant (then the library, now the testing center). New buildings were desperately needed to accommodate the growing student body. So were new professors.

In his letter to BYU President Howard S. McDonald, Widtsoe praised Hugh as "one of the ablest scholars among us," and "a good Latter-day Saint, [who] remembers his tithing and other obligations." Among Hugh's academic and linguistic qualifications, Widtsoe mentioned his mission but not his war experience nor who his grandfather was. Widtsoe, former president of both Utah State University and the University of Utah, personally spoke German, Danish, Norwegian, Swedish, French, and Latin. There is perhaps a proprietary note, maybe even a touch of patronage, in his description of Hugh: "He is a book-worm of the first order. He will probably annoy his wife, when he marries, all his life, by coming home late at night—too late for dinner—and by sitting up all night with his books. . . . Do you not think that the B.Y.U. should gather this young scholar into its fold? He would not be an expensive man, but might become a most useful one." At the

---

[22] Ernest L. Wilkinson, Brigham Young University: The First One Hundred Years, 4 vols. (Provo, Utah: Brigham Young University Press, 1975-76) 2:429; 457. The Servicemen's Readjustment Act of 1944, better known as the "GI Bill of Rights," was signed into law by President Franklin D. Roosevelt on 22 June 1944. During the legislative debate, some felt the bill would create a multitude of slothful veterans, while still others feared that it would lower educational standards. However, the fear of another depression if thousands of soldiers began competing for jobs in an economy no longer running at wartime capacity encouraged Congress to pass the bill. Honorably discharged veterans who had served a minimum of ninety days were eligible for one year of fulltime education plus a period equal to their time in service, up to a maximum of forty-eight months. The bill paid the educational institution up to $500 a year for tuition, books, and fees, plus a subsistence allowance of up to $65 a month, prorated to accommodate dependents. At its peak year of 1947, veterans accounted for 49 percent of college enrollment. The total cost of the program was $14.5 billion, but it played an important role in eliminating unemployment during the postwar period. When veterans did enter the job market, they were better trained, able to find higher-paying jobs, and, in turn, paid higher taxes, thus repaying the investment. "The GI Bill: From Roosevelt to Montgomery," Department of Veterans' Affairs, Education Service Home Page, downloaded 1 March 2002, http://www.gibill.va.gov/education/GIBill.htm

bottom of letter, Widtsoe scrawled an afterthought, "I believe we must keep this man for our use."[23]

McDonald immediately wrote back, requesting Hugh's address so he could contact him directly.[24] When Widtsoe replied, he stressed, "We must keep Hugh Nibley near us because of his erudition. . . . He is the type that we find once in a generation."[25] Soon thereafter, McDonald requested that Widtsoe provide the requisite ecclesiastical interview for Hugh. Widtsoe responded:

> I have examined Dr. Hugh Nibley, carefully, as to his Gospel faith and practice, though I have long known him, even from the mission field [Widtsoe had been president of the European Mission, which supervised the Swiss-German Mission], to be thoroughly trustworthy. He is a good Latter-day Saint, who can be trusted to instill faith into the hearts of students and colleagues.
>
> He has, as I have already said to you, an unusual foundation of scholarship in fields in which we are sadly lacking in the church. And faith accompanies his work. You will find him very useful. At this end of the line, we are already drawing upon his unusual technical knowledge.[26]

Apparently Hugh and McDonald had a preliminary interview on 2 April 1946, since Hugh's diary notes: "Howard S. McDonald, Pres. at BYU." Nine days later, he "saw JAW [John A. Widtsoe] and [Richard L.] Evans," presumably to inform them that he was being considered for a BYU position. On 28 April 1946, Hugh sent his vita along with a "credo and propositum"—his statement of teaching philosophy—to McDonald. In addition to his employment history and list of publications, his vita listed speaking ability in French, German, Arabic, Spanish, Latin, Greek, Russian, Dutch, Italian, and a reading ability in Old Icelandic, Hebrew, Babylonian, Hieroglyphic, as well as the dialects of Old Bulgarian, Old English, and Flemish. Hugh's statement of philosophy was one that did, in fact, guide him throughout his career. He stated an overwhelming concern for historical (presumably ancient) documents. "Originally I took to the documents because I felt this responsibility was being gravely neglected by our age," wrote Hugh. "But upon nearer acquaintance with some of the sources it has become apparent to me that they really have something to tell us." These documents, Hugh writes, contain "vital" information that needs to be disseminated "by publication, teaching, and every other means." Hugh also revealed how his faith in the gospel guided his research. "The greatest privilege a man can enjoy is to receive revelation, but he has no claim to such as long as he ignores that form of revelation which is in his power to enjoy at will. For in the scriptures, ancient and modern, we have a clear declaration that there is a kind of validity in the written word—that

---

[23] John A Widtsoe, Letter to Howard S. McDonald, 14 March 1946, Howard S. McDonald Presidential Papers L. Tom Perry Special Collections, Harold B. Lee Library, Brigham Young University, Provo, Utah. Widtsoe may have also been suppressing a pang of wistfulness for his own foregone academic career. Certainly, he saw himself as discovering and mentoring new intellectual talent that could be useful to the Church.

[24] Howard S. McDonald, Letter to John A. Widtsoe, 23 March 1946, McDonald Collection, Perry Special Collections.

[25] John A. Widtsoe, Letter to Howard S. McDonald, 25 March 1946, McDonald Collection, Perry Special Collections.

[26] John A. Widtsoe, Letter to Howard S. McDonald, 22 April 1946, McDonald Collection, Perry Special Collections.

some part of the spirit may actually be caught and preserved by written symbols." Hugh's three-page "discourse" is most unusual, but he begged for McDonald's "indulgence," "trusting you will attribute an apparent weakness for preaching to an honest zeal in the cause."[27]

About a month later on 23 May 1946, McDonald interviewed Hugh and promptly offered him a joint position as assistant professor of history and religion.[28] Hugh jubilantly wrote to Springer: "When the leaves begin to fall I shall repair to Provo, for brother Brigham's celebrated academy has charms that make the blandishments of Claremont seem positively repulsive by comparison."[29] These charms, as Hugh later stated, were geographic—the beauty of Utah Valley, framed on the west by Utah Lake and the desert, and on the east by the rugged Wasatch Range. He

Phyllis Ann Hawkes Draper, ca. 1943, about age seventeen.

confessed to Lucien Goldschmidt: "The mountains have greatly taken my fancy,"[30] and to Paul Springer "I am elated beyond description at the local variety of mountains, which presents no end of wonders to the curious. Life is a perpetual picnic here."[31]

The only concern that Widtsoe or BYU's administration had about hiring Hugh, a thirty-six-year-old bachelor, was his marital status. Widtsoe pressed Hugh to find a wife; and Hugh, though no doubt listening politely and agreeing, privately chafed a little. He described his encounter with Widtsoe to Paul Springer as "the rising admonition of the brethren that I get me espoused."[32] But to the apostle himself, Hugh gave an obedient response with a witty edge: He says he told Widtsoe to work it out with the Lord and "I

---

[27]Hugh Nibley, Letter to Howard S. McDonald, 28 April 1946, McDonald Presidential Papers, Perry Special Collections, Lee Library.

[28]Hugh Nibley, Appointment Book, 23 May 1946; Hugh Nibley, Letter to Agnes Sloan Nibley, 23 May 1946. This journal is a pocket appointment book for 1946 in which Hugh kept sporadic entries jotted down mostly in Gregg shorthand but interspersed with notations in English, German, Arabic, and Greek. BYU hired more than twenty new faculty members in 1946, half of whom had doctorates. In 1946, this was a very high number of hires for the school. Wilkinson, *Brigham Young University*, 2:439.

[29]Hugh Nibley, Letter to Paul Springer, n.d., early summer 1946.

[30]Hugh Nibley, Letter to Lucien Goldschmidt, 5 June 1946.

[31]Hugh Nibley, Letter to Paul Springer, n.d., ca. 5 August 1946.

[32]Ibid.

would marry the first girl I met at BYU."³³

Although this story is part of the Hugh folklore, it is also part of the Nibley factual history. On one of his first days on campus, 25 May 1946, Hugh walked into the housing office. Phyllis Draper—the receptionist—was literally the first girl he met at BYU. Phyllis, majoring in English with a French minor, was working for B. F. Cummings, a professor of French who was head of both the Language Department and the Housing Office. Phyllis assisted Cummings in both capacities, grading French papers some days and filing housing applications on others. Phyllis remembers meeting Hugh. It was a "rainy, gloomy" Saturday; and normally she would not have been there, "but commencement was coming up the next week and summer school would start the week after that, and Professor Cummings had asked me if I would stay in the office that Saturday." When Hugh came in the office, Phyllis was doing some filing. Hugh, noticing her cello in the corner of the outer office, came to the inner office to ask whose it was. "When I told him it was mine, we started a conversation," Phyllis recalls. "The orchestra had played in the Assembly Hall just the week before, or two or three days before. He had heard us, and he was quite impressed that a small college orchestra could have played what we did."³⁴

Phyllis Draper ca. 1936, about age ten.

Phyllis was sixteen years younger than Hugh and had lived a very different life. Where Hugh had come from wealth and status, Phyllis had seen only hardship and misfortune. But she had the native intelligence, will, and determination to rise above trials; and her background left her forever sympathetic and charitable toward those less fortunate. As Hugh wrote his mother: "Phyllis is a child of adversity who has accomplished wonders against great odds; she has a phenomenal noodle and is universally adored for her heavenly disposition and almost foolish generosity."³⁵

Phyllis was born on 2 August 1926 to Fredrick Pratt Hawkes and Edla Kristina Charlotte Peterson Hawkes. Fredrick was born and raised in Idaho in an established

---

³³Todd F. Maynes, "Nibleys: Pianist, Scholar, Brilliant But Different," *Daily Universe*, 1 November 1982, 7.
³⁴Phyllis Nibley, "Faith of an Observer," 421.
³⁵Hugh Nibley, Letter to Agnes Sloan Nibley, n.d., postmarked 23 August 1946. To Paul Springer, six weeks after the wedding, he wrote: "My devoted spouse is one who has acquired an infinitely angelic disposition in the process of being kicked around by fate . . . . [is] most delectably feminine, is celebrated for her fabulous I.Q. but stupid enough to think I'm hot potatoes. . . . She plays a mean cello and cooks with great skill and dotes [on] belle lettres in any form." This letter is not dated; Springer wrote "28 October 1946" on the first page.

Mormon family; his mother was a distant relative of Parley P. and Orson Pratt.[36] Edla, a second-generation Swedish Mormon, had immigrated as a young girl eight years after her mother's death. Edla and Fredrick were married on 5 August 1925, but the differences between them proved too great. They divorced when Phyllis, their only child, was a year old. Edla worked to support her daughter and herself, at one time, coincidentally, working as hired help in the home of Charles W. Nibley. But life was always a struggle, and Phyllis was boarded with various relatives throughout her early years.

When Phyllis was five, Edla married Otto Draper, a widower with a son, Billy, from his previous marriage. Soon afterward, the family moved to Portland, Oregon, where Otto had a job as a U.S. Government surveyor. Otto treated Phyllis like his own child. Two more sons, Raymond and Otto Jr., were born, but this stable family life ended when Phyllis was almost nine. Otto was surveying a piece of land when he fell while crossing a small stream. He struck his head and died almost instantly. Rumors circulated that he had been murdered. Edla sold the house in Portland. Otto's parents came and got Billy while Edla was out of the house. Edla took Phyllis, Raymond, and Otto Jr. back to Utah where she lived frugally on Otto's pension. Phyllis, who was a voracious reader, did well academically and learned the cello, first in Midvale, then at Jordan High. Upon graduation in 1944, she earned an academic scholarship to Brigham Young University.[37] She supported herself as a secretary while going to school full time. When spring semester ended during her sophomore year, she decided to stay in Provo and keep working in the Housing Office.

When Hugh came in to inquire about a place to stay on that dreary day in May, Phyllis had no idea that he was looking for anything more than an apartment to rent. However, Hugh had already decided, based on that single encounter, that he was going to marry Phyllis. He didn't mention it to her; however, two months later, he was hinting to Paul Springer that he was exerting every effort to make a good impression:

> All that the smartest pomades and the most lavish applications of Shinola can do to redeem the defects of nature [are] being thrown into the balance against the blandishments of youth, wealth, and collegiate glamour to put the belated Hugo on a footing with some of the less dashing also-rans in the celebrated Provo love-mart. Wish me well, sweetling, and when we meet again, who knows . . . ?[38]

Hugh returned to southern Utah, perhaps for two or three trips, during parts of June and July, which deflected his attentions from Phyllis. Perhaps he also felt insecure about the difference in their ages. For whatever reason, he did not take the fateful step of asking her out for two months, but he "kept coming into the office every few days to ask for 3x5 note cards," recalls a still-amused Phyllis. "And he wouldn't take very many, just a few, which would get him through the next couple of days, and then he'd come and ask for another one."[39] Finding her welcome warm enough, Hugh took the next step on 27

---

[36]Fredrick's mother, Florence Arabella Pratt (28 July 1874), was the granddaughter of William Dickinson Pratt, brother of Parley P. and Orson Pratt.

[37]Personal History of Phyllis Hawkes Draper Nibley, 17 February 1985, holograph, photocopy in my possession.

[38]Hugh Nibley, Letter to Paul Springer, n.d., ca. 5 August 1946.

[39]Phyllis Nibley, "Faith of an Observer," 421.

July—again, with a typically unconventional invitation. "He said, 'Look, I've got a real problem and maybe you can help me out,'" remembers Phyllis. "My cousin's husband is on the faculty here and they've invited me to a party up in the canyon, and I have to have a girl and I don't know any girls but you, so will you go?" Phyllis "said yes because I liked him."[40]

Thereafter, Hugh and Phyllis took long walks together, ate dinner in the campus cafeteria, and had lengthy discussions. "We just seemed to be together most of the time," remembers Phyllis. On 18 August after another Allen family picnic, Hugh asked Phyllis to marry him and she accepted.[41] The entry in his diary for that date is in shorthand, but the words "Silver Lake Flats," "Allens," and "Phyllis" can be deciphered. The following day, he wrote to his mother, "I am going to get married at the earliest possible date to Miss Phyllis Draper of Midvale, Utah, who is an amiable young lady with excellent references. The manifold excellences of Mlle. D. must be seen to be appreciated."[42] Sloanie undoubtedly felt that it was more than high time he married but simultaneously was sure that no woman was good enough for him, and she may have expressed worries that Hugh was rushing into matrimony with a comparative stranger, for he reassured her about his "delectable and ever-sensible" fiancée: "We have had a number of long walks in the mountains and I think I have become thoroughly acclimatized."[43]

Hugh's mother sent an engagement present, an heirloom pin that she had received when Hugh was born. Phyllis wrote her redoubtable future mother-in-law a shy thank-you note, obviously anxious to please: "Thank you again for everything, and most of all for Hugh. I hope I can make him the kind of wife he wants; I shall certainly do everything I can do to please him."[44] About their whirlwind courtship, Hugh later quipped, "That's why it's called BYWoo, I guess."[45]

After knowing each other for less than four months and dating for less than two, Hugh and Phyllis were married in the Salt Lake Temple on 18 September 1946 on a chaotic day. Only Phyllis's mother and Hugh's parents were present. Elder Widtsoe had agreed to perform the ceremony but, for some reason, did not show. El tracked down Joseph Fielding Smith, a family friend, and invited him to officiate. Bypassing the usual prenuptial counsel, Elder Smith whisked briskly through the sealing ceremony. After the ceremony, the wedding party was milling about in the hallway with their party when Elder Smith, remembering that a short lecture of counsel was traditional, stopped them and delivered a short speech on the spot which neither of them have remembered. Phyllis's mother had scheduled a wedding breakfast at the Hotel Utah, but the arrangements got mixed up. The unprepared restaurant staff seated them in the dining room with the regular patrons, and they ordered from the menu. The two mothers did not hit it off, although they were civil. After the meal, Hugh and Phyllis drove away in El's car, which Hugh had borrowed for the honeymoon. They had no reception or wedding party.

---

[40]Ibid., 422. The cousins were the Allen family.
[41]Nibley, Appointment Book, 18 August 1946; Hugh Nibley, Letter to Agnes Sloan Nibley, 19 August 1946.
[42]Hugh Nibley, Letter to Agnes Sloan Nibley, 19 August 1946.
[43]Hugh Nibley, Letter to Agnes Sloan Nibley, postmarked 23 August 1946.
[44]Phyllis Draper, Letter to Agnes Sloan Nibley, 31 August 1946, Hugh Nibley Papers.
[45]Maynes, "Nibleys," 7.

The couple honeymooned for a week, exploring Hugh's favorite retreat: the desert around Zion National Park. The day after the wedding, while walking along the main street of Hurricane, Hugh and Phyllis met a family of gypsies who were traveling in the area. An old gypsy woman asked to look at their hands so she could tell their future and told them that they would both live long lives.[46]

Although Hugh joked about their courtship, he felt strongly that he had been directed to Phyllis by the Lord. Despite the fact that they were so far apart in age and came from such different backgrounds, Hugh and Phyllis shared many interests: a love for classical music, the theater, and the arts; a passion for good books and good conversation; and a commitment to similar political causes. Most importantly, they shared one thing that had been missing in Hugh's previous romantic relationships: they were both solidly dedicated to the gospel, and this proved to be the strongest glue of all.

The couple returned to Provo on 26 September, in time for the beginning of classes. Hugh began teaching, while Phyllis did what all new wives were supposed to do in those days: she quit school. She did, however, sit in on Hugh's Greek class and also continued to play the cello in the BYU orchestra. The couple set up their first home in a small apartment on 800 East in Provo. After a few contented weeks of marriage, Hugh wrote to Paul Springer: "I displayed immeasurable wisdom in waiting until the happy present to get married," and joked, "Of me [Phyllis] expects nothing and I must admit for once I have risen magnificently to the occasion."[47]

Hugh's income was humble, but he was also so oblivious to physical comforts that even if he had plenty of money they would have lived in spartan conditions. This must have been frustrating for Phyllis, particularly when she became pregnant in October with their first child. They had neither car nor telephone. Their only furniture, remembers Hugh, was "this mattress which went on the floor and we had two orange crates for the table. . . . And that's the only furniture we had for almost two years. It never occurred to me that we'd need any more."[48] The "decor" reflected Hugh's self-proclaimed "knack as well as a passion for plastering walls with maps and charts," as he put it to his mother.[49]

To make matters worse, the front door swelled from the moisture until it literally could not be closed. Instead of repairing the door, the landlord took it off its hinges and replaced it with a blanket. Apparently the housing shortage was so acute and Hugh's disinterest so complete that he simply mentioned it as a quaint element in their lives to Paul Springer: "Would you believe it, we actually have a blanket for a front door, and we still pay rent? If it were not that the air of Zion even at 20 below is purest nectar to infatuate lungs I would stop breathing it out of sheer spite."[50]

They endured these conditions until the spring of 1947, when they moved to BYU's Wymount Village student housing complex, a group of military surplus two-story

---

[46] Hugh Nibley, Journal, 19 September 1946.

[47] Hugh Nibley, Letter to Paul Springer, n.d., Springer wrote "28 October 1946" at the top of the letter.

[48] Hugh Nibley, "Faith of an Observer," 29. He is embellishing his nonchalance somewhat. Phyllis remembers that their furnitureless state lasted only "several months." Sloanie had promised the newlyweds some furniture but, for unknown reasons, never delivered it.

[49] Hugh Nibley, Letter to Agnes Sloan Nibley, postmarked 23 August 1946.

[50] Hugh Nibley, Letter to Paul Springer, 29 January 1947. Hugh wrote this letter after finally reaching home following a long train ride. He jokingly dates this letter: "en route 4-29 January 1947"; I am assuming that the last date is the actual date of the letter.

barracks located on the east side of upper campus where the J. Reuben Clark Law School is today. Here they were definitely more comfortable. Not only was there a working front door, but these apartments were furnished, which made homemaking more tolerable for Phyllis.

Hugh's teaching assignments were heavy those first few years. For the fall quarter 1946, Hugh taught elementary Greek, second-year Greek, first-year Russian, two sections of world religions, and a survey course in early Christian church history during the first quarter. For winter quarter 1946-47, he taught elementary modern Greek, two sections of his church history survey, first-year Russian, and second-year Greek. For spring quarter, he again taught two sections of Christian history, world religions, first-year Russian, and second-year Greek. During the summer of 1947, he taught a course titled "Builders of Early Christianity" and another in Greek classics.[51] Other classes were Greek and Roman history, the literary history of Greece and Rome, the early Christian church and the church fathers, the medieval church, and Greek language and literature.[52] BYU's language department was severely limited at this time, so having Hugh join the faculty with a strong background in Greek and Arabic and a proficiency in several other languages kept him in heavy demand. In addition to his teaching schedule, he was also the faculty advisor of the BYU Russian Club. One of Hugh's first (and at the time only) students in Greek, Marian Robertson, remembers that Hugh announced at the beginning of the semester, "'I just got married. Usually when you start out with Homer you read the *Iliad*, but I don't feel like reading the *Iliad*. That's too bloodthirsty. So let's do the *Odyssey*.' So we spent the beginning of that year reading about Odysseus who took eighteen years to get home to his wife."[53] Hugh infected her with his own enthusiasm: "We often went outdoors; and as I chanted aloud mighty lines, carefully prepared, from Homer, Hesiod, Aeschylus, Sophocles, and many many others, we both would gaze northward to imperial Mount Timpanogos, or southwestward to hazy, distant Mount Nebo."[54]

Happily married and happily hired, Hugh loved the state, the campus, the students, and the residents of Provo. It was idyllic, an anodyne that finished cancelling out the futility and horror of war. He wrote to Paul Springer, "I teach seven courses plus Sunday School and social life in Utah must be seen to be believed. Nevertheless a gay spirit pervades everything and a good time is had by all."[55] After he and Phyllis visited California for the Christmas holidays in 1946, Hugh wrote to Lucien Goldschmidt, contrasting Utah positively to the home of his youth:

> I had almost forgotten how cynical and drab the world could be away from the zealots of Zion. If the total absence (rather than conscious ban) of all smoking, drinking, and everything that "isn't nice" seems prudish, such limitations are more than offset by

---

[51] Hugh Nibley, Course Schedule and Clipping File, 1946-47, Perry Special Collections.

[52] Hugh Nibley, *Curriculum Vita*, n.d., ca. 1959.

[53] Marian Robertson Wilson, Interviewed by Boyd Petersen, 5 January 1990. Marian and Phyllis shared the same music stand in the orchestra.

[54] Marian Robertson, "Which Came First, The Music or the Words? (A Greek Text and Coptic Melody: Musical Transcription and Analysis of the Setting)." *By Study and Also By Faith: Essays in Honor of Hugh W. Nibley on the Occasion of his Eightieth Birthday 27 March 1990*, edited by John M. Lundquist and Stephen D. Ricks, Vol. 1 (Salt Lake City: Deseret Book/FARMS, 1990), 417-27.

[55] Hugh Nibley, Letter to Paul Springer, n.d., Springer wrote "28 October 1946" at the top of the letter.

the earnest, free and unaffected manners of the students, nearly all of whom are from very rural places indeed, call each other brother and sister and think nothing of opening and closing every meeting with prayer. You might find such people oversimple . . . but in these times simplicity if it is honest and not just stupid is indeed a pearl of great price.[56]

Almost wonderingly a year later, Hugh confided to Paul: "This nuthouse attracts strange people. . . . I think to myself (I think) Hugo, you *can't* be normal to like this sort of place, and yet I do like it. Even to chunks"—a Nibleyism meaning "a lot."[57]

Hugh also noted the academic dedication of BYU students, claiming that they surpassed those at Claremont. In a letter to Lucien Goldschmidt, Hugh commented, "This almost empty part of the world is strangely prolific of great talents. One of the things that has astonished me most is the high perfection of language and spelling on examination papers—I never knew anything like it in California."[58] To his parents, Hugh wrote "I would say it is a rare teacher here who is not excelled by at least half his pupils."[59] However, the library at BYU was not at all up to the standards Hugh expected. In 1960, he reflected on his first impressions of the school and its library:

> I well remember the amazement and delight with which I perused the BYU catalogue as I waited for my first interview with President McDonald. Never had I ever beheld such a sumptuous offering in Classical Antiquity; there were advanced courses in Greek and Roman literature, philosophy, religion, archaeology, language and what-not. "You must have a splendid Classical library," I observed to President McDonald, who, in his curt, blunt way replied, "The Brigham Young University has no library!" "Come again?" quoth I in astonishment, and he repeated the brutal phrase. At once I rushed to the stacks and discovered that he was right—I found on the shelves just one Greek book (Homer) and one Latin book (Manilius), and I soon found out that nobody in Provo could read a line of either one. Yet we were offering the youth of the Church an unparalleled selection of courses, along with higher degrees, in Classical Studies.[60]

Hugh set out to remedy that problem, becoming an unofficial acquisitions librarian for the school. Not only did Hugh know what titles the school needed to bring itself up to par, but he also had contacts who could help him do it. Both Lucien Goldschmidt and George Allen, his comrades-in-arms, were managing bookstores.[61] Hugh wrote

---

[56] Hugh Nibley, Letter to Lucien Goldschmidt, 10 January 1947.

[57] Hugh Nibley, Letter to Paul Springer, n.d., ca. fall 1948.

[58] Hugh Nibley, Letter to Lucien Goldschmidt, 10 January 1947.

[59] Hugh Nibley, Letter to Alexander and Agnes Nibley, n.d., ca. January 1947.

[60] Hugh Nibley, Letter to "Brother Bergen," 29 July 1960, 1. This ruthless nine-page appraisal of education, especially at BYU, was titled "Nobody to Blame." Hugh circulated it with a cover letter addressed to "Dear Brother" dated 3 August 1960.

[61] In 1937, Goldschmidt opened a New York branch of Pierre Berès's antiquarian bookstore in Paris. After managing this store through World War II, he opened his own gallery in 1953 at 1117 Madison Avenue, with his wife, Marguerite Studer Goldschmidt. Obituary of Lucien Goldschmidt, *New York Times*, 18 December 1992; *New York Times Biographical Service*, December 1992, 23:1626. Also dealing in specialized and rare books, George Allen managed his father's bookstore, the William H. Allen Bookstore, located at 2031 Walnut Street in Philadelphia. The business was founded in 1918 in Temple, a community north of Reading. William Allen moved it to Philadelphia two years later. Obituary of George R. Allen, *Philadelphia Inquirer*, 25 November 1998.

temptingly to Goldschmidt: "This institution intends to spend large sums on its library in the near future: if you should happen to run on to a stray Patrologia, Pauly Wissowa, or such little item in the Classical or Religious line, we would be most grateful to hear from you in a business way—large collections will be especially welcome."[62] Soon thereafter, Goldschmidt discovered a set of the Patrologia in a Belgian attic, and Hugh arranged for the school to purchase it. During the next two decades, Hugh arranged for BYU to purchase more than five hundred volumes which eventually made their way to the Ancient Studies Reading Room in the Harold B. Lee Building. "I brought them to BYU," Hugh says, "and I've never been lonesome since."[63]

Despite the thinness of the library, Hugh continued his language study. "During the intersession lull I have been driving my little licorice-root [Phyllis] half mad by playing the Linguaphone records in the language department's collection," wrote Hugh to Springer. "The most gratifying are the Dutch and Italian, every word of which is perfectly understandable."[64]

In early 1948, Hugh discovered a family of Palestinian immigrants, the Mose Kader family, living in the mouth of Rock Canyon, just above BYU. Soon he was frequenting their house to practice his Arabic. "They exceed my wildest expectations," wrote Hugh to Springer. "Especially the wife . . . . who pours vials of her wrath upon the world and its inhabitants indiscriminately (though it must be confessed with a slight bias in the direction of the father of her ten children) and in a language the purity and richness of which she is justly proud."[65] After another visit, Hugh exclaimed: "Their kids are amazingly bright—no one can ever tell me that the Arab is the intellectual inferior of anyone on earth . . . . Think of it, Mrs. Kader can't read or write a line of any language, poor woman: so . . . she learns a book by heart when it is read to her once, and since she cannot read epic poetry . . . she just perforce speaks it."[66]

That same year, Hugh discovered a group of people who spoke Icelandic, as well as an "immense trove of Old Icelandic books" in Spanish Fork, just twenty miles south of Provo. "Spanish Fork is the oldest Icelandic settlement in the western hemisphere [outside of Iceland], and most of the community still speak Icelandic more or less," Hugh wrote excitedly to Goldschmidt. "The old woman who keeps the books is a veritable Edda, who knows all the sagas by heart and speaks, I am told, flawlessly."[67] Hugh was able to arrange for BYU to purchase the Old Icelandic library.

In addition to his conversational practice, he focused on reading texts, using his system of rotating from language to language each week. "It is far the best system I have found yet," he commented to Springer. "This week is Old Norse again."[68] He soon added Persian, convinced that "nothing (barring Arabic and Greek) is quite so important as

---

[62] Hugh Nibley, Letter to Lucien Goldschmidt, 10 January 1947.
[63] Quoted in Arnold J. Irvine, "Hugh Nibley: Profile of a Scholar," *Utah Magazine: Deseret News Magazine*, 15 April 1984, 5. See also Wilkinson, *Brigham Young University*, 2:441.
[64] Hugh Nibley, Letter to Paul Springer, 15 June 1947.
[65] Hugh Nibley, Letter to Paul Springer, n.d., ca. fall 1948. It begins "Vos Pitons, Monsieur!"
[66] Hugh Nibley, Letter to Paul Springer, n.d., ca. late summer or fall 1948.
[67] Hugh Nibley, Letter to Lucien Goldschmidt, 3 June 1947 [sic]. The year should be 1948.
[68] Hugh Nibley, Letter to Paul Springer, n.d., ca. fall 1948. It begins "Vos pitons, Monsieur!"

Persian: a terribly controversial field in which the major relationships still have to be established, but one that promises a bedizzening bouquet of surprises."⁶⁹

In June 1947, Hugh announced to Springer that he and Phyllis were expecting the imminent arrival of their first child. "Only one other sport is more popular in these parts," than "the great perennial matehunt," wrote Hugh, "and that is baby having. Phyllis is way out ahead in this."⁷⁰ On 19 July 1947, the baby was born: "male gender, large and mighty of limb and voice," as Hugh related in another letter. "We walked for miles and miles that night and polished off an enormous cake (our anniversary), after which [Phyllis] said, *eh bien, mon vieux, je vais m'enfanter!* and she did." The moral of the story, according to Hugh, is that "if you are poor and don't have a car blessed events are no more trouble than putting up peaches."⁷¹

Phyllis and Hugh with their newborn son Paul in the summer of 1947.

To decide on a name for the new baby, Hugh and Phyllis stuffed a jar full of possibilities and then drew one out. They kept pulling names out until the one they both had already decided on actually emerged: Paul. "We didn't even put Hugh into the drawing because of obvious complications," wrote Hugh to his mother.⁷² They gave him the middle name of Sloan, in honor of Hugh's maternal grandparents. Hugh did not comment to Paul Springer about naming the baby for him, and no letters about it from Paul to Hugh have survived. Although Phyllis did not get on easily with Paul, she liked his name and respected his friendship with her husband.

It could not have been an easy time for Phyllis. They had been married less than a year and were living in primitive circumstances. They had no car, had to walk to church at the Joseph Smith Building and also had do their grocery shopping on foot, which meant that Phyllis had to push Paul there in the baby buggy and then bring back him and the groceries in the same way, wait for Hugh to get home, or send him and trust that he wouldn't get absorbed in something else either coming or going. But they were happy, and Hugh marveled to Paul Springer: "Strangely enough for all that I am tied up with summer school, a new infant, a load of Church activities, and no end of extra duties, I

---

⁶⁹Hugh Nibley, Letter to Paul Springer, n.d., ca. late spring 1949.

⁷⁰Hugh Nibley, Letter to Paul Springer, 15 June 1947.

⁷¹Hugh Nibley, Letter to Paul Springer, 20 July 1947. Hugh's French can be roughly translated as "Well, old man, I am going to have myself a baby!"

⁷²Hugh Nibley, Letter to Agnes Sloan Nibley, 27 July 1947.

can't escape the impression that it is all a holiday—day after day bringeth fun and night after night sheweth forth entertainment: we live in an atmosphere of three cheers though to be frank I can't imagine why."[73]

Following Christmas 1947, Hugh left Phyllis and the baby while he dashed to Berkeley to "look up a few dubious points in the library." When a former professor invited him to attend the "first big get-together of the American Historical Association since the war," Hugh was thrilled to visit with old acquaintances and make new friends—"which, I announce with pleasure, shall never have the slightest mercenary value," Hugh wrote on the return train to his parents. "There was a good deal of eyebrow-raising when I announced that I was at the B.Y."[74]

In the summer of 1948, they made a major purchase—a second-hand car. Hugh wrote to Lucien Goldschmidt: "We have a car now, and put it under punishing contribution in ranging the little known corners of the state." Phyllis and the baby accompanied him on these explorations of Utah, and Hugh wrote delightedly: "Little Paul has become a confirmed *Naturfreund*. He sits on my shoulders all day long, singing and beating time on my head, and never grows tired on the trail. Though only ten months old he can drink very well from the swift stream without any help from me and he loves to play on the hole of the asp and the brink of the cataract."[75]

In fall 1948, the Nibleys bought a small pioneer-era home just south of the upper BYU campus at 612 North 400 East, across the street from Manavu Ward. (The house has since been razed and replaced by apartments, but the chapel is still standing.) Hugh blithely described their new home to Springer: "It is about the oldest building in the valley: a one story affair with tremendously thick adobe walls." He was delighted that "there is nothing about it even remotely reminiscent of the bourgeois; it is straight pioneer stuff, all atmosphere and no affectation."[76] A few months later, Hugh added, "I am quite in love with the main part of the house, which lets you know in a dozen pleasant ways that it is a hundred years old, and as far as it is concerned another hundred years won't make much difference."[77]

What Hugh describes as a comfortable pioneer home was a nightmare to Phyllis. Once again, they started without furniture. "It started snowing the day we moved in and didn't stop for four days; the snow was three feet deep all winter long," she remembers. Although they had a crib for the baby, they were still sleeping on a mattress on the floor. The house was heated by a coal-burning stove, and they dragged their mattress and Paul's crib into the living room in front of it; but the deep snow blocked access to the root cellar where the coal was stored. Phyllis remembers waking up to ice in the bathtub.[78] And

---

[73] Hugh Nibley, Letter to Paul Springer, n.d., summer 1947.

[74] Hugh Nibley, Letter to Agnes and Alexander Nibley, 4 January 1948. Although Hugh occasionally addressed his letters to both parents, who lived apart for the rest of their lives, the content of his letters makes it clear that he was thinking of Sloanie as the only audience.

[75] Hugh Nibley, Letter to Lucien Goldschmidt, 3 June 1948. This letter is misdated as 3 June 1947. Since Paul was ten months old at this time in 1948, the date is an obvious typo.

[76] Hugh Nibley, Letter to Paul Springer, n.d., ca. fall 1948. It begins "Vos pitons, Monsieur!"

[77] Hugh Nibley, Letter to Agnes Sloan Nibley, 17 October 1948.

[78] Phyllis Nibley, Interviewed by Boyd Petersen, 24 September 2001.

of course, since Hugh was on campus all day, she had to deal with the discomfort, the drafts, and the uncomfortable baby alone.

Hugh also began churning out articles for both scholarly and Church publications. But Hugh did not compartmentalize his research. His articles aimed at the scholarly community were certainly written in an academic style, but they often reached conclusions that supported what he was doing in his Church writing. And while he was more open about his gospel approach in writing for a Mormon audience, Hugh did not attempt to speak down to his audience nor was he any less rigorous in his research. "I am writing a lot of stuff for the Church these days," he reflected to Springer, "and it is surprising how much more one gets read in the process of looking things up than by any honest and straightforward method."[79] It also demanded just as much systematic thought: "I am doing a piece of work for the Cause that requires considerable concentration."[80] And it demanded just as much work: "At present I am working furiously day and night on a really exciting study for the Church."[81]

Hugh published his first attempt at linking the Book of Mormon to an ancient setting in 1948 with "The Book of Mormon as a Mirror of the East,"[82] then wrote an extended series on "Baptism for the Dead in Ancient Times," both of which ran in the *Improvement Era*.[83] His first article for a peer-reviewed publication since Claremont, "The Arrow, the Hunter, and the State," appeared in 1949, followed two years later by "The Hierocentric State," both in *Western Political Quarterly*, which was then being edited by Francis Wormuth at the University of Utah.[84]

Interestingly, it was the Mormon publication that attracted the most outside attention. Bernard Foschini, a Franciscan priest, discussed Hugh's *Improvement Era* article on baptism for the dead in a lengthy analysis of 1 Corinthians 15:29 "Else what shall they do which are baptized for the dead, if the dead rise not at all? Why are they then baptized for the dead?" Foschini's essay ran to five installments (1950-51) in the *Catholic Biblical Quarterly*, a publication of the Washington Catholic Biblical Association.[85] Among the many interpretations of this scripture that Foschini reviewed was the Mormon interpre-

---

[79] Hugh Nibley, Letter to Paul Springer, n.d., ca. spring 1948. It begins "Dear Impatient."

[80] Hugh Nibley, Letter to Paul Springer, n.d., ca. 1949. It begins "My Throssel."

[81] Hugh Nibley, Letter to Paul Springer, n.d., ca. late 1949. It begins "Dear Bunnymouse."

[82] Hugh Nibley, "The Book of Mormon as a Mirror of the East," *Improvement Era*, April 1948, 2024, 24951. Much of this essay was incorporated into *Lehi in the Desert, The World of the Jeredites and There Were Jeredites*, edited by John W. Welch, Darrell L. Matthews, and Stephen R. Callister [*Lehi in the Desert and The World of the Jeredites* originally published without *There Were Jeredites* in 1952 by Bookcraft] (Salt Lake City: Deseret Book/FARMS, 1988), 25-42.

[83] Hugh Nibley, "Baptism for the Dead in Ancient Times," *Improvement Era* (December 1948): 786-88, 836-38; (January 1949): 24-26, 60; (February 1949): 90-91, 109-10, 112; (March 1949): 146-48, 180-83; (April 1949): 212-14; reprinted in *Mormonism and Early Christianity*, edited by Todd M. Compton and Stephen D. Ricks, Vol. 4 in *The Collected Works of Hugh Nibley* (Salt Lake City: Deseret Books/FARMS, 1987), 100-167.

[84] Hugh Nibley, "The Arrow, the Hunter and the State," *Western Political Quarterly* 2 (1949): 328-44; reprinted in *The Ancient State*, edited by Donald W. Parry and Stephen D. Ricks, Vol. 10 of *The Collected Works of Hugh Nibley* (Salt Lake City: Deseret Books/FARMS, 1991),132; "The Hierocentric State," *Western Political Quarterly* 4 (1951): 226-53, reprinted in *The Ancient State*, 99-147.

[85] Foschini discusses Hugh Nibley's article in "'Those Who Are Baptised for the Dead,' 1 Cor. 15:29," *Catholic Biblical Quarterly* 13 (1951): 52-55, 70-73. The full article was serialized in five parts, beginning two issues prior to this one.

tation, which he drew from Hugh's essay, describing it as "the arguments which the Mormons use to defend" the practice (53). "To answer the Mormons is difficult," Foschini conceded, "not because of the strength of their arguments, but because they are not on common ground with us. We must depend on research and reason; they depend on the light of their 'revelations.'" He rejected the Mormon interpretation as contradicting Hebrews 9:27—that "it is appointed unto men once to die, and after this the judgment."[86] Thus, for Foschini, post-death decisions about salvation are not possible.

Hugh had argued that proxy baptism should not be any more objectionable to Christians than infant baptism, since "those offering the child for baptism, we are told 'answer for it' and the little one believes 'through another' (in altero) 'because he sinned through another.'"[87] Foschini countered, "There is no parity here because in Baptism for the dead the sacrament is administered to another person, whereas in infant Baptism it is the person himself who is baptized." Foschini admits that the Bible nowhere states that infants should be baptized but then argues, somewhat contradictorily, that the practice "is in perfect conformity" with the Bible while baptism for the dead is not because "scripture nowhere says that a man is to be baptized through a proxy," even though it does specifically mention baptism for the dead.[88] A Mormon reading Foschini's essay comes away with the feeling that the "research and reason" Foschini depends on have very little to recommend them.

Phyllis spent another winter pregnant and overseeing the remodeling of the house to suit their needs more comfortably. On 31 March 1949, she gave birth to Christina, "a fat and sassy daughter" whom Hugh described as "alarmingly beautiful."[89] Hugh's mother arrived just before the birth to help Phyllis with child care and housekeeping. Hugh was dismayed by the disruption and confessed candidly to Springer:

> This relieves me of the responsibility of taking care of little Paul during the day, but it loads me with Herculean house-cleaning assignments, for of course the good lady immediately turned everything upside down amid clouds of dust and an unceasing torrent of good if caustic advice. After about ten minutes her high-powered tirades and Augean energy began to weary us; at present it is only aspirin that keeps me sane. And now goes Phyllis to the Krankenhaus [hospital]—the last barrier between me and the full tide of momism which is already subduing the fiercely joyful and spontaneous character of my only begotten son.[90]

But Phyllis's dismay matched Hugh's. "She gave me lessons on how I was supposed to take care of [Hugh]," remembers Phyllis. "I was supposed to lay out his clothes for him; I was supposed to have his dinner ready the minute he came in the house, even if I had no idea when he was coming in; I was supposed to do everything for him—to treat him like a king or a god or whatever, because that was how she believed he should be treated." Hugh, fortunately, "had a much more realistic view of things than his moth-

---

[86]Ibid., 53, 70.

[87]Nibley, Mormonism and Early Christianity, 146.

[88]Foschini, "'Those Who Are Baptised,'" 72.

[89]Hugh Nibley, Letter to Paul Springer, 1 April 1949; Hugh Nibley, Letter to Paul Springer, n.d., ca. summer 1949. It begins "Your problem is mine, kiddo."

[90]Hugh Nibley, Letter to Paul Springer, 1 April 1949.

er did." Phyllis's mother came just before Sloanie's stay of about ten days was up, and the combination of the two grandmothers was explosive. It would be hard to say who was more relieved when Sloanie finally left—Hugh or Phyllis—and Sloanie remained one of Phyllis's "severest critics," a policy that assured an unbridgeable distance.[91]

Hugh had made some radical adjustments in the course of only four years, adjustments that must have been as difficult as those he faced in war time. He had gone from witnessing war and genocide to witnessing peacetime domesticity, from traveling throughout Europe in a jeep to exploring Utah's outdoors and the library stacks, and most importantly, from being a thirty-six-year-old bachelor to being husband and father. "Having a house and family is turning me into what I swore I would never be—one of those fat, sleek, domesticated, handymen who thinks himself a second Leonardo," wrote Hugh reflectively in late 1949.[92] The children were "a ball and chain, but much worth all the trouble they make—a source of perpetual glee."[93] Hugh adored his small children; he related to them in ways he never could once they got older. They were simple, loving, and loveable. "Little Christina is devastatingly pretty and little Paul is devastatingly wild—two such delightful little pipples, it does mine heart good."[94]

---

[91] Phyllis Nibley, "Faith of an Observer," 426-27. Both El and Sloanie visited many times, always at their initiative. Although Phyllis and Hugh were welcoming and good-mannered, they found the visits trying. Sloanie "just plowed into" their lives with little sensitivity about the hurt feelings her high-handedness caused.

[92] Hugh Nibley, Letter to Paul Springer, n.d., ca. summer 1949. It begins "Your problem is mine, kiddo." Phyllis counters that he "never" took on a handyman's tasks.

[93] Hugh Nibley, Letter to Paul Springer, n.d., July 1949.

[94] Hugh Nibley, Letter to Paul Springer, n.d., ca. late 1949. It begins "Dear Utz."

Hugh and Sidney Sperry (left) examine copies of ancient manuscripts, ca. 1950.

Photo courtesy of L. Tom Perry Special Collections,
Harold B. Lee Library, Brigham Young University.

No one in the history of Mormon scholarship has done more to establish rational grounds for belief in the Book of Mormon than Hugh Nibley. . . . Nibley's legendary erudition, fluency across a spectrum of languages, and prodigious output . . . have lent his work a weight that is unprecedented in Mormon studies. . . . Nibley has done more than any Mormon of his era to further the intellectual credibility of the Book of Mormon.

--Terryl L. Givens [1]

---

[1] Terryl L. Givens, By the Hand of Mormon: The American Scripture That Launched a New World Religion (Oxford: Oxford University Press, 2002), 118, 124.

Chapter 16

"Something to Move Mountains": Hugh Nibley and the Book of Mormon

Hugh Nibley has had a revolutionary influence on the way we read the Book of Mormon. In *Lehi in the Desert, An Approach to the Book of Mormon,* and *Since Cumorah,* as well as in his many related articles, Hugh Nibley has set the Book of Mormon in an ancient Middle Eastern context and helped three generations of readers realize the book's relevance and importance to our day. The effect of Hugh's writings has been fundamental and far-reaching; our understanding of the Book of Mormon has deepened and our appreciation of the book has grown. As John W. Welch, BYU law professor and Book of Mormon scholar, puts it, "We are warned but reassured" by Hugh's work.[2]

Hugh finds the Book of Mormon compelling in three fundamental ways: First, the uncanny parallels to other writings from the ancient Middle East have called forth Hugh's respect for the Book of Mormon's ability to fit comfortably within that historical and cultural milieu. Second, this, in turn, has caused him to see the book as a significant witness for the prophetic calling of Joseph Smith; these connections confirm the Prophet's story about the coming forth of the Book of Mormon and witness to his divine calling as a translator. Most importantly, Hugh Nibley venerates the book for its relevance to our day and its prophetic nature, for its accuracy in depicting the sins and

---

[2] Welch, "Hugh Nibley and the Book of Mormon," *Ensign,* April 1985, 56. I read a version of this chapter, titled "Something to Move Mountains": Hugh Nibley's Devotion to the Book of Mormon," at the Literature and Belief Symposium, 28 March 1997 at Brigham Young University. It appeared in the *Journal of Book of Mormon Studies* 6, no. 2 (1997) 1-25, and *Colloquium: Essays in Literature and Belief,* edited by Richard H. Cracroft, Jane D. Brady, and Linda Hunter Adams (Provo, UT: Center for the Study of Christian Values in Literature, 2001), 489-513.

trials of our generation and its reassuring guidance on how to survive these last days. In short, Hugh Nibley really believes that the Book of Mormon is the word of God.

Hugh Nibley's Life with the Book of Mormon

Hugh Nibley has been interested in the Book of Mormon from a very early age. In our modern Church, this really does not seem so strange, but at the time of Hugh's youth, the Book of Mormon was largely ignored. Significantly this change is somewhat his doing. In his essay "The Coming Forth of the Book of Mormon in the Twentieth Century," Noel Reynolds, BYU political science professor, demonstrates that our present concern with the Book of Mormon is a very recent phenomenon. "The early Saints valued the Book of Mormon as evidence of the Restoration, but by the Nauvoo period, focus on the book had already decreased."[3] And in the twentieth century, Reynolds documents that in general conference addresses, Church manuals, books published for the LDS audience, courses of study both at BYU and throughout the Church Educational System, and even the lessons given by our missionaries, focus on the Book of Mormon has been cursory and sporadic until very recent times. "Not long ago you would find stake presidents who had never read the Book of Mormon," states Hugh Nibley.[4] The reason for the previous generations' neglect of the book may be understandable. Hugh Nibley commented to one correspondent: "Our ancestors for example, spent little time reading the Book of Mormon—even for the youthful President Grant it was nothing but a bore. People tried to get interested in it from a romantic point of view; its strangeness exercised a kind of fascination. It was a happy generation to which the abominations of the Nephites and Jaredites seemed utterly unreal."[5]

Reynolds documents the dramatic shift in perspective: "The last few decades have produced a significant revolution in the LDS community in terms of the increased understanding and competent appreciation for the Book of Mormon as an inspired work of ancient scripture."[6] Both scholars and the general populace of the Church, Reynolds demonstrates, "strive to understand the Book of Mormon as an ancient document and to give diligent heed to Christ's gospel that it contains."[7] Hugh Nibley has certainly inspired much of this change in focus. Elder Neal A. Maxwell has stated that Hugh's influence on the new generation of Book of Mormon scholars—his "intellectual reconnaissance," as Elder Maxwell has called it—is among Hugh's greatest contributions to the Church. Elder Maxwell compares Hugh to "an early explorer" who has staked claims on various mine shafts, sampled the ore, and signaled to his students where the ore lies. Maxwell continues, "What's now happening is that his . . . students are coming on and they go all the way into the mine and come out and say, 'Yes, it

---

[3]Noel B. Reynolds, "The Coming Forth of the Book of Mormon in the Twentieth Century," *BYU Studies* 38, no. 2 (1999): 7.

[4]Hugh Nibley, interviewed by Allison Clark, June 1996; photocopy of transcript in my possession.

[5]Hugh Nibley, Letter to Parley H. Merrill, 18 June 1957. Unless otherwise noted, photocopies of all correspondence are in my possession.

[6]Reynolds, "The Coming Forth of the Book of Mormon," 39-40.

[7]Ibid., 40.

really was a rich vein to be explored.'"[8] But Hugh has also inspired the rest of us to take the Book of Mormon more seriously—to look at the text more closely, to reevaluate our assumptions, and to pay closer heed to its teachings.

Hugh's earliest written reference to the Book of Mormon appears in a letter to his mother from the Swiss-German Mission when he was eighteen. He quoted Ether 12:4, then commented jubilantly: "Great stuff, the Book of Ether."[9] Eight months later, he would comment at greater length on what he called the "marvelous paradox" of 1 Nephi: "I started to pick it to pieces this evening, pruning with colored pencils. As a result I am, at the moment, beside myself with enthusiasm. What boundless hope!—True, true, rings thru the whole thing. Everything ignored that would stand between the reader and the Idea. That is a library of history & philosophy in the little account of Nephi's vision."[10] Shortly afterward, he confided to his journal, "The Book of Mormon is giving me greater joy than anything ever did" (25 March 1929).

His fellow-missionaries, however, typically traded only on the book's novelty, approaching people with the query: "This is about the American Indians. Don't you want to know where the American Indians come from?"[11] This approach had little appeal in the Swiss-German Mission. In contrast, when Hugh served a short-term mission to the Northwestern States, President William Sloan, Hugh's uncle, made the Book of Mormon the central message of the mission. Hugh recalls: "We really hit it hard and had great success."[12]

It wasn't until World War II, however, that Hugh became preoccupied with the Book of Mormon. He has told how the potency of the Book of Mormon struck him with full force as he drove one of the first jeeps onto Utah Beach during the invasion of Normandy.[13] His correspondence from that period confirms that he was indeed consumed by the Book of Mormon at that time. In a letter to his mother as preparations for D-Day accelerated, Hugh commented, "Of course, there is little time to relax in the Airborne at a time like this, but when I can snatch a moment or two off it is devoted to a single engrossing item: at this late date I have discovered the Book of Mormon, and live in a state of perpetual excitement—that marvelous production throws everything done in our age completely into the shadows."[14]

Five months later, after witnessing the battles of Normandy and Holland from the front lines, Hugh lamented that he had lost his triple combination: "I would give anything to get one. I can't tell you how badly I miss not having those three books, though I do have plenty of others."[15]

---

[8] Neal A. Maxwell, interviewed by Boyd Petersen, 29 December 1989.

[9] Hugh Nibley, Letter to Agnes Sloan Nibley, 16 July 1928, Charles W. Nibley Collection, Mss 1523, Box 1, fd. 4, L. Tom Perry Special Collections, Harold B. Lee Library, Brigham Young University, Provo, Utah.

[10] Hugh Nibley, Journal, 17 March 1929. In Nephi's vision, which replicated his father's vision, he saw the tree of life that was "exceeding all beauty" and "precious above all." When Nephi asked the significance of the tree, he was shown Christ's birth, baptism, ministry, and death. Nephi also witnessed the persecution of the early church as well as the history of his people in the New World (1 Ne. 11-14).

[11] Hugh Nibley, Interviewed by Allison Clark, June 1996.

[12] Ibid.

[13] Welch, "Hugh Nibley and the Book of Mormon," 50-56.

[14] Hugh Nibley, Letter to Agnes Sloan Nibley, 8 April 1944.

[15] Hugh Nibley, Letter to Agnes Sloan Nibley, 5 November 1944.

An important step in Hugh's development as a defender of the Book of Mormon came in his monograph-length rebuttal of Fawn McKay Brodie's dismissal of Joseph Smith as translator of an authentic ancient record. She explained the Book of Mormon as a result of Joseph Smith's creative mind working on biblical motifs and nineteenth-century American concerns.[16] Hugh countered Brodie's argument that the Book of Mormon contained nineteenth-century parallels with an argument about parallels of his own: "Oriental literature bristles with parallels to the Book of Mormon that are far more full and striking than anything that can be found in the West."[17]

As a faculty member at BYU, Hugh pursued these parallels from Arabic and Egyptian literature, breaking new ground in Book of Mormon thought. His first article about the Book of Mormon appeared in the Improvement Era in April 1948. "The Book of Mormon: A Mirror of the East" cited the episode of the Nephites' change of political systems from a monarchy to judges and compares it to a similar historical change in Egypt around 1085 B.C. Hugh notes that "the eagerness and ease with which the [Book of Mormon] people adopted the system imply that they were familiar with it." It was also in this article that Hugh first noted similarities between Book of Mormon names and those from the ancient Middle East.[18] Two years later, Hugh evaluated this approach in a letter to Paul Springer:

> I am enclosing herewith a few excerpts from a Book of Mormon speculation in which I indulged a couple of years back. It is very premature, but subsequent researches have shown me that I was on the right track almost without knowing it. . . . You can ignore most of my nonsense about the proper names: at the time I had not gone through Lieblein or Ranke, and so failed to realize that the case for the Book of Mormon was really ten times as strong as I supposed.[19]

Hugh extended this new approach into a series of articles called "Lehi in the Desert," which appeared in the Improvement Era between January and October of 1950. In the series, Hugh compared the culture, social customs, and language in the first forty pages of the Book of Mormon with Middle East documents from the same milieu. He notes, for example, that 1 Nephi 1-3 is a "typical colophon," a common Egyptian literary device. He also expanded material on politics and personal names he had originally used in "The Book of Mormon: A Mirror of the East." He provided a plausible character study on Lehi (a "model sheikh of the desert") and challenged Book of Mormon critics to write a history of eleventh-century Tibet without doing any research, without making any absurd or contradictory statements, and without making any changes to the text. "The ablest orientalists" must have full access to examine the text. He concluded: "It would have been quite as impossible for the most learned

---

[16] As she stated in a later interview, "I think there is no question that the Book of Mormon was fraudulently conceived." Shirley E. Stephenson, "Fawn McKay Brodie: An Oral History Interview," Dialogue: A Journal of Mormon Thought 14, no. 2 (Summer 1981): 99-116.

[17] Nibley, "No, Ma'am, That's Not History": A Brief Review of Mrs. Brodie's Reluctant Vindication of a Prophet She Seeks to Expose, in Tinkling Cymbals and Sounding Brass, edited by David J. Whittaker, Vol. 11 of The Collected Works of Hugh Nibley (Salt Lake City: Deseret Book/FARMS, 1991), 8.

[18] Hugh Nibley, "The Book of Mormon as a Mirror of the East," Improvement Era, April 1948, 202-4, 249-51. The quotation is on p. 202.

[19] Hugh Nibley, Letter to Paul Springer, n.d., 1950.

man alive in 1830 to have written the book as it was for Joseph Smith." Such tests, he affirmed, proved that the Book of Mormon was an authentic ancient document.[20]

In his letter to Paul Springer, Hugh described his method: "For an experiment I decided a year ago to confine all my attention to a couple of chapters and simply tear them to pieces. This has entailed an enormous lot of looking up . . . but has been very rewarding."[21]

Hugh followed "Lehi in the Desert" with a second series, "The World of the Jaredites," issued serially between September 1951 and July 1952, in which he examined the book of Ether in light of the cultural/historical milieu of early Asiatic civilization. Both series were combined and published as a book later that year. Then, in 1956-57, the *Improvement Era* ran Hugh's series, "There Were Jaredites," comparing the book of Ether to other ancient epics.[22]

President McKay was so impressed by Hugh's approach in these essays that he suggested a similar series of lessons for the 1957 Melchizedek Priesthood manual. Hugh was then absorbed by the twin themes of the apostasy and the early Christian church. He countered by proposing a manual "more abstruse and unfamiliar than that treated by Brother Barker" in his manual *Apostasy from the Divine Church*.[23] However, President McKay's wishes won out and Hugh began working on a Book of Mormon study manual. Once he accepted the job, Hugh's commitment was wholehearted. In a letter to his mother, he stated: "It has been a steady diet of Book of Mormon and no other food is so invigorating. It is the bread of life in the most digestible form."[24]

Making a virtue of necessity, he made a strong case to Henry D. Moyle, chair of the committee, that he would need to complete his research in a number of specialized libraries outside Utah:

---

[20] Hugh Nibley, "Lehi in the Desert" in *Lehi in the Desert, The World of the Jeredites, There Were Jeredites*, edited by John W. Welch, Darrell L. Matthews, and Stephen R. Callister (Salt Lake City: Deseret Book/FARMS, 1988), 43, 119, 123.

[21] Hugh Nibley, Letter to Paul Springer, n.d., 1950.

[22] Hugh received very little financial recompense for these articles; usually Church magazines did not pay contributors. If he received anything at all, it was very little, and he received so little from his published books that one goal of the Foundation for Ancient Research and Mormon Studies (FARMS) in printing Hugh's collected works, beginning in the 1980s, was to compensate him more fairly for his intellectual labor.

[23] Henry D. Moyle, Letter to Hugh Nibley, 6 May 1955. Moyle quotes from Nibley's earlier letter to him. At this time, Nibley had completed a series "The World and the Prophets," which on KSL Radio aired between March and October 1954 and was published that year in book form. "The Way of the Church," another series, ran in the *Improvement Era* between January and December 1955, when the Era canceled it. Nibley used material from the remaining articles in other articles; all are compiled in *Mormonism and Early Christianity*, edited by Todd M. Compton and Stephen D. Ricks, Vol. 4 of *The Collected Works of Hugh Nibley* (Salt Lake City: Deseret Books/FARMS, 1987). James L. Barker, chair of BYU's Language Department and professor of German, French, Spanish, and Italian, wrote three Melchizedek Priesthood quorum manuals. The three manuals were titled: *The Divine Church: Down Through Change*, *Apostasy Therefrom*, and *Restoration* (Salt Lake City: Church of Jesus Christ of Latter-day Saints, Council of the Twelve Apostles, 1952, 1953, 1954). They were later combined and published as *Apostasy from the Divine Church* (Salt Lake City: Deseret News Press, 1960).

[24] Quoted by LeGrand Richards, "Be Ready Always to Give a Reason of the Hope that Is in You," address to BYU student body, 10 February 1960, BYU *Speeches of the Year, 1960*, 7, on *LDS Collectors Library*, CD-ROM (Orem, UT: Infobase, 1995). Elder Richards says that Sloanie Nibley provided him with a copy of the letter.

> I can fill up paper as well as the next man, but you can readily see that a half-baked treatment of this great subject would be far worse than none at all. When attempted proof falls short it but adds to the burden of suspicion already held against the Book of Mormon. Since the rate of discovery has been breaking all records since the War and is now moving at an accelerating pace, it is extremely important to be up to date on everything. I am sure you would be as reluctant to accept as I would be to write a sloppy defense of the most important book in the world. So what can we do about it? There is no point to postponing the business, since the complete returns are never in, and today's evidence is as up-to-date as it ever will be.[25]

Hugh explained his modus operandi to a correspondent while the manual was being prepared:

> It was Brother McKay's express and repeated request that the Melchizedek manual for 1957 be based on Lehi in the Desert. From what I was told at various committee meetings, it was to be the old opus with almost no changes. As I am constitutionally incapable of redoing anything without completely rewriting it, the eight lessons we have turned out so far resemble the original about as closely as the Book of Mormon resembles the Spalding manuscript—it is a completely new thing.[26]

Hugh sent off a sample lesson to the reading committee on 2 March 1956, with a letter that combined both an aggressive defense of his scholarly method and humble trepidation about how it would be received:

> You will notice that this lesson is too long and swarms with the vices of the pedant. It is clear that the author can no more keep from lapsing into moral tirades and personal reflections than he can voluntarily stop breathing. It is for you to decide whether you want that sort of thing or not; unfortunately it is not for me to decide whether I will write that way or not—I can do no other. I have always been impressed by the intelligence of the average priesthood member, and to ask me to write for his benefit a text-book for backward ten-year-olds is to ask the impossible. . . . The evidences for the Book of Mormon are simply overwhelming; they leave me breathless, but I have learned only too well in my few years in Utah that they excite great anger and resentment in certain quarters, and I should be most reluctant to write a whole priesthood manual for the waste-basket. To write a typical priesthood manual is totally beyond my powers: the question is, can the Lord's work be helped by a new approach? If so, we've got a million of them—and a couple may be pretty good.[27]

Hugh's misgivings were prescient. Elder Richard L. Evans of the Quorum of the Twelve, even though he was not on the committee overseeing production of the manual, recommended that Hugh write for an uneducated and uninformed audience. "Always think of yourself as addressing the tiredest farmer in Koosharem," was Evans's counsel, as Hugh recalled it.[28] Predictably, Hugh rejected such advice. When the review-

---

[25]Hugh Nibley, Letter to Henry D. Moyle, 3 February 1956.
[26]Hugh Nibley, Letter to M. W. Wellin, 6 July 1956.
[27]Hugh Nibley, Letter to Henry D. Moyle, 2 March 1956.
[28]Nibley, "Mediocre Meditations on the Media," in Brother Brigham Challenges the Saints, 394.

ing committee turned down Hugh's lessons, he unburdened himself to Paul Springer: "When the massive work was done, the two stooges appointed by the Committee to read it took one look and decided to save themselves the time and eyestrain by turning thumbs down. I was understandably peeved."[29]

Responding to an unrelated letter from Elder LeGrand Richards, Hugh took the opportunity to defend his lessons:

> My own belief is that they are by far the best thing I have ever written and the only really compelling stuff ever brought forward on the Book of Mormon. But Brother Moyle informs me that the committee is sure I would not be willing to let such writings appear under my signature. The committee knows best, but THIS IS CERTAINLY THE LAST THING I WILL EVER WRITE FOR THE CHURCH. Excuse the emotion, but I am sick of committees that pass the buck to other committees that pass the buck to others, and so on, while nobody really pays attention to what is going on. I would recommend a careful reading of these invaluable lessons in their final form. . . . But as things stand, it is doubtful whether there will ever be a final form.[30]

Hugh's priesthood manual almost certainly would have been shelved had not President McKay intervened personally. There is no evidence that Hugh approached him on this issue, although Hugh's letter to Richards may have prompted Richards to take up the matter with McKay. As Hugh tells it: "Then one night a Very Important Person could not sleep and decided in sheer desperation to look at the mountain of type that had been so long and so gingerly bandied about. After an hour he was having fits, calling me up long distance from the end of the world at an unearthly time to shout hosannah over the wire."[31] Hugh rejoiced in the excited President McKay's reasoning, based on his career as an educator: "Well, if you think it's over their heads, let them reach for it. We have to give them something more than pat answers."[32] When the final version of the lessons was completed, Hugh wrote, relieved but realistic: "Unless it is completely emasculated by those members of the Committee who are afraid of offending the Gentiles it should (but won't) cause quite a stir."[33] The orange, paperbound *Approach to the Book of Mormon* was published by the Council of the Twelve for use as the 1957 course of study for all Melchizedek Priesthood holders. The unnamed editor wrote in the foreword that the course "needs diligent and prayerful study" (vii); and in the preface, Joseph Fielding Smith invited readers to "show their gratitude to Dr. Nibley by taking a deep interest in these lessons" (x). A second, clothbound edition appeared in 1964.

To a correspondent in 1982, Hugh told what may be a hyperbolic version of this same experience:

---

[29] Hugh Nibley, Letter to Paul Springer, 17 September 1956.
[30] Hugh Nibley, Letter to LeGrand Richards, 1 September 1956.
[31] Hugh Nibley, Letter to Paul Springer, 17 September 1956.
[32] Hugh Nibley, interviewed by Allison Clark, June 1996.
[33] Hugh Nibley, Letter to Paul Springer, 20 December 1956.

The objection to an "over-intellectual" approach to the Gospel runs entirely counter to the long tradition of learning in the Church. When I wrote the Melchizedek Priesthood Manual for 1957, the "Reading Committee" rejected each and every lesson as it was submitted week by week; and in each and every case without exception President McKay overruled the Committee, saying, "If it is over their heads, let them reach for it—that is what we need!" Every lesson was printed without any alteration; the Manual was reprinted many times and with all its "mistakes of men" is still in print. So much for study that is "too advanced" for our people.[34]

Hugh's work on the Book of Mormon has been praised by many. Elder John A. Widtsoe wrote to Hugh in 1952, "We have looked upon the Book of Mormon too much as something apart from flesh and blood. You have opened a new course of thinking about the book and the characters it contains."[35] Spencer W. Kimball, then an apostle, wrote that Hugh's Book of Mormon volumes represent "real contributions to our literature, and open up a new field untouched by anyone else that I know of."[36] Ezra Taft Benson, also an apostle at the time, called the priesthood manual "a practical, scholarly and timely work."[37]

But Hugh downplayed his own contribution. Writing the next year to Spencer W. Kimball, then an apostle, he demurred:

The main purpose of the Manual is to show what anybody is up against who undertakes a serious questioning of the Book of Mormon: especially we wish to demonstrate how easy it is to be wrong about the Book—and to do that we don't have to be right much of the time! Moreover, we have merely scratched the surface, and anyone who wants to is welcome to dig further. Our business is to raise questions, not to answer them. After a vast expenditure of time and money, our Book of Mormon archaeologists have failed to produce a single clinching argument for the book in the last thirty years: it is time to try a fresh approach. . . . This is the very beginning of Book of Mormon research, not the end: it would be a paralyzing and a foolish thing to start making pontifical pronouncements at this early date. On to the fray![38]

And on to the fray Hugh went, tapping out article after article about the Book of Mormon on his typewriter, without secretarial assistance until at least the 1970s. *Since Cumorah* appeared in 1967, and most of the twenty-three articles and talks he has produced on the Book of Mormon over the years have been compiled in *The Prophetic Book of Mormon*. Throughout, his focus has steadfastly remained fixed on establishing the ancient Middle Eastern setting for the Book of Mormon.

---

[34] Hugh Nibley, "To Whom It May Concern" (letter of recommendation for Avraham Gileadi), 16 February 1982.
[35] John A. Widtsoe, Letter to Hugh Nibley, 1 July 1952.
[36] Spencer W. Kimball, Letter to Hugh Nibley, 16 September 1959.
[37] Ezra Taft Benson, Letter to Hugh Nibley, 2 January 1958.
[38] Hugh Nibley, Letter to Spencer W. Kimball, 1 November 1957.

The Book of Mormon as a Middle Eastern Book

Hugh began his career studying patterns between cultures—how the writings and rituals of one culture compare with those of another. The focus of his Ph.D. work was year-rites and coronation assemblies throughout the ancient world, and later he noticed patterns in religious ceremony and myth, preceding the efforts of Mircea Eliade.[39] Hugh described the inspiration for his first article fourteen years after the fact in a letter to his friend and Egyptian teacher Klaus Baer:

> It was certain Egyptian undertones which seemed to me to be more than accidental that first got me interested in the Book of Mormon years ago. I refer to the episode of the judges, in which it is reported how the people in the New World set up a system of courts after the Old World pattern; how one Korihor challenged the system as introducing dangerous "ordinances and performances which are laid down by ancient priests, to usurp power and authority" (Alma 30:21-24); how the new chief judge charged one Nehor with being "first to introduce priestcraft among this people" and warned that such a thing "would prove their entire destruction" (Alma 1:12); how Korihor was seized as an agitator by a particularly pious community known as "the people of Ammon"; how finally the rivalry among three brothers called Pahoran, Paanchi, and Pacumeni finally wrecked the system, etc. Well, it seemed to me that the names, the situations, and the conscious harping back to unhappy experiences in the Old World were something beyond the ingenuity of a young yokel writing in upper New York State in 1829. Just now what intrigues me is the old Israelite apocryphal stories that turn up in the Book of Mormon as popular tales.[40]

More of these parallels could be found in sources that came to light in 1947 when Bedouin shepherds discovered scrolls in the caves on the shores of the Dead Sea. Although these scrolls would not be translated for decades, their existence was immensely provocative. In 1967 Ernest L. Wilkinson, BYU president, asked Hugh to review an article on the Dead Sea Scrolls that he had received from a syndicated columnist in 1967. Hugh responded:

> Away back in 1957 I included in the Melchizedek Priesthood Manual a chapter entitled UNWELCOME VOICES FROM THE DUST. The idea was that the Dead Sea Scrolls are unwelcome both to Jews and Christians for the same reason that the Book of Mormon is, namely because they give a picture of ancient Judaism AND Christianity which is totally at variance with that of conventional Christianity and Judaism alike. The picture they give, however, is identical with that of the Book of Mormon, and that should make them doubly welcome to the Latter-day Saints.[41]

---

[39] Hugh Nibley, *The Ancient State*, edited by Donald W. Parry and Stephen D. Ricks, Vol. 10 of *The Collected Works of Hugh Nibley* (Salt Lake City: Deseret Books/FARMS, 1991).

[40] Hugh Nibley, Letter to Klaus Baer, 2 August 1962, Klaus Baer Collection, Archives of the Oriental Institute, University of Chicago.

[41] Hugh Nibley, Letter to Ernest L. Wilkinson, 10 January 1967, Ernest L. Wilkinson Collection, Box 403, fd. 13, Perry Special Collections.

As the parallels Hugh discovered became apparent, he marveled at how numerous and how conspicuous they were. He wrote Paul Springer in 1964:

> I have been sort of overseeing the translating of the Book of Mormon into Greek (it is now finished), while at the same time working on my Moslems[42] and consorting with the Hasidic Jews, meantime faithfully plodding through the Coffin Texts and preparing an article on the new Christian Coptic texts for a very serious journal.[43] Doing all this at once has addled the old brains more than ever, but forced me to recognize the common pattern behind things. I say recognize, not invent, because other people are beginning to recognize it too. This whole apocryphal world is brought together in the Book of Mormon, a veritable handbook of motifs and traditions. As a work of fiction, as a mere intellectual tour-de-force, nothing can touch it—but along with that it is full of old Jewish lore that very few Jews have ever heard of, handles the desert situation in a way that delights my Meccans, and gives a picture of primitive Christianity that is right out of the Dead Sea Scrolls and the Nag Hammadi texts.[44]

As Hugh mentions, the enthusiastic response of Moslem students in his Book of Mormon class was living "proof" that his parallels were justified. Proudly he claimed that they often related to the book better than Westerners:

> I always get at least a dozen Iranians in my Book of Mormon class for Moslems—had eight students from Mecca this year!—and since they have all seen the golden plates and the stone box in Ispahan they are properly impressed. In teaching several hundred Arabs—well, maybe ONE hundred real Bedouins—over the past several years I have found that they universally approve of Lehi in the Desert and have only one criticism to make, viz., WHY did Nephi wait so long to cut off Laban's head? For them that is the one false note.[45]

When he began teaching at BYU, Hugh also came in contact with further "living proof" of the ancient authenticity of the Book of Mormon in his associations with the Hopi of northeastern Arizona. (See chap. 18.) He visited their mesas many times throughout his career. Hugh's respect for the Hopi derives from their having managed to preserve ancient lore and customs that he had previously only read about in books. And like Hugh's Arab students, the Hopi developed an appreciation for the Book of Mormon which caused, as Hugh delightedly reported, Protestant missionaries and clergy on the reservation to evolve some complicated explanations for the parallels the Hopi found between the Book of Mormon and their oral lore. Writing to Paul Springer, he confided:

---

[42] For several years during the 1960s, Hugh taught a special Book of Mormon class to Moslem students.

[43] Hugh lectured on "The Early Christian Church in Light of Some Newly Discovered Papyri from Egypt" on 3 March 1964. It probably reflected the work he was doing at this time. The essay was published by the BYU Extension Publications and most of it was later incorporated into *Since Cumorah*, edited by John W. Welch (1967; reprinted Salt Lake City: Deseret/FARMS, 1988).

[44] Hugh Nibley, Letter to Paul Springer, 2 February 1964.

[45] Hugh Nibley, Letter to Paul Springer, 5 July 1963.

As far as I was able to find out, every Hopi we talked with was quite frank in stating that he knew the Book of Mormon was perfectly true and told the very same stories that have always been told in the tribe. The other missions, justly alarmed, have now spread abroad the interesting fiction that old Chief Tuba (after whom Tuba City was named) when he became a Mormon and went to Salt Lake with Jacob Hamblin cir. 1870 was buttoned-holed by Joseph Smith, wheedled into telling the tribal secrets which were then written down & published as the Book of Mormon. That is how the Protestant missionaries now explain to the Hopis how their sacred & secret legends all got into the Mormons' book. There is a slight matter of chronology to be adjusted, but at least it is a frank admission by the opposition that the Book of Mormon does contain the real stuff.[46]

In 1958, Ezra Taft Benson sent Hugh a letter of "gratitude and congratulations" for the priesthood manual, and Hugh responded: "Wishing to be fair in the matter, I have just compiled what I believe to be a complete list of all important arguments AGAINST the Book of Mormon. Not one new argument has been added since 1840! This shrinking list makes a significant contrast to the growing list of arguments in the book's favor."[47]

In the four decades since Hugh launched his impressive reconstruction of the Book of Mormon's ancient world, the evidence in its favor, documented both by Hugh and by other Mormon scholars, has grown exponentially. Hugh has influenced a whole new generation of Book of Mormon scholars. John Welch has examined literary evidence, in particular the use of the ancient poetic form of chiasmus in the Book of Mormon and has published a book exploring the temple rituals preserved in the book. Stephen Ricks, professor of Hebrew, has followed Hugh's lead in examining kingship in the Book of Mormon. William Hamblin, a history professor, has further considered warfare in the Book of Mormon, while Paul Hoskisson, professor of ancient studies, has looked more attentively at proper names in the Book of Mormon. Donald Parry, a professor of Hebrew, has focused on Hebraisms in the Book of Mormon.

Perhaps the most significant change occurred in 1980 when the Foundation of Ancient Research and Mormon Studies (FARMS) was founded as a clearing-house of scholarly materials on the Book of Mormon. This organization, which became part of BYU in 1998, fulfilled a desire that Hugh had expressed to Wilkinson in 1952 that "the BYU should be the Information Center for the Church," compiling files and "information-sheets" to answer questions for "members who passionately desire" such information. He continued, "The dissemination of well-documented, scholarly, pertinent information throughout the Church would contribute substantially to its strength."[48]

---

[46] Hugh Nibley, Letter to Paul Springer, 29 April 1957.

[47] Hugh Nibley, Letter to Ezra Taft Benson, 9 January 1958. He did not include this list in his letter.

[48] Hugh Nibley, Letter to Ernest L. Wilkinson, 13 April 1952, Wilkinson Presidential Papers, Perry Special Collections, Lee Library; emphasis Hugh's.

The Book of Mormon as Witness of Joseph Smith's Calling

A logical outgrowth for Hugh Nibley of the authenticity of Middle East traces in the Book of Mormon is the conclusion that Joseph Smith really was who he claimed to be—the translator of an ancient document "by the gift and power of God" (Book of Mormon, title page) and a divinely called prophet. Writing at age sixty-eight, Hugh sounded the same note that he had in his thirties about Joseph Smith: "What Joseph Smith gives us bears none of the marks of the careful researcher, and even less of the wild and undisciplined imagination to which Ms. Brodie attributes the Book of Mormon. Research is a way of life, and Joseph Smith lived under a relentless spotlight: he might have gotten away with a little bit—but with research and note-juggling on such a scale?"[49]

For Hugh, the brilliance of Book of Mormon's literary achievement confirms that Joseph Smith could not have written the book—he wasn't capable of writing it. But this does not decrease Joseph's stature; rather it raises it. Joseph is not a "religious genius" with a brilliant "religion-making imagination," as Harold Bloom has declared him,[50] but a prophet of God.

"What a theme for a kid of 23 to attempt," Hugh marveled to Paul Springer.

> It makes all the honors papers I have ever read look painfully jejeune and unbeholden: I have never met or heard of anyone in college or out who could turn out a piece of work of such boldness, sweep, variety, precision, complexity, confidence, simplicity, etc. Put it beside any work in our literature for sheer number of ideas, situations, propositions and insights. . . . It makes me mad the way they act as if this was nothing at all and then turn out a million pages of pompous froth about a literature that has hardly given the world a dozen interesting ideas or characters in 200 years. Open the Book of Mormon every ten or twenty pages and see what it is talking about—a bedizzening [sic] variety of stuff; open any other big work, James Joyce or the 1001 Nights, and you will find largely variations on a theme, a round of safely familiar matter given largely stereotyped treatment. Shakespeare has that kind of variety, but Shakespeare does not have to be telling the truth, does not have to combine his things in a single package, and can take thirty years to tell his story; also he is free to borrow at will without apologies to anyone. When you start listing the problems Joseph Smith had to face just to get his book down on paper you will see that writing about a biblical people does NOT automatically take care of everything, in fact it raises more questions than it solves.

Recognizing his own frenetic tone, Hugh queries, with a charming lapse into domesticity: "You ask why I am going on like this? Because [fourteen-year-old] Christina is making such a damnable racket with the vacuum cleaner around my feet,

---

[49]Hugh Nibley, Letter to John W. Welch and other *Festschrift* contributors, 20 September 1978. The material from this *Festschrift* was later compiled with other materials in *By Study and Also By Faith: Essays in Honor of Hugh W. Nilbey on the Occasion of his Eightieth Birthday, 27 March 1990*, edited by John M. Lundquist and Stephen D. Ricks, Vol. 1 (Salt Lake City: Deseret Book and FARMS, 1990).

[50]Harold Bloom, *The American Religion: The Emergence of the Post-Christian Nation* (New York: Simon & Schuster, 1992), 96-97.

cleaning up our rumpus-room-salon-library-ante-room-dining-music-conservatory-nursery-playschool-parlor for company, that I can't think as is fiercely apparent."[51]

The Book of Mormon, Hugh argues, is truly the keystone of our religion: "Some object that the Book of Mormon does not contain the fullness of the Gospel but I find such elements as the preexistence and the Temple spread all over it—sometimes thinly and by inference, but always lurking nearby."[52]

In short, even though it is not always evident, Hugh saw the Book of Mormon as containing the full doctrines, ordinances, and covenants of God. For all its marvelous antiquity, he also saw it as an up-to-date handbook containing answers for the problems of our day.

The Book of Mormon as Prophecy for Our Day

It is the Book of Mormon's relevance to our day and prophetic accuracy that makes the book so important in Hugh's life, even though that relevance and accuracy is a source of both comfort and fear. As he commented to Paul Springer in the mid-fifties: "Poverty keeps me off many a sucker list, [but] the nature of my writings has brought me into direct and heated correspondence with every crackpot in the country. . . . What brings me back to earth is the good old Book of Mormon, the book that really tells you what goes on in the world."[53] Hugh was always willing to give even a crackpot a hearing, even when he knew that said crackpot probably simply wanted the validation of being able to say that he had had a conversation with Hugh. But his respect for the Book of Mormon's ability to help us understand the absurdity of the contemporary world and provide the stability of anchoring in eternal principles never wavered.

---

[51] Hugh Nibley, Letter to Paul Springer, 2 February 1964. In a letter to his missionary sons, Paul and Tom Nibley, n.d., ca. 1971, Hugh wrote similarly: "Consider once more the Book of Mormon. There are thousands of points at which it can be tested against real historical evidence, but in the world of science nothing is settled until the last reports are in. Meanwhile if one would put the Prophet to a truly rigorous test, let him compare his performance with that of other men who have created fanciful civilizations out of their heads. One thinks at once of Tolkien, then of Homer, Dante, James Joyce, Galsworthy, Dickens, Thomas Mann, etc., men who have conjured societies, mythical nations, whole worlds into existence by the power of their imaginations. How does their performance compare with Joseph Smith's? It is completely different: They all had age and experience, reading and training and all the literary and historical sources they needed at their disposal; they were all free to put down anything they chose, without having to answer for it as fact or history. But Joseph Smith goes far beyond any of them as he blocks out his geography, builds his cities, names and clothes his strange people, arranges his battles and elaborate campaigns, follows his migrations and explorations, evolves his social unrest, his dynastic intrigues, invents ingenious weights and measures, describes plagues and the upheavals of nature, while telling a religious story of great moral impact, with heavenly visitations, inspired prophecies, cosmological discourses and eschatological significance. With it all, his book must have something to tell people that they did not know before, something extremely important for the world to know. And all this done without the aid of scholarship, age, experience, and literary or historical sources or assistance, in a situation tense with hostility and danger, and completed in a matter of weeks. Since there is in the annals of human attainment no performance to equal this, I think it entitles Joseph Smith to a patient and respectful hearing free from the ridiculous nit-picking which has always been fashionable where the Book of Mormon is concerned."

[52] Hugh Nibley, Letter to John W. Welch and other Festschrift contributors, 20 September 1978.

[53] Hugh Nibley, Letter to Paul Springer, June 1956.

Noting that one of the principal themes of the Book of Mormon is the fall of civilizations, Hugh finds its note of doom inescapably appropriate for our contemporary world: "I cannot imagine a more powerful, prophetic document or one more obviously going into fulfillment at the present time," he told a correspondent in the mid-seventies. "If you look at the big picture, the Book of Mormon is as up-to-date as tomorrow's newspaper."[54]

As already noted, previous generations of Mormons had not understood or appreciated the Book of Mormon because genocide was simply unthinkable, emotionally unfathomable, until the lessons of World War II's holocaust and the possibility of a nuclear winter sank into the consciousness of the nation. "It was a happy generation to which the abominations of the Nephites and Jaredites seemed utterly unreal," Hugh wrote trenchantly. To make his point, Hugh posed an enigmatic question in *An Approach to the Book of Mormon* at the end of a chapter on the downfall of Jerusalem: "Explain the saying: 'Wo to the generation that understands the Book of Mormon!'"[55] He received many calls and letters asking him if he had gotten the question backwards; some wondered if it was, in fact, even his question. In a response to one such letter, Hugh writes: "The [question] you asked about is my own and to it I might add another: 'Woe to people who make up enigmatic [questions]!' But although Hugh turned the question aside with a jest, he was in deadly earnest and continued: "For our generation the story [of the Book of Mormon] rings painfully familiar. . . . The generations that understand the Book of Mormon must needs be in much the same situation that the ancient Americans were in, and people in such a predicament are to be pitied."[56]

In another letter, Hugh quotes 1 Nephi 22:15-19 about the events to take place in the last days—how the time will soon come when "the fulness of the wrath of God shall be poured out upon the children of men" and "blood, and fire, and vapor of smoke must come," but "the righteous shall not perish; for the time surely must come that all they who fight against Zion shall be cut off." He then writes: "A display of force is going to be necessary, and the world is going to get it in terms described—NOT fire from heaven, but their own dirty work: 'for they shall war among themselves, and the sword of their own hands shall fall upon their own heads,' etc. How did I get on this track? Rather how can I get off? It haunts me."[57]

The pervasiveness of the Book of Mormon's cataclysmic and catastrophic worldview shows up in details. For example, the eruption of Mount St. Helens in Oregon in May 1980 proved to Hugh that the calamities described by the Book of Mormon are not that far fetched. "I have read the Book of Mormon twice this week—a revelation; infinitely cheering and reassuring, this saddest of stories that is coming closer to home every day," he wrote hastily to his son Alex, then serving a mission to Japan. "The cheering thing is that we were right all along in believing its extravagant story—mountains do blow up and great nations do destroy each other."[58]

---

[54]Hugh Nibley, Letter to Jan Taylor, 24 April 1975.

[55]Nibley, *An Approach to the Book of Mormon*, edited by John W. Welch, Vol. 6 in *The Collected Works of Hugh Nibley* (1957; Salt Lake City: Deseret Book/FARMS, 1988), 119.

[56]Hugh Nibley, Letter to Parley H. Merrill, 18 June 1957.

[57]Hugh Nibley, Letter to Paul Springer, 20 May 1961.

[58]Hugh Nibley, Letter to Charles Alexander Nibley, n.d., ca. May 1980.

Yet despite such apocalyptic musings, Hugh remains hopeful because the Book of Mormon's dire warnings are always accompanied by an open door showing the way to escape—repentance. Responding to a letter from a detractor, Hugh wrote cheerfully:

> Anyway, it's lucky you wrote me when you did, it is *still* not too late; the Lord has extended the day of our probation: you would be insane to waste this priceless reprieve, and you could still be one of the few really happy men on the earth, but you'll have to stop being a damned fool. I could find as many faults as you do without half trying, but a committee of characters like us couldn't produce the Book of Mormon in 140 years. Why do you worry so much about what *other* people think? They don't know anything about it. Ask the Lord for a change![59]

Writing from the war front, Hugh Nibley seemed to prophesy of our day: "The potential power of [the Book of Mormon] is something to move mountains; it will only take effect when everything is pretty far gone, but then it will be dynamite. That leaves room for optimism."[60]

---

[59] Hugh Nibley, Letter to LeMar Petersen, 17 July 1961.
[60] Hugh Nibley, Letter to Agnes Sloan Nibley, 26 July 1944.

Hugh Nibley, ca. 1950.

Photo courtesy of L. Tom Perry Special Collections, Harold B. Lee Library, Brigham Young University.

In 1950 the Dead Sea Scrolls began to come out, along with the equally interesting Coptic texts from Nag Hammadi in Egypt, fusing early Judaism and Christianity in a way that conventional churches and scholars found very disturbing but which fitted the Book of Mormon like a glove. Then in 1951 Brigham Young University acquired both the Greek and Latin Patrologiae and the Egyptian collection of the venerable S.A.B. Mercer, he who had spearheaded the attack on the Book of Abraham back in 1912. Here indeed was a treasure trove of hints, including some very enlightening ones about Mercer himself. At last we had something to work with in the Patrologiae. But to be taken seriously one must publish, and I soon found that publishing in the journals is as easy and mechanical as getting grades: I sent out articles to a wide variety of prestigious journals and they were all printed.[1] So I lost interest: what those people were after is not what I was after. Above all, I could see no point to going on through the years marshalling an ever-lengthening array of titles to stand at attention some day at the foot of an obituary. That is what they were all working for, and they were welcome to it. But there were hints I could not ignore and answers I must seek for my own peace of mind.[2]

---

[1]The only rejection letters I have found in Hugh's correspondence are two from Mormon periodicals: one from *The Instructor* (see chap. 19) and another from the *Ensign* (chaps. 14, 23).

[2]Hugh Nibley, "Intellectual Autobiography," *Nibley on the Timely and Timeless* (Provo: BYU Religious Studies Center, 1978), xxv.

Chapter 17

Poor-Man's Plato and Paterfamilias, 1950-59

In February 1951, Ernest L. Wilkinson became President of Brigham Young University.[3] Wilkinson was outspoken, ultraconservative, and confrontational. Right from the start, Wilkinson offended most of the faculty with his "paternalistic, dictatorial, and inconsiderate" leadership style.[4] Most notably, he violated university tradition by making decisions himself which had been customarily made after consulting with faculty. During the first weeks of Wilkinson's tenure, tension mounted to the point where a petition was circulated among faculty protesting this autocratic management style. Unfortunately, Wilkinson intercepted it before it could be delivered formally. At an emergency faculty meeting, Wilkinson blustered in and demanded, "Who is responsible for this?" Although Hugh had not drafted the petition, he *had* signed it and promptly stood up; no one else followed him. He recalls that his colleagues' eyes were all on him, and some whispered, "Goodbye, Hugh."

Deflecting some of the tension to himself, Brigham Madsen, a professor in the History Department, asked Wilkinson what role faculty would play in formulating policy under his leadership. "None whatsoever," was Wilkinson's curt reply. Wilkinson then denounced the petition's signers as cowards for going behind his back and ordered Hugh to come to his office after the meeting.[5]

---

[3]After bitter disputes with the BYU Board of Trustees over funding issues, President Howard S. McDonald accepted a position as president of the combined schools of Los Angeles State College and Los Angeles City College in October 1949. Professor emeritus Christen Jensen served as acting president during the interim between McDonald's departure and Wilkinson's inauguration. Gary James Bergera and Ronald Priddis, *Brigham Young University: A House of Faith* (Salt Lake: Signature Books, 1985), 21-22.

[4]Ibid., 24.

[5]Hugh Nibley, Conversation with Boyd Petersen, 1 July 1996. Brigham D. Madsen, *Against the Grain: Memoirs of a*

Hugh naturally feared he would be fired for his audacious confrontation with the new BYU president. However, when he arrived at Wilkinson's office the two talked for a long time in quite friendly terms, although Hugh no longer remembers the topic. The subject of the petition never came up again. Thereafter, Wilkinson invited Hugh to his office quite often to discuss such issues as library acquisitions and the direction and scope of the Religion Department. "Wilkinson was a lawyer who liked confrontation," remembers Hugh. "He respected people with whom he disagreed." It may have also helped that Hugh's mother and Wilkinson's mother were close friends.

But it was not long before Hugh had another run-in with the new president. During the first few months of his administration, Wilkinson began to surround himself with people he could trust, and he began to solicit favors from certain faculty members. Hugh felt as if he were being invited into that inner circle when Wilkinson asked him to write a speech for him. It made Hugh uncomfortable, but he solved the problem with characteristic wit and verve. Instead of turning down the request and alienating the prickly president, he wrote "a first-rate speech on 'doing your own work' and the importance of not plagiarizing." Wilkinson got the message and never asked Hugh to write a speech for him again.[6]

Although campus politics created so much dissonance for some faculty members that they left BYU, Hugh tended to ignore such episodes and concentrate on his work. Hugh quipped to Paul Springer, "Gone are the happy days when we had time to sin" and catalogued: "With writing, endless committees, teaching, constant speech-making, and a large and growing family I have my hands full."[7] He was still teaching ancient history and literature, the early Christian church, and Greek language and literature, meanwhile squeezing out spare moments for language study. "This fall my salvation has been the possibility of constant conversation in Hebrew and Persian with exchange students from those countries," he wrote Springer. "After Arabic, Persian is almost embarrassingly easy, and philologically it is very enlightening."[8]

The publication of his priesthood manual, *An Approach to the Book of Mormon*, which was used during 1957, generated "a steady rain of letters upon my head—and they all have to be answered—hundreds and hundreds of them."[9] He also responded to an increasing load of mail, most of it from Church members asking obscure gospel questions. Although it was burdensome, it acknowledged his growing role as the Church's preeminent scholar. To respond to the avalanche of mail he began to receive in the 1950s, Hugh began compiling a series of what he called "G-2 Reports," most giving quotations from classic texts or leading authorities on topics like "The Religious World," "Religious Scholarship," "Evolution," and "Eschatology." Throughout the 1950s and early 1960s,

---

Western Historian (Salt Lake: Signature Books, 1998), 208, recalls that the precipitating incident was Wilkinson's proposal to hold campus-wide devotional assemblies three days each week, while Hugh remembers that it was Wilkinson's granting an honorary doctorate to one of his close friends without consulting with faculty. However, both agree that Wilkinson had not consulted with faculty before making a decision about an issue that directly affected them and about which the faculty would have traditionally been consulted.

[6] Hugh Nibley, Conversation with Boyd Petersen, 1 July 1996.

[7] Hugh Nibley, Letter to Paul Springer, ca. 1952. Hugh writes "Lovely Provo, Ghastly February, Year of Doom" as a dateline at the top of the page.

[8] Hugh Nibley, Letter to Paul Springer, n.d., ca. 1952.

[9] Hugh Nibley, Letter to Paul Springer, 29 April 1957.

Hugh sent these prepared reports to individuals who wrote in about a related gospel question. He also sent "G-2 Reports" to a group of interested General Authorities.[10]

Moreover, he continued to read, research, write, and publish at a ferocious pace, living up to the "Nibley maxim," as he wryly put it, of having "no word without three footnotes."[11] As his reminiscences suggest, he published a burst of articles in scholarly journals during this period but thereafter tended to concentrate on articles for general LDS audiences. "The Hierocentric State," a comparative approach examining ancient religious shrines, appeared in 1951 in *Western Political Quarterly*, which also published "The Unsolved Loyalty Problem: Our Western Heritage," a historical response to the McCarthy era loyalty oaths, in 1953.[12] "Victoriosa Loquacitas: The Rise of Rhetoric and the Decline of Everything Else" appeared in *Western Speech* in 1956, and helped earn Hugh a sabbatical at Berkeley at the close of the decade.[13] Finally, "Christian Envy of the Temple" ran in two installments during 1959 and 1960 in the *Jewish Quarterly Review*.[14] He also published four substantive book reviews.[15]

The writings in the second category—those aimed at the Mormon audience—were even more abundant, with Church members receiving almost uninterrupted monthly installments from Hugh throughout the 1950s. The series "Lehi in the Desert" ran in the *Improvement Era* from January through October 1950. "The World of the Jaredites" followed from September 1951 through July 1952. "The Stick of Judah and the Stick of Joseph" appeared from January through May 1953, and "New Approaches to Book of Mormon Study" spanned November 1953 through July 1954.

In 1954, Hugh shifted his focus from the Book of Mormon to the early Christian apostasy and moved from the printed page to the radio airwaves when he was invited to deliver the message for KSL's weekly Sunday night radio devotional. Similar to today's "Music and the Spoken Word," the Sunday evening devotionals were hosted by Elder Richard L. Evans of the Quorum of the Twelve and included "sacred songs and organ recitations." Hugh's series of thirty talks, "Time Vindicates the Prophets," were heard from

---

[10]Louis Midgley, "Hugh Winder Nibley: "Bibliography and Register," in *By Study and By Faith: Essays in Honor of Hugh Nibley*, edited by John M. Lundquist and Steven D. Ricks, 2 vols. (Salt Lake City: Deseret Book/FARMS, 1990), 1: lxxxvi-lxxxvii. "G-2" was the intelligence branch of the U.S. Army, and Hugh wrote hundreds of genuine G-2 reports during the course of World War II. They were destroyed when the government storage facility in which they were housed in St. Louis burned to the ground in the 1950s.

[11]Hugh Nibley, Letter to Paul Springer, n.d., ca. March 1951.

[12]Hugh Nibley, "The Hierocentric State," *Western Political Quarterly* 4 (1951): 226-53; republished in *The Ancient State* (Salt Lake City: Deseret Book/FARMS, 1991), 99-147; and "The Unsolved Loyalty Problem: Our Western Heritage," *Western Political Quarterly* 6 (1953): 631-57. Republished in *The Ancient State*, 195-242.

[13]Hugh Nibley, "Victoriosa Loquacitas: The Rise of Rhetoric and the Decline of Everything Else," *Western Speech* 20 (1956): 57-82; republished in *The Ancient State*, 243-86.

[14]"Christian Envy of the Temple" *Jewish Quarterly Review* 50 (1959-60): 97-123, 229-40; reprinted in *Mormonism and Early Christianity*, edited by Todd M. Compton and Stephen D. Ricks, Vol. 4 of *The Collected Works of Hugh Nibley* (Salt Lake City: Deseret Books/FARMS, 1987), 391-434.

[15]Hugh's review of Joseph Ward Swain's *The Ancient World* was published in *The Historian* 13 (1950): 79-80; his review of Philip K. Hitti's *History of Syria* was published in *Western Political Quarterly* 5 (1952): 312-13; his review of *Near Eastern Culture and Society* by Philip K. Hitti et al. was published in *Western Political Quarterly* 5 (1952): 315-16; and his review of Edward A. Shils's *The Torment of Secrecy: The Background and Consequences of American Security Policies* was published in *American Political Science Review* 50 (1956): 887-88.

March through October 1954.[16] Mining BYU's new copy of the Patrologia, Hugh documented how the church established by Christ and led by inspired prophets and apostles devolved into an institution directed by secular scholarship. As R. Douglas Phillips, a professor of classics and first associate director of the Institute of Ancient Studies, stated in the preface to the 1987 FARMS edition of *The World and the Prophets*, Hugh "shows how prophets were replaced by scholars, revelation by philosophy, inspired preaching by rhetoric."[17]

Like many of Hugh's other works, the series also contained some not-too-subtle social commentary, especially criticizing the modern education system. Shortly before the series concluded, Hugh wrote mischievously to Paul Springer: "As a desperate resort to force the authorities to curtail my endless radio series, I am beginning to speak up with a frankness that is winning me enemies everywhere among the educationists. I trust the series will come to an end this month; if not, I will have to go all the way and give it to them straight."[18] Only recently, two evangelical Christians evaluating Mormon scholarship and apologetics commented that "the breadth of learning displayed in these lectures is intimidating."[19] The series was well received within the Church, but it also caught the attention of Woodrow Borah, a former Berkeley classmate who was now on its speech faculty and editor of *Western Speech*. Borah wrote to Hugh on 1 March 1956 requesting permission to publish "Rhetoric and Revelation" from the series. Hugh felt that, since it was already in a book, he wanted to do a different article for the journal; the result was "Victoriosa Loquacitas: The Rise of Rhetoric and the Decline of Everything Else" ("The Victory of Loquacity").

In January 1955, another series began in the *Improvement Era*. "The Way of the Church" focused on the apostasy.[20] "There Were Jaredites" ran from January 1956 through February 1957. And rounding out the decade, Hugh produced "Mixed Voices: A Study in Book of Mormon Criticism," which ran from March through November of 1959. Early in the decade, Hugh lamented to Springer the challenge of having "five masterpieces all preparing at once and all with shoot-to-kill deadlines. It's been moider."[21] That rigorous schedule did not let up throughout the decade.

Hugh's monthly installments in the *Improvement Era* so impressed President McKay that he invited Hugh to write the Melchizedek Priesthood manual for 1957. Elder Henry D. Moyle wrote Hugh in 1955: "In keeping with President McKay's initial suggestion, we would like to recommend that you turn your thoughts to the Book of

---

[16]The series was published as *The World and the Prophets* that same year, in 1962 with two additional chapters as *The World and the Prophets*, and for a third time under the same name, edited by John W. Welch, Gary P. Gillum, and Don E. Norton, Vol. 3 of *The Collected Works of Hugh Nibley* (1954; reprinted Salt Lake City: Deseret Books/FARMS, 1987).

[17]"Foreword," *The World and the Prophets*, 1987, x-xi.

[18]Hugh Nibley, Letter to Paul Springer, n.d., ca. October 1954.

[19]Carl Mosser and Paul Owen, "Mormon Scholarship, Apologetics, and Evangelical Neglect: Losing the Battle and Not Knowing It?" *Trinity Journal* 19 (1998): 196.

[20]The editors dropped this series at the end of the year, but Hugh recycled the remaining materials into "The Passing of the Church," in *Church History* 30 (1961): 131-54. Both "The Way of the Church" and the *Church History* article with a modified title, "Passing of the Primitive Church," are reproduced in *Mormonism and Early Christianity*, 168-322.

[21]Hugh Nibley, Letter to Paul Springer, n.d., ca. 1950.

Mormon" and suggested that he produce "something along the lines of 'Lehi in the Desert and the World of the Jaredites.'"[22]

Hugh did not spend all of his productive life leafing through dusty volumes and hunched over his typewriter. He delivered a steady stream of addresses at various wards and branches, seminars and lectures throughout the western states and even in Canada on one occasion. "Comes the brief weekend," described Hugh to Springer, "and I must [be] off to some conference or other calling for a painful expenditure of time and energy but usually quite rewarding in experience and adventure."[23] With the publication of the priesthood manual, these invitations became even more numerous. "I have to give talks everywhere, explaining what I am trying to say in the book," he explained. "It has wiped out what remained of privacy in this part of the country, though it has the compensating virtue of opening doors wherever I go."[24]

On some of these travels, Hugh accompanied General Authorities, part of Wilkinson's plan to "encourage Latter-day Saint boys and girls to attend our church schools"[25] by having faculty members and representatives attend stake conferences with General Authorities. Hugh recalls "making a number of visits with quite a few General Authorities—S. Dilworth Young, young Milton R. Hunter, and others."[26] The most memorable trip came in 1952 when he traveled to Safford, Arizona, and then to Los Angeles with Apostle Spencer W. Kimball. "Brother Kimball was such a delight," remembers Hugh. "He knew all the plants and the animals in the Southwest where we went. He knew all the people; he knew all the Indian members, in particular. And he could play the piano, and he sang and he danced and he was merry." Elder Kimball was also an extremely active General Authority. Hugh remembers: "He got up at five o'clock in the morning to hold meetings, and we were still going at ten o'clock in the evening. And he pounded along and wore everybody out. What a man!"[27] Hugh was awed by Elder Kimball's dedication, zeal, and humility. (See also chap. 3.) Likewise, the General Authority "came to have considerable admiration" for Hugh, and wrote home to his wife, Camille, that "we are fortunate to have such men of his scholarly attainment and sweet faith in our University."[28]

---

[22]Henry D. Moyle, Letter to Hugh Nibley, 6 May 1955. For a discussion of the adventure of producing this manual, see chap. 16.

[23]Hugh Nibley, Letter to Paul Springer, 16 December 1952.

[24]Hugh Nibley, Letter to Paul Springer, 29 April 1957.

[25]Quoted in Bergera and Priddis, Brigham Young University, 26.

[26]Hugh Nibley, "Criticizing the Brethren," in Brother Brigham Challenges the Saints, edited Don E. Norton and Shirley S. Ricks, Vol. 13 in The Collected Works of Hugh Nibley (Salt Lake City: Deseret Books/FARMS, 1994), 444. I have found no reference to travels with S. Dilworth Young in Hugh's correspondence. However, Milton R. Hunter of the First Council of Seventy wrote to Hugh on 12 November 1953: "I enjoyed very much the trip [to New Mexico] with you good brethren from the Brigham Young University." This trip may not have been to recruit BYU students, since Hunter describes its purpose as being to evaluate some "Hebrew writings" which Hugh believed to be quite recent and "therefore not genuine as pertaining to Book of Mormon evidence," but about which Dr. Sidney Sperry was "not so definite." Hunter, who had been a member of the First Council of Seventy since 1928, was only eight years Hugh's senior, so it is not clear why Hugh calls him "young."

[27]"Hugh Nibley in Black and White," BYU Today, May 1990, 38-39.

[28]Spencer W. Kimball, Letter to Camilla Eyring Kimball, 20 May 1952, photocopy courtesy of Edward L. Kimball.

Hugh's visits to various wards and stakes throughout the West, along with his monthly articles in the *Improvement Era*, each with its accompanying photograph, brought him regional celebrity, a status that surprised and sometimes dismayed him. "Already I am becoming fairly well known in these parts," wrote Hugh in the early 1950s. "I suppose in time [I] may even become a character." In 1952 when he and his family set out to deliver a series of lectures in Lethbridge, Alberta, he realized in Logan that he had left his wallet, containing his driver's license and all forms of identification, at home. "So here we were going to a foreign country without a scrap of identification," wrote Hugh. It was a gamble, but Hugh decided to press on. When the family entered Yellowstone Park, they encountered a sign that said "identify yourself." But there was no need. "The ranger rushed out and greeted us with noisy glee—'Why Brother Nibley, of all people, fancy meeting you here!'" And when they crossed the border into Canada, a place they had never visited before, the attendant at a gas station also immediately recognized him. "This floored me," exclaimed Hugh. "I have not been able to buy a beer anywhere in Utah for over a year because every storekeeper in the state spots me half-way down the block. But to be called by name less than an hour after breathing the free air of a foreign land was too much. And I was wearing two pair of dark glasses! (I find this very restful for the eyes)." Hugh complained with mock-irritation: "If Hollywood celebrities and international jewel thieves can travel incognito, why can't I?"[29]

On the home front, Phyllis had her hands full with a rapidly growing family. Five more children were born during the 1950s, joining Paul and Christina: Thomas Hugh (17 August 1950), Michael Draper (16 January 1953), Charles Alexander (3 January 1956), and Rebecca (7 July 1958). Phyllis's poor nutrition during her childhood made her health precarious. These pregnancies were difficult for her, and the deliveries were prolonged and strenuous. An Rh factor mismatch between her and Hugh made childbirth particularly dangerous. Between the births of Michael and Charles Alexander, a late-stage miscarriage on 11 November 1954 nearly cost Phyllis's life when the doctors had difficulty in arresting the hemorrhaging. Three weeks later when she was out of danger, Hugh wrote: "Phyllis staged a spectacular miscarriage. It was a puzzle how she stayed alive without any blood in her. The worst was that every attempt to give a transfusion produced a violently negative reaction, which would have been fits in anyone of a less placid and philosophical nature."[30] Hugh and Phyllis surely noted the significant date of their loss—Armistice Day, the commemoration of war's end and the beginning of peace. The stillborn son was never officially given a name and blessing, but Hugh and Phyllis grieved his loss and subsequently referred to him as Isaac.

Despite this sorrowful episode, life in the Nibley home was an adventure. Hugh often took the children on excursions with him, a practice Phyllis encouraged. As a mere toddler, Paul rode in the handlebars basket on Hugh's bicycle as he peddled from Provo to Spanish Fork to visit its Icelandic residents.[31] The children also accompanied Hugh on visits to the Kader home. Eventually Hugh was taking his own chil-

---

[29] Hugh Nibley, Letter to Paul Springer, n.d., ca. 1952.

[30] Hugh Nibley, Letter to Paul Springer, 1 December 1954.

[31] Hugh Nibley, "Faith of an Observer," 56, compilation of interviews, ca. 198384 for a video documentary of the same name aired in 1985, photocopy of typescript in my possession, pagination added; Paul S. Nibley, Interviewed by Boyd Petersen, 7 October 2001.

dren and the Kader children on long drives, insisting that the Kader children speak Arabic and hoping that his own offspring would absorb its essentials.

When Hugh came home and took an impulse to set out an excursion into the canyons or desert, he would gather up two or three of the oldest children to accompany him. For these spur-of-the-moment trips, Hugh would throw a loaf of bread and some cheese along with blankets and sleeping bags into the back of the car and they would take off, leaving Phyllis holding the newest baby and waving good-bye. In 1950 Hugh reported to Lucien Goldschmidt: "We have had some wonderful times and got lost in eery places. I think Paul now gets bored if he suspects that I know where we are or have the faintest idea how we are going to get back to the car."[32]

Friends Don Decker and Stanley Hall, both more than ten years Hugh's junior, were eager collaborators in such adventures, though not always with the children. Don had been a student in one of Hugh's first Greek classes at BYU and had drawn Stan, his own friend, into Hugh's circle. Both were veterans from the Marine Corps, in love with the rugged outdoors. "We all wanted to go to the mountains," remembered Hugh. On these outings, the three men would compare notes on the war—conversations that probably served as a sort of rough-and-ready therapy. Of these trips Hugh wrote to Springer, "We DO have fun—and then there is the wonder and surprise of getting home alive after all."[33] Hugh spoke at both men's funerals, Hall's on 25 November 1972 and Decker's on 11 August 1982.[34]

The family also gained a reputation for being a bit eccentric. Hugh described their home in 1956 as "more and more of an enclave, a foreign colony, in the midst of Provo." He had refused to buy a television, which "marks us queer to the point of defiance."[35] Hugh wanted his children to receive their education from books rather than television: "I'll see them in jail before I expose them to that," he wrote.[36] But Hugh was no Luddite, and he and Phyllis thoroughly relished the relatively recent invention of an electric blanket. "On these cool nights we turn it up to 75 and it buzzes and throbs all night, sending off occasional showers of sparks and billows of colored smoke, superbly illuminated by a restless play of truly Byronic lightning. It makes us realize how dull our nights have been in the old prescientific days."[37]

The house was awash with books, many of them the children's. But Hugh blithely assumed that his children could handle the classics from babyhood. Although he often stayed up past midnight working, he made every effort to eat supper with the family and considered bedtime stories to be his inviolable time with the children unless he had a speaking engagement. In 1950, Hugh wrote to his mother that Paul, who had not yet turned three, demanded nightly: "Daddy, read me some

---

[32]Hugh Nibley, Letter to Lucien Goldschmidt, 11 November 1950.

[33]Hugh Nibley, interviewed by Zina Petersen, 5 March 2002; Hugh Nibley, Letter to Paul Springer, August 1952; emphasis Nibley's.

[34]"Stanley Hall's Funeral Service," 25 November 1972, photocopy of transcript in my possession; "Don Decker's Funeral Service," 11 August 1982, published as "Funeral Address," in *Approaching Zion*, edited by Don E. Norton, Vol. 9 of *The Collected Works of Hugh Nibley* (Salt Lake City: Deseret Book/FARMS, 1989), 290-307.

[35]Hugh Nibley, Letter to Paul Springer, 28 March 1956.

[36]Hugh Nibley, Letter to Paul Springer, October 1953.

[37]Hugh Nibley, Letter to Paul Springer, August 1952.

Shakespeare!" Hugh added proudly, "We haven't the slightest intention of forcing him. A kid that smart doesn't need to be forced."[38] He also read Homer in Greek to them, translating as he went along. "The program of serious literature which has kept the kids amused all winter, and the wild informal 'jaunts' we take whenever the weather allows have set people to wondering if we are quite all right. My religious rantings serve to balance the books." Hugh added, "Thank God for Phyllis, who thinks exactly as I do on all essentials."[39]

Hugh took almost annual trips to the library in Berkeley. He probably did not feel guilty about leaving Phyllis to cope alone, since both of them accepted the standard gender roles of the 1950s without much question; but there is a certain amount of relief in his comment to Springer after one such trip: "What I found on getting back to Provo was an unanswerable argument for matriarchy: Phyllis had everything running smoothly for the first time in history."[40]

However, as the children got older, Hugh became more distant. Hugh enjoyed spending time with the babies and toddlers, but the older the children got, the less attention they received from their father. Phyllis remembers that "as [the children] got older and became more responsible and they had personal problems that they wanted to talk about with him, [Hugh] closed off."[41] This distance likely resulted from a combination of factors. First, Hugh was raised by nineteenth-century parents, a generation who could barely acknowledge emotion and who largely dealt with it by suppression. Hugh's mother, while pushing him intellectually and manipulating his life, gave only passing thought to Hugh's social and emotional development. Furthermore, as demands on Hugh's time increased, he had less time to spend with his family; and, in many ways, it probably became less rewarding as the children grew into more complicated personalities. As the size of the family grew, the noise level at home rose, breaching even Hugh's famed ability to concentrate. He frequently spent Saturdays and evenings working at his office. This focus on work was not seen as a personality defect. On the contrary, American social values placed the provider role at the top of the list for responsible manhood. It is only in our generation that "workaholism" is seen as dangerous to emotional health. The pressure was particularly acute on Mormon men with time-demanding positions like stake president and bishop to literally serve two masters: their employer and the expectations of excellent Church service. This message likewise was one that Hugh had internalized from babyhood. It is only the current generation that has stressed fatherhood first for men as it has long stressed motherhood first for women. As a result, nearly all of Hugh's children grew up closer to Phyllis than they did to Hugh. As sad as such generation gaps are, they were relatively common for baby boomers.

Another family complication from which Hugh may have sought refuge in his work was his parents' declining health. Hugh's father, still eking out a hand-to-mouth existence, had become increasingly desperate to make back the family fortune and resorted to using his connections with Church leaders and dropping his now-famous

---

[38]Hugh Nibley, Letter to Agnes Sloan Nibley, 28 April 1950.
[39]Hugh Nibley, Letter to Paul Springer, 28 March 1956.
[40]Hugh Nibley, Letter to Paul Springer, August 1952.
[41]Phyllis Nibley, "Faith of an Observer," 435.

sons' names to potential clients to build trust in him so they would invest in high-risk schemes. Hugh was clearly the best-known of the Nibley boys, but Reid and Richard were also known for their music. Beginning in 1956, people who had been on the losing end of these schemes began contacting Hugh and his brothers and sister to solicit their help in reclaiming the lost funds. In 1958, Hugh received a notice from a lawyer explaining that he had obtained judgments against Hugh's father for two of his clients for over $5,000. Hugh wrote the attorney back, stating that he did not "doubt for a moment the good faith" of his clients and assuring the lawyer that he would "do all in my power to assist them in reclaiming what is rightfully theirs." Hugh admitted, however, that he had little influence on his father. "Mr. Alex Nibley has always keenly resented any inquiry by me . . . concerning his business affairs," wrote Hugh and called his father "the most secretive man on earth."[42] The older children remember being taken to visit El when he lived in Salt Lake City, and the father and son still talked to each other; but the relationship was definitely a distant one. On Hugh's part, it was both chilly and wary. Hugh must have felt both angry and ashamed that his father was hurting other families, trading on Hugh's name and reputation to gain their trust. Furthermore, exploiting the common bond of the gospel to make money hurt and angered Hugh greatly.

Sloanie's problems were medical rather than legal, but they were equally difficult. Her relationship with El had deteriorated to endless bickering and they had not lived together since at least the early 1940s. Hugh and Phyllis both felt that, although his parents loved each other, they couldn't live together. In 1956 after visiting Sloanie, El wrote to Hugh and his brothers that Sloanie "has not been able to take a step, nor stand on her feet for four or five months. I don't blame her if she 'blows her top' now and then."[43] At that moment, Sloanie was living in the home of an LDS nurse who was caring for her, but she wore out her welcome quickly and had to move often. The children passed her around among themselves; her brief stay with Hugh and Phyllis—of whom she never approved—was such a disaster that it was never repeated.

In 1959, Hugh's brother Sloan wrote him that there was "not much we can do here except feed Mud and try and make her as comfortable as possible."[44] Only two days later, Sloan wrote Hugh again, absolutely at his wits' end. Sloanie could no longer live independently, but "she has gotten sore at everyone here"—by which he meant not only his own home but Sloanie's network generally in Los Angeles—"who has tried to help her. . . . As her best friend here told me, 'who will put up with it?'"[45] The family tried several rest homes; but she was so disruptive that after only a few days either the personnel at the rest home, exhausted by her tirades, would insist she be removed, or Sloanie would fabricate stories that she was being abused by her attendants. In addition to her severe rheumatoid arthritis, she was obviously suffering from

---

[42] Hugh Nibley, Letter to Dwight L. King, 13 January 1958.

[43] Alexander Nibley, Letter to Hugh Nibley, Richard Nibley, and Reid Nibley, 9 February 1956. The letter was not addressed to either Sloan or Barbara since they both were living in Los Angeles at the time and were both aware of their mother's situation.

[44] Sloan Nibley, Letter to Hugh Nibley, 8 February 1957. Sloan and his wife, Linda Stirling Nibley, were living in Los Angeles.

[45] Sloan Nibley, Letter to Hugh Nibley, 10 February 1957.

acute paranoia. Her tales circulated so widely that Hugh eventually had to write to a family friend, Elder LeGrand Richards, to assure him that they were without foundation. "If we did not love her these things would not break us down as they do," wrote Hugh. "As it is, nothing we have done pleases her, though we keep on trying."[46]

By 1958, Hugh reported to Springer with mingled pity and exasperation that Sloanie was "a complete invalid and total physical wreck who insists that the only reason she can't do as much as anyone else is that those who should be devoted to her (especially meaning me) have carried on a campaign of systematic abuse and neglect." Hugh wrote that his mother, who "has always had a genius for wrapping everybody around her finger and dominating every waking and sleeping moment in the lives of her Loved Ones," had "become somewhat trying" since she still "refuses to yield an inch of authority, though quite helpless to do anything but phone, write letters (WHAT letters!) and bawl the hell out of nurses." He admitted: "It is no easy matter to find a place that will take her. One place after another refuses to keep mamma—in a matter of weeks she can get any place completely upset, with everybody taking sides and going at it hammer and tongs."[47]

After three years of fractiousness and emotional turmoil, Sloanie died on 28 May 1959, leaving mixed feelings of sorrow and relief behind her. She was buried at Forest Lawn cemetery in Los Angeles near the grave of her fourth son, Philip. Paradoxically, despite El's tempestuous relationship with her, he was devastated. Although his own health was good, he died only three months later on 30 August 1959. He was buried in the Logan, Utah, cemetery. "He just couldn't stay after she left," recalls a mystified Hugh. "I guess they were as different as anything and yet they were alike as anything."[48]

Given this emotional turmoil as his parents aged gracelessly, it is easy to see why Hugh turned with relief to the absorption of his work during the decade of the 1950s. He used a sabbatical in the spring of 1953 to blitz East Coast libraries, both for his own research and also, as he reported to Wilkinson after his return, to "interview . . . those who can impart the most information and wisdom on the subject of libraries and curriculums."[49] After researching at Harvard University, he moved on to Philadelphia where he stayed with his friend George Allen, then ended up in Baltimore at Johns Hopkins University. "Baltimore was a tepidarium during rush-hour," wrote Hugh. "Stuck it out ten days and after making sure I had consulted all the people and books not to be found in Berkeley, I made a dash for the opposite shore."[50] One of the people Hugh consulted at Johns Hopkins was the renowned scholar of ancient Near Eastern studies, William F. Albright, whom he was meeting for the first time. Their conversations focused on recent discoveries in Egypt which, according to Hugh, Albright believed were "so revolutionary in nature as to render utterly worthless

---

[46]Hugh Nibley, Letter to LeGrand Richards, 19 June 1957.
[47]Hugh Nibley, Letter to Paul Springer, 24 May 1958.
[48]Hugh Nibley, "Faith of an Observer," 107.
[49]Hugh Nibley, Letter to Ernest L. Wilkinson, 12 June 1953, Wilkinson Presidential Papers, L. Tom Perry Special Collections, Harold B. Lee Library, Brigham Young University, Provo, Utah.
[50]Hugh Nibley, Letter to Lucien Goldschmidt. He was obviously distracted in writing the date. "July" is crossed out and June is hand-written over it. He gives the year as "1952/3." The correct year is 1953.

This photograph was taken at Forest Lawn Cemetery near Los Angeles on 1 June 1959, the day Sloanie was buried. Left: Barbara Nibley Richards, Hugh Winder Nibley, Reid Neibaur Nibley, Fred Richard Nibley, Alexander (El) Nibley, and Alexander Sloan Nibley.

everything that has been written on [Christian] Church History for the past 200 years!"[51] Additionally, Hugh identified several Egyptian parallels with the Book of Mormon for Albright, who was evidently quite impressed with some of the evidence.[52] Hugh stopped briefly in Provo, where he found it "hard to leave my noisy little house" when he left for more research at Berkeley. On these research trips, Hugh geared his schedule to the hours the library was open, leaving for campus at seven each morning and returning every night "just before midnight[.] The intervening hours are spent in a dark and dusty paper-mine where every moment must be beaten flat and squeezed out."[53]

All the work Hugh was doing paid off in 1953 when he was promoted to full professor, but he felt sufficiently dissatisfied with his position at BYU that he seriously considered an offer from the University of Utah where he had lectured at least twice. Francis Wormuth, a non-Mormon professor of political science, was greatly

---

[51]Ibid.

[52]In 1966 Albright wrote to an outspoken critic of the Book of Abraham, alluding clearly to Hugh Nibley's discovery that the Book of Mormon names Paanchi and Pahoran were Egyptian: "It is all the more surprising that there are two Egyptian names, Paanch and Pahor(an) which appear together in the Book of Mormon in close connection with a reference to the original language as being 'Reformed Egyptian.'" While Albright states that he does not believe Joseph Smith's story about the coming forth of the Book of Mormon, he does state emphatically that he does not believe Joseph Smith was trying to mislead anyone. William F. Albright, Letter to Grant S. Heward, 25 July 1966, photocopy in my possession.

[53]Hugh Nibley, Letter to Lucien Goldschmidt, July [crossed out] June [overwritten] 1952/3 [1953].

impressed by Hugh's work, had published his writings in *Western Political Quarterly*, and may very well have been responsible for the offer. Ernest L. Wilkinson noted in his diary that, on 1 February 1955, he arrived at his office and found that "Dr. Hugh Nibley had come in to resign to transfer to the University of Utah." Wilkinson asked him to return the next day for a more detailed discussion. According to his diary:

> I had a conference with Hugh Nibley, who had been sold on going to the University of Utah on the strange theory that he could do more for the Church there than he could at the Brigham Young University. It was quite apparent that his main grievance, however, was that we had "not made enough of him" at the B.Y.U. He had never been invited to give any university-wide lectures to the student body, whereas they always made a "fuss" over him whenever he went to the University of Utah. In a two hour talk I am satisfied I made progress, for we parted on the terms that the sole question was that of where he could do the most good for the Church.[54]

Although Wilkinson's somewhat impatient tone suggests that he found Hugh's complaint immature, it is true that Hugh had received a great deal of attention when he lectured at the U.[55] Still, Wilkinson had correctly gauged Hugh's weak point by appealing to his sense of loyalty—where he could do the most good for the Church.

It is unclear who at the University of Utah was encouraging Hugh to transfer; however, on 1 February 1955, Sterling McMurrin, then dean of the College of Letters and science, and G. Homer Durham, then chair of the Political Science Department, asked University of Utah President A. Ray Olpin what his "attitude would be toward hiring Hugh Nibley." Olpin told McMurrin and Durham that "I would like to take his letters of application to President [David O.] McKay before contacting the BYU, for he is one of their prize teachers. A real scholar in the field of languages and history and one whom, I am sure, the BYU would not be happy to lose."[56]

Meanwhile, Wilkinson was concerned enough at Hugh's dissatisfaction that he reported the possibility of Hugh's leaving to the Executive Committee of the Church Board of Education two days after meeting with Hugh. The committee asked J. Reuben Clark of the First Presidency to take up the matter with Hugh; and President Clark asked Nibley to call at the Clark home the very next day, 5 February, at 11:50 A.M. Clark evidently reported the results to Wilkinson, who recorded them in his diary: "President Clark pointed out to him that, if he went to the University of Utah, he

---

[54] Wilkinson, Journal, 1 February 1955, Wilkinson Presidential Papers, Perry Special Collection.

[55] Francis Wormuth, Letter to Hugh Nibley, 20 December 1949; Hugh Nibley, *Mormonism and Early Christianity*, 377. Hugh read an early version of "The Hierocentric State" at the Pi Sigma Alpha National Political Science Honor Society lecture during the University of Utah's centennial celebration in 1950. The invitation to deliver this annual lecture was itself an honor. Louis Midgley, Neal Maxwell, and Truman Madsen have all reported in conversations to me that Wormuth thought Hugh was "one of the two great scholars west of the Mississippi." (He himself was the other.) Hugh doubtless delivered less formal speeches, firesides, class lectures, and faculty forums, the records of which have not survived. In 1952, he described lecturing at a "rodeo staged by the philosophy department which has received great publicity and in which I am to play a prominent if unpopular role." Hugh Nibley, Letter to Paul Springer, n.d., ca. 1952. He delivered the Pi Sigma Alpha lecture again at the University of Utah on 21 May 1964, where he read his "Tenting, Toll and Taxing."

[56] A. Ray Olpin, Office Diary, 1 February 1955, Olpin Papers, ACC 219, Box 4, fd. 11, Special Collections, Marriott Library, University of Utah, Salt Lake City.

could not under any circumstances openly proclaim the Gospel and publish treatises on the Gospel as part of his professorial duties, as he would be permitted at the B.Y.U."[57] Clark's desk journal records that he "gathered the impression from [Hugh's] observations that he had quite made up his mind to go." Clark summarized Hugh's reasons: "Our scholarship was way down at the Y," the U was "offering him advantages . . . that he did not have at the Y," and "he seemed to feel that he was not appreciated at the Y."

Clark pointed out to Hugh that he could not "write articles and work in the way of supporting Mormon doctrine away from BYU," but he also dangled a tempting carrot of four specific projects that "I had in mind that needed to be done for our Church that could be and should be done at the Y," presumably by Hugh. The first was Clark's hope to see the Bible "gone over and studied with reference to the ancient manuscripts . . . so that we might have our own translation." This proposal was an interesting one from a man who was such an ardent advocate of the King James Version that he published *Why the King James Version* (Salt Lake City: Deseret Book, 1956) only a year later, defending it as the only authoritative translation that the Church should use. He proposed as a second project "reading the works of the early 'heretics,'" whose ideas were often, he believed, "statements of true principles which the [Catholic] Church had thrown away." The third project was the flip side of the second project: "the works of the [early Church] Fathers should be gone over with great care, to get an idea of their early teachings." Fourth, Clark stated that "there was work to be done . . . in cracking the Aztec Codes [translating the Aztec Codices]." Clark also brushed aside Hugh's complaint about BYU's scholarship: "Our graduates were making records everywhere in the United States in other institutions and that did not spell poor scholarship." He paid Hugh a backhanded compliment by stating that "the mere teaching of languages was of no particular value. . . . Anybody could teach languages," but the "research work which [Hugh] was fitted to do was the thing that he ought to be doing and for that work we were in a better situation at the Y."[58]

Between them, Wilkinson and Clark apparently presented persuasive arguments, and Hugh dropped his plans to switch schools, though not without mixed feelings. He wrote to Paul Springer:

> I got some pretty good propositions from other schools and we were all set to leave our Siberian fastness but who should stand squarely in our path blocking all escape but a stern-faced damsel with the word 'DUTY' embroidered in neon lights across her *embonpoint* [bosom]. So duty it is and we stay here—but not without having wrung some concessions from our employers. Not money, of course—you told me all about churches the last time—but tangible benefits none the less.[59]

---

[57] Wilkinson, Journal, 5 February 1955.

[58] J. Reuben Clark, Desk Journal, 5 February 1944, dictated 21 February 1955, J. Reuben Clark Papers, Perry Special Collections. Hugh may have done more listening than being listened to during this conversation. Clark's report of the meeting is three single-spaced pages long and is primarily a quotation of Clark's comments.

[59] Hugh Nibley, Letter to Paul Springer, n.d., ca. February 1955.

Wilkinson's chief concession was agreeing to let Hugh take two trips each year to visit libraries at the nation's larger schools at the university's expense. However, the school apparently never fully honored that agreement. A year later, while working on his priesthood manual, *An Approach to the Book of Mormon*, Hugh reported to Elder Henry D. Moyle, head of the Church Education Committee: "When I agreed to stay on at the Y last spring, it was with the understanding that I would be allowed two trips to the Coast each year, but recently I received the long-expected note from the Treasurer's office, informing me that there has been a misunderstanding, and I should not count on receiving the agreed amount."[60] Although he did not say so directly, Hugh may have been asking Moyle to intervene. He had already agreed with Wilkinson that he would need access to other libraries to complete this project, but Wilkinson seems to have fulfilled this unwritten agreement only occasionally—or at least understood it differently.

Although no record exists of whether Phyllis favored the move or was disappointed by its abandonment, she must have been relieved that Hugh decided to move into a larger house. He wrote cheerfully to Springer in February 1955: "Since we have decided to stick it out in Provo until the Big Bang we are selling the house as a museum piece and getting a bigger one."[61] The arrangements were not completed until the next winter and the new house was only a couple of blocks away at 285 East 700 North. A small brick three-bedroom house on a modest lot, it was just south of campus, with Hugh's office an easy dash up the hill. Built by an early Mormon polygamist, the house had two front doors to accommodate his two families. One of these doors was nailed shut and the two living rooms were joined by an arch, with the partition between them knocked out to provide more room inside. Phyllis later had a second story added with four bedrooms and another bathroom. One downstairs bedroom, halved, provided space for the stairwell (which suggests their size). After the non-stairwell half did duty as a nursery for many years, Phyllis eventually took it over as a sewing room. Hugh's and Phyllis's bedroom was always on the ground floor. Hugh and Phyllis still live in that house as of this writing (summer 2002).

Only six weeks after deciding to remain at BYU, Hugh visited the University of Utah on 23 March 1955 for a highly publicized debate with Sterling McMurrin, a professor of philosophy. As part of the school's "Great Issues Forum," the debate topic was "Do History and Religion Conflict?" (See chap. 11.) Arguing that nothing poses as great a challenge to religion as historical scholarship, McMurrin stated that no religion could be understood without looking at it historically. McMurrin later characterized Hugh's position as "non-rationalist," and paraphrased Hugh's position as: "There really is nothing important to be learned from history as far as religion is concerned."[62] Although the audience was predominantly Mormon, Hugh's style was less overtly Mormon than usual. He spoke of "my religion" and "my own church," and there was a much more distant—some would call it objective—tone in his presentation. It is as if President Clark's words were still ringing in his ears, telling him that he could not openly preach the gospel at the University of Utah. Still, after the debate

---

[60]Hugh Nibley, Letter to Henry D. Moyle, 3 February 1956.
[61]Hugh Nibley, Letter to Paul Springer, n.d., ca. February 1955.
[62]Sterling McMurrin, "Faith of an Observer," 545.

Hugh may have felt somewhat conflicted about his decision to remain at BYU. Perhaps he enjoyed the open exchange of the debate and the attention he received on the U of U campus, but he probably also felt some relief about his decision to remain in a setting where he could be openly and passionately Mormon.

At the end of the decade, Hugh summarized his life: "I must play the backwoods Ranke, domestic martinet, stern paterfamilias and poor man's Plato, nursing my frustrations with lemonade." His "brutal regime" consisted of "21 hours of teaching, two books due, two articles, sick kids, a new baby, an old house to be kept up, administrative nonsense."[63] But the immediate future offered a change of pace for the entire family. "Day before yesterday came a letter which told me I could consider it as a formal invitation to spend the Academic Year 1959-1960 at Berkeley." Hugh was to spend his sabbatical teaching in the Speech Department, while studying Egyptian and Coptic with one of the few certified Egyptologists in the nation. "So now the problem," wrote Hugh, "is to find a cheap used station-wagon and see how much junk we can pile into it."[64]

---

[63]Ibid.
[64]Hugh Nibley, Letter to Paul Springer, 7 March 1959.

Hugh Nibley and Bill Muse stand at the Hopi "prophecy rock" on 27 July 1996. This records a prophecy of the last days but is not the Hopi Stones that *Massau'u*, the Great Spirit, gave to the Hopi.

What I most admire about Nibley's response to Native Peoples is that he takes their sacred narratives and ritual activities seriously. Nibley's vast knowledge of ancient sacred texts and languages prepared him to recognize not only the profound integrity of Hopi myth and ritual but also the actual contribution Hopi myth and prophecy make to the world's body of knowledge. What Nibley recognizes is that Native Peoples have much to offer dominant cultures. Until more humans can dialogue across cultural boundaries the way Nibley does, I think we will continue to have mythological wars throughout the world between Muslim and Christians, Catholics and Protestants, Natives and Christians. I can't tell you how deeply troubled I am about the failure on the part of so many "scholars" to imagine that God is "no respecter of persons." James Treat's *Native and Christians: Indigenous Voices on Religious Identity in the United States and Canada* (New York: Routledge, 1996) contains essays about "The Old Testament of Native America." I see Nibley as a person who has the critical capacity to receive such testaments from others.

—Suzanne Evertsen Lundquist[1]

---

[1] Suzanne Evertsen Lundquist, e-mail to Boyd Petersen, 9 May 2002.

Chapter 18

The Home Dance: Hugh Nibley Among the Hopi

Hugh Nibley lives in a world of serendipity. I have discovered that, time and time again, he has miraculously avoided some catastrophe or dropped in on some fortunate eventuality. Call it happenstance, fate, or divine will, but these moments of pleasant coincidence have followed him throughout his life. Psychiatrist M. Scott Peck believes that these "miracles of serendipity," as he calls them, are "amazingly commonplace" and usually "in some way beneficial" to the recipient.[2] Those who don't experience them, he argues, are simply not aware of them—"serendipitous events occur to all of us, but frequently we fail to recognize their serendipitous nature; we consider such events quite unremarkable, and consequently we fail to take full advantage of them."[3] While this may be true, I have never known anyone who experiences these moments of serendipity to the degree Hugh Nibley does. More importantly, not only do they *happen* to him, but he makes himself *aware* of them.

Although Hugh would not dismiss the significance of any good fortune, to me the most thrilling instances are the times during World War II when, through fortunate synchronicity, his life was spared, sometimes by mere inches. (See chap. 13.) Less dramatic, but no less important, are countless instances of providence in which he has just "happened" upon an important source exactly when he needed it in his research and writing. What is surprising to me is that, despite his gratitude and delight at the happenstances of his life, he never seems shocked or even surprised. Instead, he cheerfully attributes such blessings to God, perhaps as a reward for paying his tithing, doing his home teaching, or performing some other modest act of righteousness. As Hugh wrote to his

---

[2]M. Scott Peck, *The Road Less Travelled* (New York: Touchstone, 1978), 255. This chapter was first published in *Dialogue: A Journal of Mormon Thought* 31, no. 1 (Spring 1998): 23-35.

[3]Ibid., 257.

friend and teacher Klaus Baer, "A hundred times a week I ask myself in amazement: What am I doing here? Well, if that's the way the Lord wants it—he knows what he's doing; it's a cinch I don't. But that's what makes it interesting."[4] Hugh wrote to a prospective graduate student who had asked for advice about what career to pursue: "In all of this, there is only one rule to follow, and that is, 'Let the Spirit guide.'"[5] I believe that Hugh takes that rule farther and more seriously than most of us dare.

Knowing of Hugh's encounters with serendipity, I haven't been terribly surprised when these same types of coincidences have accompanied my efforts to chronicle his life. It's been very difficult not to notice them. For example, while my family and I were living in Maryland, Hugh and Phyllis came east in 1990 for the wedding of their son, Michael, who also lived in Maryland. The day before the wedding, Zina asked me to take Hugh sightseeing while everyone else worked on pre-wedding preparations. I knew Hugh would rather see something off the beaten path, so I took him to one of my favorite Civil War sites: the battlefield of Antietam. On the way there I learned that Hugh had spent many hours conducting maneuvers at Antietam battlefield during World War II while he was stationed at Camp Ritchie. That day I was treated to a dizzying account of his adventures during World War II and of parallels drawn from ancient history, the Civil War, and the then-current Gulf War. The day we spent at that battlefield was also, "coincidentally," the anniversary of the battle of Antietam.

On another occasion, when I called the University of Chicago's Oriental Institute to gain access to Klaus Baer's papers, the curator just about dropped the telephone. He said he couldn't believe that I had called on the very day he had finished cataloguing Baer's papers—everything was in apple-pie order, completely available, and fresh in his mind. More recently, while searching in the papers of BYU presidents, I came across a letter to Hugh from former BYU President Jeffrey R. Holland. He was answering a letter from Hugh, which I couldn't find. I searched every logical place in the vast collection without success. Just before I left for the day, on a whim I pulled an unmarked box off the shelf. The first letter in the first folder in that box was the missing letter.

After moving back to Utah, I wanted some way to explore Hugh's fascination with the Hopi of northeastern Arizona. I knew he used to travel there with his sons, and I enviously thought how interesting it must have been to visit the Hopi with Hugh.[6] I

---

[4] Hugh Nibley, Letter to Klaus Baer, 12 February 1968, Klaus Baer Papers, Archives of the Oriental Institute, University of Chicago.

[5] Hugh Nibley, Letter to Gary B. Keeley, 15 March 1982.

[6] It is impossible to determine exactly how many times Hugh visited the Hopi, but at least ten can be documented. If his first visit was, as he has stated, soon after he arrived at BYU, may have been as early as 1947 or 1948. His first mention in writing occurs in a letter to Paul Springer, 12 June 1951: "I am quite unintentionally becoming an Indian man, having already attended a number of dances by invitation and spoken to groups of Navajos and Utes on the Book of Mormon; they eat it up." On 16 December 1952, he wrote Springer: "I have been hobnobbing with the Navahos again: they have a remarkable insight into many things and that without the slightest trace of mysticism." He may have been including the Hopi with the Navajo, although he observed the tribal distinction scrupulously later in his life. His son Paul remembers visiting the mesas with Hugh twice in the mid to late1950s. A letter to Paul Springer on 29 April 1957 mentions another visit, and a receipt from the Hopi Indian Agency shows that he rented a room on 26 July 1957. On 1 June 1964, he wrote to Klaus Baer that he had been invited to view the Hopi "prophecy stone" and has confirmed that he was given this opportunity twice. On 12 August 1968, Hugh invited Klaus Baer to observe the Snake Dance with him on the reservation. I have found no documentation of visits beyond this point, although it is

yearned to experience first-hand what had captivated him so about their culture and lifestyle. A few days later, my brother-in-law, Paul Nibley, telephoned to say that a man he knew had mentioned Hugh on one of his own visits to the Hopi mesas. Some members of the Hopi tribe remembered Hugh, wanted to visit with him, and invited him to stay in the village. So Paul and his contact, Bill Muse, arranged the details while I worked out the logistics of getting us to Hotevilla in July 1996.

The serendipity continued—the Hopi invited us to visit during their annual "Home Dance." It was singularly appropriate that we would take Hugh Nibley back to visit the Hopi during the Home Dance, or the *Niman Kachina*. The Home Dance is held at the time of the summer solstice to honor the *kachinas*, the spirits who represent the invisible forces of life, who have been on earth since the winter solstice ensuring the success of the creation process. Now that the harvest is in full bloom, the *kachinas* can return to their home in the San Francisco Mountains, and this dance is their send-off. It is a dance, like many of their ritual dances, completely concerned with cosmology—with the four forces of creation: germination, heat, moisture, and air—and with "the harvesting of the winter's prayers and planning."[7] But the going home of the *kachinas* is also rich in deeper cosmological meaning, for where the *kachinas* go to abide is where the Hopi believe all the righteous go when they die. What the *kachinas* are, the Hopi people can become.

Naturally, the cosmological nature of this dance was ideal for Hugh's return to the Hopi, since he has always been preoccupied with cosmology, whether Mormon, Egyptian, or Hopi. Yet this was also a homecoming of sorts for him. Hugh had first visited the Hopi soon after being hired at Brigham Young University. He recalled this event:

> When I first came to Provo shortly after World War II, I was approached by Brother Virgil Bushman, who had been called to revive the mission to the Hopi Indians after it had languished during the war. He urged me to go with him and promised me that I would see an ancient world probably much like the kind I would like to have found in the ancient Near East. I eagerly complied, and on a cold, bleak morning in March we approached the Third Mesa from the west.[8]

What he found there was a culture both ancient and timeless. But it was the ritual dances of the *kachina* that really caught his attention:

---

likely that he took at least another trip or two. Our 1996 trip was the first time Hugh had visited the mesas for over twenty years.

Hugh has mentioned the Hopi in seven articles, beginning in 1963: "Three Shrines: Mantic, Sophic, and Sophistic" (*Ancient State*, 369); *Since Cumorah* (220); "The Mormon View of the Book of Mormon (*Prophetic Book of Mormon*, 263), "Myths and the Scriptures" (*Old Testament and Related Studies*, 43), "The Law of Consecration" and "But What Kind of Work" (*Approaching Zion*, 455, 274), and "The Book of Mormon: Forty Years After" (*The Prophetic Book of Mormon*, 543). Hugh refrained from writing at length about his fascination with the Hopi, perhaps out of respect for their culture or perhaps because he felt that the subject matter was out of his area of expertise. A departure from this policy was his 1992 speech "Promised Lands," an address to BYU law students that reflected on the work of the lawyer he had known best: former BYU president Ernest L. Wilkinson. Wilkinson had won $30 million dollars for the Utes, who preferred land to money, in a settlement with the government over Ute tribal lands. For Hugh's recollection of Wilkinson's legacy, see "Promised Lands," in *Brother Brigham Challenges the Saints*, edited by Don E. Norton and Shirley S. Ricks, Vol. 13 in *The Collected Works of Hugh Nibley* (Salt Lake City: Deseret Books/FARMS, 1994), 8990.

[7] Frank Waters, *The Book of the Hopi* (New York: Penguin, 1963), 198.
[8] Nibley, "Promised Lands," 76.

> Here, on a high, bleak rock, surrounded by nothing but what we would call total desolation in all directions, was a full-scale drama in progress in the grand manner of the Ancients. . . . I told Brother Bushman that there should be fifty-two dancers, and that is exactly what there were. Fifty-two was not only the sacred number of the Asiatics and the Aztecs, but it was also the set number of dancers in the archaic Greek chorus. The dancing place was the bare plot which the Greeks called the *konistra*, the sand patch where this world came in contact with the other, at the crucial periods of the year. That was the time when the *orcus mundi* was open—*mundus patet*; that is, when the mouth of the other world was open and the spirits of the ancestors attended the rites. By the altar, of course, was the *sipapuni*, the mouth of the lower world, the *orcus mundi*, at which the spirits from above and below could meet with their relatives upon the earth. This was the essential year-rite, found throughout the world from the earliest times. On either side of the altar was a small evergreen, adorned like a Christmas tree with prayer feathers, for as in countless ancient societies these dramas were sacred. . . . Suffice it to say, it was a miracle of survival, commonly recognized as the only surviving instance of the fully celebrated year-cycle.[9]

In a letter to Klaus Baer, Hugh emphasized why he thought these rites preserved by the Hopi were so important:

> But I cannot get it out of my system that we have here in these people who dance all day in animal masks, feathers, paint, and fox-skin aprons something that is a) fundamental in the world's experience, and which is b) all but extinct in most parts of the world today. This is the sort of people that the old Libyans or the 'Amu might have been—I feel relaxed and happy with them.[10]

In a letter to Baer four years later, Hugh reiterated: "By the latest count, the Hopi are the only people in the world who still preserve a full annual cycle of full-dress protological, eschatological and cosmological ceremonies."[11]

The reason Hugh felt so comfortable among the Hopi was not simply their preservation of ancient cultural patterns which he studies but also their lifestyle. "Since I toured the Hopi mission last week nothing can bring me back to this world," he wrote Paul Springer after one of his 1950s visits. For the Hopi, as Hugh states:

> success means simply survival—they are so glad just to be alive that life is a perpetual holiday with them. Something should be done to make them more rank-conscious, but how can you teach people to get ahead in life if their whole life is confined to five acres on the top of a rocky mesa? They are where they want to be, and those who have been

---

[9] Ibid., 77-78.

[10] Hugh Nibley, Letter to Klaus Baer, 1 June 1964, Klaus Baer Papers. In his "Intellectual Biography," *Nibley on the Timely and Timeless* (Provo, Utah: BYU Religious Studies Center, 1978), xxv, Hugh reinforces this point: "Here at our doorsteps among Arizona Indians lies the world's best clue to the spiritual history of the race; nowhere else on earth will one find the old cycle of the Year Rites still observed in full force and unbroken continuity from the beginning." He praised "the devotion and courage with which a little band of less than five thousand people had kept alive a language and a culture which preserved the practices and beliefs of our own ancestors from prehistoric times until nineteenth-century industrialism severed the umbilical cord."

[11] Hugh Nibley, Letter to Klaus Baer, 12 August 1968, Klaus Baer Papers.

in the army and seen the world prefer the top of the mesa to anything else they have seen; they put on gorgeous but not too strenuous dances at which everybody has all kinds of fun, they refuse vehemently to be photographed or to allow anything of theirs to be photographed, they grind their corn and make their peekee fresh every morning, but they just will not enter into the spirit of our modern, progressive, competitive society. They have poisoned my little mind.[12]

To another correspondent, Hugh described: "Sitting with the missionaries and sharing the gospel with a group of Hopis you will find them to begin to loosen up very late at night, sharing what they really believe because they know that you really believe it."[13] Summing up his visits to the Hopi mesas, Hugh wrote, "My own connections with the Hopi . . . are exhilarating, puzzling, and faith-promoting."[14]

Hugh had to earn his intimacy with the Hopi. On his second visit to the Hopi, again accompanying Virgil Bushman, Hugh recounts with unqualified delight that "they apologized profusely to me for their coolness and aloofness on my first visit: 'Forgive us,' they said, 'we thought you were an anthropologist.'"[15] Hugh enjoys relating anecdotes of how the Hopi respond with straight-faced nonsense to patronizing anthropologists who have seen the Hopi merely as subjects for their publications rather than as people. The Hopi "will not tell [anthropologists] a thing, except to lead them down the garden path," he comments. He quotes them as saying that they "'always know Spring is here . . . when we see the beetles and the anthropologists come out.'"[16]

Hugh returned many times to visit the Hopi people, to compare their culture to those he was studying from the ancient Near East, and to experience the dramas of the dances. But it was the Hopi vision of life that took his heart. My trip with him and Paul was no different. Even the heavens seemed prepared for our arrival. For as we approached the third mesa on 25 July 1996, we saw a short rainbow directly over the village of Hotevilla. An American Indian would read it as a sign: "Short Rainbow links the sky and earth, having power over the atmosphere when the sun is shining and power over the earth when rain falls upon it."[17] With such a connection between the earth and the heavens, we were confident that our experience would indeed be significant.

During our visit, Hugh discussed with our hosts the parallels between their dances and those of the ancient Greeks and Egyptians. He read from the Egyptian *Book of the Dead* and quoted Greek epic poetry to illustrate. He cited the similarities in apparel among the different ritual dramas: the two eagle feathers on the headdress, the foxtail hanging down from the waist in back, the masks which both conceal and create identities, the bandoleer over the shoulder, the apron, and the sash. He noted the cosmic importance of the turtle shell (which the Hopi use as a rattle strapped to their right calf). He also noted the parallels in staging these drama-dances: the symbolic significance of the number of dancers, of the two spruce trees decorated with prayer feathers, of the all-male

---

[12] Hugh Nibley, Letter to Paul Springer, 29 April 1957.
[13] Hugh Nibley, Letter to Steven Epperson, 11 March 1982.
[14] Hugh Nibley, Letter to Fay Campbell, 22 June 1982.
[15] Nibley, Letter to Steven Epperson, 11 March 1982.
[16] Hugh Nibley, Letter to Klaus Baer, 1 June 1964, Klaus Baer Papers.
[17] Waters, *Book of the Hopi*, 59.

cast being dressed as both male and female dancers, and of the orientation of the dancers with the four directions.

These comparisons were not lost on the Hopi. They believe that they are the keepers of ancient traditions, and Hugh's words confirmed their beliefs. Like most of us, they were amazed by Hugh's ability to read these ancient documents and to understand their relevance, but they were more impressed by his vision—both by his ability to understand the deep religious significance of their traditions and his ability to see the sacredness of the world around him.

Of course, what amazed us were the parallels between Mormon rituals and those of the Hopi. In addition to those Hugh showed us were others called to our attention by Robert C. Bennion, an emeritus BYU professor of psychology, who accompanied us. Bob had served his mission among the Hopi and Navajo, and is a long-time friend of the Nibley family. He told us about witnessing the initiation ritual of a young woman in which the Hopi priest touched each of her sense organs with a feather dipped in corn meal, blessing them that they would function properly. Parallels appear between the language of the Mormon temple ceremony and the Hopi myths of origin in Frank Water's *Book of the Hopi*. Responding to someone who asked about similarities between the Mormon temple endowment and the Masonic ceremony, Nibley wrote that the parallels between the Mormon endowment and the rites of the Hopi "come closest of all as far as I have been able to discover—and where did they get theirs?"[18]

Like Mormons, the Hopi are a covenant people. They believe that the Great Spirit Maasaw met them at Oraibi some eight hundred years ago and gave them three things: warnings, prophecies, and instructions on how they were to live, recorded on four stone tablets.[19] For a covenant people like believing Mormons, to study the Hopi is to see further evidence that Joseph Smith did in fact restore ordinances and scriptures that were had previously in their purity but which, in time, were diluted, lost, or corrupted.

The fact that Hugh twice viewed the sacred Hopi tablets is also significant,[20] for the Hopi believe that at some future time a white man will come who can read these stones and he will be their leader. Clearly, the Hopi viewed Hugh with high esteem, but they also recognized that he was not the one they were to follow.

The poignancy of the theme of "going home" was further emphasized by the fact that most of the people Hugh had known on the mesas had themselves returned home. None of the old people he remembered were still alive at our visit. In the village of Moenkopi, Leroy Ned Shingowitewa, then in his thirties, remembered Hugh staying with his family on a visit in 1964. Our host, Silas Hoyungowa, had a childhood recollection of Hugh visiting the village. However, none of the Hopi whom Hugh remembered as friends were there. On the morning of our first full day in Hotevilla, Hugh and I walked around the old city. He recalled buildings that were no longer standing where he remembered them, remarked on how few of the people he had known were still alive, and seemed confused by these evidences of time's passage in a place that had always seemed timeless to him.

---

[18] Hugh Nibley, Letter to Howard S. Rhodes, 4 March 1980.
[19] Thomas E. Mails and Dan Evehema, *Hotevilla: Hopi Shrine of the Covenant, Microcosm of the World* (New York: Marlowe, 1995), 85; Waters, *Book of the Hopi*, 31-36.
[20] Nibley, "Promised Lands," 82-84.

Yet on that walk, Hugh also noted how many things had not changed. Life in the village of Hotevilla goes on much as it has for hundreds of years. He called my attention to the similarities between the sacred city of the Hopi and the ancient cities of the Middle East. He was right. Even the houses resembled those I had seen in the old city of Jerusalem two years earlier. He also mentioned that the scent of burning cedar, which perfumes the air in Hotevilla, is a recurrent theme in Greek poetry.

Hugh also noted the two main differences between the Hopi city and other ancient cities: Among the Hopi there are neither palaces nor large assembly halls. Hugh explained that the Hopi are such democratic people that they don't even have kings; they simply look to their wisest men as their leaders. And in a manner that recalls the rule of King Benjamin, the Hopi leader works alongside his followers and shares their fortunes. For assembly halls, the men meet in their *kivas*, which are underground ceremonial chambers that symbolically represent the Earth Mother—the small hole in the floor (the *sipapuni*) is symbolic of the womb while the ladder leading out through the roof is the umbilical cord. Another parallel can be drawn between the Hopi *kiva* and the labyrinth of Daedalus, a design of which appeared on early Cretan coins.[21]

I had been prepared for very primitive conditions; however, when we arrived, our host, Silas Hoyungowa, was watching the Olympics on television. Silas is among the very last and most conservative of the "traditional" Hopi. His son Manuel is the leader and spokesperson for many of the traditionals at Hotevilla and some from the other mesas.[22] There has been a long history of division between the "progressives"—those who would like to accommodate the white people (or *Pahanas*) and accept modern technology—and the "hostiles" or "traditionals"—who want to preserve the traditional way of life. Many have adopted the ways of the white man and see the conveniences of in-door plumbing and electricity as particularly appropriate for their aging elders. While many of his neighbors now have electric lines, telephone lines, and running water in their houses, Silas Hoyungowa uses solar panels to gather energy to run his television, refrigerator, and electric lights. He hauls water, storing it in private tanks to supply drinking and bath water to the house. And the outhouse is still a fact of life on the mesas, even in more progressive villages.

Despite the resistance of the traditionals, however, contact between our culture and theirs is eroding Hopi culture to the vanishing point. The traditionals see this trend in apocalyptic terms. They see the water and power lines now being constructed on the mesa not only as destroying their way of life, but also as desecrating the sacred lands of their heritage. Manuel Hoyungowa has stated: "We know that these [water pipelines, electric lines, and phone lines] cannot come into our sacred village. Hotevilla, the last traditional stronghold, in prophecy is connected to the four directions. We have always rejected these conveniences and in this, the final phase, we must remain Traditional and Strong." According to prophecy, if their village "allow[s] these conveniences to come in, then we face sudden destruction and purification in this world."[23]

---

[21] Waters, *Book of the Hopi*, 24.

[22] Mails and Evehema, *Hotevilla*, 12.

[23] Manuel Hoyungowa, (no title), statement delivered at the United Nations conference "Cry of the Earth: The Legacy of the First Nations," General Assembly, United Nations, 22 November 1993; photocopy in my possession. At this conference, leaders from seven Native American nations delivered prophecies about the environment to an audience of U.N. delegates and guests.

Part of this apocalyptic fear comes from the belief that the bulldozers would destroy shrines, cut across sacred pathways, and injure the earth. But the traditionals have an even greater fear. At the founding of Hotevilla, a sacred object was buried—an obvious parallel to the consecration of cities in ancient times. It is believed that disturbing that object will bring the end of Hotevilla, the punishment of its desecrators, and the final stages of the end of the world.[24] As Mircea Eliade has shown (and as Hugh noted six years prior to Eliade in "The Hierocentric State"[25]) the ancient city was consecrated around a sacred center. "For the pole to be broken denotes catastrophe; it is like 'the end of the world,' reversion to chaos."[26]

One thing is certain: the traditional Hopi world *is* ending. Today they purchase much of their food at the grocery store, and most adults seek employment in Flagstaff. To further complicate this picture, a drought in 1996 was so devastating that many Hopi simply did not even plant crops that season. The drought took a tremendous toll on the Hopi lifestyle and gave the traditionals further evidence that the world is ending. It is the harvest of the Hopi corn that allows the Home Dance to take place. Without a traditional Hopi harvest, there can be no dance. The rituals cannot be continued in the same ways without the existence of the traditional culture. And it is the rituals, the Hopi believe, that hold the world together.

Nevertheless, in the summer of 1996 during our visit, the dance went on. After four days of fasting, the village men who become the *kachinas* emerged from the *kivas* early in the morning and gathered just below the Hoyungowa residence. We were awakened by the sound of their singing, beginning as a low monotonous chant, then swelling with the sounds of the turtle shell rattles. It was eerie. When we walked down to the plaza where the dance was to take place, the entire village was assembled—some sitting on chairs and benches, some standing, and some on the rooftops of the pueblo houses.

Then the *kachinas* entered the plaza. I had seen pictures of the *kachinas* but nothing prepared me for the actual sight. The Home Dance requires some thirty *hemis kachinas* and eight or more *kachina-manas*. The *hemis kachinas* are the male *kachinas* ("hemis" means "far away"—they have come from far away and must now return). Their bodies are painted black with white symbols on the breast and back, and tufts of spruce branches are tucked in their blue arm bands, in the belts at their waist, and in a wreath around their necks. They wear beautiful, handwoven, multicolored aprons and sashes. Black and white bandoleers are tied over their right shoulders. Each *kachina* has a turtle-shell rattle strapped to his right calf. He holds another rattle in his right hand, and a spruce twig and a downy feather in his left hand. But the most overwhelming sight is their headdress. The face mask is yellow or red on one side and blue on the other. A brightly decorated blue *tablita* rises above the face mask. On it is painted a frog or butterfly in the middle of a red rainbow. The *tablita* has three terraces which are topped with downy feathers and tufts of wild wheat; two eagle tail feathers and two parrot feathers adorn the top terrace. Jutting out from the sides are still more feathers. The dress of the *kachina manas*, the female *kachinas*,

---

[24] Mails and Evehema, *Hotevilla,* 21.

[25] Hugh Nibley, "The Hierocentric State," in *The Ancient State,* edited by Donald W. Parry and Stephen D. Ricks, Vol. 10 in *The Collected Works of Hugh Nibley* (Salt Lake City: Deseret Book/FARMS, 1991), 99–147.

[26] Mircea Eliade, *The Sacred and the Profane,* translated by Willard R. Trask (New York: Harcourt Brace Jovanovich, 1959), 33.

is more subdued. They wear an orange face mask and their hair, after the fashion of unmarried Hopi women, whirls into buns on the sides of their heads. This design represents the squash blossom, a fertility symbol.

When entering the plaza, the *kachinas* carry armloads of corn stalks, cattails, *piki* bread, gourds, melons, toy bows and arrows, and *kachina* dolls which will all be distributed as gifts at the midday dance. As they arrive, they make a cooing noise like the sound of a dove, only more unearthly. When they are assembled, the chief sprinkles each *kachina* with cornmeal and blows smoke at them from a pipe. Then he speaks to them in welcome, encouraging them to dance. The leader of the *kachinas* begins to shake his rattle and the dance begins. Each of the *kachinas* stamps his right leg and shakes the rattle in his right hand in time to the very monotonous chant of the song. Meanwhile, the *kachina manas* kneel on blankets and place large gourds in front of them which resonate when they rub a bone over a notched stick placed on the gourd. The sound produced by the resonating gourds also defies description, but it somehow resembled the grunting of pigs. The entire spectacle is completely otherworldly.

The dance itself doesn't seem terribly demanding—it is very simple in form and involves stamping the right foot, shaking the rattles, and turning from one direction to another. Yet it is quite complex in meaning. Embodying the patterns of the Hopi cosmology, the dance is oriented to the four directions and each section represents a reenactment of the Four Worlds of Hopi mythology. For each Home Dance a new song is composed which also expresses the Hopi belief system. The dance is performed throughout the entire day, in three separate performances—one at dawn, one after noon, and the third in a final performance that continues after sunset. The Hopi believe that these rituals help to preserve order in this Fourth World where we currently reside, date their migration story and settlement of the mesas to thousands of years ago, and have a tradition of performing these rituals with only minor variations.

Yet despite the continuity of this ritual, we witnessed a further disintegration of the Hopi way at the dance. Two eagles should have been tethered to the post at the center of the plaza and then sacrificed immediately following the dance. No eagles could be found in the summer of 1996 and the ritual could not be completed. Some at Hotevilla believed that the dance we witnessed would be the final Home Dance.[27] They believe the world is ending. The world is out of balance (*koyaanisqatsi*) and will continue to spiral downward to chaos unless there is a substantive change in human hearts. The words of the Hopi traditionals are too similar in both style and content to the words of Mormon prophets for a Latter-day Saint like Hugh Nibley to dismiss them lightly. In language reminiscent of Doctrine and Covenants 87, Martin Gashweseoma, a traditional spiritual elder, delivered an apocalyptic warning to the United Nations: "[When corruption has covered the earth,] then the wars will come about like powerful winds, and will spread from country to country and bring Purification or Destruction to this world. The more we turn away from the instructions of the Great Spirit, *Massau'u*, the more signs we see in the form of earthquakes, floods, drought, fires, tornadoes, as Nature makes ready her revenge."[28]

---

[27] Although I have not had an opportunity to return, I understand the Home Dance is being continued.

[28] Martin Gashweseoma, (no title), statement delivered at the United Nations conference "Cry of the Earth: The Legacy of the First Nations," General Assembly, United Nations, 23 November 1993; photocopy in my possession.

At that same meeting, Manuel Hoyungowa spoke in similarly apocalyptic language:

> [The] Great Spirit, *Massau'u*, who we firmly believe is here with us, listening to us and watching over us, long ago gave to all races of people a good Life Plan to follow. His commandment to all was, "Be faithful always for I am the First and I will be the Last." Then in very clear and simple words [he] told us to love one another, to be kind to all people, animal and plant life on this Mother Earth. . . . But what happens today? Mankind is doing exactly the things the Great Spirit told us not to. For material gains many people have killed, lied, stolen, robbed their neighbors' property and heaped falsehood upon their fellow beings. There is hardly any true love, only hatred in the hearts of men today. . . . The more we turn away from the Great Spirit, the more He will punish us either with earthquakes, floods, lightning, great winds or all kinds of sickness or drought.[29]

The Hopi elders see things as either being *Hopi* or *Ka-Hopi*. *Hopi* not only means "peace," as it is commonly translated, but also "to obey and have faith in the instructions of the Great Spirit, and not to distort any of his teachings for influence or power."[30] For his part, Hugh Nibley has repeatedly described the ancient doctrine of the Two Ways—the way of the Lord and the way of Satan. He has also urged us to learn from people like the Hopi how to establish the Zion for which we yearn. Referring to the Book of Mormon, he writes, "Throughout these explicit prophecies it is the Gentiles who join 'the Lamanites and those who have become Lamanites,' not the other way around. If we are to be saved, we must move in their direction."[31] But to move in their direction means learning to see from a completely new perspective.

I believe Hugh Nibley represents a model of one who has moved in their direction. For not only does he take their world seriously, he sees our world in the same way they do. While he is not the least bit sanctimonious, everything about him is deeply religious, and he sees all things as spiritual. With this perspective, he has an awareness and an openness to miracles of serendipity—a form of grace which, Scott Peck argues, is available to all, but which only a few notice and take advantage of. In this, Hugh Nibley is very much like the Hopi. Both Hugh and the Hopi see meaning in the seemingly meaningless and the extraordinary in the seemingly ordinary.

A few weeks after my stay with the Hopi, I was canoeing on Tibble Fork Lake in American Fork Canyon. With the influence of my visit to Hotevilla still fresh in my mind, I was more aware of my surroundings than ever. The morning air was brisk; the sunlight sparkled on the water; and the gentle breeze smelled of campfires. The only sounds were those of my paddle as it moved gently through the water at the side of the boat, and of a fisherman's fly line as it settled onto the smooth water. I watched him; the grace and rhythm of the fly line were spell-binding. Then, as delicately as a ballet, two deer stepped into the clearing behind the fisherman and stopped only a few feet away from the him. They lowered their heads and drank from the stream that feeds into the lake, then lifted their heads and watched the weaving of his flashing line. Time seemed to stop in a

---

[29] Manuel Hoyungowa, (No title).

[30] Mails and Evehema, *Hotevilla*, 48.

[31] Nibley, "Promised Lands," 100-101.

moment of hypnotic beauty, of holy awareness. Then the deer returned serenely into the woods and disappeared. Even though the fisherman's casting created a rhythm that beautifully accompanied the movements of the deer, he was completely unaware of his role in the ritual dance. The incident was a spine-tingling episode of heightened awareness, underscoring how little intent I usually give to my actions and of how many small miracles that go unnoticed because I don't make the effort to become aware of them.

To be aware is the Hopi way—recognizing our place in the world and our relationship with creation. It is also a quality seriously absent in our modern world. That absence is at the root, I believe, of the violence, crime, and cruelty that are destroying us. But awareness is something that can be learned. As Scott Peck promises, "With this capacity, we will find that our journey of spiritual growth is guided by the invisible hand and unimaginable wisdom of God with infinitely greater accuracy than that of which our unaided conscious will is capable."[32] The key to our own survival may well be found on the humble, arid, and desolate mesas of Arizona's Hopi reservation.

---

[32] Peck, *The Road Less Travelled*, 309.

Hugh Nibley, already white-haired in his fifties. This photograph often accompanied his writings during the 1960s.

Courtesy L. Tom Perry Special Collections,
Harold B. Lee Library, Brigham Young University.

The fifties ended in Berkeley as a visiting professor in humanities, with Classical Rhetoric as the main subject.... Along with teaching I sweated for a year at Egyptian and Coptic with a very able and eager young professor. The Coptic would be useful, but Egyptian? At my age? As soon as I got back to Provo I found out. People in Salt Lake were preaching around that Joseph Smith's fatal mistake was to commit himself on matters Egyptian—safe enough in his own day, but now that Egyptian could be read it was a trap from which there was no escape.... In 1966 I studied more Egyptian in Chicago ... but still wondered if it was worth all the fuss. When lo, in the following year came some of the original Joseph Smith papyri into the hands of the Church; our own people saw in them only a useful public relations gimmick, but for the opposition they offered the perfect means of demolishing Smith once and for all. Not yet confident in Egyptian, I frankly skirmished and sparred for time, making the most of those sources which support the Book of Abraham from another side, the recent and growing writings, ancient and modern, about the forgotten legends and traditions of Abraham: they match the Joseph Smith version very closely.[1]

---

[1] Nibley, "Intellectual Autobiography," *Nibley on the Timely and Timeless* (Provo, Utah: BYU Religious Studies Center, 1978), xxv-xxvi.

Chapter 19

Fighting Academic Battles and Gaining the Brethren's Trust, 1959-69

As Hugh Nibley's 1959-60 sabbatical began, the Nibley family arrived in Berkeley in September and settled into a large, four-story home which "backed up against a deserted quarry where the sun never appeared before eleven a.m."[2] The Bay Area offered a great adventure for the Nibley children. Four of the six children—twelve-year-old Paul, ten-year-old Christina, nine-year-old Tom, and six-year-old Michael—would be adjusting to new schools in California. Shuttling her children back and forth to their various after-school activities, Phyllis would be learning the roads of the quaint but sometimes maddening college town where the large hills and deep valleys can make access to a relatively close destination a complicated process. For her own part, Phyllis brought her cello with her, took lessons from Margaret Rowell, a very prominent musician, and joined the faculty wives at their socials. At home she cared for three-year-old Charles Alexander and one-year-old Becky.

Hugh had to make adjustments of his own. Not only would he be teaching a subject he had never taught before—classical rhetoric in the Speech Department—to students quite different from those at BYU, but he would also experience life from the other side of the desk, as a student. Hugh had accepted the appointment at Berkeley, not for the nostalgia of returning to his alma matter, but for the express purpose of resuming "the study of Egyptian, even if it had to be with old Lutz." Henry L. F. Lutz had been professor of semitics at Berkeley when Hugh was a graduate student. Hugh didn't have a lot of respect for Lutz's scholarship, and he also got the

[2]Hugh Nibley, Letter to Paul Springer, 12 December 1960.

impression that Lutz didn't like Mormons; but Hugh was grimly determined to learn Egyptian no matter what.³ However, when he stopped by Lutz's office on his first day in town, Lutz had retired and was packing. "He told me the person I should see was a young man from Chicago, whom the University had been very fortunate in acquiring." That man was Klaus Baer. Getting to work with Klaus instead of Lutz was "manna from heaven," as Hugh put it.⁴

Baer was new to teaching. He had just completed his Ph.D. in Egyptology at the University of Chicago's Oriental Institute in December 1958 and was facing his first semester as a teacher in the fall of 1959. Klaus, twenty years Hugh's junior, found it a bit awkward to have Hugh, a senior professor, enrolled in his class that first semester. As Baer's wife, Miriam, later recalled, "Nibley was a very experienced teacher who wanted to learn hieroglyphs, while Baer was a brand new teacher who knew all about Egyptology." Hugh, an avid student, learned quickly, while Klaus began to seek advice from Hugh about teaching. Miriam says that Hugh advised him to "slow down, [to give] students a little more time to digest material."⁵ This as strange advice coming from Hugh, whose lecture speed approached the speed of sound.

Despite the "helpfulness and long-suffering patience" that Klaus showed his students, Hugh was the only student who remained in his Coptic class after the first few weeks, and one of only two who stuck it out in Egyptian. "That does not mean that [Klaus] enjoyed making things hard," remembers Hugh. "He put himself out for everyone and went to no end of trouble to be helpful to every student." In such an intimate setting, Hugh and Klaus got to know each other quite well. "There was no academic barrier between [Klaus] and anyone else, not the slightest trace of stuffiness or pretense," Hugh recalled in a nostalgic letter to Miriam after Klaus's death in 1987.⁶ The Coptic class was more of a student-student relationship, with each keeping the other on his toes. He remembered the two-student Egyptian class as grueling: "I was badgered and bullied six hours a week by a fellow twenty years my junior, who was trying to knock the simple elements of Egyptian and Coptic into my head," as he later put it.⁷

Hugh and Klaus discovered they had more in common than a love for Egyptian. Klaus had an "enthusiasm for mountains matching my own," Hugh recalls, and the two became good friends, eventually spending many hours together in nature. Klaus later visited the Nibleys in Utah, while Hugh visited Klaus at his summer cabin in Estes Park, Colorado. "A series of delightful summers followed," remembers Hugh. "Camping with my boys in the dramatic retreats of Capital Wash, penetrating the mysterious and endless windings of Chimney Rock Canyon, collect-

---

³Hugh Nibley, interviewed by Boyd Petersen, 11 August 2001. Hugh stated that Lutz was very unhappy because his only son had converted to Mormonism.

⁴Hugh Nibley, Letter to Miriam Reitz Baer, n.d., ca. June 1987.

⁵Miriam Reitz Baer, "Reminiscences of Hugh Nibley and Klaus Baer," 24 November 1989, 1; typescript in my possession.

⁶Hugh Nibley, Letter to Miriam Reitz Baer, n.d., ca. June 1987.

⁷Hugh Nibley, Letter to "Bro. Bergen," 29 July 1960. This ruthless nine-page appraisal of education, especially at BYU, was titled "Nobody to Blame." Hugh circulated it with a cover letter addressed to "Dear Brother" dated 3 August 1960.

Family portrait in Berkeley, 1959. Phyllis is holding Rebecca with Christina standing behind them. Michael is sitting between Phyllis and Hugh holding his telescope. Thomas is standing behind Hugh, Charles Alex is perched on the arm of Hugh's chair, and Paul stands at the far right holding a book and his car for the Cub Scout pinewood derby.

ing gems at Topaz Mountain, wearing out the trails of Bryce and Zion's Canyons, visiting old Hopi friends on the Mesas and witnessing the Snake Dance—all before those places had been discovered by the public or the developers."[8]

Hugh enjoyed teaching at Berkeley but could not avoid talking about religion—and perhaps he did not try too hard. "I gave them the law of the gospel in there too," concedes Hugh. While his preaching in a public school among "the liberal Berkeley crowd" may have raised some eyebrows, it also converted one young student named Brown, whom Hugh remembers as "a very fine young man." He consulted Hugh on "a serious problem. He said he was raised by good parents in a good family and they wanted to give him the right upbringing. They'd done everything they could to teach him the right things and now he didn't know how to break the news to them that there really is a God."[9]

For Hugh, the academic climate at Berkeley was seductive; the school was likewise impressed with Hugh. By the end of the first semester, Berkeley made Hugh an offer to stay on as a full professor at a salary considerably higher than the one he

---

[8] Hugh Nibley, Letter to Miriam Reitz Baer, n.d., ca. June 1987.
[9] Nibley, "Faith of an Observer," 67-68, compilation of interviews, ca. 1983-84 for a video documentary of the same name aired in 1985, photocopy of typescript in my possession, pagination added.

made at BYU. Hugh began to seriously contemplate the offer. Surely the fact that he had helped one student believe in the existence of God must have been an encouraging sign that he could have an influence for good perhaps even larger than he had at BYU. On 3 December 1959, Hugh wrote to Apostle Joseph Fielding Smith asking for his advice. Within a week, Elder Smith wrote back: "This is a matter that you must decide for yourself. If you feel that you have greater opportunities and a larger field where you are then perhaps that should be your decision. Of course I would regret to lose you."[10]

The tug of duty again won out. When he wrote the head of the Religion Department about his schedule, he asked to teach "nothing but the gospel from here out"—in other words, no more language classes. The dean of the Religion Department complied and sent Hugh a tentative schedule for the 1960-61 school year that had him teaching classes on the primitive church, comparative world rites and liturgy, readings in Christian history, readings in the history of world religions, Christianity in the second and third centuries, Islam, and early oriental history, which he co-taught with Richard Poll.[11]

As the new school year began, Hugh reported to the Religion Department about his "very strenuous and energetic year" at Berkeley, particularly focusing on the similarities and differences between BYU and Berkeley. Departmental lines were disappearing at Berkeley, Hugh noted, with professors teaching across the disciplines. And while teaching standards were no better at Berkeley than at BYU, he stated that faculty benefits were "unbelievable"; however, publication was required of "anyone who might get anywhere." Students at Berkeley, Hugh reported, "have a great sense of high endeavor." Hugh also commented on anxiety about the Cold War: "The people there are frightened and are storing food and planning routes of escape." Beyond that, he sensed a general malaise among faculty and students that he felt could only be satisfied by religion.[12]

To his enduring friend Paul Springer, he reported that "the year in Berkeley was most profitable for us all" but that it was good to be back in Utah. "The terrible tension of Berkeley has gone and we are in a position (as we never could be there) of preparing for any eventuality with confidence and assurance."[13] Not surprisingly, he had missed his decade-long immersion in the Book of Mormon: "I have spent the past year far from the Book of Mormon, and now, returning to it after a bout—an orgy—of strictly orthodox 'scholarship,' I find it looks better than ever," he wrote to Louis Midgley, a BYU professor of political science and major Nibleyophile. Hugh stated that his revised philosophy for dealing with secular scholarship was to "let the

---

[10] Joseph Fielding Smith, Letter to Hugh Nibley, 9 December 1959.

[11] David H. Yarn Jr., Letter to Hugh Nibley, 20 May 1960. Although I have not found Hugh's letter to Yarn, Yarn quotes from it in his response.

[12] College of Religious Instruction Faculty Meeting, Minutes, 20 September 1960, 3, Ernest L. Wilkinson Presidential Papers, Department of Religion, L. Tom Perry Special Collections, Harold B. Lee Library, Brigham Young University, Provo, Utah.

[13] Hugh Nibley, Letter to Paul Springer, 12 December 1960. Although Hugh's use of the royal "we" sometimes obscures his meaning, this sentence seems to refer to his family.

Gentiles go their way in some things, go along with them in others, and make no concessions where the Gospel is concerned."[14]

Hugh ended up using this philosophy among his peers in the Religion Department before he had the occasion to use it on "Gentiles." Even before he returned from Berkeley, battle lines were forming about a change in BYU's religion requirements. A special General Education Committee had recommended that all students should take a survey course called "Doctrines and Principles of the Gospel and Practical LDS Living" that would outline fundamental Church tenets.[15] Several Religion Department faculty countered with a proposal that all students should take a course on the Book of Mormon instead because it is "the pivot and anchor of everything in our faith." Other faculty resisted, feeling that such a policy would put the Book of Mormon "above the other scriptures."[16] The lines were drawn in the department between what some characterized as the conservative faction—those for the Book of Mormon—and the liberal faction—those wanting the doctrinal survey course. Hugh often disagreed with the way many of the more conservative faculty members taught the Book of Mormon. He characterized their approach reading the book as a "tract against Socialism," adding, "This was a theme they aimed at all the way through. . . . That was very discouraging at times because they wouldn't let up on it."[17] Nevertheless, Hugh always agreed with them that the Book of Mormon should receive more attention, and so he naturally sided with those who thought that the Book of Mormon should be the one required religion class at BYU. The debate continued through the academic year of 1960-61, becoming so rancorous that Elders Harold B. Lee and Marion G. Romney were finally asked in early 1961 to settle the issue for the school. The apostles recommended that the Book of Mormon become the required course, and the Board of Trustees accepted that proposal.[18]

Such acrimonious debates did not sit well with Hugh. "It is the same here as in Berkeley, institution-wise—the University is part of a world that is passing away," he wrote to Paul Springer.[19] Hugh felt that the faculty was not taking the gospel seriously, nor was it offering the high caliber of education that a university should offer. Immediately after returning from Berkeley, Hugh was asked to give the prayer at the June 1960 graduation exercises. Because of the bitter curriculum debate, Hugh was "feeling very strongly . . . that there was a lot of hypocrisy going on. There was so much fakery, so much bluff going on." He was so discouraged that he later confessed, "I wanted to cry."[20] He gave utterance to that pain in an unforgettable opening sentence: "We have met here today clothed in the black robes of a false priesthood."[21]

---

[14] Hugh Nibley, Letter to Louis Midgley, 1 July 1960.

[15] Gary James Bergera and Ronald Priddis, Brigham Young University: A House of Faith (Salt Lake City: Signature Books, 1985), 70.

[16] Glenn Pearson, Letter to Hugh Nibley, 26 May 1960.

[17] Hugh Nibley, "Faith of an Observer," 138.

[18] Bergera and Priddis, Brigham Young University, 70.

[19] Hugh Nibley, Letter to Paul Springer, 12 December 1960.

[20] [no author], "Hugh Nibley in Black and White," BYU Today, May 1990, 38.

[21] Nibley, "Leaders to Managers: The Fatal Shift," in Brother Brigham Challenges the Saints, edited by Don E. Norton and Shirley S. Ricks, Vol. 13 in The Collected Works of Hugh Nibley (Salt Lake City: Deseret Books/FARMS,

Hugh's prayer created a storm of conversation, but it remained a salutary call for academic humility for a generation.

The topic was still on his mind a month later when a potential student inquired about getting a Ph.D. at BYU. Hugh's written response, addressed to "Dear Brother Bergen," was a brutal critique of education in general and of BYU in particular. "It is high time I was explaining my reluctance to assist people in getting Ph.D. degrees in Religion or anything else here at the BYU," wrote Hugh. "It is expensive, unnecessary, and not really honest for us to pretend to duplicate the work of firmly established and far better equipped instructors and institutions."[22] Hugh charged that BYU faculty had neither the fundamental knowledge to foster intellectual greatness nor the spiritual depth to nurture testimonies. "Only in Utah can you take advanced courses in the fine points of Greek literature from a man who does not know a word of Greek but who, in the name of scholarship, has driven hundreds of young people from the Church," Hugh wrote.[23] Hugh acknowledged that there has always been a fundamental conflict between "intellectuals" and the Church. Alluding to his commencement prayer, Hugh wrote, "A university is a substitute for the Church; its doctorate is a substitute for the priesthood; its discussions and techniques a substitute for revelation; its robes and rituals a substitute for lost ordinances." Hugh's solution for the problem would be to return to "the program of the School of the Prophets and the University of Nauvoo, which was the acquisition of basic knowledge (especially languages) for the avowed purpose of aiding the spreading of the Gospel."[24]

Hugh not only sent the letter to its intended recipient but circulated it widely among friends and associates with a cover letter lamenting, "What one most misses in our Utah institutions is that air of intellectual candor, that free and searching discussion of the schoolmen, their ways and their foibles which is the principal delight and, in the end the main justification, of institutions of higher learning." After pointing out that people can either take themselves or the gospel seriously, but not both, Hugh continued, "At our Utah universities we take ourselves very seriously." Hugh stated that the Bergen letter "is the present state of things, to keep silent could only be harmful, and speaking out might do some good." Marion G. Romney, then an apostle, read the letter "twice with great interest," and stated, somewhat noncommittally, "I think you have given us food for thought."[25] The lengthiest response—thirteen pages—came from Sterling McMurrin at the University of Utah. Also widely circulated, it saluted Hugh for "the way in which you have driven home some very basic things that need to be driven home." But McMurrin also took Hugh to task, claiming that the "air of intellectual candor" and "free and searching discussion" that Hugh lamented was absent from Utah schools was, in fact, present at the U. McMurrin pointed out that attacks on religion do not come expressly from universities, and he criticized Hugh for placing too much emphasis on language acquisition

---

1994), 491. In "Leaders to Managers," his famous 1983 commencement address, Hugh retold the story of his prayer, of which no tape or transcript apparently exists.

[22]Hugh Nibley, Letter to "Brother Bergen," 29 July 1960, 1.

[23]Ibid., 4.

[24]Ibid., 8, 7.

[25]Marion G. Romney, Letter to Hugh Nibley, 7 September 1960.

as a means of obtaining knowledge. "For you, apparently, one who does not know the dead antique languages can know little of human culture, certainly little of religion."[26] There is no record that Hugh answered this letter (or any others he received on the topic).

It was part duty and part desperation that made Hugh decide to remain at BYU after being offered a position at Berkeley. He knew that the General Authorities valued his input and his efforts at defending the faith. He also knew that only at BYU could he openly discuss the gospel. Yet upon returning, Hugh evidently felt that BYU was just like Berkeley in all of the ways he had come to abhor: the same academic one-up-manship, professional arrogance, and faculty in-fighting. But he also saw very few of the factors he had come to love at Berkeley: the intellectual candor and rigorous inquiry. He clung idealistically to the notion that the gospel demands better from faculty at a Church school. This is the stated reason for his scathing criticism of BYU; but beneath his tirade, Hugh may have been having second thoughts about his decision to stay at BYU. He surely must have worried that he had traded the intellectual exhilaration of Berkeley for obscurity in the intellectual backwaters of Provo.

During the 1961-62 school year, Hugh's attitude about being at BYU smoothed out. "This has been the happiest and most profitable year we have ever had," Hugh wrote happily to Springer. Teaching only religion classes particularly pleased him, and he considered teaching a special class on the Book of Mormon to non-Mormon Middle Eastern students a plum assignment. Hugh was truly in his element, teaching his favorite book to a group of Arabic- and Farsi-speaking students. "The whole of my teaching time has been spent with Moslems," he described. "They took to the Book of Mormon like ducks to water—especially the Arabs; Nephi was their boy, and they knew his story was true from the opening gun."[27] Hugh also delighted in his budding friendship with a Coptic scholar who had just arrived to teach at the University of Utah. "The celebrated Arab scholar Aziz Atiya is now teaching at the University of Utah, and we have become good friends."[28]

An outlet for his ironic humor was the skit for the annual faculty banquet that he was assigned to plan with Cleon Skousen, who occupied the opposite ends of the political spectrum from Hugh. They both enjoyed this assignment for many years, clear evidence that Hugh did not require ideological conformity from people he liked. The entire faculty would meet together in the banquet hall of the old Joseph Smith Building (since razed and replaced by a building with the same name in the 1990s) and, following the meal, would engage in a Saturnalia of skits and comedy roasts of faculty members across the campus.[29] "We would spoof, oh, would we spoof," remembers Hugh. "We cooked up some real skits that were absolutely devastating. With Wilkinson, we were unsparing, and we'd do that with everyone in the school."[30] Wilkinson never missed a performance if he could help it.

---

[26]Sterling McMurrin, Letter to Hugh Nibley, 1 November 1960, 1, 8, Sterling McMurrin Papers, Special Collections, J. Willard Marriott Library, University of Utah, Salt Lake City.

[27]Hugh Nibley, Letter to Paul Springer, 20 May 1961.

[28]Ibid.

[29]Hugh Nibley, interviewed by Boyd Petersen, 1 July 1996, transcript.

[30](no author), "Hugh Nibley in Black and White," 38.

Hugh's grueling publishing schedule continued unabated through the 1960s. In 1961, "The Liahona's Cousins" appeared in the *Improvement Era*. The essay was prompted by a letter from Elder Spencer W. Kimball in 1959 asking whether "in any of your writings you have given much consideration to the Liahona found by Lehi at the tent door."[31] The resulting article kicked off another series about the Book of Mormon, which was published in 1967 as *Since Cumorah*. In the series, Hugh paid specific attention to the newly published sections from Dead Sea Scrolls which, as he stated in a letter to Elder Ezra Taft Benson, "Christian and Jewish scholars alike are increasingly annoyed by their teachings which, as more than one scholar has pointed out, are all too much like Mormonism."[32] Hugh felt that there were divine reasons why the scrolls were then receiving so much attention. "The enormous and unprecedented interest in the Dead Sea Scrolls, kept constantly warm by the prestige battle that is now waging around them is, I suspect, the Lord's way of preparing men's minds for new light."[33]

In 1961, Hugh boldly published "The Passing of the Church: Forty Variations on an Unpopular Theme," in the scholarly journal *Church History*, a periodical sponsored by the American Society of Church History, a group focused on the study of Christianity. This article began a short but intense skirmish within the journal's pages. Hugh took a strong but tacitly Mormon position, outlining forty historical indications that the Church established by Christ had fallen into apostasy.[34] Hans J. Hillerbrand, a historian of modern Christianity at Duke University, wrote a letter to the editor protesting Hugh's article. Hillerbrand underscored that for him this was a "bread and butter" issue: If Hugh's arguments were taken seriously, Hillerbrand would be out of a job. He argued that Hugh had not taken into account the insights of the Protestant Reformers, nor had he acknowledged that a church had continued, even if it was not the true church.[35] The journal's editors asked Robert M. Grant, a professor of New Testament from the University of Chicago, to comment on the exchange. Grant "admired both the vigor of [Hugh's] work and the style of his presentation," but said he disagreed with Hugh's conclusions. Grant stated that Hugh had

---

[31] Spencer W. Kimball, Letter to Hugh Nibley, 16 September 1959.

[32] Hugh may have been engaging in hyperbole on this point. Some Jewish scholars may have perceived the scroll as "too Christian," and some Christians were equally troubled by their "Jewishness," but I know of no scholar who publicly expressed the opinion that they were "too Mormon."

[33] Hugh Nibley, Letter to Ezra Taft Benson, 21 January 1965. Hugh was responding to Benson's letter, 4 January 1965, suggesting that Hugh prepare a book similar to Werner Keller's *The Bible as History* (2d ed. rev. [New York: Morrow, 1981]) which "would pull together the archaeological and scientific knowledge as a confirmation of the Book of Mormon." Hugh responded that, since the Nephites were a "numerically small society lost in the vastness of two continents," the best evidence for the Book of Mormon's authenticity would come from newly discovered documents in the Old World, a project Hugh undertook in *Since Cumorah*, edited by John W. Welch (1967; reprinted Salt Lake City: Deseret Book/FARMS, 1988).

[34] Nibley, "The Passing of the Church: Forty Variations on an Unpopular Theme," *Church History* 30 (1961): 131-54; republished as "The Passing of the Primitive Church," pamphlet, *When the Lights Went Out* (Salt Lake City: Deseret Book, 1970), 1-32; and "The Passing of the Primitive Church: Forty Variations on an Unpopular Theme," in *Mormonism and Early Christianity*, edited by Todd M. Compton and Stephen D. Ricks, Vol. 4 of *The Collected Works of Hugh Nibley* (Salt Lake City: Deseret Books/FARMS, 1987), 168-208.

[35] Hans J. Hillerbrand "The Passing of the Church: Two Comments on a Strange Theme," *Church History* 30 (1961): 481-82.

not "taken into account the context of the Fathers' statements" or "their homiletical rhetoric" but gave no examples of where Hugh erred. On the other hand, Grant argued that Hillerbrand was wrong to look for Reformers' thought in Hugh's essay since "they knew practically nothing" about the early church. Nor did Grant believe Hugh could be faulted for distinguishing between a "true" church and the church that had survived to the present, since to do otherwise turns "the object of church history" into a "history of interpretation" or a "history of ideas."[36]

Philip Hefner, a professor of theology at the Lutheran School of Theology in Chicago, next jumped into the fray, taking the position that the very job of a church historian is to link the events of the church in a "continuous tradition" that "moves from Christ to Saint Paul to Luther" and in this way make church history serve the needs of theology.[37] Albert C. Outler, a professor of theology and Wesleyan Scholar at Perkins School of Theology at Southern Methodist University and president of the American Society of Church History, concluded the discussion in his 1964 presidential address. As Hugh had predicted, he terminated the discussion by assertion: "Can the church in history be delineated?" asked Outler. "If this is impossible, then more than the enterprise of church history is at stake, for the Christian faith itself will not long outlive its major premise: God's real presence in human history—past, present, and future."[38]

Reviewing that debate in 1970, William A. Clebsch wrote:

> On the basis of his study of patristic writings, Hugh Nibley scored all church historians since Eusebius for describing rather than questioning the survival of the church through the early centuries. That Nibley took a Mormon's viewpoint on the nascent Christian movement does not make any easier the defense of its identity and continuity against attack.[39]

Hugh responded to none of these discussants. He never commented on his silence, but it seems highly unlikely that so articulate a man had nothing to say on the topic. More likely, he was giving his attention to war on another front. In 1961, Bookcraft published his *The Myth Makers*, responding to anti-Mormon claims against Joseph Smith. A series of articles in the *Improvement Era*, "Censoring the Joseph Smith Story," spoke to the same theme.[40] As historian David J. Whittaker showed in his introduction to the FARMS-produced compilation of these writings, Hugh follows in

---

[36] R. M. Grant, "The Passing of the Church: Comments on Two Comments on a Strange Theme," *Church History* 30 (1961): 482-82.

[37] Philip Hefner, "The Role of Church History in the Theology of Albrecht Ritschl," *Church History* 33 (1964): 338-55. The quotation is from p. 352.

[38] Albert C. Outler, "Theodosius' Horse: Reflections on the Predicament of the Church Historian," *Church History* 34 (1965): 261.

[39] William Clebsch, "History and Salvation: An Essay in Distinctions," in *The Study of Religion in Colleges and Universities*, edited by Paul Ramsey and John F. Wilson (Princeton, NJ: Princeton University Press, 1970), 40-72. The quotation is on p. 68.

[40] Both are reprinted in *Tinkling Cymbals and Sounding Brass*, edited by David J. Whittaker, Vol. 11 of *The Collected Works of Hugh Nibley* (Salt Lake City: Deseret Book/FARMS, 1991): "Censoring the Joseph Smith Story," 55-101, and *The Myth Makers*, 103-406.

both the tradition of early Mormon pamphleteers who defended Joseph Smith from accusations made by angry dissenters and the tradition of early Christian writers who defended Catholicism from similar attacks. Whittaker finds that Hugh "functions as a classical apologist in the highest sense (that is, as one who responds, clarifies, or defends) as he explains and vindicates the life and teachings of the prophets."[41] After beginning to read *The Myth Makers*, Elder Marion G. Romney warmly commended Hugh "for the work you are doing and hope the Lord will preserve you many years to continue it."[42] Likewise, Elder Gordon B. Hinckley genially commented: "No one has quite the same capacity as you to burst bubbles—and no one seems to take more Puckish delight in doing it."[43]

The response from Church authorities to Hugh's apologetics was so positive that, soon after Irving Wallace's *The Twenty-Seventh Wife*, a one-sided biography of Brigham Young's estranged wife Ann Eliza Webb Dee Young Denning, appeared in print, the First Presidency asked Hugh to write a response.[44] Hugh began a thorough study of anti-Mormon literature focusing on Brigham Young, as well as an exhaustive and careful study of Brigham Young's own words as reported in the *Journal of Discourses*, contemporary newspapers, and manuscript sermons in the LDS Church Archives. Hugh revered Brigham Young as "a man who knew where he was going; no other figure in American history is quite like him—what he accomplished single handed without any fuss or hysterics and in high good humor is simply incredible; the cards were stacked against him in every game, and he always came out on top, with no hard feelings."[45] Reading anti-Mormon literature, in contrast, was very depressing. In a letter explaining that a lecture he had been invited to give at Oklahoma State University had been canceled, Hugh told President Henry D. Moyle that it was all for the best. "Frankly, after five solid months of Ann Eliza Dee Young Denning I am in no mood to be sweet to Gentiles, and so I see the hand of the Lord in this."[46] He also complained to Elder Richard L. Evans about how negative this task was; Elder Evans responded: "I feel guilty that you have given it so much time" and suggested that Hugh turn his attention to other things unless his "findings will have general and continuing use."[47]

As a bright spot, the First Presidency urged BYU President Ernest Wilkinson to temporarily reduce Hugh's teaching load so that Hugh could "be free to devote

---

[41] David J. Whittaker, Introduction, *Tinkling Cymbals and Sounding Brass*, xvii. Whittaker explains (xx) that the first satirical essay published by a Mormon author was Parley P. Pratt, *An Epistle of Demetrius, Junior, The Silversmith* . . . (Manchester, England: n.pub., 1840).

[42] Marion G. Romney, Letter to Hugh Nibley, 26 July 1961.

[43] Gordon B. Hinckley, Letter to Hugh Nibley, 27 July 1961.

[44] Nibley, "Faculty Load Report," Fall 1961, wrote that he was engaged in responding to "critics of Brigham Young (by request of 1st Presidency)." Confirming the First Presidency's involvement are memos from Ernest L. Wilkinson to Dean Bryan West Belnap, 27 June and 21 July 1963; from Belnap to Wilkinson, 28 June and 12 August 1963; from Wilkinson to David O. McKay, 5 July 1963; from McKay and Henry D. Moyle to Wilkinson, 15 July 1963, Wilkinson Presidential Papers, Religion Department, Perry Special Collections.

[45] Hugh Nibley, Letter to Paul Springer, 5 July 1963.

[46] Hugh Nibley, Letter to Henry D. Moyle, 30 January 1962.

[47] Richard L. Evans, Letter to Hugh Nibley, 16 April 1962. Evans refers to a letter from Hugh, 13 April 1962; I have been unable to find this letter.

such time as may be necessary to research work along lines that may be considered urgent and vital to the work that he is engaged in, and to the welfare of the Church."[48] Wilkinson wrote back to "David O. McKay and counselors" on 5 July 1963, stating that the school needed Hugh to teach three courses which no one else was qualified to teach (the primitive church, Christianity in the second and third centuries, and Christian rites and liturgy), but that the administration would stagger these classes so that Hugh would teach only one two-hour class per semester. However, the faculty load reports for 1963 and 1964 show Hugh teaching a full load. Only the fall schedule has survived from both 1964 and 1965. In 1964, he taught Book of Mormon for Mideast students (2 hours), the primitive church (2 hours), and Christian ritual and liturgy (2 hours). The next fall, he taught the primitive church and two sections of the Book of Mormon.

Hugh published his results in 1963 as *Sounding Brass*, with an engaging subtitle: "Informal Studies in the Lucrative Art of Telling Stories about Brigham Young and the Mormons." Hugh went beyond Wallace's book to survey virtually all of the claims made by anti-Mormons against Brigham Young. One of Hugh's most timeless chapters analyzes anti-Mormon rhetoric broadly in a strongly satirical chapter titled "How to Write an Anti-Mormon Book (A Handbook for Beginners)."[49] Hugh's book did indeed provide what Elder Evans wanted: material of a "general and continuing use."

Despite his productivity designed for LDS audiences, Hugh also published a significant number of articles in scholarly journals. In 1965, he published "Qumran and the Companions of the Cave," comparing narratives found in both Muslim sources and in the Dead Sea Scrolls, in *Revue de Qumran*. In 1966, he published in *Vigiliae Christianae* "Evangelium Quadraginta Dierum" which looked at apocryphal accounts of Christ's teachings during his post-resurrection forty-day ministry. That same year, he published in *Western Political Quarterly* "Tenting, Toll and Taxing," which looked at the historical roots of political power. In 1967 "The Mormon View of the Book of Mormon" appeared in a special edition of *Concilium: An International Review of Theology* devoted to the study of Christian scripture.[50]

In 1963 the editors of the newly proposed *Encyclopedia Judaica* asked him to write the entry on the meaning of Jerusalem for Christianity and were so impressed by Hugh's work that, in January 1964, they offered him the position of departmental editor for sections dealing with Christian Latin biblical exegesis. The *Encyclopedia*

---

[48]David O. McKay and Henry D. Moyle, memo to Ernest L. Wilkinson, 15 July 1963.

[49]Thomas G. Alexander, "Toward the New Mormon History: An Examination of the Literature on the Latter-day Saints in the Far West," in *Historians and the American West*, edited by Michael P. Malone (Lincoln: University of Nebraska Press, 1983), referred to Nibley's style as "intellectual overkill," but Hugh was simply following in the tradition of early Mormon pamphleteers whose satire is often stronger and less respectful than Hugh's.

[50]Hugh Nibley, "Qumran and the Companions of the Cave," *Revue de Qumran* 5 (1965): 177-98; reprinted as "The Haunted Wilderness" in *Old Testament and Related Studies*, edited by John W. Welch, Gary P. Gillum, and Don E. Norton, Vol. 1 of *The Collected Works of Hugh Nibley* (Salt Lake City: Deseret Book/FARMS, 1986), 253-84. "Evangelium Quadraginta Dierum," *Vigiliae Christianae* 20 (1966): 1-24; reprinted as "Evangelium Quadraginta Dierum: The Forty-Day Mission of Christ: The Forgotten Heritage," in *Mormonism and Early Christianity*, 10-44; "Tenting, Toll, and Taxing," *Western Political Quarterly* 19 (1966): 599-630; reprinted in *The Ancient State*, edited by Donald W. Parry and Stephen D. Ricks, Vol. 10 of *The Collected Works of Hugh Nibley* (Salt Lake City: Deseret Books/FARMS, 1991), 33-98.

was to be a "highly scholarly" publication devoted to "all subjects of interest concerning Jews and Judaism," and the editors sought "the cooperation of the best scholars available for the various departments." As a departmental editor, Hugh would need to propose the list of subjects which would appear under his broad subject heading, write on any subjects within his "editorial scope," and solicit scholars to write on the other entries.[51] Flattered by the offer but daunted by the task, Hugh wrote back, modestly demurring, "I am probably not up to it." In the same letter, however, he proposed a list of possible subtopics.[52] After several weeks of contemplating the offer, he tried to rearrange his schedule to accommodate the extra work. He asked President Hugh B. Brown, First Counselor to President David O. McKay, about the reaction of the General Authorities were he to take on this departmental editorship. President Brown wrote back that President McKay "is of the opinion that he should leave this decision entirely in your hands. We think there is an opportunity to do a lot of good, but with your present heavy load unless some adjustments can be made it would seem to be inadvisable."[53] Hugh wrote back that he was "grateful for the counsel of President McKay, which settled all doubts in my mind." Unable to find a place to squeeze his hard-pressed schedule any tighter, he finally declined the offer on 4 May 1964: "It is with a heavy heart and a guilty mind that I return your generous contract unsigned after abusing your patience with long delays."[54] Hugh was likely most sincere when he wrote that turning down the invitation gave him a "heavy heart." Again he was giving up an opportunity that promised much more national and international prestige than any of his Mormon writings and would have been intellectually rewarding. Hugh must have felt deeply conflicted; yet out of a sense of duty, he passed it up. His Church leaders had called the project "inadvisable" and were not offering to make accommodations in his teaching schedule as they had when they needed him to defend the faith.

Only a little over a year after this highly distinguished offer, Hugh received his first rejection—and it came from a Mormon periodical. The editors of *The Instructor*, the successor to the *Juvenile Instructor* (1866-1929), then the monthly magazine (1930-70) published by the Deseret Sunday School Union, asked him for an article on "Archaeology and Our Religion" for a series titled "I Believe." Hugh had long felt that the best evidences for the Book of Mormon are in its text, rather than in the archaeological record. He had concluded that Book of Mormon peoples were a relatively small segment of the total population in ancient America and that archaeological evidences were a particularly shaky form of proof given the general uncertainty about the location of Book of Mormon events. Furthermore, he found it exas-

---

[51]B. Netanyahu, Letter to Hugh Nibley, 15 January 1964. Netanyahu was one of the editors of the *Jewish Quarterly Review*, which published Hugh's essay, "Christian Envy of the Temple," in 1959-60. See B. Netanyahu, Letter to Hugh Nibley, 28 March 1960.

[52]Hugh Nibley, Letter to B. Netanyahu, 4 February 1964.

[53]Hugh B. Brown, Letter to Hugh Nibley, 30 April 1964.

[54]Hugh Nibley, Letter to Samuel T. Lachs, 4 May 1964. Another member of the editorial board, Abraham A. Neuman, wrote on 12 June 1964, asking Hugh to reconsider his decision. Hugh did not. His article, "Jerusalem: In Christianity," appeared in the *Encyclopedia* when it was finally published in 1972, was later reprinted as a pamphlet by the Israeli Foreign Ministry, and was finally republished in *Mormonism and Early Christianity*, 323-54.

perating that critics used the dearth of archaeological evidence supporting the Book of Mormon against the Church. Consequently, his article, instead of supplying the desired list of "evidences," delineated the overall weaknesses of archaeology as a science. After reviewing Hugh's article, Lorin F. Wheelwright, the *Instructor's* associate editor, wrote to tell Hugh that he was recommending against publication. "I realize now that this is a very sensitive area for you," wrote Wheelwright with considerable sympathy:

> I feel very much like a patron of a great composer who has asked him to compose a symphony featuring the percussions, only to learn that the man hates percussions and particularly the cymbal. Therefore the work turns out to be an "anticymbal symphony." Not only does he feature the percussion, he proceeds to take vengeance upon the cymbal by pounding it, smashing it, hitting it, and fragmenting it. All of this is done to [the] rhythm of a most sophisticated style. There is no question but what it is an effective piece, but in the process the ears of the listener also take a beating. As a composition it is unique, but not suitable for programming before the intended audience.[55]

Overlooking the good humor, Hugh wrote back a scathing five-page response: "You would be justified in rejecting it on the basis of my renowned incompetence had you suggested any other title for the thing than 'I Believe.' That happens to be the one theme on which, right or wrong, I am beyond all doubt the world's foremost authority." He continued by raising a valid question: "What could be of greater importance in discussing Archaeology and Our Religion than the indisputable fact that archaeology has been used and is being used as a tool against Our Religion? Or the equally indisputable fact that archaeology is by no means the precision tool that some people think it is?"[56] Despite the point's validity, it was not relevant to the issue of suitability that Wheelwright had raised. Reading between the lines reveals Hugh's shock and indignation at being rejected for the first time in his life by any publisher.

Hugh mimeographed copies of the article, his letter to Wheelwright, and a cover letter, all of which he distributed widely. Elder Marion G. Romney wrote positively: "I agree with you that [the rejection] called for a rejoinder, and I think you more than adequately answered it."[57] Elder LeGrand Richards speculated that the editors thought the article "might be offensive to some of the brethren who have paid so much attention and given so much time to the study of archaeology that they felt might add additional testimony of the divinity of the Book of Mormon." He was no doubt thinking of men like Milton R. Hunter, a member of the First Council of the Seventy, who was deeply engaged in precisely such efforts. Richards poured oil on the troubled waters of Hugh's equanimity: "Now, Dr. Hugh, I wouldn't let this worry you too much. You have contributed so much valuable information that you cannot hope to please everybody."[58] Mormon archaeology enthusiast Paul Cheesman, then teach-

---

[55] Lorin F. Wheelwright, Letter to Hugh Nibley, 2 September 1965.
[56] Hugh Nibley, Letter to "Mr. W.," 16 September 1965.
[57] Marion G. Romney, Letter to Hugh Nibley, 25 October 1965.
[58] LeGrand Richards, Letter to Hugh Nibley, 21 September 1965.

ing in BYU's Religion Department, congratulated Hugh on the essay, generously calling it "one of the best articles you have written" and stating that it "helped my thinking."[59]

In the 1960s, Hugh also gave many speeches, primarily throughout the Intermountain West, although no record has been kept. In 1963 he participated in Religious Emphasis Week at Oklahoma State University where, as he reported to the First Presidency, in three days he "gave 13 formal addresses, each followed by a question period and consultations."[60] That same year, he also gave a series of lectures to the Deseret Club at Yale University, arranged by Truman Madsen, president of the New England Mission. Hugh's lectures focused on the integration of Christian revelation (the Mantic) with Greek philosophy (the Sophic) which resulted in a church beguiled by the philosophies of men (the "junkyard" of the Sophistic).[61]

Likely the most celebrated of his public appearances in the 1960s was his encore debate with Sterling McMurrin, this time at BYU. After the Academic Emphasis Committee set up the encounter, Hugh mischievously wrote to McMurrin, "Let's teach the rascals a lesson by giving them not a disputatio but a joint recital. Everybody will learn more that way. Having become as mellow as last Halloween's pumpkin (and about as significant), I am beyond taking issue on anything, while my own opinions are as set as a geologist's."[62] On the evening of 13 May 1963 an overflow crowd assembled in the George Albert Smith Fieldhouse to hear the disparate views of Utah's two most prominent thinkers. The debate got off to a light-hearted start when, in introducing McMurrin, Hugh made a sly quip at President Wilkinson's right-wing political stand against government-sponsored welfare with an allusion to tithing as the basis of BYU's funding: "Welcome to this welfare institution."[63] The topic of the debate was "The Nature of Man," and, like their encounter eight years earlier, Hugh took the side of revelation while McMurrin took the side of reason. "How can you know if what I'm telling you is the truth?" asked Hugh, paraphrasing Brigham Young. "You can't unless you've received revelation." McMurrin responded: "Even revelation must be judged at the bar of reason, and a failure to understand this is a failure to understand Mormonism." Furthermore, he doubted that BYU was established "for the purpose of encouraging revelation" over reason.[64]

In December 1964, Hugh was invited by a well-connected Mormon family to fly to the Middle East to "determine the extent, location, and accessibility of docu-

---

[59]Paul R. Cheesman, Letter to Hugh Nibley, n.d., ca. 1965.

[60]Hugh Nibley, Letter to A. Hamer Reiser, 11 March 1963. Reiser was Assistant Secretary to the First Presidency. Hugh had been invited to attend the same conference a year earlier; but the invitation had been withdrawn at the last minute for an unspecified reason.

[61]B. West Belnap, Letter to Truman G. Madsen, 20 March 1963; B. West Belnap, Letter to Hugh Nibley, 27 March 1963; Earl C. Crockett, Letter to Hugh Nibley, 9 May 1963, Ernest L. Wilkinson Presidential Papers, Religion Department, Perry Special Collections.

[62]Hugh Nibley, Letter to Sterling McMurrin, 12 February 1963. If McMurrin responded, the letter has not survived.

[63]Nibley, "Faith of an Observer," 138.

[64]Bergera and Priddis, *Brigham Young University*, 349; "Revelation vs. Reason Viewed at AEC Debate," (BYU) *Daily Universe*, 14 May 1963. Unlike the 1955 encounter, no published transcript of the debate was made. Only excerpts appeared in the newspaper.

ments relevant to the study of the Gospel and in particular of the Book of Mormon." During the almost three weeks that he spent in Jordan, Syria, and Israel, Hugh met with dignitaries and scholars from many countries, visited many newly discovered archaeological sites including Qumran, and viewed the Dead Sea Scrolls both at the Amman Museum in Jordan and at the Palestine Archaeological Museum (now the Rockefeller Museum). He got a first-hand glimpse of the politics involved in acquiring and translating the scrolls. The Jordanian government was jealously guarding the scrolls after seven scrolls ended up in Israel, and scholars suspiciously hoarded their individually assigned fragments, denying access to other scholars. Hugh noted that the trip was "very instructive and from a professional point of view most rewarding, but it was NOT a pleasant experience." Political tensions between Israel and its neighboring Arab nations were on the boil. Only days before Hugh visited Qumran, the site was closed for military maneuvers and he had personally "heard a lot of shooting in the area, and nobody ever seems to know what is going on." Because his Arab hosts in Jordan and Syria assumed that Hugh and the other Americans in his party did not speak Arabic, Hugh "was able to understand a good deal of what was said. We were suspected of sinister motives in Syria and Jordan and watched all the time." In contrast, Hugh felt that the streets of Jerusalem were "a haven of calm" and that the Israelis were "a law-abiding people." The visit made him reverse his assumptions, and "I came away convinced that the Jews and NOT the Arabs have right on their side."[65]

Not long after Hugh returned home, the First Presidency wrote Hugh to report that Dr. Joseph Saad, director of the Palestine Museum, through antiquities dealer Khalil Kando, had offered several "vases, jars, and artifacts" related to the Dead Sea Scrolls. They asked for Hugh's opinion on the purchase.[66] Hugh wrote back assuring them that "Mr. Saad's reputation cannot be rated too highly" and that "Kando is not only a reliable dealer but has been from the beginning the ONLY official outlet of sales of Jordanese antiquities."[67] The Church acquired several pieces, one of which, a jar like those containing the Dead Sea Scrolls, was used as an illustration in *Since Cumorah*.[68]

Although Hugh had complained a decade earlier that his peers at BYU did not appreciate him, they honored him in 1965 with the invitation to give the Second Annual Faculty Lecture. (Professor H. Tracy Hall had been honored with the first the previous year.) The honor went to "the faculty member whose achievements transcend local or regional boundaries" and are recognized by colleagues within the discipline. At the time, it was the highest recognition that could be paid to a BYU faculty member.[69] On 17 March 1965, Hugh spoke on "The Expanding Gospel," showing parallels with the gospel as found in sources like the Dead Sea Scrolls, the

---

[65] Hugh Nibley, Letter to First Presidency, 28 December 1964.

[66] David O. McKay, Hugh B. Brown, and N. Eldon Tanner, Letter to Hugh Nibley, 18 January 1965.

[67] Hugh Nibley, Letter to the First Presidency, 25 January 1965. James C. Vanderkam, "The Dead Sea Scrolls and Christianity," *Understanding the Dead Sea Scrolls*, edited by Hershel Shanks (New York: Random House, 1992), 204, describes Kando as "the Bethlehem and East Jerusalem antiquities dealer who had served as middleman for the purchase of most of the Dead Sea Scrolls from the Bedouin shepherds."

[68] Nibley, *Since Cumorah*, 78.

[69] Earl C. Crockett, Letter to Hugh Nibley, 10 December 1964.

Christian apocrypha, the Old Testament pseudepigrapha, Jewish mystical texts, and ancient Egyptian texts.[70]

An unpublicized but increasingly important fraction of his scholarly energies throughout the decade went to special assignments from the General Authorities, whose trust in him was steadily increasing. Individually or collectively, they consulted Hugh for information about a particular topic or solicited his views on a current issue. For example, in 1966 Apostle Ezra Taft Benson asked Hugh's opinion about the newly established independent Mormon quarterly *Dialogue: A Journal of Mormon Thought*.[71] Hugh's response was respectful and balanced. He stated that he felt the editors were as "faithful and devoted" to the Church as he was; that the editors' intention of dealing with both sides of issues could be good since "there are some issues, such as evolution, which can most profitably be treated by hearing from both sides"; and that the journal might "reawaken the Saints to that interest in things of the mind which was so characteristic of the early leaders of the Church." On the other hand, Hugh noted that the journal may be tempted to "steady the ark" and try to counsel the leaders of the Church; that nothing was hampering the Saints from achieving greatness in the arts and sciences without the journal; and that nothing good could come of creating dialogue about controversial issues. "For me, the title of the journal displays both its strength and its fatal weakness. Christ often rebuked his Apostles both before and after the Resurrection, for making a Dialogue of the Gospel. The word occurs 31 times in the New Testament and always in a bad sense."[72]

This increasing confidence Hugh had earned with the General Authorities also allowed him to offer unsolicited suggestions when he felt they might prove useful. After Elder Marion G. Romney gave a speech at BYU on the evils of communism, Hugh commented:

> That was the best talk I have heard on Socialism. But doesn't it produce a dangerous imbalance to warn against Scylla while ignoring Charybdis? The Devil was delighted when the millions rushed from the abuses of Capitalism right into the

---

[70] It was published in *BYU Studies* 7, no. 1 (Autumn 1965): 3-27; reprinted in *Temple and Cosmos: Beyond This Ignorant Present*, edited by Don E. Norton, Vol. 12 of *The Collected Works of Hugh Nibley* (Salt Lake City: Deseret Book/FARMS, 1992), 177-211. See "Nibley on 'Expanding Gospel' at Second Annual Faculty Lecture," (BYU) *Daily Universe*, 16 March 1965, 1.

[71] Ezra Taft Benson, Letter to Hugh Nibley, 18 January 1966.

[72] Hugh Nibley, Letter to Ezra Taft Benson, 28 January 1966. Hugh is referring to the Greek root *dialogismos* from which we get our English word "dialogue." In the New Testament, it can mean a neutral concept like "thoughts" or "imaginations," but it is more often a negative term. For example, it is translated in Romans 14:1 as "doubtful disputations," in Philippians 2:14 as "disputing," in 1 Timothy 2:8 as "doubting," and in James 2:4 as "evil thoughts." It is interesting to note, however, that Hugh sent a memorandum to Chauncey Riddle, a professor in the Philosophy Department, on 29 October 1963 expressing the need for a journal of the very sort that *Dialogue* hoped to become: "All churches but ours publish serious journals frankly dealing with things from their own point of view." Church magazines like the *Improvement Era*, "being family magazines cannot give space to overly 'technical' or controversial material. . . . A journal of Mormon studies would not have to be official or even connected with an institution; it would simply be a publication willing to deal with Mormonism from all sides." Hugh concluded: "It is the right and duty of those who have a word to say for the Gospel above the adolescent level to publish their findings: even the World expects that much of us, and interprets our silence as a declaration of bankruptcy. This condition should be corrected and could be very effectively."

The Nibley family in 1966. Front left: Paul, Hugh holding Zina, Phyllis holding Martha, and Thomas. Back left: Charles Alex, Christina, Rebecca, and Michael.

gently smiling jaws of Socialism; is he not equally delighted to see the Saints rushing from the evils of Socialism into the enticements of Gracious Living and the Quick Buck? . . . In observing the students here I cannot but ask myself if we are not selling whisky to the Indians—telling many spoiled and selfish young people exactly what they want to hear. They would like nothing better than to believe that it is wicked to yield to any of the foolish and generous impulses of youth (that made so many of us radicals in our younger days), and that the very quintessence of righteousness is a zealous aspiration to acquire worldly status and success.[73]

Elder Romney did not ignore this strong but respectful perspective. He wrote back thanking Hugh for his "thoughtful letter," agreeing that his own words had been one sided, and promising to "better balance my talks in the future."[74] It is obvious that Elder Romney was not threatened by Hugh's advice, nor did he consider Hugh out of line for having written. Hugh's long-standing commitment to the Church and repeated attempts to defend the faith gave him a great deal of latitude to express his opinions with the Brethren.

---

[73]Hugh Nibley, Letter to Marion G. Romney, 2 March 1966. In Homer's *Odyssey*, Scylla was a nymph who changed into a monster and terrorized Odysseus and other mariners in the straits of Messina. Charybdis was the daughter of Poseidon and Gaea, whom Zeus threw into the sea off Sicily. By swallowing and spewing water, she created a dangerous whirlpool. Thus, to choose "between Scylla and Charybdis" is to choose between two equally hazardous alternatives.

[74]Marion G. Romney, Letter to Hugh Nibley, 21 March 1966, dictated 18 March 1966.

Elder Boyd K. Packer, an Assistant to the Twelve who was then serving as president of the New England Mission and was soon to become an apostle, wrote Hugh in 1966:

> Recently a non-member, a protestant clergyman as a matter of fact, attended one of your classes at the university [presumably BYU]. In reporting the experience to me he was very much impressed, and then consenting [sic] to your scholarship he concluded by saying the thing incredible to him was that here was a man who was a scholar and yet was a believer. He said in his seminary and in his circles a man so trained was never open in any declaration of his faith. The impression you made on this man was all together wholesome and he stands now in admiration of the Church because of this opportunity to meet with you and others there.[75]

Meanwhile throughout the decade of the 1960s, Phyllis continued to manage the home and children, largely on her own. On 29 November 1962, Martha was born. The following winter, Phyllis was pregnant again. Just prior to their final child's birth, Hugh explained to Paul Springer: "Years ago [Phyllis] had a very vivid dream or impression and ever since we have been convinced that we would have nine (9) children—and now No. 9 is on the way." Hugh added that he and Phyllis had "no objections as long as they are superior, and our last one, Martha, is a whole quatorze juillet of fireworks."[76] On 15 August 1964, another daughter was born and Hugh and Phyllis named her Zina—chosen partly because, since it began with the letter "Z," it symbolized the last baby. At this point, the children ranged from the newborn to seventeen-year-old Paul.

With eight surviving children, the Nibleys' modest house was "busting out at the seams," wrote Hugh, "but everybody seems to be having a good time."[77] The next year, however, eighteen-year-old Paul joined the Coast Guard, which Hugh confided "relieved the pressure slightly at home, but our small house with seven kids is still no haven of celestial calm, though I rather enjoy the seething turmoil."[78] In 1965, sixteen-year-old Christina was beginning to date. All of the older children—Christina, fifteen-year-old Tom, twelve-year-old Michael, nine-year-old Charles, and seven-year-old Becky—were busy with school and involved in drama, music, and art. Hugh and Phyllis always tried to support their children in their various endeavors and became frequent patrons of high school theatrical productions and concerts. And all of the children doted on the little girls—three-year-old Martha and year-old Zina.

Hugh continued to encourage Phyllis to play the cello in the Utah Valley Symphony and would babysit the children whenever she went to rehearsals. Hugh played the piano, usually in the evenings to unwind. He and Phyllis also ensured that each child had music lessons. As a result, the house was filled with music—a sonata on the stereo, Hugh playing the piano, or Phyllis and the children practicing their

---

[75] Boyd K. Packer, Letter to Hugh Nibley, 27 April 1966.

[76] Hugh Nibley, Letter to Paul Springer, 2 February 1964. "Quatorze Juillet," 14 July, is the French national holiday. When counting their children, Hugh and Phyllis always included their stillborn son, Isaac. Thus, with Zina's birth the family had nine children even though only eight survived.

[77] Hugh Nibley, Letter to Paul Springer, 2 February 1964.

[78] Hugh Nibley, Letter to Klaus Baer, 28 September 1965.

instruments. Sometime after 1958, Phyllis was invited to join a small group of musicians and their spouses. Calling themselves Musicians Anonymous, the group met every three or four weeks to play music and socialize. What started out as a quartet grew to an ensemble as new members were added, eventually including such notable Utah Valley musicians as Robert and Charlotte Cundick, Ralph and Margaret Woodward, Harold and Naomi Goodman, Darrell and Eva Stubbs, Clinton and Grace Nordren, Jim and Lynne Mason, Glenn and Barbara Williams, Merrill and Janet Bradshaw, and three Nibley couples: Reid and Marjorie, Richard and Nadine, and Hugh and Phyllis. "Those parties were really something," Reid remembers. But the music was often upstaged by the laughs. "Get Richard and Hugh together and the wit that sparked between those two was just unquenchable."[79]

Hugh served in the seventies quorum (then a local calling), for a short time as president. He also taught priesthood and Sunday School classes. Phyllis managed the chaotic family schedule and stretched the budget by canning fruit and sewing clothes for the children. She also taught or served in the presidencies of the Primary or Relief Society. After reporting to his friend Lucien Goldschmidt about his family's many activities, Hugh wrote, "So when the END comes it will find us all busy if not prepared."[80]

Hugh's already-scarce time at home evaporated completely when he was given a sabbatical to study Egyptian at the University of Chicago's Oriental Institute in 1966-67. Phyllis and the children stayed in Provo, while Hugh studied with Egyptologists John A. Wilson and Klaus Baer.[81] Hugh took Baer's class on Middle Egyptian biography; and in Wilson's class, he studied techniques of textual analysis and collation, focusing on five different manuscripts of some of the earliest Egyptian texts available. "Towards the end of the semester I was pulling ahead very nicely," Hugh appraised his progress in his sabbatical report. It was a gratifying experience to throw himself completely into the role of student: "Every seven years I am reminded what real study is like, and it is refreshing."[82]

While Hugh was in Chicago, he received an offer to teach in the Department of History at Clarion State College in eastern Pennsylvania. "They offered me far more than I was getting at BYU," said Hugh. "They had a very special dinner for me. I didn't realize it was special, but afterwards the Dean told me, 'You realize we had lobster tonight. That's the first time we've had that in years. That means you're a very special guy.'" The Dean asked him how much the school was offering him and when Hugh told him, the Dean stated, "You can get three times that much. Just ask them, you'll get more than that." Hugh was tempted by the move; however, his family was not anxious to be uprooted and neither the General Authorities nor President

---

[79] Reid Nibley, "Faith of an Observer," 478.

[80] Nibley, Letter to Lucien Goldschmidt, 28 December 1969; emphasis his.

[81] Hugh wrote to Baer, who had transferred back to his alma mater from Berkeley, on 28 September 1965: "We were in Berkeley last month and are in a position to inform you that you are sorely missed there; we felt rather conspicuous since we were wearing shoes and I had thoughtlessly shaved that morning, and so it was a relief to get away. Whatever the Oriental Institute is like, you made a wise move."

[82] Hugh Nibley, untitled transcript of a tape reporting on his sabbatical, 14 March 1967, 1, 2; photocopy of transcript in my possession.

Wilkinson wanted him to leave.[83] Phyllis, later recalling Hugh's three offers to leave BYU, commented supportively: "I think there was always the conflict between the material, the worldly success, and the gospel. And the gospel always won out. When he weighed things in the balance, it was where could he accomplish his work in supporting Joseph Smith and the scriptures. And the gospel always won out, but there were tremendous pulls from his friends, from his colleagues, and from other people who knew his abilities."[84]

Hugh's abilities in Egyptian were put to the test when, soon after his return to BYU on 27 November 1967, the Church acquired the Joseph Smith Papyri—the Egyptian texts from which Joseph Smith said he had received the Book of Abraham. Although not totally confident of his Egyptian, Hugh nevertheless felt pressure to publish something about the documents. As he put it, he "skirmished and sparred for time."[85] Monthly installments on the Book of Abraham began to appear in the Church's *Improvement Era*.[86] Klaus Baer read the series consistently, observing trenchantly, "They don't have much to do with the point at issue" but still were "a delight and should be compulsory reading for budding Egyptologists. They might be an effective inoculation against the pompous ass syndrome."[87]

Hugh had hoped to follow his studies in Egyptian with a trip to Libya in 1968 where he was awarded a Fulbright to teach ancient history to scholars in the king's palace. However, when U.S. relations with Lybia soured that year, his plans were canceled.[88] Hugh was likely frustrated by the cancellation but also grateful that he could continue to study the newly discovered papyri and write about the Book of Abraham.

Nor did he abandon his Brigham Young research. Gordon C. Thomasson, his graduate research assistant, drove frequently with him to the Church Historian's office in Salt Lake City where they sat in the "cage" to "read the original brittle volumes of Brigham's Manuscript History and make notes of anything of significance." The two filled out "stacks of 3x5's [note cards] all day long." On the first trip, Thomasson says Hugh asked him if he could take "accurate but indecipherable word

---

[83] Hugh Nibley, "Faith of an Observer," 65.

[84] Phyllis Nibley, "Faith of an Observer," 428.

[85] Nibley, "Intellectual Autobiography," xxvi. By "skirmishing and sparring" Hugh is evidently referring to "A New Look at the Pearl of Great Price," *Improvement Era*, serialized from January 1968 through May 1970. However, in 1968, Hugh also produced the following essays about the Book of Abraham and the recovery of the Joseph Smith Papyri: "Phase One" in *Dialogue: A Journal of Mormon Thought* 3, no. 2 (Summer 1968): 99-105; "Prolegomena to Any Study of the Book of Abraham," *BYU Studies* 8, no. 2 (Winter 1968): 171-78; "Fragment Found in Salt Lake City," *BYU Studies* 8, no. 2 (Winter 1968): 191-94; "Getting Ready to Begin: An Editorial," *BYU Studies* 8, no. 3 (Spring 1968): 245-54; and "As Things Stand at the Moment," *BYU Studies* 9, no. 1 (Autumn 1968): 69-102.

[86] The First Presidency asked Hugh to respond to the papyri and had requested that Wilkinson reduce Hugh's course load so he could spend "most of his time doing research." N. Eldon Tanner, Letter to Hugh Nibley, 29 March 1968. His faculty load reports show that his load was, in fact, reduced for the 1968-69 academic year. In fall 1968, he taught only one class (religions of the ancient Near East), and in the spring of 1969, he taught only Christian rites and liturgy.

[87] Klaus Baer, Letter to Hugh Nibley, 10 August 1968, Archives of the Oriental Institute, University of Chicago; photocopy in my possession.

[88] "Hugh Nibley: If He's Got it All Together, Why Does He Stand All Alone?" *BYU Today*, May 1974, 13.

for word notes." Thomasson suggested using Spanish equivalents for English words but writing them using the Greek alphabet. Hugh thought that would be fine. Hugh has always done his own notes in Gregg shorthand, with assorted Arabic, Hebrew, Greek, or Egyptian notes thrown in. As they left the archives each day, they handed over their note cards to A. William Lund, the senior assistant to the Church historian, who would "dutifully and carefully" inspect each one of their note cards, though as Thomasson puts it, "it was all Greek to him." Thomasson states that Lund was doing his best to protect the Church. "No one else was going to embarrass the Church by exploiting the Historian's Office as Fawn Brodie had, if [Lund] could do anything about it." Thomasson added somewhat remorsefully: "Neither of us enjoyed the subterfuge. That was simply a reality of working there."[89] Hugh incorporated this material into several articles and speeches during the late 1960s and early 1970s.[90]

As the 1960s came to a close, the political climate at BYU was becoming even more conservative. President Wilkinson, who had become the darling of far-right Republicans in Utah, had taken a year off to run for the U.S. Senate in 1964, was soundly defeated, and returned feeling that the school was becoming much too liberal. "I am going to do what I can to reverse [this] trend, which may mean the elimination of certain faculty members," he vowed in his journal.[91] Soon after Hugh returned from Chicago, an administration-backed student spy ring was exposed. "Sixteen students confessed to being employed as spies by the Administration," wrote Hugh lightly to Klaus Baer, "since when things have been considerably easier for the spyees."[92]

While campuses throughout the country were vehemently protesting the Vietnam War, many Religion Department faculty members were openly advocating John Birch ideology in their classrooms, anti-communist speakers were regularly brought to campus, and "moderate" or "liberal" speakers were banned.[93] At the same time, the "hippie" movement influenced youthful dress styles. Hair got longer. Men sported beards and moustaches. Blue jeans, dashikis, sandals, and peasant dresses brought a new look to college campuses. In reaction, Wilkinson tightened BYU's

---

[89] Gordon C. Thomasson, e-mail to Boyd Petersen, 21 July 2001.

[90] In 1967, Hugh produced "Brigham Young as a Leader," "Brigham Young as a Statesman," "Brigham Young as an Educator," and "Brigham Young as a Theologian." In 1970, he wrote "Brigham Young and the Enemy" and "Educating the Saints: A Brigham Young Mosaic," a more polished version of "Brigham Young as an Educator." In 1971, he wrote "Brigham Young on the Environment." In 1976, he delivered "More Brigham Young on Education" at the BYU Sperry Lecture. All but "Brigham Young as a Theologian" and the redundant "Brigham Young as an Educator" have been reproduced in *Brother Brigham Challenges the Saints*.

[91] Quoted in Bergera and Priddis, *Brigham Young University*, 197.

[92] Hugh Nibley, Letter to Klaus Baer, 12 February 1968, Archives of the Oriental Institute Archives, University of Chicago. Bergera and Priddis, *Brigham Young University*, 207-17. Hugh later stated that he was among the group that was spied on. "They were opening my mail, and tapping the telephone wires, and stealing manuscripts; they stole the whole manuscript for that book *Since Cumorah*." (He later explained that the book was published from his carbon copy of the manuscript.) Nibley, "Faith of an Observer," 64. As a Democrat, Hugh was likely suspect during the Wilkinson years, since those known to be targets of spies were all moderate Republicans who had publicly supported Wilkinson's opponent in the election. However, I have found no documentary evidence that proves Hugh's assertions.

[93] Bergera and Priddis, *Brigham Young University*, 180-98.

dress and grooming policy, announcing: "At this institution we must resist even the appearance, not only of evil, but also of the emulation of undesirable contemporary characters." By fall 1969, beards were outlawed and the length of sideburns was specified.[94]

Although Utah had joined the rest of the nation in handing Republicans a resounding defeat during Franklin D. Roosevelt's administration in the 1930s and 1940s, it had drifted back into the Republican camp during Eisenhower's administration in the 1950s. Sloanie was a Democrat and El was a Republican. Hugh had deliberately chosen to lean politically toward the Democrats, feeling that they addressed humanitarian and social issues better than the Republicans. For him, it fit his views better of how the gospel should be lived.[95] The political climate at BYU increasingly distressed Hugh. While he didn't agree completely with the "counter-culture"—especially with its open acceptance of drugs and liberal attitudes about sexuality—he felt that the school was overreacting.

On 8 May 1969, Republican Vice President Spiro Agnew spoke at BYU.[96] Hugh called him "an authentic Rhetor—Greek, political, ostentatious, and not overly scrupulous," an insightful observation about one of the nation's highest officers who would resign on 10 October 1973 after being convicted of income tax evasion. Commemorating Agnew's visit, Hugh published an article titled "How to Have a Quiet Campus, Antique Style," which appeared immediately following Agnew's address in BYU Studies. In it, Hugh compared the reactionary conservatism of the 1960s with that of ancient Greece.[97] "The century before Christ was a time of chronic and mounting social unrest," wrote Hugh. "It was a world gone mad," with political power consolidated in the controlling hands of Augustus Caesar. "But the cornerstone of his grand design for preserving peace and order was education."[98] As culture declined, Hugh argued, "scholarship does not go down with the ship. It torpedoes it."[99] Satirically, Hugh summed up the five rules for keeping students in line:

---

[94]Ibid., 109.

[95]President James E. Faust, another Democrat, takes this position: "I am a conservative on fiscal and property matters and I am a liberal in terms of human values and human rights. I believe what is said in the Book of Mormon, that the Lord values all of his children equally—black and white, bond and free, male and female, Jew and gentile—and that the Lord likewise has compassion for the heathen. As a result, I like to see all people enjoy every advantage, every blessing, every opportunity that comes to them by reason of citizenship. I also support what has been said by the Brethren—that it is in the interest of the Church to have a two-party system and not to have one party that is exclusively LDS and the other party exclusively non-LDS. Both locally and nationally, the interests of the Church and its members are served when we have two good men or women running on each ticket, and then no matter who is elected, we win." Quoted in James E. Bell, In the Strength of the Lord: The Life and Teachings of James E. Faust (Salt Lake City: Deseret Book, 1999), 86.

[96]His remarks, "Some Answers to Campus Dissent," appeared in BYU Studies 9 (Summer 1969): 433-39.

[97]Nibley, "How to Have a Quiet Campus, Antique Style," BYU Studies 9 (Summer 1969): 440-52, reprinted in The Ancient State, edited by Donald W. Parry and Stephen D. Ricks, Vol. 10 of The Collected Works of Hugh Nibley (Salt Lake City: Deseret Books/FARMS, 1991), 287-302.

[98]Nibley, The Ancient State, 290.

[99]Ibid., 297.

    1. Free the student from the necessity of any prolonged or strenuous mental effort.
    2. Give him a reasonable assurance that the school is helping him toward a career.
    3. Confine moral discipline to the amenities, paying special attention to dress and grooming. The student will have his own sex-life anyway.
    4. Keep him busy with fun and games—extracurricular activity is the thing.
    5. Allay any subconscious feelings of guilt due to idleness and underachievement by emphasis on the greatness of the institution, which should be frequently dramatized by assemblies and ceremonies; an atmosphere of high purpose and exalted dedication is the best insurance against moments of honest misgiving.[100]

These rules worked for Greece, Hugh pointed out with heavy irony. True, they brought about the collapse of Greek civilization, but at least they kept the students from rioting, just as they were doing at BYU.

For Hugh, who was then in his fifties, the 1960s were a decade of verbal sparring, both in academic circles and in Church circles. But these battles earned him the confidence of Church authorities, which, in turn, allowed him to criticize what he believed was an unbalanced approach to dealing with the radicalism of the decade. He had received and rejected his last invitation to relocate to another university; and it was within the BYU community that he balanced his scholarship, his cutting social commentary, and his committed defenses of gospel principles.

---

[100]Ibid., 302.

Hugh looks over a reproduction of Facsimile #1 from the Joseph Smith Papyri ca. 1967, his desk covered by stacks of his trademark notecards.

Photo courtesy L. Tom Perry Special Collections,
Harold B. Lee Library, Brigham Young University.

In looking at Hugh Nibley's work on the Pearl of Great Price, one is simply awestruck by the feat. Most good scholars will produce a couple of scholarly articles a year; a prolific one will produce half a dozen. When Hugh was working on the Pearl of Great Price, he was producing about one a month in addition to his regular publishing and teaching load. Given the rate he was writing one would expect that much of it would not have held up over the years—and some of it has not—but so much of it has held up so well that a quarter of a century or so later they are still the standard works on the subject. Even where his information is dated, he was asking the right questions and answering them to the best of the knowledge available to him.

—John Gee[1]

---

[1]John Gee, e-mail to Boyd Petersen, 24 April 2002.

Chapter 20

"The Book That Answers All the Questions": Hugh Nibley and the Pearl of Great Price

During the summer of 1962, Klaus Baer, then professor of Egyptian at Berkeley, wrote to Hugh asking about Egyptian connections to the Pearl of Great Price. No doubt he had received inquiries from Mormons searching for information about the Book of Abraham. Even during Hugh's 1959-60 sabbatical when he had studied Egyptian and Coptic with Baer, they had not discussed the Pearl of Great Price. "I have always steered clear of the Pearl of Great Price which, as you can well imagine, has been a Happy Hunting-Ground for crack-pots," Hugh wrote to Baer. "However, I would not be human if I were not guilty of speculating at times."[2] Hugh then launched into a seven-page, single-spaced technical discussion of the three facsimiles which accompany the text of the Book of Abraham. A few weeks later, Hugh wrote, exhilarated, to his friend Paul Springer that he and Baer "have been corresponding at some length about the Pearl of Great Price—he brought it up; I wouldn't dare."[3] While Hugh's letter to Baer was lengthy, it was the first of many exchanges that would follow between the two men.

Indeed, Hugh did not publish on the Pearl of Great Price until the discovery of the Joseph Smith Papyri in 1967.[4] It is clear, however, that he had a keen interest in the book and had indeed engaged in much speculation. In fact, it was the relationship

---

[2]Hugh Nibley, Letter to Klaus Baer, 2 August 1962, Klaus Baer Collection, Archives of the Oriental Institute, University of Chicago. I have not yet discovered the letter from Baer that prompted Hugh's response, but it is clear in Hugh's letter that Baer had initiated the discussion.

[3]Hugh Nibley, Letter to Paul Springer, 20 August 1962.

[4]While Hugh's first publication about the Pearl of Great Price did not come out until after the papyri were discovered, he gave at least one lecture, "On the Pearl of Great Price," earlier. On 13 May 1965, Hugh dis-

between the Book of Abraham and Egyptian that prompted Hugh to study Egyptian in the first place. Although he did not begin working with the Pearl of Great Price until he was in his late fifties, he certainly made up for lost time. As with the Book of Mormon, Hugh has defended the Book of Abraham and the Book of Moses as ancient texts, seeing in them strong evidence of Joseph Smith's divine calling. "I consider the Pearl of Great Price no less a marvelous work and wonder than the Book of Mormon," he wrote to one correspondent.[5] However, while it is the prophetic warning about the sins and conditions of our modern days that Hugh finds so compelling in the Book of Mormon, it is the profound doctrinal insights found in the Pearl of Great Price that Hugh believes make the book so important for the Church.

Hugh's interest in the Pearl of Great Price has been primarily directed toward the Book of Abraham and the Book of Moses.[6] He began working on both almost accidentally—on the Book of Abraham only after the 1967 discovery of the Joseph Smith Papyri and on the Book of Moses after he noticed significant parallels between it and some apocryphal documents he was teaching about in 1971.[7]

The papyri that Joseph Smith purchased in July 1835 which gave rise to the Book of Abraham were sold by Joseph's family after Lucy Mack Smith's death in 1856 and reportedly ended up in the Wood Museum in Chicago. For years most people assumed that they had been destroyed in the Chicago Fire of 1871.[8] Dale Morgan apparently had heard otherwise. In 1953, he passed on the report that one of Fawn Brodie's readers had

---

cussed the 1912 controversy when scholars, without really examining the book or the facsimiles, dismissed the Book of Abraham as a fraud. As Klaus Baer wrote to anti-Mormon publisher Jerald Tanner on 8 August 1968, "Nibley is perfectly right when he says that none of the 1912 scholars actually tried to translate the inscriptions and that Mercer is talking nonsense when he claims that 'they condemned it on purely linguistic grounds,' etc. The opinions (I'm sorry) are snap judgments." Photocopies of Baer's correspondence with everyone but Nibley courtesy of David J. Whittaker.

[5]Hugh Nibley, Letter to Bruce E. Holmes, 22 May 1985.

[6]For example, in the transcript of lectures for his 1986 Pearl of Great Price class, Hugh spends only one lesson each of twenty-six on Joseph Smith's translation of Matthew and on Joseph Smith's history. Nibley, *Ancient Documents and the Pearl of Great Price*, "Personal Development 80" (Provo, UT: BYU Press, 1986); published as *Teachings of the Pearl of Great Price* (Provo, UT: FARMS, 1986).

[7]*Apocrypha*, a Greek word which literally means "secret" or "hidden away," is a term used to describe primarily early Christian texts that did not make it into the Bible. *Pseudepigrapha* literally means "with false superscription." But the term is used to describe texts that are Jewish or Christian in origin, often attributed to biblical characters of Old Testament times, claim to contain God's word, often build upon an Old Testament theme or story, and almost always were composed between 200 B.C. and 200 A.D. See James H. Charlesworth, "Introduction for the General Reader," *The Old Testament Pseudepigrapha*, 2 vols. (Garden City, NY: Doubleday, 1986), 1:xxiv-xxv.

[8]Apparently William Smith, Joseph Smith Jr.'s brother, sold the mummies and papyri to one Abel Combs on 26 May 1856. It was believed that the entire lot was acquired by the Wood Museum, which later moved from St. Louis to Chicago. For a scholarly history of the papyri from 1841 until their discovery in 1966, see Stanley B. Kimball, "New Light on Old Egyptiana: Mormon Mummies, 1848-71," *Dialogue: A Journal of Mormon Thought* 16, no. 4 (Winter 1983): 72-90. For a broader history tracing the papyri's provenance from their origins in Egypt to Joseph Smith and finally to their discovery in 1966, consult H. Donl Peterson's *The Story of the Book of Abraham: Mummies, Manuscripts and Mormonism* (Salt Lake City: Deseret Book, 1995) and Jay M. Todd, *The Saga of the Book of Abraham* (Salt Lake City: Deseret Book, 1969). Despite their less scholarly approaches, both books, especially Todd's, include information about and reproductions of many significant documents, letters, and news articles. Yale-trained Egyptologist and FARMS resident scholar John Gee is presently working on a book that will likely become the authoritative source for this history.

written to her: "Did you ever see the evidence in the files of the curator of Egyptology of the Museum of Fine Arts in N.Y. which might prove that all of the papyri were not destroyed in the Chicago fire?"[9] Almost a decade later, while searching every possible location in 1962 for evidence that the papyri might have survived, Walter Whipple wrote to the Metropolitan Museum in New York. Soon thereafter museum officials responded that the museum indeed had papyri from the Smith collection and sent him a photograph of one part of the collection. It was Facsimile 1 from the Book of Abraham. Whipple did not try to keep the discovery a secret but did little with the information aside from showing the photograph to fireside and seminary groups.[10] Hugh, evidently hearing of Whipple's discovery, wrote Baer in 1962: "It is commonly believed that the originals of the [Joseph Smith Papyri] were destroyed in the Chicago fire, though recent evidence has been claimed that they escaped the fire and are still kicking around somewhere."[11] By March 1963, Hugh told Baer, "Somebody here has just located a pile of unpublished and unknown Egyptian manuscripts that were in the possession of Joseph Smith. I haven't seen them yet, but there may be something significant, one way or the other. They await the attention of the competent."[12]

Klaus Baer was intrigued by Hugh's letters, but he had made a discovery of his own:

> Your note about the Joseph Smith papyri has interested me immensely. In the meantime, I have received a lead on some other papyri definitely originating from his collection that are still in existence, unfortunately in hands that want to be kept quiet about (I practically had to take an oath). However, it seems to me by now reasonably certain that the Pearl of Great Price MSS are probably still in existence, and that the story of their being burned is just that, a story.[13]

Most likely the rumors Hugh was hearing and the discovery Baer had made were about the same set of papyri, then owned by the Metropolitan Museum.[14] During the 1966-67

---

[9] Dale Morgan, Letter to Stanley S. Ivins, 9 June 1953, in *Dale Morgan on Early Mormonism: Correspondence and a New History*, edited by John Phillip Walker (Salt Lake City: Signature Books, 1986), 199. Morgan suggested to Ivins that these papyri "would be of interest to you" and had obviously received the information from Brodie; but as far as I have been able to determine, neither Brodie, Morgan, nor Ivins followed up on the information, nor do I have more information on Brodie's reader, Edward Bowditch.

[10] Todd, *The Saga of the Book of Abraham*, 350-51. Whipple received his M.A. degree in Church history and Semitic languages from BYU in 1958 and went on to become vice-president of a transportation company in southern California and coauthor with Keith Terry of *From the Dust of the Decades: A Saga of the Papyri and Mummies* (Salt Lake City: Bookcraft, 1968). This Walter Whipple is not the same man as the current professor of Germanic and Slavic Languages at BYU.

[11] Hugh Nibley, Letter to Klaus Baer, 10 August 1962, Klaus Baer Collection, Archives of the Oriental Institute, University of Chicago.

[12] Hugh Nibley, Letter to Klaus Baer, 29 March 1963. Ibid.

[13] Klaus Baer, Letter to Hugh Nibley, 1 April 1963. Baer was assuming that there were perhaps two different collections of papyri—the one he had learned of and the one Hugh had mentioned. In the same letter. He asked Hugh if he could see the collection Hugh had learned of but phrased his request sensitively: "I know how ticklish matters regarding these documents can get and don't want to intrude."

[14] The Metropolitan had first seen the papyri when their owner, Mrs. Alice C. Heusser, the daughter of a woman who worked for the Abel Combs family, offered them for sale in 1918. The museum decided against acquisition at that time but finally bought them from Heusser's husband, Edward, in 1947. Peterson, Story

school year, Hugh used his sabbatical to study Egyptian at the Oriental Institute at the University of Chicago, where Klaus Baer was then teaching. Baer told a correspondent soon after Hugh's return to Provo that the papyri had not been mentioned between them after their 1962-63 exchange of correspondence "and I doubt very much that his stay in Chicago had anything to do with purchasing the papyri" since "none of the principals or intermediaries are anywhere around" Chicago.[15]

Baer later wrote: "The Metropolitan Museum was fully aware of what the papyri were when they first saw them in 1918, and they knew what they were doing when they acquired them [in 1947]. I saw photographs of them for the first time in 1963, I believe, and was asked at the time, on my honor not to tell anyone where they were and to keep the whole thing confidential."[16] In hindsight, Baer believed that "it may very well be that the Metropolitan Museum was dropping hints about the papyri to everyone they could think of that had some sort of Mormon connections (come to think of it, I was known to be a friend of Nibley's) in the hope that they'd do something about it—and we all took the request to keep the matter confidential too seriously."[17] It is difficult to untangle the reasoning of the museum officials. They may have been concerned that the museum would be inundated with visitors. Or they may have believed that the Church would want to suppress the documents. Evidently they wanted the documents discovered, but not before the Church knew about them. As Baer put it, "It is pretty clear to me" that the museum "didn't want anyone to find out about the papyri before the Mormon Church did, at least not publicly, and that [the museum] took their own sweet time about it." He added, "The situation evidently was handled in the manner that would least embarrass anybody, and the general attitude seems to have been to wait until an auspicious moment."[18] Or as Henry Fischer, Curator of Egyptian Art at the Metropolitan Museum, later wrote: "The matter is a very sensitive one, and we want to avoid becoming involved in doctrinal disputes that have nothing to do with our subject."[19]

In 1966, the Metropolitan finally found an emissary to take news of the papyri to Church authorities: Aziz Atiya, professor of Coptic and director of the University of Utah's

---

of the Book of Abraham, 242-45.

[15] Klaus Baer, Letter to Wesley P. Walters, 29 August 1967.

[16] Klaus Baer, Letter to Jerald Tanner, 13 August 1968.

[17] Klaus Baer, Letter to Jerald Tanner, 16 August 1968. Fellow Egyptologist John Wilson, in a letter to Glen Wade dated 31 August 1967, confirms that a museum in the United States had acquired the papyri but that he had been asked to not reveal the source. Wade summarized this letter and also a conversation with Atiya in an article reporting the papyri's discovery, "A Conversation with Professor Atiya," *Dialogue: A Journal of Mormon Thought* 2, no. 4 (Winter 1967): 54. Because this background was not central to the book, an examination of the Metropolitan's records and correspondence and interviews with its staff remains a future project for some scholar.

[18] Klaus Baer, Letter to Jerald Tanner, 13 August 1968. Evidently, someone, whom Baer does not identify, had given Hugh photos of the papyri several years before the Church acquired them. Klaus Baer, Letter to Wesley P. Walters, 29 August 1967, wrote: "In the summer of 1966, Prof. Nibley showed me enlargements of the photographs; they had been obtained by a third party and passed on to Prof. Nibley, who was evidently interested in purchasing the papyri." In another letter, Baer gave a different date: "Nibley has had photos since 1965 (that's when he showed them to me)." Klaus Baer, Letter to Jerald Tanner, 8 August 1968. Klaus Baer, Letter to Jerald Tanner, 13 August 1968, affirmed that Hugh "did not know where the originals were."

[19] Henry G. Fischer, Letter to Wesley P. Walters, 4 December 1967, photocopy courtesy of David J. Whittaker.

Middle East Center. He was working in the museum's Egyptian collection in the early spring of 1966 when he "discovered" the papyri.[20] Although not a member of the Church, he was certainly a friend of the Church and became an intermediary in transferring the papyri. After over a year of negotiations, on 27 November 1967 the Church announced that it had acquired eleven papyri that had been part of Joseph Smith's original collection.[21] Hugh commented on the transfer of the papyri from the Metropolitan Museum to the Church:

> This [acquisition] was a far more momentous transaction than might appear on the surface, for it brought back into play for the first time since the angel Moroni took back the golden plates a tangible link between the worlds. What we have here is more than a few routine scribblings of ill-trained scribes of long ago; at least one of these very documents [the original Egyptian papyrus of Facsimile No. 1] was presented to the world by Joseph Smith as offering a brief and privileged insight into the strange world of the Patriarchs.[22]

The Church published, "with commendable promptness" as Klaus Baer put it, photographic reproductions in the *Improvement Era* of February 1968.[23] Hugh was immediately drawn into the debate that followed. The same month that the papyri were published, Hugh wrote to Klaus Baer, "I had to give up a perfectly lovely research project when the Pearl of Great Price stuff turned up; naturally I am extremely reluctant to be drawn out on these matters, for reasons you will understand better than anybody else—mainly that I don't know anything about it."[24]

Hugh does not state what research project he gave up; but during this period, he was deeply involved in Brigham Young research and may have postponed it. It is likely that Hugh had bigger things planned for the Brigham Young material he was gathering from Church archives than the series of speeches and articles he produced in the late 1960s and early 1970s. Even though he admitted feeling unprepared to deal with the Egyptian papyri, he must have also relished the fact that the language skills he had been working to acquire since youth would now be put to the test. One thing Hugh did know was that

---

[20] According to Klaus Baer, Letter to Jerald Tanner, 13 August 1968, Atiya "'discovered' them because the Metropolitan Museum wanted them 'discovered.' Atiya played an indispensable role as mediator and middle man in helping the Church acquire the papyri."

[21] Peterson, *Story of the Book of Abraham*, 236-43. While the Metropolitan Musuem gave the papyri to the Church as a "gift," an unnamed donor made the gift possible by donating an artifact to the museum in exchange. According to Nibley, Letter to Roy W. Doxey, 26 May 1987, "The Joseph Smith Papyri were acquired in an exchange such as museums practice in the proper pursuit of their interests. The Metropolitan got an Egyptian head paid for by a generous donor in exchange for giving us the papyri." Klaus Baer, Letter to Jerald Tanner, 8 August 1968, added: "I am sure the Metropolitan Museum profited very handsomely on the papyri." I have no other information on the donor or on the artifact, but John Gee has told me that he has spent considerable time going through the acquisition files at the Metropolitan Museum and was not able to pinpoint this exchange.

[22] Nibley, "Prolegomena to Any Study of the Book of Abraham," *BYU Studies* 8, no. 2 (Winter 1968): 171.

[23] Klaus Baer, Letter to Jerald Tanner, 13 August 1968, described the photos as "quite good ones" and stated that the timely publication was especially impressive "when you consider that such an important Egyptological discovery as the Abusir papyri was jealously guarded by assorted public and private owners for 75 years during which they neither studied them nor let anyone else work with them."

[24] Hugh Nibley, Letter to Klaus Baer, 12 February 1968, Baer Collection, Archives of the Oriental Institute.

the connection between Egypt and the Church was important. Hugh wrote to Baer that Joseph Smith "believed that the Egyptians had an inside track on something, and invited others to enter the paths he was not able to follow."[25]

Hugh later stated that, since he was "not yet confident in Egyptian," he "skirmished and sparred for time."[26] Almost certainly part of Hugh's reluctance stemmed from the fact that the papyri fragments did not contain the same text as the Book of Abraham itself, as Hugh himself could tell at a glance. However, he made several early contributions to the debate, not the least of which was to involve Baer, whose competence in Egyptian and fairness was above question. Baer also pointed out: "Let's face it; it was Nibley and not the Egyptologists who noticed that the sensen fragments were not from the Book of the Dead."[27] Hugh confessed to one inquirer, "The documents are NOT hard to translate, but they are VERY hard to understand; so much so that Egyptologists today do not by any means agree as to what they are talking about."[28]

Translations of the papyri appeared rapidly, the first two from Modern Microfilm of Salt Lake City, the printing arm of Jerald and Sandra Tanner's anti-Mormon ministry. The first to appear came from Grant S. Heward, who was self-trained in Egyptian and had a personal quest to prove the Book of Abraham to be fraudulent.[29] The second came from Dee Jay Nelson, a pseudo-academic from Billings, Montana, whose claims to have a Ph.D. from the Oriental Institute were later proved to be fraudulent. He later claimed a Ph.D. from Pacific Northwestern University, a notorious diploma mill. Hugh immediately dismissed Heward's translation as relying too heavily on E. A. W. Budge's translation of the Book of the Dead. "Mr. Heward has simply followed Budge's translation of the Ani Papyrus all the way, even when it differed radically from the LDS Papyrus which he was supposed to be translating," wrote Hugh in his review for *BYU Studies*. In contrast, he found the translation by Nelson, then a member of the Church, a "conscientious and courageous piece of work."[30] Baer was less impressed by Nelson's work—"not because he makes a lot of mistakes (who doesn't?) but because he seems so convinced of the infallibility of his judgment." Baer continued, "It is just as easy, if not easier, to find places where Nelson has followed Budge against the manuscript as in Heward's attempt."[31] Hugh may have been so approving about Nelson's work and so harsh about Heward's because of Heward's

---

[25]Ibid.

[26]Nibley, "Intellectual Autobiography," *Timely on the Timeless* (Provo, Utah: BYU Religious Studies Center, 1978), xxvi.

[27]Klaus Baer, Letter to Jerald Tanner, 8 August 1968.

[28]Hugh Nibley, Letter to "Bro. Baldwin," 3 February 1968, Aziz Atiya Papers, Special Collections, J. Willard Marriott Library, University of Utah, Salt Lake City; emphasis Nibley's.

[29]Heward, "The Fall of the Book of Abraham," *Salt Lake City Messenger* (Modern Microfilm Co.), March 1968, 4. Grant S. Heward, Letter to I.E.S. Edwards, 14 March 1967, confessed that it was his hatred of what he considered the blind authoritarianism and the "racism" implicit in the Church policy of not ordaining African American men to the priesthood that motivated his efforts to prove the Book of Abraham false, since many Mormons used its description of the curse of Cain to justify the ban. He had been excommunicated from the Church by 1968 for, according to him, "questioning the accuracy of the translation of the Book of Abraham from Egyptian." Grant S. Heward, Letter to Klaus Baer, 8 January 1968. However, his association with the notoriously anti-Mormon Tanners may have had a greater impact on his Church status than his views on the Book of Abraham.

[30]Nibley, "Getting Ready to Begin: An Editorial," *BYU Studies* 8, no. 3 (Spring 1968): 245, 247.

[31]Klaus Baer, Letter to Jerald Tanner, 13 August 1968.

association with the Tanners, for whose work of discrediting Mormonism Hugh had no sympathy.[32] Both translations were published by the Tanners, but Nelson's came out as a pamphlet, *The Joseph Smith Papyri*, and only someone who knew that Modern Microfilm was the Tanners' press would make the connection. In contrast, Heward's was published in the Tanners' newletter, the *Salt Lake City Messenger*, under the headline, "The Fall of the Book of Abraham." Hugh knew that Nelson was a member of the Church but probably did not know that Nelson was also associated with the Tanners.

Nelson had written to Hugh in 1967, shortly before confirmation of rumors about the papyri's existence, evidently detailing his credentials and accomplishments. Hugh responded warmly, "Brother, you HAVE been around!" and added encouragingly: "I see no reason in the world why you should not be taken into the confidence of the Brethren if this thing ever comes out into the open; in fact, you should be enormously useful to the Church." Hugh confessed to Nelson that "I don't consider myself an Egyptologist at all, and don't intend to get involved in the Pearl of Great Price business unless I am forced into it—which will probably be sooner than that."[33] After the Church procured the papyri, Hugh wrote a short note introducing Nelson to Church archivists: "I think it would be wise to permit Prof. Dee J. Nelson to obtain copies of the photographs of the 11 papyrus fragments acquired from the Metropolitan Museum."[34]

Not long afterwards, Nelson began to tour the area, giving lectures to LDS audiences on the Book of Abraham. At these lectures he would often make claims about his background and credentials that seemed extreme. Hugh, irritated by this obvious attempt to milk the Mormon market, wrote an open letter of challenge that was widely circulated. In it, he detailed some of Nelson's more improbable claims: that "he [spoke] Egyptian with his family at the breakfast table," had made several TV appearances, and had been commissioned by the General Authorities to translate the Joseph Smith Papyri.[35] For his part, Nelson dismissed Hugh's writings on the subject as amateur and incompetent. As Klaus Baer pointed out to Jerald Tanner with some asperity: "Nelson is not a skilled Egyptologist; I think he is the last person to accuse Nibley of a 'superficial' knowledge of Egyptian. At least Nibley was sufficiently aware of his limitations not to rush into print with a translation."[36] Nelson began to dispute the authenticity of the Book of Abraham, accuse Joseph Smith of fraud, and claim that General Authorities asked him to lie about his findings. In 1975, Nelson left the Church. In 1978, he threatened to sue Hugh for challenging his conclusions and questioning his qualifications.[37] Nothing came of this threat. Robert and Rosemary Brown, a husband and wife investigating team from Mesa, Arizona, exposed Nelson as a fraud three years later.[38]

---

[32]Hugh did not mention the Tanners in *Sounding Brass* or any of his other books; but when they asked him for access to the journal of his great-grandfather Alexander Neibaur, Hugh returned an icy refusal on 8 March 1961.

[33]Hugh Nibley, Letter to Dee Jay Nelson, 27 June 1967. Hugh also gave some indication of the genuineness of his reluctance: "I actually don't know where the original Pearl of Great Price manuscripts are, though I could find out easily enough; so far my ignorance has served me well."

[34]Hugh Nibley, unaddressed note, 4 January 1968.

[35]Hugh Nibley, Letter to "Brother, Sister, Friend," 20 July 1977.

[36]Klaus Baer, Letter to Jerald Tanner, 13 August 1968.

[37]Dee Jay Nelson, Letter to Hugh Nibley, 7 January 1978.

[38]Robert and Rosemary Brown, *They Lie in Wait to Deceive: A Study of Anti-Mormon Deception*, Vol. 1 (Mesa, AZ:

Should Hugh have become more suspicious sooner? Perhaps, but Nelson fooled many, both within and outside of the Church. Hugh's sponsorship was confined to recommending that Nelson receive photos of the papyri, something he would have done for anyone knowledgeable about Egyptian.[39] In a letter to Robert Brown, Hugh commented: "In the short time I spent with [Nelson], it became immediately apparent that he *did* know something about Egyptian; more at least than any of our local scholars. Also, he claimed to be a good member of the Church—and what reason was there for disputing it?"[40] The episode illustrates both Hugh's generosity toward fellow scholars (misplaced though it was, in this case) and a touching naivete about human greed and ambition.

As the translations by more competent authorities made clear, the papyri contained an Egyptian text known as the Book of Breathings.[41] "There is really very little new here to shed light on the Book of Abraham," wrote Hugh. "As far as I can see their main value is still in calling the attention of Latter-day Saints to the existence of scriptures which they have studiously ignored through the years."[42] What the papyri confirmed was that Joseph Smith had owned them, that he spent many hours studying them, and that they are somehow related to the Book of Abraham.

Hugh held out the possibility that the text of the Book of Abraham may have come from papyri that are still lost. This was not a far-fetched speculation. According to Klaus Baer, at a "conservative estimate," the Church had acquired only eleven of possibly forty-one documents, leaving least thirty still missing, and Mormon scholar John Gee estimated that the acquired fragments represented at most 13 percent of Joseph Smith's total.[43] Baer did not personally accept Hugh's hypothesis, however, writing to one correspondent: "Despite what Nibley tries to argue, there can be no question in my mind that we know and now have the ancient Egyptian papyrus that Joseph Smith thought he was translating in the Book of Abraham: the Egyptian characters found running down the margin of several manuscripts of the English text of the Book of Abraham are on a fragment of papyrus that immediately adjoins the original of Facsimile No. 1."[44] This observation did not lead him to conclude that Joseph Smith was engaged in deception: "Joseph Smith's EAG [Egyptian Alphabet and Grammar] is not the kind of thing a man does who

---

Barnsworth Publishing, 1981).

[39]Hugh Nibley, Letter to Steven L. Mayfield, 14 April 1980: "I have never spent more than half an hour with Mr. Nelson altogether. I like him. A jolly and interesting character. Also, there is no reason why an amateur should not obtain a good knowledge of Egyptian. But the lavish reports of credentials by which he rests his case, instead of supplying the precise references to sources, which the public has a right to expect, have been recently checked by interested parties and found wanting on all points. The policy when the papyri came into possession of the Church was to let anyone see them who wanted to. When they were here at the BYU I showed them to Mr. Nelson who spent 20 minutes or so looking at them, we discussed things and that was that."

[40]Hugh Nibley, Letter to Robert L. Brown, 9 April 1981.

[41]*Dialogue: A Journal of Mormon Thought* 3, no. 2 (Summer 1968) published two articles: Richard A. Parker, "The Joseph Smith Papyri: A Preliminary Report," 86-88, 98-99; John A. Wilson, "A Summary Report," 68-85, followed by Klaus Baer, "The Breathing Permit of Hor," ibid., 3, no. 3 (Autumn 1968): 109-33.

[42]Nibley, "Phase One" *Dialogue: A Journal of Mormon Thought* 3, no. 2 (Summer 1968): 102.

[43]Baer, Letter to Jerald Tanner, 16 August 1968; John Gee, "A History of the Joseph Smith Papyri and the Book of Abraham," 3 March 1999, FARMS *Book of Abraham Lecture Series*, transcript, 11.

[44]Klaus Baer, Letter to a Mr. Gelling, 6 June 1982.

is perpetrating a fraud, Nibley is quite right there."[45] While Baer did not accept Joseph Smith as a prophet nor the Book of Abraham as the translation of an ancient document, he also pointed out in a letter to a man who was investigating the Church:

> Remember that the truth or falsehood of a religion does not depend on whether or not Joseph Smith was a competent Egyptologist. He thought that he could read Egyptian papyri and it is evident that he could not—but does that mean that the Book of Abraham (I am talking about the English text now) could not be inspired scripture? He thought he was translating a papyrus while actually his ideas were coming from somewhere else. The Book of Isaiah does not say "Behold a virgin shall conceive," yet all Christians believe that that mistranslation of the Hebrew text was divinely inspired. Both those who, like me, do not believe that Joseph Smith was a prophet and those who, like Nibley, believe that he was, will translate the papyri the same way. But they come to different conclusions regarding the validity of Joseph Smith's writings as sacred scripture. Ultimately the answer to your doubts will have to come from somewhere else.[46]

Baer took this stance because he didn't want "to attack the faith of a man to whom his faith was a very meaningful part of his existence, without my being able to replace it by anything else; and I am not in the business of making life meaningless for people. And as you are undoubtedly aware, the Mormon's faith does much more to make his life meaningful, purposeful, and satisfying than that of most persons in this country."[47]

Hugh also presented, right from the first, an argument that Klaus Baer stated "will get the Mormons out of the dilemma"[48]—namely, that it is not the Egyptian text but the English one that manifests Joseph Smith's prophetic gift. "We are completely in the dark as to how it was produced," wrote Hugh in 1968, "but we are anything but helpless with the wealth of detailed material it offers us to test it by." He continued, "The great mass of Abraham legends preserved in Jewish, Muslem, Christian, and even Classical sources are known to few Egyptologists, but as we read through them we find Egypt coming into the picture again and again in new and strange relationships." Since the Book of Abraham "is a book of legends about Abraham," Hugh concluded that it can only be "tested in the light of other such legends."[49]

At this early stage of the debate, Hugh also noted a tangential connection between the Book of Breathings and the Book of Abraham:

> With what subject matter does it have recognizable connection, bearing in mind that "the underlying mythology must be largely inferred"? Even the casual reader can see that there is cosmological matter here, with the owner of the papyrus longing to shine in the heavens as some sort of physical entity along with the sun, moon and Orion; also he places great importance on his patriarchal lineage and wants to be pure, nay baptized, so as to enter a higher kingdom, to achieve, in fact, resurrection and eter-

---

[45] Baer, Letter to Jerald Tanner, 8 August 1968. The Egyptian Alphabet and Grammar, was a failed attempt by early Church leaders to create an Egyptian grammar based on Joseph Smith's translation.
[46] Baer, Letter to Gelling, 6 June 1982.
[47] Baer, Letter to Wesley P. Walters, 2 September 1967.
[48] Baer, Letter to Jerald Tanner, 8 August 1968.
[49] Nibley, "Phase I," 102-3.

nal life. And these teachings and expressions are secret, to be kept scrupulously out of the hands of the uninitiated. And all these things have nothing to do with the subject matter of the Pearl of Great Price? What else, then?[50]

Despite his initial reluctance, Hugh wrote a series of articles that ran in the *Improvement Era* monthly between January 1968 and May of 1970. The series began, not by looking at the papyri themselves, but by looking at the credibility of Egyptologists who were involved in the 1912 controversy. In 1912, Rev. Franklin Spencer Spalding, the Episcopal Bishop of Utah, solicited the opinions of a group of scholars, including the famous Eduard Meyer, S.A.B. Mercer, Wallis Budge, and James Henry Breasted, about Joseph Smith's translation of the Book of Abraham. Since this work was published before the papyri had been discovered, all the team had to work with were the English text of the book and the accompanying Egyptian facsimiles. The scholars universally condemned the Book of Abraham but also spent very little time actually analyzing the book. Nor did the scholars all have the training and competence necessary to make such judgments.[51]

Klaus Baer frankly felt that some of Hugh's early installments in the *Improvement Era* were a red herring, but he also told a correspondent: "I find Nibley's *Era* articles among the most amusing reading that has come out of the whole business." Baer continued, "There is something to be said for not taking a serious matter too seriously; it prevents the development of rigid, ossified stands and is more likely to lead to the truth in the end."[52] But Baer also warned those who might be tempted to take Hugh's writings lightly:

> Nibley should not be underestimated. He is not a fully trained Egyptologist, but he knows a great deal in a great many fields, writes well, and is a skilled debater. His articles in [the *Improvement*] *Era* hit very close to home if you know something about the field. It is, unfortunately, true that Egyptologists have behaved like pompous asses with a claim to infallibility, that they have restricted themselves to ill-considered snap judgments in dealing with Mormons that they never would have ventured to produce if there had been a risk of critical examination by their colleagues, evaded problems, and insisted that the layman accept their opinions without question.[53]

But Hugh was also frustrated by the attitudes of contemporary Egyptologists, who were not able to see deeper ritual meanings in Egyptian texts. As late as 1980, he scoffed to his son Alex that some Egyptologists were only interested in the money and status of their high-titled positions, not in Egypt or Egyptians: "Some of them have admitted that freely,

---

[50]Ibid., 103-4.

[51]Spaulding published *Joseph Smith, Jr., As a Translator* (Salt Lake City: Arrow Press, 1912). Hugh discussed this work at great length in his *Improvement Era* series, much of it reproduced in the 2000 FARMS edition of *Abraham in Egypt* in chapters on "Joseph Smith and the Sources" and "Joseph Smith and the Critics." See Hugh Nibley, *Abraham in Egypt*, edited by Gary P. Gillum, Vol. 13 in *The Collected Works of Hugh Nibley* (1981; Salt Lake City: Deseret Books/FARMS, 2000).

[52]Klaus Baer, Letter to Jerald Tanner, 13 August 1968.

[53]Klaus Baer, Letter to Jerald Tanner, 3 August 1968. In a letter to Tanner ten days later, Baer lightheartedly defined "an 'authority' [as] a person who agrees with me" while "a 'pedantic, pompous ass' is one who disagrees."

but for all of them it is perfectly clear in the questions they ask, in which the first rule is, never under any circumstances hint that there might be something in any way out of the ordinary connected with anything the Egyptians ever said or did; just like us, they must never go beyond the acceptable little things of everyday life."54

Hugh wrote to Klaus Baer out of the same frustration: "I do believe that if the Egyptologists would spend a little time with the Hopis they would understand a lot of things about Egyptian religion that they can't even make decent guesses about now. Fact is, the documents are NOT self-explanatory."55 In 1970, Hugh told one correspondent that he was "concentrat[ing] on some relatively tidy and clear-cut Egyptian problems (as if ANYTHING Egyptian could be tidy and clear-cut!) and leav[ing] the rest alone."56 The next year, he wrote that he was

> doing this commentary to go with a very "literal" (oi) translation of the Book of Breathings. . . . And since I am too old to care in the least what anybody thinks about me, I have confined my observations to things of interest only to Mormons and Hopis. The footnotes are really essays on special subjects in which LDS practice closely parallels Egyptian, meaning of course things not for public delectation.57

This approach, while unquestionably reflecting Hugh's deepest personal interests, was also a way of sidestepping some of the difficult problems raised by the Joseph Smith Papyri.

Hugh did not rush into print. It was eight years after the discovery of the papyri that Hugh published his own translation of and commentary on the Joseph Smith Papyri in *The Message of the Joseph Smith Papyri: An Egyptian Endowment* (Salt Lake City: Deseret Book, 1975).58 Just before it came out, Hugh told a correspondent: "Though the manuscripts now available

---

54 Hugh Nibley, Letter to Charles Alexander Nibley, 27 June 1980.

55 Hugh Nibley, Letter to Klaus Baer, 12 August 1968, Baer Collection, Archives of the Oriental Institute; emphasis Hugh's. Writing to Baer again on 2 September 1969, Hugh commented: "As to the Big Ritual Picture which has been my obsession for years, it is gratifying to see how many experts in how many fields are sort of coming into line. Some of the most die-hard positivists are beginning to see that there IS a rather uniform pattern of ritual and doctrines in the Old World. Though I may have been over-eager in detecting parallels and pushing analogies (the understatement of the year, you will say!), still it is becoming clearer to more and more people every day that there is 'something there.' It is because I have been aware of this all along that I have not been disturbed by what I have considered more or less irrelevant attacks on the Pearl of Great Price."

56 Hugh Nibley, Letter to Robert F. Smith, 18 February 1970; emphasis Nibley's.

57 Hugh Nibley, Letter to Robert F. Smith, 28 October 1971.

58 The debate about the significance of the Joseph Smith Papyri continues today, most recently in a cluster of articles published in *Dialogue: A Journal of Mormon Thought* 33, no. 4 (Winter 2000). Speaking as the objective outsider, Robert K. Ritner, professor of Egyptology at the University of Chicago, gives a new translation of the papyri, updating and correcting previous translations by Klaus Baer and Hugh Nibley "in light of Egyptological advances" ("The Breathing Permit of Hor: Thirty-Four Years Later," 97-119). A non-Mormon, Ritner taught John Gee at Yale and is now employed at Chicago's Oriental Institute, the same institution where James Henry Breasted, John A. Wilson, and Klaus Baer had taught earlier. Second, Edward H. Ashment takes a perspective critical of the Book of Abraham's authenticity. A former Nibley student who did Ph.D. work in Egyptian philology at the University of Chicago, Ashment evaluates the implications of Joseph Smith's authorship of one version of the Egyptian Alphabet and Grammar ("Joseph Smith's Identification of 'Abraham' in Papyrus JS 1, the 'Breathing Permit of Hor,' 121-26). Third, taking a position similar to Hugh's and employing a similar strategy, Bradley J. Cook, a Ph.D. in Middle East Stud-

do not contain the text of the Book of Abraham as described by Joseph Smith, the matter they do contain can be related to Abraham at many points. Taken by themselves, the contents of these papyri are of peculiar interest to Latter-day Saints."[59] That "peculiar interest" was the Mormon temple ceremony. Hugh spent little time in the book arguing a connection between Abraham and the text of the Book of Breathings. Rather he argued, implicitly, for a connection between the Book of Breathings and the Mormon temple ceremony—not that Joseph Smith derived the endowment from the Book of Breathings but that he restored rituals present from the foundation of our world, traces of which are also found in the Book of Breathings as well as in other places, such as Hopi ceremonies.[60]

Hugh followed *The Message of the Joseph Smith Papyri* with *Abraham in Egypt* in 1981, a closer look at parallels between the Book of Abraham and ancient lore. Abraham has continued to be the main focus of Hugh's work to the present.[61] In his later writings especially, Hugh combines sources from apocryphal literature to provide a fuller picture of Abraham—frustratingly failing, sometimes, to acknowledge the provenance, date, and background of these often late and sometimes dubious sources. Regardless, Hugh believes that likely elements of true Abraham lore have been preserved intact in these later texts. As he noted about Egyptian stories in Jewish and Christian documents, "Many recent studies confirm . . . that much authentic Egyptian matter was carried over into Judaism and Christianity, but that such Egyptian stuff instead of being the spoiled and rancid product of a late and degenerate age, represented the best and oldest the Egyptians had to offer."[62] Intriguingly, nearly all of this material was "unknown to the scholars of the last century," and he stated that anti-Mormon critics "all insist[ed] that [Joseph] Smith himself invented his wild stories about Abraham, never suggesting that he might have stolen them. Indeed where would he have gotten them?" Hugh describes. "In my own searching I found here a piece and there a piece, tidbits, but only in texts published in the present century did I find them put together in a single story."[63] Hugh spent the rest of the decade working to show that, not only were these parallels significant, but they also could not have been known to the young prophet on the Ohio frontier. As Hugh stated his position in 1979, "I can assure you [the Book of Abraham] is a true and faithful history translated by the gift and power of God. I have never had the slightest reason for doubting this but find everyday new evidence for its truth and divinity."[64]

---

ies from Oxford University who currently serves as the Vice President of College Relations at Utah Valley State College, examines significant parallels between the Book of Abraham and Islamic sources ("The Book of Abraham and the Islamic *Qisas al-Anbiya* (Tales of the Prophets) Extant Literature," 127-46).

[59]Hugh Nibley, Letter to Sharon Sartian, 24 April 1975.

[60]Much later, Hugh tied Abraham to this picture even more clearly in his 6 April 1999 lecture "Abraham's Creation Drama," a reading of the Book of Abraham as a temple text. It was published as "Abraham's Temple Drama," in *The Temple in Time and Eternity*, edited by Donald W. Parry and Stephen D. Ricks (Provo, UT: FARMS, 1999), 1-42.

[61]See Chapter 25, "One Eternal Round, 1990-Present" for Hugh's continuing preoccupation with Abraham.

[62]Hugh Nibley, "What Is 'The Book of Breathings'?" *BYU Studies* 11, no. 2 (Winter 1971): 159.

[63]Nibley, "Some Reasons for the Restored Gospel," 13. Hugh is right about the inaccessibility of the Abraham material. *The Apocalypse of Abraham* was translated into German in 1897 but not into English until 1918.

[64]Hugh Nibley, Letter to "Sister McQuiddy," 30 April 1979. In this letter and several others composed about this time, Hugh responded to rumors that he had left the Church because he believed the Book of Abraham was a fake. Hugh was outraged by the rumors: "Nothing could be further from the truth than the reports

In 1976, Hugh got his first chance to visit the land where Abraham lived: Egypt. "In the late '70s I discovered that Hugh Nibley had never been to Egypt," remembers Truman Madsen. Although Egypt had been Hugh's central concern for a decade, he had been forced to rely on "his own thorough reading," says Madsen. Coincidentally, Madsen was arranging a tour to the Holy Land for a group of Mormon travellers, so he invited Hugh to join them as a guest. Hugh was already going to be in Greece on university business,[65] so he and Phyllis were able to join Madsen's group in Israel. But Egypt was definitely the highlight of the tour. "One of the delights of that trip was to see the wonder and the boyish euphoria that emerged from his seeing these things," recalls Madsen. "He was as happy and euphoric as a child on Christmas morning." Madsen also said that, while the group was happy to have Hugh along, they were not thrilled with his selection of the archaeologists' "hang-out" for accommodations. "We were in the oldest hotel," remembers Madsen. "He loved it [but] my group almost lynched me. . . . It was the old Shepherd Hotel, and [Hugh] was physically and psychologically at ease in Egypt, and everybody else was saying, you know, 'Fried tarantula for breakfast?' And the smell of cockroaches and the oil and so on." Despite Hugh's choice of hotels, the tour group enjoyed having Hugh along to explain the sites to them. They ended up asking so many questions that Hugh spent much of his time lecturing. At the end of each day, he was hoarse after speaking so much. Of this "free" trip, he later ruefully commented, "'I earned it,'" recalls Madsen.[66]

During the 1970s, Hugh took a brief but substantial detour from Abraham to look at the Book of Moses. During a course he was teaching in fall 1971 on apocryphal literature, which, he complained, the administration had "thrust upon" him, Hugh noticed parallels between the Book of Moses and the pseudepigraphal Enoch literature. The discovery led to several articles as well as another series in the *Ensign*, the successor to the *Improvement Era*, titled "A Strange Thing in the Land: The Return of the Book of Enoch," running from October 1975 to August 1977.[67] In a letter discussing Moses 1, Hugh commented, "I think the Apocryphal connections of that first chapter are simply staggering. It seems to combine the four qualities which Matthew Arnold says are combined only in Homer: eminent rapidity (brief, vigorous and to the point), simplicity, nobility of subject, and nobility or exaltation of treatment."[68]

Hugh also discussed the Enoch literature in "The Book of Enoch as a Theodicy,"[69] a paper he presented at the joint regional meeting of the Society for Biblical Literature and the American Academy of Religion held in Denver 3-5 April 1974. It was the first academic conference in which Hugh had participated since teaching at Claremont. Two of

you hear about my leaving the Church."

[65]The exact nature of this business is not clear. He was actually on assignment from the General Authorities. Hugh recalls it as an unsuccessful attempt to work out some kind of exchange with the University of Athens, but the only documentation consists of two memos about who would cover his classes while he was gone. Ellis Rasmussen, long-time dean of Religious Studies, called the trip "something of a mission in the Mediterranean area, particularly in Greece. Ellis T. Rasmussen, Memo to Robert K. Thomas, 1 September 1976, Oaks Papers, Robert K. Thomas Subcollection.

[66]Truman G. Madsen, "Faith of an Observer," 461-63, 469-70.

[67]This series was republished in *Enoch the Prophet*, edited by Stephen D. Ricks, Vol. 2 of The Collected Works of Hugh Nibley (Salt Lake City: Deseret Books/FARMS, 1986), 91-301.

[68]Hugh Nibley, Letter to Robert F. Smith, 11 January 1976.

[69]Republished in *Enoch the Prophet*, 66-88.

Hugh's colleagues from BYU's Department of Ancient Scriptures, S. Kent Brown and Wilfred Griggs, had noticed that there was a proposed section at the conference on "The Apocalyptic." Knowing that Hugh had been working on Enoch, they persuaded him to submit a paper. Kent Brown remembers that Hugh read his paper at a morning session of the conference. "It was a very nice paper and I think people appreciated it; but it was during the questions and answers that little by little the amazing knowledge Hugh had was revealed to every attendee."

In response to one question, Hugh quoted a lengthy passage from Shakespeare; in response to another he quoted from the *Odyssey* in Greek, tapping out the cadence with his knuckles on the table, and then translating for his audience. "That was sort of the first piece of bedazzlement for those who were there," remembers Brown. The same erudite fireworks continued during question-answer periods and during breaks as the conference continued. "Hugh was in the middle of them," recalls Brown, "and he'd cite passages from Egyptian literature. He was pulling stuff from Ancient Near Eastern sources, Babylonia and Assyria, and so on, plus the Classical world in addition to scriptural passages, the New Testament and Old Testament." Everyone present soon recognized that Hugh was someone to be reckoned with. Graduate students clustered around Hugh during breaks, peppering him with questions and listening in stunned admiration. At one point George MacRae, then professor of religion at Harvard, commented, amazed, "It is simply obscene that a person knows this much." Brown grinned at the memory: "George had simply been knocked off his chair. He was a very big guy, but he had really been swept up by this whole thing." Brown summarized: "It was an astonishing set of exchanges, and it was clear that Hugh wasn't just a point of light. He was a concentration of light. It was clear that he had a grasp of things that nobody else possessed."[70]

Most of Hugh's research on the Pearl of Great Price has focused on demonstrating that the Book of Abraham and the Book of Moses are ancient texts, restored through revelation by Joseph Smith. As evidence for this claim, Hugh has looked at ancient lore preserved in apocryphal and pseudepigraphal sources. Two principal works have provided ample parallels for the Book of Abraham: "The Apocalypse of Abraham" and "The Testament of Abraham." "The Book of Abraham is right at home in the world of the Apocalypse and Testament of Abraham," wrote Hugh in *Abraham in Egypt*.[71] The Apocalypse of Abraham, a first-person tale, tells how Abraham rejects his father's idols after he sees several stone idols crushed and a wooden idol consumed by fire. Abraham then searches for the true God, who reveals himself to Abraham and commands him to offer sacrifices. As he does, an angel appears and takes Abraham on a tour of the cosmos where he sees all of God's works, witnesses the creation, and sees Adam and Eve in the Garden of Eden.[72] Hugh has demonstrated both thematic and linguistic parallels between the Book of Abraham and the Apocalypse of Abraham.[73] But he has also found comparisons in other "nonbiblical but very ancient stories about Abraham, most of them fairly

---

[70] S. Kent Brown, interviewed by Boyd Petersen, 26 September 2001.

[71] Hugh Nibley, *Abraham in Egypt*, edited by Gary P. Gillum, Vol. 13 of *The Collected Works of Hugh Nibley* (1981; Salt Lake City: Deseret Books/FARMS, 2000), 57.

[72] James H. Charlesworth, ed. and trans., *The Old Testament Pseudepigrapha*, 2 vols. (Garden City, NY: Doubleday, 1983), 1:681-705.

[73] Nibley, *Abraham in Egypt*, 13-26.

recent discoveries, the rest long despised by normative Judaism and ignored by scholars but at last receiving serious attention in some quarters." He sums up this lore:

> The dominant theme of these stories is the jealousy of a great king who fears for his priesthood and kingship—both threatened by Abraham—from the time Abraham's birth is foretold by the king's wise men to the time the king finally recognizes the true God, after an unsuccessful attempt to put Abraham to death on an altar. Being placed on an altar at the urging of the king's courtesans, Abraham prays for deliverance, an angel of the Lord appears, and at the last moment the altar is overthrown and the erstwhile sacrificing priest becomes the victim.[74]

Hugh has also found evidence for the Book of Moses from this extracanonical lore, focusing particular attention on the figure of Enoch. "It is strange that the man to whom the Bible gives only a few brief sentences should be the colossus who bestrides the Apocrypha as no other," wrote Hugh.[75] Significantly, the Book of Moses also devotes a great deal of attention to Enoch. Hugh has found much in the apocryphal Books of Enoch that parallels what Hugh has called "the Book of Enoch section of the Pearl of Great Price."[76] As Hugh wrote to one correspondent, "As far as I am concerned it goes far beyond coincidence: in those two chapters alone, 6 and 7, you have an epitome of the Enoch literature."[77] In 1977, he told a correspondent, "Last night for Family Night, I got into the first chapter of Moses—a prelude to everything and having just found some interesting Enoch passages in Odeberg's book on John was enormously impressed by the parallels it produces with the Moses passages."[78]

Additionally, Hugh has noticed many details in the Enoch sections of the Book of Moses that are also found in the pseudepigrapha. "Here is a neat test for Joseph Smith," challenged Hugh. "The 'Son of Man' title does not occur once in the Book of Mormon . . . and in the Pearl of Great Price it is confined to one brief section of the Book of Enoch where it is used no fewer than seven times." Significantly, the expression is common in the Enoch literature. As Hugh stated, "The prophet [Joseph Smith] is right on target."[79] Likewise, the Book of Moses detail of God weeping over his creation prior to the flood (Moses 7:28-29), a moving but radical theological contribution, is also found in the ancient Enoch literature.[80]

One detail that Hugh noted impressed even a non-Mormon specialist in Enoch literature. Hugh had noticed that the only nonbiblical name that appeared in the Book of Moses is Mahijah, the man who demands that Enoch tell the people who he is and where he came from (Moses 6:40). Enoch also says that he heard the voice of the Lord in the

---

[74] Nibley, *Abraham in Egypt*, 78-79. For a more extensive overview of noncanonical Abraham lore, see Louis Ginzberg, *The Legends of the Jews*, 7 vols. (1909; Baltimore: Johns Hopkins University Press, 1998), 1:185-308.

[75] Nibley, *Enoch the Prophet*, 19.

[76] Hugh Nibley, Letter to Robert F. Smith, 28 October 1971.

[77] Ibid.

[78] Hugh Nibley, Letter to Robert F. Smith, 11 January 1977. Hugh is referring to Hugo Odeberg, *The Fourth Gospel: Interpreted in Relation to Contemporaneous Religious Currents in Palestine and in the Hellenistic-Oriental World* (Chicago: Argonaut, 1968).

[79] Nibley, *Enoch the Prophet*, 37.

[80] Ibid., 69.

land Mahujah (Moses 7:2). Hugh had "a shock of recognition" when he discovered in the Aramaic Enoch fragments from Qumran "the name Mahujah leaping out of the pages again and again."[81] Hugh wrote about this discovery to Matthew Black, professor of divinity and biblical criticism at the University of St. Andrew's and principal at St. Mary's College in Scotland.[82] Black had translated and done a commentary on the Ethiopic Book of Enoch. When Black later visited BYU, Hugh observed: "He brought my letter with him, but all he would say was that whoever produced the Book of Moses was 'saturated' in pseudepigraphal Enoch literature."[83]

For Hugh, the parallels between the Book of Abraham and the Book of Moses on the one hand and the ancient extracanonical texts on the other are strong evidence of Joseph Smith's divine calling. No matter how the translation process worked, it is clear to Hugh that the texts came by inspiration. "Joseph Smith translated books from a number of ancient languages, none of which he could read," wrote Hugh to one inquirer. "The translations were given to him by revelation, an imponderable process. There is no way of testing the translations by analyzing the method. But there is a virtually foolproof way of testing the authenticity of all those translations, namely, by comparing them with the larger body of literature to which they are supposed to belong."[84] The Book of Abraham and the Book of Moses are the work of genius. But it is spiritual genius, not intellectual genius that gave us these texts. When one reader expressed concern that the papyri's discovery proved Joseph Smith did not understand Egyptian, Hugh responded robustly, "Of course Joseph Smith didn't know Egyptian. That is why we can safely say that the Book of Abraham is inspired. He did not know Nephite, but gave us the Book of Mormon, the detailed history of a nation covering a thousand years. In each case the only question that can be directly and positively addressed is whether the book itself is authentic or not. There is no shortage of evidence supporting an affirmative answer in both cases."[85]

The Book of Moses likewise bears witness of Joseph Smith's inspiration as a prophet. As Hugh stated, the Enoch section of that book "offers the nearest thing to a perfectly foolproof test—neat, clear-cut, and decisive—of Joseph Smith's claim to inspiration."[86] But Hugh is particularly impressed by the doctrinal richness of the Pearl of Great Price texts. As Hugh stated in his 1989 Pearl of Great Price class, Joseph Smith "has really given the world something it did not have."[87]

In "A Strange Thing in the Land," Hugh noted that the four books contained in the Pearl of Great Price paradoxically form a whole, even though Apostle Franklin D. Richards more or less had simply gathered up four conveniently available texts in England and printed them as a pamphlet in 1851.[88]

---

[81]Ibid., 277-78.

[82]Born in 1908, Black was a professor at St. Mary's College from 1954 to 1978, his expertise well recognized on both the Old and New Testament and on apocryphal literature. He published *The Ethiopic Book of Enoch* (Leiden: Brill, 1985), a translation and commentary on the text. He died in November 1994. Obituary, *Daily Telegraph* (London), 8 November 1994, 23.

[83]Hugh Nibley, Letter to Robert F. Smith, 11 January 1976.

[84]Hugh Nibley, Letter to Michael R. Alder, 12 December 1984.

[85]Hugh Nibley, Letter to "Brother Baker," 30 October 1986.

[86]Nibley, *Enoch the Prophet*, 94.

[87]Nibley, *Ancient Documents and the Pearl of Great Price*, Lecture 5, 14.

[88]According to Robert L. Millet, "Pearl of Great Price," *Encyclopedia of Latter-day Saint History*, edited by Arnold

> The Pearl of Great Price should be read as a single work, an epitome of world history, summarizing and correlating in the brief scope of less than sixty pages the major dispensations of the gospel, past, present, and future. The story is told largely by excerpts, which announce themselves as fragments of original books written by Adam, Enoch, Abraham, Moses, and Joseph Smith, all centering about the figure of Christ and his mission in the meridian of time, with a preview of the millennium thrown in.[89]

The purpose of the Pearl of Great Price, as Hugh stated during an interview, is to serve as "a linch pin that ties together . . . the experience of the human family, and it takes us to cultures and to times far removed from our own."[90]

Prior to the discovery of the papyri in 1967, the Pearl of Great Price was often underrated or ignored by members of the Church. Hugh recalls that it was not taught as a separate class when he first came to BYU because "many professors felt that you couldn't possibly find enough in the Pearl of Great Price to fill a whole quarter of instruction. So they divided it up with the Doctrine and Covenants."[91] Hugh has always found it difficult to get through even one book of the Pearl of Great Price during the course of a semester. At the conclusion of one semester, Hugh mused to twenty-three-year-old Alex, then on a mission in Japan in 1979:

> This is the last day of the semester; I had a good class in the Book of Abraham and barely touched the subject. That little book of only five chapters fills an immense void in our knowledge and is an incomparable admonition to faith. A performance quite as marvelous in its way as the Book of Mormon, and as evidence even more potent than the Book of Enoch [in the Book of Moses]. Which comes as a surprise, though it should not.[92]

In *Enoch the Prophet* Hugh stressed the worth of this "small" book:

> It's been assumed, because the Pearl of Great Price is a little, thin book, that anybody can handle it and write a commentary about it. Actually it is the most difficult and portentous of our scriptures, and we can't begin to approach the ancient aspects of this

---

K. Garr, Donald Q. Cannon, and Richard O. Cowan (Salt Lake City: Deseret Book, 2000), 900-902, these selections were "some of his [Richards's] favorite documents. They included some revelations already in the Doctrine and Covenants and the poem, "O Say What Is Truth?""

[89] Nibley, *Enoch the Prophet*, 154-55. Hugh emphasized the unity of the Pearl of Great Price: "The Pearl of Great Price might well be called the Book of Six Testaments, namely: (1) the Book of Moses, including the Visions of Moses and the Writings of Moses, designated in the ancient manner as 'the words of God which he spake unto Moses' (Moses 1:1); (2) A Revelation of the Gospel unto Our Father Adam, excerpted from his Book of Remembrance and quoted in (3) the Prophecies of Enoch; (4) the Book of Abraham Written by His Own Hand upon Papyrus [this is the title of the book after the ancient fashion, not merely the colophon of one particular manuscript only]; (5) an Extract from the New Testament, 'being the 24th Chapter of Matthew,' also called 'the Little Apocalypse' and with equal propriety 'the Little Enoch'; (6) Extracts from the History of Joseph Smith, the Prophet (54-55).

[90] Nibley, "Faith of an Observer," 347.

[91] Nibley, *Ancient Documents and the Pearl of Great Price*, Lecture 1, 11.

[92] Hugh Nibley, Letter to Charles Alexander Nibley, n.d., ca. 1979. It begins "On the matter of letter writing."

most difficult of books unless we know a lot more than we do now. The Prophet Joseph says, "The things of God are of deep import; and time, and experience, and careful and ponderous and solemn thoughts can only find them out." It's no small thing to approach a writing like the Pearl of Great Price.[93]

Fourteen years later, Hugh again stressed the doctrinal significance of the book in another letter to Alex, then running a dance studio in Guam. "I have chosen to teach the Pearl of Great Price this Fall—it is the book that answers all the questions. Seven covenants, handed down by the founders of Seven Dispensations, each telling it in the First Person, and each now matched by an apocryphal writing of great importance that was not even known to exist in Joseph Smith's day."[94]

Among the problems that the Pearl of Great Price answers are those that Hugh refers to as "the Terrible Questions."[95] The questions are terrible because their answers can only be found by revelation: Will there be life after death? What is it like? Will I be myself or turn into some other creature? Where did I come from? Why am I here? Hugh insists that "only our Pearl of Great Price can answer" these questions, and, in his Pearl of Great Price class, refers to the book as "our handbook [for the] terrible questions," because it restores material that has been lost from the Bible. He quoted Old Testament scholar William F. Albright as saying: "Our Hebrew texts have suffered more from losses than from glosses" and also pointed out that R. H. Charles, one of the principal editors of the Book of Enoch, said that nearly all writers of the New Testament were familiar with Book of Enoch. Even the early Church Fathers and apologists quoted from the book. For all of them, "it had all the weight of scripture." As Hugh summarized: "It is the Pearl of Great Price alone to date that restores precious parts that were removed from the scriptures."[96]

Hugh sees, as one of the most significant doctrinal contributions of the Pearl of Great Price, its restoration of the link between religion and cosmology—in other words, the study of the physical universe. "Without cosmology in religion, an important ingredient is missing," Hugh stated. "This is what the Pearl of Great Price restores with a vengeance."[97] Hugh has called cosmology "an indispensable element of ancient wisdom literature, and one which abounds in the Book of Moses . . . and the Book of Abraham."[98] He expanded this thought in a letter to Alex: "What the Book of Abraham shows is that we are in the midst of eternity. We are surrounded by evidences of it."[99] Furthermore, Hugh believes that these teachings "command greater respect at the present time than ever before," since the idea of other worlds like ours is no longer viewed as impossible.[100]

---

[93]Nibley, *Enoch the Prophet*, 3.

[94]Hugh Nibley, Letter to Charles Alexander Nibley, 28 August 1993. In fact, Hugh's eagerness for symmetry betrays him; the Book of Moses is written in the third person, not the first person.

[95]Nibley, "The Terrible Questions," *Temple and Cosmos: Beyond This Ignorant Present*, edited by Don E. Norton, Vol. 12 of *The Collected Works of Hugh Nibley* (Salt Lake City: Deseret Book/FARMS, 1992), 336-78.

[96]Nibley, *Ancient Documents and the Pearl of Great Price*, Lecture 2, 2; ibid., Lecture 4, 1.

[97]Ibid., Lecture 5, 3.

[98]Nibley, "The Book of Mormon: Forty Years After," *The Prophetic Book of Mormon*, edited by John W. Welch, Vol. 8 of *The Collected Works of Hugh Nibley* (Salt Lake City: Deseret Book/FARMS, 1989)551.

[99]Hugh Nibley, Letter to Charles Alexander Nibley, n.d., ca. 1979. It begins "On the matter of letter writing."

[100]In "Getting Ready to Begin," 254, Hugh notes that Walter Sullivan (*We Are Not Alone* [New York: Signet,

Not only does the Pearl of Great Price reunite religion with cosmology, but it also gives us a better understanding of the creation. As Hugh summarizes these insights: "The creation process as described in the Pearl of Great Price is open ended and ongoing, entailing careful planning based on vast experience, long consultations, models, tests, and even trial runs for a complicated system requiring a vast scale of participation by the creatures concerned. The whole operation is dominated by the overriding principle of love."[101] As a result, Latter-day Saints cannot agree with either creationists or evolutionists. "Today one feels obliged to be either a fundamentalist or a Darwinist," Hugh stated to his Pearl of Great Price class. "Well, the gospel rejects both."[102] The Pearl of Great Price gives us "a story to tell before Adam. [Conventional] religion and science have none, absolutely none."[103]

Because of the doctrinal content of the Pearl of Great Price, Hugh believes, its message is highly relevant to our age. Both the Book of Abraham and the Book of Moses show us a people living in a world similar to ours with similar concerns. In the concluding chapter of *Abraham in Egypt*, Hugh pointed out that Abraham lived in "a wicked world very much like our own. From childhood to the grave, he was a stranger in his society because he insisted on living by the principles of the gospel and preaching them to others wherever he went, even if it meant getting into trouble." Abraham's life, wrote Hugh, "was a series of trials or tests, and by example and precept he tells us how to come through victorious." Abraham's chief desire was simple but profound: "to bless all with whom he [came] into contact." Because of this righteous desire, Abraham became known as "the magnanimous, the great-hearted, the ever-hospitable Abraham, who always does the fair and compassionate thing no matter how badly others may behave toward him; he is the friend of God because he is the friend of man, pleading for Sodom and Gomorrah. That is the moral pattern for all men to follow."[104] We must follow Abraham's example because "he's the father of the faithful; we're his descendants. We must do his work and follow his path."[105]

One of the principal lessons Abraham teaches us is to always seek to be more virtuous. Not only is Abraham a "follower of righteousness" but he wants to be a "greater follower of righteousness" (Abr. 1:2). "Notice there's your gospel of repentance—to be a greater follower. He's not doing well enough."[106] Furthermore, Abraham is on a quest "to

---

1966], 280), includes a lengthy quotation from the Pearl of Great Price—"not, of course, to prove that there is life on other worlds, but to show that the Mormons have long been teaching what scientists are now coming around to." See also Nibley, *Temple and Cosmos*, 366: "In our own times, it has been widely assumed that the discovery of life on other worlds would be an end to a belief in God. Mormons believe just the opposite: such life would be additional evidence for the existence of God." Sullivan, longtime science editor at the *New York Times*, was the first popular writer to report on the growing movement among such scientists like Guiseppe Cocconi and Philip Morrison to consider using radio telescopes to pick up signals from space in an effort to determine whether life exists on other planets. The program became known as SETI (the search for extraterrestrial intelligence).

[101] Nibley, "Before Adam," in *Old Testament and Related Studies*, edited by John W. Welch, Gary P. Gillum, and Don E. Norton, Vol. 1 of *The Collected Works of Hugh Nibley* (Salt Lake City: Deseret Book/FARMS, 1986), 69.

[102] Nibley, *Ancient Documents and the Pearl of Great Price*, Lecture 6, 2. See also Nibley, "Before Adam," 49-85.

[103] Nibley, "Before Adam," 51.

[104] Nibley, *Abraham in Egypt*, 651-52.

[105] Nibley, "Faith of an Observer," 361.

[106] Ibid., 288.

possess a greater knowledge" (Abr. 1:2). We should follow Abraham's example, "ever seeking more light and knowledge, and we leave the temple as we close the scriptures with that commitment. We are guaranteed instruction and guidance at every step and are advised to ask for it and to follow it."[107]

Likewise, Enoch's world was much like our own, full of grim sophistication and wickedness. And while Enoch could not save everyone from the impending destruction of the flood, he did gather a group of righteous individuals from among the world—a call we also have been given. The Zion which he built became a haven from wickedness where all "were of one heart, one mind, and dwelt in righteousness; and there was no poor among them" (Moses 7:18). This is our present goal: "It is Enoch who presides when all things are gathered in one," writes Hugh.[108] "Enoch, the supermissionary, was sent out and was able 'in [the] process of time' (Moses 7:21) to draw many after him into his city of Zion, which was then totally segregated from the rest of the world, pending the world's destruction."[109]

The Pearl of Great Price shows both the good news and the bad news that have been on the earth from the beginning to these last days: "The good news is that the gospel is here; the bad news is the people aren't going to accept it. It's going to be rejected."[110] But the ones who do accept it have the duty and blessing to move into a different world:

> Enoch, Abraham, and Moses all sought against frightful opposition to restore the order that alone offers happiness to earth's inhabitants. Their program is renewed in full force in the law of consecration. To consecrate is to set aside, to dedicate to a particular purpose; what has been dedicated is no longer at the donor's disposal. Happily, the Latter-day Saints have agreed to consecrate here and now everything with which they have been blessed in order to establish on earth Zion.[111]

One of the most moving parts in the documentary, *Faith of an Observer*, shows Hugh retelling a story from the Jewish Midrash. While Abraham was sitting in his tent on the plain of Mamre in the heat of the day, he had the impression that someone might be lost and suffering out in the heat. "It was a hot day," states Hugh. "It says it was a day like the breath of *Gahinum*, like the breath of hell." So Abraham sent his servant Eliazer out to search the surrounding area, but Eliazer found no one. Still worried that someone might perish in the burning heat, Abraham finally went out to search himself. By the end of the blistering day, he still had found no one. When he finally returned to his tent, there were three people waiting for him. "It was the Lord and the two with him," said Hugh. "And he went up and threw himself on his knees, 'Lord of the universe, what makes me worthy that you should visit me?' he says. It is then that the Lord promises him Isaac, as a reward for what he had done, you see. The supreme offer." Hugh continues, "He'd gone out to look for his fellow man in that dusty hell, all alone. Eliazer couldn't find anyone, and he said 'I think I can find somebody.' Well, he found something. He found the answer

---

[107]Nibley, "But What Kind of Work?," in *Approaching Zion*, edited by Don E. Norton, Vol. 9 of *The Collected Works of Hugh Nibley* (Salt Lake City: Deseret Book/FARMS, 1989), 263.
[108]Nibley, *Enoch the Prophet*, 150.
[109]Nibley, "We Will Still Weep for Zion," in *Approaching Zion*, 341.
[110]Nibley, "Faith of an Observer," 376.
[111]Nibley, "The Utopians," in *Approaching Zion*, 520.

to the thing he'd prayed for all his life: his son Isaac." As Hugh tells the story, he begins to choke up. "I have never been able to get through that story without that happening," confessed Hugh in the filming. "It's a very moving story." The story is poignant, and it shows us the extent to which we are called to do the works of Abraham. "Remember, we are told that Abraham was tested to the last extreme, to the ultimate extremity," summarizes Hugh. "Unless you are willing to give everything you cannot claim eternal life. It's not to be cheaply bought."[112] But for Hugh, the poignancy of this story is even more real: His own Isaac was the stillborn son whom Phyllis delivered on 11 November 1954. (See chap. 17.) When he speaks about being willing to "give everything," he is speaking as one who has felt the pain of loss and undoubtedly longs for eventual reunion with that son.

It is clear that, for Hugh, Abraham was not just a man and not just a model for righteous living. Abraham is his hero. A recent article in the *New Yorker* states that Hugh "seems weary of the effort to authenticate the Book of Abraham."[113] Nothing could be further from the truth. Hugh has spent the last thirty-five years of his life defending the Book of Abraham and the Book of Moses as ancient texts. Certainly, at age ninety-two, Hugh is weary; but he is not weary of the Book of Abraham. Each weekday for as long as I've known him, he has gone to his office to work on *One Eternal Round* which is about the hypocephalus, Facsimile 2, from the Book of Abraham. (See chap. 25.) Hugh continues to focus his energy on Abraham, but he is also committed to living like Abraham, seeking "more light and knowledge" and continually working to be a better "follower of righteousness." Hugh takes Abraham seriously.

Hugh believes that both the Book of Abraham and the Book of Moses show us a world like our own, full of treachery, wickedness, and sin. But they offer us a way out. The Book of Moses shows us the goal we should be striving for: to establish Zion on this earth, a place where the whole community shares love, vision, virtues, and possessions. The Book of Abraham shows us the way to accomplish this goal: to do the works of Abraham, humbly seeking for greater righteousness and knowledge, all the while caring for and ministering to those in need.

---

[112]The description of Hugh's story-telling comes from *Faith of an Observer*, video documentary, directed, and photographed by Brian Capener; coauthored by Brian Capener and Alex Nibley (Provo, Utah: Brigham Young University and the Foundation for Ancient Research and Mormon Studies, 1985). Most of the language, however, is quoted from the interview transcript, "Faith of an Observer," 296-99. The story of Abraham's hospitality can be found most readily in Ginzberg, *The Legends of the Jews*, 1:240-45.

[113]Lawrence Wright, "Lives of the Saints," *New Yorker*, 21 January 2002, 53.

Hugh Nibley in the 1970s.

Photo courtesy L. Tom Perry Special Collections,
Harold B. Lee Library, Brigham Young University.

The reading of the Abraham apocrypha inevitably led to Enoch documents and the discovery that Joseph Smith had given us among other things a perfectly good Book of Enoch which rang up an astonishing number of stunning parallels when I started to compare it with the growing catalogue of newly discovered Enoch manuscripts. But my obsession of the 1970s has been the Temple.

The essential information for solving almost any problem or answering almost any question is all *brought* together in the scriptures; but it is not *put* together for us there. Learned divines for sixty generations have argued about that, and the vast bulk of their writings is eloquent witness to their perplexity. And this is where the *Temple* comes in. Without the Temple any civilization is an empty shell, a structure of custom and convenience only. The churchmen, posting with too much dexterity to accommodate their teachings to the scientific and moral tenets of the hour, present a woeful commentary on the claims of religion to be the sheet anchor of civilization and morality. Where is the unshakable rock, the *shetiyah*? It is the Temple.[1]

---

[1] Nibley, "Intellectual Autobiography," *Nibley on the Timely and Timeless* (Provo: BYU Religious Studies Center, 1978), xxvi-xxviii.

Chapter 21

Politics, Basketball, Patriarchs, and Temples, 1970-79

As the 1970s began,[2] Hugh Nibley saw BYU's condition as deplorable. Under the continuing presidency of the aging Ernest L. Wilkinson, BYU had reacted to tensions and outbreaks on other college campuses by moving even farther to the right. In March 1971, Wilkinson retired; and Dallin H. Oaks was appointed to replace him on 4 May. Hugh responded to the new administration with hope that the change meant a more moderate political emphasis and an increase in serious scholarship. A few months into the new administration, Hugh told a correspondent: "The BYU is in some sort of transition and nobody knows just which direction it will take; the main issue is whether or not it should turn to serious study."[3]

Wilkinson's positive legacy was a formidable physical plant. During his twenty years as president, he had more than doubled the size of the campus and erected more than two hundred buildings, including a library, a fine arts center, several classroom buildings, an administration building, a stadium, a physical education building, student housing, and a student center. Student enrollment increased six-fold to more than 25,000 students; the faculty quadrupled; and library holdings increased almost 500 percent.[4]

---

[2]Unfortunately for a biographer, the volume of Hugh's personal correspondence with friends and family dropped sharply during the 1970s. Particularly lamentable is the fact that the regular exchange between Hugh and Paul Springer essentially stopped at this time, probably because Hugh was too absorbed in his Book of Abraham studies to continue writing his regular, lengthy letters and partly because the two men, despite their long friendship, had simply drifted apart. Instead, Hugh's correspondence files are filled with hundreds of short letters to individual Church members responding to their gospel questions. Not surprisingly, Hugh reveals little about his personal life in these letters. As a consequence, I am forced to rely more on interviews and Hugh's published writings from this point.

[3]Hugh Nibley, Letter to Robert F. Smith, 28 October 1971.

[4]Gary James Bergera and Ronald Priddis, *Brigham Young University: A House of Faith* (Salt Lake: Signature Books,

While size had been the preoccupation of the Wilkinson administration, the incoming president promised to place more emphasis on intellectual growth. Dallin H. Oaks, a law professor at the University of Chicago, was not only a savvy administrator but a strong intellectual talent. Above all, faculty found Oaks's quick wit and moderate tone endearing.[5]

In January 1973, President Oaks began to consider a proposal by Chauncey Riddle of BYU's Philosophy Department and dean of the graduate school, to create an Institute of Ancient Studies. The idea had been around for several years, but it picked up speed at this point. Riddle envisioned it as "an interdisciplinary organization designed to promote the development and dissemination of information relating to ancient manuscripts of religious significance."[6] When Oaks met with Hugh to discuss the proposal, Hugh was ecstatic. Hugh felt, as Oaks recorded in a memo, that such an institute would "focus interest and give significant persuasive outside expression of our commitment and our expertise."[7] But when he asked Hugh to consider serving as the institute's director, Hugh refused: "For nothing do I thank my Heavenly Father more fervidly than his singular bounty in sparing me all the days of my life from the toils and distractions of Administration," he wrote.

> I am sure that the greatest possible contribution I could make right now would be NOT to blight such a worthy project with my type of timid and inept direction. At the moment I stand in a critical position, with a painfully long period of often unproductive but indispensable preparation behind me, and a time of senile imbecility not far ahead of me. If I don't exploit the present brief interval to the fullest, I shall be losing my whole laborious investment. This is no time for the added frustrations of administration![8]

Undeterred by Hugh's refusal, Oaks asked him to reconsider on condition that he be appointed director in name only, with an associate director "who would be responsible for all of the day to day administration." Resorting to flattery, Oaks stated that he and others felt that "we cannot launch a successful 'Institute for Ancient Studies' without being able to use the enormous prestige and past and future accomplishments of Hugh Nibley as the headliner and pace-setter for the Institute."[9] Hugh finally agreed, largely because "it would be churlish to do otherwise."[10] On 4 April 1973, Hugh accompanied Oaks to the meeting of the Board of Trustees when they approved the proposal.[11] Hugh never presented himself as anything other than a reluctant draftee and soon afterwards wrote to a

---

1985), 26-30.

[5]Ibid., 33.

[6]Ernest L. Wilkinson, ed., *Brigham Young University: The First 100 Years*, 4 vols. (Provo, UT: Brigham Young University Press, 1976), 4:191.

[7]Dallin H. Oaks, Memo to File, 11 January 1973, Dallin H. Oaks Presidential Papers, Department of Religious Instruction, L. Tom Perry Special Collections, Harold B. Lee Library, Brigham Young University, Provo, Utah.

[8]Hugh Nibley, Letter to Dallin H. Oaks, 1 March 1973, ibid.

[9]Dallin H. Oaks, Letter to Hugh Nibley, 5 March 1973, ibid.

[10]Hugh Nibley, Letter to Dallin H. Oaks, 12 March 1973, ibid.

[11]Dallin H. Oaks, Letter to Hugh Nibley, 14 March 1973, ibid.

friend: "The Authorities have decided, much against my advice and consent, to set up here what is humorously called an 'Institute of Ancient Studies,' which reaches the point of high comedy with me in the role of 'Director.'" He conceded, however, that the mission of the institute was noble: "The idea is that SOMETHING should be done about all these documents and all the smart young men that are turning up to tell us about them."[12]

The institute began full operation on 1 September 1973, with R. Douglas Phillips, associate professor of classical languages, assuming the role of associate director in charge of the business administration of the new organization. Associate members of the institute were Richard Lloyd Anderson, a professor of history and ancient scriptures; S. Kent Brown and Wilford Griggs, both assistant professors of ancient scriptures; Thomas W. Mackay, assistant professor of classical languages; and Ellis T. Rasmussen, assistant dean of the College of Religious Instruction and professor of ancient scriptures. "The scholarly world is being flooded with newly discovered manuscripts, many of which have a direct bearing on the Church of Jesus Christ of Latter-day Saints," Hugh was quoted in the press release announcing the institute's creation. "It is important that LDS scholars have and know these manuscripts. The new Institute will give them an important means of acquisition, loan, and use of manuscripts and contact with authorities in the field throughout the world."[13] This organization is still a vital institute. Brown recently succeeded Griggs as director.

Despite this solid encouragement of scholarship in Hugh's most passionately loved area, conservative extremism continued to characterize BYU and Mormon culture in general, and Hugh continued to raise a warning voice about what he saw as a dangerous trend. The early 1970s were a volatile time in American culture. The Vietnam War was expanding into Cambodia and Laos, and protests against the war exploded on America's college campuses. At Kent State, jittery National Guardsmen killed four student protesters on 4 May 1970. A great divide opened up between those who wanted the war to end and distrusted the intentions of the nation's political leaders and those who felt that the protesters were unpatriotic rebels against law and order. In June 1972, Democrats discovered that their campaign headquarters at the Watergate Hotel in Washington, D.C., had been bugged. Later revelation that President Richard M. Nixon's administration was involved resulted in his eventual resignation and a great cynicism on the part of many about the government and other institutions. At BYU and within the Mormon culture, people often reacted to this cynicism with a reactionary shift rightward. BYU students were more likely to protest *for* the Vietnam War than *against* it, and many dismissed the revelation of Nixon's involvement in Watergate as the liberal media pestering the president.[14] Around one-third of Hugh's writings during the decade were scathing social commentary aimed at BYU and Mormon culture. He denounced the culture's unquestioning support for the Vietnam War, chastised Mormons' lack of respect for the environment, and decried unthinking loyalty to political parties. Most of all, he called for a renewed goal of seeking Zion.

---

[12] Hugh Nibley, Letter to Robert F. Smith, 27 April 1973; emphasis Hugh's.
[13] Brigham Young University News Bureau, (no title), n.d., Oaks Presidential Papers, Department of Religious Instruction, Perry Special Collections.
[14] Bergera and Priddis, *Brigham Young University*, 180-89.

Hugh's criticism of BYU was particularly harsh as he saw a concern with dress and grooming replacing a concern with academic achievement. In 1973, he critiqued "the haircut" as "the test of virtue in a world where Satan deceives and rules by appearance."[15] In 1975, he commented: "The penalty we pay for starving our minds is a phenomenon that is only too conspicuous at Brigham Young University."[16] In that same talk, he denounced Mormon culture for rewarding

> zeal alone, zeal without knowledge—for sitting in endless meetings, for dedicated conformity and unlimited capacity for suffering boredom. We think it more commendable to get up at five A.M. to write a bad book than to get up at nine o'clock to write a good one—that is pure zeal that tends to breed a race of insufferable, self-righteous prigs and barren minds. One has only to consider the present outpouring of "inspirational" books in the Church that bring little new in the way of knowledge: truisms and platitudes, kitsch, and clichés have become our everyday diet.[17]

Another social issue that Hugh addressed during the 1970s was the Church's official policy of excluding black male members from holding the priesthood. Lester Bush, a member of the Church who was then medical officer with the U.S. embassy in Saigon and also a member of the Saigon Branch presidency, spearheaded an effort to air the issue in the pages of *Dialogue: A Journal of Mormon Thought*. Bush treated it from a historical perspective, outlining the origins and development of the policy from Joseph Smith to the present. To round out the discussion, *Dialogue's* editor Robert Rees proposed that Richard Bushman, Truman Madsen, and Hugh Nibley write articles on the subject. When approached, Bushman declined, stating that his contribution as a historian would be redundant. Hugh was asked to trace the scriptural origins of the ban, especially focusing on the Book of Abraham, which many members and leaders of the Church used to justify the official policy.

According to Bush's memoir on this episode, when word got out that the topic was to be discussed in *Dialogue*, Rees received a phone call from Robert K. Thomas, academic vice president at BYU, urging him to cancel the article. According to Rees, Thomas said that "there would be absolutely no sympathy for those involved in the publication." Madsen soon backed out. Rees remembered him being "very frightened by the whole thing," stating that the issue "was a tar baby and he didn't want to get stuck."[18]

Hugh sent Rees an essay, but it was not the one requested. In a handwritten note dated 20 June 1973, Hugh told Rees, "I junked the [my] article—you will have to settle for these few generalities. Do with them what you will. No time to pretty things [up]."[19] Rees remembers being impressed that Hugh had not been scared off by the political pressure that was being placed on Church members, especially BYU scholars, not to touch this

---

[15] Nibley, "What Is Zion? A Distant View," originally given as part of the Joseph Smith Lecture Series at BYU on 25 February 1973, *Approaching Zion*, edited by Don E. Norton, Vol. 9 of *The Collected Works of Hugh Nibley* (Salt Lake City: Deseret Book/FARMS, 1989), 57.

[16] Nibley, "Zeal Without Knowledge," in *Approaching Zion*, 69. This paper was originally given as the Academic Awareness Lecture at BYU on 26 June 1975.

[17] Ibid., 75. I have found no record of any immediate reaction to this talk.

[18] Quoted in Lester Bush "Writing 'Mormonism's Negro Doctrine: An Historical Overview' (1973): Context and Reflections, 1998," *Journal of Mormon History* 25, no. 1 (Spring 1999): 261.

[19] Ibid., 262.

topic. In a letter to Lester Bush about a week after receiving Hugh's note, Rees commented:

> It's refreshing to find someone like Nibley who is so good and so independent that he doesn't have to worry about such political concern. It is the difference, I think, between a true intellectual and scholar and one who only has the trappings. In a sense, what Nibley did was write the article that Madsen should have written, so we still don't have a significant discussion of the Cain/Ham/Canaan tradition. Nibley wrote an article along the lines but scrapped it for the personal response which he makes. I feel that the personal response is in some ways much better although I hope that he gets around to doing the other as well.[20]

Bush's essay appeared in the spring 1973 issue of *Dialogue*, with accompanying essays by Eugene England, a founding editor of *Dialogue* and then dean of academic affairs at St. Olaf College, a Lutheran institution in Northfield, Minnesota; Gordon C. Thomasson, associate editor of *Dialogue*; and Hugh Nibley.[21] Hugh's essay, "The Best Possible Test," briefly discussed the Book of Abraham and implied that, although the Pharaoh spoken of may have been black, he was "a just and righteous man, blessed with wisdom and earthly knowledge." Hugh's main thesis, however, was that members of the Church really didn't know why the ban on priesthood was instituted, but knew only the justifications made for it, which were chronicled in Bush's study. He concluded: "So now the whole issue boils down to asking whether it is really God and not man who has ordered this thing. . . . And so it gives me great pleasure to be in a position to answer the question with an unequivocal affirmative: it is indeed the Lord's doing. How do I know it? By revelation—which I am in no position to bestow upon others; this goes only for myself."[22] Among other things, Hugh proposed that the Abraham passages support the idea that blacks should seek and be elected to public office. Throughout the essay, however, Hugh—rather uncharacteristically—never attempted to give a reason for the ban or marshal evidence to support it.

In 1976, Lester Bush met with Hugh while visiting Utah and discussed the issue with him face-to-face. Bush said Hugh confessed that his 1973 essay was nothing more than an effort to "stall for time." Bush recorded a detailed account of the conversation:

> We went through the story in fairly great detail from Adam on down and though [Hugh] doesn't feel the final word is in, he says: He does not find any clear support for the priesthood denial/Book of Abraham relationship in early texts or "I would be shrieking it from the house tops." He does not think the blacks are related to Cain, or the early Canaan, and probably not to Ham, Egypt, Canaan or Pharaoh. He's unsure

---

[20]Ibid., 263.

[21]Lester Bush, "Mormonism's Negro Doctrine: An Historical Overview," *Dialogue* 8 no. 1 (Spring 1973): 1168, was reprinted in *Neither White Nor Black: Mormon Scholars Confront the Race Issue in a Universal Church*, edited by Lester E. Bush Jr. and Armand L. Mauss (Midvale, UT: Signature Books, 1984), 531-29. Responses to the essay by Gordon C. Thomasson (69-72), Hugh Nibley (72-77), and Eugene England (78-85) appeared in the same issue. England's essay, "The Mormon Cross," was reprinted in his collection *Dialogues with Myself* (Midvale, UT: Orion Books, 1984), 121-34. Hugh's "The Best Possible Test" was reprinted in *Temple and Cosmos: Beyond This Ignorant Present*, edited by Don E. Norton, Vol. 12 of *The Collected Works of Hugh Nibley* (Salt Lake City: Deseret Book/FARMS, 1992), 532-40.

[22]Nibley, "The Best Possible Test," in *Temple and Cosmos*, 539.

but would guess that Brigham Young was "wrong" relating blacks to Cain. He said "we all have Negro blood" there was intermixture everywhere. I asked about the accounts of the early patriarchs marrying apparent blacks. He exclaimed yes[.] I mentioned Moses Yes. But the real "irony" was Joseph marrying a daughter of the priest of On who he says by definition had to have been a Hamite and their sons were Ephraim and Manasseh, who[m] we are all so proud to claim. He said it was as though the Lord was trying to tell us something.

I asked about the notion that the doctrine was a mistake initially but that the Lord was not interceding at present even if we ask "Is it time?" He said he would be "very uncomfortable" with that.[23]

Bush felt "disappointed" that Hugh had not explored these concepts in his *Dialogue* essay, but Hugh did write about some of them after the ban had been lifted in 1978, in his 1981 *Abraham in Egypt*. (See chap. 23). This incident is revealing. Hugh had clear and scripturally based views on this issue, even though his claim to know that the Church's priesthood ban was inspired is somewhat puzzling. However, since these beliefs conflicted with the Church's official position, he loyally remained silent on those particular points but courageously wrote on the aspects of the topic that he felt had not been placed off limits for him at a time when other BYU professors declined the controversial challenge.

The early 1970s also brought a very unlikely friendship for Hugh. In 1969, BYU recruited a basketball player from Yugoslavia to play center on the BYU team. His name, soon to be a household word among BYU fans, was Kresimir Cosic, nicknamed "Kreso." Kreso already had a distinguished sports career prior to coming to BYU and had been a member of the Yugoslavian basketball team that won the silver medal in the 1968 Olympics. He was not Mormon, but two Finnish basketball players who were attending BYU approached him at a European All-Star game and persuaded him to give BYU a try. He made up his mind and arrived at BYU on little notice in 1969. A BYU coach and Zdravko Mincek, a Yugoslav tennis player, met Kreso's plane when he arrived the Salt Lake airport. Mincek and Kreso immediately hit it off and became roommates.[24]

Kreso soon became the star of the BYU basketball team. Not only did he average 19.1 points per game, becoming for a time the school's all-time leading scorer with 1,512 points, but Kreso's unorthodox style was a crowd-pleaser.[25] *Sports Illustrated* called Kreso's "zest for the game" "something to behold," and stated that he was "forever clapping his hands, raising fists high, laughing, shouting 'Opa! Opa! (I'm open, I'm open),' jackknifing for layups, dribbling through his legs, passing behind his back, and joyfully firing all manner of shots from improbable positions and angles."[26]

Hugh's and Phyllis's oldest daughter, Christina, who turned twenty-one in 1970, was dating Kreso's roommate, Zdravko ("Z") Mincek, whom she would later marry. She remembers that she and Kreso "were really confidants. Kreso knew that I was Z's girlfriend and he was very honorable about it. It was just a friendship, but we got to know each other very well." Sometime during the 1970-71 school year, Kreso became so disillu-

---

[23]The meeting, arranged by Omar Kadar, occurred on 24 October 1976 in Ray Hillam's home. Bush wrote his account the next day. Bush, "Writting Mormonism's Negro Doctrine," 269.

[24]Bergera and Priddis, *Brigham Young University*, 283.

[25]AP Newswire, (no headline), 26 May 1995, printout in my possession.

[26]Quoted in Bergera and Priddis, *Brigham Young University*, 283.

sioned about playing basketball in Provo and so homesick that he told Christina he was leaving. "Nobody knows because I'm not coming back," he told her. She was very worried; but the next day he called to say that his plans had changed. The coaches had somehow known he was going to the airport and had headed him off. Rather than being angry, Kreso was actually resigned to his "fate." He had seen the mountains east of campus in a dream even before coming to BYU and knew that he was meant to be at BYU, so he was not surprised when his attempt to leave had failed. Christina interpreted it as a vision: "He never told anybody in his own country about his feelings—these dreams and visions." She reassured Kreso, who was feeling puzzled by his dream, that Mormons accepted such spiritual guidance. Her own father had experiences like this all the time. "This got him so excited," Christina remembers. "We talked for two or three hours and I told him that the Church teaches these things and you should check it out, but what he wanted to do was talk to my dad." Christina thought the idea of sending a basketball player to talk with her father was a particularly bad one. "I was thinking, Dad with a basketball player? Are you kidding? Dad's not going to want to talk to him."

But Kreso "did not talk to the second in command."[27] When Christina's reluctance to bring the two together became obvious, Kreso simply showed up at Hugh's office door. He spilled out his concerns and confusion without holding anything back. Hugh remembers that Kreso "was greatly distressed" because life "seemed perfectly empty." He had not taken BYU's Honor Code seriously—and, naturally, had had little training in understanding what "honor" meant in a religious context. He was an ardent party-goer. He was quickly attracted to the segment of the student body that lived for "the hanky-panky that went on," as Hugh put it, and "had one coed after another in his bedroom," as Christina put it. According to Christina, he was disgusted by what he saw as their total hypocrisy. They wouldn't "smoke, drink, or swear," but they never rejected his amorous advances, either. Z had been known to take an occasional beer, but he was a serious student who tried to pull Kreso away from the party scene. Christina, off limits because of Kreso's respect for Z, as well as her own strong assertion of Mormon values, was perhaps the one important woman in Kreso's life who was not a sex object.

So Kreso confronted Hugh Nibley with an artless but sincere question. His life was not making him happy, so what was the problem? Christina had alerted Hugh, but he probably would have given the same answer regardless. He quoted the Book of Mormon: "Men are, that they might have joy" (2 Ne. 2:25). Kreso wrinkled up his face in bewilderment. His still-small English vocabulary did not include the word. "*Radost*," said Hugh, trying the Russian word on him. Kreso "responded with a smile of immense satisfaction—joy was his element, not the dreary and laborious pleasures of sophisticated celebrities, but the spontaneous childlike happiness of sharing an eager awareness of each other."[28]

Kreso returned often to discuss the gospel with Hugh, and improbably, the two became very close friends. It was truly a sight to behold five-foot-seven-inch Hugh walking around campus with six-foot-eleven-inch Kreso. The topic of conversation was always the gospel. One day Kreso told Hugh, "There are a hundred reasons why I should not join the Church, and only one reason why I should—because it is true." After being interviewed by his bishop, Kreso asked Hugh to baptize him. Hugh agreed at once. He found

---

[27]Christina Nibley Mincek, Interviewed by Boyd Petersen, 13 September 2001.

[28]Hugh Nibley, remarks prepared to be read at the funeral of Kresimir Cosic, n.d., ca. 26 May 1995.

it touching that, despite Kreso's campus celebrity, "he did not want to make a public relations gimmick of a sacred ordinance."[29] To keep the ordinance private, Hugh arranged for the ceremony to occur in the font in the basement of the Tabernacle on Temple Square in November 1971. Only a few people were in attendance. The elderly sisters who maintained the baptismal clothing at the Tabernacle began to laugh when they saw him. Only a few days earlier, they had been prompted to sew an extra-tall baptismal outfit, baffled the whole time about who would ever wear it. It fit perfectly.[30] In the months following Kreso's baptism, Kreso and Hugh continued to discuss the gospel, and Kreso began attending the Nibleys' family home evening on Mondays. Frequently, other Mormon players from the BYU basketball team joined them up through 1973 when Kreso graduated. Family home evening at the Nibley home was always more like a devotional than the traditional family conference with a floating population of the children and Kreso's friends.

Hugh's and Phyllis's children were vigorously exploring new paths for themselves. After serving in the Coast Guard, Paul served a mission in Italy (1970-72), then majored at BYU in theater technical design. On 10 November 1972 he married Bronia Janousek, a native of Czechoslovakia who had been his language lab instructor in a Russian class he took at BYU. Throughout the 1970s, Paul worked as a prop designer for several films and television series and for the BYU scenery shop.

Christina married Zdravko Mincek on 26 May 1971 and, after Z graduated from BYU, moved to Ponte Vedra Beach near Jacksonville, Florida, where Z became a tennis coach at a country club. After Christina's two children were born, she returned to BYU in 1973 and finished her B.A.

Tom was called in late 1969 to serve a mission to Singapore but was transferred to the Philippines after the Church could no longer obtain visas for its missionaries. In 1973, he revisited his missionary areas in Singapore and the Philippines, then toured Yugoslavia in company with the Yugoslavian basketball team for which Cosic was playing. Tom returned to BYU in 1975-76 and served as the school's official mascot, Cosmo.

Michael completed his B.A. degree in English at BYU and spent a year studying at the University of Grenoble in France, then earned his M.A. in English at BYU. On 26 February 1976, he married Margaret Trimble; they later divorced.

Charles Alex (he began using Alex soon after high school) attended the American Conservatory Theater in San Francisco from ages eighteen to twenty where he received his Master's of Fine Arts (he later earned a baccalaureate degree in fine arts), then joined several performing arts organizations, danced with the Pacific Ballet Company, and served a mission to Japan (1978-80).

Becky graduated from high school in 1976, attended the Pacific Conservatory for the Performing Arts in Santa Maria, California, and also worked in the summer theater at Sundance. Martha and Zina, who graduated from high school in 1980 and 1982 respectively, both both participated in their school's drama, debate, and music programs, Martha singing in the school choir and Zina playing in the orchestra.

In the late 1960s and early 1970s, attendance at BYU's forums, a weekly hour when all students and faculty were supposed to attend lectures by noted local, national, or international figures, dwindled to the point that President Oaks appointed a Forum

---

[29]Ibid.

[30]Kresimir Cosic, Interviewed by Carol Petranek, 2 May 1994, photocopy of transcript in my possession.

Subcommittee in 1973 to consider ways to improve attendance. One recommendation was to invite more BYU professors to speak on topics more relevant to the students. One of the professors invited to participate was sixty-three-year-old Hugh Nibley, whose reputation among students earned him the students' "Professor of the Year" award in April 1973.[31] To take advantage of Hugh's quick wit and to foster more spontaneity, the committee decided on an interview format, rather than a formal paper, and asked Louis Midgley, professor of political science and a Nibley devotee for the previous decade, to conduct the interview. Although Hugh's spontaneity and candor in the classroom were legendary, he was not completely comfortable with the interview format. "He wanted to be able to know the questions beforehand and have something written out, something that he had thought through beforehand," recalls Midgley. "But in the couple of instances where I tried questions that I had been fashioning, I thought that spontaneity was what we needed with him."[32]

Hugh Nibley and Louis Midgley, discussing the forum interview they planned to present on 21 May 1974.

Photo courtesy of Perry Special Collections, Lee Library, Brigham Young University.

On 21 March 1974, students crowded the Marriott Center for "A Personal Encounter with Hugh Nibley." Midgley and Hugh gave the program a private run-through in a nearby room before the 10:00 A.M. meeting. "I went over some of the questions and you've never seen anything more brilliant," remembers Midgley. "He was just fabulous. He was funny and quick witted and incisive and not lengthy and not wandering around. It was just absolutely fabulous." But when the interview got underway, Midgley could tell something was wrong. "I thought at first that he was just uncomfortable with me asking him questions where it's all extemporaneous for him; but after a couple of questions I thought, 'No, there's something more to this.'" The audience probably didn't notice, but Midgley felt that Hugh was not responding to his questions as quickly, and his answers became shorter. At one chilling point, Midgley had to remind Hugh of an article he had published only two years before. "What is man's dominion?," Midgley asked, referring to Hugh's October 1972 New Era essay "Man's Dominion."[33] Hugh responded cheerfully but

---

[31] Bergera and Priddis, Brigham Young University, 350.
[32] Louis C. Midgley, Interviewed by Boyd Petersen, 19 September 2001.
[33] Reprinted as "Man's Dominion, or Subduing the Earth" in Brother Brigham Challenges the Saints, edited Don

mystified: "By George, I should remember that. Do I remember, I don't even remember what it was. Boy—I'm pretty far gone."³⁴ "At that point I thought, 'We are in big, big trouble,'" said Midgley. But Hugh was still coherent, and Midgley realized: "With a clogged carburetor, on three cylinders he was better than most everyone else on all eight. He was still good."³⁵ Likely few noticed that he was having difficulty answering the questions.

In retrospect, Midgley probably should have settled for getting through the forum; but he gamely tried to keep the ball rolling during the question-and-answer session in the Varsity Theater that followed the forum. By this time, Hugh was much less coherent. When a question was asked, Hugh, still cheerful, would turn to Midgley and ask, "Well, what do you think about that?" No doubt many of the students simply saw it as Hugh's famous willingness to involve everyone in the scholarly enterprise; and fortunately Midgley, from his close acquaintance with Hugh's works, could take over smoothly. "I would say, 'Well, Brother Nibley thinks the following thing, and I would explain and I took over." But he was becoming increasingly anxious and was relieved when the session ended.

Following the question and answer session, a special luncheon was held in the President's Room of the Wilkinson Center for those involved in putting the program together. By now, Phyllis had recognized that Hugh was largely unresponsive. Unable to extricate him without considerable turmoil, Phyllis deftly seated him at the end of the table while she sat next to him, fielding questions and giving responses if he was asked a direct question. Most of the guests, though recognizing that his behavior was atypical, probably chalked it up to fatigue or his famous professorial distraction.

When Hugh and Phyllis finally returned home, Phyllis hoped that all Hugh needed was a nap. But he picked up the manuscript to the book he was working on—*The Message of the Joseph Smith Papyri*—and did not recognize it. Phyllis announced that they were going to the hospital and would not listen to his protest. With the help of Marvin Robeson, a family friend and BYU athletic trainer, she got Hugh checked into Utah Valley Hospital. After evaluation, he was listed in fair condition. Phyllis later told the BYU newspaper that her husband had suffered a "breakdown from fatigue and overwork."³⁶ It actually seems to have been a mild stroke.

Midgley felt intensely guilty about the episode, wondering if he had caused the episode by putting Hugh in a stressful situation. "He wanted to have the thing more scripted. He wanted to see a list of questions and have actually prepared answers so that it wasn't spontaneous. . . . [But] he wouldn't know what I would ask. . . . I wondered if that had put him under some kind of pressure." The following day when Midgley visited Hugh at the hospital, Hugh exclaimed, "Oh I'm just humiliated to see you. I can remember everything and I made a total fool of myself." Hugh confided to Midgley that, when he had awakened, he worried about his mental faculties, but had felt reassured when he was able to remember the central argument of *The Joseph Smith Papyri*. "If I can do that I'm on top of my faculties," he told Midgley.

E. Norton and Shirley S. Ricks, Vol. 13 in *The Collected Works of Hugh Nibley* (Salt Lake City: Deseret Books/FARMS, 1994), 3-22. ³⁴"Nibley the Scholar," Forum address, 21 May 1974, transcript, 11.

³⁵Louis C. Midgley, Interviewed by Boyd Petersen, 19 September 2001.

³⁶"Dr. Nibley in Hospital," (BYU) *Daily Universe*, 28 May 1974; photocopy of clipping, Oaks Presidential Papers, Religion Department Papers, Perry Special Collections, Lee Library.

But Midgley could tell that Hugh was not completely optimistic. Hugh worried that the stroke had smitten him as divine punishment because he was revealing too much about the Mormon temple ceremony in *The Joseph Smith Papyri*. Midgley was amazed that the circumspect Hugh could even think such a thing. "I remember him saying, 'I may be a damn fool. I may have just had too much in there,'" Midgley remembers. "He was stewing about that." In particular, Hugh was concerned about a quotation from Brigham Young that the endowment is designed to give the initiate all the key words, signs, and tokens needed to "pass by the angels" guarding the way to Heavenly Father's presence.[37] This statement is now nearly always quoted in descriptions of the endowment, but Hugh was agitated. Brigham Young "knew what he was talking about," Hugh said, according to Midgley, "and that's the key, but I don't know whether that should be in there."[38]

Hugh became more coherent, detailed memories returned, and he was soon released from the hospital. Phyllis insisted that her workaholic husband take a vacation to get a "much needed rest." She booked a flight and they travelled to Ponte Vedra Beach, Florida, to visit Christina and Z. Phyllis thought that was far enough away from Hugh's office. There Hugh got plenty of rest. He would walk to the ocean—only a block from his daughter's house—and stroll up and down the beach, observing the animal life, searching for sea shells, and listening to the natural rhythm of the ocean tide. He didn't carry a book with him to the ocean; and for the first time in his married life, he didn't take a book with him to bed at night. "This is the one time he actually did rest," remembers Christina. "He seemed to be pretty determined to recover." By the time he returned to Utah two weeks later, Hugh had made a full and complete recovery.

Knowing that Klaus Baer, Hugh's friend and teacher, spent his summers in Colorado, Hugh invited Baer to participate in BYU's Education Week of August 1975. "Every summer we have at the BYU what is optimistically called 'Education Week,' a sort of chautauqua for stirring up the rubes, both on the faculty and off," wrote Hugh. "We voted to bring in somebody who carries real weight, and does it lightly. . . . You could do it all blindfolded, and would bring great comfort to them that sit in darkness." Hugh added temptingly, "Aside from sheer educational uplift a lot of people in Provo would find your presence during the Dog Days exhilarating."[39] The university offered only a small honorarium and travel expenses, but Baer could not resist the high-energy experience of a visit with Hugh. The two discussed topics for the three talks Baer would give, and Hugh pungently but accurately advised Baer that "there is a real interest, if no real

---

[37]*Discourses of Brigham Young*, edited by John A. Widtsoe (Salt Lake City: Deseret Book, 1925), 416; Brigham Young, 6 April 1853, *Journal of Discourses*, 26 vols. (London and Liverpool: LDS Booksellers Depot, 1855-86), 2:31-32.

[38]Louis C. Midgley, Interviewed by Boyd Petersen, 19 September 2001. Hugh omitted this quotation from the published version but included it in "Temple," the essay he wrote at the General Authorities' request in 1985 (see chap. 22), a published version of which appeared titled "On the Sacred and the Symbolic," in *Temples of the Ancient World: Ritual and Symbolism*, edited by Donald W. Parry (Salt Lake City: Deseret Book/FARMS, 1994), 535-621. See the passage in question on pp. 537-38.

[39]Hugh Nibley, Letter to Klaus Baer, 16 April 1974, Klaus Baer Collection, Archives of the Oriental Institute, University of Chicago.

knowledge, in your subject here and anything you might say would be appreciated and discussed as well as widely misinterpreted."[40]

During the course of his visit, Baer delivered, not three, but four lectures followed by long question-and-answer sessions. Hugh also spent many hours talking with Baer. "We had not talked together for some years," Hugh wrote to a correspondent, "and I was much impressed by the changes in his point of view."[41] Hugh does not specify what changes he noted in Baer, but clearly he was hoping for more. Hugh had never been subtle when talking with Baer about his Mormon beliefs, and he hoped one day to persuade Baer of the truthfulness of the gospel. During Baer's visit, Hugh delivered a lecture of his own titled "Some Reasons for the Restored Gospel." He began: "What I wish to talk about tonight is the coming forth, since I have been at the BYU, of a vast mass of evidence and interpretations which, in my opinion, require one to look at Joseph Smith with increasing respect. My opinion, of course, is not worth a straw, but I would like to call your attention to the type of evidence that might influence anyone's opinion."[42]

Hugh surveyed evidence he had accumulated over his lifetime, citing parallels between apocryphal Enoch literature and the Book of Moses, comparing Jewish legends of Abraham with the Book of Abraham, showing points where contemporary scholarship agreed with passages in the Book of Mormon, demonstrating similarities between some of the "Forty Day" literature and Third Nephi, illustrating the "epic milieu" of Ether, and concluding with the prophetic warnings that Mormon scripture delivers to the world. Hugh's speech was a tour-de-force summary of his twenty years of gospel scholarship. Clearly he was hoping that this evidence would have an impact on his friend. But to a correspondent soon after Baer's visit, Hugh admitted: "While he was here last, Baer repeatedly stated that evidence can have nothing whatever to do with faith: his faith as a dedicated Lutheran is not to be touched by any evidence. By the same token no amount of evidence will ever, ever change his opinion of Joseph Smith. For those who consider evidence, however, each item must be considered on its own merits."[43]

The Message of the Joseph Smith Papyri: An Egyptian Endowment, which had occupied most of Hugh's time during the early 1970s, finally appeared in 1975. To Jewish scholar Jacob Neusner, who had spoken several times at BYU, Hugh wrote: "What justifies the book is that the most important and instructive of the [Joseph Smith Papyri] happens to be an Egyptian papyrus upon which Joseph Smith placed particular value, without saying what it contains."[44] What the papyri contained was the Egyptian Book of Breathings. The Church's own *Improvement Era* had published color reproductions of the papyri almost immediately after they were discovered, and the independent Mormon journal *Dialogue* had published translations of the papyri soon thereafter.[45] The translation that Hugh provides in his book was not very

---

[40] Hugh Nibley, Letter to Klaus Baer, 9 May 1974, ibid.

[41] Hugh Nibley, Letter to Noel Hausler, 25 September 1974.

[42] Nibley, "Some Reasons for the Restored Gospel," n.d., ca. August 1974, 8. Hugh made notes all over his original typescript—in the margins and interlinearly. I have a photocopy of a photocopy of this original, courtesy of Gary Gillum.

[43] Hugh Nibley, Letter to Noel Hausler, 25 September 1974.

[44] Hugh Nibley, Letter to Jacob Neusner, 12 January 1977.

[45] Improvement Era, February 1968, supplement paginated 40-41 with the intervening pages designated by letter; Richard A. Parker, "The Joseph Smith Papyri: A Preliminary Report," *Dialogue: A Journal of Mormon Thought* 3, no. 2 (Summer 1968): 86-88, 98-99; John A. Wilson, "A Summary Report," ibid., 67-105; and

different from the translations that had already appeared, but his interpretation was. Unlike many Egyptologists at the time, Hugh believed that the Book of Breathings was a ritual text that described the initiatory rites preceding induction into the mysteries of the Egyptian religion. He saw these ancient rites as paralleling Mormon temple rites in many ways—hence his subtitle. To underscore his point that such ritual texts were common in antiquity, Hugh appended six ancient texts with common temple motifs. (See chap. 22.)

Without describing Mormon temple ceremonies in any detail, Hugh interpreted the ancient texts, allowing the knowledgeable reader to draw his or her own parallels. Undoubtedly, the technically dense analysis put off many Mormon readers; however, those who persevered through the book to the appendices found it extremely rewarding. As Hugh told Neusner, "Many Latter-day Saints have found the book instructive and enlightening, though the parallels are, for the most part, by no means glaringly obvious."[46]

With this publication, Hugh was again breaking new ground in Mormon studies. It was the first major study demonstrating that Mormon temple ceremonies had an ancient origin. While the book was written for a Mormon audience, it received a favorable review in the *Annual Egyptological Bibliography* of 1977. After thoroughly outlining its contents, the reviewer noted that while the book "shows clear traces of Mormon viewpoints," it employs "a serious scientific attempt to make full use of Egyptological literature."[47]

In March 1975, Hugh celebrated his sixty-fifth birthday and, as sixty-five-year-olds did in his day, officially retired from BYU.[48] However, Hugh could not imagine doing anything else for the rest of his life and, unlike most retirees, he still had three children to support: seventeen-year-old Becky, thirteen-year-old Martha, and eleven-year-old Zina. Without missing a beat, he continued teaching part-time.

Retirement was hardly restful. As he complained to Alex, "Day and night (and I MEAN day and night—the hour means nothing) the phone calls, the knock on the door, the letters, the steady line of visitors, each assuming that an aged retiree finds the time heavy on his hands."[49] Daughter Zina remembers a virtual parade of strangers showing up on their doorstep. Once a man dressed in business suit and a turban, speaking with a Utah accent came to the door asking if the "master" was home. "I didn't even blink," remembers Zina, "but just called 'Daddy!' and went back to my book." Hugh

---

Klaus Baer, "The Breathing Permit of Hor," *Dialogue: A Journal of Mormon Thought* 3, no. 3 (Autumn 1968): 109-34.

[46]Hugh Nibley, Letter to Jacob Neusner, 12 January 1977.

[47]L. M. J. Zondhoven, Review No. 77562, *Annual Egyptological Bibliography* 1977, compiled by Jac. J. Janssen, Inge Hofmann, and L. M. J. Zonhoven (Warminster, England: Aris and Phillips, 1981), 181.

[48]John W. Welch edited a *Festschrift* in 1975 honoring Hugh on the occasion of his sixty-fifth birthday. Because publishers feared the venture would lose money, the manuscript was never officially published. However, the bulk of the essays were "casually published" and "modestly circulated," according to John W. Welch, Letter to Robert K. Thomas, 4 October 1976, Oaks Presidential Papers, Robert K. Thomas Papers, Perry Special Collections, Lee Library. Three of the essays appeared in *BYU Studies*: Michael Dennis Rhodes, "A Translation and Commentary of the Joseph Smith Hypocephalus," 17, no. 3 (Spring 1977): 259-74; Stephen E. Robinson, "The Apocalypse of Adam," 17, no. 2 (Winter 1977): 131-53; and Richard L. Bushman, "The Book of Mormon and the American Revolution," 17, no. 1 (Autumn 1976): 3-20. The rest were "printed by off-set from typed pages," according to Welch, and privately circulated. Several of the essays from this first *Festschrift*, along with additional essays, later appeared in the two-volume *Festschrift By Study and Also by Faith* (Salt Lake City: Deseret Book/FARMS, 1990), on the occasion of Hugh's eightieth birthday.

[49]Hugh Nibley, Letter to Charles Alexander Nibley, n.d., ca. 1979.

didn't altogether dislike these presumptuous interruptions. "I know of no harried executive who gets more imperious letters and phone calls and visits than I do," Hugh wrote in another letter to his son. "Being retired I am at everybody's beck and call. The strange thing is that I enjoy it. Every summons is just another chance to strike for Zion—and I have learned that one never knows what will come of it. So far nothing bad has come of any of it, because the Lord turns all things to good if our hearts are right."[50] Furthermore, he had already turned with great relish to his next book, *Abraham in Egypt*. (See chap. 20.)

Three years later in 1978, Truman Madsen was responsible for bringing some of Hugh's lesser-known work to a wider audience. BYU's newly established Religious Studies Center planned to launch a monograph series to publish, among other things, essays delivered at its annual symposia. Madsen wanted to begin the series with a compilation of Hugh's essays, ranging in scope from scholarly approaches to Mormon scriptures to trenchant social commentary. To select the twelve to fifteen essays that would eventually be included in the book, Madsen organized an ad hoc committee consisting of Terry Warner, Arthur Henry King, Louis Midgley, and Douglas Phillips. The goal of the project was to "enable Nibley to showcase materials which are presently scattered" with the possible future goal of publishing "all of his papers in a series"; to guarantee Hugh "a royalty which is better than his often abusive pittance from certain other printing establishments which shall remain nameless"; and to "front for the publication with cold cash which we have already half-raised."[51] The book was to be named *The Nibley Legacy*.[52] Hugh, of course, knew about the project, but not its details.

As the book neared publication, Madsen wanted to show Hugh and Phyllis a mock-up of it. "I invited him to the house and I had it on the coffee table, remembers Madsen. "And he comes up with Phyllis, and I say, 'There's the book!' And I thought, you know, it was like announcing it with trumpets and he would jump for joy." But Hugh's response was instant repulsion. According to Madsen, he exclaimed: "'Oh no! You can't do that. I don't like it; it won't do!'" Hugh absolutely hated the title of the book. "'For one thing, it sounds like I'm dead and gone, and I'm not, and for another, legacy, legacy, legacy, What does that mean?'"

Dismayed, Madsen telephoned Hugh the next day with information that he thought would make Hugh reconsider: "I said, "Hugh, it's on the spine; it's on the cover; it's on the jacket; and it's on every page of the galleys. And if we change it now, it will cost eleven hundred dollars.' And I thought he'd say, 'Okay, go ahead.' You know what he said? This is typical Nibley. He said, 'Change it and take it out of my royalties!' And I gasped, and I said, 'Hugh do you care that much about a title?' and he said, 'No, I care that little about royalties!'[53] The book finally appeared in 1978 under the title *Nibley on the Timely and the Timeless*.

---

[50]Hugh Nibley, Letter to Charles Alexander Nibley, 22 October 1979.

[51]Truman Madsen, Letter to Robert K. Thomas, 19 July 1976, Oaks Presidential Papers, Religious Studies Center, Perry Special Collections.

[52]Ellis T. Rasmussen, Letter to Robert K. Thomas, Oaks Presidential Papers, Robert K. Thomas Papers, Perry Special Collections.

[53]Truman Madsen, "Faith of an Observer," 468-69, compilation of interviews, ca. 1983-84 for a video documentary of the same name aired in 1985, photocopy of typescript in my possession, pagination added.

The decade closed on a sorrowful note. Hugh's brother, Richard Nibley, an accomplished violinist who had been teaching music at Snow College in Ephraim, Utah, was diagnosed with amyotrophic lateral sclerosis, better known as Lou Gehrig's disease, a fatal neuromuscular disease characterized by progressive muscle weakness which results in paralysis. Richard's "body eroded away completely and at an astonishing rate," reported Hugh to Alex. "Yet he showed not the slightest sign of mental decline, even up to the last moment."[54] On 22 September 1979, Hugh started a letter to Alex: "We are all sitting in a waiting room in the LDS Hospital in Salt Lake, adjoining the intensive care room where we have just said our goodbyes to your Uncle Richard. Everyone is in high spirits, the Spirit having assured one and all (there are some 20 people present) that this should be a cheerful missionary farewell." A little later, he continued:

> One o'clock now, and Rich still on the life-sustaining system; whatever vitality is there comes from the machines, his body is completely gone—and yet his spirit is obviously as whole and vigorous as ever, a thing we all took note of; if the spirit does not fade with the body to the slightest degree—and Richard is too weak even to move his lips or blink an eye (a sudden smile or nod of the head just at the right time shows that he really is all there)—it is glaringly apparent that the spirit does not die with the body. How little we have to fear beside our own weaknesses.[55]

Richard died peacefully that evening. In addition to the outpouring of the Spirit that Hugh documented, he also had a sweet personal experience that gave him inner peace. "A week before he died, Richard called me to say that he had something urgent to tell me," remembers Hugh. Hugh drove down to the hospital in Mount Pleasant, and Richard confided that he had been worried that "his work on earth was not satisfactorily completed." But three visitors dressed in white had come to see him as he lay in his hospital bed. Richard told Hugh that these strangers assured him that he had "passed the test" and could leave this world at any time. "It is quite right for us to feel inadequate," wrote Hugh. "Anything else in our present condition would be self-deception."[56]

Richard's funeral, held a few days later in Ephraim, Utah, was, in Hugh's terms, "highly satisfactory." Continuing his description to Alex, he commented, "That is not the wrong word to use, for the last five days have been a series of clear demonstrations of the reality of the spirit and the after-life."[57] Certainly he was comforting his distant son for the loss of a beloved uncle, but Hugh was also affirming, in the face of his own inevitable aging, the spiritual strength that he in turn would draw on when his time came.

---

[54]Hugh Nibley, Letter to Charles Alexander Nibley, 22 October 1979.
[55]Hugh Nibley, Letter to Charles Alexander Nibley, 22 September 1979.
[56]Ibid.
[57]Hugh Nibley, Letter to Charles Alex Nibley, 22, 27 September 1979.

Hugh and Phyllis stand outside the Salt Lake Temple, May 1984.

Nibley's name is synonymous with temple studies, due to his solid contribution to the field over the past five decades. In fact, Nibley produced several groundbreaking articles on subjects related to ancient temples for years before other notable temple scholars came on the scene. His writings have gone far in defining the temple from an ancient Near Eastern and Mediterranean perspective. He has examined sacred vestments, ritual drama, initiation, the temple's cosmic significance, ancient prayer circles, the temple as a house of glory, ritual enactment of curses, ancient Egyptian temple rituals, temple "spin-offs," and a number of related topics. Most significantly, Nibley's studies have brought many to understand and appreciate Latterday Saint temples and to participate in sacred temple worship.

—Donald W. Parry[1]

If one studies Nibley's writing output not chronologically but thematically, one can see a pattern, both in the foreground and in the background. It is the temple. . . . He has shown that Joseph Smith's fullbodied presentation of ordinances, with the temple as their climactic apex, could not have been simply a nineteenth-century aberration nor warmedover Masonry. By and large, and point for point, what takes place in Mormon temples is closer to presently describable ancient practice than to any modern ritual.

—Truman Madsen[2]

---

[1]Donald W. Parry, e-mail to Boyd Petersen, 9 May 2002.
[2]Truman Madsen, "Foreword," *Nibley on the Timely and the Timeless* (Provo, UT: Brigham Young University Religious Studies Center, 1978), xvxvi.

Chapter 22

"The Source of All Good Things": Hugh Nibley and the Temple

Prefacing his address at FARMS Symposium on Ancient Temples at Brigham Young University on 20 February 1993, Elder Marion D. Hanks joked that, as president of the Salt Lake Temple, he had been asked some questions so deep that only "Hugh Nibley and the Almighty might know how to answer them." Elder Hanks mentioned his respect and admiration for Hugh's knowledge of temples, as well as Hugh's sensitivity in discussing the topic: "I love the freshness and the beauty of [his] labors and utterances."[3] In a later interview, Elder Hanks acknowledged: "Hugh's awareness, his knowledge, his linguistic and historical strength permitted him to know more about many things than many others of us know or will likely know in this world." He also expressed his "affection and appreciation and admiration for Hugh's knowledge of the temple," which comes not only from Hugh's understanding of history and languages but also from his "great personal experiences, which you can't leave out when you try to understand something. He has been a temple goer and observer."[4]

It is impossible to overemphasize Hugh's contribution to our understanding of the temple. His research represents the first scholarly comparative analysis on the Mormon temple endowment. Importantly, Hugh has maintained the confidence of General Authorities by writing about the temple in a highly respectful way that also preserves the sacred nature of the subject matter. Hugh's writings about the temple provide not only new insights and knowledge but also deeper inspiration and motivation. Indeed,

---
[3]Marion D. Hanks, "Christ Manifested to His People," delivered at the FARMS Symposium on Ancient Temples, 20 February 1993, was published in *Temples of the Ancient World*, edited by Donald W. Parry (Salt Lake City: Deseret and FARMS, 1994), 3-28. The introductory remarks (transcript in my possession) were not included in the published version.

[4]Elder Marion D. Hanks, Interviewed by Boyd Petersen, 20 March 1998.

with both his words and his deeds, Hugh has inspired both templegoers and a whole generation of scholars to take the temple more seriously.

Just before leaving on his mission, Hugh attended the dedication of the Mesa Arizona Temple on 23 October 1927. Nine days later on 1 November, he was endowed in the Salt Lake Temple. "I was very serious about it," remembers Hugh. "And the words of the initiatory [part of the endowment] I thought those were the most magnificent words I have ever heard spoken!"[5]

Although the temple has always been a crucial part of Mormon theology and covenant-making, in 1927 it was far from occupying its current position as "the great symbol of our membership" that it became under the administration of President Howard W. Hunter and has continued to be under President Gordon B. Hinckley.[6] In 1927, instead of more than a hundred temples dotting the globe, there were only seven.[7] The Salt Lake Temple was open only four days a week in 1927. Prior to the 1920s, Church members were not expected to attend the temple regularly and were expected to do temple work only for their own relatives.[8] Before he moved to Utah following World War II, Hugh himself had only attended the temple twice, "both times in something of a daze."[9] His second visit to the temple came after his mission in 1930, and it was at this time that the ceremony really overwhelmed Hugh. "At that time I knew it was the real thing. Oh boy, did I!"[10] Seventy-five years later, Hugh has proved his dedication both as a temple student and temple participant. Likewise, our attitudes about the temple have greatly changed, and some of that change may be attributed to his words and example.

Truman Madsen, now emeritus professor of philosophy and religion at BYU, has called Hugh a "ritualist" because he has stressed that "one way to study cultures is to look at their rites" that "somehow these rites tie in to the ideas of the temple, and finally even to the foundations of civilization."[11] This statement accurately represents

---

[5]Hugh Nibley, "Faith of an Observer," 297, compilation of interviews, ca. 1983-84 for a video documentary of the same name aired in 1985, photocopy of typescript in my possession, pagination added.

[6]Howard W. Hunter used this phrase in his first press conference after becoming the fourteenth president of the Church. Quoted in Jay M. Todd, "President Howard W. Hunter: Fourteenth President of the Church," Ensign, July 1944, 5. He used the phrase again in his First Presidency message, "The Great Symbol of Our Membership," Ensign, October 1994, 2-5.

[7]In addition to the Mesa Temple, temples in use at this time were located in St. George (dedicated in 1877), Logan (1884), Manti (1888), Salt Lake City (1893), Hawaii (1919), and Alberta (1923).

[8]Thomas G. Alexander, Mormonism in Transition: A History of the Latter-day Saints, 1890-1930 (Urbana: University of Illinois Press, 1986), 299. Indeed, Alexander notes that Apostle Reed Smoot had testified in 1905 that he had not attended the temple since his marriage and that President Heber J. Grant attended the temple infrequently prior to the 1920s. Alexander also gives a very interesting account of temple clothing and ordinance changes that were made in the early to mid-1920s (299-302).

[9]Nibley, "What Is a Temple," in Mormonism and Early Christianity, edited by Todd M. Compton and Stephen D. Ricks, Vol. 4 of The Collected Works of Hugh Nibley (Salt Lake City: Deseret Books/FARMS, 1987), 377.

[10]Nibley, "Faith of an Observer," 297. Hugh did the temple work for his deceased brother Philip in 1933, but he has also stated that he attended the temple immediately following his mission when he visited his Grandfather Nibley in 1930. In interviews he has usually combined the two events, stating that he was in Utah to do Philip's temple work when he visited his grandfather; however, the dates make this combination of events impossible. Either Hugh attended the temple three times before World War II (1927, 1930, and 1933) or only twice (1927 and 1933). Either way, it does not affect Hugh's point that he did not attend the temple regularly until he moved to Utah in 1945.

[11]Truman Madsen, "Faith of an Observer," 453-54.

Hugh's position. "All the arts and sciences began at the temple," stated Hugh at BYU's Sesquicentennial Symposium on the Humanities in 1980. "Dance, music, architecture, sculpture, drama, and so forth—they all go back to the temple."[12] As Hugh has translated the last lines of the Shabako Stone, the temple is "the source of all good things."[13]

While the topic didn't become a preoccupation for Hugh until the 1970s, his study of ancient temples and rituals goes back many years. His doctoral thesis on "The Roman Games as a Survival of an Archaic Year-Cult" (1939), as well as several essays he wrote before World War II looked at ancient rites as "foundational."[14] One of his earliest examinations of Mormon rituals was "Baptism for the Dead in Ancient Times," a series in the *Improvement Era* that ran from December 1948 through April 1949. There he gave evidence, primarily from early Christian texts, supporting the LDS practice of baptisms for the dead.[15] Although intended for a Mormon audience, the series was quite erudite and even prompted a response in the pages of *Catholic Biblical Quarterly*.[16] A decade later, to celebrate the 1958 dedication of the London Temple, Hugh wrote "The Idea of the Temple in History" for the *Millennial Star*.[17] Using what Truman Madsen characterized as, "comparative and patternistic methods which show a diffusion of temple ideas throughout all the cultures of the world," Hugh demonstrated that the "complex of Mormon temple architecture, symbolism, and ritual process cannot be found in the milieu of Joseph Smith's own time and place," but are found in abundance in the ancient world.[18]

---

[12] Hugh Nibley, in panel discussion with Eliot Butler, Robert Rees, and Dennis Smith, in *Letters to Smoother, Etc. . . . Proceedings of the 1980 Brigham Young University Symposium on the Humanities*, edited by Joy C. Ross and Steven C. Walker (Provo, UT: Brigham Young University Press, 1982), 104.

[13] Nibley, "The Expanding Gospel," in *Temple and Cosmos: Beyond This Ignorant Present*, edited by Don E. Norton, Vol. 12 of *The Collected Works of Hugh Nibley* (Salt Lake City: Deseret Book/FARMS, 1992), 192. The Shabako Stone is one of the oldest written records. It contains the creation myth from the first Egyptian dynasty (3100 B.C.), but the language and the inscription technique reveal it to be even older.

[14] In 1983, Hugh recounted his early work looking at comparative approaches to ritual: "In 1940 a section of the Pacific Coast Meeting of the American Historical Association slept through a discourse on the feasting of the multitudes at the holy places and in the following year a like gathering of the American Archaeological Association in San Diego listened with remarkable composure to a paper on "National Assemblies in the Bronze Age." . . . An article comparing the earliest Roman rites to those all over the ancient world was held up by World War II (which was then considered more urgent), not appearing until 1945." Nibley, "Sparisones," *Classical Journal* 40 (1945): 515-43; reprinted in *The Ancient State*, edited by Donald W. Parry and Stephen D. Ricks, Vol. 10 of *The Collected Works of Hugh Nibley* (Salt Lake City: Deseret Books/FARMS, 1991), 148-94. The quotation is from "What Is a Temple," *Mormonism and Early Christianity*, edited by Todd M. Compton and Stephen D. Ricks, Vol. 4 in *The Collected Works of Hugh Nibley* (Salt Lake City: Deseret/FARMS, 1987), 377.

[15] Reprinted in *Mormonism and Early Christianity*, 100-167.

[16] Bernard M. Foschini, "Those Who are Baptized for the Dead: I Cor. 15:29," *Catholic Biblical Quarterly* 12 (1950): 260-76, 379-88, and 13 (1951): 46-79, 172-98, and 278-83.

[17] Nibley, "The Idea of the Temple in History," *Millennial Star* 120 (1958): 228-37, 247-49. The essay was published several times in English and German, renamed "What Is a Temple," and was printed with an additional short essay, "Looking Backward," in *The Temple in Antiquity*, edited Truman G. Madsen (Provo, UT: BYU Religious Studies Center, 1984), 19-37, 39-51. The two essays were subsequently combined into one article and printed as "What Is a Temple?" in *Mormonism and Early Christianity*, 355-90.

[18] Truman G. Madsen, Preface to "What Is a Temple," in *The Temple in Antiquity*, 19.

By the 1970s, the temple had assumed new importance for Hugh, and he produced a stream of articles on the topic specifically for LDS audiences.[19] In 1972 Hugh summarized much of his efforts to show how ancient cultures were "hierocentric" and the harmony of that worldview with LDS teachings in "Ancient Temples: What Do They Signify?" which appeared in the *Ensign*.[20] In "Genesis of the Written Word" the following year, Hugh demonstrated how the oldest written texts are temple documents.[21] And in 1978, he published an intriguing study of ancient prayer practices in his "The Early Christian Prayer Circle."[22] But Hugh's most important work during the 1970s also contained his most detailed examination of the temple. *The Message of the Joseph Smith Papyri: An Egyptian Endowment* gave not only a detailed analysis of the papyri once owned by Joseph Smith which the Church acquired in 1967, but also showed how these papyri contain a ritual similar to the Mormon temple endowment.[23] While many Mormon readers were perplexed by its highly technical material, subtle references to the LDS temple make it a page turner. The most interesting section of the book was a series of appendices which reproduced six ancient Jewish and Christian texts that show striking parallels with the Mormon temple ceremony.[24] (See chap. 21.)

In all of these studies, Hugh has been respectful of the covenants of secrecy safeguarding specific portions of the LDS endowment, usually describing parallels from other cultures without talking specifically about the Mormon ceremony. This approach earned him a great deal of trust from both General Authorities and from Church members. In the

---

[19]Hugh also dealt with the temple in secular, non-Mormon journals. Without mentioning Mormon temples, Hugh argued that the temple, rather than being an exclusively Jewish institution, is a logical and necessary part of Christianity, deeply rooted in antiquity. In "The Hierocentric State," *Western Political Quarterly* 4 (1951): 226-53; reprinted in The *Ancient State*, 99-147, Hugh positioned rituals and temple-like edifices at the very foundation and center of ancient civilization. In "Christian Envy of the Temple," *Jewish Quarterly Review* 50, no. 2 October 1959: 97-123 and 50, n. 3 (January 1960): 229-40, reprinted in *Mormonism and Early Christianity*, 391-434, Hugh documented a deep longing for the temple in Christianity, which retains temple elements in its symbols, rituals, and architecture. "Tenting, Toll, and Taxing," *Western Political Quarterly* 29, no. 4 (December 1966): 599-630, reprinted in *The Ancient State*, 33-98, discusses "migratory temples" which travelled around ancient Asia. "Evangelium Quadraginta Dierum," *Vigiliae Christianae* 20, no. 1 (1966): 1-24, reprinted as "Evangelium Quadraginta Dierum: The Forty Day Mission of Christ—The Forgotten Heritage," in *Mormonism and Early Christianity*, 10-44, lays out apocryphal sources about Christ instructing his disciples in secret rituals during the forty-day ministry after the resurrection. "Jerusalem in Christian Thought," *Encyclopedia Judaica*, 16 vols. (Jerusalem: Macmillan, 1972), edited by Cecil Roth, 9:1568-75, reprinted as "Jerusalem: In Early Christianity," in *Mormonism and Early Christianity*, 323-54, documented the role of Jerusalem as a holy center for Christians, Muslims, and Jews because of its temple heritage.

[20]Nibley, "Ancient Temples: What Do They Signify?" *Ensign*, September 1972, 16-19, reprinted in *The Prophetic Book of Mormon*, edited by John W. Welch, Vol. 8 of *The Collected Works of Hugh Nibley* (Salt Lake City: Deseret Book/FARMS, 1989), 265-73.

[21]Nibley, "Genesis of the Written Word," *New Era*, September 1973, 38-50. The essay appeared in several publications, most notably in *Temple and Cosmos*, 450-90.

[22]Nibley, "The Early Christian Prayer Circle," *BYU Studies* 19, no. 1 (Fall 1978): 41-78, reprinted in *Mormonism and Early Christianity*, 45-99.

[23]Nibley, *The Message of The Joseph Smith Papyri: An Egyptian Endowment* (Salt Lake City: Deseret Book, 1975).

[24]Several of Hugh's informal lectures from this period have been reprinted in *Temple and Cosmos*. They include "The Meaning of the Temple," given on several occasions between 1973 and 1975, pp. 1-41; a discussion of ancient parallels to LDS temple clothing in "Sacred Vestments" (1975), pp. 91-138; and "The Circle and the Square," n.d., pp. 139-73.

mid- to late-1960s the BYU Religion Department began asking Hugh to address its faculty members in the temple during their regular temple excursions. Hugh spoke on topics like "anointings and washings in ancient manuscripts" and "ancient Near Eastern temple rites."[25] When Jeffrey R. Holland, who had a Ph.D. in American Studies from Yale, became president of BYU in 1980, he asked Hugh to address the members of BYU's administration in the temple during a special temple trip.[26]

Likewise, Church leaders were so impressed with Hugh's insights and so appreciative of the respectful way he had addressed the topic that, when the First Presidency and Quorum of the Twelve began to consider changes to the endowment, they asked Hugh to prepare a report on the "history and significance of the endowment."[27] Hugh received the assignment on 31 March 1985 in a Sunday meeting with the Quorum of the Twelve,[28] a project that, he happily wrote, "animated me with a wild sense of work to be done and the gratifying discovery that what I have been engaged in [for] the past two years is right on target."[29] Holland responded, "I do know that the Brethren are very enthused about your assignment to bring together the temple material." He continued, "both Elder [Howard W.] Hunter and Elder [James E.] Faust have spoken to me about it within the week and they are anxious that I give you all the support I can. Please know that I am committed to doing that and I'm asking your secretary to give that project her highest priority. Let me know how I can help. My guess is that any help I give will be Alexander-like: simply staying out of the light."[30]

In March 1986, Elders Hunter and Faust asked Holland to write Hugh for an update on his progress.[31] Hugh replied, "The fact is that everything I do these days is endowment." He continued humbly, "Whether I have anything of value to contribute remains to be seen. Thank you for the reminder and the intimidating opportunity."[32]

The result was two essays. He read the first, "Temple," to the First Presidency and Quorum of the Twelve in a special three-hour Sunday meeting in the Salt Lake Temple in

---

[25]College of Religious Instruction, Minutes of Faculty Meetings, 12 January 1965, 10 March 1967, and 27 October 1967, College of Religious Instruction Collection, Department Chairman's Meeting, Minutes, 13 December 1967, L. Tom Perry Special Collections, Harold B. Lee Library, Brigham Young University, Provo, Utah.

[26]Jeffrey R. Holland, Interviewed by Boyd Petersen, 20 December 1989.

[27]Jeffrey R. Holland, Letter to Hugh Nibley, 18 March 1986, Holland Presidential Papers, Perry Special Collections.. Although this letter was written almost a year after the assignment was given, it is the first letter that stated the exact nature of Hugh's assignment. In a letter to Hugh soon after the assignment was given, Holland referred to it less specifically as an "assignment to bring together the temple material."

[28]Hugh mentions the meeting in an undated letter to Holland thanking him for the party BYU had hosted commemorating Hugh's seventy-fifth birthday. Thus, the letter must have been written after his birthday on 27 March 1985 and before 22 April 1985 when Holland responded. In the letter, Hugh states that his meeting with the General Authorities occurred "on the Sunday before Conference." Conference that spring was 6-7 April 1985, thus dating the meeting at 31 March.

[29]Ibid.

[30]Jeffrey R. Holland, Letter to Hugh Nibley, 22 April 1985, Holland Presidential Papers, Perry Special Collections.

[31]Jeffrey R. Holland, Letter to Hugh Nibley, 18 March 1986, ibid.

[32]Hugh Nibley, Letter to Jeffrey R. Holland, 13 May 1986, ibid.

June 1986 and, at the same time, submitted a much longer written essay, "Endowment History."[33]

Stressing the value Church leaders placed on Hugh's temple-related studies and their gratitude for his approach, Elder Dallin H. Oaks later wrote Hugh: "It also seems desirable for me to express, in behalf of my brethren, our admiration and appreciation for the sensitive way in which you have done your scholarly work and expressed your views on subjects related to the temple ceremonies."[34] Oaks included with that letter "The Temple Ceremonies," a talk he had recently given to "an audience of General Authorities" in which he addressed the manner and extent to which temple ordinances should be discussed outside the temple. Oaks assured Hugh that "nothing in this talk is intended to be a criticism or a discouragement of efforts as sensitive as yours. The talk has some targets, but you aren't one of them."[35]

Hugh's passion for the temple has continued in recent years even though his publication rate has declined. At the 20 February 1993 FARMS symposium on Ancient Temples, Hugh delivered an essay, "House of Glory," analyzing Doctrine and Covenants 109, which is the dedication prayer for the Kirtland Temple.[36] In 1997, he spoke at a fireside "On the Meaning of Temples."[37] And on 6 April 1999 Hugh examined the Book of Abraham as a temple text in "Abraham's Creation Drama."[38] But more importantly, Hugh has continued to attend the temple regularly. Since the Provo Temple's completion in 1972, Hugh has attended the temple weekly on Saturday mornings, not so much as a manifestation of duty as prompted by a desire for further light and knowledge. As he wrote in his "Intellectual Autobiography," "If I went to the temple five times and nothing happened, I would stop going. But I've gone hundreds of times, and the high hopes of new knowledge with which I go up the hill every week are never disappointed."[39] Upon hearing Hugh's claim that he learns something new every time he attends the temple, some have felt daunted. Even Elder Marion D. Hanks confessed that this statement "has discouraged me significantly, as indeed many things he says do, simply because I'm so ignorant."[40]

---

[33] Hugh Nibley, Interviewed by Allison Clark, June 1996. "Temple" was published as "Return to the Temple," in Temple and Cosmos, 42-90. "Endowment History" was published as "On the Sacred and the Symbolic" in Temples of the Ancient World, 535-621. Although explicit references to the Mormon temple endowment were deleted from these manuscripts, they are essentially identical to the originals.

[34] Dallin H. Oaks, Letter to Hugh Nibley, 4 November 1988.

[35] Ibid.; Elder Dallin H. Oaks, "The Temple Ceremonies," address at the General Authority Training Meeting, 2 November 1988, photocopy of transcript in my possession. Oaks cited James E. Talmage and Boyd K. Packer as models of what can and cannot be discussed; however, he specifically quotes Hugh's writings in several places throughout the talk.

[36] Nibley, "House of Glory," in Temples of the Ancient World, 29-47.

[37] Hugh Nibley on the Meaning of Temples, taped ca. May 1997, Hugh Nibley Videotape Collection, FARMS, Provo, Utah.

[38] Reprinted as "Abraham's Temple Drama," in The Temple in Time and Eternity, edited by Donald W. Parry and Stephen D. Ricks (Provo, Utah: FARMS, 1999): 1-42.

[39] Nibley, "An Intellectual Autobiography," Nibley on the Timely and the Timeless, xxviii.

[40] Marion D. Hanks, "Christ Manifested to His People," typescript, 1. These introductory remarks were not published.

While I share Hanks's discouragement when considering Hugh's experience, I am comforted by two factors. First, what Hugh has taken from his temple trips is more often an insight than a revolutionary discovery. In 1987, Hugh told a correspondent:

> I do continue to learn something new every time [I go to the temple]. Last Saturday, for example, I was struck by "the need for constant nourishment to body and spirit." We go on feeding ourselves with calories and vitamins from day to day, even though we have already been stuffing for years. Why don't we carry on with the same elan in nourishing the spirit instead of chewing the same tired bubble gum that we did as children?[41]

This insight, though important, is not earth-shaking. Most Latter-day Saints have had similar insights in the temple. On another occasion he commented: "Last Saturday I left the temple loaded with instructions, specific instructions." And then he revealed his secret for gaining knowledge from temple work: "I found it all laid out for me, because I was looking for it. That is always the case when you are going to the temple."[42] This is the second comforting factor: Hugh gets out of his temple trips what he puts into them. When he attends the temple, he actively seeks knowledge and insight rather than just hoping for it. And he rejoices in whatever insight or knowledge he gains.

Much of what Hugh has learned through temple attendance is, however, quite profound. It is a direct result of the rich background he has as a student of ancient cultures and languages. And fortunately for us, he desires to share these insights and has found appropriate ways to do so. Hugh has had a great impact on our understanding of the temple. First, just as he has done with the Book of Mormon and the Pearl of Great Price, he has begun his research with the firm conviction that Joseph Smith, far from creating these rituals from his own imagination, restored the temple and its ordinances through divine revelation. He believes that God revealed these same rituals anciently to prophets in previous dispensations but that they were lost as the world fell into apostasy. Since these ordinances were once on earth in their totality, it makes sense that fragments would survive in ancient texts and even in contemporary religions. As Hugh wrote to one inquirer: "In a book called An Egyptian Endowment, I analyzed an Egyptian temple endowment at length and in an appendix supplied half-a-dozen parallels from the earliest Christian and Jewish writings. I think you will find there truly impressive resemblances to our own temple ordinances throughout, as well as an indisputable common pattern among them all."[43]

Hugh found inadequate the parallel between the rites of Freemasonry, to which Joseph Smith once belonged, to explain the depth and richness of the endowment: "The undoubted parallels between our temple ordinances and certain Masonic rites can be easily explained," he told an inquiring correspondent. "But ours makes a consistent theological and historical whole and is much closer to some of the older rites than they are to Freemasonry."[44] Or, as Hugh has also stated, Masonry is the "shadow," while the LDS tem-

---

[41]Hugh Nibley, Letter to Ghent Graves, 22 July 1987.
[42]Hugh Nibley, "But What Kind of Work?" in *Approaching Zion*, edited by Don E. Norton, Vol. 9 of *The Collected Works of Hugh Nibley* (Salt Lake City: Deseret Book/FARMS, 1989), 261.
[43]Hugh Nibley, Letter to Howard S. Rhodes, 4 March 1980.
[44]Ibid.

ple endowment is the "substance." Ours is "literal," while theirs is "allegorical."[45] "The LDS endowment was not built up of elements brought together by chance, custom, or long research," wrote Hugh in the introduction to his *The Message of the Joseph Smith Papyri*. "It is a single, perfectly consistent organic whole, conveying its message without the aid of rationalizing, spiritualizing, allegorizing, or moralizing interpretations."[46] In fact, Hugh noted more significant parallels to rituals from cultures where Joseph Smith had no contact, some of which continue today. "The Hopi Indians, for example, come closest of all as far as I have been able to discover—and where did they get theirs?"[47] (See chap. 18.)

The parallels Hugh has cited from ancient texts not only testify of Joseph Smith's calling as a prophet, but they are often staggering to an endowed LDS reader. The abundant examples of ancient prayer circles compiled in "The Early Christian Prayer Circle" are a case in point. For example, Hugh mentions that in the "Pistis Sophia," the Lord gathered his disciples and their wives around him, all clothed in white, and, "taking the place of Adam at the altar, called upon the Father three times in an unknown tongue." The prayer he uttered was in a strange language but was interpreted to mean "Hear me Father, the Father of all fatherhood, boundless light!"[48]

In another essay, Hugh describes two veils that Sir Aurel Stein, a nineteenth-century archaeologist, discovered in a Central Asian tomb in 1925. One was hung on the wall, while the other was draped over a coffin. Both had similar marks: "We see the king and queen embracing at their wedding, the king holding the square on high, the queen a compass. . . . Above the couple's head is the sun surrounded by twelve disks, meaning the circle of the year or the navel of the universe." Illustrator Michael Lyon reproduced these marked veils in Hugh's *Temple and Cosmos*.[49] Any endowed Latter-day Saint who saw these illustrations would immediately recognize the parallels to their own temple symbols.

While Hugh has ably demonstrated that ancient cultures had these ordinances and lost them, he also recognizes that we have them but do not fully understand them. His knowledge of these ancient cultures has helped us better understand what we have by looking at what these rituals meant to the ancients. One of Hugh's first contributions is to help us understand what a temple is. *Temple*, Hugh has noted, comes from the root *tem*, which in both in Greek and Latin, means "a cutting or intersection of two lines at right angles," the point "where the four regions come together." A temple is "a scale-model of

---

[45]Nibley, "What Is a Temple?" in *Mormonism and Early Christianity*, 389 note 71. See also Hugh's discussion of Masonry, "One Eternal Round," in *Temple and Cosmos*, 419-23.

[46]Nibley, *The Message of the Joseph Smith Papyri*, xii.

[47]Hugh Nibley, Letter to Howard S. Rhodes, 4 March 1980.

[48]Nibley, "The Early Christian Prayer Circle," in *Mormonism and Early Christianity*, 57. See also Edgar Hennecke and Wilhelm Schneemelcher, eds., *New Testament Apocrypha*, trans. R. McL. Wilson and Henri-Charles Puech, Vol. 1 of *Gospels and Related Writings* (Philadelphia: Westminster, 1963), 258-59. Puech renders what Nibley calls "wives of the disciples" as "the women disciples." At the conclusion of the "Pistis Sophia," Jesus gives his disciples "names," "passwords," and "formulae" which "allow free passage through each of their spheres" and charges them to preserve and not give these "mysteries" to any man "except he be worthy of them" (263).

[49]Hugh Nibley, "Sacred Vestments," in *Temple and Cosmos*, 111-12. Michael Lyon's exact renderings of the veils from Stein's *Innermost Asia*, 3 vols. (Oxford: Clarendon, 1928), 2:707 are found on pp. 114-15.

the universe" and "a sort of observatory where one gets one's bearings on the universe."[50] Thus its form is cosmically oriented, while its function is to serve as an intersection between the celestial and the terrestrial worlds, "the one point on earth at which men could establish contact with other worlds."[51]

Hugh summed up this cosmic orientation and interworldly function of ancient temples in a lengthy letter to the Church Architectural Services, a division in the general Church Building Department), in 1981, in which he discussed what he considered essential elements of temple design:

> In all of the literature you will find two basic patterns for ancient temples . . . the circle and the square, which represent the same thing, and in Jewish lore are often combined. There are also certain standard ways of representing the progression or steps of initiation: the straight processional way from room to room through a series of gates or the mounting up by stairways either circular or straight—you find both at Chichen-Itza. The circular Tawwaf is negotiated three times by the pilgrim at Mecca around the Qaaba, which is a great square; in fact, the word Qaaba is cognate with our Cube.
>
> You will note that there is not a curved line on the exterior of the Salt Lake Temple, except for windows and doors. The Cosmic cycle or circle is clearly indicated, however, by the Dipper and Pole Star on the main west tower, for Ursa Major and Polaris have always represented to all peoples the rotation of the heavens and the earth. The cosmic cycle is also represented in the circular font at the bottom and center of everything—the Tehom of the Old Testament. All temples express in one way or another the idea of the divine mountain, the mountain of the Lord. Which makes the tower principle indispensable, even if the tower is a low-profile mountain and includes the whole temple as in Cardston.
>
> The three levels or three degrees are essential both inside and out. In a single room they could be presented by taking a step up upon entering, another step up at the prayer circle, the altar standing on a slight rise, and a final step up at the veil. Or the walls could have panelling at three levels, indirect lighting displaying successively the blank walls of "matter unorganized" (appropriate designs for such would be only too easy to find among our present-day artists), a panel set back with stars, another behind and above it with phases of the moon, and finally the sun and its rays.
>
> The tower would be a central one over a celestial room, resembling the main tower of the Salt Lake Temple, clearly displaying the three degrees and four-square principle. The lowest and broadest level could have horns at the corners representing the law of sacrifice in our telestial kingdom, the next level could have a stylized stairway indicated on four sides like ancient American temples or a Hopi kiva, indicating the covenants by which we mount up. The top crowned with Moroni or some celestial symbol. These are the things that occur to me most forcefully in reviewing many studies on the "hierocentric structure." Whatever else one adds or subtracts they represent the historical minimum.[52]

---

[50]Nibley, "What Is a Temple?," 357-58.

[51]Ibid., 359.

[52]Hugh Nibley, Letter to Leland A. Gray, in the LDS Architectural Services and Standard Plans Section, 19 May 1981. Evidently Church Architectural Services had contacted Hugh for information on temple architecture because Hugh's letter appears to be a response to specific questions. I have not, however, found Gray's letter to Hugh.

In addition to explaining the symbolism of the temple edifice itself, Hugh has also explained the symbolism of our temple ritual. He has noted that "the rites of the temple are always a repetition of those that marked its founding in the beginning of the world, telling how it all came to be in the first place."[53] That is, the ritual drama that is always associated with temples recounts the creation of the world. The Egyptian rituals that Hugh discusses in *The Message of the Joseph Smith Papyri*, as well as the six ancient texts in the appendices, are all creation narratives. In looking at these ancient ritual dramas, Hugh has noted: "It is now generally held that mythology is simply an attempt to explain the origin and meaning of rituals that men no longer understand."[54]

Hugh has also occasionally noted new ways of reading scriptures. "I have always had a weakness for seeking out ritual indicators in the Scriptures," wrote Hugh in 1971.[55] One such case is, as Hugh describes it, "one of the most puzzling episodes in the Bible," in which Jacob wrestles with an angel (Gen. 32:24-30). Hugh notes that "the word conventionally translated by 'wrestled' (*yeaveq*) can just as well mean 'embrace,' and that it was in this ritual embrace that Jacob received a new name and the bestowal of priestly and kingly power at sunrise. . . . Shu, the lord of thrones, embraces the new king and confers power on him." Hugh sums up, "The parallel to the Egyptian coronation embrace becomes at once apparent."[56] What he leaves for the astute Latter-day Saint reader to fill in is the parallel with the Mormon endowment.

In addition to helping us understand the significance of our temples and the endowment, Hugh has also worked to help us overcome some of the obstacles that might prevent us from loving temple attendance. For example, Hugh's address "Patriarchy and Matriarchy," delivered at the BYU Women's Conference in February 1980, has helped many women overcome the sexism they have seen in the Adam and Eve narrative which is central to the LDS temple endowment. In the spirit of the biblical scholar Phyllis Trible, Hugh "rescued" the biblical narrative for a modern audience.[57] "In the Eden story [Eve] holds her own as a lone woman in the midst of an all-male cast of no less than seven supermen and angels," wrote Hugh.[58] He viewed Eve as more progressive than Adam—"she takes the initiative, pursuing the search for ever greater light and knowledge while Adam cautiously holds back."[59] He also stated that the curses placed on the pair were roughly equivalent—both are forced to labor and suffer to survive, the man in the field, the woman in childbearing. "Both of them bring forth life with sweat and tears, and Adam is not the favored party. If his labor is not as severe as hers, it is more protracted."[60] He has specifically addressed the inequality that many see in the temple covenants:

---

[53] Nibley, "What Is a Temple?," 361.

[54] Ibid., 365.

[55] Hugh Nibley, Letter to Robert F. Smith, 9 January 1971.

[56] Nibley, *The Message of the Joseph Smith Papyri*, 242-43.

[57] See Phyllis Trible, *God and the Rhetoric of Sexuality* (Philadelphia: Fortress, 1978), particularly Chapter 5, "A Love Story Gone Awry," in which Trible reaches conclusions about the Adam and Eve narrative similar to Hugh's in "Patriarchy and Matriarchy." There is, however, no evidence that Trible had any influence on Hugh's reading, and her approach is a more sustained close reading than Hugh's.

[58] Nibley, *Old Testament and Related Studies*, edited by John W. Welch, Gary P. Gillum, and Don E. Norton, Vol. 1 of *The Collected Works of Hugh Nibley* (Salt Lake City: Deseret Book/FARMS, 1986), 90.

[59] Ibid., 92.

[60] Ibid., 90.

> [Adam and Eve] supervise each other. Adam is given no arbitrary power; Eve is to heed him only insofar as he obeys their Father—and who decides that? She must keep check on him as much as he does on her. It is, if you will, a system of checks and balances in which each party is as distinct and independent in its sphere as are the departments of government under the Constitution—and just as dependent on each other.[61]

In the LDS culture, in which the Adam and Eve narrative is not only scripture—and scripture three times since it appears in both the Book of Moses and the Book of Abraham in addition to Genesis—but also a central part of the temple ceremony, Hugh's reading of the narrative had a great liberating function for many women in the Church.[62]

Hugh has also noted that our promise to keep the temple endowment secret is not so much to keep it from the world as to test our own ability to be trusted. "In revealing sacred things one gives away nothing but one's integrity, though that is everything," Hugh has written. "It is significant that none of the 'frightful disclosures' of the temple ordinances made in the sensational literature of the nineteenth century had the expected impact—they all fizzled, as indeed they must, since to one who does not understand their significance, these sacred things have no interest at all."[63] Furthermore, Hugh has stated that the scriptural expression that we should not "cast pearls before swine" (Matt. 7:6; 3 Ne. 14:6; D&C 41:6) "is not an expression of contempt, but a commentary on the uselessness of giving things to people who place no value on them, have no use for them, and could only spoil them."[64] Thus, even though many "exposés" have been published about the temple, we need not be overly concerned: "The more the truth of these things is known the better we look."[65] In a letter to the Jewish scholar Jacob Neusner, Hugh joked that Mormons may hide behind the obligation of secrecy from the responsibility of fully implementing temple covenants: "What the Mormons like best about their temples is the obligation of secrecy that exonerates them from ever having to speak, and hence to think, about what they have learned by the ordinances and teachings. So strict are they in observing the confidential nature of those teachings that they, for the most part, scrupulously avoid dropping so much as a hint to outsiders by putting any of them into practice."[66]

---

[61] Nibley, "Patriarchy and Matriarchy," in *Old Testament and Related Studies*, 92.

[62] Hugh's article has been cited in a wide range of Mormon feminist articles. See, for example, Beverly Campbell, "Eve," *Encyclopedia of Mormonism*, 4 vols. (New York: Macmillan Publishing Company, 1992), 2:475-76; Campbell, "Mother Eve: A Mentor for Today's Woman: A Heritage of Honor," *Collegium Aesculapium*, 1994, 36-49; Suzanne Evertsen Lundquist, "The Repentance of Eve," in *As Women of Faith*, edited by Mary E. Stovall and Carol Cornwall Madsen (Salt Lake City: Deseret Book, 1989), 88-106; Jolene Edmunds Rockwood, "The Redemption of Eve," *Sisters in Spirit: Mormon Women in Historical and Cultural Perspective*, edited by Maureen Ursenbach Beecher and Lavina Fielding Anderson (Urbana: University of Illinois Press, 1987), 3-36; Alison Walker, "Theological Foundations of Patriarchy," *Dialogue: A Journal of Mormon Thought* 23, no. 3 (Fall 1990): 77-89. For a history of how the Adam and Eve narrative has been interpreted by contemporary feminist literary critics, see my "Feminism in the Garden: Can Modern and Postmodern Literary Theory Redeem Eve?" (M.A thesis, University of Maryland at College Park, 1995).

[63] Nibley, "On the Sacred and the Symbolic," *Temples of the Ancient World*, 572.

[64] Ibid., 553.

[65] Hugh Nibley, Letter to Mada Edstrom, 25 November 1986.

[66] Hugh Nibley, Letter to Jacob Neusner, 12 January 1975.

Another of Hugh's contributions to temple scholarship is the generation of students who are now doing their own research and producing other illuminating studies. People like Stephen D. Ricks, Donald W. Parry, and John W. Welch are writing books and articles that continue the tradition that Hugh started.[67]

One of the most important contributions Hugh has made to our understanding of the temple has been, I believe, to show us how Christ is at the very center of our temple symbolism. In his essay "What Is a Temple?," Hugh notes that Cyril, bishop of Jerusalem, saw ritual washing as "the antitype of the anointing of Christ himself" and a way of "making every candidate as it were a Messiah." The initiatory ritual is described, Hugh writes, as "an imitation of the sufferings of Christ in which we suffer without pain by mere imitation his receiving of the nails in his hands and feet."[68] He has also noted how the "magnificent gesture" of praying with both hands raised above the head in a prayer circle was viewed anciently as "a natural gesture both of supplication and submission" as well as a "conscious imitation of the crucifixion," where, at a crucial moment, the Lord cried out in a strange tongue a prayer similar to that found in Psalms 54:2: "Hear my prayer, O God; give ear to the words of my mouth."[69] In "The Meaning of the Atonement," Hugh demonstrated that the reconciliation we hope to achieve is inextricably linked to the temple. "The embrace," states Hugh, "is the imagery of the Atonement," and he cites several significant illustrative scriptures: "The Lord hath redeemed my soul from hell; I have beheld his glory, and I am encircled about eternally in the arms of his love" (2 Ne. 1:15). "O Lord, wilt thou encircle me around in the robe of thy righteousness!" (2 Ne. 4:33). "Behold, he sendeth an invitation unto all men, for the arms of mercy are extended towards them, and he saith: Repent, and I will receive you" (Alma 5:33).[70] Such words are not only strikingly beautiful but also deeply consoling.

When Hugh wrote his "Intellectual Autobiography" in 1978, he observed:

> Five days a week between three and four o'clock in the morning, hundreds of elderly people along the Wasatch Front bestir themselves to go up and begin their long hours of work in the Temple, where they are ready to greet the first comers at 5:30 A.M. At that time, long before daylight, the place is packed, you can't get in, so I virtuously wait until later, much later, in the day. Whatever they may be up to, here is a band of mortals who are actually engaged in doing something which has not their own comfort, convenience, or profit as its object. Here at last is a phenomenon that commands respect in our day and could safely be put forth among the few valid arguments we have to induce the Deity to spare the human race: thousands of men and women putting themselves out for no ulterior motive. There is a touch of nobility here.[71]

---

[67] Articles by these scholars and others can be found in Truman G. Madsen, *The Temple in Antiquity: Ancient Records and Modern Perspectives* (Provo, UT: BYU Religious Studies Center, 1989) and in the FARMS compilations *Temples of the Ancient World: Ritual and Symbolism*, edited by Donald W. Parry (Salt Lake City: Deseret Book/FARMS, 1994) and *The Temple in Time and Eternity*, edited by Donald W. Parry and Stephen D. Ricks (Provo, UT: FARMS, 1999). See also John W. Welch, *The Sermon at the Temple and the Sermon on the Mount: A Latter-day Saint Approach* (Salt Lake City: Deseret book, 1990).

[68] Nibley, "What Is a Temple?," 364.

[69] Nibley, "The Early Christian Prayer Circle," 58.

[70] Nibley, "The Meaning of the Atonement," in *Approaching Zion*, 559.

[71] Nibley, "Intellectual Autobiography," xxvii.

And if there is a touch of nobility in the LDS commitment to temple worship, then I would argue there is a great deal of nobility in the words and deeds of Hugh Nibley. Certainly, the understanding that Hugh has shared with us of fragments of rituals and symbols similar to ours in other traditions has inspired us. These parallels underscore the reality of Joseph Smith's prophetic mission. And from Hugh's insights, based on his knowledge of ancient cultures, we have also gained a better understanding of the design and function of our temples and ordinances. But his humble example of dedicated temple attendance is the most inspiring of all. There truly is, as Elder Marion D. Hanks has stated, a "freshness and beauty" in Hugh's labors and words, for he has helped us to better understand and appreciate the "source of all good things."

Hugh Nibley, ca. 1980.

Photo courtesy of L. Tom Perry Special Collections,
Harold B. Lee Library, Brigham Young University

I sense someone digging deep beneath my crumbling battlements to blow me at the moon in some apocalyptic indiscretion. I can't imagine anything exciting or edifying in the life and times (and even less in the works) of an uncomplicated Beach Boy.[1]

I can't conceive of there being anything the least bit interesting in what a person has to say who has lived in Provo for 37 years. He couldn't have done anything, he couldn't have seen anything, he couldn't have thought about anything in such an environment.[2]

---

[1]Hugh Nibley, Letter to Paul Springer, 3 January 1983. Hugh was responding to a letter (which I have not found) from Paul Springer in which Springer gave Hugh "broad hints and well justified jibes" about the filming which was just beginning on the documentary, Faith of an Observer. Springer knew about the planned documentary because Hugh's son Alex had arranged to interview him. Hugh states in the letter that Springer's letter "is the first definite information that I have on this insane project." In fact, Hugh had been told about the project before Springer wrote him, but had conveniently "forgotten" about it.

[2]Nibley, "Faith of an Observer," 215, compilation of interviews, ca. 1983-84 for a video documentary of the same name aired in 1985, photocopy of typescript in my possession, pagination added. Hugh, with his customary modesty, was protesting about that the video documentary, Faith of an Observer, was unnecessary.

Chapter 23

Consecration and Recognition, 1980-89

The 1980s brought Ronald Reagan to the White House, a chill in the Cold War with the former Soviet Union, an accompanying military buildup, and a self-contented "me-generation" which was more concerned with financial gain than with social activism. At BYU, the Oaks administration had earned a reputation as being academically strong, less confrontational, and much more moderate than Wilkinson's. As Jeffrey R. Holland took over the presidential reins in September 1980, he continued that same tradition. The affable Holland had served as dean of Religious Instruction from 1971 to 1976, where he had come to have great respect for Hugh. That respect is underscored in a 1975 memorandum that Holland, as dean, wrote to Oaks. Holland praised the great work "Hugh Nibley has done for the Church in an almost totally unique way."[3] Likewise, Hugh developed a great respect for and cordial relationship with President Holland, just as he had with President Oaks.

Although Hugh was officially retired, he was an ongoing presence on the BYU campus. Each semester, he taught at least one class—usually an honors section on the Pearl of Great Price or the Book of Mormon. As he wrote to Lucien and Marguerite

---

[3]Jeffrey Holland, Memo to Dallin H. Oaks, 14 May 1975, Dallin H. Oaks Presidential Papers, Department of Religious Instruction, L. Tom Perry Special Collections, Harold B. Lee Library, Brigham Young University, Provo, Utah. Holland was arguing that, while he felt the "affective, inspirational mold" of some professors in the department was of primary importance, the "scholarly skill" of professors like Nibley "is nevertheless an important one for the Church, and probably the university as well. . . . Religious Instruction at BYU simply must have the former, but I think the Church will always need something of the latter," wrote Holland. To that end, Holland proposed that a special section of the Religion Department—"something like our present Institute of Ancient Studies (which has no faculty per se)"—be created "to keep us abreast of religious developments outside our traditional LDS undergraduate curriculum." Apparently nothing came of this proposal.

Goldschmidt in 1982, "I have been officially retired for seven years now, but am still teaching almost as much as ever and enjoying it more—age cannot wither nor custom stale what is already a preshrunk apple."[4] Continuing to teach the same classes he had taught for over thirty years would be no problem for most teachers. But Hugh was not like most teachers. "Since I make it a policy NEVER to teach the same thing I have taught before," wrote Hugh to Paul Springer in 1983, "it keeps me humping. Which is good for the circulation."[5]

Although Hugh's publication rate was slower than his prolific output during the 1950s and '60s, he turned out a large number of articles and speeches. Particularly impressive is the fact that Hugh's writing schedule was constantly punctuated by the intrusion of unannounced visitors, phone calls, and letters. "Life in this goldfish bowl" wrote Hugh to Paul Springer, "is just one uninterrupted interruption."[6] "I have published a lot of stuff," Hugh confessed to the Goldschmidts in 1982. "My playful pedantry disturbs local sensibilities, and my tactless and frequent references to religion scare off the academicians. Which does not worry me, since I know that they never read each other's writings either."[7]

What "disturbed local sensibilities" most were his frequent speeches lambasting Mormon culture for its preoccupation with wealth and lack of concern for the poor—a theme he had begun stressing during the 1970s—all while affirming his allegiance to the gospel. As he witnessed monstrous homes being built higher and higher up the mountains overlooking campus while poverty simultaneously became more evident in Utah Valley, Hugh turned repeatedly to the law of consecration for a speech theme during the 1980s. In 1982, Hugh challenged prevailing attitudes about work and wealth in "Work We Must But the Lunch Is Free."[8] That same year, he also delivered the sardonically titled "How to Get Rich" and showed how the Old Testament law required people to care for the poor or be cursed. In a sequel to his 1973 talk, "What Is Zion?: A Distant View," Hugh continued to explore the battle between Zion and Babylon in his 1984 "We Will Still Weep for Zion." Hugh expounded on the theme three years in a row for BYU's Spheres of Influence Lecture Series. In 1984, he spoke of the law of consecration as one of the "Breakthroughs I Would Like to See." In 1985, he compared the unchanging, stable, consecrated civilizations to our ever-changing and constantly declining world in "Change Out of Control." In 1986, he compared the United Order to other utopian enterprises in "The Utopians." In 1986, he elaborated on "The Law of Consecration" to a group of temple

---

[4]Hugh Nibley, Letter to Lucien and Marguerite Goldschmidt, 20 May 1982. Photocopies of Nibley's correspondence with the Goldschmidts are in my possession courtesy of Marguerite Goldschmidt.

[5]Hugh Nibley, Letter to Paul Springer, 2 January 1983, emphasis Nibley's. Alex's documentary project had briefly revived the correspondence between the two old friends. Springer worked as a San Francisco Superior Court probate commissioner (1963-78), then started a private practice in probate law which he maintained until his death on 28 May 1993 at age seventy-nine. This short exchange and a 1984 letter from Paul ends the correspondence that has been preserved.

[6]Hugh Nibley, Letter to Paul Springer, 3 January 1983.

[7]Hugh Nibley, Letter to Lucien and Marguerite Goldschmidt, 20 May 1982.

[8]On the bottom of his copy of "Work We Must But the Lunch Is Free," Sterling McMurrin scrawled, "If Hugh goes political or economic he'll get his butt in a sling yet. I like this piece." Sterling McMurrin Papers, MSS 32, 1990 Agenda, Box 41, fd. titled "Hugh Nibley," Special Collections, Marriott Library, University of Utah.

workers at the Church Office Building. And in 1987, he delivered a sequel to "Work We Must" titled "But What Kind of Work?"[9]

Given the forcefulness with which he denounced materialism, Hugh was often surprised by the favorable response these talks generated. After "unloading" "Work We Must But the Lunch is Free" to a group of lawyers and businessmen in Irvine, California, Hugh commented, amazed, to President Holland: "'This is just what we need!' was the usual response, which in some cases I believe was sincere."[10] In 1984, Hugh told the Goldschmidts that "for some reason our most pointed and tactless commentaries are tolerated and even applauded in the most unlikely quarters." He continued: "I think my teaching and writing and Phyllis' valued counselling are beginning to have some effect—locally, of course, but Mormons get around."[11]

In addition to the law of consecration, Hugh also turned his attention again to the Book of Mormon. Although he spent some time on evidences for the book's antiquity, as he had done in the 1950s and 1960s, his preoccupation in the 1980s was the book's message. In 1980, Hugh delivered a thinly veiled response to the Freeman Institute called "Freemen and Kingmen in the Book of Mormon." Hugh's reading of relevant Book of Mormon passages, in which he sees the Freemen as pacifists who were supporting the government, called into question the appropriation of the term "Freemen" by a right-wing political organization founded by Cleon Skousen. In a 1981 address titled "The Prophetic Book of Mormon," Hugh mapped out the Book of Mormon's social polarization and drew parallels with the polarization occurring between the Soviet Union and the United States. "In my youth," confessed Hugh, "I thought the Book of Mormon was much too preoccupied with extreme situations, situations that had little bearing on the real world of everyday life and ordinary human affairs. What on earth could the total extermination of nations have to do with life in the enlightened modern world? Today no comment on that is necessary."[12]

Hugh continued this theme in his apocalyptic essay "Scriptural Perspectives on How to Survive the Calamities of the Last Days" which appeared in BYU Studies in 1985. "Last Call: An Apocalyptic Warning" followed in 1986, expanding on the topic, but also stressing that pride resulting from wealth was the downfall of Book of Mormon peoples and would likewise be our own. "Repentance, and repentance alone, can save [the] land," wrote Hugh.[13] In 1988, Hugh celebrated the fortieth anniversary of his first class spent teaching the Book of Mormon with the retrospective "The Book of Mormon:

---

[9]These essays are all reprinted under these titles in *Approaching Zion*, edited by Don E. Norton, Vol. 9 of *The Collected Works of Hugh Nibley* (Salt Lake City: Deseret Book/FARMS, 1989).

[10]Hugh Nibley, Letter to Jeffrey R. Holland, 29 June 1982, Jeffrey R. Holland Presidential Papers, L. Tom Perry Special Collections, Harold B. Lee Library, Brigham Young University, Provo, Utah.

[11]Hugh Nibley, Letter to Lucien and Marguerite Goldschmidt, n.d. December 1984. The "valued counselling" Hugh mentions is probably Phyllis's Church service. At this point, she had served as a counselor in two Relief Society presidencies, as Relief Society president, and also on the Relief Society stake board, in addition to teaching in the Primary, Young Women, Sunday School, and Relief Society.

[12]Nibley, *The Prophetic Book of Mormon*, edited by John W. Welch, Vol. 8 of *The Collected Works of Hugh Nibley* (Salt Lake City: Deseret Book/FARMS, 1989), 468.

[13]Ibid., 520.

Forty Years After." Again, after looking at several recent historical and archaeological evidences supporting the historicity of the Book of Mormon, Hugh zeroed in on the "economic matters" of the Book of Mormon and the polarizing dangers they lead to. "Teaching the Book of Mormon class last semester, I was brought to my senses with a shock," relates Hugh. "The Book of Mormon has become alarmingly, terrifyingly, relevant."[14]

Hugh challenged traditional Mormon attitudes about evolution when he delivered his speech "Before Adam." In this talk, Hugh argued that Mormons cannot fully support either the creationist view or the view of secular science since our doctrine does not align with either position. Unlike creationists, asserted Hugh, we believe that all animal life has a spirit, that there is life on other worlds, and that matter was not created out of nothing. Unlike evolutionists, we believe that God was the creator of the universe and that humans are His divine offspring. According to creationists, it is an insult to be too closely associated with animals, while for evolutionists, "if animals are mere 'things' then so is man." For creationists, "man's life on earth [is] a one-act drama: Adam fell, Christ redeemed us, and that is the story. Before Adam there was nothing. Science tells us that the drama is pointless, because there is really nothing after it." Hugh believed that "this futile quarrel should be no concern of ours. For one thing, we have a story to tell before Adam. Religion and science have *none*, absolutely none." As for ape-like beings that existed before Adam, Hugh cautioned, "Do not begrudge existence to creatures that looked like men long, long ago, nor deny them a place in God's affection or even a right to exaltation—for our scriptures allow them such." Nor need we worry about whether we evolved from such creatures since, as Hugh argued, "Adam becomes Adam, a hominid becomes a man, when he starts keeping a record."[15]

In 1981, *Abraham in Egypt*, on which Hugh had been working since the mid-seventies, finally appeared. "The Book on *Abraham in Egypt* went up to Salt Lake today—they are going to rush publication," Hugh wrote to his son, Alex in 1980. "I am the one who has been holding it up from week to week as I dig up and load on more information—all information that has NOT been available until now. The Lord does time these things, and it seems to be more apparent every day that we are running on an increasingly tight schedule."[16] In another letter at about the same time, Hugh again reported to Alex: "By the time Deseret Book gets through reading the manuscript of *Abraham in Egypt* it will be my third revision coming up; well, my object is to satisfy myself on certain matters and things will keep changing."[17]

In addition to supporting the Book of Abraham as an ancient text by comparing the narrative with similar narratives from ancient Near Eastern texts, the book challenged the folk belief used by many members and leaders of the Church to jus-

---

[14]Ibid., 551-52.

[15]Hugh Nibley, "Before Adam," in *Old Testament and Related Studies*, edited by John W. Welch, Gary P. Gillum, and Don E. Norton, Vol. 1 of *The Collected Works of Hugh Nibley* (Salt Lake City: Deseret Book/FARMS, 1986), 50, 77, 51, 83.

[16]Hugh Nibley, Letter to Charles Alexander Nibley, n.d., ca. summer 1980.

[17]Hugh Nibley, Letter to Charles Alexander Nibley, 27 June 1980.

tify the official pre-1978 policy of excluding black men from being ordained to the priesthood. As Hugh asked:

> Why was Pharaoh, "a righteous man . . . blessed . . . with the blessings of wisdom" (Abraham 1:26), denied that priesthood, which he "would fain claim it from Noah, through Ham" (Abraham 1:27)? Certainly not because of Ham, "a just man [who] walked with God" (Moses 8:27).

Rather, Hugh argued, Pharaoh was denied the priesthood because he claimed it through the "matriarchal line" rather than the "patriarchal."[18] Hugh concluded: "There is no mention of race, though enemies of the Church have declared with shock and outrage that these passages are proof of Mormon discrimination against blacks."[19] Although Hugh was being tactful in ascribing such attitudes only to "enemies of the Church," many Latter-day Saints needed no other justification for racist attitudes. Equally unfortunately, many Mormon members are still not aware of Hugh's argument, and prejudiced readings of the Book of Abraham continue.[20] Lester Bush, who wrote the most detailed historical examination of the Church's policy denying blacks the priesthood, was disappointed that Hugh "unfortunately failed ever to publicly address Church teachings on blacks in the context of his Book of Abraham studies" until after "the point [was] moot."[21]

---

[18]Evaluating Hugh's argument is difficult since I have no background in Egyptology. Yale-trained Egyptologist John Gee, in a consultation with me, says that Hugh's assertion that Pharaoh claimed his authority through matriarchal lines was in agreement with much of the pre-1980s scholarship, which saw Egypt as a matriarchal culture. Contemporary scholarship has moved away from this position. Nevertheless, while the race of the Egyptians is a touchy topic, given the desire of many African Americans to tie their culture to the greatness of ancient Egypt, there is little evidence that the Egyptians themselves were concerned about race. Some Pharaohs were definitely black, others definitely were not; however, the race of most has not been determined. There is no scriptural or historical evidence to support the notion that Egyptus (the woman who, according to Abraham 1:23, "discovered" Egypt) was black. Gee also finds flaws in Hugh's chapter, "The Trouble with Ham," in which Hugh dismisses the idea that the curse of Ham was associated with a black skin; his argument is based on "a one-hundred year misreading" of khem (shrine) and min (an Egyptian god). This error, however, does not directly affect Hugh's argument that racism has been read into the text rather than out of the text. Hugh's scholarship on Egypt has been vindicated in one significant way: Hugh argued in The Message of the Joseph Smith Papyri that the Book of Breathings and other Egyptian documents are ritual texts that were used to induct a novice into the religion. Gee stresses that few if any Egyptologists at the time read these texts as Hugh did but that is no longer the case. Egyptologists have discovered that the texts show up in temples as well as tombs and what were once classified as funerary objects actually have a broader cultic function. John Gee, telephone conversation with Boyd Petersen, 7 March 2002.

[19]Nibley, Abraham in Egypt, edited by Gary P. Gillum, Vol. 13 in The Collected Works of Hugh Nibley (1981; Salt Lake City: Deseret Books/FARMS, 2000), 426-28.

[20]The Mormon folk tradition that Egyptus was black is most recently continued in the highly entertaining but ultimately disappointing musical The Ark, written by Michael McLean and Kevin Kelly, which was featured in the Festival of New Musicals on Broadway in New York City in September 2000 and performed in Utah soon thereafter.

[21]Lester E. Bush Jr. "Whence the Negro Doctrine? A Review of Ten Years of Answers," in Neither White Nor Black: Mormon Scholars Confront the Race Issue in a Universal Church, edited by Lester E. Bush Jr. and Armand L. Mauss (Midvale, UT: Signature Books, 1984), 212. Bush's assertion that Hugh never addressed the issue in context of the Book of Abraham is not exactly true. Bush wrote a lengthy and detailed essay, "Mormonism's Negro Doctrine: An Historical Overview," Dialogue: A Journal of Mormon Thought 8, no. 1 (Spring 1973): 11-68, later reprinted in Neither White Nor Black, 53-129. Hugh was one of three scholars invited to respond in

In a jovial moment, BYU President Jeffrey R. Holland (right) confers an honorary degree on Hugh Nibley during the 1983 commencement exercises. Fully in the mood, Ezra Taft Benson, president of the Quorum of the Twelve, laughs in the background.

Photo by George Frey, *Daily Universe*.

Although Hugh expressed surprise, as we have seen, at the general agreement that greeted his strong social commentary, he also faced a certain amount of backlash. Disgruntled readers wrote letters in which they expressed disagreement freely. Signs on the Nibleys' lawn supporting unpopular candidates or causes occasionally prompted someone to dump garbage in their yard. Other irrational responses were threatening mail and messages. The threats usually were mailed to his BYU office, and Hugh seldom told his family about them; but in 1980, an unidentified man telephoned, threatening to harm sixteen-year-old Zina. Hugh had been receiving menacing letters at his office from what he characterized as an anti-Mormon militia group and suspected that the caller was associated with this same group. Although they were not certain about the source of the threat, they took it seriously. Both Zina's parents and her school assured that she did not walk alone anywhere for the rest of the year. Fortunately, nothing came of it.

But for such events, the decade was marked much more consistently by recognitions of Hugh's scholarly achievements. On 7 June 1983, President Holland told several BYU administrators that the university would award Hugh an honorary doctor of letters degree during August commencement. "I am pleased about that and I believe Hugh is," reported Holland.[22] As the 19 August ceremony drew near, Hugh prepared what would become his most famous speech. He was officially retired, he had established a reputation as being loyal to the Church, and he saw the opportunity to speak directly to his greatest concerns about Mormon culture. "I am giving a commencement address this summer," wrote Hugh to Paul Springer. "I intend to

---

the same issue of *Dialogue* and there briefly addressed the Abraham text. (See chap. 21.)

[22] Jeffrey Holland, Memo to Noel B. Reynolds, Robert J. Matthews and Truman G. Madsen, 7 June 1983, Holland Presidential Papers, Perry Special Collections, Lee Library. Some of the candidates whom the Board of Trustees had "approved" in May 1982 as possible choices for the degree included the distinguished sociologist Bruno Bettelheim, Supreme Court nominee Robert Bork, and literary theorist Northrup Frye. Seven weeks later, Hugh and the Mormon Tabernacle Choir were added to the list. Jeffrey Holland, Memo to Neal Lambert, 5 May 1982; Holland, memo to file, 30 June 1982.

make myself irretrievably obnoxious."[23] In fact, Hugh fully expected to be fired and ostracized for what he was about to say, but he would not pass up the chance to speak his mind.

On the day of commencement exercises, President Holland read the citation while Hugh stood next to him, fidgeting awkwardly and bouncing on the balls of his feet. "The contributions of Professor Hugh W. Nibley to the University, the Church, and the world are too numerous to list or even summarize in this brief introduction," President Holland intoned. "To the extent that BYU has them, [Hugh] is an institutional treasure. Heaven only knows there has never been one quite like him before, and we worry lest there should never be one quite like him again." Then President Holland conferred the degree upon Hugh, "Because of our profound gratitude to Hugh Winder Nibley for demonstrating that the life of scholarship is best lived as a life of faith, and pursuant to the authority conferred upon me as president of the university by the Board of Trustees, I hereby confer upon you, Hugh W. Nibley, the degree of Doctor of Letters, honoris causa."[24]

Hugh allowed himself to be draped in the honorary hood, then stepped to the microphone to address the audience of BYU and Church dignitaries, including Apostles Ezra Taft Benson, Howard W. Hunter, and Thomas S. Monson, Jacob de Jaeger of the presidency of the First Quorum of Seventy, and Relief Society President Barbara B. Smith (all members of the Board of Trustees), as well as the graduating BYU students. Hugh's first words riveted everyone's attention: "Twenty-three years ago today, if you will cast your minds back, on this same occasion I gave the opening prayer in which I said: 'We have met here today clothed in the black robes of a false priesthood. . . .' Many have asked me since whether I really said such a shocking thing, but nobody has ever asked what I meant by it. Why not? Well, some knew the answer already; and as for the rest, we do not question things at 'the BYU.'"[25] The entire audience erupted into laughter. Hugh described how the contemporary graduation robes, which, as Hugh quipped, "produce the well-known greenhouse effect,"[26] had descended to us from the robes worn in the ancient Jewish temple, and how in that same way the true leadership of early Christianity devolved into the uninspired managers of the later church. Hugh went on to contrast the inspired leadership of Moroni with the managerial machinations of Amalickiah. He quoted Brigham Young: "There is too much of a sameness in this community . . . . Away with stereotyped 'Mormons!'" And Hugh interjected a wry, "Goodbye, all" for the benefit of the Marriott Center audience. "'If you love me,' said the greatest of all leaders, 'you will keep my commandments.' 'If you know what is good for you,' says the manager, 'you will keep my commandments and not make waves.'" And then, in one of the most

---

[23]Hugh Nibley, Letter to Paul Springer, 3 January 1983.

[24]Hugh Nibley Citation, 19 August 1983, Holland Presidential Papers, Perry Special Collections.

[25]Hugh Nibley, "Leaders to Managers: The Fatal Shift," in Brother Brigham Challenges the Saints, Vol. 13 of The Collected Works of Hugh Nibley (Salt Lake City: Deseret Book/FARMS, 1994), 491. Before this final publication, the essay was printed in Dialogue: A Journal of Mormon Thought 16, no. 4 (Winter 1983): 12-21; Fireside and Devotional Speeches, 1982-83, edited by Cynthia M. Gardner (Provo, UT: University Publications Press, 1983), 184-90; BYU Today, February 1984, 16-19, 45-47, accompanied by several photographs; and Personal Voices: A Celebration of Dialogue, edited by Mary L. Bradford (Salt Lake City: Signature Books, 1987), 179-91.

[26]This aside never made it into the published versions of the talk.

trenchant passages of his speech, Hugh summed up the managerial zeal that was eroding national and local Mormon culture:

> The rise of management always marks the decline, alas, of culture. If the management does not go for Bach, very well, there will be no Bach in the meeting. If the management favors vile sentimental doggerel verse extolling the qualities that make for success, young people everywhere will be spouting long trade-journal jingles from the stand. If the management's taste in art is what will sell—trite, insipid, folksy kitsch—that is what we will get. If management finds maudlin, saccharine commercials appealing, that is what the public will get. If management must reflect the corporate image in tasteless, trendy new buildings, down come the fine old pioneer monuments.

Hugh concluded his speech by referring to President Kimball's bicentennial address "The False Gods We Worship," which called for the Saints to "leave off the worship of modern-day idols."[27] Hugh summarized, "In a forgotten time, before the Spirit was exchanged for the office and inspired leadership for ambitious management, these robes were designed to represent withdrawal from the things of this world—as the temple robes still do. That we may become more fully aware of the real significance of both is my prayer."[28] Response to the speech was strong but mixed. Most were inspired and motivated by his words. However, some felt that Hugh was tactless in making such a speech, especially with administrators from the Marriott School of Management present.[29]

President Holland was not among those who expressed concern. In 1982, after Hugh sent him a copy of his speech "Work We Must But the Lunch Is Free," Holland wrote back: "You probably heard me quote you last February when I spoke to the student body about the damage dollars do. If this is as good as I think it is going to be, I may quote you again this year."[30] Two years later, Holland suggested to Truman Madsen that a second volume of *Nibley on the Timely and the Timeless* might be

---

[27]Spencer W. Kimball, "The False Gods We Worship," *Ensign*, June 1976, 3-6.

[28]Nibley, "Leaders to Managers," in *Brother Brigham Challenges the Saints*, 498, 497, 507.

[29]In *The Mormon Corporate Empire* (Boston: Beacon, 1985), 213. John Heinerman and Anson Shupe reported that, after the speech was published in *BYU Today* "a number of businessmen who were known to be generous donors to the school threatened to withhold gifts if some 'corrective measures' were not taken." Since they could not touch "someone of Nibley's status," BYU administrators, "as a facesaving gesture," decided instead to fire "one of the people responsible for publishing Nibley's speech (then quietly rehired him later)." Heinerman and Shupe cite as their source "George Boy" [sic]. They may mean George Boyd, a former seminary and institute instructor who retired to Provo after a lengthy teaching career in California. However, George Boyd was never a BYU administrator nor associated with *BYU Today* and would have no firsthand information about this incident. However, according to "Editor Dismissed at BYU," *Sunstone Review* 3, no. 6 (June 1983): 5, *BYU Today* editor Ken Shelton was fired, rehired after administrators determined that correct dismissal procedure had not been followed, and then refired because administrators did not like his "candid" publishing record. According to the article, Shelton maintained that one reason for his dismissal was that he ignored instructions not "to publish articles or profiles about certain professors whose thinking is considered 'too much out of the ordinary.'" Shelton added that publishing a condensed version of Hugh Nibley's speech "Work We Must But the Lunch Is Free," *BYU Today* 36, no. 6 (November 1982): 812, "fanned the flames" that led to his final dismissal.

[30]Jeffrey R. Holland, Letter to Hugh Nibley, 2 July 1982, Holland Presidential Papers, Perry Special Collections.

welcome: "As I look at the Nibley corpus," wrote Holland, "it seems to me unfortunate that more of those are not available. Is there any way in which a second volume might be pursued?"[31] Madsen wrote back a reluctant refusal: Although "the Nibley volume has done better than any of the monographs" produced by the Religious Studies Center, its officers did not want to "tie up further funds for a new edition. They want to underwrite new and other volumes in the series. Hence, no more Nibley."[32]

Holland may not have known that another group was already planning an even more ambitious publishing project. John W. Welch, one of Hugh's former students, was practicing tax law in Los Angeles. He had learned about chiastic structures as an undergraduate, discovered them in the Book of Mormon, and remained strongly interested in Book of Mormon research.[33] During the 1970s, he addressed many LDS audiences about Book of Mormon research and found a great interest among Mormons in articles, including many by Hugh, that his audience had either never heard of or had no idea how to obtain. Welch began to photocopy articles and send them to interested members. The demand soon became greater than Welch could handle on his own, so he organized the Foundation for Ancient Research and Mormon Studies (FARMS), with the principle task of making research on the Book of Mormon available at a minimal cost. By 1982, FARMS put out a catalogue of articles which it sent to subscribers. Soon thereafter, the organization established the goal of bringing together Hugh's collected works. As Welch puts it, "We knew that FARMS needed to build directly on the scholarly work of Hugh Nibley, who had taught many of us as students, and we knew that our future was closely aligned with his past."[34]

In 1983, FARMS board members divided up the entire Nibley corpus by subject and assigned editors for projected volumes. A team of volunteers tirelessly assembled materials, typed manuscripts, checked footnotes, and proofread hundreds of essays which would appear in the projected nineteen-volume *Collected Works*. Welch negotiated an agreement with Deseret Book to co-publish the series; and by March 1986, the first volume, *Old Testament and Related Studies*, appeared in print. The second volume, *Enoch the Prophet*, appeared later that same year.

Giving the series a degree of authority that other LDS books lacked, Gordon B. Hinckley, then First Counselor to President Ezra Taft Benson, commented on the

---

[31] Jeffrey R. Holland, Letter to Truman Madsen, 21 February 1984, ibid.

[32] Truman Madsen, Letter to Jeffrey R. Holland, 23 February 1984, ibid. There is no record about how well the volume had sold or if the center had, as Nibley insisted, taken the costs of retitling the edition out of his royalties.

[33] Chiasmus is a literary device found in ancient documents, in which a given unit replicates ideas (and may repeat key words) in an hourglass format. In other words, the first and last lines are a pair, the second and next-to-last lines are a pair, and so forth. Chiastic units can be either a single verse or even whole chapters in length. Welch was the first to identify chiasmus in the Book of Mormon.

[34] John W. Welch, e-mail to Boyd Petersen, 27 November 2001, printout in my possession. Welch moved FARMS to Provo when he accepted a position on the faculty of the J. Reuben Clark Law School at BYU in 1980. FARMS always had a close relationship with BYU (most scholars working on FARMS projects have been BYU faculty), but in 1998 LDS Church President Gordon B. Hinckley invited FARMS to become a part of the university.

series in the April 1986 general conference.³⁵ After the fourth volume came out, Elder Neal A. Maxwell in a more private setting called the series "a blessing for the Church," and Elder Dallin H. Oaks called it an "epic contribution."³⁶ By 1990, ten volumes of the collected works had appeared in print, and FARMS had also produced many other volumes of Mormon scholarship, including John Sorensen's *An Ancient American Setting for the Book of Mormon*, Welch's *Sermon at the Temple*, *Sermon on the Mount*, and collections of essays by various scholars in *Warfare in the Book of Mormon*, *The Allegory of the Olive Tree*, *Re-exploring the Book of Mormon*, and *Rediscovering the Book of Mormon*. "Those years were incredibly productive," remembers Jack Welch. "Linked together was a tidal wave of new material, rising out of the huge ground swell of Nibley's lifetime of precocious and prodigious publications."³⁷ The collected works of Hugh Nibley never could have happened without FARMS, and likewise FARMS could never have happened without Hugh Nibley. Both FARMS and Hugh benefitted from the venture. "FARMS could not have arisen without the foundation laid by Hugh Nibley," states Welch. "And the new discoveries coming out of FARMS proved that Nibley was on the right track, that there was more where he was coming from, that he wasn't the only one who saw the things he was claiming to have spotted."³⁸

During the early stages of FARMS, Jack Welch began to consider producing a documentary about Hugh's life and work. Jack felt that a good production could be done for the modest sum of about five thousand dollars. The idea took on a life of its own, led to hundreds of hours of personal interviews with Hugh, his family, friends, and associates, and consumed a budget of a quarter-million dollars. Welch approached Hugh's son, Alex, who had studied at the American Conservatory Theater and was working at Sundance on what would later become the Sundance Film Institute. Alex liked the idea and talked it over with his supervisor at Sundance, Sterling Van Wagenen. Soon they added a cinematographer named Brian Capener to the team. As they began to plan the film, Alex hoped it would show the more conversational side of his father. "I wanted to show the public part of what I saw in private," stated Alex.³⁹

Although Alex had informed Hugh about the project, Hugh didn't fully appreciate that the project would actually become a reality until Paul Springer wrote him giving "broad hints and well-justified jibes." Needless to say, Hugh was furious: "What in hell is going on? Charles (Alex) is being maddeningly uncommunicative. Here I was, sinking into the grateful obscurity of a somewhat benign old age, and this thing breaks loose. I must put a stop to whatev-

---

³⁵"The other evening I picked up a new publication of the writings of Dr. Hugh Nibley, a man of my age whom I have known and admired for many years," President Hinckley began. He then read from the dust jacket of the book. Gordon B. Hinckley, "Come and Partake," *Ensign*, May 1986, 46.

³⁶BYU Religious Studies Center, Quarterly Meeting Minutes, 14 December 1987, Holland Presidential Papers, Perry Special Collections.

³⁷John W. Welch, e-mail to Boyd Petersen, 27 November 2001, printout in my possession.

³⁸Ibid.

³⁹Charles Alexander Nibley, Interviewed by Boyd Petersen, 2 November 2001.

The filming crew for *Faith of an Observer* poses on location in Egypt in January 1984. Hugh's son Alex stands next to him on the right.

er Charles is up to. I did not settle in and for the suffocating obscurity of Provo to attract public notice."⁴⁰

Alex was eventually able to coax Hugh into cooperating, and filming began in earnest in late 1982. The crew set up the sound stage so the cameras were hidden behind sound baffles to keep Hugh from getting overly nervous. The problem was not that Hugh sulked and refused to talk on camera. On the contrary, his machine-gun-rapid delivery and encyclopedic knowledge made it virtually impossible to keep him focused systematically on any one subject. As Welch later commented, "Any subject mentioned, for Nibley, is an open invitation to discuss matters of universal significance."⁴¹ To help with this problem, Alex and Sterling "double-teamed" him as interviewers to try to keep the conversation on track. Sterling later stated that "Hugh's mind works rather like one trajectory of Halley's Comet. You may start with a question that pinpoints his thinking at one location next to the sun, but his erudition quickly draws the question into an orbit that goes out past Pluto and finally circles back to the point at which you began, if you give him enough time."⁴² The team also discovered that Hugh would come prepared with his own material to discuss, whether it was what the team wanted on film or not. To capture the elements that they wanted, they finally learned to simply let the cameras roll until Hugh finally ran out of prepared material. Then they could start asking him more personal and focused questions.

---

⁴⁰Hugh Nibley, Letter to Paul Springer, 3 January 1983.

⁴¹Jack [John W.] Welch, "The Timelessness of Hugh Nibley," *This People*, April 1987: 39.

⁴²Ibid.

After shooting hundreds of hours of film in Provo, in January 1984 the filming team makers accompanied Hugh to Egypt. Here another set of problems dogged them. Hugh's passion for Egyptian culture and history were apparent, but he would seldom hold still long enough to be filmed unless he was lecturing. Furthermore, he kept talking about the hypocephalus (the round Facsimile 2 accompanying the Book of Abraham), but they could not get Hugh to define it on film. As the time in Egypt wound down, they were worried that they would not capture anything really usable from the trip. But as they rested on the banks of the Nile one hot afternoon, Hugh began, spontaneously and emotionally, to tell the story from the Midrash about the Lord promising Abraham his long-sought-after son Isaac after Abraham had gone into the desert fearing lest a stranger might be lost. (See chap. 20.) "That was the one moment when you see something besides the scholar," stated Alex. "There was real emotion, a real human being there." On the way back from Egypt, the party detoured through France to drive out to Utah Beach, where Hugh had landed during the Normandy invasion.[43]

One of the individuals interviewed for this documentary was Elder Neal A. Maxwell. Responding to a question, he explained how, a few years earlier, the Brethren had asked Hugh to compile material on the Savior's atonement. "It was a feeling I had as well as some others—Truman Madsen, President Hinckley, and the Brethren—that he can take all of the manuscripts, ancient and modern, and integrate them into a wholeness such as no one else could do," explained Maxwell.[44] Hugh responded by writing "The Meaning of the Atonement," which he read at a lecture sponsored by FARMS and Deseret Book in Riverton, Utah, on 11 November 1988. Hugh described the atonement as a state in which "one rejoins the family, returns to the Father, becomes united, reconciled, embracing and sitting down happily with others after a sad separation." Hugh constructed this meaning from ancient Near East rituals and their endowment parallels. "This is the imagery of the Atonement, the embrace," stated Hugh. "This is the *hpet*, the ritual embrace that consummates the final escape from death in the Egyptian funerary texts and reliefs."[45]

After Hugh had finished the speech, Maxwell expressed the hope that "some wider use might be made" of the material, "perhaps several articles in the *Ensign*. . . . I would like [it] to be shared as widely and appropriately as possible. As is so often the case with you, Hugh, you have spun off so many fine things for so many different audiences." As to the many allusions to the temple, Elder Maxwell cautioned: "You may want to let any temple-related imagery speak for itself, as you have always done so adroitly." He concluded: "Thanks again for what seems to me to be the crescendo of your own marvelous ministry in which the focus, so appropriately, is on Christ as the centerpiece of the atonement."[46] With Elder Maxwell's support, an edited version of the lecture later appeared in a four-part *Ensign* series.[47]

---

[43] Charles Alexander Nibley, Interviewed by Boyd Petersen, 2 November 2001.
[44] Neal A. Maxwell, "Faith of an Observer," 523.
[45] Nibley, "The Meaning of the Atonement," *Approaching Zion*, 581, 559.
[46] Neal A. Maxwell, Letter to Hugh Nibley, 21 December 1988.
[47] This series was: "The Atonement of Jesus Christ," July 1990, 18-23; August 1990, 30-34; September 1990, 22-26; October 1990, 26-31.

It was during the filming of *Faith of an Observer* that Hugh first began to experience uncharacteristic fatigue and shortness of breath. He had always led an extremely active lifestyle, hiking at great speed up the steep hill on the south side of campus to his office. He had started swimming daily as soon as the Richards P.E. Building pool was constructed and kept it up religiously. He also took frequent walks around town and hikes in the neighboring mountains. "I refuse to ride anywhere in a small place like Provo," wrote Hugh to Paul Springer.[48] For a man whose work was performed at the typewriter, Hugh was far from sedentary. Ever since his stroke in 1975, Hugh had made regular visits to the doctor. However, he was going into the doctor's office in the summer of 1982 when "it suddenly occurred to me that I was NOT sick but feeling great—so why go to a Doctor (all this I said to myself, none other knowing) so I turned on my well-worn heel (I wear only running shoes—a luxury allowed the ancient in our society) and have not gone since to pine away in the waiting room."[49]

After the weakness and shortness of breath did not disappear, Hugh had a series of tests that revealed major arterial blockage. He had quadruple bypass surgery from Dr. Russell M. Nelson, a cardiac surgeon at LDS Hospital, on 10 April 1984. Only three days prior to the surgery, Dr. Nelson had been called as an apostle, but he carried out his previously scheduled surgeries—among them Hugh and former Church Historian Leonard J. Arrington. Nelson later commented: "I have always enjoyed studying [Hugh's] scholarly works. Then when it became my privilege to help him in a surgical way, I felt a keen sense of responsibility. I could appreciate even more the importance of prolonging the health of Hugh W. Nibley to further the work that I had been called to lead."[50] Nelson added: "The privilege that I have enjoyed, not only with being a surgical servant, but being [Hugh's] confidant and friend, I regard among the precious privileges of my life."[51] The surgery was a success, and Hugh's recovery was quick and complete. He was again walking to his office and swimming within weeks of the operation. Hugh later quipped that Elder Nelson had touched his heart more profoundly than any other General Authority.

By the mid-1980s, there were no children left in the Nibley home and Hugh finished taking over the four upstairs bedrooms to lay out his research. In 1982 Paul went to Columbia University to get an MFA in film directing and screen writing, then taught film at BYU from 1985 to 1989. He and Bronia have five children: David, Anna, Miriam, Philip, and Kristina. In 1980, Christina earned an M.A. in English from Jacksonville University in Florida and began teaching high school English in Florida. She and Z have two children, Natalie and Alex. Tom married Cynthia Smily on 21 June 1980 and the couple moved to Los Angeles where he has been working as an actor, with parts in several television shows, commercials, and movies. He and Cindy have five daughters: Aurora, Alethea, Athena, Celeste, and Sarah. After completing his MA at BYU, Michael began working for WICAT, a Utah-based company specializing in computer-assisted education. Margaret and Michael

---

[48]Hugh Nibley, Letter to Paul Springer, 3 January 1983.
[49]Ibid.
[50]Russell M. Nelson, Letter to Boyd Petersen, 21 May 1990.
[51]Russell M. Nelson, Letter to Boyd Petersen, 12 April 1990.

were divorced in 1985. In 1986 he was transferred to New York City and three years later he moved to the Washington, D.C., metropolitan area. During Alex's mission to Japan (1978-80), he met Carol Eliason, also serving a mission. They married on 20 December 1980 and had three children: Angela, Joseph, and Marianna before their divorce. After Alex finished his B.A. at the University of Utah, the family moved to Guam in the late 1980s where Alex opened a ballet studio. Becky performed with the Milwaukee Repertory Theater during the late 1970s and early 1980s, while completing an MFA at the University of Wisconsin in Milwaukee and, like Alex, later completed a baccalaureate degree in fine arts. She also worked in the summer theater at Sundance and the Utah Shakespearean Festival in Cedar City. She married Richard Tingey on 7 August 1981. In 1982, she performed with a Japanese acting company in Japan. She and Richard had one child, Jonathan, before they divorced in 1985. Martha earned her B.A. in Asian studies and her Ph.D. in sociology from Harvard and married John Beck on 21 June 1983. They are the parents of Katherine, Adam, and Elizabeth. Zina graduated from BYU in English. We were married on 25 May 1984, and she completed her M.A. and Ph.D. at Catholic University in Washington, D.C.

On 27 March 1985, Hugh turned seventy-five. To his embarrassment BYU hosted a special party in his honor attended by friends, associates, and family. After a banquet in one of the Wilkinson Center dining rooms, Jack Welch and Elder Dallin Oaks gave brief addresses. Welch acknowledged wryly that "the last person in the world who is interested in celebrating Hugh Nibley's seventy-fifth birthday is Hugh Nibley." Elder Oaks recalled taking a class from Hugh when he was at BYU. "It was a course in whatever Dr. Nibley was studying at that time," Oaks stated. Hugh responded to the celebration by stating, "While I love and respect you, I'm not impressed with your judgment." When a large birthday cake with seventy-five blazing candles was wheeled into the room, Hugh lifted his water glass and feinted dousing the flames, but then blew out all seventy-five candles with one breath.[52]

After the formal program was over, the entire assembly walked over to the Joseph Smith Building for the premiere of the sixty-minute *Faith of an Observer*. Elder Neal A. Maxwell introduced the film by calling Hugh "a scholar and a warrior," quipping that Hugh is the only person he knows who can "be silent in sixteen languages."[53] The film itself was beautifully done. Covering five major themes in Hugh's life and teachings, it touched on wealth, the environment, education, war, and Egypt. Even Hugh was quite impressed by the production. "I must say I was very much surprised at what I saw—very surprised," Hugh conceded.[54]

Following the birthday celebration, Hugh wrote President Holland a characteristic thank-you note of self-deprecation and appreciation:

> A large part of being a college president, I have observed, is to suffer fools gladly: you gave a superb demonstration. Consider me grateful. On the whole, I don't

---

[52] Arlene Shutt, "Nibley's 75th Celebrated Despite His Own Protests," (BYU) *Daily Universe*, 28 March 1985, 10.

[53] Ibid.

[54] Quoted in Welch, "The Timelessness of Hugh Nibley," 39.

think there was much mischief done, and best of all it made everybody but me feel younger—what more could one ask? On me too the event had a salutary effect: "All these years (thus to myself) and what have you got to show for it?" Since then I have been working with frantic zeal to make up lost ground, and at last I have a subject worthy of unlimited effort—just wait and see whether I muff it this time."[55]

President Holland replied warmly, "If you felt motivated and we felt entertained, it was exactly the right BYU teacher-student response. (That is what we do isn't it—motivate the teacher and entertain the students?)"[56]

Hugh gained additional motivation in his studies in 1985, when Egypt came to Utah. BYU hosted the Ramses II exhibit, which was touring the United States, for several months, displaying it in an elaborate and beautiful setting. Hugh was delighted by the opportunity to have the exhibit in Provo, and it also gave him an excuse to bring Klaus Baer back to Provo for a brief visit. A series of lectures coinciding with the exhibit began with Hugh delivering "The Greatness of Egypt" on 12 March 1986. Hugh argued that "the size, manifest age, and splendor of the Egyptian show is after all only a facade." Rather, what makes the Egyptians great was their faith in and unceasing search for an afterlife. "In spite of everything, they never shut the door on other worlds."[57] Baer visited the exhibit and delivered a series of lectures later that month. He had married Miriam Reitz only eight months earlier. It was Hugh's first meeting with Miriam and his last visit with Klaus, who died on 14 May 1987. During the visit, Miriam Baer saw first-hand that "the relationship between the two was one of mutual respect and affection. I know that Klaus Baer thought that Hugh Nibley is absolutely one of a kind."[58] On his evaluation form at the end of his visit, Baer praised BYU for the "immense strides" it had taken in "recent years to turn itself into a place that has a substantial international reputation for work in Egypt." He continued, "It ultimately goes back to Professor Nibley's foresight many years ago, when he saw to it that BYU has the necessary library resources to make it a place where a scholar studying ancient Egypt can work—the only one between Chicago and the West Coast, so far as I know."[59]

---

[55]Hugh Nibley, Letter to Jeffrey R. Holland, n.d., 1985. Jeffrey R. Holland Presidential Papers, Perry Special Collections, Lee Library.

[56]Jeffrey R. Holland, Letter to Hugh Nibley, 22 April 1985, ibid. Hugh also sent an appreciative letter to Elder Neal A. Maxwell who had spoken at the premiere of *Faith of an Observer*. In that letter, Hugh commented that the "whole show did have the effect of making everybody present feel younger." Quoted in Bruce C. Hafen, *A Disciple's Life: The Biography of Neal A. Maxwell* (Salt Lake City: Deseret Book, 2002), 513-14. In 1997 when Elder Maxwell was hospitalized, battling leukemia, "Brother Nibley was one of the few people he had strength to call on the telephone. Neal honestly thought he might not see him again, and he wanted to thank Hugh one more time for all that he had done to build the Lord's kingdom" (514).

[57]Hugh Nibley, "The Greatness of Egypt," 23, 36, photocopy of typescript in my possession.

[58]Miriam Reitz Baer, "Reminiscences of Hugh Nibley and Klaus Baer," 24 November 1989, 3, prepared at my request.

[59]Klaus Baer, Evaluation Form for Participating Scholars, Ramses II Lectures, 13 February 1986, Holland Presidential Papers, Perry Special Collections, Lee Library. Baer continued, "The fact that the Ramses II Exhibit was offered to BYU is indicative of its reputation; the way it was handled shows that it deserves it."

At the conclusion of the Ramses exhibit, on 25 October 1985, Hugh delivered a final lecture, titled "There Is Always Egypt," at the Church Office Building for an audience of Church officials, BYU administrators, and Egyptian government representatives. He discussed the importance of ancient Egypt to culture, charged Egyptologists with dismissing the serious concern in ancient Egypt for the afterlife, and drew parallels between Mormonism and ancient Egyptian concerns for family, eternity, and cosmology. "Joseph Smith knew there had been a real archaic wisdom, and regarded the restored gospel as going back to the beginning," stated Hugh. Again, he spelled out the central role of the temple in Mormon theology.[60]

In August 1989, Hugh again spoke his mind. Concerned after several essays and talks criticizing the Church and its leaders were published or read at Sunstone symposia,[61] Hugh wrote "Criticizing the Brethren" which he delivered both at the Church Education System symposium at BYU on 18 August 1989 and at the independent Mormon Sunstone Symposium on 29 August 1989. In the essay, Hugh shows how Joseph Smith was frustrated by, yet gently tolerated, criticism from the early members of the Church. "Let us be faithful and silent, brethren," Hugh quotes the Prophet as saying. "Do not watch for iniquity in each other, if you do you will not get an endowment, for God will not bestow it on such." In this essay Hugh told of travelling with President Kimball, then an apostle, in 1952, and how President Kimball had unself-consciously dusted Hugh's shoes. (See chap. 3.) "That has conditioned my attitude toward the Brethren," Hugh affirmed. "I truly believe that they are chosen servants of God."[62] Writing to me about the talk two months later, Elder Maxwell wrote that it was "just what was needed," adding, "Some of the Sunstone constituency would not have appreciated the full significance of his remarks, but many others did!"[63]

As the 1980s drew to a close, FARMS produced a two-volume *Festschrift* to honor Hugh on his eightieth birthday.[64] The volumes were impressive for both the quality and breadth of the essays as well as the calibre and credentials of the Mormon and non-Mormon authors. It was a fitting tribute to a man who had faithfully served both the academy and the Church for over forty years, who had chal-

---

[60]Hugh Nibley, "There Is Always Egypt," typescript, 17. See Chapter 22, "'The Source of All Good Things': Hugh Nibley and the Temple," for an assignment from the Brethren to prepare briefings for them about the history of the endowment.

[61]For an overview of the period Hugh is writing about, see Lavina Fielding Anderson, "The LDS Intellectual Community and Church Leadership: A Contemporary Chronology," *Dialogue: A Journal of Mormon Thought* 26, no. 1 (Spring 1993): 7-64.

[62]Nibley, "Criticizing the Brethren," *Brother Brigham Challenges the Saints*, 433, 444.

[63]Neal A. Maxwell, Letter to Boyd Petersen, 3 October 1989. Elder Maxwell was responding to my request for an interview.

[64]John M. Lundquist and Stephen D. Ricks, eds., *By Study and Also by Faith*, 2 vols. (Salt Lake City: Deseret Book/FARMS, 1990). According to BYU's Religious Studies Center, Quarterly Meeting Minutes, 14 December 1987, Holland Presidential Papers, Perry Special Collections, Lee Library. The issue of the *Festschrift*, which had been first proposed and for which some papers had been written in 1978, came up again. Jack Welch stated that the project "needs to be pushed ahead to avoid embarrassment" (he does not say to whom). Elder Maxwell urged the group to complete the project during Nibley's lifetime, even though Elder Oaks questioned the need for a two-volume set "since we only have one tombstone."

lenged both to better live the principles each espoused, and who had become recognized by both as a leading authority.

The Nibley family has lived in this modest residence at 285 E. 700 North in Provo since 1953, underscoring Hugh's and Phyllis's lack of ostentation. The 1976 Datsun parked in the driveway was Hugh's vehicle until 2002 when he gave up driving himself.

> I keep telling him, "Your grandfather gave the Church $500,000. Do you think it would have been better if he hadn't?" Hugh almost talks like a Franciscan. It would be better if we were all poor. Then we wouldn't be tempted to think God gave it to us and we can use it the way we want. God didn't give it to us; and if he did—honorably—we'd better use it for Him and not for feathering our own nest. Boy, he's tough on that.
> —Truman Madsen[1]

---

[1] Truman Madsen, "Faith of an Observer," 469, compilation of interviews, ca. 1983-84 for a video documentary of the same name aired in 1985, photocopy of typescript in my possession, pagination added.

Chapter 24

"Joy Lies in Another Direction": Hugh Nibley's Call to Leave Babylon and Build Zion

On 27 March 1915, to celebrate his fifth birthday, Hugh went with his family to the boathouse of his Uncle Louie on the Willamette River. "That was the biggest treat in the world, going down to the boathouse on the river," remembers Hugh.[2] There he received a birthday present that most five-year-olds at that time would have surely considered a fine gift: five shiny new pennies. But Hugh was not like most five-year-olds. In a private moment of contemplation, Hugh took his birthday pennies to the water's edge and dropped them into the river "solemnly one by one, reflecting on each one, 'There's no loss there: what's money?'"[3] "That's how I spent my fifth birthday," Hugh later recalled, "Philosophyzing."[4]

Hugh Nibley's attitude about money has changed little over the years. He has had little use for it; and as a young man when he saw its effects on his parents, he came to regard money as a corrupting influence. Yet it wasn't until rather late in his life that Hugh forcefully addressed the theme in his writings. And despite his negative feelings about materialism, he has usually taken a position of hope and optimism for the future. Whether anticipating the subject of his last public discourse as he did in his contribution to the 1971 Last Lecture Series, or contemplating break-

---
[2]Hugh Nibley, "Faith of an Observer," 26-27. Lou West, known by the courtesy title of "Uncle Louie," was the brother of Hugh's uncle by marriage, Richard Ballantyne West, husband of Ruth Sloan. I read an early version of this chapter at the Sunstone Symposium, 15 July 1999, in Salt Lake City.
[3]Hugh Nibley, interviewed by Boyd Petersen, 9 June 1996.
[4]Hugh Nibley, "Faith of an Observer," 27.

Hugh's grandmother, Margaret Violet Reid Sloan, in her older years.

throughs he would like to see as he did in his 1984 "Spheres of Influence" speech, both delivered at BYU, when Hugh Nibley has looked to the future the theme has always been the contemporary "affluenza" binding the Latter-day Saints to Babylon and the hope that we will begin living the law of consecration and working to establish Zion. It was not until 1989, however, that the publication of *Approaching Zion* made his writings fully accessible to members of the Church outside the BYU community. Since then, Hugh's words, springing from a personal quest to approach Zion that began in childhood, have had an immense influence on many individual lives.

Tracing the influence on Hugh's decided skepticism about wealth is anything but easy. He was born in a family that was affluent for the times, and the adults in that family prized and respected wealth. In this, they were rather typical of the cult of self-made men who dominated American business and politics of their generation. Yet instead of absorbing these values, Hugh countered them.

He has recalled on several occasions the significant influence of his Grandma Sloan, whom he has described as having been both "very practical" and very generous. "She just gave everything to everybody," is how he characterizes her. "She didn't keep anything . . . . She was just helping everybody all the time."[5] After reading the tender letters he sent to her, I know that she was one of the earliest and deepest influences on Hugh's life.

Very early in his youth, Hugh also read Thoreau and the transcendentalists. As a teenager, he spent two summers trying to get back to nature, roaming around the forests of Oregon and California. As Hugh stated in *Faith of an Observer*, "I read the Concord school and thought that all you had to do was go back to nature, and I really believed that."[6] Certainly, if Hugh took Thoreau's message of getting back to nature so literally, he must also have taken to heart Thoreau's message of living simply.

Likely the person who had the greatest influence on Hugh next to his Grandmother Sloan was his Grandfather Charles W. Nibley. At the turn of the century, C. W. Nibley made a fortune in lumber and sugar beets and became one of the richest men in Utah. He was also the Presiding Bishop and a member of the First Presidency. But Hugh remembers him as being a very divided man. "He was very

---

[5]Ibid., 27.

[6]Ibid., 131.

smart and he had a passion for knowledge and his real love was the theater," but business took him away from his deepest loves.[7] C. W. had grown up in the abject poverty of the Scottish mines where the family had had to subsist on oatmeal and potato soup. As Hugh recalls, his grandfather was "determined that [his] kids would never have to go through what [he] went through . . . . He didn't want them to grow up in poverty." So C. W. felt that making money was absolutely essential, yet at the same time "he felt very guilty about it."[8]

Hugh drew this conclusion from what amounted to his grandfather's deathbed confession in November 1931. The ailing man confessed that, if he were to see an angel personally, he would feel so guilty that he would plunge through the window to escape.[9] (See chap. 1.) Charles W. Nibley died one month later. These parting words from his grandfather, coupled with Charles's repeated advice to "forget . . . business," made an indelible impression on Hugh's life.[10]

In a letter to a correspondent written when he himself was seventy-four, Hugh compared his Nibley and Sloan grandparents:

> The passion for succeeding and making something of one's self was nowhere as strong as among the poor Scotts laborers of the 19th Century, and that is the tradition I grew up in. My canny grandparents had seen enough of the world to know two things: 1) that nothing can hold you back like poverty; and 2) that nothing can fool and beguile you like wealth. That was their rock-and-a-hard-place situation. My grandfather passionately sought for both prizes, became very rich and was a general authority, but he was always ashamed of his concern for money. He was obsessed with feelings of guilt and warned me against taking that way even though that is where the world's rewards lie. Did he do the right thing? My other grandfather who was Irish and gave up all his wealth when he joined the church and continued to distribute whatever he got for ever after never achieved a high office. But when the two men were together, which happened sometimes at our house in Portland, everyone including the two men themselves knew who the really successful man was.[11]

There is some irony in this appraisal. Hugh was essentially assigned to fulfill the values and dreams that Charles W. Nibley cherished but could not act on, pursuing C. W.'s love of learning and his interests in literature and the sciences. Because C. W. had built a family fortune that he assumed would keep Hugh comfortable for his entire life, he urged Hugh to remain unspotted from the dirty business dealings he himself had been involved in. But the relationship was a complicated one. Hugh seemed to not only accept the advice his grandfather gave him but also to reject, on some psychological level, his grandfather's money. For example, Hugh wrote what can only be considered a highly ambiguous letter to thank his grandfather for the check he received on his seventeenth birthday: "As to the check—I can only honest-

---

[7]Ibid., 17. See also Charles W. Nibley's *Reminiscences: 1849-1931* (Salt Lake City: Stevens & Wallis, 1934), 152.
[8]Hugh Nibley, "Faith of an Observer," 27, 17.
[9]Hugh Nibley quoting Charles W. Nibley, "Faith of an Observer," 248.
[10]Hugh Nibley, "Faith of an Observer," 249.
[11]Hugh Nibley, Letter to J. Byron Flanders, 16 May 1984.

ly say that I shall be glad to be finally rid of the profound obligation incurred in the piece of paper—signed by the backbone of the imposing 'Nibley Company.'"[12] There is no indication in family papers or lore that C. W. found such a cavalier attitude offensive. Certainly Hugh not only avoided business strenuously but also became less and less concerned with money.

He lived out this philosophy, not only through his spartan lifestyle as a missionary and a student (see chaps. 6, 8, 10), but in his steadfast fidelity to a life of scholarship, accepting with apparently little concern the frugal salary BYU chose to pay him. I found nowhere in his papers an appeal for a raise or more than a humorous complaint about straitened finances. Although it is true that Phyllis proved to be marvelously successful in managing their income, Hugh's dismissive attitude toward money was certainly consistent with his earlier perspective.

Hugh probably found reinforcement for this attitude in the shape of his parents' lives after their bankruptcy. For eighteen years, Hugh watched his father's increasingly desperate but always futile attempts to recover the family's wealth and status, the subterfuges and sleight of hand he resorted to, and what must have been painful compromises of integrity for a son to witness. One of his few comments about El's choice of values was: "My father was a very good man and could have been very spiritual, but he was totally sunk in [business]."[13] Sloanie's deepening bitterness, high-handedness, and marital disharmony must have further reinfoced Hugh's horror of putting material values first.

As early as 1941, Hugh staked out an anti-materialistic position that he adhered to for the rest of his life:

> I'm broke now and expect to stay that way—the austere life is the only one I can enjoy; you may think it strange, but I find the good, homey atmosphere simply suffocating. May I be boiled in oil if I force a congenial and comfortable home on anyone; if the war keeps up even this plush-bottom generation may learn that joy lies in another direction and a world far removed from cozy beds and double-rich Sundaes.[14]

Hugh's letters home from the European theater during World War II revealed an unfaltering contempt for money per se. Except for the money he sent home to his mother, he almost certainly spent all of his meager master sergeant's pay on the 150 volumes of Arabic literature and other books he sent home. He once characterized money as "nothing but congealed wickedness."[15] In another letter home, he dispassionately described his father's practice of investing in risky business deals: "Dad seems remarkably persistent in his attempts to grab a disproportionate share of the riches of the earth: it has taken millions of years to produce that stuff, and the supply is limited; in an earlier day almost anyone could pull it off, but now it

---

[12] Hugh Nibley, Letter to Charles W. Nibley, 13 March 1927.
[13] Hugh Nibley, "Faith of an Observer," 27.
[14] Hugh Nibley, Letter to Agnes Sloan Nibley, postmarked 3 November 1941.
[15] Hugh Nibley, Letter to Agnes Sloan Nibley, 5 February 1945.

requires a wolf—like cunning and boldness—in which papa's qualifications are happily in far arrears of his intentions."[16]

Following the war, Hugh spent the winter of 1945-46 hiking in southern Utah's red-rock country, writing to Paul Springer: "There are so many things of real importance in life that I never can bring myself to face the nauseating trivialities that, unfortunately, pay off."[17]

In April of 1946, Hugh signed a contract to teach at BYU—his first "permanent" job. At that time, teaching at BYU didn't pay much (then as now, salaries are confidential), but it did allow Hugh to work at something that he felt had real significance. Paul Springer marveled at Hugh's abstemious lifestyle: "The only time I've ever known him to splurge is when he hit a good bookstore."[18]

Unlike Hugh, Phyllis had not been brought up in a wealthy family. Raised for the most part in a single-mother household, often passed around to live with aunts and uncles, Phyllis's childhood circumstances had been so meager that she got a case of rickets from malnutrition. Thus, Hugh's modest income and lack of concern for material goods did not put much of a strain on their relationship.

She agreed with Hugh in principle that material things do not create happiness and has been mostly content with the modest lifestyle he provided. "I always felt that we had enough to eat. We had enough to make the payments on the house," she reflected. "We didn't have a big income, but it was steady. And if you want to manage things, you can manage within that income."[19] However, in the early years of the marriage, she grew frustrated when Hugh spent money on books without leaving her sufficient to run the household. She also discovered that her husband would, as she put it, "prefer not to have anything to do with money at all"—in fact, suffered from "denial [about] the need to manage money."[20] Although managing money was the traditional task of the husband in 1950s America, the Nibley household ran more smoothly with less stress for all concerned when Phyllis simply took over everything related to finances.

Phyllis was frugal and resourceful. She canned fruit and bought as much food in bulk as she could store. An elegant and speedy seamstress, she sewed clothes for the girls, which made the descent from oldest to youngest. Hugh bought most of his wardrobe from the Deseret Industries thrift store. And he entertained the children on the cheap, taking them to BYU productions of plays and concerts. (They attended dress rehearsals until the children were old enough to be decorous members of the audience.) He also took them hiking, camping, and swimming at the local pools, walked to work, and came home for lunch each day. Usually he would walk or bicycle when he needed to go across town. The Nibley family wasted little and got a lot of mileage out of what they had.

Early in his faculty career at BYU, Hugh spent a stint staffing the telephones for a BYU fund-raiser. While none of the other volunteers that day was successful,

---

[16] Hugh Nibley, Letter to Agnes Sloan Nibley, 5 November 1944.
[17] Hugh Nibley, Letter to Paul Springer, n.d.
[18] Paul Springer, "Faith of an Observer," 515.
[19] Ibid., 430-31.
[20] Ibid., 436.

Hugh had about $1,500 worth of pledges in only an hour. He was quite impressed with himself. But he says he paid for it later: "That night at 3:00 in the morning, I had the most awful cramps I'd ever had in my life and I knew instantly why. Because I'd been lying over that phone and leading them on, you see. I wanted them to contribute and I knew how" to influence them.[21] On another occasion, when asked to speak at a seminar about leadership, Hugh refused the invitation with characteristic candor:

> Aside from the fact that I am the world's worst leader, the thing smacks of business, which I find (I might as well admit it) violently repugnant. So you can imagine what kind of speech I would give, even if I had the time and inclination. It would be full of spite and make your every particular hair to stand on end like quills upon the fretful porpentine. That might not be desirable.[22]

Needless to say, Hugh did not make many points with local businessmen. On another occasion, an LDS publisher contacted Hugh, desiring to list him in a book of "successful people." Hugh's response was typical:

> I was flattered by your invitation and exhilarated by your sense of humor. To put me in a book of successful people is high comedy indeed. The first time I succeed in anything I shall let you know, but don't hold your breath.
> Might I suggest a book of Born Losers which I honestly believe would contain some far more interesting characters than any top management. . . . The church archives are full of obscure nobodys whose achievements rank with those of Enoch's people. I am not thinking of the usual heroic pioneers but those who disappeared in obscurity after leaving tracks in the wilderness.[23]

Hugh Nibley has lived a very contented life. He has been, as Paul Springer noted, content to "eat regularly, and have a place to sleep, and get his books."[24] He has provided an income and a home for his family of eight children which has been sufficient for their needs. Despite better offers from more prestigious universities, Hugh has remained at BYU because the financial inducements of salary do not, in and of themselves, hold any appeal to him.[25] Paul Springer once tried to persuade him to consider moving up academically. Paul and Lucien Goldschmidt wrote to him, stating, "We see in you one of the few really first class minds of these muddled times voluntarily consigning itself to oblivion."[26] (See chap. 11 for Hugh's answer to this letter.) Eventually, Springer came to feel that Hugh had made a better career choice than he himself had: "He's doing what he wants, and he gets paid for it. I get

---

[21]Ibid., 31.

[22]Hugh Nibley, Letter to Boyd Ware, 27 February 1989. "Fretful porpentine" is an allusion to *Hamlet*, 1.5.19-20 and one of Hugh's favorite quotations.

[23]Hugh Nibley, Letter to Ronald A. Millett, 16 May 1984.

[24]Paul Springer, "Faith of an Observer," 515.

[25]Truman G. Madsen, interview, "Faith of an Observer," 444, commented: "I happen to know that he has had invitations and offers and some of them both prestigious and, what's the proper word?, 'well-oiled' in terms of financial reward, and he has turned them down."

[26]Paul Springer, Letter to Hugh Nibley, 15 May 1958.

paid for doing what I don't want and I don't get paid for doing what I want. So in the end, I think his choice was much more wise than my own."[27]

Perhaps Hugh's attitude toward money is, at times, a bit extreme. I think Phyllis Nibley's position that money does need to be managed and cannot be completely avoided is much more practical. However, Hugh has done us all a great service by calling to our attention the corrosive influence money can have on our lives and urging us to seek instead to build Zion.

While Hugh's lack of interest in and disgust toward money have remained consistent throughout his life, they also remained primarily in the realm of personal philosophy. His early writings and speeches rarely addressed the topic. He first developed this theme in print in *An Approach to the Book of Mormon*, the 1957 Melchizedek Priesthood manual. In a chapter titled "The Way of the Wicked," he wrote that the Book of Mormon is "speaking to our own society" when it warns that "the people of the land have been destroyed because of their concern for the vain things of the world" (395).[28] Hugh returned to the topic in his 1967 book *Since Cumorah*. In summing up the message of the Book of Mormon in his chapter "Good People and Bad People," Hugh described what he termed the "Nephite disease" as an obsession with wealth and ambition that leads to secret combinations. "Wealth is a jealous master," wrote Hugh, "who will not be served halfheartedly and will suffer no rival—not even God" (356).[29] Nevertheless, it wasn't really until the 1970s that Hugh began to address the subject forcefully in his speeches and writings. Perhaps he saw less need for it earlier among the Wasatch Front Mormons where he lived. Or perhaps it was there all along but was eliminated from his work by his publishers. Hugh has stated that censorship on this topic did, in fact, occur: "There is only one thing [publishers] censor [from my writings]. You can say anything you want about anything but you must never, never, never say anything disrespectful about money. Even if it were a verse of scripture, they would cut it right out."[30]

For whatever reason, Hugh became increasingly obsessed about this topic, and his message began to appear more and more often in print. He made what may be considered his opening salvo in his speech "Our Glory or Our Condemnation" which he delivered as part of BYU's Last Lecture Series, sponsored by the Associated Students, in 1971. This invitational series was framed around the question: "What would you say if this were your last lecture?" It invited academics to reflect broadly and to share what they would consider the wisdom they had acquired. Hugh focused on the Tenth Article of Faith[31] in an expression of passionate longing for the

---

[27] Paul Springer, "Faith of an Observer," 504.

[28] Hugh W. Nibley, *An Approach to the Book of Mormon* (Salt Lake City: Church of Jesus Christ of Latter-day Saints, 1957; reprinted Salt Lake City: Deseret Book/FARMS, 1988), 397-98.

[29] Hugh W. Nibley, *Since Cumorah*, edited by John W. Welch (Salt Lake City: Deseret Book, 1967; reprinted Salt Lake City: Deseret Book/FARMS, 1988), 354-61.

[30] "Nibley Talks about Contemporary Issues," *Sunstone Review* November/December 1983, 14. In Hugh Nibley, "Faith of an Observer," 17, Hugh repeated that publishers "don't censor except when you speak disrespectfully of money. . . . That will be cut out just like that. They will not listen to anything that questions the beauty or perfection of money."

day when the Saints would build up Zion and abandon the clamor of greed. It was here that he first contrasted Zion with Babylon and lamented: "Saints start out building up Zion and end up building Babylon."[32]

Two years later, he returned to and expanded the theme in his 1973 discourse, "What Is Zion?: A Distant View" delivered at the Joseph Smith Lecture Series at BYU. In that speech he confessed:

> All my life I have shied away from these disturbing and highly unpopular—even offensive—themes. But I cannot do so any longer, because in my old age I have taken to reading the scriptures and there have had it forced upon my reluctant attention that, from the time of Adam to the present day, Zion has been pitted against Babylon, and the name of the game has always been money—"power and gain." (58)

Perhaps it was the nationwide emerging trend toward seeking personal affluence that caused Hugh to focus on this theme in his public discourses. In a letter he wrote to his son Alex in 1979, Hugh repeated: "The winning philosophy throughout the land today, and especially in Utah, is simple and to the point: Whatever takes money from me for whatever purpose is bad; whatever brings me money by whatever means, is good."[33]

Obviously this trend disturbed Hugh—an antimaterialism proponent from childhood—a great deal. But he was also responding to the promptings of the Spirit. After giving his speech "How Firm a Foundation! What Makes it So" at the 1979 Sesquicentennial Lectures on Mormon Arts, Hugh confided in a letter to Alex: "Yesterday I gave the opening talk of a set of Sesquicentennial addresses. The last moment, under strong promptings of the Spirit, I changed the subject and spoke about something that has suddenly become very important to me—the Law of Consecration."[34]

His identification of the law of consecration is significant. Being against greed and money-grubbing, while a worthy stance, is essentially negative. Being for the law of consecration is to take a powerfully spiritual stance in relation to God as creator, stewardship over the earth's resources, and charity toward fellow human beings. It became a dominant theme for Hugh during the 1980s, a decade characterized by the "me generation." Hugh delivered a steady stream of speeches—"How to Get Rich," "Work We Must, But the Lunch Is Free," "But What Kind of Work?" "Leadership to Management," "We Will Still Weep for Zion, ""Breakthroughs I Would Like to See," and other essays—all describing the perils of seeking after riches and urging the Saints instead to seek to build up Zion.

---

[31]"We believe in the literal gathering of Israel and in the restoration of the Ten Tribes; that Zion (the New Jerusalem) will be built upon the American continent; that Christ will reign personally upon the earth; and that the earth will be renewed and received its paradisiacal glory." In 1981 edition of the Pearl of Great Price.

[32]Hugh W. Nibley, "Our Glory or Our Condemnation," in *Approaching Zion*, edited by Don E. Norton, Vol. 9 of *The Collected Works of Hugh Nibley* (Salt Lake City: Deseret Book/FARMS, 1989), 17. References to the essays in this book are hereafter cited parenthetically in the text.

[33]Hugh Nibley, Letter to Charles Alexander Nibley, 1 April 1979.

[34]Hugh Nibley, Letter to Charles Alexander Nibley, 22 September 1979.

In these speeches, Hugh warns that ultimately the Saints have only two choices in this life: to seek treasure here or to seek treasure in heaven. As he learned when his father lost the family fortune, Hugh knows that "the only secure treasures we have are in heaven, and we have no right or reason to be concerned with the other treasures—they don't mean a thing; but the real treasure means everything."[35] For Hugh, seeking for wealth is a distraction from the quest for spirituality. In a letter he wrote in 1988, Hugh describes the dilemma:

> We have been instructed to read the Book of Mormon with scrupulous care and close analysis. If we do that, we will discover that the acquisition of wealth often rewarded the zeal of the Saints but invariably led to pride, ambition and the increase of inequality among the Saints. It was the inequality that bothered the prophets—let me refer you to the Concordance for checking on these things statistically. Match up, for example, "riches" and "angels," both of which are mentioned many times. The riches tell one story, the angels another. The riches don't bother me because they don't concern me, but the absence of angels on the present scene may be significant. As you know, Joseph Smith said "the heavens have often been sealed up because of covetousness in the Church." But the [primitive] Church still went on—without angels or revelations, the channel being pretty well closed off. The degree of inspiration in the Church is not always the same; the Book of Mormon is a barometer in which it goes up and down in astonishingly short periods. If you examine it, you will find that there is a definite correlation between wealth and revelation—a negative correlation. You will also find that at every period there are humble servants of Christ who go their way without trying to control anything but their own behavior; they are the ones who really benefit by the Gospel and enjoy it.[36]

Furthermore, Hugh maintains that any material thing we acquire in this life is a gift: "[The Lord] gives us everything we need as a gift and is not at all pleased when we spend our days fighting among ourselves to see who can grab the most. That is not what he intended us to be doing either here on earth or in the eternities."[37] Those who choose not to seek the Lord's gifts will get other gifts from another source. In a highly scriptural letter to Alex, Hugh pointed out:

> Well, it is not a question of whether we will accept gifts or not, but whom we accept them from. Deny not the gift of God! cries Moroni to our generation, to which he adds, "Touch not the evil gift, nor the unclean thing!" and so he ends the Book of Mormon (Moroni 10:30). Unclean gift? I believe that the name "filthy" is applied to Satan's wonderful package gift that brings you "anything in this world."[38]

The problem, as Hugh would describe it, is that the evil gifts are often disguised as good gifts, and Babylon always puts on a respectable and proper front:

---

[35] Hugh Nibley, Letter to Charles Alexander Nibley, n.d., ca. 1979.
[36] Hugh Nibley, Letter to Brent Lewis, 24 February 1988.
[37] Hugh Nibley, Letter to Stuart C. Reid, 11 December 1979.
[38] Hugh Nibley, Letter to Charles Alexander Nibley, 1 April 1979. Hugh typed letters to his missionary sons at the same ferocious speed with which he typed his articles, and the content was frequently similar. In his

> Babylon is always there: rich, respectable, immoveable, with its granite walls and steel vaults, its bronze gates, its onyx trimmings and marble floors (all borrowed from ancient temples, for these are our modern temples) and its bullet-proof glass—the awesome symbols of total security. Keeping her orgies decently private, she presents a front of unalterable propriety to all. (54-55)

In Mormon communities, Hugh identifies, with aesthetic repugnance, a persistent pattern in which Babylon tries to masquerade as Zion:

> The label game reaches its all-time peak of skill and effrontery in the Madison Avenue master stroke of pasting the lovely label of Zion on all the most typical institutions of Babylon: Zion's Loans, Zion's Real Estate, Zion's Used Cars, Zion's Jewelry, Zion's Supermart, Zion's Auto Wrecking, Zion's Outdoor Advertising, Zion's Gunshop, Zion's Land and Mining, Zion's Development, Zion's Securities. All that is quintessentially Babylon now masquerades as Zion. (53-54)

And while Babylon presents itself in the disguise of Zion, it also presents itself as a productive part of society. In fact, argues Hugh, "the ancient teaching that the idler shall not eat the bread of the laborer has always meant that the idle rich shall not eat the bread of the laboring poor, as they always have" (240).

The business of Babylon "is based on the exchange of life for property." This Hugh calls "the Mahan Principle"—which is the secret Satan taught Cain (Moses 5:29-31): "that I can kill and get gain." But Hugh sees this phenomenon at different levels throughout our economy. While drug dealers, hit men, and weapons dealers are certainly one manifestation of the Mahan Principle, so too are businesses which pollute, force employees to work under dangerous conditions, or use chemicals that are noxious to human life. "The fearful processes of industry," denounces Hugh, "shorten and impoverish life at every level, from forced labor to poisonous air and water. This is the world's economy, for Satan is 'the prince of this world'" (436-37).

The only hope for our world is to establish Zion, and Hugh sees the law of consecration as a "minimal requirement" (52) for our exaltation —"the last and hardest requirement made of men in this life" (168). Hugh ranks sexual temptations second to temptations of wealth because lust "subside[s] with advancing age, while desire for the security and status of wealth only increases and grows through the years" (168). If we see ourselves as God does as members of a world family, then "to take more than we need is to take that which does not belong to us" (50).

Ultimately, Hugh sees this life as a school:

---

letters, he developed, clarified, or expanded on ideas he was working on for articles or speeches, seldom including family news. Relatively few letters have survived from the early 1970s when Paul and Tom were serving their missions; but Alex saved most of his, probably because their content was urgently contemporary. World and local conditions prompted Hugh to write on apocalyptic themes like the end of the world, the temptations of wealth, and the establishment of Zion. The United States was in the middle of an intensifying cold war with the Soviet Union, the nation was heading into Reagan-era conservatism, and Wasatch-Front Mormons were becoming more socially divided, with huge, expensive homes climbing up the Provo hillsides while the modest pioneer homes in the town deteriorated into slums or were demolished for outrageously overpriced student housing.

We have been sent to school upon the earth with all our room and board freely provided; if we spend the time we should be devoting to our studies planning how to get and secure more room and board, and more room and board, he will say to us, as he did to the highly successful entrepreneur who expanded his business and achieved delightful security for the future, "thou fool, this night shall thy soul be required of thee."[39]

But Hugh has not only called on us to seek Zion, he has reminded us that the Law of Consecration is simultaneously a practical way of life and a covenant we've already made:

We forget today how well the United Order worked in many places. *United* means by definition team-work, cooperation, necessarily requiring a number of people involved in the same project. (As in Zion's [sic] Cooperative [sic] Merchantile [very] Institution [you name it].) *Order* means that people are following a common rule. All of which says that you can only live the United Order in a cooperative group; you cannot play it alone. The thing must be planned, directed and controlled from a head; it is an organization, and as such must be properly directed by the head of the Church.[40]

True, the law of consecration and the United Order are not the same thing. We cannot live the United Order until the Church returns to such planned communities. But we *can* consecrate all that we have to the Lord. Hugh flung down a personal challenge to every temple-going Saint by asking, "What is there to stop me from observing and keeping the law of consecration at this very day as I have already covenanted and promised to do without reservation?" (173) "The plain fact is," Hugh reminds the Saints, "that I have promised to keep a law, and to keep it now. I know exactly what I am supposed to consecrate, exactly how, exactly why, exactly when, and exactly where" (388). We often assume that external events will motivate the change in our individual practices—that the establishment of Zion will bring about the revival of the Law of Consecration. Hugh stands the equation on its head: It is by living the Law of Consecration that we will establish Zion. "We do not wait until Zion is here to observe [the law of consecration]; it is rather the means of bringing us nearer to Zion" (390).

As Hugh stated in a personal letter, consecration can occur in an institutional setting but only an individual can practice it:

Consecration . . . is most intimate, personal and private. You cannot consecrate what belongs to somebody else and nobody else can consecrate what belongs to you without first taking it away from you. Consecrate as you know means to set apart, take out of circulation, literally put within an enclosure or behind a fence . . . or cut off from the profane world.

It is quite possible to give out all you have except what you need to live on— ". . . having food and raiment, etc." and that is what I do. I leave things to my wife who is a fanatical giver. Needless to say, there is no shortage of takers, but as

---
[39] Hugh Nibley, Letter to Stuart C. Reid, 11 December 1979.
[40] Hugh Nibley, Letter to Russell Stewart, 24 January 1986; brackets Nibley's.

"He's been like this ever since he read Nibley's 'What Is Zion?'"

Cartoon by Kent and Janet Christensen,
Sunstone, August 1992, No. 88.
Used by permission.

Joseph and Brigham both said it is better to give to ten imposters than run the risk of turning down one worthy person.[41]

Hugh's words seem confirmed by the vision of the General Authorities when they speak of Zion. Elder Marion G. Romney once stated that we would establish Zion only when we start living its laws:

> From the very beginning I felt that the [welfare] program would eventually move into the Law of Consecration and that this is the trial pattern. Until I can pay my tithing and make liberal contributions of my money and labor . . . I will not be prepared to go into the United Order, which will require me to consecrate everything I have and thereafter give all my surplus for the benefit of the kingdom. I think the United Order will be the last principle of the gospel we will learn to live and that doing so will bring in the millennium.[42]

And President Kimball once stated that "the Lord's timetable is directed a good deal by us. We speed up the clock or we slow the hands down and we turn them back by our activities or our procrastinations."[43] It is only when we are indi-

---

[41]Ibid.

[42]Quoted in Dean L. May, "The Economics of Zion," Sunstone 14, no. 4 (August 1990): 22.

vidually living up to the covenants we have already made that we will be able to live those covenants in unison as communities and, finally, to establish Zion.

While Hugh Nibley's strong and uncompromising voice has not been heard by all, many individuals are listening. Numerous people have told me that Hugh's words have effected a tremendous change in their lives. If, as Hugh has stated, "every step in the direction of increasing one's personal holdings is a step away from Zion" (37), then Hugh Nibley has been approaching Zion for many years. His words are a call to join him and, by so doing, to discover greater peace and happiness by living simple, holy, and committed lives.

---

[43] Edward L. Kimball, ed., *Teachings of Spencer W. Kimball* (Salt Lake City: Bookcraft, 1982), 441-42.

Hugh with his grandson, Nathanael Hugh Petersen, age eight and a half months, in July 2002.

The Lord has made me small and insignificant so, since both Joseph and Brigham have said that minding one's own business is the credo of the Latter-day Saints, I have been content to creep into the background and observe things. What I have seen is vastly more interesting than anything I have done. But the things that would make the most interesting opus are the very ones I have no intention of telling. "I could a tale unfold," but I leave it there. A bland list of conventional doings would be unobjectionable and dull. I seek only one kind of influence—to induce people to appreciate and love the Gospel, so we can all have a good time.[1]

---

[1] Hugh Nibley, Letter to Dallin H. Oaks, 7 May 1997. Hugh was responding to Oaks's request to tell his life story.

Chapter 25

One Eternal Round, 1990-Present

During the 1990s, Hugh finally began to pace himself less recklessly. He spoke less frequently in public. His correspondence, which had, since the 1970s, consisted mainly of responses to church members' questions rather than intimate letters to personal friends, tapered off radically as Hugh began to refer many requests for information to FARMS. He wrote less but, thanks to FARMS, was publishing a great deal. *The Collected Works of Hugh Nibley* had reached ten volumes by 1990, and four more had rolled off the press as of the spring of 2002.

Despite the slowing of his work schedule, Hugh's mind has remained as active and vital as ever. As he wrote to Alex in 1993, "The feeble old brain, by special request, is as clear and active as it ever was, and the memory was never more reliable."[3] As I've interviewed Hugh over the course of writing this book, I have been repeatedly astonished at the acuity and comprehensiveness of his memory. His preoccupation during this time has been his *magnum opus*, a book he has already titled *One Eternal Round*. It continues Hugh's work on the Book of Abraham, but focuses on the hypocephalus (Facsimile 2 in the Book of Abraham). Hugh began the project during the early 1980s and has been constantly engaged in working and reworking the book over almost two decades.[4] Those who have spent any time around Hugh during this period have often heard him delight in some new detail that he has discovered or

---
[2]*Tinkling Cymbals and Sounding Brass* was published in 1991, *Temple and Cosmos* in 1992, *Brother Brigham Challenges the Saints* in 1994, and *Abraham in Egypt* in 2000.

[3]Hugh Nibley, Letter to Charles Alexander Nibley, 28 August 1993.

[4]Hypocephalus (lit. "under the head") is a class of Egyptian funerary documents in the shape of a small disk that was placed under the head of a mummy, as Hugh puts it, to "preserve a flame in the head, putting the body on hold, as it were, without hanging up, to leave a connection between the spirit above and the body in the tomb pending the day of resurrection." Hugh Nibley, "Approach to Facsimile No. 2," unpublished manuscript, 17 May 1985, 1.

comment on how wonderful the material is that he is working on. They have also felt frustrated by the fact that the book is taking so long to appear in print. But few have wanted to wrest the book away from Hugh when it keeps him motivated and gives him such undisguised pleasure. Since the early 1990s, Hugh has been keenly aware of pressure to finish the book. When he drifts away into the library stacks to look up sources and someone catches him doing more research, Hugh acts "like a boy caught with his hand in the cookie jar," comments his secretary, Pat Ward. But he is always excited by the information he discovers or rediscovers in these brief bouts of research. "This is good stuff; I'd forgotten about this; I've got to go over this!" Pat hears Hugh exclaim.[5]

Along the way, Hugh has provided several clues about the book's content. In 1980, Hugh wrote a lengthy unpublished article, "The Three Facsimiles from the Book of Abraham" in which he argued that "the best approach to Facsimile No. 2 is surprisingly supplied by an episode in the Testament of Abraham, discovered in 1880, supported by the Apocalypse of Abraham, which first appeared in English in 1898 in the pages of the *Improvement Era*." Both are pseudepigraphic works from the first to second century.[6] On 17 May 1985, Hugh spoke at the first regional Sunstone Symposium in Washington, D.C. on "[An] Approach to Facsimile No. 2." In it he discussed this hypocephalus and others like it as a work of "sacred geometry" and stated that after his "extensive and coordinated studies," he had determined that they are "an expression of the unity of all life with the cosmos itself in the eternal processes of death and rebirth."[7]

---

[5]Pat Ward, interviewed by Boyd Petersen, 26 September 2001.

[6]Hugh Nibley, "The Three Facsimiles of the Book of Abraham," 9, unpublished manuscript, 1980, photocopy in my possession. I have been unable to determine this manuscript's original audience. It is too long for a speech, but it has never appeared in print except as an unpublished paper offered through FARMS. The Apocalypse of Abraham and the Testament of Abraham are in James H. Charlesworth, ed., *The Old Testament Pseudepigrapha*, 2 vols. (Garden City, NY: Doubleday, 1983), 1:681-705 and 1:871-902 respectively. R. Rubinkiewica and H. F. Lunt translated the Apocalypse of Abraham, and E. P. Sanders translated the Testament of Abraham.

[7]Hugh Nibley, "Approach to Facsimile No. 2," 2, unpublished manuscript, 17 May 1995; photocopy of typescript in my possession. Clayton Chandler, speaking in August 2001 in a session at the Sunstone Symposium honoring retiring Sunstone editor Elbert Peck, recalled this speech, made at the first of the regional Sunstone symposia held on the East Coast in Washington, D.C. "It was a grand affair. It was remarkable. None of us knew what to expect. . . . ," describes Chandler. "On opening night, Hugh Nibley was the speaker. Six hundred people were there. This ballroom was packed. It crackled with excitement as all these people from Washington, D.C., were sitting there waiting to hear from Hugh Nibley. He proceeded to give the most incredible . . . un-understandable talk ever given. I was sitting in the back with my brother Neal [Chandler] and [his wife] Becky. Neal was [leaning forward] the whole time, straining to understand. Becky was knitting. She just gave up. I perked up when he started talking about the Golden Triangle because I'm an architect. I knew about that; but within minutes, I was totally lost again. Years later I talked to Elbert about this [evening] and confessed, 'You know, Elbert, I really didn't understand.' He just looked at me. 'No one did.' But it was marvelous, a big success, and I was looking forward to doing it again the next year, and so was Elbert. He planned a marvelous event for the next year. There was just one problem. He assumed that the same number would come, but Nibley [had] scared them off. It [the second symposium] was such a financial disaster." "Sunstone Celebrates Elbert Peck," Audio cassette SL 01 #291. The drop in attendance may, however, be less attributable to Hugh "scaring off" attendees than to Hugh's drawing an unusually large crowd for the first year.

Between 27 June and 26 September 1990, Hugh delivered a series of twelve FARMS-sponsored lectures at BYU: "One Eternal Round."[8] He began the series by addressing criticisms of the Book of Abraham from Egyptologists past and present. He next showed how the emphasis in Egyptology has shifted from seeing the Egyptians as preoccupied with death to seeing them as preoccupied with resurrection. Then he turned to discussing the hypocephalus as a work of cosmic design which was thought to create a connection between higher and lower beings. After making a detailed reading of the hypocephalus and comparing it to other extant hypocephali, Hugh examined parallels between the Book of Abraham and ancient narratives from Egypt and the Near East.[9] On 14 June 1995, Hugh read "Abraham" at the Institute of Religion at Utah Valley State College. In his paper, he used biblical and extra-biblical sources about Abraham to assemble a biography of the ancient patriarch.[10] Finally, on 6 April 1999, Hugh read a paper titled "Abraham's Creation Drama" at the FARMS-sponsored Abraham Lecture Series. In this speech, Hugh again painted a portrait of Abraham and showed his relationship to the temple. In a highly interesting reading of Abraham's vision, Hugh argued that the text contains stage directions for a ritual drama that closely parallels the Mormon temple endowment.[11]

It becomes clear, especially in these later writings, that Abraham is more than a preoccupation for Hugh. He is, for Hugh, the quintessence of the righteous man. Hugh describes him as "squarely in the middle" of all dispensations of time, a man who "binds all things together and gives meaning and purpose to everything that happened" but also as a man who held no office, performed no miracles, and lived in a heroic time without being involved in any "mighty combats, blow-by-blow, or challenges boasting heroic genealogy." Hugh points out: "His ten trials were Everyman's trials." He was a poor businessman who "seemed to be generous to the point of lacking common sense," but Abraham was also capable of "extreme independence of thought and action, . . . eager to exchange ideas with the greatest thinkers of his time."[12] While Hugh's description of Abraham may not be hyperbolic, it is certainly glowing and conveys the high degree of veneration Hugh feels for this ancient father of nations.

In addition to working on his book, Hugh also continued to teach one honors religion class (either Book of Mormon or Pearl of Great Price) each semester. When he first came to BYU and was teaching a grueling five classes each quarter, Hugh hated the interruptions to his research that teaching interposed. But Hugh

---

[8]FARMS sponsored the lecture series with the express purpose of helping Hugh assemble the material he had been working on in order to get a working manuscript of the book. However, Hugh would not let go of the project after the lecture series ended. FARMS recorded the lectures and made them available as a set of audio cassettes.

[9]Hugh Nibley, "One Eternal Round: The Significance of the Egyptian Hypocephalus," 12 audio cassette tapes (Provo, UT: FARMS, 1990).

[10]Hugh Nibley, "Abraham," unpublished manuscript, 14 June 1995, photocopy in my possession.

[11]This essay was later published as "Abraham's Temple Drama," in *The Temple in Time and Eternity*, edited by Donald W. Parry and Stephen D. Ricks (Provo, UT: FARMS, 1999), 1-42.

[12]Hugh Nibley, "Abraham's Temple Drama," 2-6.

enjoyed being in the classroom, preparing material, and presenting it to his students. Pat Ward describes him returning to the office thoroughly energized after a class. Despite his advancing years, "he would come in here all excited about some scripture that he'd found and then they hadn't been able to get past five verses because there was so much information there." She continued, "He was so excited about it, he lit up. Even though he would be a little tired sometimes, he'd go to class and he'd have that light in his eye after teaching."

Hugh traditionally required only three things from his religion students: attendance, participation, and a term paper. During the winter semester 1994, Hugh was teaching an honors class on the Pearl of Great Price. Toward the end of the semester he gave his students their paper topic and told them that they could either prepare it in advance or write it during the final exam period. When the papers came in, Hugh was not impressed. "They really weren't that good," recalls Pat Ward. Hugh gave mostly C's, perhaps a few B's, maybe one or two A's, and "even gave some D's." "They got what they deserved," Pat insists, "but they were upset." To be fair to the students, Hugh's classes always focused on his on-going research and were therefore highly theoretical, esoteric, and abstruse. No wonder students could be mystified about his expectations for their term papers. However, instead of confronting Hugh directly with their complaints, the students went over his head to the chair of Ancient Scripture in the Department of Religious Education. Without consulting Hugh, the chair reviewed the students' complaints and changed their grades across the board.

Like any professor faced with such high-handed administrative action, "that didn't go very well with Hugh," Pat Ward states. He stormed into the office and announced: "They [students] don't want to work anymore; I'm not going to teach." He was as good as his word. At age eighty-four, Hugh had taught his last class.

The mid-1980s through the 1990s proved to be a time of Job-like tribulations for Hugh, but he emerged from them tried and tested, a better man. Most of these trials fell upon the people he loved best. During this turbulent fifteen years, three of Hugh's children experienced the trauma of divorce. Some drifted away from the Church. Such events were an assault on Hugh's deep-rooted traditional Mormon values, but he never shunned his children. Instead, he worried, prayed, and wept for his sons and daughters. The most distressing incident occurred in 1991, when, after reading several popular self-help books, visiting a poorly trained therapist, and using self-hypnosis, Hugh's daughter Martha accused him of abuse. While no one in the family took these allegations lightly, Phyllis and all of Martha's siblings eventually concluded that Martha's "memories" were false. Martha went on to sever her relationships with most of her family and eventually leave the Church. For his own part, Hugh knew Martha's accusations were false and felt great pain that they had come between his daughter and him.[13]

---

[13] I must confess that I have spent considerable time stewing over how to approach this topic, or even whether I should approach this topic. I find myself in a no-win situation, especially since we live in a cultural atmosphere where doubting the story of an alleged victim is frequently seen as blaming the victim. However, even though Martha has not published an exposé about her alleged abuse, she has not kept silent. So to not deal

But despite these difficulties, Hugh and Phyllis have always deeply enjoyed the diversity of their children, supported their achievements, and loved them through hard times. Paul resigned his position at BYU in 1989 and started his own general contracting company, specializing in furniture building and cabinet-making. He, Bronia, and their children live in Provo. Christina retired from teaching high school in 1989, earned a J.D. from the University of Florida at Gainesville, and practiced immigration and family law until 2000 when she left her practice to support their daughter, Natalie, whose husband, Joel Myres, was diagnosed with terminal cancer. She and Z still live in Florida, where Z is a corporate executive. Tom and Cindy continue to live in the Los Angeles area, where Tom works as an actor and writer. Michael married Sandy Desautel in 1990; he works as an expert in communication with new technologies in the Washington, D.C., area. Alex, divorced in 1992, married Junalee Jarque and resides in the Salt Lake area where he works as a writer and in arts production. Becky is a costume and clothing designer in the Los Angeles area. Martha and John currently live in Phoenix, where Martha works as a writer and life coach. Zina and Boyd have lived in Provo since 1995. Zina is an assistant professor of English at BYU. She and Boyd have four children: Mary, Christian, Nathanael, and Andrew Reid.

In 1988, Hugh's eleven-year-old granddaughter Miriam, (Paul's daughter) was paralyzed from the waist down when a sand cave she was playing in just above Timpview High School collapsed on her, crushing her back. Miriam recalls that she was greatly touched when her grandfather came to visit her, bringing her a paperback copy of Tolkein's *Lord of the Rings*. (She was also greatly amused to discover that,

---

with this episode would lead some to believe that I'm covering up a family secret. But here are the facts: Martha was one of eight children who grew up in the Nibley household; two of her sisters shared a room with her until she was a teenager; yet only Martha believes Hugh was abusive. No one witnessed any inappropriate activities between Martha and her father, and the Nibley home was too small for the family to keep many secrets from each other. Martha's siblings range from active Latter-day Saint to completely disengaged, from believing to agnostic. And all have some complaints about the way Hugh fulfilled his role as father, so their rejection of Martha's story does not come from a desire to preserve the reputation of their father or the Church. Furthermore, it can be documented that Martha has not been very consistent in reporting on her own past. For example, in their book *Breaking the Cycles of Compulsive Behavior* (Salt Lake: Deseret Book, 1990), she and her husband John write that they "accept as inspired the teachings of The Church of Jesus Christ of Latter-day Saints" (xi), while in her book *Expecting Adam* (New York: Times, 1999), she states plainly that she hadn't believed in God since she was a teenager and describes the very people who bought her first book as "religious fanatics" (50). It must also be remembered that False Memory Syndrome was part of the general *zeitgeist* of the early 1990s, with many noted celebrities publicly confessing their status as victims of abuse and a whole subculture of primarily women using hypnotherapy to "uncover" the buried abuse in their past. Thousands of families were shattered during this witch hunt. Since then, reputable psychologists and psychiatrists, while maintaining that abuse is a significant and often over-looked problem in America, now distrust the use of hypnosis for uncovering memories, understand better the malleable and inaccurate nature of memory, and advocate some real life confirmation in cases where accusations of abuse are made. The American Medical Association has officially declared that it "considers recovered memories of childhood sexual abuse to be of uncertain authenticity, which should be subject to external verification," and the American Psychological Association has asserted that "at this point it is impossible, without other corroborative evidence, to distinguish a true memory from a false one." For a good overview of the history behind FMS see Julia Gracen's "Truth and Reconciliation: Incest Accusations of the Recovered-Memory Craze Tore Families Apart. Now One of its Leaders Wants to Let Bygones be Bygones." 22 May 2002 at http://www.salon.com/books/feature/2002/05/22/davis/index.html or visit the False Memory Syndrome Foundation website at www.fmsfonline.org.

typical of the Nibley household's level of disorganization, the book had been due at the Provo High School library twenty years earlier.) Hugh awkwardly asked to give her a blessing, Miriam remembers, and promised her that she would be able to walk again, a prophecy that did in fact come true as Miriam is now able to walk with the aid of canes and braces. This crisis revealed to Miriam the depth and genuineness of her grandfather's love for her. He has continued to cheer her achievements as a wheelchair athlete.[14]

On 3 April 1990, Hugh's older brother Sloan died. Hugh had not spent much time with his brother since childhood, nor did they share much in common after their brief passage at UCLA as students in the 1930s.[15] Hugh was deeply affected by Sloan's passing, a reaction that surprised even him, but comfort finally came to him after he sensed Sloan's presence in his room one night, a highly spiritual experience that Hugh will not discuss. In April 1995, Hugh's close friend Kresimir Cosic was diagnosed with non-Hodgkins lymphoma. Hugh and Phyllis flew to Maryland to visit with Kreso at Johns Hopkins Medical Center in Baltimore. Even though Kreso slipped in and out of unconsciousness, Hugh talked to him for many hours and gave him a priesthood blessing. Kreso died while Hugh was flying back to Utah.

Nor was Hugh spared health problems of his own. In 1991, he was diagnosed with prostate cancer, and the prognosis "did not look too promising," as he confessed in a letter to Alex. Despite this disheartening news, the tumor "vanished totally in seven weeks of fifteen-second painless radiation. So the radiation raised hell, but the treatment for that is simple and easy even if it is embarrassing and inconvenient, and it is working."[16] As Hugh approached his ninetieth year, Phyllis began "having a hard time getting around," as Hugh wrote to Alex. Hugh stepped in to do more of the household chores and also took over the grocery shopping. With concern, he wrote to Alex, "I am going to have to use more of my own faith-and-prayer treatment. I can assure you with absolute certainty that it never fails."[17] In 2000, Phyllis had cataract surgery, then got a serious infection in one eye that almost cost her its sight. Even this dark cloud had a silver lining. While she was in the hospital recuperating from the infection, doctors noticed that she had an irregular heart beat. They put her on a monitor and installed a pacemaker that greatly improved her cardiac functioning.

All of these events, and many more among colleagues and relatives made Hugh reflect on his life, take stock of his efforts as a father and husband, and commit to living more connectedly with his family. Those close to him saw a real mellowing in his personality. Hugh became more attentive to his family's needs, more thoughtful about remembering birthdays or anniversaries, and more expressive of

---

[14]Miriam Nibley, interviewed by Boyd Petersen, 13 March 2002, transcript in my possession.

[15]After World War II, Sloan made his career as a screenwriter for Republic Motion Picture Studio. He wrote many Hollywood westerns, including *Springfield Rifle* (1952) starring Gary Cooper and *The Far Frontier* (1949), starring Roy Rogers, and worked on several TV series such as the 1964-66 comedy *The Addams Family*, the 1958-61 Lloyd Bridges drama *Sea Hunt*, and for the Hanna-Barbera cartoons during the 1960s. He married Linda Stirling, a leading lady of popular 1940s action films.

[16]Hugh Nibley, Letter to Charles Alexander Nibley, 28 August 1993.

[17]Ibid.

Hugh and Phyllis celebrate their fiftieth anniversary with most of their children and grandchildren.

his love and appreciation to his children, twenty-two grandchildren, and one great-grandchild. But perhaps the most important legacy of these years was not a reorientation but an acceleration along a path he had already chosen: his faith in the gospel and in the plan of salvation. He expressed some of these sentiments in a 1993 letter to Alex:

> I have often walked through frightfully perilous situations blissfully at ease and unsuspecting . . . , while at other times I have been in panic and dread and apprehension of something than which nothing could be more harmless.
> The Buddhists and Zen people are right in writing off this world as less than nothing much, but dead wrong in dismissing the next one—the advance notices on it alone are enough to satisfy me. Picking our way through this obstacle-course of nasty surprises makes perfectly good sense to me.[18]

Although these years were difficult for Hugh, he also celebrated several milestones: On 18 September 1996, Hugh and Phyllis celebrated their fiftieth wedding anniversary with an open house for friends and relatives. Later that weekend, Hugh's children and grandchildren gathered for a celebration at a Provo hotel. Phyllis felt that the two social gatherings more than made up for the fact that she and Hugh had had no party to celebrate their actual wedding fifty years earlier. And while Hugh seemed bemused by the fuss, he also seemed to recognize that fifty years of marriage is a landmark to be celebrated.

---

[18]Ibid.

Hugh opens presents at his ninetieth birthday party in March 2000. The button, a gift from a grandchild, reads: "Getting Better with Age."

On 27 March 2000, Hugh celebrated his ninetieth birthday. His children hosted one open house celebration, while FARMS and BYU hosted a second small gathering at which his colleagues, friends, and family expressed their appreciation for his life and work. For his part, Hugh paid a glowing tribute to Phyllis. He expressed his love and appreciation for her support through the years, stating that, out of the two of them, she was really the smart one.

Finally on 14 November 2001, after having been relocated and remodeled during the renovation of the Harold B. Lee Library, the Ancient Studies Reading Room was dedicated and renamed the Hugh Nibley Ancient Studies Reading Room. The reading room was established in 1974 to support the work of the newly founded Institute of Ancient Studies. Hugh was largely responsible for the collection housed in the reading room. Since his arrival at BYU, he had recommended, sought out, and procured many volumes of ancient and classical texts. Thanks to his efforts, the school acquired the *Patrologiae Latinae* and *Graecae* (The Writings of the Early Church Fathers in Latin and Greek), a set of more than four hundred volumes.

Also thanks to Hugh's efforts, the library achieved such visibility in the scholarly world that in 1958 it successfully procured the Egyptological collection of the late Samuel A. B. Mercer.[19] Today the reading room houses over 4,400 titles (many of them multi-volume works), with over 20 ancient languages represented, plus reference works in English, French, German, Latin, and Italian. It also includes 2,700 microforms of collections from libraries like St. Catherine's Monastery in Mount Sinai, the Coptic Museum in Cairo, several church archives in Jerusalem, and the monastery at Mount Athos, Greece. Thankfully, many of these rare works are now being digitalized by the newly created Institute for the Study and Preservation of Ancient Religious Texts at FARMS.[20]

As of this writing (spring 2002), Hugh Nibley just celebrated his ninety-second birthday. He says he is now turning in chapters from *One Eternal Round* to his editor, but those of us who have learned patience over the past twenty years suspect that he will still be tinkering for some time to come. He still goes up to work in his office for three or four hours every week day. When he is home, he can most frequently be found sitting in his well-worn, comfortable chair with piles of manuscripts surrounding him, poring over a book of Egyptian hieroglyphs, or taking time out to watch an episode of *West Wing* or a PBS show with Phyllis. His life is quieter now, but still full, made richer by a lifetime of accumulating the treasures of a mind consecrated to the service of the gospel, a heart grateful for its blessings, and a spirit keenly alive to unseen realities.

---

[19]Hugh confirms the date that the library acquired Mercer's collection in a letter to Paul Springer on 24 March 1958: "Our library has bought up some pretty good collections recently, including a really excellent Egyptian library, so I will not be starved for footnotes." Mercer's was the only major Egyptian collection acquired during this period.

[20]My thanks to Gary Gillum for this information.

Hugh Nibley, with a characteristic twinkling smile, stands outside BYU's Maeser Building in the early spring of 2001. He taught most of his honors sections in this building until his final class in 1994.

Photo by Brent Orton.

Chapter 26

Conclusion: Constancy Amid Change

Hugh Nibley has lived a rich life and witnessed almost the entire twentieth century. His amazing memory has stored a stunning share of it. He can remember hearing about the *Titanic* sinking in 1912, when he was only two years old. He recalls family conversations about World War I. He witnessed first-hand the devastating effects of the Great Depression and of World War II. It was a century of tremendous change. When Hugh was a boy, tall ships were sailing into the harbor of his hometown of Portland, Oregon, the Model-T Ford was rolling off the assembly line, and the Wright Brothers' famous flight had launched aviation only seven years before Hugh's birth. He has witnessed the move from airplanes to jetliners to spaceships. He also witnessed first-hand the transition of Mormonism from a Utah church to a world church. When Hugh was born there were only 398,000 members, sixty-two stakes, twenty-one missions, and four temples. Today there are more than 11 million members, more than 2,500 stakes, in excess of 300 missions, and 107 temples with 18 more planned.

In addition to witnessing this explosive growth, Hugh has significantly influenced the direction the Church has taken in its approach to the Book of Mormon, the Pearl of Great Price, and the temple. He has touched many individual lives as he has urged the Saints to take the law of consecration more seriously, to respect the environment, and to work for peace. Finally, he has set a wonderful example of faithful discipleship, all the while demonstrating how taking the gospel seriously liberates believers to feel joy, laugh at themselves, and relish the gifts of mortality.

Church leaders have praised him as a loyal defender of the faith who has challenged the Saints to take their religion more seriously. President Gordon B. Hinckley has "respected him highly for his great scholarship and for his quiet and humble manner. He knows what he is talking about, but he does not shout it."[1] Elder Boyd K. Packer called

---

[1] Gordon B. Hinckley, Letter to Boyd Petersen, 5 October 1989. I read part of this chapter at the FARMS Brown Bag Lunch Lecture Series, 20 November 1996. It appeared as "Youth and Beauty: The Correspondence of

Hugh "one of a kind—it is a very good kind."[2] And Elder Neal A. Maxwell has stated how grateful he is that "the Lord didn't put Hugh in some monastery in the middle ages to plow through the parchments, when, instead, he has been such a rich part of the Restoration's forward movement."[3]

As I've researched his life over the past fourteen years, I have decided that what is truly extraordinary about Hugh Nibley is the consistency between the public and the private man. What he says in his books he also says in private letters and interviews. Even more extraordinary, there has been little evolution in his writing style, intellectual rigor, interests, or beliefs. His writings as a teenager reflect similar themes, ideas, and interests to those he wrote in his eighties or nineties. His writings, both public and private, are almost seamless in their consistency.

The young Hugh Nibley was certainly precocious. His intellect, wisdom, and self-deprecating humility are evident from his teenage years. And his family quickly recognized this precocity. Grandfather Charles W. Nibley, writing on Hugh's fourteenth birthday, praised Hugh for his abilities and at the same time warned him against vanity:

> We all think you are gifted and talented above many of your fellows. The Lord has blessed you greatly. . . . Surely you are favored of the Lord. You must use your ability in His service in all humility and faithfulness. Do not ever allow yourself to get big-headed. Always be humble, always be prayerful. Do not forget to pray. . . . I am going to keep my eye on you and see what you do, whether you are going to be a success or whether it is all make-believe.[4]

Hugh's response to this sober warning illustrates not only Hugh's imaginative wit but also his characteristic tendency to draw parallels:

> Few things turn out to resemble what they're cracked up to be. Cleopatra was irresistible in the moonlight, but when that Egyptian sun scorched that hideous map, Antony, no doubt, turned a little pale and asked to be excused. The same will hold true in my case and, if you weren't exercising your, or your stenographer's, imaginative ability in that birthday letter, there is going to be an awful shock, not unlike the kind produced when the Lord Mayor of Dublin joins the Shriners. . . . As to getting "bigheaded", it is in my case as that of a pin. It does not have a big head because it is unnecessary and foolish. Although there are some exceptions on the part of a pin, there is none with persons.[5]

Responding to another of Grandpa Nibley's congratulatory letters on his seventeenth birthday, Hugh was equally deprecatory about his accomplishments:

> Why do you suppose one would think his efforts anything but futile—who minces about in "The Beginner's Greek Book," "First Steps in German," or "Anglo Saxon for

---

Hugh Nibley," BYU Studies 37, no. 2 (1997-98):6-31.
[2]Boyd K. Packer, Letter to Boyd Petersen, 4 October 1989.
[3]Neal A. Maxwell, Letter to Boyd Petersen, 3 October 1989.
[4]Charles W. Nibley, Letter to Hugh Nibley, 25 March 1924, Charles W. Nibley Collection, Family Correspondence, LDS Church Archives.
[5]Hugh Nibley, Letter to Charles W. Nibley, (no date) 1924, Charles W. Nibley Collection, Family Correspondence.

Grammar Schools"? How can one get the big head over "Easy Lessons in Latin"? Not a day passes but what I am completely silenced by some urchin who knows what every urchin should know—and I don't—a little Arithmetic.[6]

Hugh's remarkable erudition and self-conscious humility have remained surprisingly consistent.

I also discovered something I believe is even more remarkable about Hugh Nibley: Not only is the private man consistent with the public man, but Hugh's actions have been consistent with his words. As a member of the Nibley family, I have had the opportunity to observe Hugh Nibley at close range for almost twenty years. Hugh is constantly curious and has an abiding hunger for knowledge, yet is genuinely accepting of individuals without advanced degrees or credentials. I have been astonished by his complete lack of materialism but equally astonished by his generosity. I have been impressed by his commitment to preserving our environment, not only by speaking out against pollution and in favor of wilderness, but by consuming less, wasting less, and conserving more. I have likewise seen his deep commitment to the gospel—worrying as much about his home teaching as he does about his next book. And I have witnessed his deep faith in the Lord.

While he certainly isn't perfect, Hugh Nibley is the one of the most consistent people I have ever met. If, as Brigham Young once said, consistency is "one of the fairest jewels in the life of a saint,"[7] Hugh Nibley is a rich man indeed.

---

[6]Hugh Nibley, Letter to Charles W. Nibley, 13 April 1927, photocopy in my possession.
[7]Brigham Young, 1-10 August 1865, "Summary of Instructions" delivered in Box Elder and Cache counties, *Journal of Discourses*, 26 vols. (London and Liverpool: LDS Booksellers Depot, 1855-86), 11:136.

Appendix A

A Chronology of the Life of Hugh Winder Nibley

7 May 1876	Alexander ("El") Nibley is born to Charles W. Nibley and his first wife, Rebecca Neibaur Nibley.
17 Oct. 1885	Agnes Sloan ("Sloanie") is born in Manti to Hugh Russel Sloan and Margaret Violet Reid Sloan.
17 June 1902	El Nibley marries Constance Thatcher.
1905	Constance dies in giving birth to a daughter, Connie, who is raised by the Thatchers.
1906	El, on a mission in Holland, meets Agnes Sloan ("Sloanie") in Berlin.
4 Dec. 1907	Charles W. Nibley is sustained as Presiding Bishop.
27 June 1907	El and Sloanie are married and move to Portland, Oregon, where El manages his father's lumber interests.
23 June 1908	Alexander Sloan Nibley is born to El and Sloanie in Portland.
27 Mar. 1910	Hugh Winder Sloan is born to El and Sloanie Nibley in Portland, Oregon.
29 Apr. 1913	Fred Richard Nibley is born in Portland.
early 1917	The Nibley family moves to Medford, Oregon, where El manages Utah-Idaho Sugar Company for his father.
25 July 1917	Philip Gordon Nibley is born.
27 Mar. 1918	Hugh is baptized at Medford, Oregon.
1919	The Nibley family moves back to Portland, Oregon, where El is a purchasing agent for a sugar company.

Oct. 1920	Heber J. Grant defends Charles W. Nibley at general conference against charges of financial irresponsibility in a government anti-trust action against the sugar companies in which the Church had a financial interest.
16 Jan. 1921	The Nibleys move to Los Angeles.
1921-23	Hugh attends Alta Loma Middle School.
5 Jan. 1923	Reid Neibaur Nibley, the fourth child, is born.
	Hugh completes ROTC as a high school program.
28 May 1925	Charles W. Nibley is sustained as Heber J. Grant's second counselor.
6 June 1925	Hugh spends part of summer vacation in the wilderness of Big Bear Lake in Southern California with a friend.
Aug. 1925	Hugh works at the Nibley-Stoddard lumber mills in Oregon.
Apr. 1926	Hugh writes his first surviving poem, a birthday tribute to his Grandmother Sloan. Charles W. Nibley has it published in the *Improvement Era*. Also in 1926, his poem "The Freight Train" is published in the literary journal *The Lyric West*, probably as a result of his English teacher's sponsorship.
2 Apr. 1926	Barbara Nibley, El's and Sloanie's only daughter, is born.
15 May 1926	The family moves to Glendale, California, where El is developing real estate and participating in civic organizations.
Summer 1926	Hugh camps out in the Crater Lake wilderness for about six weeks.
1927	Hugh's poem "Two Stars" is published in *LA High School Anthology of Student Verse*.
Spring 1927	Hugh graduates from Los Angeles High School.
Summer 1927	Hugh attends summer school at BYU's Aspen Grove, giving him a lifetime love for Utah's mountains.
Oct. 1927	Hugh attends the Mesa Temple dedication with his parents.
1 Nov. 1927	Hugh receives his endowment in the Salt Lake Temple.
9 Nov. 1927	Melvin J. Ballard sets Hugh apart for his mission to Germany. He reaches Cologne on 27 November. He serves in Ludwigshafen (Dec. 1927-Jan. 1928), Frankenthal (Feb.-Dec.1928), to Bruchsal and Karlsruhe (Dec.-Oct. 1928), and mission home in Basel (Oct-Nov. 1928).
2 July 1928	Rebecca Neibaur Nibley, Hugh's paternal grandmother, dies.
July 1928	Ill with the mumps, Hugh studies the writings of Brigham Young.
July-Aug. 1929	Sloanie visits Hugh and Sloan in Germany. She is concerned about his emaciation and general health.
6 Nov. 192	Hugh is released from his mission. He visits Greece and Italy before returning home.
1 Jan. 1930	Hugh rejoins his family in Glendale, California, and registers at the University of California, Los Angeles, with Sloan. He earns his best grades in history, philosophy, and languages.
11 Dec. 1931	Charles W. Nibley dies.
1932	Responding to the real estate slump in California as part of the Great Depression, El Nibley diversifies into mining with temporary success.
31 Dec. 1932	Hugh's brother Philip dies at age fourteen after a lingering illness.
22 June 1934	Hugh graduates summa cum laude (AB) in history from UCLA.

25 June 1934	Hugh serves a short-term mission in Portland, Oregon, where he serves as stenographer in the Northwestern States Mission until September.
1934-38	Hugh attends graduate school at Berkeley where he meets Paul Springer during the 1934-35 school year and studies languages.
Fall 1936	Hugh receives a fellowship that will pay all of his expenses but loans it to his father, who loses it in a poor investment. Hugh survives on a meager wage translating Latin texts for Herbert Bolton.
Dec. 1936	Hugh has a near-death experience while undergoing an appendectomy. It gives him a first testimony of the afterlife.
29 Nov. 1938	El and Sloanie are served with a notice of default for being in arrears on their mortgage payments.
Dec. 1938	Hugh completes his Ph.D. dissertation, "Roman Games as a Survival of an Archaic Year Cult."
1939-40	Hugh visits the Golden Gate International Exposition in San Francisco.
1939-42	Hugh becomes a lecturer in history and social philosophy at Claremont Colleges, Claremont, California: modern European history (Pomona College); U.S. history (Claremont); junior humanities (Scripps College); history of education, Greek, German (Claremont Colleges).
Dec. 1940	Hugh delivers his first paper to a professional conference, "The Origin of the Roman Dole" at the annual meeting of the Pacific Coast Branch of the American Historical Association at Stanford.
[Spring?] 1941	Hugh delivers second first paper to a professional conference, "Acclamatio," at the Southwest Archaeological Foundation, San Diego.
Apr.-Nov. 1941	Hugh is briefly engaged to Herta Pauly, a German emigrée.
July 1941	El's and Sloanie's palatial home is auctioned off to pay their mounting debts.
1942	Hugh's first scholarly article, "New Light on Scaliger," is published in *Classical Journal*.
Summer 1942	Hugh spends time in area near Zion National Park.
28 Sept. 1942	Hugh enlists in the U.S. Army and is inducted at Fort MacArthur, California.
Oct-Dec. 1942	Hugh completes basic training at Clearwater, Florida.
Mar. 1943	Hugh graduates from twelve weeks of weather observer training, Air Forces Technical School, Chanute Field, Illinois.
12 June 1943	Hugh graduates from interrogation training at the Military Intelligence Training Center, Camp Ritchie, Maryland.
June-Oct. 1943	Hugh courts Anahid Iskian, an Armenian bookseller, in New York City. She refuses him.
23 Sept. 1943	Hugh graduated from training in German Order of Battle Intelligence, still at Camp Richie.
21 Nov. 1943	Hugh arrives in England with other American soldiers. He is stationed at Whittington Barracks of the South Staffordshire regiment near Lichfield. His assignment is to compile a catalogue of German general officers in preparation for the Normandy invasion.

21 Jan. 1944	Hugh is assigned to the U.S. 101st Airborne where he conducts training sessions on German strategy and tactics.
6 June 1944	Hugh drives one of the first Jeeps onto Utah Beach during the Allied invasion of France.
July-Nov. 1944	Hugh plans for and participates in the disastrous Operation Market-Garden invasion of Holland (17 Sept.-27 Nov.).
22 Oct. 1944	Margaret Violet Reid Sloan, Hugh's maternal grandmother, dies.
Nov.1944-Jan.1945	Hugh is stationed at Mourmelon-le-Grand before the Ardennes offensive, predicts the breakthrough, is transferred to Paris, then serves in counter-intelligence in the Ardennes. The remainder of his squad is killed.
1945	Hugh spends the occupation in Luxemburg, Belgium, Paris, and Heidelberg. He also travels widely.
27 Oct. 1945	Hugh returns to the United States and is discharged 19 November 1945 at Fort Macarthur.
Winter 1945-46	Postwar recovery in Hurricane, Utah.
ca. Mar.-Apr. 1946	Hugh moves to Salt Lake City and is employed briefly at the *Improvement Era*. John A. Widtsoe encourages BYU president Howard S. McDonald to hire him.
1946	Bookcraft publishes pamphlet *No, Ma'am, That's Not History: A Brief Review of Mrs. Brodie's Reluctant Vindication of the Prophet She Seeks to Expose*. It is a response to Fawn McKay Brodie's biography of Joseph Smith, published in 1945, for which she was excommunicated.
28 Apr. 1946	Hugh sends his vita and statement of teaching philosophy to Howard S. McDonald, president of Brigham Young University.
May 1946	Hugh signs a contract with Brigham Young University as an assistant professor of history and religion.
25 May 1946	Hugh meets Phyllis Ann Hawkes Draper, a French major and cellist, at the BYU Housing Office where she is employed.
27 July 1946	Hugh takes Phyllis on a family picnic with his Allen cousins.
18 Aug. 1946	Hugh and Phyllis become engaged.
18 Sept. 1946	Hugh and Phyllis are married in the Salt Lake Temple by Joseph Fielding Smith. Hugh begins teaching on 26 September 1946. His classes include Greek, Russian, early Christian history, and world religions.
19 July 1947	Paul Sloan Nibley, the first of Hugh's and Phyllis's nine children, is born.
ca. 1948	Hugh first visits the Hopi reservation with Virgil Bushman. He returns frequently until at least 1964.
Dec. 1948	Hugh spends Christmas vacation in research at Berkeley.
Apr. 1948	*Improvement Era* publishes "The Book of Mormon as a Mirror to the East," which grew into several series on the Book of Mormon.
1948-49	"Baptism for the Dead in Ancient Times" runs as a series in the *Improvement Era* and is critiqued in *Catholic Biblical Quarterly* (1951).
1949	"The Arrow, the Hunter, and the State," Hugh's first scholarly article since Claremont, is published in the *Western Political Quarterly*.
31 Mar. 1949	Christina Nibley is born.
Jan.-Oct. 1950	The *Improvement Era* serializes "Lehi in the Desert."

17 Aug. 1950	Thomas Hugh Nibley is born.
1951	Hugh's "The Hierocentric State" is published in the *Western Political Quarterly*. Ernest L. Wilkinson becomes president of Brigham Young University in February.
Sep.1951-July 1952	The *Improvement Era* serializes "The World of the Jaredites."
May 1952	Hugh travels with Spencer W. Kimball to Arizona for stake conferences and BYU recruiting.
16 Jan. 1953	Michael Draper Nibley is born.
1953	Hugh's "The Unsolved Loyalty Problem: Our Western Heritage," a historical response to the McCarthy era loyalty oaths, appears in the *Western Political Quarterly*.
Jan.-May 1953	Hugh's "The Stick of Judah and the Stick of Joseph" is published in the *Improvement Era*.
Nov.1953-July 1954	Hugh publishes "New Approaches to Book of Mormon Study" in the *Improvement Era*.
1953-54	Hugh spends a sabbatical doing research at Harvard, Johns Hopkins, and Berkeley.
1953	Hugh is promoted to professor of history and religion.
Mar.Oct. 1954	Hugh delivers a series of thirty talks, "Time Vindicates the Prophets," broadcast over KSL Radio broadcast of "The World and The Prophets." They are published as *The World and the Prophets* in 1954.
11 Nov. 1954	Another son, Isaac Nibley, dies at his premature birth.
Jan.Dec. 1955	The *Improvement Era* serializes "The Way of the Church" on the apostasy but does not finish the series.
2 Feb. 1955	Hugh announces his desire to resign and transfer to the University of Utah to President Wilkinson. Wilkinson arranges for Hugh to talk with J. Reuben Clark the next day. Clark persuades him to stay at BYU.
23 Mar. 1955	Hugh debates Sterling McMurrin on the question, "Do Religion and History Conflict?" at the University of Utah.
Winter 1955-56	The Nibleys move into the home near campus that they still (2002) occupy.
3 Jan. 1956	Charles Alexander is born.
1956	Hugh's "Victoriosa Loquacitas: The Rise of Rhetoric and the Decline of Everything Else" appears in *Western Speech*.
Mar. 1956	"More Voices from the Dust" is published in the *Instructor*.
19 June 1956	Hugh lectures on "The Historicity of the Bible" to Seminary and Institute faculty at BYU.
1957	At President David O. McKay's request, Hugh writes *An Approach to the Book of Mormon*, which is the Melchizedek Priesthood manual.
7 July 1958	Rebecca Nibley is born.
1958	Hugh's "What Is a Temple?" is published in *Millennial Star*.
Mar.-Nov. 1959	The *Improvement Era* publishes "Mixed Voices: A Study in Book of Mormon Criticism."
28 May 1959	Hugh's mother, Agnes Sloan Nibley, dies in California.

30 Aug. 1959	Hugh's father, Alexander Nibley, dies in Oregon.
1959-60	Hugh and his family spend his sabbatical in Berkeley where he lectures on ancient rhetoric and studies Coptic. Although invited to stay on at Berkeley, he decides to return to BYU. At his request, he teaches only scripture-related classes.
1959-60	Hugh's "Christian Envy of the Temple" is published in two installments in *Jewish Quarterly Review*.
June 1960	Hugh's opening prayer for BYU commencement exercises begins, "We have met here today clothed in the black robes of a false priesthood."
Feb. 1961–Dec. 1966	Another *Improvement Era* series (not published continuously) eventually will become *Since Cumorah* (Deseret Book, 1967).
June 1961	Hugh's "The Passing of the Church: Forty Variations on an Unpopular Theme" appears in *Church History*, sparking a short debate.
1961	Bookcraft publishes *The Myth Makers*, responding to critics of Joseph Smith. Another series in the *Improvement Era*, "Censoring the Joseph Smith Story," deals with the same topic.
29 Nov. 1962	Martha Nibley is born.
March 1963	Hugh gives thirteen lectures during Oklahoma State University's Religious Emphasis Week.
1-3 May 1963	Hugh delivers three lectures on "The Three Shrines: Mantic, Sophic, and Sophistic" to LDS students at Yale University, sponsored by the LDS Deseret Club at Yale.
13 May 1963	Hugh and Sterling McMurrin debate "The Nature of Man" at BYU. It is the fourth annual "liberal-conservative debate" sponsored by BYU's Academic Emphasis Committee.
1963	*Sounding Brass*, Hugh's response to Irving Wallace's *The Twenty-seventh Wife*, is published by Bookcraft. He wrote this book at the request of Elder Mark E. Petersen and other General Authorities.
Jan. 1964	Impressed by Hugh's "Jerusalem: In Early Christianity," the editors of *Encyclopedia Judaica* invite him to edit the department dealing with Christian Latin biblical exegesis. Hugh declines.
15 Aug. 1964	Zina Nibley, the last of Hugh's and Phyllis's nine children, is born.
Dec. 1964	Hugh travels to Jordan where he examines the Dead Sea Scrolls.
17 Mar. 1965	Hugh delivers BYU's Second Annual Faulty Lecture, then the university's highest honor for a faculty member. His topic is "The Expanding Gospel."
Apr. 1965	*Revue de Qumran* publishes "Qumran and the Companions of the Cave: The Haunted Wilderness."
1966-67	Hugh uses his sabbatical for advanced studies in Egyptian at Chicago's Oriental Institute under Professors Klaus Baer and John A. Wilson.
1966	Hugh considers a professorship at Clarion College in Eastern Pennsylvania but decides to stay at BYU.
1966	Hugh's "Evangelium Quadraginta Dierum" ("The Forty-day Mission of Christ") appears in *Vigiliae Christianae*. He also publishes "Tenting, Toll and Taxing" in the *Western Political Quarterly*.

Spring 1966	Aziz Attiya "discovers" the Joseph Smith papyri at the Metropolitan Museum of Art in New York City and informs LDS leaders about them.
1967	Hugh's "The Mormon View of the Book of Mormon" appears in a special edition of *Concilium: An International Review of Theology*.
19 Mar. 1967	Provo Stake President Roy W. Doxey ordains Hugh a high priest.
27 Nov. 1967	The Church announces its acquisition of eleven pieces of the Joseph Smith papyri.
Jan. 1968–May 1970	The *Improvement Era* runs Hugh's series on critics of the Book of Abraham.
1968	Hugh is awarded a Fulbright to teach in Libya, but it is cancelled because of political tensions.
Summer 1968	*Dialogue* publishes Nibley's "Phase One," with other views on the Joseph Smith Papyrus.
May 1971	Dallin H. Oaks becomes president of Brigham Young University. Hugh receives BYU's David O. McKay Humanities Award.
Nov. 1971	Hugh baptizes Kresimir Cosic, a Czechoslovakian basketball star whom he had befriended and to whom he taught the gospel.
Feb. 1972	With the dedication of the Provo Temple, Hugh begins attending sessions weekly.
Oct. 1972	The *New Era* publishes Hugh's "Man's Dominion," one of Mormonism's first environmental essays.
Apr. 1973	Hugh is named BYU Professor of the Year.
Apr. 1973	BYU's Board of Trustees approves Hugh as director of its newly formed Institute of Ancient Studies, which began full operation that fall.
Spring 1973	Hugh publishes "The Best Possible Test" in *Dialogue*, an essay on blacks and the priesthood to accompany Lester Bush's important survey "Mormonism's Negro Doctrine: An Historical Overview."
21 May 1974	Hugh has a mild stroke during an interview by Louis Midgley for a BYU devotional. After a month in Florida, he recovers fully.
3–5 Apr. 1975	Encouraged by Wilfred Griggs and S. Kent Brown, Hugh presents "The Book of Enoch as a Theodicy" at the Rocky Mountain–Great Plains regional meeting Society for Biblical Literature and the American Academy of Religion in Denver. It is his first academic conference since graduate school.
1975	Deseret Book publishes *The Message of the Joseph Smith Papyri: An Egyptian Endowment*.
Spring 1975	Hugh "retires" from BYU but continues to teach a class or two each semester and maintain his office.
Aug. 1975	At Hugh's invitation, Klaus Baer lectures at BYU's annual Education Week.
Oct. 1975–Aug. 1977	The *Ensign* publishes Hugh's "A Strange Thing in the Land: The Return of the Book of Enoch."
22 Nov. 1975	Hugh lectures on "Enoch the Prophet" at BYU's Pearl of Great Price Symposium.
1976	Hugh and Phyllis join a BYU tour group in Egypt led by Truman G. Madsen. It is Hugh's first visit to Egypt.

1977	The Ensign's editors invite Hugh to write an article on "The Uses and Abuses of Patriotism" for its special edition celebrating the bicentennial of the Declaration of Independence, then reject it.
1978	Hugh's "Early Christian Prayer Circle" is published in BYU Studies.
1978	BYU's Religious Studies Institute publishes some of Hugh's popular lectures in Nibley on the Timely and the Timeless. Hugh wrote "An Intellectual Autobiography" as its foreword.
1979	Hugh is honored with BYU Alumni's Distinguished Service Award.
21 Sept. 1979	Hugh delivers "How Firm a Foundation! What Makes It So" at BYU's Sesquicentennial Lectures on Mormon Arts.
22 Sept. 1979	Hugh's brother Richard dies of Lou Gehrig's disease.
1 Feb. 1980	Hugh delivers "Patriarchy and Matriarchy" at BYU's Women's Conference.
1 Apr. 1980	Hugh lectures on "Before Adam" at BYU.
1980	Hugh lectures on "Freemen and Kingmen in the Book of Mormon" as a critique of Cleon Skousen's Freeman Institute.
Sept. 1980	Jeffrey R. Holland becomes president of BYU. He asks Hugh to address the faculty on the temple during a special temple session.
1981	Deseret Book publishes Abraham in Egypt.
23 Sept. 1981	Hugh speaks on "The Prophetic Book of Mormon" at BYU.
20 Apr. 1982	Hugh speaks on "Work We Must But the Lunch Is Free" to the Cannon-Hinckley Club in Salt Lake City as well as to other groups. This speech began an emphasis on consecration that continued through the 1980s with "How to Get Rich" (1982), "We Will Still Weep for Zion" (1984), in BYU's Spheres of Influence Lecture Series for three years, "Breakthroughs I Would Like to See" (1984), "Change Out of Control" (1985), "The Utopians" (1986), "The Law of Consecration" (1986), and "But What Kind of Work?" (1987).
Fall 1982	With significant participation from Alex Nibley, interviews and filming for the video documentary Faith of an Observer begin.
1983	The Foundation for Ancient Research and Mormon Studies (FARMS), organized by John W. Welch, undertakes the project of preparing Hugh's collected works for publication. The first volume appears in 1986.
19 Aug. 1983	BYU awards Hugh an honorary Doctor of Letters degree and he delivers the commencement address "Leaders to Managers: The Fatal Shift."
Jan. 1984	Hugh goes to Egypt again, this time with the film crew of Faith of an Observer.
10 Apr. 1984	Hugh undergoes quadruple bypass surgery, one of the last cardiac operations performed by Russell Nelson, newly called as an apostle.
27 Mar. 1985	At Hugh's seventy-fifth birthday party, the documentary Faith of an Observer premieres.
31 Mar. 1985	The First Presidency and Quorum of the Twelve ask Hugh to prepare a report on the history and significance of the temple.
29 Apr. 1985	Hugh receives BYU's 6th annual Religious Education Service Award.

17 May 1985	Hugh addresses the first regional Sunstone Symposium in Washington, D.C. on "[An] Approach to Facsimile No. 2."
1985	"Scriptural Perspectives on How to Survive the Calamities of the Last Days" appears in *BYU Studies*.
25 Oct. 1985	Hugh delivers an address, "There Is Always Egypt," to Egyptian delegates at ceremonies commemorating the arrival of the Ramses II exhibit to BYU.
12 Mar. 1986	Hugh gives the final talk, "The Greatness of Egypt," in the Ramses II lecture series.
June 1986	Hugh reads "Temple" to the Twelve and First Presidency at a three-hour meeting in the temple and delivers a longer written report, "Endowment History."
Aug. 1986	Hugh gives "Last Call: An Apocalyptic Warning from the Book of Mormon" at the Sunstone Symposium.
6 Feb 1987	Hugh speaks on "The Law of Consecration" to temple workers in the Church Office Building Auditorium.
19 May 1987	Hugh delivers "But What Kind of Work?" to the Cannon-Hinckley Club in Salt Lake City.
10 May 1988	At the Sunstone Book of Mormon lecture series in Salt Lake City, Hugh reflects on teaching the Book of Mormon for forty years in "The Book of Mormon: Forty Years After."
11 Nov. 1988	Hugh delivers "The Meaning of the Atonement" as part of a Deseret Book/FARMS Nibley lecture series.
16 Feb. 1989	Hugh speaks at a "Clean Air Symposium" at BYU protesting pollution from Geneva Steel.
19 Aug. 1989	Hugh delivers "Speaking Evil of the Lord's Anointed" at BYU's Church Education System annual conference and gives the same lecture on 26 August at the Sunstone Symposium in Salt Lake City.
1990	A *festschrift* in Hugh's honor, *By Study and Also by Faith*, edited by John M. Lundquist and Stephen D. Ricks, is published by Deseret Book/Farms.
3 Apr. 1990	Hugh's older brother Sloan dies.
June-Sept. 1990	Hugh delivers twelve FARMS-sponsored lectures at BYU on the Book of Abraham called "One Eternal Round."
1991	Hugh is diagnosed with prostate cancer but the tumor disappears after radiation therapy.
11 Apr. 1991	Hugh receives the "Exemplary Manhood Award" at BYU Associated Students Awards Assembly.
20 Feb. 1993	Hugh delivers a paper, "House of Glory," analyzing Doctrine and Covenants 109 (dedication prayer for the Kirtland Temple) at the FARMS symposium on Ancient Temples.
1994	Hugh teaches his last class at BYU during winter semester.
May 1995	Kresimir Cosic dies in Maryland after Hugh spends hours at his bedside and gives him a priesthood blessing.
Apr. 1996	Hugh delivers a speech "Assembly and Atonement" at the FARMS King Benjamin Symposium.

14 June 1995	Hugh reads a paper, "Abraham," at the Institute of Religion at Utah Valley State College.
25 July 1996	Accompanied by Boyd Petersen and Paul Nibley, Hugh again visits the Hopi reservation.
18 Sept. 1996	Hugh and Phyllis celebrate their fiftieth wedding anniversary.
May 1997	Hugh speaks at a fireside "On the Meaning of Temples."
6 Apr. 1999	Hugh examines the Book of Abraham as a temple text in "Abraham's Creation Drama."
27 March 2000	Hugh celebrates his ninetieth birthday.
Fall 2000	Phyllis's sight is threatened by an eye infection after cataract surgery, but her hospitalization identifies a heart problem that is corrected with a pacemaker implant.
14 Nov. 2001	After the renovation of the Harold B. Lee Library, the Ancient Studies Reading Room is dedicated and renamed the Hugh Nibley Ancient Studies Reading Room.

Appendix B

Genealogy of Hugh Winder Nibley

James Nibley (1810-76) and Jean Wilson Nibley (1815-89)
   James Nibley (1837-37)
   Mary Nibley (1838-77)
   James Nibley (1840-96)
   Margaret Wilson Nibley (1843-1930)
   Henry Nibley (1845-51)
   Charles Wilson Nibley (1849-1931)
   Henry Wilson Nibley (1851-1923)
   Euphemia Nibley (1855-1930)

Charles W. Nibley and Rebecca Neibaur Nibley (1851-1928)
   Ellen N. Nibley (1870-71)
   Charles W. Nibley, Jr. (1872-1959)
   Jean Nibley (1874-74)
   Alexander Nibley (1876-1959)
   Joseph F. Nibley (1880-1953)
   James O. Nibley (1881-1964)
   Merrill Nibley (1884?)
   Rebecca Nibley Whitney (1886?)
   Grover Nibley (1888-88)
   Alice Nibley Smoot (1890?)

Charles W. Nibley and Ellen Ricks Nibley (1856-1935), married 30 March 1880.
   Joel Nibley (1881-1958)
   Preston Nibley (1884-1966)
   Esther Nibley (1887-89)
   Edna Nibley Cannon (1890-1973)

Florence Nibley Hatch (1894-1947)
Nathan Nibley (1899-1981)

Charles W. Nibley and Julia Budge Nibley (186-1938), married 14 October 1885.
    Julia Nibley Howell (1886-1977)
    Annie Nibley Bullen (1888-1972)
    Margaret Nibley Meldrum (1891-1976)
    William Budge Nibley (1893-1895)
    Carlyle Nibley (1895-1956)
    David Jesse Nibley (1897-1898)
    Oliver Nibley (1900-00)
    Ruth Nibley Grant (1905)

Hugh Russel Sloan (1856-1920) and Margaret Violet Reid Sloan (1857-1944)
    John Samuel Sloan (1879-1946)
    William Reid Sloan (1881-1961)
    Hugh Russel Sloan Jr. (1883-1963)
    Agnes Sloan (1885-1959)
    Maggie Sloan (1887-88)
    Clara Sloan (1889-1979)
    Ruth Sloan (1891-1928)
    George Peacock Sloan (1894-95)
    Edward Louden Sloan (1896-96)
    Rayman Reid Sloan (1899-99)
    Edgar Lloyd Sloan (1902-38)

Alexander Nibley (1876-1959) and Agnes Sloan Nibley (1885-1959), married 27 June 1907
    Alexander Sloan Nibley (1908-90)
    Hugh Winder Nibley (1910)
    Fred Richard Nibley (1913-79)
    Philip Gordon Nibley (1917-32)
    Reid Neibaur Nibley (1923)
    Barbara Nibley Richards (1926)

Alexander Nibley married Constance Thatcher (1880-1905), 17 June 1902
        Connie Nibley (1905-?)

Hugh Winder Nibley (1910) and Phyllis Ann Hawkes Draper Nibley (1926)
    Paul Sloan Nibley (1947)
    Christina Nibley Mincek (1949)
    Thomas Hugh Nibley (1950)
    Michael Draper Nibley (1953)
    Isaac Nibley (1954-54)
    Charles Alexander Nibley (1956)
    Rebecca Nibley (1958)
    Martha Nibley Beck (1962)
    Zina Nibley Petersen (1964)

Appendix C

Letter from the Front, 1945

Note: This is one of Hugh's lengthiest letters written during World War II, to his mother, Agnes Sloan Nibley. It is not dated, but from internal evidence was written during the summer of 1945 and, because of earlier censorship, the most detailed. I have standardized punctuation and capitalization and added minimal paragraphing.

Dear Mother,

You mentioned in your last that I had never told you anything about my activities. Come to think of it, I haven't. Of course not: your old Hugh isn't one to go around sinking ships. But now that it doesn't make much difference whether ships are sunk or not I might as well ring off a bare chronicle of events as noted down in my little red appointment book, just to let you know what's been going on all this time.

The latter part of November and early December were passed in the barracks of the South Staffordshire regiment near Lichfield. The place was called Whittington Barracks—very cold, dark and stony, with a 150-years' deposit of coal smoke and Empire tradition. Incidentally, the more you see of this sort of thing the clearer it becomes that the Empah is nothing but a cheeky bit of window-dressing; top to bottom, it is pure eyewash. This impression was first borne upon me, however, in the British War Office, where I worked alone on a little project for a few weeks in December and January.

The little book says I reached the HQ of the 101 on an unbelievable dark and stormy night, January 21. We lived in tents without light or heat on top of a very windy hill with gliders tied down all around us. The mud was pelasgic, the food unspeakable vile and very scarce. (At the foot of the hill a negro supply company lived on chicken and ice cream, but we never saw any of that unless we had some excuse to visit them.) I was quickly informed of what the role of the division was to be in the invasion, namely to spearhead the whole operation, landing 4 hours ahead of anyone else; and after being sworn to undying secrecy, [I] set about wising everyone up on the strength, disposition, and honest intentions of the Germans. To get this information we had to break all the rules of priority and procedure (this was the first Order of Battle team ever to work with a division) and became adept at falsification and intrigue, plain and fancy gate-crashing and advanced prevarication.

Since our undertaking was to be something unique in its kind, a great many practice runs had to be gone through—after each one things looked blacker: it is fantastic how many things there are to to go wrong in an airborne operation; everybody was worried to pieces, and I was wistfully envious of the simple linesmen who had no idea what they were in for. I gave lots of lectures to all the units about the German army, and the questions the boys asked on those occasions called for all the comfort I could give them—I lied until I even cheered myself up.

The other member of the team artfully managed to get himself transferred, after months of string-pulling, just before the invasion, but my luck was almost as good. They had me down as number 2 man in number 1 glider when a lone unescorted jeep called for a driver, and I was told to take it in seaborne. The murderous British Horsa gliders were used in the invasion with disastrous effect: the crowd in my glider were all banged up and captured; my lieutenant was never heard from again.

We sailed from Bristol on June 4 and on the sixth were off Vierville. My fate seems always to have been first in line. Our ship headed the convoy and as if that were not enough our party was to be the first ashore when contact was made with the division. The ship was bombed repeatedly but never hit. I stood at the head of the rope ladder for half an hour and then went down to the LCT without orders. Presently the very spot where I should be waiting was hit by an 88 and half a dozen tankmen blown up; the chaplain with whom I had been talking was wounded.

When we put in for shore the 88s tried hard to stop us, first landing in front and then behind. The ship was sunk. This sort of thing goes on and on. Who should be our naval artillery liaison man but one of my old Claremont pupils? After a lot of noise and excitement we moved into Carentan against the protest of the Germans who repeatedly tried to overrun our very thinly held position. Came the big storm and we found ourselves cut off from any support; it was what the British call a very sticky time.

On July 13 we went back to England: that was running back for another try. A period of frantic preparation followed. The objective would be chosen, the whole operation rehearsed, everyone resigned to fate and all set for the take-off, and then would come word that Patton had already reached the place, or was so near it that we would not have to go in. This happened again and again and was very trying. Finally the fantastic Holland Operation [Market-Garden], which everybody saw would be a bust unless the British commander acted his age: he gave a speech which set an all-time high for silliness and failure to grasp the most elementary aspect of the situation.[1] The first flight went late on September 17 and the pilots came back with the worst possible news: terrible weather, murderous flak, and waiting for us in the landing zone a division of German tanks. But it was too late to turn back—regardless of weather, we would have to make a try for it at dawn the next day.

---

[1] Possibly Sir Bernard Law Montgomery, first Vicount Montgomery of Alamein.

Again I was number 2 man in number 1 glider on the right—the one the Germans always try for: our tow plane was the only one with a bathtub—a new and very secret device which the enemy was dying to get hold of; it was called a bathtub because it was a huge, bulky underslung affair that nobody could miss and the pilot said the Jerries would give anything to shoot it down.[2] With this cheering prospect, we took to the air; and of course I became very sick as I always do in a glider. There was an old piece of armor plate lying on the floor and out of curiosity I wondered how it would be to sit on: just as I slipped it on my little chair with a characteristically witty remark, it absorbed three machine-gun bullets while another went between my feet. This particular escape became proverbial in headquarters company.

The Dutch campaign was touch and go, with our people scattered all over the land and surrounded and outnumbered most of the time. The other member of the team was run over by a tank while he was bringing in our jeep and the lieutenant was wounded, but he stayed on the job—otherwise I would have had to do everything single-handed as in Normandy. But I was pretty good at Dutch, which meant a lot of extra work and extra excitement, of course.

On November 27 we were back in training again, getting all steamed up for another operation. It was not a pleasant atmosphere and people started committing suicide.[3] Then came the breakthrough (exactly as I predicted weeks ahead) while the same day I got an order to come to Paris, for with the order came a team which was to relieve me. I showed them the ropes and they took over: both were killed the next day. After Paris came Luxemburg, where the big boys at Army Group insist that the breakthrough took them totally by surprise: an unpardonable state of affairs. At that exalted level. no one ever thinks of anything but his career; and they are worlds removed from the war—spend all their time pinning decorations on each other, the Lord knows for what.

After Luxemburg, Belgium for a few weeks, and then Paris again. Paris becomes a terrible habit. For the past month I have been in Heidelberg, which has not been scratched by the war. Mannheim and Ludwigshafen have simply ceased to exist. The weeks with the 6th Army Group have been delightful: we live in sumptuous quarters and have a club that makes the pavilions of the Golden Horn look like something on the wrong side of the tracks.

What the future holds is up to nobody. All I control is my own mental process, which simply ignores the army, and that is all the power I ever want to have. Hereafter, when anything important transpires I will be allowed to let you know immediately. Meanwhile we are moving with unerring compliance to prophecy straight into the Next War: nobody seems to believe even half heartedly that the peace is permanent. We never will learn that there is no point to being clever: every sharp operator in Europe has walked right into his own trap. If we know what's good for us we won't tangle with the Russians—ever: in one week the German breakthrough in the Ardennes had us scraping the bottom of the barrel, though we were dealing with less than a third of the German

---

[2] When I asked Hugh what this top-secret "bathtub" was, he responded that he never did find out.

[3] In addition to the suicide Hugh witnessed that is reported in Chapter 14, Hugh also reported that a commanding officer, a Colonel Milner, killed himself just after Hugh had left his office. He did not see the two suicides as connected, however. See Hugh Nibley, "Faith of an Observer," 155-56.

Army. Unlike other armies the Russians have an unbelievable capacity for learning; unhampered by pride or tradition, they have a positive veneration for truth and never seem to be able to learn enough; their vitality is fabulous, and their birth-rate is simply out of sight. I think the Lord has big things in mind for them.

Love,
Hugh

Appendix D

Letter to Sterling M. McMurrin, 23 August 1967

Note: On 31 July 1967, Sterling McMurrin wrote Hugh about plans for *"a piece on Mormon philosophy"* that he was working on that would feature the views of Orson Pratt, W. H. Chamberlin, B. H. Roberts, E. E. Erickson, Hugh Nibley, and W. P. Read. McMurrin invited Hugh to list *"those writings which you regard as most effectively representing your position with respect to philosophy matters in general and in particular the philosophy of religion"* or to *"jot down a few paragraphs that epitimize"* his position.[1] So far as I know, McMurrin's essay was never completed, but this letter was Hugh's response.

August 23, 1967

Dear Sterling,

I have been away—first visit to southern California in 20 years—so here we are back again and forced to think about a religious philosophy. I can see that there would be a place for my peculiar views in your interesting Roman salad if only for contrast: "If a man will compare the richness and variety of the universe," wrote A. E. Housman, "and inspire his mind with a due measure of wonder and of awe, he must contemplate the human intellect not only in its heights of genius but in its abysses of ineptitude." Let that be my passport to your august company while I list, in no particular order, a few propositions that express my religious position at the moment.

Proposition No. 1. We are participating in a vivid little drama being enacted in empty space. If blind chance can set this stage, put the characters on it, and set the plot in motion, then there is nothing that blind chance cannot do, including the staging of innumerable other plays on other worlds; and blind chance may very well have arranged to

---

[1] Sterling McMurrin, Letter to Hugh Nibley, 31 July 1967, Sterling McMurrin Papers, Special Collections, Marriott Library, University of Utah, Salt Lake City.

have this particular world quarantined to provide a testing situation in which we find ourselves—strained and awkward, but just the test for those particular qualities which are going to be needed in the really long run.

Proposition No. 2, etc. Blind chance isn't a force. at all, but a term denoting an unknown X. Just as Newton could never bring himself to believe that gravity could be a force operating across a completely empty gap, so I can't believe in a directing force which is itself completely without any sense of direction or an organizing force which itself has no concept of organization. That idea stopped even Darwin, you may recall.

3. From the tiny segment of the play I have studied, I like to think that things have been following the script recommended by Joseph Smith more closely than the other scripts written by scientists and scholars and altered from time to time. I really believe that the unfolding of the human comedy has shown a consistent tendency to adhere to the ancient script, and at present gives every indication of following it out to the bitter or glorious end.

For me religion to be convincing must be nonspeculative. If it were the sort of thing we could figure out for ourselves, I would strongly suspect that we had invented it (C.S. Lewis). Mormonism has the great virtue of being, along with Judaism, early Christianity, and Islam, a nonspeculative religion. It accepts the moral law within and *also* the starry heavens above, the latter being something we do NOT make up ourselves and yet somehow part of the religious picture.

My present religious mood is an all, out literalism. If the history of Christianity has been one long undignified retreat, one continual process of accommodation to the science of the hour (Whitehead), the time has come to reverse the process, since the science of the hour has brought us to a most dismal slough in which it is no delight to dwell (Kozyrev). If the discussion is to be kept alive, it must move away from its old perennial game of de-mythologizing and de-eschatologizing, in the opposite direction, which I call de-rhetoricizing. So today, just for kicks, I read the Scriptures AS IF everything in them was meant to be taken in the most literal sense, as if no such thing as a symbol, allegory, or type even existed. And in doing that I find that there begins to build up within my personal computer a mass of data that has a totally different power and thrust from anything I have known before. Granted that the new deposit in its naive literalism will in time need radical correction, still I am convinced that the correction will not have to be nearly so radical as that required by the opposite view—that of the doctors of the church, who insisted on reading the scriptures as if nothing in them was to be taken literally, and instructed their students never to give a literal interpretation to a passage if any other interpretation was possible

I deplore the authoritarian, Baconian structure on which the entire edifice of modern learning is built (the schoolmen are even worse than the churchmen—when they are not actually the same), and have always been a passionate devotee of the openended discussion in which nothing is ever proven *except* for the individual. Whenever anything is proven, it is because some individual has been convinced, having acquired a personal, noncommunicable testimony of the truth of the proposition (Popper).

A testimony is a gift and a talent (I Cor 12:7ff); *man muss ein Organ dafür haben.* [A person must have a sense organ for it.] It functions like any of the senses, e.g., like hearing, it is an "absolute" thing. You either have it or you don't; but like hearing, it may be strong at one time and weak at another; it is never in ailing mortals in perfect operating condition (Heraclitus), and may vanish altogether at times, be nonoperative at times, and at times return with astonishing force and vigor. But it does NOT produce the things it hears. It would be hard to explain to one devoid of those senses that seeing and hearing are not functions of the imagination and are only in part self-induced—that there would be no seeing and hearing at all if some sort of stimulus did not come from the outside (Kantish). All this is commonplace enough, but I am trying to say that when I "bear my testimony" I am really talking about something, whether you get it or not.

We are here to use our brains, but the most important impressions that come to us do so directly and without any conscious cerebration. We may work over the data of such experiences in our minds, but we do not produce the impressions in the first place. An interview with John the Baptist led Oliver Cowdery to declare that whatever the doings of men may be, "one ray of glory from the upper world, or one word from the mouth of the Savior, from the bosom of eternity, strikes it all to insignificance, and blots it forever from the mind!" I have not had Oliver Cowdery's experience, but I have had some like it, and this puts any discussion of my religious "philosophy" on a difficult plane. For if I were to tell you that on a particular day I had such and such an experience, you would write me down as a mental case, and rightly so, in case you had not had the same experience or one like it. I see no reason why I should prejudice and offend you by telling you stories you can't believe and have no means of testing. But such experiences as I refer to are bound to affect one's behavior if only in subtle ways, and I find for one thing that there are some things that I simply cannot take seriously, and other things which I must take seriously even at the risk of giving offense to my more rational colleagues. It is surprising how many people have thought me to be merely spoofing—just having a little fun, like Joseph Smith when he got up the Book of Mormon. I wonder if they realize what a price one must pay for that kind of fun? I say to hell with careers and the things of the world; but if I thought there was the remotest possibility that this was my only life and my only world I would most assuredly NOT say it, and I would not throw away invitations to serious accomplishment for the sake of a monotonous series of pranks.

I include acceptance of the Gospel among the basic bodily functions like sleeping, eating, and breathing. They are not rational but spontaneous; without them we would die, but that is not why we engage in them. We eat, breathe, and sleep long before we are in danger of dying of hunger, suffocation, or exhaustion; if we had to have a rational explanation for doing those things before we were willing to invest any effort in them we would not be long for this world. The eye it cannot choose but see, *l'ame pense toujours,* [the soul thinks always], and as far as I can see, faith is inseparable from the awareness of existence. Existence, the Egyptians said, is a marvel compared with which all other marvels pale into insignificance: it is something not to be explained but accepted; and to accept it is to feel a surge of gratitude—to what, for what? We cannot shake off the wonder and delight of being, the indefinite prolongation of which is but a minor problem once we have got over the original obstacle, namely, the enormous odds against existing at all. Our reaction to being here must be a religious one, because the only principle of continued being is holiness. One cannot maintain an even level of folly. Each act is a step downward unless it is a righteous act, and the concept of righteousness cannot be divorced from the idea of holiness.

I have written too much and said too little. This is no religious philosophy at all. It is a situation in which I find myself: I am stuck with the gospel, I know perfectly well that it is true; there may be things about the Church that I find perfectly appalling—but that has nothing to do with it. I KNOW THE GOSPEL IS TRUE.

Yours as ever,
/s/ Hugh Nibley

If all this sounds trite, I can't help it.

Appendix E

Shalamar

Note: This skit was given 24 April 1970 at a Brigham Young Women's Program.

Bashir: (in loud chanting tone) He comes! He comes (that's a rough translation, but you get the idea)—the august, the magnificent, bottomless Sea of Wisdom, Fountain of Charity, unplumbed Sink of Sanctity. Behold, he cometh—it's him all right; it's he. Kiss the earth, infidels, before the ineffable, the unspeakable Hadji Baba! (Fanfare).

Ali: Here he comes, sure enough, the Great Hadji Baba, the Carbuncle on the Brow of Wisdom, the Paragon of the East and elsewhere, trailing clouds of glory from his journey to the lands of the West. I, Ali, must prepare myself for his coming.

Hadji: This is an inspiring sight. Where else in all the world will you find a larger gathering of BYU professors and their wives at this moment?

Ali: (shocked) Master, your tempest is raging! What kind of a greeting is that—so unknown to the canons of Oriental Eloquence? What has happened to you?

Hadji: The Western touch, my boy. I thought we had pretty much of a corner on decadence. For lo, these many years the name of Hadji Baba has been the symbol of Oriental degeneracy—but brother, I had a lot to learn. There I went under contract to teach Intermediate and Advanced Decadence, Sections 101 and 244; but with the first faculty meeting I knew that the gorgeous East had met its match. You've heard of him, of course.

Ali: Ernest the King? Who hasn't? Isn't he the one who says, "The faculty that decays together stays together"?

Hadji: That's him.

Ali: And doesn't he have a branding iron that says, "In your heart you know I'm right, ELW."

Hadji: Well, maybe. But he's really quite a modest fellow. They put his name on the letterheads when he wasn't looking.

Ali: But weren't you able to teach those barbaric Westerners anything in the arts of decadence?

Hadji: Well, first I thought they would sort of be impressed by my threads. These are about as decadent as you can get, you know: Everything for appearance. But they were already way ahead of me.

Ali: What do you mean, O Hugh Nibley of the East, O author of rare and out-of-print books, marathon page-filler of the Improvement Era?

Hadji: Well, there is this matter of clothing. Take one look at the average human body, and you know it was made to be hidden. We know that it's what's on the outside that counts. Inside there is just a lot of charts, plumbing, and things like that. Any TV ad can show you that—which is one of the things that TV has taught us. So we want to see either the inside or the outside—and the inside is out; the outside's in. But how do you think they do it?

Ali: Who?

Hadji: Those people where I came from—that BYU. They make a ghastly compromise.

Ali: Shocking.

Hadji: No inside; no outside—just the worst parts of both. The damsels cover their legs, yes indeed, but with see-through stockings; they insist on making their skirts long enough to be not revealing (though they do believe in revelation) but suggestive; they don't dance decently segregated as we do, but with promiscuous mingling of sexes, and the most meaningless and disorganized gyrations. Oh, how I longed to see a decently decadent belly-dance!

Ali: By the most sublime good fortune we have arranged such dancing for your homecoming. See if this does not bring coolness to your eyes.

DANCE TO KAHLIL GIBRAN POEM[1]

Ali: Not bad, eh?

Hadji: It might be improved by just a touch of Janie Thompson—a little sand in the salad, as it were, to give it body.[2]

Ali: Master, Master. Are you not aware that we are being watched?

Hadji: So we are. My, my. I only wish that each of you could stand where I am standing to look into your sea of upturned faces. A sight, as the poet says, to remember for years—to remember with tears. Five ducks on a pond, that's it. Look Ali:, how different from the unwashed, grimy, sullen, long-haired, red-eyed, sneering, pot-smoking, dirtyfooted, guitar-playing, naked, drug-conked, bead-wearing, hop-heads that make up the faculties of other universities. All it would take is a little learning to make them a model faculty.

---

[1] Lebanese poet/philosopher Kahlil Gibran was enjoying international fame at this time, especially for his short romantic essays in *The Prophet*.

[2] Janie Thompson was, for many years, head of BYU's Program Bureau (the name changed over time) and the indefatigable coach of a series of popular student singing and dancing groups who mounted USO-type variety shows characterized by snappy choreography, energetic dancing, colorful costumes, and big production-number finales. These groups toured extensively both nationally and abroad in peppy performances that showcased BYU's students as happy, patriotic, wholesome youth.

Ali: I'm afraid you're asking for the impossible there—too risky. You get people reading books and before you know it—poof, you've got an egghead. They can't afford the risk.

Hadji: Well, as Karl G. Maeser used to say, "Show me your egghead, and I'll show you mine." But they have pretty well licked this reading threat. Would you believe it—in a city holding a hundred-year-old university with 25,000 students, there is not one single bookstore?

Ali: Amazing. But aren't you exaggerating?

Hadji: Well, they have what they *call* a bookstore—a state bookstore, but it's really a suq—a real bazaar like one of ours: There's a good olde gifte shoppe, a record shop, a photography emporium, a men's wear shop, a women's wear shop, candy counters, and—yes, come to think of it, there are some racks of paperbacks—almost enough for one of the better supermarkets or a Walgreen's Drugstore.

Ali: But surely, the school has a library.

Hadji: Yes, and a pretty good one. They had to have that—no choice.

Ali: Why do they have to have a big library?

Hadji: Because books are something you can count, and as the President says, "If you can count it, we got it!" Well, books are something you can count—like students—and so whether they like it or not, they are all out to get more books than somebody else has.

Ali: Isn't that dangerous?

Hadji: Not a bit. That's the clever part of it. They put all these voluptuous lounge chairs and loveseats around the place so that any student who sits down with a book is slugged into delicious unconsciousness, but there is little danger that the books will be touched by anybody—they are kept in open stacks, and the sight of all that reading to be done simply scares them out of it. The kids wear out warehouses full of easy-chairs, but the books are safe. Outsiders are encouraged to walk away with books, and that decreased the danger still more. I carried a whole truckful out with me and nobody stopped me.

Ali: Didn't the people at the door look in the trunk to see if you might be taking anything?

Hadji: What, and insult my honor? Man, are you crazy?

Ali: The honor system, eh?

Hadji: Yes, at other schools they sneak around as if they suspected students of cheating. But there is none of that unpleasant suspicion at the BYU. They *know* they're cheating. And then it gives you a kind of nice feeling to know that your books, clothes, and bicycles are being stolen by clean-cut LDS types.

Ali: But don't they have any treasures among their books, things they really guard?

Hadji: Of course—and nobody ever gets to see them. They are guarded by a demon of whom all stand in awe: The Green Hornet.

Ali: What are these books? Are you free to speak?

Hadji: Well, it's dangerous, but I can give you a few hints. There is *Dialogue* (shortly to be renamed *Monologue*), the *New Yorker*, *Sports Illustrated*, *New York Times*, the University of Utah's *Chronicle*—unmentionables like that. And in a safe within the vault is an old BYU humor magazine edited by Ernest L. Wilkinson.

Ali: But what do the faculty read?

Hadji: Every word that proceedeth from the mouth of the President. Then the office keeps everybody well supplied with speeches and offprints from the *Reader's Digest*, a much more congenial document than the scriptures (which are liable to give people ideas). Ladies and Gentlemen: We wish to make clear at this point that in this election year we wish to avoid all reference to politics. The administration has set us an excellent example by suppressing all manifestations of the divisive two-party system. There is to be one party only.

Ali: Will an intelligent faculty stand for that?

Hadji: If it is wisely chosen. The BYU recruits its faculty on a mathematically and scientifically sound basis. Say they want a professor for a certain subject. He is not cheap and his I.Q. is 160. Nothing is easier than to get two professors with I.Q.'s of 80 apiece—it adds up to the same thing, and it is much cheaper. They are much easier to handle, too. That's how I went there, you know.

Ali: No, I didn't know.

Hadji: It was their recruiting literature that got me: "You too can be a professor or a dean. No experience or training required. Amaze your friends. Degrees cheerfully granted on request. See your local bishop for requirements." Who can resist a come-on like that?

Ali: But how do you teach and publish and all that if you really don't know anything? Aren't you afraid of being exposed?

Hadji: Ho, there is a trick to that: you threaten to expose them first. By the way, did you know that communists don't wear clothes? That's what you call nondress standards.

Ali: I have heard that their College of Religion is hard on liberals.

Hadji: Now that is hardly a fair statement. They are really a very charitable group. In fact, the whole lot of them are on welfare themselves. Broad-minded isn't the word for it. The college is a very haven for the unemployables and the dropouts from the effete -ologies of other institutions.

Ali: Yes, I've heard about them—the President's speeches, you know.

Hadji: That's right. They don't go for that sort of thing at the BYU. As we say in my college, "Never mind if a man is a slob as long as he has character." But the President isn't proud; he will even admit that he went to that awful Harvard. In fact, he has been known to admit it as much as forty times a day. So you see, there's nothing proud about him. It's those effete snobs back at Cambridge who won't admit it. But don't you want to hear the rest of the brochure? "The Cumulative Intelligence Quota at the BYU is twice again the distance in pyramid inches between Calcutta, which has the largest university in the world and Paris, Idaho, divided by a third of the number of pages in the *Nautical Almanac* for 1966, which was the fourth largest issue of the *Nautical Almanac* between 1937 and 1970, or more than 3,000 percent more than the number of ostrich eggs which, if placed end to end, would reach more than 45 times around the base of the Washington Monument and more than 18 times the gross tonnages displacement of the battleship Missouri multiplied by one-third the kilowatt hours of electricity required to lift 13,499 Shetland ponies from the third story of the Empire State building, the tallest building in the world, to the seventy-first floor of the Incorporated—

Ali: O master, the musicians are here to render a number.

Hadji: A number, did you say? We can do miracles with numbers. If you want to get yourself a first-class university, numbers are the answer. Do you know that if all the stitches used in all the footballs used in practice in just three and a half seasons at the BYU —

Ali: Yes, yes, but right now a little music might do you good. Bend an ear, O ocean of perspicacity.

PERSIAN PLAYERS

Hadji: Now that was beautiful, but I believe Janie would have made it just a bit more abrasive, shall we say?

Ali: I'm afraid my revered master hath flipped. I must do what I can to get him back into the swing of our authentic Oriental decadence, though I must say that BYU has something. Master, O Elliot Cameron of the mystic East, I have something that may turn your weary mind away from contemplating Squaw Peak and the dismal Rockies to your native palms and sands.

GYPSY DANCE

Hadji: Perfectly delightful. Kind of decadent, too. But you know as well as I do that we cannot match the progressive spirit of the West. Their decadence is far in advance of ours. Ah, if you only knew the strenuous freedom of the Janie Thompson school—*there's* culture.

Ali: Speaking of freedom—it's a word they use a lot, isn't it? They have freedom, I suppose.

Hadji: O yes, quite a bit. There are places where radar and security police never reach, wire-tapping doesn't always work, and letters are often unopened. There are controls, of course, such as increasing the speeding net to pay for raises in salaries.

Ali: Oh, salaries.

Hadji: Hold on. Perhaps I shouldn't have said that. It might make a lot of trouble. You're not supposed to mention that sort of thing. Well, some of the commerce and engineering people get something, but it all comes out of their tithing and radar tickets. Of course there are the intangibles: the view of Timpanogas when the wind is blowing right, free concerts by the electric chimes in the middle of classes; and there is that intellectual caviar, the President's speeches, which he bestows in unmeasured bounty and endless prodigality.

Ali: Oh, those lucky people. To hear the same stately refrains again, and again, and again, and again. Now about this freedom . . .

Hadji: Well, it has its limits like everything else. There are crimes too heinous to name—for them, naturally, license must be curtailed.

Ali: Crimes such as . . .

Hadji: Walking across the grass, if you must know the worst. After all, what is that but a form of demonstration and protest?

Ali: But why do they shoot them for it?

Hadji: So you're one of these gun-control nuts, eh? Well, we'd better change the subject right now and hear the voice of Elaine Clark.

ELAINE CLARK[3]

---

[3]Elaine Clark, a vocalist and musician, was well-known in Utah Valley, and her entertainment was not satiric. Her husband, Dallan, and his brother owned and operated Clark's Department Store, an institution in downtown Provo through the 1970s.

Hadji: Not bad. But still . . .

Ali: But still what?

Hadji: A little touch of Janie—a dance routine between verses, some artillery and bugles here and there, a couple hundred all-American kids singing their hearts out. . . Little things like that—none of your vulgar hippie stuff.

Ali: Patriotic, eh?

Hadji: That's it—and making damn sure everybody knows it, in a modest way, of course. By the way, why don't you apply for one of their honorary degrees?

Ali: Are you serious?

Hadji: Of course it can be easily arranged. What are your politics?

Ali: But I have no qualifications. I have never done anything of an intellectual nature. I'm completely unknown. Nobody on the faculty has ever heard of me. I just work in my shop and make my pile. I don't know the back of a book from the front.

Hadji: Man, you're in! You're a natural!

Ali: You mean I've got what it takes?

Hadji: Every penny of it. With the right personal connections, of course.

Ali: How about grades, examinations, a thesis, and all that sort of stuff?

Hadji: They're going to give that up. They are grading by the alphabet now. If your name begins with an A, you get an A. And if your name begins with a B, you get a B, and so on. It's much easier on the computers.

Ali: But what if your name begins with T or J?

Hadji: Well, you can't help that, can you? There is no prejudice against you.

Ali: But do I have to flunk?

Hadji: I'm sorry about that. We didn't invent the alphabet.

Ali: But it seems so unfair.

Hadji: Oh, one of those trouble makers, eh?

Ali: Well, I'll have to think it over. Meanwhile let's meditate to the sweet notes of the khammandja—that's violin to you clods.

VIOLINS

Hadji: Glorious. It reminds me of the time Miss Thompson had 76 administration members marching on the basketball floor and singing "76 Trombones Led the Whole Parade," while 76 professors of Religious Economy led the faculty in singing "When Those Saints Come Marching In," accompanied by 76 high-school marching bands, as the President performed his 76 pushups—one for each year—left-handed.

Ali: What was he doing with the other hand?

Hadji: Pointing at the kid in the audience who threw the balloon. There's always a trouble-maker. I have written a poem about that. One of the secrets of good, solid conservative Oriental decadence is knowing whom to blame when anything goes wrong. That is why I have written "Hadji Baba's Lament" or "What's Wrong with the World: H. B.'s Lament." Neat, huh?

HADJI BABA'S LAMENT

Ali: Frightening, isn't it? Here are some Pakistani dancers to take our minds off such things.

PAKISTANI DANCERS

Ali: There, you see, you're relaxed. You're soothed—you like them.

Hadji: Yes—but there's that Janie—"You're a Grand Old Flag," "It's My Country," and all of that—

Ali: Say, they must have really got to you at BYU.

Hadji: Yes indeed, as the saying goes, "BYU! Love it or leave it—but how?"

Index

101st Airborne, 182, 188, 196, 210, 220, 423

A

Abraham, 331-333
Agnew, Spiro, 33, 310
Albright, William F., 270-271, 330
Allen, George, 201, 237, 270
Ancient Studies Reading Room (BYU), 404-5
Anderson, Richard Lloyd, 337
Anti-Semitism, 133-135
Antietam Battlefield, 278
Apocalypse of Abraham, 326
Arbuckle's Coffee, 4
Arches National Park, 74
Arrington, Leonard J., 119
Ashment, Edward H., 159, 323
Aspen Grove summer school, 64, 69
Atiya, Aziz, 153, 295, 316
Atomic Bomb, 206
Avebury, England, 189

B

Baer, Klaus, xxvi, 121, 151, 154, 253, 278, 280, 290-291, 307, 313, 315-317, 319-323, 345-346, 379
Baer, Miriam Reitz, 379
Bailey, George, 174-176
Ballard, Melvin J., xxv
Barker, James L., 249
Barr, Mr. (principal and tutor), 28
Battle of the Bulge, 202, 210, 425
Battle of Leipzig Monument, 94
Beck, Martha Nibley (daughter), xviii, 305-306, 342, 347, 378, 400
Bell, Elouise, 96
Bennion, Lowell, 119

Bennion, Robert C., 282
Benson, Ezra Taft, 216, 219, 252, 255, 296, 304, 370-371
Bernard, Robert J., 146
Bernay, David, 220-221
Berry, Wendell, 82
Black, Matthew, 328
Bolton, Herbert, 113
Book of Abraham, 288, 308, 313-315, 318, 320-321, 324, 326, 328, 338, 346
Book of Moses, 314, 325-328, 346
Book of the Dead (Egyptian), 281
Book of Breathings, 320-321, 324, 346
Borah, Woodrow, 264
Bradley, Omar, 213
Bradshaw, Janet, 307
Bradshaw, Merrill, 307
Breasted, James Henry, 139-140, 322
Brigham Young University, 150, 164, 237, 240, 292, 295, 387, 400
Brigham Young Women's Program, 100, 431
Bristol, England, 192
British War Office, 166, 179
Brodie, Fawn McKay, 119, 154, 160-161, 222, 225, 248, 256, 314
Brooks, Juanita, 227-228
Brown, Hugh B., 300
Brown, Robert, 319-320
Brown, Rosemary, 319
Brown, S. Kent, 326, 337
Bruchsal in Baden, Germany, 91
Budge, E.A.W., 318, 322
Burckhardt, Jacob Christopher, 212
Burns, Robert, 5
Bush, Lester, 338-340, 369
Bushman, Richard, 338

Bushman, Virgil, 279-281
Buzz Bombs, 197
BYU Studies, 310

C

Cache Valley, 4
Cameron, Elliot, 435
Camp Ritchie, 33, 40, 71, 173-181, 210-211, 278
Campbell, Beverly, 361n
Capener, Brian, 374
Capitol Reef, 76
Cardston, Canada, 19, 24
Carentan, France, 197, 220, 424
Carson, Rachel, 78
Cassandra, 46
Chanute Field, Illinois, 171
Charles, R.H., 330
Charlesworth, James, 153
Cheesman, Paul, 301
Christensen, Janet, 394
Christensen, Kent, 394
Christensen, P.A., 64
Claremont Colleges, 132, 136, 140, 146, 156
Clarion State College, 307
Clark, Elaine, 435
Clark, Herald R., 64
Clark, J. Reuben, 14, 212, 272-274
Clawson, Rudger, xxiii, 109
Clearwater, Florida, 70, 169-171
Clebsch, William A., 297
Cold War, 35, 42, 77, 152, 214, 217, 258, 365
Collected Works of Hugh Nibley, 373
Cologne, Germany, 88
Committee on War Objectives and Peace Aims, 139
Compton, Todd, 163
Cook, Bradley J., 323
Cooley, Everett, 154, 160
Corvin, Edward S., 132
Cosic, Kresimir, 340-342, 402
Coughlin, Charles, 133, 135
Cowdery, Oliver, 429
Cowley, Matthias F., 115
Cracroft, Richard H., 100, 103
Crater Lake, 63
Crawford, Miss, 166, 179, 187-188
Cundick, Charlotte, 307
Cundick, Robert, 307

Cutler, Douglas, 89

D

D-Day Invasion, 191-197, 210, 220, 247, 425
Dachau, 40-41
Danahy, Paul, 220
Darwin, Charles, 428
de Jaeger, Jacob, 371
Dead Sea Scrolls, 253-254, 260, 296 303
Decker, Donald, 128, 267
Denning, Ann Eliza Webb Dee Young, 298
Desegregation, 35n
Deseret Club at Yale University, 302
Dialogue: A Journal of Mormon Thought, 304, 338-339, 346, 433
Doctrine and Covenants, 36, 82, 98, 285, 329
Dorson, Richard, xxiv
Draper, Edla Kristina Charlotte Peterson, 232-233, 243
Draper, Otto, 233
Durham, G. Homer, 272

E

Eccles, David, 19
Egypt, 325
Egyptian Alphabet and Grammar, 320
Einstein, Albert, 138, 151
Eliade, Mircea, 154, 284
Encyclopedia Judaica, 299-300
England, Eugene, xxix, 31, 220, 339
Enoch, 327-328, 332, 334, 346
Epic poetry, 249, 281, 346
Evans, Richard L., 225, 250, 263, 298-299
Eyring, Henry, 46

F

Faith of an Observer (documentary), xiii, 332, 364, 374-378, 384
Farr, Cecelia Konchar, 220
Faust, James E., 310n, 355
Festschrift, 347n, 380-381
Fischer, Henry, 316
Folklore, xxiii-xxxi
Ford, Henry, 133, 135
Fort MacArthur, 167-168, 207
Forum (BYU), 343
Foschini, Bernard, 241-242

Foundation for Ancient Research and Mormon Studies (FARMS), 219, 255, 351, 356, 373-374, 380, 403
Frankenthal, Germany, 89
Freeman Institute, 367
Freemasonry, 282, 357
Fulbright, 308

G

Gashweseoma, Martin, 285
Gee, John, 312, 323, 369n
Generation of Vipers, 42
Geneva Steel, 78-79
Germany, 133
Gibran, Kahlil, 432
Givens, Terryl L., 244
Gliders, 189, 191-192, 198-199, 424-425
Godman Field, Kentucky, 172
Goldschmidt, Lucien, 33, 175-178, 237-238, 388
Golf, 62
Goodman, Harold, 307
Goodman, Naomi, 307
Goodspeed, Edgar J., 132, 139, 156
Gordon, Cyrus, 153
Grand Staircase-Escalante National Monument, 83
Grant, Heber, J., 13, 22-23, 86, 109, 127
Grant, Robert M., 296
Greece, xxvii, 95
Greenville, Rhode Island, 3
Grenham Lodge, 189
Griggs, Wilfred, 326, 337
Gulf War, 220

H

Haddock Nibley Real Estate Company, 50
Haddock, Lon J., 50
Hall, Stanley, 267
Hamblin, William, 255
Handley, George, 66, 82
Hanks, Marion D., 351, 356
Harmon, David, 209
Hawkes, Fredrick Pratt, 232
Hefner, Philip, 297
Heidelberg, Germany, 124, 204, 213, 425
Hemingway, Ernest, 193
Heraclitus, 429
Heward, Grant S., 318

Heym, Stefan, 175
Higgins, Gerald, 201
Hillerbrand, Hans J., 296
Hinckley, Gordon B., 298, 352, 373-4, 407
Hölderlin, Friedrich, 204n
Holland, Jeffrey, 79, 278, 355, 365, 370-373
Holocaust, 40-41, 258
Horace, 99
Hoskisson, Paul, 255
Hotel Utah, 13
Housman, A.E., 427
Hoyungowa, Manuel, 283, 286
Hoyungowa, Silas, 282-283
Hunter, Howard W., 352, 355, 371
Hunter, Milton R., 265, 301
Hurricane, Utah, 71, 223
Hypocephalus, 376

I

Improvement Era, xxv, 222, 225, 228, 248, 322, 346, 353, 398, 432
Independent Company, Pioneers, 4
Institute of Ancient Studies, 336
International House, Berkeley, 110
Iskian, Anahid, 178, 180, 186, 224
Ivins, Anthony W., 226
Ivins, Stanley S., 161, 226-227

J

Jackson, Kent P., 226
Jaeger, Werner, 112
Johnson, Howard R., 209
Joseph Smith Papyri, 308, 313, 315, 317, 319, 323
Joyce, James, 48
Juvenile Instructor, 300

K

Kader, Mose, 238
Kader, Omar, 216n
Kant, Immanuel, 90
Karlsdorf, Germany, 92
Karlsruhe, Germany, 91, 92
Kimball, Camille Eyring, 265
Kimball, Heber C., 127
Kimball, Spencer W., 45-46, 81, 127, 218, 252, 265, 296, 372, 395
King, Arthur Henry, 348
Klamath and Umpqua forests, 62-63, 68

Korean War, 35

L

Last Lecture Series, 69
Lee, Harold B., 293
Lee, J. Bracken, 128
Lermontov, Mikhail Yuryevich, 208
Lethbridge, Canada, 266
Lewis, C.S., 428
Libya, 308
Limburg, Germany, 89
Lindbergh, Charles A., 133, 135
Logan Temple Association, 9
London, England, 197
Longley, Snow, 68
Los Angeles, 49, 105
Lou Gehrig's disease, 349
Lund, A. William, 309
Lundquist, Suzanne Evertsen, 276, 361n
Lutz, Henry L.F., 289
Luxembourg, 203, 425
Lyon, Michael, 358

M

MacArthur, Douglas, 198
MacCrae, George, 326
MacKay, Douglas, 74-75
MacKay, Thomas W., 337
Madsen, Brigham, 261
Madsen, Truman, 30, 148, 302, 325, 338, 348, 350, 352-353, 373
Maeser, Karl G., 433
Mahan Principle, 182, 212-213, 392
Manavu Ward, 240
Mann, Klaus, 175
Mann, Thomas, 132, 138
Martin, Everett Dean, 132, 138-139, 156
Mason, Jim, 307
Mason, Lynne, 307
Maxwell, Neal A., 44, 161, 246-247, 374, 376, 408
McAuliffe, Tony, 201
McCarthy Loyalty Oaths, 32
McCrae, John, 195
McCune, A.W. and Elizabeth, 12
McDonald, Howard S., 227, 229
McDonald, Myrtle, 102,
McKay, David O., 225, 227, 249-252, 264, 272, 299-300
McKay, Thomas E., 225
McMurrin, Sterling, 119, 120, 149-150, 159-161, 272, 274, 294, 302, 366n, 427
Medford, Oregon, 26
Mercer, S.A.B., 260, 322, 404
Merrill, Marriner, xxiii
Mesa (Arizona) Temple, 86, 352
Metropolitan Museum, 315-316
Meyer, Eduard, 322
Midgley, Louis, 45, 119, 292, 343-344, 348
Milgrom, Jacob, 153
Mincek, Christina Nibley (daughter), 242, 256-257, 266, 289, 291, 305-306, 340, 342, 377, 401
Mincek, Zdravko, 340
Monson, Thomas S., 371
Mont Calm, 87-88
Morgan, Dale, 227, 314
Moslems, 254
Mosser, Carl, 162
Mount St. Helens, 43, 258
Mount Timpanogos, 73-74
Mourmelon-le-Grand, France, 201, 209
Moyle, Henry D., 249, 264, 274, 298
Mumford, Lewis, 132
Muse, Bill, 276, 279
Musicians Anonymous, 307
Musseburgh, Scotland, 2
Myres, Joel, 401
Myres, Natalie Mincek, xix, 401

N

Nag Hammadi, 254, 260
Neibaur, Isaac, 6
Nelson, Dee Jay, 318-320
Nelson, Russell M., 377
Neusner, Jacob, 153, 346, 361
Newton, Isaac, 428
Nibley, Agnes "Sloanie" Sloan (mother), 17, 19-20, 22-23, 50-51, 59, 93-94, 105, 109, 114, 144-145, 185, 223, 242-243, 269-271, 310
Nibley, Alexander Sloan (brother), 20, 106, 184-185, 269, 271, 402
Nibley, Alexander "El" (father), 17-20, 22, 50, 105, 109, 112, 144-145, 185, 199, 268-271, 310

Nibley, Charles Alexander (son), 266, 289, 291, 305-306, 342, 374-376, 378, 401

Nibley, Charles Wilson (grandfather), 1-15, 19, 23, 26, 62, 85, 108, 127, 187, 226, 233, 384, 386, 408

Nibley, Ellen Jane Ricks, 9, 10

Nibley, Fred Richard (brother), 25, 185, 271, 307, 349

Nibley, Hugh, attitudes and characteristics, consistency, 408-440, curiosity, 21, eating habits, xix, 93, 109, 114, fame and awards, xiv, 152, 303, 343, fashion, xxviii, money, 90, politics, xviii, 310, wit, xvii, 96-103, 431-437

Nibley, Hugh, family life, xiv-xv, 239, 242, 266-268, 289, 291, 305-306, 342, 377-378, 401-402, Family Home Evening, xviii, 342

Nibley, Hugh, interests and influences, xx, art, 53-54, astronomy, 52-54, Grandmother Sloan, 24-25, 121, language study, 54-55, 91, 107, 114, 141-143, 152-153, 158, 170, 199, 200, 202, 203, 228-230, 236, 238, 409, music, xii, 50-51, poetry, 55-58, popular culture, xi,

Nibley, Hugh, life events, birth, 17, 20-21, baptism, 27, education, 28-29, 90, 92, 104-117, moved to California, 29, ROTC, 60-61, 166, 210, Swiss-German Mission, xxiv-xxv, xxvii, xxviii, 36-37, 84-95, 247, Northwestern States Mission, 109, 247, depression, 114-115, near-death experience, 115-116, 121-122, Ph.D. dissertation, 116, 353, teaching at Claremont, 133-147, family's financial collapse, 144-145, Army service, 38-41, 145, 147, 166-207, BYU appointment, xxv-xxvi, 229-231, courtship and marriage, xxv-xxvi, 124, 231-235, seeking employment at University of Utah, 271, Berkeley sabbatical, 151, Director of Institute of Ancient Studies, 336-337, Honorary Doctorate, 370, Bypass surgery, 377, Seventy-fifth birthday, 378-379, quitting teaching, 400, Fiftieth wedding anniversary, 403, Ninetieth birthday, 404

Nibley, Hugh, on Abraham, 397-405, on Adam and Eve, 360-361, on Babylon, 382-395, on Book of Mormon, 91, 97, 112, 160, 194, 214-215, 218-219, 220, 222, 245-259, 292-293, 295, 302-303, 346, on Blacks and Priesthood, 338-340, 368-9, on cosmology, 330, on creation, 331, on dress standards, 309-311, 338, on education, 148-165, 264, 338, on environment, 16, 66-83, on evolution, 368, on faith, 118-131, 402-403, 427-430, on gifts, 126-127, on Hopi, 254, 276-287, 324, 358, on humor, 96-103, on hunting, 80-81, on kitsch, 98, on last days, 33-35, 258-259, on Law of Consecration and Zion, 332-333, 366-367, 393, on the Pearl of Great Price, 312-333, on repentance, 129, 331, as social critic, 31-47, on the temple, 257, 334, 350-363, on the "terrible questions," 330, on war, 39-41, 134, 208-221, on wealth, 48, 122-123, on Word of Wisdom, 198, on Zion, 382-395

Nibley, Hugh, writings and speeches, "Abraham," 399, *Abraham in Egypt*, 326-327, 331, 348, 368, "Abraham's Creation Drama," 356, 399, "Acclamatio," 140, "An Approach to Facsimile No. 2," 398, *An Approach to the Book of Mormon*, 245, 249-252, 258, 262, 264, 274, 389, "Ancient Temples," 354, *Approaching Zion*, 47, "Archaeology and Our Religion," 300-301, "The Arrow, The Hunter, and the State," 241, "Baptism for the Dead in Ancient Times," 241-242, 353, "Before Adam," 368, "Bird Island," 99-100, "Book of Enoch as a Theodicy," 325-326, "Book of Mormon as a Mirror of the East," 241, 248, "The Book of Mormon: Forty Years After," 367-8, "Breakthroughs I Would Like to See," 366, 384, 390-91, "Brigham Young and the Enemy," 216, "Brigham Young and the Environment," 82, "Brother Bergen Letter," 294, "But What Kind of Work?" 390, "Censoring the Joseph Smith Story," 297, "Change Out of Control," 366, "Christian Envy of the Temple," 263, 354n, "Criticizing the Brethren," 380, "The Early Christian Prayer Circle," 354, *Enoch the Prophet*, 329, 374, "Evangelium Quadraginta Dierum," 299, 354n, "The Expanding Gospel," 303, "Freemen and Kingmen in the Book of Mormon," 367, "Genesis of the Writen Word," 354, "Gifts," 217-218,

"Hierocentric State," 241, 263, 284, 354n, "House of Glory," 356, "How Firm a Foundation," 218, 390, "How to Get Rich," 366, 390, "How to Have a Quiet Campus," 310, "The Idea of the Temple in History," 353, "Last Call," 218, "The Law of Consecration," 366, "Leaders to Managers," 44-45, 371-372, 390, *Lehi in the Desert*, 245, 249, "Liahona's Cousins," 296, "Man's Dominion," 80, 343, "The Meaning of the Atonement," 376, *Message of the Joseph Smith Papyri*, 323-324, 344-347, "Mixed Voices," 264, "The Mormon View of the Book of Mormon," 299, *Myth Makers*, 99, 102, 297-298, "New Light on Scaliger," 141, *Nibley on the Timely and the Timeless*, 348, 372-3, *No, Ma'am, That's Not History*, 161, 225-228, *Old Testament and Related Studies*, 373, "On the Meaning of Temples," 356, *One Eternal Round*, 127, 397-405, "One Eternal Round" (series of speeches) 399, "Origin of the Roman Dole," 140, "Our Glory or Our Condemnation," 389, "Passing of the Church," 296, "Patriarchy and Matriarchy," 360, *Prophetic Book of Mormon*, 252, "Qumran and the Companions of the Cave," 299, "Scriptural Perspectives on How to Survive," 367, "Some Reasons for the Restored Gospel," 346, *Since Cumorah*, 245, 252, 296, 389, *Sounding Brass*, 99, 298-299, "Sparisones," 141, "Stewardship of the Air," 79, 82, "A Strange Thing in the Land," 325, 328, "Subduing the Earth," 80, 343, *Temple and Cosmos*, 358, "Tenting, Toll, and Taxing," 299, 354n, "There Were Jaredites," 264, "The Way of the Church," 264, "The Utopians," 366, "Three Facsimiles from the Book of Abraham," 398, *World and the Prophets*, 263, "The Unresolved Loyalty Problem," 263, "Victoriosa Loquacitas," 263, "We Will Still Weep for Zion," 390, "What Is Zion?," 366, 390, "Work We Must But the Lunch is Free," 366, 390

Nibley, Isaac (stillborn son), 266, 333
Nibley, James, 2-3
Nibley, Jean Wilson, 2-3
Nibley, Julia Budge, 10
Nibley, Marjorie Doolittle, 307
Nibley, Michael Draper (son), 266, 278, 289, 291, 305-306, 342, 377-378, 401
Nibley, Miriam, 401-2
Nibley, Nadine Monson, 307
Nibley, Nathan, 18
Nibley, Paul Sloan (son), 239, 242, 266, 279, 289, 291, 305-306, 342, 377, 401
Nibley, Philip Gordon (brother), 27, 108-109, 270
Nibley, Phyllis Draper (wife), xxvi, 72-73, 77, 124, 232-235, 239, 242, 266, 274, 289, 291, 305-308, 325, 333, 344, 386, 387, 402-403
Nibley, Rebecca Neibaur (grandmother), 6-7, 10, 14
Nibley, Rebecca (daughter), 266, 289, 291, 305-306, 342, 347, 378
Nibley, Reid Neibaur (brother), 58-59, 107, 114, 167, 185, 271, 307
Nibley, Thomas Hugh (son), 266, 289, 291, 305-306, 342, 377, 401
Nibley-Stoddard Lumber Company, 61, 68
No Substitute for Victory, 216
Nordren, Clinton, 307
Nordren, Grace, 307

O

Oaks, Dallin H., 335-336, 356, 374
Operation Market-Garden, 198-200, 209, 211, 424
Oppenheimer, Max, Jr., 168, 177, 180, 185, 205
Order of Battle, 178-180, 212
Oregon Lumber Company, 19, 26
Oriental Institue (University of Chicago), 139, 278, 307
Outler, Albert C., 297
Owen, Paul, 162

P

Packer, Boyd K., 306, 407
"Parallelomania," 162-163
Parry, Donald, 255, 350, 362
Patai, Raphael, 153
Patrologia, 238, 260, 264, 404
Pauly, Herta, 143-144
Pearl of Great Price, 312-333
Peck, M. Scott, 277, 286
Penrose, Charles W., 14
Petersen, Zina Nibley (daughter), xi, 131, 278, 305-306, 342, 347, 370, 378

Petronius, 99
Phillips, R. Douglas, 264, 337, 348
Pistis Sophia, 358
Polygamy, 7, 9-11
Pope, Alexander, 103
Popper, William, 111-112
Portland, Oregon, 17, 27
Powers, Francis Gary, 77
Pratt, Don F., 192
Pratt, Parley P., 127

Q

Queen Mary, 185
Qumran, 303

R

Ramses II exhibit (BYU), 379-380
Rasmussen, Ellis T., 337
Raye, Martha, 216
Redford, Robert, 82
Rees, Robert, 338
Reid, John Patrick, 23
Reid, Margaret Kirkwood, 23
Religion Department (BYU), 262, 293, 309, 355, 434
Religious Studies Center, 348
Reynolds, Noel, 246
Richards, Barbara Nibley (sister), 61, 185, 223, 271
Richards, Franklin D., 328
Richards, LeGrand, 109, 251, 301
Ricks, Stephen E., 32, 255, 362
Riddle, Chauncey, 336
Ritner, Robert K., 323
Roberson, Marvin, xviii, 344
Roberts, Brigham H., 119
Roberts, Tomi Ann, 220
Rock Canyon, 73
Rockwood, Jolene Edmunds, 361n
Romanov, Vladimir Kirillovich, 206
Romney, Marion G., 162, 293-294, 298, 301, 304-305, 394
Rosenbaum, Morris, 6
Rowell, Margaret, 289
Rushforth, Sam, 220

S

Saad, Joseph, 303

Salmon, Douglas F., 163
Salt Lake Mission Home, 87
Scaliger, Joseph Justus, 141
Scottish Highlands, 71, 190, 197, 203
Serendipity, 277-279
Sesquicentennial Symposium on the Humanities, 353
Shabako Stone, 353
Shakespeare, William, 5, 48, 54, 69, 256, 268
Sherman Anti-trust Act, 13
Shingowitewa, Leroy Ned, 282
Silent Spring, 78
Skousen, Cleon, 295
Sloan, Hugh Russel (grandfather), 19, 24
Sloan, Joann, 109,
Sloan, Margaret Violet Reid (grandmother), 16, 19, 23-24, 33, 55, 200, 384
Sloan, William Reid, 109, 247
Smart, William B., 82
Smith, Gibbs M., 82
Smith, Joseph Fielding, 162, 217, 234, 251, 291
Smith, Joseph, 98, 127, 160, 222, 225, 245, 256-257, 357
Smith, Joseph F., 8, 11, 19, 26, 80, 127
Smith, T.V., 132
Smith, Winslow Whitney, 88
Smoot, Reed, 11
Snow, LeRoi C., 87
Snow, Lorenzo, 87
Socrates, 90
Spaulding, Franklin Spencer, 322
Springer, Paul, 100, 110-112, 114, 128, 134-135, 335n, 374, 388
Spy ring (BYU), 309
St. Petersburg, Florida, 169
Standard Oil, 213
Ste. Mère Eglise, France, 197
Stein, Aurel, 358
Steindorff, George, 139
Stendahl, Krister, 130
Story, Russell M., 132, 137-139, 143, 146
Stratford, Richard, 94
Stubbs, Darrell, 307
Stubbs, Eva, 307
Sunstone Foundation, 380, 394, 398
Swearing Elders, 160
Swensen, Russel, 64
Swiss-German Mission, 85

T

Tadje, Fred, 84, 88, 93-95
Tanner, Jerald, 318-319
Tanner, Sandra, 318-319
Taylor, Maxwell, 190-191, 196, 219
Testament of Abraham, 326
Thatcher, Constance, 19
Thatcher, Moses, 19
Thomas, Robert K., 148, 338
Thomasson, Gordon, 154, 208, 308-309, 339
Thompson, Janie, 432, 436
Thoreau, Henry David and Transcendentalists, 384
Titanic, 407
Toelken, Barre, xxvii
Torquay, England, 191
Trible, Phyllis, 360
Tucker, Mr., 166, 179
Twain, Mark, 22,
Twenty-Seventh Wife, 298

U

Uintas, 75-76
Ulysses, 48
United Order Lumber Company, 9
University of California, Los Angeles, 104, 106, 107, 140
University of California at Berkeley, 104, 110, 164, 240, 275, 288, 291-292, 293, 295
University of Utah, 271-275

V

Vade Mecum, 188
Van Wagenen, Sterling, 374-375
Vierville, France, 197, 424
Vietnam War, 214, 216-217, 309, 337
von Clausewitz, Karl, 179, 210, 217, 219

W

Wallace, Irving, 298
Wallace, Kent, 153
War Crimes, 203-205
Ward, Pat (secretary) 398, 400
Warner, Terry, 348
Wasden, Brooks, 137
Watergate, 337
Wayne, John, 216
Weiland, Kurt, 219
Welch, John W., 102-103, 214, 245, 255, 362, 373-375
Wellsville, Utah, 4
West, Lou ("Uncle Louie"), 383
Weyland, Raymond, 115
Wheelwright, Lorin F., 301
Whipple, Walter, 315
Whitney, Orson F., 58
Whittaker, David J., 297-298
Whittington Barracks, 186, 423
Widtsoe, John A., xxv-xxvi, 72, 86, 227-229, 231, 234, 252
Wilkinson, Ernest L., 100, 253, 255, 261-262, 265, 272-274, 279, 295, 298-299, 308, 309, 335, 431, 434
Willamette River, 383
Williams, Barbara, 307
Williams, Glenn, 307
Williams, Terry Tempest, 82
Wilson, John A., 307, 316n
Wilson, Marian Robertson, 236
Wilson, William A., xxiv, xxx
Winder, John R., 12, 14, 17
Wood Museum, 314
Woodruff, Wilford, 127
Woodward, Margaret, 307
Woodward, Ralph, 307
World War I, 23, 133, 210
World War II, xxv, xxvii, 123, 133-134, 166-214, 220-221, 277, 386, 407
Wormuth, Francis, 272
Wright, Curtis, 97
Wylie, Philip, 42

Y

Young, Brigham, 90, 98, 127, 130, 215, 298, 308, 317, 345, 409
Young, Orson Whitney, 91
Young, S. Dilworth, 265

Z

Zion National Park, 70, 147, 235